리딩이노베이터
기본편

박지성

고려대학교 언어학과 및 영어영문학 졸

현 | 해커스 편입 독해전임
　　마공스터디 온라인 강사
　　대치동 용인외대부고·휘문고·숙명여고 내신
　　목동 용인외대부고 내신

전 | 강창용편입 독해전임
　　이패스편입 독해전임
　　리스공 공무원 강사

저서 | 리딩이노베이터(기본편) 「Jonghap Books」
　　퍼펙트 편입독해 「Jonghap Books」
　　영어독해 개념이해 「Jonghap Books」
　　영어독해 문제원리·풀이이해 「Jonghap Books」
　　매그너스 MAGNUS 고등영어 서술형 기본편 6주완성 「오스틴북스」
　　매그너스 MAGNUS 서술형 시리즈 고등영어 서술형 실전편 「오스틴북스」

리딩이노베이터 (기본편)

발 행 일　2025년 3월 7일 (개정2판 2쇄)
　　　　　2024년 9월 2일 (개정2판 1쇄)
저　　 자　박지성
발 행 인　이도경
발 행 처　JH press
주　　 소　13558 경기도 성남시 분당구 느티로 16, 9층
홈페이지　www.booksellers.co.kr
전자메일　proper002@properenglish.co.kr
대표전화　070-4454-1340
팩　　 스　031-718-0580

정가 23,800원

ISBN　979-11-984391-9-2

리딩이노베이터
기본편

박지성 지음

JH press

머리말

'영문독해'라고 하면 학습자들은 일반적으로 문장 단위별 해석을 떠올리게 된다. 그리고 대부분 이것을 독해방법의 전부라고 생각한다. 그런 배경에는 과거 문법을 강조하는 교육풍토와 무관하지 않다. 특정 언어와 관련된 규칙의 집합을 문법이라 하는데, 문법을 배우는 과정에서 대부분의 학습자는 여러 문장으로 구성된 단락이 아닌 특정 문법규칙이 들어간 하나의 독립된 문장을 다룬다. 처음에는 대개 개별 문장에 대한 해석도 버거울 뿐 아니라, 상당한 시간 투자를 필요로 한다. 이런 상황에서 학습자는 독해가 안 되는 원인을 개별 문장에 대한 해석으로 돌리게 되며, 자연스레 더욱 많은 시간을 문법에 투자하게 된다. 그러면서 문법이 되면, 독해가 잘 될 것이라는 막연한 생각을 품는데, 어찌 보면 이는 투자대비 보상심리가 작용한 것이라 볼 수 있다. 하지만 시간이 흘러 문장 단위에 대한 해석능력을 익혔다 해서 독해가 잘 되는 것이 아님을 곧 알게 된다. 학습자의 입에서 "해석은 되는데, 전체 글의 의미를 잘 모르겠다"라는 말이 아무 이유 없이 나오는 것이 아닐 것이다. 이는 개별 문장에 대한 문법적 지식을 단락독해에 적용한 꼴로 이를 공부하지 않은 상황에서 나오는 당연한 결과다.

그렇다면 단락독해를 위해선 무엇을 배워야 하는가? 영문독해란 영어권에서 쓰인 글을 읽는다는 것을 의미하므로 각 문화권마다 다른 글쓰기 방식에 대한 이해가 선행되어야 한다. 응용언어 학자인 Robert Kaplan은 문화가 다르면 사고방식이 다르고, 이는 곧 글쓰기 방식에도 차이가 보임을 아래와 같이 제시했다.

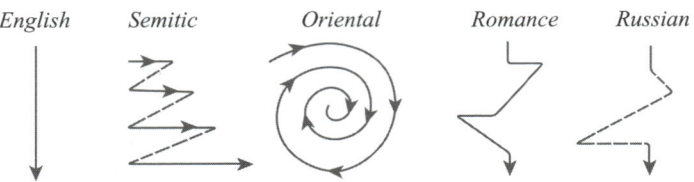

| Kaplan의 문화권에 따른 글쓰기 전개방식 |

위 도식화에서 제시된 각 문화권에 따른 고유한 글쓰기 방식을 보면, 영어(English)의 경우 글쓴이가 전달하고자 하는 요지를 글의 도입부에서 먼저 제시하고 뒷받침 진술로 이어지는 두괄식 구조를 취함을 알 수 있는데, 이는 영어권의 글의 가장 큰 특징인 "주장 – 뒷받침 근거"의 직선적(연역적) 사고를 의미한다. 이와 달리, 동양(Oriental)의 글 전개방식은 글의 요지와는 관련이 적은 주변적 이야기로 시작한 후 글의 중·후반부에서 글의 의도를 드러내

는 경향을 보인다. 이마저도 타당한 근거를 바탕으로 결론을 이끌어내는 영어권의 미괄식 구조와 현격한 차이를 보인다. 이런 차이점에 대한 인식의 중요성은 만약 동양권 문화에 익숙한 사람(즉, 한국 학습자)이 영어권에 대한 글쓰기 방식에 대한 선행학습이 부재한 상황에서 영문지문을 접할 경우 동양식 사고를 바탕으로 글을 분석하려는 성향을 보인다는 점이다. 그러므로 이런 상황을 인식하고 영문지문의 특성에 대한 체계적인 학습이 이뤄지지 않은 상태에서 지금까지의 "문제-해설-어휘-해석"이라는 단순 문제풀이 방식에 의존하는 것은 바른 대안이 될 수 없다. 그렇다면, 영문 글쓰기 방법에 대한 이해와 문제풀이와의 연관성은 무엇인가?

모든 문제풀이의 시작은 철저한 지문(원문)분석이다. 영문지문을 바르게 분석하기 위해선 이미 언급했듯이 그 문화권에 특수화된 글쓰기 방법을 익혀야 한다. 영어권에서 가장 흔히 사용되는 구조(structure of writing)를 보통 두괄식이라 하는데, 이런 구조에 대한 이해는 단순히 글을 잘 분석할 수 있는 차원을 넘어 문제풀이와 직접적인 연관성을 지닌다. 예를 들어, 모든 공인영어 시험에 출제되는 주제를 묻는 문제는 주제문과 뒷받침 문장의 관계를 파악하는 능력과 연관된다. 주제문과 뒷받침 문장을 구별할 수 있을 경우 문제풀이 시 다음과 같은 효과를 얻을 수 있다. 첫째, 주제문은 중심소재와 중심내용을 담는 문장이기에 글 전체를 읽지 않아도 주제 문제를 신속·정확하게 풀 수 있다. 둘째, 주제문 파악은 "예측하며 글 읽기"를 가능케 한다. 가령, "문화권마다 글쓰기 방법은 다르다"라는 주제문을 파악했을 경우 주어진 지문에는 다양한 문화권에 따른 나름의 독특한 글쓰기 방법이 제시되었으리라는 것을 예상할 수 있다. 곧 주제문과 뒷받침 문장을 파악하는 능력은 제시된 지문에 대한 깊이 있는 분석을 가능케 해 주므로 글 전체에 대한 이해를 높여 주제를 묻는 문제 뿐 아니라 수험생이 까다롭게 여기는 내용일치·불일치 문제에 대한 이해의 정확도도 높여준다. 또한 "예측하며 글 읽기"를 바탕으로 촌각을 다투는 시험장에서 속독을 가능케 한다.

앞에서도 언급했지만 기존 독해 문제집에서는 대다수 "문제-해설-어휘-해석" 방식으로 짜여져 있다. 이 책은 이러한 천편일률적인 구성에서 벗어나 영문독해를 하는 데 꼭 필요한 영어권 글쓰기에 원론적인 핵심사항들을 먼저 갖춘 후 이를 문제풀이에 어떻게 적용하는지 그 방법을 제시·설명했다. 아무쪼록 이 책을 잘 습득·활용해서 뜻하는 바를 이루기 바란다.

박 지 성

책의 구성과 특징

| 구성 |

Part 1
: 글의 구성요소 분석과 실전응용 연습문제

1. 영어권 글쓰기 방식을 총 14장으로 세분화하였는데, 각 장에서 다뤄지는 내용은 개별적 성격을 지니면서도 동시에 글쓰기를 하나의 통합적 과정으로 이해할 수 있도록 구성하여, 학습자 스스로 글쓰기가 하나의 유기적 통합과정임을 이해해서 익힐 수 있도록 했다.

2. 또한 각 장에서 배운 이론을 학생 스스로 적용해 볼 수 있는 실전응용 지문(원문)을 제시하고, 이에 대한 자세한 분석 및 해설을 달아 "이론-적용-확인"의 삼단계로 구성해 학습자가 이해한 바를 바로 적용·확인할 수 있도록 했다.

3. 특히, 개별 장의 내용과 상관없이 글 읽기의 시작인 주제파악과 예측하며 글 읽기는 모든 지문(원문)을 통해 연습할 수 있게 구성했으며, 시험에서 자주 출제되는 문제 유형과의 연관성과 풀이전략을 함께 제시하여, "이론-적용-문제풀이"로 이어질 수 있도록 구성했다.

Part 2
: 실전대비 유형별문제

1. Part 1에서 익힌 글쓰기 방법을 실제시험에 나오는 중요빈출 문제유형에 따라 적용할 수 있도록 구성했다.

2. Part 1과 마찬가지로 문제풀이 자체만으로 끝나는 것이 아니라 각 문제의 지문(원문)분석을 학습자 스스로 적용·확인할 수 있는 "본문분석"란을 두어 이를 활용함으로써 제시된 글에 따른 문제유형과의 연관성 그리고 풀이방법을 학습자 스스로 발견할 수 있도록 구성했다.

Part 3·4
: (Part 1) 실전응용 연습문제 · (Part2) 유형별 문제 분석 및 해설

1. Part 1·2에 나온 문제 원문(지문)을 하나도 빠짐없이 Part 3·4에도 각각 그대로 수록하여, Part 1에서 다룬 영어권 글의 요소별에 따른 글쓰기 방식을 적용하여 매 지문마다 분석과 문제해설을 했다.

② Part 2의 문제해설의 경우 독학생을 배려하여 최괘한 답이 아닌 보기의 내용도 설명했으며, 문제에 대한 단순 해설을 벗어나 원문(지문) 성격에 따른 문제 유형과 접근방법까지 제시하여 출제자와 같은 눈높이를 갖출 수 있도록 구성했다.

| 특징 |

① Part 1에 다뤄진 영어권 글의 구성요소를 분석·이해하여 영어권 글쓰기 방식을 파악, 원문(지문) 독해에 적용하면 독해시험 문제풀이 시 답의 정확성을 높이고 시간을 줄이게 된다.

② 각 Part별마다 원문분석 등의 자세한 설명과 함께 체계적·유기적으로 꾸몄으므로 각각의 항목마다 연계해서 학습함으로써 효율성을 크게 높일 수 있다.

③ 문제풀이를 다룬 Part 3·4에도 Part 1·2에 나오는 문제 원문(지문)을 그대로 실어놓았으므로 굳이 앞부분 원문(지문)을 대조할 필요가 없고 또한, 문제풀이집(해설·해석·정답 등)만으로의 이용뿐 아니라 전체 원문(지문)독해 복습 기회로 활용할 수 있다.

기존의 독해 방식 vs 리딩 이노베이터 비교

본서는 기존 독해 책에서 흔히 볼 수 있는 "문제-해설-어휘-해석"라는 강사 해설강의에 초점을 둔 구성이 아닌 학습자 중심으로 독학이 가능하도록 꾸몄다. 기존의 독해 방식과 본서의 접근 방식에 대한 비교를 통해 본서의 특징을 살펴보도록 하자.

[기존의 독해 방식]

[문제] 다음 글의 제목으로 가장 적절한 것을 고르시오.

> According to a new study, during most armed conflicts on the globe since the 1970s, mortality rates have actually declined. That's not to say that war, in and of itself, leads to longer life spans. Instead, a major reason for the drop is that conflict has motivated international humanitarian groups to strengthen their efforts in poor countries, and they've learned to work public health miracles in a short amount of time. In the Democratic Republic of the Congo, for instance, just 20 percent of children were vaccinated for measles in 1997, at the start of a decade-long civil war. But by 2007 that figure was 80 percent. The history of other health initiatives, from treating malnutrition to distributing bed nets, tells a similar story.

(1) A Cry for Freedom in Africa
(2) Modern Warfare's Silver Lining
(3) Young Warriors of Modern Warfare
(4) The Dark Side of African Civil Wars
(5) Deadly Epidemics Spreading Like Wildfire

| 정답 | (2)

| 해설 | 글의 도입부에서 현대전이 오히려 사망률을 낮췄다는 긍정적 효과를 이야기하므로 보기 (2)의 "Modern Warfare's Silver Lining" 이다.

| 어휘 | conflict n. 충돌, 전쟁   decline v. 감소하다   drop n. 감소
the Democratic Republic of the Congo 콩고 민주공화국   malnutrition n. 영양실조   bed net 모기장

| 해석 | 새로운 한 연구에 따르면, 1970년대 이후 전 세계적으로 무장 전쟁이 가장 많이 일어났지만, 이 기간 동안 사망률이 실질적으로 감소했다. 이는 전쟁이 그 자체로 더 오랜 수명의 결과를 가져온다는 말은 아니다. 대신, 이런 수치의 감소의 주된 이유는 전쟁으로 인해 국제 구호단체가 가난한 나라의 원조 노력을 강화하도록 장려한다는 점과 단기간에 공공 건강의 놀라운 일을 이룰 수 있다는 것을 깨닫게 되었다는 점이다. 예를 들어, 콩고 민주공화국에서 약 20%의 아이들이 10년간의 장기 내전이 시작된 1997년에 홍역 백신을 맞았다. 그러나 2007년까지 이 수치는 80%에 달했다. 영양실조를 치유하고 모기장을 배분하는 등의 건강을 위한 다른 조치에 대한 역사를 보면 이와 비슷한 이야기를 들여다 볼 수 있다.

★ 기존의 독해 책에서 가장 중시되는 부분은 바로 문제에 대한 해설 부분이다. 즉, 답을 찾는 방법을 제시하는 동시에 보기 항에 대한 오답분석을 중심으로 다루는데, 정작 본문을 어떻게 읽어내어 문제에서 요구하는 답을 이끌어 내야 하는지에 대한 내용은 전혀 다루지 않는다.

[Reading Innovator]

책에 담겨진 모든 지문(원문)에 대한 본문분석을 담아 문장과 문장 간의 유기적 관계를 밝히는 동시에 글의 종류, 전개방식, 유형 등을 제시했다.

다음 지문의 문제풀이 접근방식과 해설을 보며 앞의 기존 방식과 비교해 보자

지문(원문)과 오른쪽 본문분석의 세부사항을 번호로 표시하여 본문분석을 쉽게 파악할 수 있도록 도왔다.

[본문분석]

★ 서론, 본론, 결론의 위치에 따라 무엇에 주목하며 글을 읽어야 할지 밝혔다.

명확한 유형이 드러나는 글의 경우 "현상 - 원인 - 예시" 등 유형을 제시하고, 특징을 강조하여 한눈에 글의 흐름을 파악할 수 있도록 굵게 표시했다.

1. According to <u>a new study</u>, during most armed conflicts on the globe since the 1970s, mortality rates have actually declined. 1) That's not to say that war, in and of itself, leads to longer life spans. Instead, a major **reason** for the drop is that <u>conflict has motivated international humanitarian groups to strengthen their efforts in poor countries, and they've learned to work public health miracles in a short amount of time</u>. ① In the Democratic Republic of the Congo, **for instance**, just 20 percent of children were vaccinated for measles in 1997, at the start of a decade-long civil war. But by 2007 that figure was 80 percent. The history of other health initiatives, from treating malnutrition to distributing bed nets, tells a similar story.

글의 도입부는 글 전체의 방향성을 제시하는 부분이다. 포괄적 주제 설정과 글의 유형을 파악할 수 있다는 점에서 가장 집중해서 읽어야 한다.

1. 연구(a new study)를 통해서 밝혀진 <u>예외적 현상</u>을 언급하고 있다 : 1970년대 이래 전 세계적으로 전쟁이 일어나는 상황임에도 불구하고 사망률은 줄어들었다.

1) <u>원인(reason)</u> : 전쟁은 오히려 인도주의적 국제단체의 노력을 장려하여 가난한 국가의 건강을 높이는데 더욱 노력하도록 기여했다.

① <u>예시(for instance)</u>를 통한 부연 – 구체적 연도와 수치를 통해 근거의 객관성을 높이고 있다.

필요한 경우 문제 풀이 시 반드시 짚고 넘어가야 하는 부분(특정 문제 풀이 방법과 문제 출제 원리 등)을 제시하는 동시에 글 전체를 도식화하여 한눈에 글의 구조를 파악할 수 있도록 했다.

| 본문정리

"현상(예외적 현상) - 원인"의 패턴을 따르는 글이다. 일반적으로 현상으로 시작하는 글은 제목 문제가 나오는 경우가 많으며(실질적으로 현상의 지문에서 주제를 물어보는 경우는 극히 드물다), **현상 자체가 제목이 됨을 기억한다**

문단의 전체 구조를 한눈에 볼 수 있도록 도식화해 제시했다.

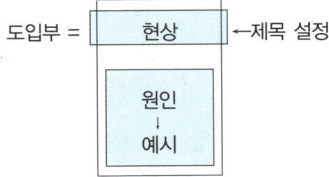

본문의 단편적 내용 이해만으로 답을 이끌어 내는 것이 아니라 특정 유형의 글의 경우 문제에서 요구하는 사항을 어떻게 이끌어 내는지 정확히 분석해 제시했다.

| 해설

특정 현상의 원인을 파악하는 글로 현대전이 오히려 사망률을 낮췄다는 긍정적 효과를 이야기하는 내용이다. 이러한 현상을 가장 잘 드러내는 보기는 "Modern Warfare's Silver Lining"이다.

| 해석

새로운 한 연구에 따르면, 1970년대 이후 전 세계적으로 무장 전쟁이 가장 많이 일어났지만, 이 기간 동안 사망률이 실질적으로 감소했다. 이는 전쟁이 그 자체로 더 오랜 수명의 결과를 가져온다는 말은 아니다. 대신, 이런 수치의 감소의 주된 이유는 전쟁으로 인해 국제 구호단체가 가난한 나라의 원조 노력을 강화하도록 장려한다는 점과 단기간에 공공 건강의 놀라운 일을 이룰 수 있다는 것을 깨닫게 되었다는 점이다. 예를 들어, 콩고 민주공화국에서 약 20%의 아이들이 10년간의 장기 내전이 시작된 1997년에 홍역 백신을 맞았다. 그러나 2007년까지 이 수치는 80%에 달했다. 영양실조를 치유하고 모기장을 배분하는 등의 건강을 위한 다른 조치에 대한 역사를 보면 이와 비슷한 이야기를 들여다 볼 수 있다.

본문 원문분석 예 및 실전 응용문제와 분석란 이용

이 책의 대표적인 특징인 단락별 원문분석의 예, 그리고 실전 응용문제 예를 먼저 살펴보자.

[원문(지문)분석 예]

원문과 해설을 같은 눈높이에 두고, 문장과 문장의 유기적 관계를 밝히는 내용을 숫자로 표시하여 학습자가 글을 읽으면서, 원문과 분석내용을 손쉽게 파악할 수 있도록 했다. 또한 원문 중 강조하고자 하는 내용은 오른쪽에 별도로 설명을 첨부했다.

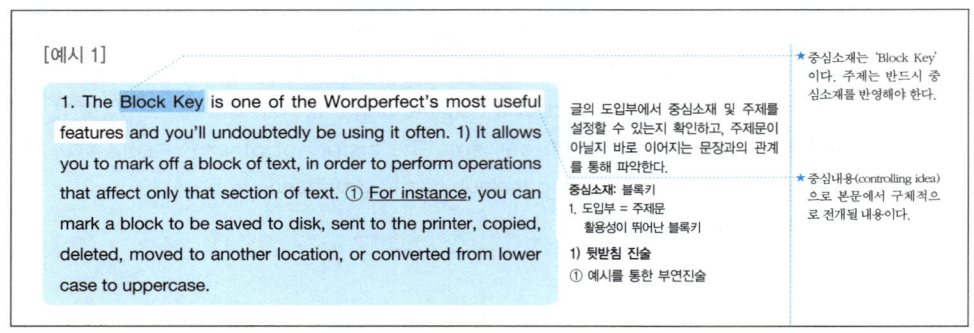

[실전 응용문제 예]

본서는 영문독해에 필요한 이론적 사항을 간략히 다룬 후 실전문제 풀이로 바로 넘어가는 시중의 대부분 교재와 달리, 각 장에 소개되는 영어권 글쓰기 이론을 학습한 후 위와 같이 예시지문을 통해서 확인하게 하는 동시에 학습자 스스로 적용해 볼 수 있는 실전응용문제를 제공했다. 또한 각 실전응용문제에는 아래와 같이 원문(지문)분석란을 두어 각 장에서 배운 사항을 학습자 스스로 적용·확인할 수 있도록 구성했다.

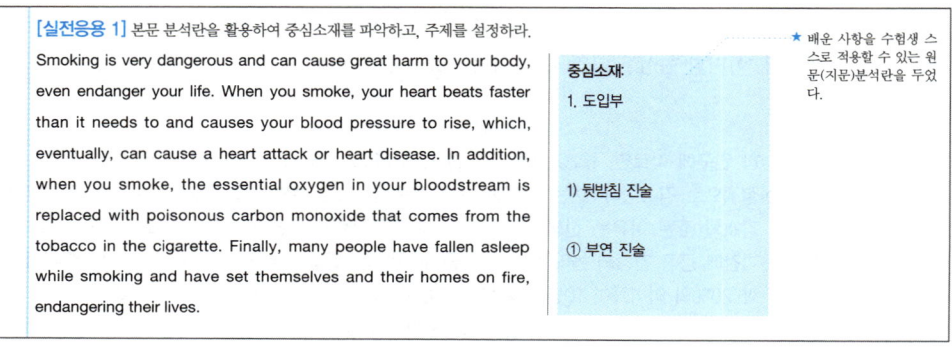

TABLE OF CONTENTS

Part 1 글의 구성요소 분석과 실전응용 연습문제 12

1. 주제와 중심소재의 폭 14
2. 중심내용 바탕으로 중심소재 범위설정 17
3. 중심소재와 중심내용을 드러내는 주제문 22
4. 글의 구조와 주제문과의 관계 28
5. 주제문과 뒷받침 문장 47
6. 부연진술 61
7. 통일성과 응집성 65
8. 일반진술과 구체적 진술 72
9. 사실·의견·신념·편견의 구별 79
10. 요지를 이끄는 시그널 연구 83
11. 글의 제목 105
12. 글 전개방식 110
13. 글의 종류 140
14. 글의 유형 152

Part 2 실전대비 유형별 문제 174

- Test 1 주제를 고르는 문제 176
- Test 2 요지를 고르는 문제 193
- Test 3 제목을 고르는 문제 202
- Test 4 내용일치·세부사항 확인 문제 216
- Test 5 실전 종합문제 233

· 별책 ·

⟨Part 1⟩ 실전응용 연습문제 분석 및 해설(원문해석·정답포함) 4
⟨Part 2⟩ 유형별 문제 분석 및 해설(원문해석·정답포함) 128

PART 1
글의 **구성요소 분석**과 **실전**응용 연습**문제**

1	주제와 중심소재의 폭 •	14
2	중심내용 바탕으로 중심소재 범위설정 •	17
3	중심소재와 중심내용을 드러내는 주제문 •	22
4	글의 구조와 주제문과의 관계 •	28
5	주제문과 뒷받침 문장 •	47
6	부연진술 •	61
7	통일성과 응집성 •	65
8	일반진술과 구체적 진술 •	72
9	사실 · 의견 · 신념 · 편견의 구별 •	79
10	요지를 이끄는 시그널 연구 •	83
11	글의 제목 •	105
12	글 전개방식 •	110
13	글의 종류 •	140
14	글의 유형 •	152

1 주제와 중심소재의 폭

일반적으로 주제란 글의 중심소재를 말하지만, 주어진 지문을 바탕으로 주제를 설정할 때, 중심소재 자체를 주제로 설정했을 경우 주제의 폭이 지나치게 포괄적일 수 있기에 본문의 중심내용을 바탕으로 좀 더 구체적인 주제를 설정할 필요가 있다. 예를 들어, 인터넷 PC방에 관한 글을 쓴다고 하자. 본문의 중심내용은 청소년에게 미치는 인터넷 PC방의 유해성을 다루고 있다. 이때, 중심소재인 '인터넷 PC방' 자체를 주제로 잡을 경우 지나치게 포괄적인 주제가 된다. 주제를 설정할 때는 중심소재를 먼저 설정하고, 중심내용을 바탕으로 제시된 지문 전체를 포괄하면서도 구체적인 주제를 설정해야 한다. 중심소재와 주제의 관계는 다음과 같다고 볼 수 있다.

주제 = 중심소재의 폭을 좁힌 것

즉, 주제를 설정한다는 말은 포괄적 개념인 중심소재를 먼저 파악하고 본문의 내용(중심내용)을 바탕으로 '중심소재의 폭'을 좁힌다는 말과 같다. 미래 내용 삽입 주제의 폭과 관련된 내용은 2장에서 좀 더 자세히 살펴보기로 하고, 다양한 예문을 통해서 중심소재와 주제를 설정해보자.

* **중심소재 찾는 방법**

도입부 | '뭘' 가지고 이야기 하는가?

연역식 사고를 지향하는 서양의 글은 포괄적/일반적 진술에서 구체적 진술로 전개된다. 글의 도입부에서 언제나 포괄적 주제인 "중심소재"를 파악해야 하는데, 이를 파악하는 방법 중 하나는 "'뭘' 가지고 이야기 하는가?"에 대한 답변을 이끌어내면 자연스레 중심소재를 파악할 수 있다.

중심소재 파악 ⇒ '뭘' 가지고 이야기 하는가?

[예시 1]

1. The Block Key is one of the Wordperfect's most useful features and you'll undoubtedly be using it often. 1) It allows you to mark off a block of text, in order to perform operations that affect only that section of text. ① For instance, you can mark a block to be saved to disk, sent to the printer, copied, deleted, moved to another location, or converted from lower case to uppercase.

글의 도입부에서 중심소재 및 주제를 설정할 수 있는지 확인하고, 주제문이 아닐지 바로 이어지는 문장과의 관계를 통해 파악한다.

중심소재: Block Key
1. 도입부 = 주제문
 - 블록키는 유용한 기능 중 하나이다.
1) 뒷받침 진술
① 부연예시

★중심소재는 'Block Key'이다. 주제는 반드시 중심소재를 반영해야 한다.

★중심내용(controlling idea)으로 본문에서 구체적으로 전개될 내용이다.

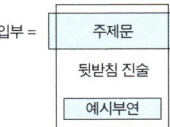

| 해설
본문은 중심소재인 '블록키'를 중심으로 다양한 기능을 설명하는 글이다. 첫 번째 문장을 주시하도록 한다. 주제 : **블록키**의 다양한 기능

| 해석
블록키는 워드퍼펙트의 가장 유용한 특징 중 하나여서, 이 키를 틀림없이 자주 사용하게 될 것이다. 이 키를 활용하여 텍스트 중의 한 블록을 표시하여 그 블록에만 관련된 작업을 수행할 수 있다. 예를 들면, 어떤 한 블록을 표시하여 디스크에 저장하거나, 인쇄기로 보내거나, 복사하거나, 삭제하거나, 다른 곳으로 이동시키거나, 소문자를 대문자로 전환할 수 있다.

[예시 2]

1. The word liberty is often interpreted incorrectly. 1) The dictionary gives many exact definitions of the word; briefly, it means "freedom from restraint or control." Such a brief definition leads to misinterpretation. ① Many people think liberty means that they may do whatever they like regardless of the effects. 2. Liberty is not uncontrolled freedom.

중심소재: 자유(liberty)
1. 도입부 = 현상
 - 자유에 대한 잘못된 통념 지적
1) 배경(원인)
① 결과
 자유 = 방종
2. **글쓴이의 견해**(요지)
 자유는 '통제' 안에서 누리는 것이다.

★중심소재는 '자유'이며, 중심내용을 고려하여 주제의 폭을 설정한다.

★일반통념의 내용은 글쓴이가 궁극적으로 반대하는 내용에 해당하는 경우가 많다.

| 해설
첫 번째 문장에서 중심소재인 "liberty"를 파악할 수 있다. 이를 중심으로 주제를 설정하는데, 본문은 자유에 대한 일반인들의 생각이 어떻게 형성되었고, 무엇이 잘못되었는지를 지적하면서 자유의 옳은 정의를 내리는 통념비판의 글이다. 주제 : **자유**에 대한 올바른 정의

| 해석
자유라는 단어는 종종 잘못 해석된다. 사전에는 이 단어에 대한 정확한 정의가 많이 나와 있지만, 간단히 말해, 그것은 '제약이나 통제가 없음'을 의미한다. 이렇게 간단하게 정의를 내리다 보면 잘못 해석하게 된다. 자유는 어떤 결과를 초래하든 자신이 하고 싶은 대로 해도 됨을 의미한다고 생각하는 사람들이 많다. 그러나 자유는 방종이 아니다.

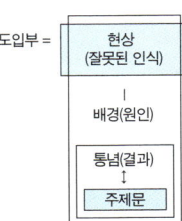

[예시 3]

'불면증'에 관한 내용으로 중심내용(controlling idea)을 고려하여 주제의 폭을 설정한다.

도입부 = 주제문

도입부에선 주제문의 여부를 떠나 중심 소재를 파악하는 데 주력한다.

> 1. Another way to fight insomnia is to exercise every day.
> 1) Muscular relaxation is an important part of sleep. Daily exercise leaves your muscles pleasantly relaxed and ready for sleep.

중심소재: Insomnia
1. 도입부 = 주제문
1) 뒷받침 진술

| 해설

첫 번째 문장에서 주제를 파악할 수 있는 두괄식의 구성을 취하는 지문이다. "Another way to fight insomnia is to exercise every day."에서 밑줄 친 문장을 통해 주제를 설정할 수 있다. 주제 : **불면증**을 퇴치하는 방법

| 해석

불면증을 치료하는 또 하나의 방법은 매일 운동하는 것이다. 근육 이완이 수면의 한 중요한 부분이다. 매일 운동을 하면 근육이 쾌적하게 이완되고 쉽게 잠을 이루게 된다.

| 핵심 정리 |

위에서 제시한 여러 예문에서 알 수 있듯이 **주제는 중심소재 중심으로 그 폭을 조절한(줄인) 표현**이라는 점을 반드시 기억한다.

[실전응용 1] 본문 분석란을 활용하여 중심소재를 파악하고, 주제를 설정하라.

Smoking is very dangerous and can cause great harm to your body, even endanger your life. When you smoke, your heart beats faster than it needs to and causes your blood pressure to rise, which, eventually, can cause a heart attack or heart disease. In addition, when you smoke, the essential oxygen in your bloodstream is replaced with poisonous carbon monoxide that comes from the tobacco in the cigarette. Finally, many people have fallen asleep while smoking and have set themselves and their homes on fire, endangering their lives.

중심소재:
1. 도입부

1) 뒷받침 진술
①
②
③

[실전응용 2] 본문 분석란을 활용하여 중심소재를 파악하고, 주제를 설정하라.

The owl and the crow prey on each other's weakness. At night, owls often make dinner of crows, which cannot see well in the dark. During the day, it's a different story. Vengeful groups of crows attack and kill sleeping owls, which are resting for another night of hunting.

1. 주제문
1) 뒷받침 진술
①
②

2 중심내용을 바탕으로 중심소재 범위설정

본 장에서는 1장에서 잠시 다룬 **주제의 범위**를 좀 더 자세히 살펴보도록 하자. 중심소재 자체를 주제로 삼았을 경우, 제시문의 내용에 비추어 지나치게 포괄적인 주제가 될 수 있다고 지적했다. 다양한 예를 통해 주제의 폭을 설정하는 방법을 알아보자.

1. Controlling Idea에 대한 이해

Controlling Idea는 본문에 전개될 중심내용을 포괄하는 문장을 말한다. 아래의 문장을 통해 Controlling Idea에 대한 개념을 먼저 잡도록 하자.

> 주제문 : There are five steps to master Math.

위 문장에서 중심소재는 'Math'이고, 글의 주제는 "수학을 정복하는 다섯 단계"인데, 본문에 전개될 내용은 다섯 단계에 대한 구체적 진술에 해당한다. 여기서 본문에 대한 예측이 가능한 정보를 제공하는 것이 바로 'Controlling Idea'이다.

```
There are five steps to master Math.

Step 1. _____.
Step 2. _____.
Step 3. _____.
Step 4. _____.
Step 5. _____.
```

★ 중심내용(controlling idea)으로 이를 바탕으로 본문 내용을 예측할 수 있다.

★ 포괄적 주제에 해당하는 중심소재이다.

★ 중심내용의 구체적 진술에 해당하는 본문이다.

2. 이제 앞에서 배운 'Controlling Idea'를 바탕으로 주제의 폭을 좁히는 연습을 하도록 하자.

[예시 1]

일반적으로 글의 도입부★에서 중심내용에 해당하는 정보, 즉 본문에서 구체적으로 다뤄질 정보를 제시하는 경우가 많다. 이 지문의 경우 첫 번째 문장에서 '맹점이란 단순히 지식의 부족에서 발생하는 것이 아니다'라는 정보를 제시하고 있다. 고로, 이후 문장에서는 맹점이 어디에서 기인하는지 그 원인을 밝혀주는 내용이 올 것을 예상할 수 있다.

도입부 = 중심소재 도출
주제문
뒷받침 예시

1. A blind spot is not the same as a simple lack of knowledge. 1) A blind spot emerges from a resistance to learning in a particular area. At the root of many of our blind spots are a number of emotions or attitudes fear being the most obvious, but also pride, self-satisfaction, and anxiety. A manager, for example, might have unsurpassed knowledge in the financial field, but her understanding of people management might be limited. Her people find her cold and aloof and want her to become more consultative and involved with the team. She, however, is not willing to accept feedback about her management style and refuses to even consider the prospect of changing her management style.

중심소재: blind spot
1. 도입부
맹점에 대한 잘못된 인식 지적
1) 주제문 : 맹점의 발생 원인(주제)
맹점은 특성 분야의 학습 거부로 '두려움, 자부심, 자기만족, 근심'과 같은 감정 또는 태도에서 발생
① 뒷받침 예시(for example)

| 해설
글의 도입부, 특히 첫 번째 문장에서 '맹점'에 관한 글임을 파악할 수 있다. 중심소재 자체를 주제로 설정했을 때, 본문에서 전개되는 구체적 내용에 비추어 지나치게 포괄적인 주제가 될 수 있으므로 이후 전개되는 중심내용(Controlling Idea)을 바탕으로 주제의 폭을 좁혀야 한다.

| 해석
맹점은 단순한 지식의 부족과는 다르다. 맹점은 특정 분야의 학습에 대한 거부로부터 나타난다. 많은 맹점의 근원에는 수많은 감정이나 태도들이 존재한다. 가장 명백한 것은 두려움이지만, 또한 자존심, 자기만족 그리고 근심도 존재한다. 예를 들어, 어떤 매니저는 재정 분야에서는 탁월한 지식을 가지고 있을지도 모르지만, 직원 관리에 대한 이해는 제한적일 수도 있다. 직원들은 그녀가 차갑고 냉정하다고 여기고 보다 상담을 잘해주며, 팀의 일에 열심히 관여하기를 원한다. 그러나 그녀는 자신의 관리 스타일에 대한 피드백을 기꺼이 받아들이려고 하지 않고 심지어는 관리 스타일을 변화시킬 가능성을 고려하길 거부한다.

[예시 2]

글의 도입부에서 중심내★용을 파악할 수 있다는 것은 글 전체의 내용이 어떤 식으로 전개될지를 예측할 수 있다는 말과 같다.

1. Mr. Brown wanted his students Ⓐ to learn math in the context of real life. 1) He felt it was not enough for them just to work out problems from a book. To show his students how math could really help them, he held several contests during the year. The contests allowed his students to have

중심소재: Math
1. 도입부 = 주제문
첫 번째 문장에서 '수학 학습'과 관련된 글임을 파악할 수 있다. 특히 본문의 경우 첫 번째 문장에서 중심내용을 함께 제시하는 주제문을 파악할 수 있다.
Ⓐ 중심내용: 실생활 측면에서의 수학 학습

fun while they practiced math and raised money. ① Once he filled a fishbowl with marbles, asked the students to guess how many marbles there were, and awarded a free lunch to the winner. ② Another time they entered a contest to guess how many soda cans the back of a pickup truck hold. To win, they had to practice their skills at estimating, multiplying, dividing, and measuring. They used most of the prize money for an end-of-the-year field trip.

1) 뒷받침 진술
주제문에서 밝힌 '실생활 속 수학 학습'에 대한 구체적 진술이 이어진다: 콘테스트를 통해 실생활에 적용할 수 있는 수학 학습에 관한 구체적 예(①, ②)를 제시하고 있다.

| 해석
브라운 선생님은 학생들이 수학을 실생활에서 배우기를 원했다. 그는 책에서 문제만 푸는 것은 충분치 않다고 생각했다. 그는 수학이 어떻게 학생들을 돕는지를 보여주기 위해서 그 해 동안 다양한 콘테스트를 개최했다. 콘테스트를 통해서 학생들은 수학을 연습하고 돈을 모으는 동안 (수학을) 즐길 수 있었다. 일단 선생님은 어항을 구슬로 가득 채우고 학생들에게 구슬이 몇 개인지를 추측해보라고 하고, 맞힌 학생에게 상으로 무료 점심을 주었다. 또 다른 콘테스트는 참여한 학생들이 픽업트럭의 뒤에 얼마나 많은 음료를 담을 수 있는지 추측하는 것이었다. 승리하기 위해서는 그들은 계산, 곱하기, 나누기, 측정에 관한 기술을 연습해야 했다. 그들은 상금 대부분을 연말 현장학습을 위해 사용했다.

[예시 3]

1. It is hard for street trees to survive with only foot-square holes in the pavement. The average life of a street tree surrounded by concrete and asphalt is seven to fifteen years. 1) Many factors underground determine if a street tree will make it. ① ⓐ If the soil is so dense that the roots cannot get in, it will surely die. If they can get in, there is a better chance of getting the water and nutrients needed to survive. ⓑ Another question is whether adequate water supplies are getting into the growing area. Some of the water comes from underground sources and some from rain, and it is hard to measure where the tree is getting it. Of course, if the roots get into the sewers, they can get everything they need.

중심소재: Street Trees
1. 도입부 ← 중심소재 도출
도심지 가로수의 열악한 생존환경 + 평균 수명.
1) 일반진술(주제문)
가로수의 생존에 필요한 요소
① 구체적 진술
ⓐ 토양
ⓑ 적절한 양의 물 공급

★ 중심내용(controlling idea)에 해당한다. 이어서 가로수의 생존에 영향을 미치는 '조건(factors)'에 관한 내용이 전개될 것을 예상할 수 있다.

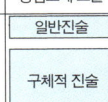

| 해석
도로에 있는 가로수는 단지 1제곱피트만 흙으로 덮여 있어 살기가 어렵다. 콘크리트와 아스팔트로 덮인 가로수는 평균 수명이 7년에서 15년 정도이다. 땅 아래 많은 요인이 가로수가 잘 살 수 있을지를 결정한다. 만약에 토양이 너무 단단하면(밀집) 나무가 뿌리를 내릴 수 없다. 만약 나무가 뿌리를 내리면 생존에 필요한 물과 영양분을 얻을 수 있다. 또 다른 문제는 나무가 자라는 곳에 적당한 물 공급이 되느냐이다. 어떤 물 공급은 지하수로부터 오고 어떤 경우는 빗물인데, 나무가 어디에서 수분을 취하는지를 측정하기는 어렵다. 물론 뿌리가 하수구에 뻗어있으면 그것은 필요한 모든 것을 얻을 수 있다.

[실전응용 1] 주제를 설정하시오.

These days, it is important to know something about computers. There are a number of ways to learn. Some companies have computer classes at work. Also, most universities offer day and night courses in computer science. Another way to learn is from a book. There are many books about computers in book stores and libraries. Or, you can learn from a friend. After a few hours of practice, you too can work with computers. You may not be an expert, but you can have fun!

중심소재:
1. 도입부

1) 주제문

① 뒷받침 진술

[실전응용 2] 주제를 설정하시오.

There are at least four things which are more or less under our own control and which are essential to happiness. The first is some moral standard by which to guide our actions. The second is some satisfactory home life in the form of good relations with family or friends. The third is some form of work which justifies our existence to our own country and makes us good citizens. The fourth thing is some degree of leisure and the use of it in some way that makes us happy. To succeed in making a good use of our leisure will not compensate for failure in any one of the other three things to which I have referred, but a reasonable amount of leisure and a good use of it is an important contribution to a happy life.

중심소재:
1. 도입부

1) 뒷받침 진술
①
②
③
④
Ⓐ

[실전응용 3] 주제를 설정하시오.

One way to accomplish teaching morals and values to your kids is to give them on-the-spot lessons in honesty. For example, your four-year-old has just walked out of the toy store with a car you didn't buy. You notice the car in his hand as you are buckling him into his safety seat. Do not make excuses for your child and laugh it off, saying to yourself, "He's only four—he didn't mean to steal it." That may be true—young children don't completely comprehend the notion of stealing—but if you don't deal with what he did, you are letting him know that it's okay to take something that's not his. Hold your child accountable for his action. Explain to him in a calm manner that you are disappointed in him for taking the toy from the store. Just hearing those words can have a deep effect on your child.

중심소재:

1. 도입부
1) 뒷받침 진술

Further explain that taking the car was wrong and that he needs to return it to the store manager and apologize immediately.

[실전응용 4] 주제를 설정하시오.

If there are more people in the world, then there must be more food for these people. But food is already a problem in today's world. A third of the world's population is very hungry, because there is not enough food. Ten thousand people die of hunger every day in some parts of the world. But in other parts of the world, people become ill or die because they are too fat. Some countries have no food, but others have too much, and throw it away.

중심소재:
1. 도입부

1) 주제문

2.

[실전응용 5] 주제를 설정하시오.

Collecting can open new worlds for children. Collecting stamps, for example, shows them cultures or historical events of a country. Plant or animal specimens teach them about the natural world. Collecting also gives children opportunities to learn skills that can be used every day. While playing with collections such as dolls, comic books, stickers, and so on, children can organize their treasures by size, shape, or color. This will teach them to see the world from different points of view. Thinking about the relationships among their pieces, they may realize things in the world are connected with each other.

중심소재:
1. 주제문

1) 뒷받침 진술

3 중심소재와 중심내용을 드러내는 주제문

주제문의 구성은 다음과 같다.

> Topic Sentence = Topic + Controlling Idea

주제문의 구성은 위에서 보는 바와 같이, **포괄적 주제에 해당하는 중심소재**와 **중심내용**으로 구성된다.

1) 주제를 설정하기 위해서는 앞 장에서 이미 언급했듯이, 중심소재를 파악해야 한다. 중심소재를 파악한 후 중심내용(Controlling Idea)을 고려하면서 주제의 폭을 설정한다(제2장을 참고한다).

2) 중심내용은 본문에서 다뤄질 핵심 내용을 말한다. 주제문에 드러나는 핵심내용을 바탕으로 앞으로 전개될 본문의 내용을 예측할 수 있다(제2장을 참고한다).

주제문을 파악한다는 것은 기본적으로 글의 중심소재를 중심으로 주제를 설정할 수 있는 동시에 본문에서 전개될 중심내용을 예측할 수 있다는 이야기이다. 일반적으로 수험영어의 80~90%가 비문학 영역이라는 점과 비문학 중 많게는 60~70% 이상이 두괄식 구성을 취한다는 점을 고려할 때 주제문 파악은 곧 글 전체의 내용이 어떤 식으로 전개될지 방향성을 설정할 수 있는 청사진(blueprint)의 역할을 한다는 점에서 그 중요성은 굳이 언급할 필요가 없다.

[주제문 분석의 예]

Topic Sentence : <u>Industrial waste</u> <u>harms underwater creatures</u>.
　　　　　　　　　A (Topic)　　　　B (Controlling Idea)

분석 | A: 주제(글에서 다루려고 하는 내용): **산업폐기물의 유해성**
　　　 B: 중심내용(Topic을 통해 글쓴이가 본문에서 궁극적으로 이야기하려고 하는 내용)
　　　 산업폐기물이 수중 생물에게 미치는 악영향

주제문	Industrial waste harms underwater creatures.
뒷받침 진술	산업폐기물(원인)이 수중생명체에 미치는 부정적인 현상(결과)을 구체적으로 진술한다. 인과의 글 전개방식을 예상할 수 있다.

※ 중심소재는 '산업폐기물'이고 주제는 "산업폐기물의 유해성"이다.

※ 본문에서 구체적으로 다룰 중심내용에 해당한다.

주제문은 전체 본문이 어떤 내용으로 전개될지 예측할 수 있는 중요한 근거가 된다. 위에서 보다시피, 주제문은 말 그대로 글이 다루려고 하는 내용과 구체적으로 어떤 내용이 본문에 전개될지에 대한 정보를 제공해 준다. 주제문이 문두에 위치한다는 점과 전체 내용에 대한 청사진을 그릴 수 있다는 점에서 다른 이의 글을 읽는데 가장 기본이 된다고 볼 수 있다.

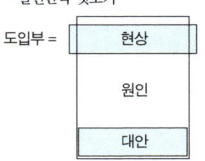

현상+원인 = 주제문
대안 + 요지

• 인과의 글 전개방식

[응용 1]

You can <u>avoid burglaries</u> by <u>taking certain precautions</u>.
　　　　　　A (Topic)　　　　　　B (Controlling Idea)

분석 | A: 주제: 강도를 피하는 방법
　　　B: 중심내용: 강도를 피하는 예방책
　　　본문의 내용 예측: 글쓴이는 '특정한 예방 조치'에 관한 뒷받침 문장(Supporting Sentence) 및 부연진술(Supporting Details)을 다룰 것을 예상할 수 있다.

주제문	You can avoid burglaries by taking certain precautions.
뒷받침 진술	강도를 피하는 구체적 예방책에 대한 내용이 자세히 다뤄진다. 글 전개방식으로 나열을 활용할 수 있다. 예방조치 1. ＿＿＿＿＿＿＿＿＿. 예방조치 2. ＿＿＿＿＿＿＿＿＿. 예방조치 3. ＿＿＿＿＿＿＿＿＿.

★ 중심소재는 '강도'이며, 주제는 '강도를 피하는 방법'이다.

★ 중심내용으로 강도를 피하는 예방책을 구체적으로 진술할 것을 예상할 수 있다.

• 실전단락 엿보기

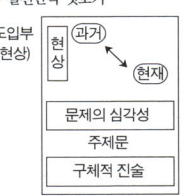

글의 도입부에서 조사를 바탕으로 과거에 비해 강도의 빈도수가 증가했다는 '현상' 제시 후 주제문으로 이어지는 글 전개를 생각할 수 있다.

[응용 2]

The cause of air pollution in Korea is the exhaust fume.
　　　　　A (Topic)　　　　　　　　B (Controlling Idea)

분석 | A: 주제: 공해의 원인
　　　B: 중심내용: 공해의 주범인 '자동차 매연'
　　　본문의 내용 예측: 자신의 주장에 대한 근거를 확보하기 위해서 이후 다양한 방법(객관적 자료 제시, 실험 등)을 통해 '자동차의 매연이 공해의 원인' 임을 설명할 것이다.

주제문	The cause of air pollution in Korea is the exhaust fume.
뒷받침 진술	현상의 결과인 공해의 심각성을 지적한 후 이에 대한 원인을 다양한 방법을 통해 밝히는 내용으로 전개된다.

• 실전단락 엿보기

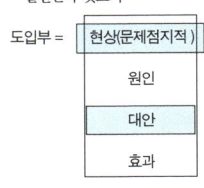

현상+원인 = 주제문
대안 = 요지

• 실전단락 엿보기

```
도입부 = 개인의 경험담을 통한
        구체적 사례
           ↓
         주제문
           ↓
        구체적 진술
```

[응용 3]

<u>Fixing a flat tire on a car</u> is easy if you <u>follow these steps</u>.
　　　　A (Topic)　　　　　　　　　B (Controlling Idea)

분석 | A: 주제: 펑크 난 자동차 타이어 수리
B: 중심내용: 여러 단계를 통해 수리할 수 있다.
본문의 내용 예측: 주제문에서 언급한 펑크 난 타이어를 고치는 구체적인 방법에 대한 내용이 전개될 것을 예측할 수 있다.

★중심소재는 펑크 난 '타이어'이고 주제는 '펑크 난 타이어 수리 방법'이다.

★본문에서 구체적으로 밝힐 중심내용에 해당한다.

주제문	Fixing a flat tire on a car is easy if you follow these steps.
뒷받침 진술	여러 단계를 거쳐 펑크 난 타이어를 수리하는 구체적 내용이 전개된다. Step 1. _____. Step 2. _____. Step 3. _____.

[응용 4]

<u>Effective leadership</u> requires <u>three qualities</u> that anyone can develop.
　　A (Topic)　　　　　　　B (Controlling Idea)

분석 | A: 주제: 효과적인 지도력의 조건
B: 중심내용: 효과적인 지도력을 위해 필요한 3가지 특징
본문의 내용 예측: 주제문에서 언급한 3가지 특징을 나열의 전개방식을 통해서 차례로 설명할 것을 예측할 수 있다.

★중심소재는 '지도력'이고 '효과적인 지도력의 조건'에 관한 내용이다.

★중심내용은 효과적인 지도력의 조건에 해당하는 세 가지 특징이며, 이에 대한 구체적 진술이 본문에서 다뤄질 것을 예상할 수 있다.

주제문	Effective leadership requires three qualities that anyone can develop.
뒷받침 진술	효과적인 지도력을 위한 세 가지 특징을 자세히 기술한다. Quality 1. _____. Quality 2. _____. Quality 3. _____.

[응용 5]

<u>Industrial waste poured into Lake Ohio</u> has led to <u>dramatic changes in its ability to support</u>
          A (Topic)   B (Controlling Idea)
<u>marine ife</u>.

분석 | A: 주제: 오하이오 호수에 유입된 산업폐기물의 영향
B: 중심내용: 산업폐기물의 영향으로 인한 수중 생명체를 유지할 능력의 급격한 변화
본문의 내용 예측: 주제문에서 밝힌 '호수에 유입된 폐기물로 인한 수중 생물을 지탱할 수 있는 호수의 능력 악화'를 본문에서 구체적으로 다룰 것이다.

주제문	Industrial waste poured into Lake Ohio has led to dramatic changes in its ability to support marine life.
뒷받침 진술	오하이오 호수가 산업폐기물로 오염된 실태(결과)를 고발하고, 이로 인해 호수에 미친 나쁜 영향력을 구체적으로 진술한다.

[실전연습] 아래 문장은 모두 주제문이다. Topic과 Controlling Idea를 구분하고, 전체 글의 구조를 파악하시오.

예제 1 | **Camping can be an inexpensive vacation.**

주제 :
중심내용 :

주제문	
뒷받침 진술	

예제 2 | Air pollution in Mexico City is the worst in the world for a number of reasons.

주제 :
중심내용 :

주제문	
뒷받침 진술	

예제 3 | There are several enjoyable ways to travel between the US and Korea.

주제 :
중심내용 :

주제문	
뒷받침 진술	

예제 4 | In order to fully explore the wreck of the Titanic, scientists must address several problems.

주제 :
중심내용 :

주제문	
뒷받침 진술	

예제 5 | **Animals in danger of becoming extinct come from a wide range of countries.**

주제 :

중심내용 :

서론	
본론	
결론	

| 참고

Good Topic Sentence와 Poor Topic Sentence의 구별

주제문에는 'Good'과 'Poor'가 있다. 이 둘을 구별하는 잣대는 주제문의 정의를 보면 쉽게 판단할 수 있다. 주제문은 이미 배운 바와 같이 'a Topic + Controlling Idea(s)'로 구성된다. 즉, '본문에서 다루는 내용'과 '본문의 핵심내용'이 바로 주제문이다. 여기서 두 정보가 제대로 제시된 것은 'Good', 빈약한 것은 'Poor'로 구분된다. 일반적으로 'Controlling Idea'를 제대로 전달하지 못할 때 'Poor'라고 말한다. 아래 예를 살펴보자.

1. It rains too much in Vancouver.

   빈약한 주제문이다. '비가 지나치게 많이 온다.'는 정보를 가지고 무엇을 이야기하려는지 불분명하기 때문이다. 단순히 '비가 많이 온다.'는 말을 하려는 것인지 아니면, 이것 때문에 발생하는 문제점에 대해 이야기를 하려는 것인지 모호하다. 만약 '밴쿠버에는 비가 많이 온다.'는 정보 자체만을 제시하는 것이라면 다른 지역과 밴쿠버의 연 강수량에 대한 객관적 자료를 제시하는 뒷받침 문장의 주제문으로 설정할 수 있다. 하지만 문제가 되는 부분은 'too much'이다. 'too much'는 일반적으로 부정적 견해가 반영된 표현이기 때문에 이에 대한 글쓴이의 견해가 드러나야 한다. 다음과 같이 바꾸어야 한다.

   → The frequent rain in Vancouver can be hard on the citizer's mood.

2. Sunny days in Vancouver are almost like a festival, since they are quite rare.

   'rare' 부분을 좀 더 명확히 할 필요가 있지만, 주제문으로 설정할 수 있다.

3. Why do people think they can save money on their clothing in Vancouver?

   중심내용을 좀 더 명확하게 할 필요가 있다. 즉, 글쓴이가 이 질문에 대해 궁극적으로 전달하려는 'Controlling Idea' 자체가 빠져 있다. 이 문장은 주제문이라기보다 글의 도입부에서 독자의 주의를 환기시키는 '문제제기'로 보아야 한다.

4. Everyone in Vancouver loves sunny days.

   'everyone'이라고 단정 지어서 말할 수 없다. 이는 밴쿠버에 사는 모든 사람이 햇볕이 드는 날을 좋아하는지 다 알아볼 수 없기 때문이다. 주제문에서는 증명할 수 없는 극단적 표현을 피해야 한다. 다음과 같이 손을 볼 수 있다.

   → Most people in Vancouver loves sunny days.

5. Summer in Vancouver is very beautiful, for there is often lots of sunshine.

   주제문으로 적절하다.

6. Why Vancouver weather can help plants to grow.

   주제문이라기보다 '제목'으로 적절하다. 주어진 문장을 바탕으로 주제문을 만들고 싶으면, 'Controlling Idea'에 해당하는 'why' 부분을 명확히 할 필요가 있다.

4 글의 구조와 주제문과의 관계

글의 구조는 주제문의 위치에 따라 결정된다.
1) 주제문이 문장 첫머리에 위치할 때는 두괄식의 구조를 취한다.
2) 주제문이 문미에 위치할 때는 미괄식의 구조를 취한다.
3) 주제문이 문장 첫머리와 문미에 위치할 때는 양괄식의 구조를 취한다. 이때 글 전체는 '서론 – 본론 – 결론'의 삼단구조를 취한다.
4) 주제문이 글의 중간에 위치할 때는 중괄식의 구조를 취한다.
5) 주제문이 본문 여기저기에 등장하는 경우 무괄식이라 한다.

각 항목을 자세히 살펴보자.

1. 두괄식

주 제 문 = 포괄적 주제(중심 소재) + 중심내용
중심내용에 대한   뒷받침 진술 구체적 진술

영어권 글에서 가장 정형화된 형태의 구조가 바로 두괄식이다. 글쓴이는 자신이 전달하고자 하는 글의 요지를 문장 첫머리에 제시한 후 이에 대한 뒷받침 진술을 제시한다. 이러한 글의 구조로 인해 Topic(주제)과 Controlling Idea(중심내용)로 구성된 주제문이 문장 첫머리에 나오며, 독자는 중심내용을 바탕으로 본문에 전개될 내용을 예측할 수 있다.

[예시 1]

1. Most people have a vase or two in a cupboard, <u>but lots of things can be turned into stylish containers for a flower arrangement</u>, so before you rush out to buy anything, look around your own home. 1) <u>For instance</u>, ① <u>goldfish bowls</u> look stunning filled with flower heads or petals, magnifying their contents. ② <u>Wine, milk, mineral water, or olive oil bottles</u> look particularly good with one or two stems in them. Try a collection of bottles in various shapes and sizes, lined up on a shelf or grouped on a table. ③ <u>An old teapot</u> which has lost its lid becomes an ideal container for a bunch of roses picked from the garden.

중심소재: Vase

1. **도입부 = 주제문**(But 이후 주제문)
집안의 많은 것들이 멋진 꽃병이 될 수 있다.

1) **뒷받침 진술**
예시(①, ②, ③)를 통해 중심내용에서 밝힌 내용을 뒷받침하고 있다.

도입부 = | 주제문 |
뒷받침 예시
①_____
②_____
③_____

| 해석
대부분 사람들은 찬장에 한두 개의 꽃병을 가지고 있지만 많은 것들이 꽃꽂이를 위한 멋진 용기가 될 수 있으므로, 무언가를 사기 위해 달려나가기 전에, 당신 자신의 집을 둘러봐라. 예를 들어, 금붕어 어항은 내용물을 확대해 보여주므로, 꽃송이나 꽃잎으로 채워지면 멋져 보인다. 포도주, 우유, 먹는 샘물, 혹은 올리브유 병의 경우 그 속에 한두 개의 꽃가지를 넣으면 특히 괜찮게 보인다. 선반에 줄지어 놓여있거나 테이블 위에 모아 놓을 다양한 모양과 크기의 병을 수집해 봐라. 뚜껑이 없어진 낡은 찻주전자가 정원에서 꺾은 장미 다발을 위한 이상적인 용기가 된다.

[예시 2]

1. In the critical area of food production, <u>new cooperative efforts in agricultural research and development are paying off</u>. 1) Food scientists are discovering that ① humankind is nowhere near the limits of plant, livestock, and soil productivity. There is still room to boost yields and learn how to use more efficiently the earth's acreage for animal and crop husbandry. ② Investigation of irrigation procedures, pest control, intercropping, and multicropping are several areas that are providing useful information for the world's farmers.

중심소재: Food Production

1. **주제문**
농업 R&D 분야에 새로운 협동적 노력이 결실을 맺고 있다.

1) **뒷받침 진술**
뒷받침 진술로 첫 번째 문장에서 제시된 새로운 연구·개발의 성과를 보고 있다는 점에 대한 구체적 진술(①, ②)이 이어진다.

| 해석
식량 생산의 중요 지역에서 농업 연구와 개발에서의 새로운 공동 노력이 성과를 올리고 있다. 식품 과학 연구자들은 인류는 식물, 가축 그리고 토양 생산성의 한계에 가까이 도달한 것은 아니라는 사실을 알아가고 있다. 생산량은 증대시키고 축산과 농사를 위해 지구의 경지를 보다 효율적으로 이용하는 방법을 알아낼 여지는 여전히 있다. 관개절차의 연구, 병충해 방제, 간작(間作) 그리고 다작은 세계의 농부들에게 유용한 정보를 제공하고 있는 여러 지역에서 이루어지고 있다.

[예시 3]

주제문의 중심 내용 (controlling idea)을 바탕으로 글 전개방식을 유추할 수 있다. ★

나열의 시그널을 확인한다. ★

역접이 아니라 강조용법의 'however' 임을 파악한다. ★

구체적 진술을 이끄는 시그널인 'when' 과 함께 'if, for' 를 기억해 둔다. ★

1. There are several things you can do to prevent your child from being bitten by insects. 1) The best protection against insect bites is ① to apply insect repellent to a child's skin and clothing. However, insect repellents should be used carefully on babies and young children. ② Another prevention technique involves avoiding areas where insects gather or nest. ③ In addition, when your child is doing outdoor activities, dress him in long pants and a lightweight long-sleeved shirt. Don't dress your child in clothing with bright colors or flowery prints which are known to attract insects.

중심소재: 곤충예방
1. 주제문
1) 뒷받침 진술
① 방법 1
② 방법 2
③ 방법 3

| 해설
두괄식 구성의 전형이다. 주제문의 위치에 따라 글의 구조가 결정되기도 하지만, 주제문의 내용을 바탕으로 글 전개방식을 유추할 수 있다는 점도 기억하도록 한다.

| 해석
아이가 곤충에 물리지 않도록 예방하는 방법이 몇 가지 있다. 곤충에 물리지 않도록 보호해주는 최선의 방법은 해충 퇴치제를 아이의 피부와 옷에 바르는 것이다. 하지만 해충 퇴치제는 아기와 어린아이들에게 주의해서 사용해야 한다. 또 다른 예방책은 해충이 모이고 알을 낳는 장소를 피하는 것이다. 또한, 당신의 아이가 야외 활동을 할 때에는 긴 바지와 가벼운 긴 팔 셔츠를 입히도록 한다. 해충을 유인한다고 알려진 밝은 색깔의 옷이나 꽃무늬 문양의 옷을 입히지 않도록 한다.

[보충학습]

구체적 진술을 이끄는 시그널 'when'
1. Living things naturally return to a state of balance. 1) When we are disturbed by forces acting on us, our inner machinery kicks in and returns us to a balanced state of equilibrium.

1. 일반진술
1) 구체적 진술(when)

| 해설
위의 제시된 지문에서 보다시피, 'when' 이 이끄는 문장은 바로 앞에 진술된 문장의 구체적 진술에 해당한다. 만약 글의 시작이 'When' 으로 시작할 경우, 구체적 진술로 시작하는 글로 파악할 수 있으며, 요지가 직접 드러나는 일반진술의 시점이 언제 시작하는지 파악하는 데 주목하도록 한다.

| 해석
생명체는 자연적으로 평형의 상태로 돌아가려는 성향을 보인다. 우리에게 작용하는 (외부의) 힘에 방해를 받을 때, 우리의 내부 기관이 작동하여 다시 균형의 상태인 평형으로 돌아간다.

[실전응용 1] 다음 글의 구조를 분석하시오.

Primitive man never looked out over the world and saw 'mankind' as a group and felt his common cause with his species. From the beginning he was a provincial who raised the barriers high. Whether it was a question of choosing a wife or of taking a head, the first and important distinction was between his own human group and those beyond the pale. His own group, with all its ways of behaving, was unique.

중심소재:

1. 도입부

1) 뒷받침 진술

[실전응용 2] 다음 글의 구조를 분석하시오.

As the impact of globalization spreads to every industry, business people around the world learn to expect tougher competition than they have ever faced before. Back when five or ten rivals could comfortably coexist in a single market, some would offer high-quality products at premium prices while others sold lesser goods for a discount. Today, most consumers and industrial buyers won't even consider low-quality goods, and it's hard to find a company that hasn't joined the quality movement.

중심소재:

1. 도입부

1) 뒷받침 진술

[실전응용 3] 다음 글의 구조를 분석하시오.

Even now, ancient India is still visible and accessible to us in a very direct sense. At the beginning of the twentieth century, some Indian communities still lived as all our primeval ancestors must once have lived, by hunting and gathering. The bullock-cart and potter's wheel of many villages today are much the same as those used 4,000 years ago. A caste-system whose main lines were set by about 1,000 B.C. still regulates the lives of millions, and even of some Indian Christians and Moslems. Gods and goddesses whose cults can be traced to the Stone Age are still worshipped at village shrines.

중심소재:

1. 도입부

1) 뒷받침 진술

[실전응용 4] 다음 글의 구조를 분석하시오.

The therapeutic value and healing powers of plants were demonstrated to me when I was a boy of about ten. I had developed an acute, persistent abdominal pain that did not respond readily to hospital medication. My mother had taken me to the city's central hospital on several occasions,

중심소재:

1. 도입부

where different drugs were tried on me. In total desperation, she took me to Egya Mensa, a well-known herbalist in my hometown in the western province of Ghana. This man was no stranger to the medical doctors at the hospital. He had earned the reputation of offering excellent help when they were confronted with difficult cases where Western medicine had failed to effect a cure.

1) 뒷받침 진술

[실전응용 5] 다음 글의 구조를 분석하시오.

The work of makeup artists ranges from highlighting the natural features of a film star to changing altogether actors' appearances to fit the characters they portray. In the black and white era of filmmaking, movies favored stars such as Katharine Hepburn and Lauren Bacall whose angular faces and prominent cheekbones caught the light and cast lovely shadows. With the advent of color, the emphasis shifted to the glowing complexion of Marilyn Monroe, Grace Kelly, and Kim Novak. The job of makeup artists, in either case, was to prepare these stars to face the camera by accentuating the telling features. At the same time, makeup artists have also created totally new faces for actors, making them seem older or younger and, in the case of horror films, turning normal people into vampires, werewolves, mummies, or other monsters.

중심소재:
1. 도입부

1) 뒷받침 문장

2. 미괄식

① 구체적 진술을 바탕으로 일반화를 이끌어내는 형태(일반진술은 생략되는 경우도 있음)
② 논증의 글에서 주로 사용되는 형태로 주장의 근거를 먼저 제시하고, 이를 통해 독자의 설득력을 높인 후 문미에서 글쓴이의 주장이 제시되는 형태

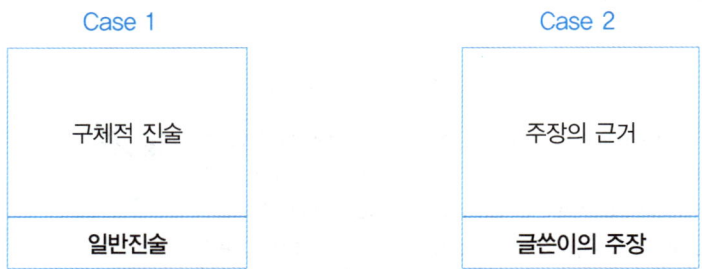

[예시 1]

1. A woman who had been receiving treatment for cancer at a clinic on a regular basis began to procrastinate about going in for periodic examinations and care. When her family asked why she had not gone in on schedule, she replied, "They gave me a new doctor, and he's not very nice. He treats me like a number, and I feel uncomfortable talking to him—he talks down to me when I ask him questions."
2. Many patients have stories about negative experiences with doctors, and these experiences can lead people to delay or stop getting the medical attention they need.

서사체의 이야기 글은 주인공과 주변 인물 사이에 발생하는 '사건'을 중심으로 이를 통해 궁극적으로 무엇을 전달하려는지 파악한다.
1. **도입부 = 구체적 진술**
한 여성의 구체적 경험담
2. **일반진술(요지)**
앞에서 언급된 구체적 경험담을 일반화하면서 요지를 이끌어내고 있다.

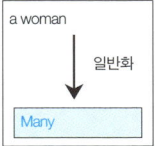

＊구체적 진술을 이끄는 시그널
① For example/ For instance
② When/ If
③ Consider/ Imagine
   Let's think(say)
   Take (an example of)
④ 구체적 대상 언급
⑤ 시간의 부사 (구/절)

| 해설
'a woman → many patients'에서 확인할 수 있듯이, 한 사람의 구체적 경험을 보편적 현상으로 파악하면서 일반화하고 있다. '구체적 진술 → 일반화 진술'의 패턴을 파악하도록 한다.

| 해석
병원에서 장기적으로 암 치료를 받고 있던 한 여자가 정기 검진과 치료를 받는 것을 미루기 시작했다. 그녀의 가족들이 왜 그녀가 예정대로 가지 않는지를 묻자, 그녀는 다음과 같이 대답했다. "병원에서 새로운 의사를 배정했는데 별로 친절하지 않아. 그는 나를 숫자 취급을 해. 그래서 그와 대화하는 것이 불편해. 즉, 내가 질문을 하면 얕보는 투로 말을 해." 많은 환자가 의사와의 부정적인 경험에 대한 이야깃거리를 가지고 있으며 이런 경험은 사람들이 자신이 필요로 하는 치료를 미루거나 중단하게 되는 결과를 가져온다.

| 참고
앞에서 살펴본, '구체적 진술(사례) → 일반진술(주제문)'로 진행되는 미괄식의 구성과 정 반대의 구조를 갖춘 '일반진술(주제문) → 뒷받침 진술'의 두괄식 구성을 비교해보자.

1. People know that honesty has its own rewards. 1) A good example is Abraham Lincoln. When he was a young man, he had a job working in a store. One day he mistakenly overcharged one of his customers. When he realized his mistake, Lincoln walked several miles to the man's house to give him the correct change. The man was surprised and delighted, and he told everyone about Lincoln's honesty. It was because of deeds like this that Lincoln became known as Honest Abe. And he got elected president of the United States.

중심소재: 정직
1. **도입부 = 주제문**
1) **뒷받침 진술**
구체적 사례(A good example)을 통해 주제문의 중심내용을 뒷받침하고 있다.

★ 글의 중심소재다. 주제를 작성할 때 반드시 포함시켜야 한다.

★ 본문에서 구체적으로 다룰 중심내용(controlling idea)에 해당한다.

★ When, one day와 같이 특정 시점을 언급하는 표현은 구체적 진술의 시작을 알리는 시그널로 활용된다.

| 해석

사람들은 정직하면 보상을 받는다는 것을 알고 있다. 좋은 예가 Abraham Lincoln의 경우이다. 젊었을 때, 그는 가게에서 일하는 직업을 갖고 있었다. 어느 날 그는 손님 중 한 명에게 실수로 요금을 더 부과했다. 자신의 실수를 깨달았을 때, Lincoln은 몇 마일을 걸어 그 사람의 집에 가서, 정확한 잔돈을 그에게 주었다. 그 남자는 놀라면서도 기뻐했고, 모두에게 Lincoln의 정직함에 대해 말했다. Lincoln이 '정직한 Abe'라고 알려진 것은 바로 이러한 행동 때문이었다. 그리고 그는 미국의 대통령으로 선출되었다.

[비교] 양괄식과의 비교

단락구조 : 양괄식
- 도입부
- 주제문
- 뒷받침진술
- 요지

1. While predictions about the future are always difficult, one can be made with certainty. 1) People will find themselves in large numbers of interactions where intercultural communication skills will be essential. ① There are **several reasons** for such prediction. Ⓐ Some reasons include increasing amounts of contact brought on by overseas assignments in the business world, the movement of college students spending time in other countries, and increasing amounts of international travel among tourists. Ⓑ Others relate to social changes within any one large and complex nation: affirmative action, the movement of immigrants and refugees, bilingual education programs, and movement away from the goal that ethnic minorities become part of a "melting pot." 2. Therefore, it is essential that people research the cultures and communication conventions of those whom they propose to meet in the future.

중심소재: 국제사회의 교역 증가
1. 도입부
미래에 닥치게 될 현상
1) 주제문(현상 – 대안)
문화 간의 상호교류 증가로 상호 문화를 바탕으로 한 의사소통 기술의 필요성 대두
① 뒷받침 근거
Ⓐ 이유 1
Ⓑ 이유 2
2. 요지(주제문 재진술)

★ 문미에 글의 주제문이 제시되고 있다. 글의 요지를 이끄는 시그널인 'therefore'와 'it is essential that'을 확인한다.

| 해설

글쓴이의 주장이 문미에 제시되는 미괄식의 구조를 취하는 글이다.

| 해석

미래에 대한 예측이 항상 어렵기는 하지만, 한 가지 예측은 분명히 할 수 있을 것이다. 사람들은 미래에 문화 간 의사소통 기술이 아주 중요한 수없이 많은 상호작용에 처하게 될 것이다. 이런 예측을 하는 데는 몇 가지 이유가 있다. 몇 가지 이유에는 사업 세계에서 국외 업무로 생기는 접촉양의 증가, 국외에서 시간을 보내는 대학생들의 이동, 그리고 국제 여행 관광객의 증가량이 포함되어 있다. 다른 이유로는 하나의 거대하고 복잡한 국가 내에서의 사회 변화와 관련이 있다. 즉, 차별 철폐 조치, 이민자와 망명자의 이동, 2개 국어 병용 교육, 그리고 소수 민족이 잡다한 인종·문화가 뒤섞인 나라의 한 부분이 되게 하려는 목표에서 멀어져 가는 추세이다. 그러므로 미래에는 사람들이 자신들이 만나고자 하는 사람들의 문화와 의사소통 관습을 연구하는 것이 필수적이다.

[예시 2]

1. It's a parent's worst nightmare. You're sitting down to dinner when, all of a sudden, your 9-month-old starts having difficulty breathing and begins swelling up around the mouth. Your child just consumed soy and is experiencing anaphylactic shock, an allergic reaction. What most people can eat freely might be fatal to someone with an allergy to that food. 2. An allergic reaction occurs when the immune system mistakes a perfectly harmless substance for a dangerous one. In response, the system launches a full-scale attack, all the while wreaking havoc on your body. If you're raising a child or even just like giving dinner parties, you should be familiar with some of the most prominent allergenic foods. Catering to someone's special dietary needs could save his or her life.

중심소재: 알레르기 반응
1. **도입부 = 구체적 진술**
아이가 특정 음식에 알레르기 반응을 일으킨 긴박한 상황
2. **일반진술(요지 도출)**
아이를 기르는 부모는 알레르기를 일으키는 일반적인 음식에 대해 잘 알아두어야 한다.

★구체적 사례를 통해 시작되는 글은 일반적으로 '구체적 진술 → 일반진술'의 미괄식 구조를 취한다. 때로 일반진술이 생략되는 경우도 있는데, 이럴 경우 구체적 진술을 바탕으로 글의 요지를 이끌어내야 한다.

★중심소재는 '알레르기 반응'이다.

★요지를 이끄는 시그널 확인

| 해석
이것은 부모에게는 악몽 같은 일이다. 저녁을 먹으려고 하는데 갑자기 당신의 9개월 된 아이가 숨을 좀처럼 쉬지 못하고 입 주변이 부풀어 오르기 시작한다. 아이가 콩을 먹고 알레르기 증상인 과민성 쇼크 증상을 보인다. 다른 사람들은 편히 먹는 것들이 그 음식에 알레르기 반응이 있는 누군가에게는 치명적일 수 있다. 알레르기 반응은 면역시스템이 실수로 지극히 안전한 것을 위험한 것으로 인지할 때 발생한다. 그에 대한 반응으로, 면역시스템은 몸을 엉망으로 만들며 전면에서 반응을 보인다. 만약 당신이 아이를 키우고 있거나, 저녁 파티를 할 때에도, 알레르기를 일으키는 음식 중 가장 두드러진 음식에 익숙해져야 한다. 누군가의 특별 식단을 마련하는 것은 그/그녀의 생명을 살릴 수 있다.

[실전응용 1] 글의 구조를 분석하시오.

Most of us believe that we can trust in technology to solve our problems. Whatever problem you name, you can also name some hoped-for technological solution. Some of us have faith that we shall solve our dependence on fossil fuels by developing new technologies for hydrogen engines, wind energy, or solar energy. Some of us have faith that we shall solve our food problems with genetically modified crops newly or soon to be developed. Those with such faith assume that the new technologies will ultimately succeed, without harmful side effects. However, there is no basis for believing that technology will not cause new and unanticipated problems while solving the problems that it previously produced.

중심소재:
1. 도입부

2. 주제문

[실전응용 2] 글의 구조를 분석하시오.

Over the past twenty years, I've asked thousands of people, "Where are you when you get your best ideas?" The most frequent answers are: 'resting in bed,' 'walking in nature,' 'listening to music while driving in my car,' and 'relaxing in the bath.' People rarely get their best ideas at work. What is so special about walking in the woods or resting in bed? Solitude and relaxation. Most people have their best ideas when they are relaxed and by themselves. Leonardo da Vinci once wrote, "If you are alone you are completely yourself, but if you are accompanied by a single companion you are half yourself."

중심소재:
1. 도입부

2. 주제문

[실전응용 3] 글의 구조를 분석하시오.

Years ago, I was involved in planning a police operation that was to take place in Lakeland, Florida. As the mission planner was describing the operation order, he seemed to have everything covered. His arms were outstretched over two chairs as he confidently explained the very detailed arrest plan. Suddenly someone asked, "Have you contacted the Lakeland ambulance crew?" Instantly the mission planner withdrew his arms and dropped them between his knees, palms together. He went from dominating a large space to being as narrow as possible, all because he had not made the necessary arrangements. He suddenly lost the initiative. This is a striking example of how quickly our behaviors ebb and flow depending on our level of confidence.

중심소재:
1. 도입부

2. 주제문

[실전응용 4] 글의 구조를 분석하시오.

Some people can learn a foreign language just by hearing it, and then trying to speak it. Other people have to read it and write it in order to learn it. So some people use their ears more, and others use their eyes more to learn new things. Take another example. I can't learn how to use a computer just by reading an instruction manual. But many people seem to learn how to use a computer just by reading the manual. In short, people learn things in different ways.

중심소재:
1. 도입부

2. 주제문(요지)

3. 양괄식

양괄식의 경우 주제문이 문두와 문미에 드러나는 형태로 '서론 - 본론 - 결론'의 삼단구성을 취한다.

[예시 1]

1. ① <u>Buildings—contrary to popular thought—are not lifeless objects</u>. From the ruins of Byzantium to the streets of New York, from the roof of a Chinese pagoda to the Eiffel Tower, ② <u>every building tells a story</u>. 1) <u>Think of it</u>: When we consider history, what we see before us are the buildings. If we look back to Rome, what we see first is the Colosseum and the Forum. Standing beside the temples of Greece or near the circle at Stonehenge, we feel the spirit of the people who created them; their spirits speak to us across the history. 2. <u>Great buildings, like great literature or poetry or music, can tell the story of the human soul.</u>

중심소재: 빌딩
1. 도입부 = 주제문(= ①+②)

1) 뒷받침 진술
구체적 예시를 이끄는 'Think of it'을 확인한다 – 로마의 콜로세움, 그리스의 신전, 영국의 Stonehenge를 통해 뒷받침 진술이 전개되고 있다.

2. 문미에서 다시 한 번 **주제문**이 제시되고 있다.

도입부 = [주제문]
　　　　　 뒷받침진술
　　　　　 [주제문]

| 해석
건물은 일반적인 생각과는 반대로 생명이 없는 사물이 아니다. 비잔틴의 유적에서부터 뉴욕의 거리에 이르기까지, 중국의 탑 꼭대기에서부터 에펠탑에 이르기까지 모든 건물은 이야기를 전한다. 한 번 생각해보라. 역사를 고려할 때 눈앞에 보는 것은 건물들이다. 만약 로마를 거슬러 올라가 보면, 우리가 가장 처음 보는 것은 콜로세움이나 포럼이다. 그리스의 신전 옆이나 스톤헨지 근처에 서면, 우리는 그것을 만들어낸 사람의 영혼을 느낀다. 그들의 영혼은 역사를 가로질러 우리에게 말을 한다. 위대한 문학 작품, 시, 음악처럼 훌륭한 건물들은 인간의 영혼에 관한 이야기를 할 수 있다.

[예시 2]

1. <u>Many large and small companies that keep and even recruit older employees report good results.</u> 1) <u>For example</u>, ① Macy's, the famous New York department store, has never practiced mandatory retirement and values its older workers. ② McDonald's now actively recruits from senior citizens clubs for its special Mc-Masters training program, offering a choice of days, hours, and jobs to trainees. ③ Travelers Insurance, a large firm in Connecticut, has created

중심소재: 고령의 직원을 고용하는 회사
1. 도입부 = 주제문
고령의 직원 고용이 큰 효과를 보고 있다.

1) 뒷받침 진술(구체적 예시)
앞에서 언급한 주제문에 대한 구체적 예시(①, ②, ③, ④)를 통한 뒷받침 진술이 이어지고 있다.

도입부 = [현상(주제문)]
　　　　　 뒷받침사례
　　　　　 ①_____
　　　　　 ②_____
　　　　　 ③_____
　　　　　 ④_____

37

개별 예에서 일반진술로 바뀌고 있다. "개별예 → All these" 확인

a number of attractive work options for its older employees. ④ A final example is Health-Wise, a small publishing house, half of whose employees are over fifty-five. 2. All these companies are profiting from the sound judgment, personal skills, and accumulated experience of older employees.

2. **결론(요지)**
주제문에서 밝힌 요지를 재차 강조하고 있다.

| 해석
나이 든 사원들을 내보내지 않고 심지어 채용하기도 하는 크고 작은 많은 회사가 좋은 실적을 얻고 있다. 예를 들어, 뉴욕의 유명한 백화점인 Macy's는 나이 든 직원들에 대해 의무적 퇴사를 실천한 적이 없으며, (오히려) 회사의 나이 든 직원을 존중한다. Mc Donald가 현재 Mc Master 특별 프로그램을 위해 고령자들을 활발히 채용하고 있는데, 훈련생들에게 날짜, 시간, 일을 선택할 기회를 제공한다. Connecticut에 있는 큰 회사인 Travelers Insurance는 회사의 나이 든 고용인들을 위해 다수의 매력적인 작업 선택권을 마련해왔다. 마지막 예는 작은 출판사인 Health-Wise인데, 직원의 절반이 55세 이상이다. 이 모든 회사는 나이 든 직원들의 올바른 판단과 개인 기술, 그리고 축적된 경험을 통해 수익을 올리고 있다.

음식 선택에 관한 글이다. 중심내용을 바탕으로 주제의 폭을 설정하도록 한다.

[예시 3]

본문에서 구체적으로 다룰 중심내용(controlling idea)이다.

1. When it comes to food choices, young people are particularly vulnerable to peer influences. 1) ① A teenage girl may eat nothing but a lettuce salad for lunch, even though she will become hungry later, because that is what her friends are eating. ② A slim boy who hopes to make the wrestling team may routinely overload his plate with foods that are dense in carbohydrates and proteins to 'bulk up' like the wrestlers of his school. An overweight teen may eat moderately while around his friends but then devour huge portions when alone. 2. Few young people are completely free of food-related pressures from peers, whether or not these pressures are imposed intentionally.

중심소재: 음식 선택
1. 주제문
1) 뒷받침 문장
① 십 대 소녀의 예
② 레슬링팀에 합류하려는 소년
2. 글쓴이의 주장을 다시 한 번 강조하면서 글을 마무리하고 있다

| 해석
음식을 선택하는 데 있어서 젊은 사람들은 특히 또래의 영향에 취약하다. 십 대의 소녀는 상추 샐러드가 그녀의 친구들이 먹는 것이기 때문에 나중에 배가 고플지라도 점심으로 상추 샐러드만 먹을지도 모른다. 레슬링팀에 들어가고 싶어 하는 호리호리한 소년은 자기 학교의 레슬링 선수들처럼 '몸집을 불리기' 위해 일상적으로 자기 접시를 탄수화물과 단백질이 많은 음식으로 가득 채울지 모른다. 과체중의 십 대는 주변에 친구들이 있을 때는 적당히 먹을지 모르지만, 혼자 있게 되면 많은 양을 게걸스럽게 먹게 된다. 음식과 관련된 압박이 의도적으로 강요된 것이든 혹은 그렇지 않은 또래들로부터 그러한 압박에서 완전히 자유로운 젊은 사람들은 거의 없다.

[실전응용 1] 글의 구조를 분석하시오.

In youth I was harshly intolerant. I remember my indignation upon hearing someone made the remark, not an original one, but new to me then, that hypocrisy was the tribute that vice paid to virtue. I thought that one should have the scourge of one's vices. I had ideals of honesty, uprightness, truth: I was impatient not of human weakness, but of cowardice, and I would make no allowances for those who hedged and temporized. It never occurred to me that no one stood in greater need of indulgence than I.

중심소재:

1. 도입부

1) 뒷받침 문장

[실전응용 2] 글의 구조를 분석하시오.

Scientists have learned to supplement the sense of sight in numerous ways. In front of the tiny pupil of the eye they put, on Mount Palomar, a great monocle 200 inches in diameter, and with it see 2000 times farther into the depths of space. Or they look through a small pair of lenses arranged as a microscope into a drop of water or blood, and magnify by as much as 2000 diameters the living creatures there, many of which are among man's most dangerous enemies. Or they can bring happenings of long ago and far away as colored motion pictures, by arranging silver atoms and color-absorbing molecules to force light waves into the patterns of original reality. Or if we want to see into the center of a steel casting or the chest of an injured child, they send the information on a beam of penetrating short-wave X rays, and then convert it back into images we can see on a screen or photograph. Thus almost every type of electromagnetic radiation yet discovered has been used to extend our sense of sight in some way.

중심소재:
1. 도입부

1) 뒷받침 문장

4. 중괄식

중괄식은 주제문이 글의 중간에 위치한다. 일반적으로 통념비판의 글에서 주로 사용된다. 'However(but)' 이후에 주제문이 등장하고, 이후 뒷받침 진술이 이어진다.

의문문은 그 자체로 주제★
문 또는 주제를 드러낸다.

도입부 = 주제(도출)
↓
문제점 지적
↓
주제문
↓
뒷받침 예시

[예시 1]

1. "What is value to the customer?" is the most important question in business, yet is rarely asked. One reason is that managers are quite sure that they know the answer. Value is what they, in their business, define as quality. 1) But this is almost always the wrong definition. 2. <u>The customer never buys a product but the satisfaction of a want</u>. 1) For the teenage girl, <u>for instance</u>, value in a shoe is high fashion. Price is a secondary consideration and durability is not value at all. For the same girl as a young mother, a few years later, what she looks for is durability, price and comfort.

중심소재: 고객이 고려하는 구매 가치 기준
1. 도입부
문제점 지적: 구매 기준에 대한 매니저의 잘못된 견해 지적
1) 논리적 반전(But)
글쓴이가 제시하는 구매 기준이 언급될 것을 예상할 수 있다.
2. 주제문
구매 물건에 대한 만족감이 바로 구매 기준
1) 뒷받침 예시(for instance)

| 해석
"고객들에게 무엇이 가치 기준(상품 구매 기준)이 될까?"는 사업에서 가장 중요한 물음이지만, 좀처럼 묻질 않는다. 한 가지 이유는 경영자들은 스스로 그 답을 알고 있다고 아주 확신하기 때문이다. 가치 기준이란 그들이 사업에서 품질로 정의하는 것이다. 그러나 이것은 거의 항상 잘못된 정의이다. 고객은 결코 필요한 것에 대한 만족감이 없이는 제품을 사지 않는다. 예를 들어, 십 대 소녀들에게 신발의 가치 기준은 최신 유행 스타일이다. 가격은 부차적인 고려사항이며, 내구성은 전혀 가치 기준이 아니다. 몇 년이 지난 후에는 젊은 엄마로서 그 소녀가 찾는 것은 내구성, 가격, 편안함이 된다.

글의 도입부에서 중심소★
재 설정은 주제, 주제문을
잡는 가장 기본이 되는 독
해의 시작이다.

도입부 = 정의(중심소재 도출)

뒷받침 1. 기능 1
- 부연 예시
뒷받침 2. 기능 2
부연예시 ①
부연예시 ②

뒷받침 1 + 뒷받침 2
= 주제문

[비교 1] 뒷받침 문장을 바탕으로 주제문을 이끌어내야 하는 유형

1. **Moles** are dark spots on human skin. They can vary in color from light to dark brown or black. Almost everyone has at least one mole. According to ancient superstitions, 2. 1) <u>moles reveal a person's character</u>. ① <u>For example</u>, a mole on one's nose means that he or she is strong-willed and trustworthy. 2) <u>Moles are also believed to foretell the future</u>. ② Having a mole over one's right eyebrow means he or she will be lucky with money and have a successful career. A mole on the hand, however, is the most desired. It forecasts talent, health, and happiness.

중심소재: 점
1. 도입부
정의: 정의로 시작하는 글을 처음부터 끝까지 특정 대상의 개념을 설명하는 글과 개념정의 후 주제의 폭을 좁혀 정의된 대상의 좀더 세부적 내용에 초점을 맞추어 전개되는 두가지 경우가 있다.
2. 1) 뒷받침 1: 첫번째 기능
① 부연예시
2) 뒷받침 2: 두번째 기능
② 부연예시 Ⓐ, Ⓑ

| 해석
점은 인간의 피부에 있는 검은 반점이다. 그것들은 밝은 갈색에서부터 어두운 갈색이나 검은색까지 다양하다. 거의 모든 사람이 적어도 한 개의 점을 갖고 있다. 고대의 미신에 따르면 점은 사람의 성격을 드러낸다. 예를 들어, 코에 있는 점은 그가 의지가 강하고 믿을 수 있다는 것을 의미한다. 점들은 또한 미래를 예언해준다고 믿어진다. 오른쪽 눈썹 위의 점은 그가 금전 운이 있을 것이고 성공적인 직업을 가질 것임을 의미한다. 그러나 손에 있는 점이 가장 좋다. 이것은 재능과 건강과 행복을 예측해준다.

[예시 2]

1. **One of** the most famous houses in the United States is Monticello. 1) It was the home of Thomas Jefferson, the third president of the United States. Located on a hill near Charlottesville, Virginia, it has a beautiful view of the surrounding countryside. 2. The house is famous, 1) ① **first of all**, because it belonged to a president. It is ② **also** a fine example of early 19th century American architecture. Jefferson designed it himself in a style he had admired in Italy. Many American buildings of that time, in fact, imitated European styles. But while most were just imitations, his Monticello is lovely in itself. ③ **Furthermore**, the design combines a graceful style with a typical American concern for comfort and function.

중심소재: Monticello
1. 도입부
중심소재 도출
1) 간략한 배경
2. 주제문
1) 뒷받침 진술
① 대통령의 집
② 19세기 초의 미국 건축의 예로 역사적 의미를 지님
③ 디자인

★ 중심소재

★ one of Ns
중심소재의 폭을 좁혀 주는 시그널

★ 뒷받침 문장에서 구체적으로 밝힐 중심내용(controlling idea)에 해당한다.

도입부 =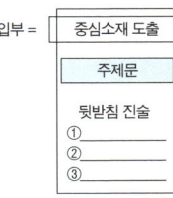

| 해석
미국에서 가장 유명한 집 중 하나는 몬티셀로다. 이것은 미국의 제3대 대통령이었던 토마스 제퍼슨의 사택이었다. 버지니아주 샬롯츠빌 부근의 언덕 위에 있는 이 집은 주위에 아름다운 전원 풍경이 있다. 그 집은 무엇보다 대통령의 소유였기에 유명하다. 또한, 그 집은 19세기 초의 미국 건축 양식의 훌륭한 본보기이다. 제퍼슨은 그가 이탈리아에서 좋아했던 건축 양식으로 자신이 직접 그 집을 설계했다. 사실 당시의 많은 미국 건물들은 유럽스타일을 모방했었다. 하지만 대부분이 단순한 모방이었던 반면, 제퍼슨의 몬티셀로는 그 자체로서 훌륭하다. 게다가, 그 디자인은 우아함과 미국인들의 전형적인 관심사인 안락함과 기능을 통합하고 있다.

[비교 2] 두괄식과 비교

1. **Advertising's main goal is**, of course, **to sell products**, but advertising also has other effects. 1) ① By increasing the demand for products, advertising encourages economic growth. ② It helps to maintain competition among businesses, and there is some evidence that this competition leads to lower prices for consumer goods. ③ A case can even be made for advertising as a source of information. Advertising frequently demonstrates how products are used and provides information on special features and prices. This information is intended to sell products, but it can also result in better informed consumers.

중심소재: 광고
1. 도입부 = 주제문
광고의 기능(유용성)
1) 뒷받침 진술
① 경제성장
② 기업 간 경쟁 유도
→ 가격 하락
③ 고객에게 유용한 정보 제공

★ 중심소재를 파악한다.

★ 중심내용(controlling idea) 이다.

| 해설

'of course A but B' 구문은 종종 등장하니 잘 염두에 두어야 한다. A는 이미 알고 있는 사실이고, 새로운 사실 B가 글쓴이가 궁극적으로 이야기하려는 주제에 해당한다. 나열을 통해 글쓴이의 요지를 뒷받침하고 있다.

| 해석

광고의 주요 목적은 물론 제품을 판매하는 것이겠지만, 광고는 또한 다른 효과도 가지고 있다. 광고는 제품에 대한 수요를 증가시킴으로써 경제가 성장하도록 자극한다. 이는 기업들 사이의 경쟁을 계속 유지시켜 주며, 이러한 경쟁이 소비자 가격을 더 낮게 이끌어준다는 일부 증거도 있다. 또 다른 경우는 정보의 근원으로 광고가 제작될 수도 있다는 것이다. 새로운 상품은 광고를 통해 자주 소개되며, 광고는 그 상품이 어떻게 사용되는지 설명해주고, 그 제품의 특별한 특징과 가격에 대한 정보를 제공해준다. 이러한 정보는 상품을 잘 팔리게 하려는 목적에서 만들어지지만, 또한 더 좋은 정보를 갖춘 구매자를 만들어 줄 수도 있다.

[예시 5]

1. The eruption of volcanoes has caused death and misery throughout the centuries. 1) Yet ① in parts of Italy, Iceland, Chile, and Bolivia, volcanic steam is used to run heat and power plants. ② Pumice, which is made from volcanic lava, is used as a grinder and polisher. ③ Sulfur produced by volcanoes is useful to the chemical industry. ④ Hawaiian farmers grow crops on land made rich by decayed volcanic material. 2) Thus, in spite of all the damage they cause, volcanoes do benefit us in various ways.

중심소재: Volcano
1. 도입부
화산의 부정적 영향력
1) Yet 이후 화제전환(화산의 유용성)
① 화력 및 발전소 에너지 공급
② 분쇄기 및 광택제
③ 화학 산업
④ 농작물
2. 요지(주제문)
화산의 다양한 혜택

| 해설

Yet 이후 글쓴이가 밝히려는 '화산의 유용성'을 나열을 통해 기술하고 있다. 'Specific → General'로 진행되는 글이다.

| 해석

화산 폭발은 전 세기에 걸쳐 죽음과 불행을 일으켰다. 그러나 이탈리아, 아이슬란드, 칠레, 그리고 볼리비아 등지에서는 화산 작용으로 생긴 증기를 열 발전소들을 가동하는 데 이용하고 있다. 화산의 용암으로 만들어지는 부석은 연마기나 광택제로 이용된다. 화산에 의해 만들어지는 유황은 화학 산업에 유용하다. 하와이 농부들은 썩은 화산 물질에 의해 비옥해진 땅에 곡식을 기른다. 그러므로 화산이 일으키는 모든 피해에도 불구하고 화산은 여러 가지 면에서 우리를 이롭게 한다.

[예시 6]

1. Farming began about 12,000 years ago and it has developed very quickly in the last 300 years. There are no signs that the speed of development will slow down. 2. Agriculture will continue to develop in three main ways. 1) ① First, farming will become even more efficient by using new types of technology. Many processes will be controlled by computers. ② Second, new ways of growing, storing and selling crops will be developed which can be used by poor people as well as rich people. ③ Third, agricultural products will be used in many ways.

중심소재: Farming
1. 도입부
농업의 기원과 급격한 발달
2. 주제문
미래에도 농업을 계속
1) 뒷받침 진술
내용을 통해 뒷받침 근거 ①, ②, ③이 제시되고 있다.

★ 중심소재다. 중심소재를 중심으로 주제의 폭을 설정한다.

★ 본문에서 구체적으로 다룰 중심내용(controlling idea)이다.

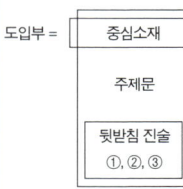

| 해설
First, Second, Third의 시그널에서 알 수 있듯이, 나열을 통한 글 전개방식을 취하고 있다.
주제: Farming in the Future

| 해석
농업은 약 12,000년 전에 시작되었으며 지난 300년 동안 급속도로 발전해 왔다. 발전의 속도가 줄어들 조짐은 보이지 않는다. 농업은 세 부문으로 계속 발전해 나갈 것이다. 첫째, 농업은 새로운 유형의 기술을 사용함으로써 보다 효율적이 될 것이다. 많은 과정이 컴퓨터에 의해 통제될 것이다. 둘째, 부유한 사람들뿐만 아니라 가난한 사람들도 이용할 수 있는 새로운 작물의 경작 및 저장, 판매 방식이 개발될 것이다. 셋째, 농산품은 여러 가지 면에서 사용될 것이다.

[실전응용 1] 글의 구조를 생각하면서 아래 지문을 분석하시오.

Most common forms of exercise, such as bicycling and swimming, rarely cause serious injury. But contact sports, such as football and judo, can cause wear on the joints that can lead to articular disease, or joint problems. The problem for most beginners is overexercise. Many people experience stiffness after the first day of exercise, but this is harmless and does not last long. People who are overweight or past middle age or who suffer from heart disease should consult a physician before starting any exercise program.

중심소재:
1. 도입부

2. 주제문
① 뒷받침 부연

[실전응용 2] 글의 구조를 생각하면서 아래 지문을 분석하시오.

Every society needs heroes, and every society has them. Some heroes shine in the face of great adversity, performing amazing deeds in difficult situations; other

중심소재:
1. 도입부

heroes do their work quietly, unnoticed by most of us, but making a difference in the lives of other people. Whatever their type, heroes are selfless people who perform extraordinary acts. The true mark of heroes lies not necessarily in the result of their actions, but in what they are willing to do for others and for their chosen causes. Even if they fail, their determination lives on to inspire the rest of us. Their glory lies not in their achievements but in their sacrifices.

1) 구체적 진술

2. 주제문

1) 뒷받침 부연

[실전응용 3] 글의 구조를 생각하면서 아래 지문을 분석하시오.

The ability to sympathize with others reflects the multiple nature of the human being, his potentialities for many more selves and kinds of experience than any one being could express. This may be one of the things that enable us to seek through literature an enlargement of our experience. Although we may see some characters as outside ourselves —that is, we may not identify with them completely—we are nevertheless able to enter into their behavior and their emotions. Thus, the youth may identify with the aged, one gender with the other, and a reader of a particular limited social background with members of a different class or a different period.

중심소재:
1. 도입부

1) 주제문

① 뒷받침 진술

[실전응용 4] 글의 구조를 생각하면서 아래 지문을 분석하시오.

A catastrophe is a sudden, often life-threatening calamity or disaster that pushes people to the outer limits of their coping capability. Catastrophes include natural disasters such as earthquakes, tornadoes, fires, floods, and hurricanes as well as wars, torture, automobile accidents, violent physical attacks, and sexual assaults. Catastrophes often continue to affect their victims' mental health long after the event has ended. For example, in 1972 a dam burst and flooded the West Virginia mining town of Buffalo Creek, destroying the town. Two years after the disaster, most of the adult survivors continued to show emotional disturbances. Similarly, most of the survivors of concentration camps in World War II (1939-1945) continued to experience nightmares and other symptoms of severe emotional problems long after their release from the camps.

중심소재:

1. 도입부

1) 주제문

① 뒷받침 진술

[실전응용 5] 글의 구조를 생각하면서 아래 지문을 분석하시오.

Several students receive poor grades on writing assignments, not because they lack the ability to communicate, but because they can not seem to manage their time when it comes to a large project. They do not know where to begin, and therefore put things off until the last minute. To solve this problem, students need to develop a timeline for completing the project. If they divide the assignment into manageable "chunks" or parts and then set a schedule for completing each part, they will be able to finish the entire project before the deadline. Without the pressure of not knowing where to begin, the students will be able to focus on the assignment and communicate their ideas effectively.

중심소재:
1. 도입부

2. 대안

[실전응용 6] 글의 구조를 생각하면서 아래 지문을 분석하시오.

Brave skydivers leap from airplanes at great heights, trusting that training, good equipment, and favorable weather will carry them safely to the ground. Still, skydiving successfully from, say, 9,000 feet involves more than courage and luck; it requires real skill. When a skydiver jumps out of a plane, he or she begins to fall, traveling through the air with the parachute tightly packed and no way to control the speed. A good skydiver, however, knows when the time is right to open the parachute. Then it's up to the diver to steer the parachute to a landing point by pulling on lines attached to the parachute.

중심소재:
1. 도입부

1) 주제문

① 뒷받침 진술

[실전응용 7] 글의 구조를 생각하면서 아래 지문을 분석하시오.

Even our most highly educated guesses often go disastrously wrong. Albert Einstein remarked, "There is no chance that nuclear energy will ever be obtainable." Why is predicting the future so difficult? Would it be smart not to try to guess what's coming next? Not predicting the future would be like driving a car without looking through the windshield. We desperately need people who can foretell the future. They help us narrow the infinity of possible futures down to one or, at least, a few. We look at the present and see the present; they see the seeds of the future. They are our advance scouts, going secretly over the border to bring back priceless information to help the world to come.

중심소재:
1. 도입부

2. 의문문

3. 주제문

5. 무괄식

글의 주제가 글 전반에 흩어져 있는 경우로 일정한 패턴을 보이지 않는다.

[예시 1]

1. Although a speech can be effective, all the words in the world cannot measure up to ① <u>the example of a leader</u>, especially in communicating new behaviors and values. There is often no more effective way to help people understand the message than ② <u>to have it modeled for them by the manager</u>. Words can yield a variety of interpretations in terms of the kind of behaviors people think they mean. ③ <u>But a manager's actions provide a clear model of exactly the kind of behavior required</u>. Managers who want people to take a more team-based approach with their people, <u>for example</u>, will almost certainly get better results by taking a more team-based approach themselves rather than just by making a speech on teamwork.

| 해설

글의 요지에 해당하는 내용이 글 전반에 드러난다. 이런 때 특정 글의 구조를 따르지 않는다 하여 무괄식이라 한다. 본문은 ①, ②, ③을 통해 모두 글의 요지를 드러내고 있다. ③ 이후 글의 구조는 두괄식의 구성을 취하고 있다.

[참고] ③ 이후 전개되는 내용은 두괄식의 "주제문 – 뒷받침 진술"의 패턴을 따르고 있다.

1. But <u>a manager's actions provide a clear model of exactly the kind of behavior required</u>. 1) Managers who want people to take a more team-based approach with their people, <u>for example</u>, will almost certainly get better results by taking a more team-based approach themselves rather than just by making a speech on teamwork.

1. 주제문
1) 예시(for example)를 통한 **뒷받침 진술**

| 해설

본문의 요지를 속담으로 표현한다면, "Actions speak louder than words." 이다.

| 해석

연설은 효과적일 수 있지만, 세상의 그 어떤 말도 지도자의 본보기에 견줄 수 없으며, 특히나 새로운 행동과 가치를 전달할 때 더욱 그러한다. 대개 관리자가 부하 직원들에게 당부하고자 하는 바를 직접 모범으로 보여주는 것보다 그들에게 그것을 더욱 효과적으로 이해시키는 방법은 없다. 말이란 사람들이 이것이 의미하는 행동의 종류의 관점에서 다양한 해석을 낳을 수 있다. 그러나 관리자의 행동은 정확히 요구되는 행동의 종류를 분명하게 모범으로 보여준다. 예를 들어, 다른 사람과 좀 더 협동에 기반을 둔 접근 방식을 취하기 원하는 관리자는 단지 협동작업에 대한 연설을 하기보다는 스스로 협동에 기반을 둔 접근 방식을 취함으로 거의 확실하게 더 나은 결과를 이끌어 낼 수 있다.

5 주제문과 뒷받침 문장

1. 주제문

주제문은 이미 3장에서 다루었으므로, 이에 관한 핵심 내용만을 간략히 정리하도록 하자. 주제문의 구성은 다음과 같다.

> 주제문 = 중심소재(포괄적 주제) + 중심내용

주제문은 포괄적 주제인 중심소재와 중심내용(Controlling Idea)으로 구성된다. 주제는 중심소재 또는 중심소재의 파악에서 시작하므로, 글의 도입부에서 이를 설정하는 연습을 꾸준히 해야 한다. 중심내용은 본문에서 다뤄지는 핵심 내용을 압축해 놓은 것이라 볼 수 있다. 때로 구체적 내용이라기보다 포괄적 내용에 해당함으로 본문을 통해 이에 대한 구체적 내용이 전개될 것을 예상할 수 있다.

2. 뒷받침 문장

뒷받침 문장이란 일반적으로 주제문에서 밝힌 내용을 'support(근거제시)' 한다는 의미에서 'Supporting Sentence(s)' 라고 한다. 주제문의 중심내용의 구체적 진술이 바로 뒷받침 진술이 된다.

[예시 1]

글의 중심소재는 '나의 고향' 이다.

1. My hometown is famous for several amazing natural features. 1) ① First, it is noted for the Wheaton River, which is very wide and beautiful. ② Also, on the other side of the town is Wheaton Hill, which is unusual because it is very steep.

1. 주제문: 자연 경관으로 뛰어난 나의 고향
1) 뒷받침 진술 – 뛰어난 자연 경관의 구체적 예를 통해 주제문을 뒷받침하고 있다.
① Wheaton River
② Wheaton Hill

중심내용(controlling idea)으로 본문에서 구체적으로 다뤄질 내용이다.

| 해석
나의 고장은 놀라운 자연적 특징으로 유명하다. 우선 우리 고장은 Wheaton 강으로 유명한데, 이 강은 폭이 아주 넓고 아름답다. 또한, 이 도시의 다른 편에는 Wheaton 언덕이 있는데, 경사가 아주 가파른 것으로 독특하다.

[예시 2]

중심소재에 해당한다.

1. People are not born with culture; they have to learn it. 1) For instance, ① people must learn how to speak and understand a particular language. ② They must learn to adapt and abide by the rules of a particular society. ③ In some areas of the world, people must learn a skill in order to earn money. Ⓐ This skill entitles them to the rights to a predetermined piece of land in which they can use at their discretion. Those who are entitled to this land usually use it to build a home for themselves and for their future families.

1. 주제문
주제: 문화의 학습성
1) 뒷받침 진술
예를 통해 주제문에서 밝힌 중심내용에 대한 뒷받침 진술이 이어진다.
① 언어
② 사회규율
③ 특정 기술
Ⓐ 부연진술(본문 끝까지)

'For instance'는 예시를 이끄는 구체적 진술이다. 일반적으로 도입부에 오면 바로 앞 문장이 주제문에 해당한다.

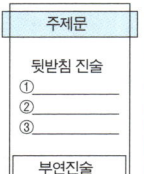

도입부 =
주제문
뒷받침 진술
①_____
②_____
③_____
부연진술

| 해설
본문의 구조는 '주제문 – 뒷받침 문장 – 부연진술'을 취하고 있다. 뒷받침 문장과 부연진술을 구별할 수 있어야 한다.

| 해석
사람들은 문화를 타고나지 않는다. 그러므로 배워야 한다. 예를 들면 사람들은 특정 언어를 말하고 이해하는 것을 배워야 한다. 그들은 어떤 사회의 규칙에 적응하는 것과 준수하는 것을 배워야 한다. 세상의 어떤 곳에서는 사람들은 돈을 벌기 위해 기술을 배워야 한다. 이런 기술 덕분에 그들은 자기 재량대로 사용할 수 있도록 결정된 특정 토지를 부여받는다. 토지를 부여받은 사람들은 주로 그 토지를 그들 자신과 미래의 가족을 위한 집을 짓는 데 이용한다.

[예시 3]

1) Like metals, plastics come in a variety of grades. ① For instance, nylons are plastics that are separated by different properties, costs, and the manufacturing processes used to produce them. 2) Also like metals, some plastics can be alloyed, or blended, to combine the advantages possessed by several different plastics. ② For example, some types of impact-resistant (shatterproof) plastics and heat-resistant plastics are made by blending different plastics together.

★ 글 전개방식 비교

중심소재: 플라스틱
1. 뒷받침 진술
1) 플라스틱의 첫 번째 특징
① 예시 부연
2) 플라스틱의 두 번째 특징
② 예시 부연

★ 중심소재는 '플라스틱'이다. 첫 번째 문장은 주제문이 아니라 뒷받침 문장에 해당한다. 주제문이 생략된 'Implicit'의 유형임을 파악하도록 한다.

| 해설

플라스틱의 두 가지 특징을 설명한 후 이후 구체적 예를 통한 부연으로 구성되어 있다. 전체 글의 주제문이 생략된 형태(Implicit)로 다음과 같은 구조를 보인다.

주제문	플라스틱은 다양한 등급(①)이 있고, 서로 다른 플라스틱의 혼합(②)이 가능하다.	생략 (Implicit)
뒷받침 문장	① 뒷받침 문장 1 – 부연진술(For instance)	
	② 뒷받침 문장 2 – 부연진술(For example)	

본문 같은 경우 주제문이 생략된 형태로 주제와 본문의 중심내용을 드러내는 주제문을 독자가 이끌어 내야 하는 'Implicit'의 유형이다.

| 해석

금속들처럼, 플라스틱도 등급이 다양하다. 예를 들면, 나일론은 다양한 특성, 비용 그리고 그것을 만들기 위한 제조과정에 따라 분리되는 플라스틱이다. 금속과 같이, 어떤 플라스틱은 몇몇 다른 플라스틱이 가진 장점들을 결합하기 위해서 합성되거나 혼합될 수 있다. 예를 들면, 특정 종류의 내구성이 강한 플라스틱과 열 저항성 플라스틱은 서로 다른 플라스틱이 합쳐져서 생성된다.

| 참고

비교/대조의 글 중 대조되는 두 대상의 특징을 전달하는 글이면 일반적으로 내용 일치의 문제가 나올 가능성이 크기에, 글을 읽을 때 각 대상의 특징을 동그라미 또는 삼각형 등으로 표시해서 문제풀이 시 다시 본문을 확인할 때 각각의 특징을 쉽게 파악할 수 있도록 해 두면 시간적 소모를 줄일 수 있다.

[예시 4]

1. The Eskimos traditionally had three types of houses. 2. 1) A summer house, which was basically a tent, 2) a winter house, which was usually partially dug into the ground and covered with earth; and 3) a snow or ice house. ① The latter

중심소재: 에스키모 → 에스키모의 집
첫 번째 문장이 주제문으로 'three types of houses'에서 나열의 전개방식으로 기술되는 설명문임을 쉽게 파악할 수 있다.
1. 도입부 = 주제문

49

was a dome-shaped dwelling constructed of blocks of snow placed in an ascending spiral with a low tunnel entrance. Although it can provide adequate protection for weeks in severe cold, it was used almost exclusively as a temporary shelter while traveling.

2. 뒷받침 문장
1) 종류 1: summer house
2) 종류 2: winter house
3) 종류 3: snow or ice house
① 부연진술
마지막 종류(snow or ice house)에 대한 부연진술이다.

| 해설

'주제문(Topic Sentence) – 뒷받침 문장(Supporting Sentence) – 부연진술(Supporting Details)'을 정확히 구별하도록 하자.

| 해석

에스키모인들은 전통적으로 세 가지 형태의 집을 가지고 있다. 기본적으로 천막인, 여름 가옥과 보통 부분적으로 지반 속으로 패여 땅으로 덮인 겨울 가옥, 그리고 눈 혹은 얼음집이다. 후자는 낮은 터널식 입구를 가진, 상승 유선형으로 놓인, 눈 벽돌로 구성된 반구 형태의 거주지이다. 비록 혹한기에 몇 주간 적절한 보호를 제공하지만, 이것은 거의 여행 중에 일시적인 피난처로써만 사용된다.

[예시 5]

뒷받침 문장에서 구체적으로 ★
진술된 중심내용(controlling idea)에 해당한다.

구체적 진술을 이끄는 시 ★
그널 확인

1. <u>A British physician-geographer used a famous map to confirm his theory that contaminated water was to blame for the transmission of cholera</u>. 1) When cholera struck England in 1842, he mapped every new case and every death in London's densely populated Soho district, marking each victim's residence with a dot. Thousands of people fell ill in Soho, and more than 500 died. His evolving map soon revealed a clustering of casualties around the intersection where Broad and Lexington Streets met. There stood a communal water pump, and he saw to it that the handle of that pump was removed, making it inoperable. Almost immediately, new cases in the area dropped to zero. This result proved the role of water in the spread of cholera, pointing the way toward protection against it.

중심소재: 콜레라 전염
1. 도입부 = 주제문
1) 뒷받침 진술
주제문에서 밝힌 중심내용은 주인공의 조사를 통해 뒷받침하고 있다.

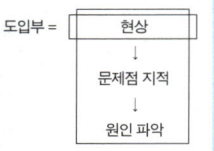

도입부 = 현상
↓
문제점 지적
↓
원인 파악

현상+원인 = 주제문

주제: 콜레라 발생 원인

| 해석

한 영국의 내과 의사이자 지리학자가 오염된 물이 콜레라 전염의 원인이라는 자신의 이론을 입증하기 위해 유명한 지도를 사용했다. 1842년에 콜레라가 영국을 강타했을 때, 그 희생자의 거주지를 점으로 표시하면서, 런던의 인구 밀집지역인 소호에서 발생하는 모든 새로운 사례와 사망을 지도에 나타내었다. 소호에서는 수천 명의 사람들이 병에 걸렸고 500명 이상이 죽었다. 점차 개선되는 그의 지도는 곧 Broad 거리와 Lexington 거리가 만나는 교차점 주변에서 사상자 집단을 보여 주었다. 그곳에는 공동 물 펌프가 있었고, 그는 그 펌프의 손잡이를 제거해서 확실히 작동되지 못하도록 했다. 거의 즉각적으로 그 지역에서 (콜레라와 관련된) 새로운 사례는 사라지게 되었다. 이 결과는 콜레라의 확산에서 물의 역할을 입증해 이를 예방하는 방향을 제시했다.

[예시 6]

1. <u>Nearly all living creatures</u> manage some form of communication. 1) ① <u>The dance patterns of bees</u> in their hive help to point the way to distant flower fields or announce successful foraging. ② <u>Male stickleback fish</u> regularly swim upside-down to indicate outrage in a courtship contest. ③ <u>Male deer and lemurs</u> mark territorial ownership by rubbing their own body secretions on boundary stones or trees. Everyone has seen ④ <u>a frightened dog</u> put his tail between his legs and run in panic. ⑤ <u>We</u>, too, use gestures, expressions, postures, and movement to give our words point.

중심소재: 의사소통을 하는 도든 생명체
1. 도입부 = 주제문
1) 뒷받침 진술
①, ②, ③, ④, ⑤를 통해 주제문에서 밝힌 중심내용을 구체적 예시를 통해 뒷받침하고 있다.

★ 중심소재다. 중심소재를 중심으로 주제를 잡을 때 이후 진술되는 중심내용을 고려하면서 주제의 폭을 고려해야 한다.

★ 본문에서 구체적으로 밝힐 중심내용(controlling idea)에 해당한다.

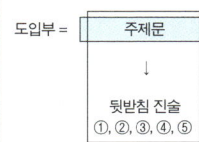

| 해석
거의 모든 생명체가 의사소통을 한다. 벌이 벌집에 돌아와 추는 춤의 형태는 먼 곳에 있는 꽃밭에 가는 길을 표지해 주고 성공적으로 꿀을 채집했다는 신호를 보낸다. 큰 가시고기 수컷은 구애 경쟁에서 자신이 화가 나 있음을 전달하기 위하여 반복적으로 거꾸로 헤엄을 친다. 수사슴과 여우원숭이는 영역 경계에 있는 바위나 나무에 분비물을 문질러 영역을 표시한다. 놀란 강아지가 꼬리를 두 다리 사이에 감추고 겁에 질려 도망가는 것은 누구나 목격한다. 우리도 역시 몸짓, 표정, 자세 또는 행동을 통해서 우리가 표현하고자 하는 주된 의도를 나타낸다.

[예시 7]

1. <u>Different people in different times have different ideas about leisure</u>. 1) ① The ancient Greek philosophers, <u>for example</u>, regarded leisure as labor of the mind, putting to use all one had learned to expand an individual's intellectual horizons and thereby make the person a better citizen. The goal was to become an educated individual. ② Today leisure is often regarded (a) <u>as time left over after caring for the needs of existence</u>, such as eating and sleeping, and for subsistence, such as work or education. This leftover time is to be used as each individual chooses. Studies suggest that the average adult spends about 80 to 85 hours weekly for existence and about 35 to 40 hours for subsistence, leaving about 40 to 50 hours of leisure time. Some people view leisure simply (b) <u>as recreation</u>. Others view it (c) <u>as an attitude or frame of mind</u>. Recent writers have defined leisure (d) <u>as a</u>

중심소재: 여가
1. 도입부 = 주제문
시대마다 여가에 대한 정의가 다르다.
주제: 여가의 다양한 의미(정의)
1) 뒷받침 진술
주제문에서 밝힌 중심내용을 구체적 예를 통해 뒷받침하고 있다.
① 고대 그리스: 여가는 개인의 지적 세계의 확장이라는 정신적 활동 → 고로 여가를 통한 이들의 목적은 교육적 인간형(여가는 필수사항임을 알 수 있다)임.
② 그리스와 다른 현대인이 바라보는 다양한 의미의 여가: (a) 존재와 생계 이외에 남는 시간 (b) 단순한 오락 또는 태도 (c) 단순히 마음가짐 (d) 자유로움 (e) 사회 계급적 기능 – 현대인에게 여가는 남는 시간 정도의 부수적 사항으로 인식됨.

★ 중심내용(controlling idea)이며, 중심소재는 '여가'이다. 주제문의 내용을 바탕으로 시대적 '대조'가 본문에 다뤄질 것을 예상할 수 있다.

★ 예시를 통한 뒷받침 진술로 바로 앞 문장이 주제문임을 드러내는 시그널이다.

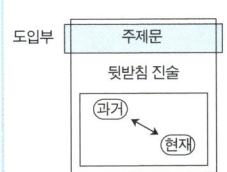

51

state of being free, an attitude of mind and condition of soul that aids in experiencing the reality of the world. Still another view defines leisure (e) as a function of social class.

| 해석

시대에 따라서 그리고 사람에 따라서 "여가"에 대한 생각이 서로 다르다. 예를 들어, 고대 그리스 철학자들은 여가란 사고의 노동으로 과거에 배운 것을 실제로 활용하고, 개인의 지적 지평선을 확장하며, 그렇게 함으로써 보다 나은 시민이 된다고 생각했다. 목표는 교육을 받은 사람이 되기 위한 것이다. 오늘날 여가는 종종 먹고 자는 것과 같은 생존에 필요한 요구를 충족시키고, 생계를 위한 일이나 교육을 하고 남는 시간으로 간주한다. 이렇게 남는 시간은 각 개인이 원하는 대로 사용한다. 연구에 따르면 평균 성인은 생존에 필요한 일로 주당 80에서 85시간을, 그리고 생계를 위해 35–40시간을 소모하여 40–50시간의 여가가 있다고 한다. 어떤 이들은 여가란 단지 오락시간이라고 생각한다. 다른 이들은 여가는 심적인 태도 또는 마음의 준거로 본다. 최근의 작가들은 여가를 자유로운 상태, 마음의 자세 또는 영적인 조건으로 이러한 것은 현실세계를 경험하는 데 도움이 된다고 정의한다. 또 다른 이들은 여가는 사회 계급의 기능이라고 본다.

[실전응용 1] 본문 분석란을 활용하여, 아래 지문의 주제문과 뒷받침 문장에 해당하는 내용을 정리하시오.

Many people do not understand that hypnosis is a natural phenomenon. It is an altered state that we frequently go into and out of. Some natural examples of hypnosis include highway hypnosis, where our sense of time and consciousness becomes altered. Have you ever taken a long trip and remembered a town you drove through? An illusion about time is a common trait of hypnotic states. Have you ever become so absorbed in a good book or a good movie that two hours rushed by like minutes? Being severely focused on something makes us enter a hypnotic state.

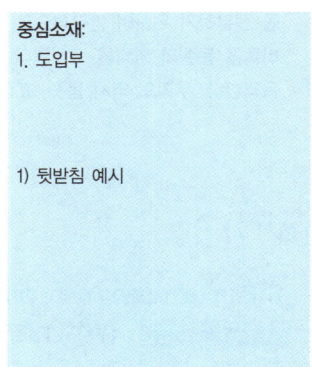

중심소재:
1. 도입부

1) 뒷받침 예시

[실전응용 2] 본문 분석란을 활용하여, 아래 지문의 주제문과 뒷받침 문장에 해당하는 내용을 정리하시오.

Windows of *hanok* reflect the traditional view that forms should be created by relying on feelings. The size and the placement of windows in *hanok* are determined by the senses, not by mathematical calculation. It is like building things with the eye, not with measuring instruments. There is no standard size or position for windows. They are installed where it feels right. This is a natural approach to creation and is based on the aesthetics of feelings. This characteristic of windows of *hanok* shows an example of the abstract beauty in traditional Korean architecture.

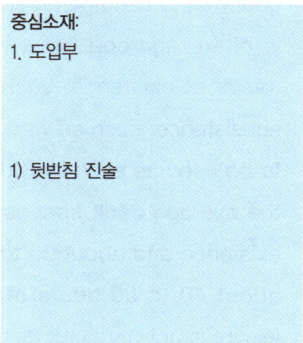

중심소재:
1. 도입부

1) 뒷받침 진술

[실전응용 3] 본문 분석란을 활용하여, 아래 지문의 주제문과 뒷받침 문장에 해당하는 내용을 정리하시오.

Statistics can tell us many things. They can help us learn more about people and places and what is happening in the world around us. We can also use statistics to help us make decisions about the things we do. For example, if you did a survey in your classroom to find out about people's favorite activities, you would be gathering statistics. If you examined these statistics to find out what they were saying, you could then use them to help you decide on the best place to go for a class trip. There are many ways in which we can use statistics to help us every day.

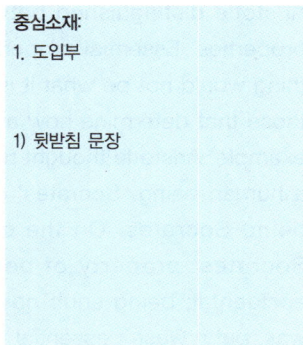

중심소재:
1. 도입부

1) 뒷받침 문장

[실전응용 4] 본문 분석란을 활용하여, 아래 지문의 주제문과 뒷받침 문장에 해당하는 내용을 정리하시오.

There is healing power in flowers—and in trees, fresh air, and sweet-smelling soil. Just walking through a garden or, for that matter, seeing one out your window, can lower blood pressure, reduce stress, and ease pain. Get out there and start digging, and the benefits multiply. While it may be basic and even old-fashioned, using gardening as a health care tool is blossoming. New or remodeled hospitals and nursing homes increasingly come equipped with healing gardens where patients and staff can get away from barren, indoor surroundings. Many also offer patients a chance to get their hands dirty and their minds engaged in caring for plants.

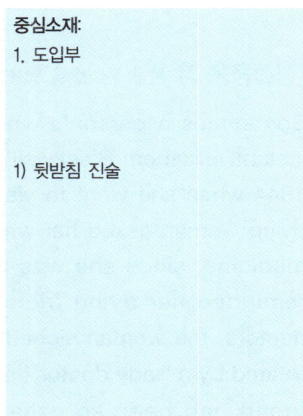

중심소재:
1. 도입부

1) 뒷받침 진술

[실전응용 5] 본문 분석란을 활용하여, 아래 지문의 주제문과 뒷받침 문장에 해당하는 내용을 정리하시오.

Conventions are the most important source of income for some hotels and motels. In the U.S., for example, it is estimated that some 10 million people attend conventions each year. Conventions assure a steady income both from sleeping accommodations and from meeting rooms, which are used for conferences and lectures. Dining facilities are the source of additional revenue through the sale of food and beverages. Local residents also use the catering services, meeting rooms, and ballrooms for social functions and business meetings.

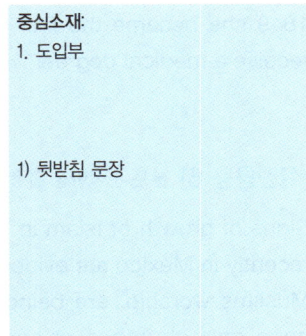

중심소재:
1. 도입부

1) 뒷받침 문장

53

[실전응용 6] 본문 분석란을 활용하여, 아래 지문의 주제문과 뒷받침 문장에 해당하는 내용을 정리하시오.

Aristotle distinguished between essential and accidental properties. Essential properties are those without which a thing would not be what it is, and accidental properties are those that determine how a thing is, but not what it is. For example, Aristotle thought rationality was essential to being a human being. Socrates' rationality was essential to his being Socrates. On the other hand, Aristotle thought Socrates' property of being snub-nosed was merely accidental; being snub-nosed was part of how Socrates was, but it wasn't essential to what or who he was. In other words, take away Socrates' rationality, and he's no longer Socrates, but give him plastic surgery, and he's Socrates with a nose job.

중심소재:
1. 도입부

1) 뒷받침 문장

[실전응용 7] 본문 분석란을 활용하여, 아래 지문의 주제문과 뒷받침 문장에 해당하는 내용을 정리하시오.

Sometimes a person's whole life can be changed in an instant. Elizabeth Blackwell's life changed one afternoon in 1844 when she went to visit a friend who was dying. The dying woman asked her why she did not think of studying medicine, since she was smart and healthy. When she reminded her dying friend that there were no women doctors, the woman sighed and said that if she had been treated by a "lady doctor," she might not be dying. Her sick friend had been so ashamed to mention her internal problems to a man that she hid her pain for too long. When she finally sought treatment, it was too late to save her life. Elizabeth couldn't get the dying woman's suggestion out of her mind. So she decided to devote her life to medicine. In 1849 she became the first woman in the United States to receive a medical degree.

중심소재:
1. 도입부

1) 뒷받침 진술

[실전응용 8] 본문 분석란을 활용하여, 아래 지문의 주제문과 뒷받침 문장에 해당하는 내용을 정리하시오.

Signs of growth of Islam in the United States, Canada, and recently in Mexico are evident everywhere. Mosques, where Muslims worship, are being built in neighborhoods where once only churches or synagogues stood. Women who wear scarves covering their hair according to Islamic

중심소재:
1. 도입부

customs are now a common sight in many towns and cities. Moreover, Muslim holidays are gaining official recognition in such places as Los Angeles, Toronto, and New York. In addition, an increasing number of employers are accommodating the religious needs of their Muslim workers in the same way they respond to the needs of their Jewish workers.

1) 뒷받침 문장

[실전응용 9] 본문 분석란을 활용하여, 아래 지문의 주제문과 뒷받침 문장에 해당하는 내용을 정리하시오.

Modern technology has now rendered many learning disabilities virtually obsolete by providing learners with access to alternative ways of getting information and expressing themselves. Poor spellers have access to spell checkers and individuals with illegible handwriting can use a word processor to produce a neat typescript. People with dyscalculia benefit from having a pocket calculator handy when a math problem comes up. Similarly, learners with poor memories can tape lectures, discussions, and other verbal exchanges. Individuals with faulty visualization skills can use computer-aided design(CAD) software programs that allow them to manipulate three-dimensional objects on screen.

중심소재:
1. 도입부

1) 뒷받침 문장

[실전응용 10] 본문 분석란을 활용하여, 아래 지문의 주제문과 뒷받침 문장어 해당하는 내용을 정리하시오.

Two hypotheses may explain why obese people eat more when anxious. One possibility is that when they were babies, their caregivers interpreted all of their distress signals as requests for food; consequently, as adults, these people have difficulty distinguishing hunger from other feelings, including anxiety. A different possibility is that some obese persons may respond to an anxiety producing situation by doing the one thing that has brought them comfort all their lives namely, eating. The two hypotheses may apply to different kinds of obese people.

중심소재:
1. 도입부

1) 뒷받침 문장

[주제문을 통해 예측하며 글 읽기 연습]

아래 문장 또는 지문은 주제문 또는 주제문을 포함한 특정 지문의 도입부(서론)에 해당한다. 주어진 문장을 바탕으로 하나의 완성된 단락 또는 글을 완성하시오.

1. Many different native American groups lived in North America, and each group had its own type of home, using the natural resources to make homes. For instance, if they lived in or near forests, they would use wood for their homes, which is why different cultures of indians had different types of homes. (도입부)

2. Scientists now understand more about the unique way spiny lobsters create sound to ward off predators. Using a method of sound production resembling that of stringed instruments, spiny lobsters startle attackers by emitting loud, raspy noises. (도입부)

3. No theory of cognitive development has had more impact than the cognitive stages presented by Jean Piaget. Piaget, a Swiss psychologist, suggested that children go through four separate stages in a fixed order that is universal in all children. Piaget declared that these stages differ not only in the quantity of information acquired at each, but also in the quality of knowledge and understanding at that stage. Piaget suggested that movement from one stage to the next occurred when the child reached an appropriate level of maturation and was exposed to relevant types of experiences. Without experience, children were assumed incapable of reaching their highest cognitive ability. Piaget's four stages are known as the sensorimotor, preoperational, concrete operational and formal operational stages. (도입부)

4. Art probably began as a form of communication or record-keeping. (주제문)

5. The term American poetry is in some ways a contradiction. (주제문)

6. Extinction is not a new phenomenon. For hundreds of millions of years, extinction has been occurring naturally as part of the evolutionary process. (주제문)

7. Yet these hunter-gatherers engaged in an array of sophisticated practices to manage their resources and enhance the yield of potential food sources. (중괄식의 주제문)

8. But diamond is extremely hard and transparent. Diamond also is much denser than an equal amount of graphite. (중괄식의 주제문)

9. Several factors contributed to the dramatic population shift from the countryside to urban areas. (주제문)

10. The eastern hognose snake is renowned for its 'death feigning' behavior. (주제문)

11. Langston Hughes was one of the most important writers and thinkers of the Harlem Renaissance, which was the African American artistic movement in the 1920s that celebrated black life and culture. (주제문)

12. Dolphins are social animals that travel in schools varying in size from small herds of 2 to 5 members to immense schools of 1,000 or more. (첫 번째 문단)

Scientists have observed dolphins displaying three types of caregiving behaviors: standing by, excitement, and supporting. (두 번째 문단)

13. Louis Sullivan is widely considered America's first truly modern architect. (주제문)

14. Historically, most periodicals have differed from newspapers in their format, publication schedule, and content. (주제문)

15. A remarkable variety of insects inhabit this planet. More species of insects exist than all other animal species together. Insects have survived on earth for more than 300 million years, and may possess the ability to survive for millions more.

16. Modern humans have a number of physical characteristics reflective of an ape ancestry.

17. The amount of carbon dioxide in the atmosphere has been increasing by 0.4 percent a year because of the use of oil, gas, and coal and the burning of tropical forests. The other gases that contribute to the greenhouse effect are increasing even faster.

18. People sometimes call the human body a machine-the most wonderful one ever built. Of course, the human body is not a machine.

[참고] 주제문의 중심내용을 뒷받침하는 다양한 장치

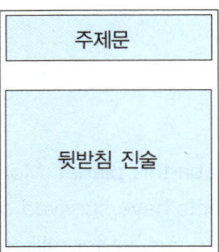

1) 예시
주제문에서 밝힌 중심내용을 뒷받침하는 가장 흔한 방법 중 하나로 For example, For instance, Take (for example)와 같은 시그널을 통해 쉽사리 파악할 수 있다. 때로, 이러한 시그널이 생략되는 경우도 있지만 주제문에 해당하는 일반진술에서 구체적 진술로 넘어가는 구분이 명확하기에 충분한 연습을 통해 구분이 가능하다.

2) 역사적 사례
역사적 사례를 통해 글의 요지를 뒷받침하는 방법은 예시의 한 형태로 개인의 경험과 같은 주관적 요소가 가미된 경우와 달리 보편적 성격이 강하기에 뒷받침 진술의 객관성을 확보하기 좋다.

3) 일화
글쓴이 본인 또는 제 삼자의 경험담을 통해 주제문에서 밝힌 중심내용을 뒷받침할 수 있다. 일반적으로 필자가 느낀 교훈담을 전달하는 경우가 많다.

4) 연구·조사·실험·관찰
연구·조사·실험·관찰을 통해 얻은 객관적 자료를 바탕으로 주제문에서 밝힌 중심내용을 뒷받침한다.

5) 권위자의 진술
글의 주제와 관련된 분야의 권위자 도는 전문가의 견해를 인용함으로 글의 요지를 강조하거나 중심내용에 대한 뒷받침 근거로 활용한다. 즉, 권위자의 진술은 글의 요지가 될 수 있는 동시에 중심내용에 내용에 대한 뒷받침 근거가 될 수 있음을 기억한다.

6 부연진술

부연진술이란?

뒷받침 문장에 대한 추가적인 정보를 제공하는 부분을 말한다. 아래의 예를 통해 적용해 보자.

[예시 1]

1. <u>Computers are helpful in many ways.</u> 1) First, they are fast. ① They can work with information much more quickly than a person. 2) Second, computers can work with lots of information at the same time. 3) Third, they can keep information for a long time. ② They do not forget things the way people do. 4) Also, computers are almost always correct. ③ They are not perfect, of course, but they usually do not make mistakes.

중심소재: 컴퓨터
1. 도입부 = 주제문
1) 뒷받침 진술 1
  - 신속성
① 부연진술
2) 뒷받침 진술 2
  한 번에 아주 많은 정보 처리
3) 뒷받침 진술 3
② 부연진술
4) 뒷받침 진술 4
  - 정확성
③ 부연진술

★ 뒷받침 진술에 대한 부연진술이다. 뒷받침 진술을 A라고 하고 부연진술을 B라고 할 때 두 관계는 언제나 A = B(같은 맥락의 진술)의 순접이 된다.

★ 나열의 글 전개방식을 확인한다.

| 해석
컴퓨터는 다양한 방면에서 도움이 된다. 첫째, 컴퓨터는 빠르다. 사람보다 훨씬 더 빠르게 정보를 처리할 수 있다. 둘째, 한 번에 많은 양의 정보를 처리할 수 있다. 셋째, 오랫동안 정보를 보관할 수 있다. 사람들이 잊어버리는 것과 같이 정보를 잊지 않는다. 또한, 컴퓨터는 거의 항상 정확하다. 물론, 완벽하지는 않지만 일반적으로 실수를 하지 않는다.

[예시 2]

1. <u>My hometown is famous for several amazing natural features</u>. 1) ① First, it is noted for the Wheaton River, which is very wide and beautiful. Ⓐ On either side of this river, which is 175 feet wide, are many willow trees which have long

중심소재: Hometown
1. 도입부 = 주제문
나의 고향은 여러 아름다운 자연적 특징으로 유명하다.

★ 주제는 'My home town'이다. 중심내용은 'several amazing natural features'이다. 앞에서 설정한 주제와 중심내용을 생각하면서 주제의 폭을 좁히도록 한다.

나열의 글 전개방식을 나타내는 시그널이다. First, Also와 Third를 확인할 수 있다.

branches that can move gracefully in the wind. In autumn the leaves of these trees fall and cover the riverbanks like golden snow. ② Also, on the other side of the town is Wheaton Hill, which is unusual because it is very steep. ⓑ Even though it is steep, climbing this hill is not dangerous, because there are some firm rocks along the sides that can be used as stairs. There are no trees around this hill, so it stands clearly against the sky and can be seen from many miles away. ③ The third amazing feature is the Big Old Tree. ⓒ This tree stands two hundred feet tall and is probably about six hundred years old. 2. These three landmarks are truly amazing and make my hometown a famous place.

1) 뒷받침 진술
① 뒷받침 진술 1
– Wheaton River
Ⓐ 부연진술
② 뒷받침 진술 2
– Wheaton Hill
Ⓑ 부연진술
③ 뒷받침 진술 3
– Big Old Tree
Ⓒ 부연진술
2. 결론(일반진술)

앞에서 언급된 개별적 사항(뒷받침 진술)을 일반화하는 시그널 These를 확인한다.

| 해설

'서론 – 본론 – 결론'의 삼단구성을 확인한다.

| 해석

나의 고장은 놀라운 자연적 특징으로 유명하다. 우선 우리 고장은 Wheaton 강으로 유명한데, 이 강은 폭이 아주 넓고 아름답다. 175피트 넓이의 이 강 다른 쪽 편에는 수없이 많은 버드나무가 있는데 아주 긴 가지가 바람에 우아하게 나부낀다. 가을에는 이 나무의 잎이 떨어져 황금색 눈과 같이 강둑을 덮는다. 또한, 이 도시의 다른 편에는 Wheaton 언덕이 있는데, 경사가 아주 가파른 것으로 독특하다. 이것이 아주 가파르지만, 이 언덕을 오르는 것은 그리 위험하진 않다. 이유는 계단처럼 사용할 수 있는 단단한 돌들이 놓여있기 때문이다. 이 언덕은 주위에 나무 없이 하늘에 우뚝 서 있어, 멀리서도 잘 보인다. 세 번째 놀라운 특징은 바로 아주 오래된 나무이다. 이 나무는 2백 피트이며, 아마도 약 6백 년 된 것으로 알고 있다. 이 세가지 특징은 아주 놀랍고, 이로 인해 우리 고장은 유명하다.

[예시 3]

중심소재는 '포플러 나무'이다. 중심내용(controlling idea)을 고려하면서 주제의 폭을 좁히도록 한다.

본문에서 구체적으로 밝힐 중심내용(controlling idea)에 해당한다.

도입부 = 통념 A ≠ B
경우 1. But A ≠ B
경우 2. But A ≠ B = C
뒷받침 진술   뒷받침 진술
본문은 경우 2에 해당한다.

1. Most people believe poplar trees can only be used for wood or paper. 1) But they can be also used for more important purposes. ① Poplar trees can be used Ⓐ to guard against water pollution. ⓐ They are planted as barriers to keep waste from entering groundwater and rivers. ⓑ Their large root systems trap waste, and help reduce the loss of soil. Ⓒ In the future, poplar trees may become important tools for cleaning the environment. ⓑ Some scientists think poplars may be a valuable resource to remove poisonous substances from the soil.

중심소재: 포플러 나무
1. 도입부 = 통념
포플러 나무는 나무 또는 종이를 만드는 데만 사용한다고 알려졌음
1) 주제문
But 이후 포플러 나무의 다른 중요한 기능 언급
① 뒷받침 진술
Ⓐ 기능 1(수질 오염방지)
  ⓐ 부연진술
Ⓑ 기능 2(토양손실 방지)
Ⓒ 기능 3(환경정화)
  ⓑ 부연진술

62

| 해석

사람들은 대부분 포플러 나무가 목재나 종이를 만드는 데만 사용된다고 믿고 있다. 하지만 이것들은 또한 더욱 중요한 목적에 사용될 수도 있다. 포플러 나무들은 수질오염을 막기 위해 사용할 수 있다. 폐수가 지하수나 강물로 흘러들어 가는 것을 막기 위한 장치로 포플러 나무를 심기도 한다. 커다란 뿌리들이 오물을 막아주거나, 토사가 유실되는 것을 감소시키도록 도와준다. 미래에, 포플러 나무는 환경 정화를 위한 중요한 도구가 될 수 있다. 몇몇 과학자들은 포플러 나무가 토양에 있는 유독 물질을 제거할 수 있는 귀중한 자원이 될 수 있다고 생각한다.

[실전응용 1] 아래 지문에서 부연진술을 구별하시오.

Drug abusers cause a great deal of damage to themselves. They may spend too much on drugs and create money problems for themselves. They may also get into trouble with police, and this can destroy their lives. And drug abusers hurt people around them as well. They cause great pain to their family and friends, who have to watch a loved one destroy his or her life. They also damage their communities. For example, many drug abusers end up in jail or in the hospital, and the community must pay for this.

중심소재:
1. 도입부
1) 뒷받침 진술 1
①

2) 뒷받침 진술 2
②

3) 뒷받침 진술 3
③

[실전응용 2] 아래 지문에서 부연진술을 구별하시오.

Psychologists who study memory tell us that our memories have three parts. First, there is short-term memory, which holds on to sights, sounds, smells, tastes and tactile experiences for only a minute or so. The second type of memory is working memory, which is where we use memory to think. We make comparisons, look for causes and effects, predict what will happen in the future. Finally, long-term memory is what we keep for many years. It is where we store the words to a song learned in childhood. We need all three kinds of memory to function well in life.

중심소재:
1. 도입부

1) 뒷받침 진술

[실전응용 3] 아래 지문에서 부연진술을 구별하시오.

It is important to use water carefully. Here are some ways you can use less water. First, be sure to turn off faucets tightly. They should not drip in the bathroom or kitchen sink. Second, do not keep the water running for a long time. Turn it off while you are doing something else. For example, it should be off while you are shaving or brushing your teeth. It should also be off while you are washing the

중심소재:
1. 도입부

1) 뒷받침 진술
① 방법 1

② 방법 2

dishes. Finally, in the summer you should water your garden in the evening. That way you will not lose a lot of water.

③ 방법 3

[실전응용 4] 아래 지문에서 부연진술을 구별하시오.

In 2003, there were already estimated to be several hundred thousand blogs on the Internet, and the number is growing by tens of thousands a month. A blog, however, differs from a traditional web site in several ways. Most importantly, it is updated much more regularly. Many blogs are updated every day, and some are updated several times a day. Also, most blogs use special software or web sites which are specifically aimed at bloggers, so you don't need to be a computer expert to create your own blog. This means that ordinary people who may find computer difficult to use can easily set up and start writing their own blog.

중심소재:
1. 도입부
1) 주제문

① 뒷받침 진술

[실전응용 5] 아래 지문에서 부연진술을 구별하시오.

In some cases, analysis of texts has shown that men and women tend to have different styles of writing. They differ, first of all, in the amount of personal pronouns they use. For instance, women are far more likely than men to use pronouns like "I," "you," and "she." On the other hand, men tend to use words like "a," "the," "that," and "these" more than women do. They also are more inclined to use numbers and quantifying words like "more" and "several." In contrast to women, men more readily modify nouns with phrases rather than single words. For example, women will probably write "rose garden" whereas men would write "garden of roses."

중심소재:
1. 도입부

1) 뒷받침 문장

7 통일성과 응집성

1. 통일성

통일성이란 하나의 문단에서는 하나의 주제만을 다루어야 하는 원칙을 말한다. 만약 하나의 문단 안에서 다양한 주제를 두서없이 기술했을 경우, 글을 읽는 사람은 글쓴이가 궁극적으로 어떤 내용을 전달하려는 것인지 알 수가 없게 된다. 통일성을 잘 따르고 있는 글인지를 알아보는 방법은 다음과 같다.

① 주제문에서 밝힌 주제와 중심내용을 뒷받침 문장에서 충실하게 전달하고 있는가?
② 주제를 전달하기에 가장 적절한 글 전개방식을 뒷받침 문장에 적용하고 있는가?
③ 새로운 정보가 없는 불필요한 문장을 재진술하고 있지는 않은가?
④ 단락별 주제는 전체 주제의 통일성을 깨고 있지는 않은가?

아래 예시를 통해 글의 통일성을 살펴보도록 하자.

[예시 1]

1. <u>Each of the Russian manned space exploration projects had specific major goals</u>. 1) ① **For example**, the Vostok project was designed to test whether or not human beings could survive and function in outer space. ② **For another example**, the Voshkhod project was intended to find out whether people could work in the weightless environment of space. Ⓐ One Voshkhod cosmonaut experimented with weightlessness by taking a "spacewalk." That is, he floated in a spacesuit outside his Voshkhod spacecraft, connected to it by a tether. ③ **Finally**, the Soyuz project, with three cosmonauts, had goals of testing spacecraft and spaceflight skills so that people could fly long missions in Earth orbit.

중심소재: 러시아 유인 우주 탐사 프로젝트
1. **도입부** = 주제문
1) 뒷받침 진술
① 첫 번째 프로젝트
② 두 번째 프로젝트
Ⓐ 부연진술
③ 세 번째 프로젝트

★ 주제는 '러시아 유인 우주탐사 프로젝트'이다.

★ 본문에서 주로 다뤄질 중심내용에 해당한다.

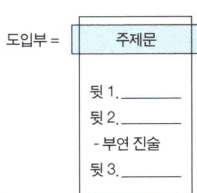

| 해설

주제문에서 밝힌 중심내용(Controlling Idea)을 뒷받침 진술에서 나열의 전개방식을 활용하여 짜임새 있는 구조를 취하고 있다. 주제문에서 밝힌 하나의 주제문을 뒷받침 문장에서 자세히 다룬다는 점에서 통일성을 잘 갖춘 지문이다. 글의 구조를 보면 다음과 같다.

	Pattern of Writing	본문의 구성
일반진술	주제문(Topic Sentence)	러시아 우주 탐사 프로그램의 특정한 목적
구체적 진술	뒷받침 문장 (Supporting Sentences)	목적 1. 뒷받침 진술 목적 2. 뒷받침 진술 – 부연진술 목적 3. 뒷받침 진술

| 해석

러시아 유인 우주 탐사프로젝트는 각각의 구체적인 주요 목표가 있었다. 예를 들어 Vostok 프로젝트는 인간이 우주 공간에서 살아남고 기능할 수 있는가에 대하여 테스트하게끔 디자인되었다. 또 다른 예로, Voshkhod 프로젝트는 우주의 무중력환경에서 사람들이 움직일 수 있는지에 대하여 알아내기 위한 것이었다. Voshkhod의 한 우주비행사는 무중력상태에서 '우주 걷기'를 할 수 있는지를 실험했다. 다시 말해, Voshkhod에 연결된 줄에 매달려 밖에서 우주복을 입고 날아다니는 것이었다. 마지막으로 Soyuz 프로젝트는 3명의 우주비행사가 우주선과 우주 비행 기술을 테스트하여 사람들이 지구 궤도에서 오랜 임무수행 기간 동안 비행할 수 있도록 하는 목적을 수행했다.

[예문 2]

★ 일반통념으로 시작하는 글이므로 이후 'But, However' 또는 유사한 표현에 주의한다.

★ 중심소재는 'skyscraper' 이다.

★ 글의 전환을 이끄는 시그널이며, 이후 글쓴이의 주장이 드러난다(통념 비판에 주로 나오는 'But, However' 대신 문장이 나왔다는 점에 주의한다).

도입부 = 통념(중심소재)
However (But) 주제문
뒷받침 근거

1. When people think of skyscrapers, they think of New York, a city with many high-rise buildings. 1) There is no other city like New York, and this is because of its great buildings that reach up into the sky. 2. It comes as a surprise then to learn that Chicago, not New York, is the home of the skyscraper. 1) The first high-rise building was built in Chicago in 1884, and it was nine stories high. This is not tall compared with today's buildings, but it was the first building over six stories. There were no tall buildings before that because the needed technology didn't exist.

중심소재: 고층빌딩
1. 도입부
통념: 고층빌딩의 기원은 뉴욕이다.
1) 근거
2. 주제문
고층빌딩의 기원은 시카고이다.
1) 뒷받침 진술
역사적 사실을 바탕으로 주제문에서 밝힌 중심내용을 뒷받침하고 있다.

| 해설

'통념 – 반전 – 글쓴이의 견해'로 진술되는 통념비판(Myth-breaking)의 글로 'It comes as a surprise'를 기점으로 이전에 언급된 통념이 옳지 않음을 지적하고, 이후 글쓴이의 견해 및 뒷받침 문장을 제시하는 글이다. 하나의 주제를 다룬다는 점에서 통일성을 잘 따른 글이라 볼 수 있다.

| 해석

사람들이 마천루를 생각할 때는 많은 고층 건물들이 있는 뉴욕을 생각한다. 뉴욕 같은 도시는 없다. 그리고 이는 하늘로 치솟아 오른 거대한 건물들 때문이다. 그러나 (사람들은) 뉴욕이 아니라 시카고가 마천루의 발생지라는 사실을 알고는 놀란다. 최초의 높은 건물은 1884년에 시카고에서 건설되었고, 9층이었다. 이것은 오늘날의 건물들과 비교하면 높지 않지만 6층 이상으로서 최초의 건물이었다. (당시) 필요한 건축 기술이 존재하지 않았기 때문에 이 건물 이전에는 높은 건물이 전혀 없었다.

[실전응용 1] 아래 지문이 통일성을 잘 따르는 지문인지 분석하시오.

Anger can make you physically sick. The next time you hear someone arguing in a raised voice, try to imagine what is happening in his body. Blood pressure builds up. A weak heart can be stressed to a dangerous point. Headaches often follow the buildup of rage. The whole internal system is stressed, ready for an emergency, and the whole digestive process is shut off or slowed down. Stomachaches, indigestion, and all sorts of trouble with digestive organs can arise from chronic anger. You can turn red, sweat, tremble, and be very uncomfortable—all because you are angry.

중심소재:
1. 도입부

1) 뒷받침 진술

[실전응용 2] 아래 지문이 통일성을 잘 따르는 지문인지 분석하시오.

In everyday conversation, there are different ways to say what we want. When we are with a group of friends, we can say to them, "Go get me that plate!" or "Shut up!" However, when we are invited to other people's house with our parents, we must say, "Could you please pass me that plate, if you don't mind?" and "I'm sorry. I don't mean to interrupt, but I'm not able to hear the speaker." We should use different expressions in different social situations.

중심소재:
1. 도입부

1) 뒷받침 진술

2. 결론

[실전응용 3] 아래 지문이 통일성을 잘 따르는 지문인지 분석하시오.

People think that English is already the international language. But English must stop being used as the international language. Scientists and business people do use English, but there are relatively few people in the world who use English conversationally. According to recent statistics, English is not spoken by more than 3.5 billion of the world's population. To put it a different way, fewer than one out of ten people in the world speak English.

중심소재:
1. 도입부

1) 주제문

① 뒷받침 진술

2. 응집성

응집성이란 일반적인 의미에서 두 가지 요소가 서로 밀접하게 연관이 있다는 말이다. 글쓰기에서 응집성이란 주제문과 뒷받침 문장, 그리고 뒷받침 문장 내 문장 간 자연스러운 흐름을 의미한다. 응집성이 깨진 글을 읽으면 독자는 '논리적 흐름(Logical flows of Ideas)'의 결함으로 글쓴이가 궁극적으로 전달하려는 내용을 이해하기가 쉽지 않게 되거나 심지어 무슨 말을 하는지 모르는 경우가 발생할 수도 있다. 주제를 효율적으로 전달하기 위해 뒷받침 문장에서 활용되는 글 전개 방식과 문장과 문장을 자연스럽게 연결해 주는 대명사, 접속사, 반복 어구 등을 통해 응집성을 유지한다.

*글전개의 단락 예시

① 나열

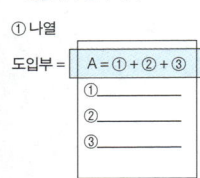

② 인과

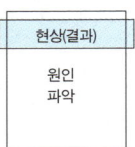

③ 비교·대조

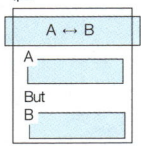

④ 순서

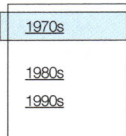

1) 글 전개방식을 활용하여 주제문과 뒷받침 문장 간의 응집성을 높인다.

글 전개방식에는 다섯 가지 종류가 있다.

① Listing(나열)

② Cause and Effect(인과)

③ Comparison and Contrast(비교·대조)

④ Order(순서)

　　– Chronological Order(시간적 흐름)

　　– Spatial Order(공간적 흐름)

　　– Order of Importance(중요도에 따른 기술)

　　– Classification(분류)

　　– Procedure(절차)

2) 대명사, 접속사, 반복 어구 등을 활용하여 글의 응집성을 높인다.

① Location

Against	Among	Away from
Beneath	Between	Beyond
In back of	In front of	Onto
Over	Throughout	Under

② Time

After	As soon as	At
Before	Finally	First
Immediately	Meanwhile	Second
Then	Third	Tomorrow
Until	When	Yesterday

③ Similarities

| Also | As | Furthermore |
| Like | Likewise | Similarly |

*응집성을 높여 주는 요소
① 대명사
② 접속사
③ a N → the N → it/ that
④ 반복어구

④ Differences

| Although | But | Even though |
| However | On the other hand | Yet |

⑤ Emphasizing a point

| Again | For this reason | In fact |
| To emphasize | To repeat | Truly |

⑥ Conclusion

| As a result | Finally | In conclusion |
| In summary | Therefore | To sum up |

⑦ Adding information

Additionally	Also	And
Another	Equally important	Finally
In addition	Likewise	Moreover

⑧ Clarification

| For instance | In other words |
| That is | To put in another way |

[예시 1 – 인과]

1. According to some scientists, one of the most serious problems for the environment is acid rain. 1) ① Acid rain is caused mainly by power plants that burn coal to produce electricity. The smoke from these power plants contains acidic substances which later fall back to earth in rain or snow. As a result, the amount of acids increases in lakes and rivers, and fish die. ② Scientists are also warning that acid

중심소재: 환경문제 → 산성비
1. 도입부 = 주제문
산성비로 인한 심각한 환경피해(현상–원인)
1) 뒷받침 진술
① 산성비의 형성 배경과 유해 성분 (원인) – 빗속의 산성 증가로 호수와 강가의 물고기 사망(결과)
② 식수 오염 → 인간의 건강 위협

★ 뒷받침 진술(본문)에서 다룰 중심내용(controlling idea)에 해당한다.

★ 글의 중심소재이다.

★ 글의 응집성을 높여주는 표현으로 결과를 나타내는 'as a result, thererfore'가 있다.

rain can damage plants and trees, and lead to the contamination of drinking water. **Therefore**, it is a danger to human health.

| 해설

인과의 글 전개방식을 활용하여 주제를 효율적으로 전달하고 있다.

| 해석

몇몇 과학자들 말에 따르면 가장 심각한 환경 문제 중 하나는 산성비라고 한다. 산성비는 주로 전력 생산을 위해 석탄을 연소하는 발전소에서 발생한다. 발전소에서 나오는 연기는 산성물질을 포함하고 있으며, 나중에 비 또는 눈으로 다시 지상으로 돌아온다. 결과적으로 호수나 강에서 산성 비율이 증가하게 되고, 물고기는 죽게 된다. 과학자들은 또한 산성비가 식물과 나무들에도 손상을 입힐 수 있으며, 식수의 오염을 초래할 수 있다고 경고한다. 그래서 이는 인간의 건강에도 하나의 위험 요소이다.

[예시 2]

★ 중심소재

1. It is commonly recognized that dogs have an extreme antagonism toward cats. 1) ① **This** enmity between **these** two species can be traced back to the time of **the early Egyptian dynasties**. Archaeologists in recent years have discovered Egyptian texts in which there are detailed accounts of canines brutally mauling felines. ② **Today this** type of cruelty between **these** two domestic pets can be witnessed in regions as close as your own neighborhood. Ⓐ For example, when dogs are walked by their masters, and they happen to catch sight of a stray cat, they will pull with all their strength on their leash until the master is forced to yield; the typical result is that a feline is chased up a tree. 2. The hatred between dogs and cats has lasted for so many centuries; it is unlikely that this conflict will ever end.

★ 본문에서 구체적으로 다뤄질 중심내용에 해당한다.

★ 구체적 예시를 통해 주제문을 효과적으로 전달하면서 글의 통일성과 함께 응집성을 높이는 역할을 한다.

중심소재: 개, 고양이
1. 도입부 = 주제문
1) 뒷받침 진술
① 과거의 사례
고대 역사적 문서에 드러난 적대감
② 현대의 사례
Ⓐ 예시부연
2. 요약 정리(주제문 재진술)

| 해설

본문은 하나의 주제인 '개는 고양이를 적대시한다.'는 내용만을 다루고 있으며, 이후 전개되는 내용은 이를 뒷받침하는 문장으로 구성되어 있다. 또한, 뒷받침 문장의 구성을 보면 'For example' 과 같은 연결사를 적절히 사용함으로 글의 응집성을 높이고 있는 동시에, 시간의 순서에 따라 글의 논리적 흐름(a flow of logic)을 잘 갖추고 있다. 글의 구조를 살펴보면,

주제문 (Topic Sentence)	Dogs have an extreme antagonism toward cats.
뒷받침 문장 (Supporting Sentences)	① 구체적 예 1. 고대 Egyptian texts showing 'detailed accounts of canines brutally mauling felines.' ② 구체적 예 2. 현대 They(dogs) happen to catch sight of a stray cat, they will pull with all their strength on their leash.
주제문 재진술	The hatered between dogs and cats has losted So many Centrie. It is likely that _____ .

해석

개가 고양이에 대해 극단적 적대감을 가지고 있다는 점은 일반적으로 잘 알려졌다. 이 두 종 사이의 적대감은 초기 고대 이집트 왕조 시대까지 거슬러 올라갈 수 있다. 최근 고고학자들은 이집트의 문서에서 개가 고양이를 잔인하게 괴롭히는 자세한 설명을 발견했다. 오늘날 이 두 애완동물 사이의 이러한 종류의 잔인성은 우리 주변만큼이나 가까운 지역에서 발견할 수 있다. 예를 들어, 개가 주인과 같이 산책할 때, 길고양이를 보게 되면, 가는 주인이 항복할 때까지 목줄을 힘껏 당기고는 결과적으로 고양이가 나무에 쫓겨 올라가는 현상이 발생한다. 가와 고양이의 적대감은 수 세기 동안 지속이 되었다. 이 싸움은 끝날 것 같지는 않아 보인다.

8 일반진술과 구체적 진술

　일반진술(General Statement)은 보편적이면서도 포괄적인 문장을 말하고, 구체적 진술(Specific Statement)은 일반진술의 내용을 상세하게 풀어쓴 내용을 말한다. 이를 단락(paragraph)의 측면에서 이해할 경우, 일반진술은 하나의 단락을 대표하는 포괄적 문장으로 글에서 전달하고자 하는 핵심내용을 담고 있다. 그런 의미에서 일반진술은 주제와 중심내용을 담고 있기에 주제문이라고 할 수 있다. 구체적 진술은 자연히 뒷받침 진술로 파악할 수 있다. 다음 예를 보고 일반진술(General Statement)과 구체적 진술(Specific Statement)을 구별해 보자.

1)

> A: The dancing bear at the circus was very entertaining.
> B: It was able to balance a ball on its nose while it was standing on one foot.

→ A는 일반진술이고 B는 구체적 진술로 서커스에서 춤추는 곰은 흥미롭다는 첫 번째 내용에 대한 구체적 예를 B에서 뒷받침 문장으로 제시하고 있다.

2)

> A: Fast-food franchises have been very successful in the U.S.
> B: At the major hamburger or chicken franchises, people know what the food is going to taste like, wherever they buy it.

→ A는 일반진술이고 B는 구체적 진술로 미국에서 패스트푸드가 성공한 원인을 구체적으로 B에서 설명하고 있다.

3)

> A: Children should be taught positive ways to interact with their pets.
> B: One positive way of interacting with a pet is to hold it correctly.

→ A는 일반진술이고 B는 구체적 진술이다. A에서 아이가 자신의 애완동물과 상호작용을 할 때 필요한 올바른 방법을 가르쳐야 한다고 말한 후, B에서 뒷받침 문장으로 애완동물을 바르게 잡는 것에 대해 언급하고 있다.

4)

> A: There are several chores that I do every day.
> B: I have to wash the dishes, make the beds, and take out the trash.

→ A가 일반진술이고 B는 구체적 진술이다. 나열의 글 전개를 바탕으로 일반진술에 대한 구체적 진술을 언급하고 있다.

5)

> A: For those who are forgetful, the following tips can make the holiday season just a little easier.
> B: One month before the Christmas or Jewish holidays, buy and mail holiday cards. Three weeks before, mail gifts to anyone you won't be seeing in person. Two weeks before, tip service providers that you use regularly. One week before, start planning the menu.

→ A는 일반진술, B는 구체적 진술에 해당한다.

[문단 적용] 아래의 지문에서 주제문과 뒷받침 문장의 관계를 고려하면서 일반진술과 구체적 진술을 구별해보자.

[예시 1]

1. Even the best listeners are unable to listen carefully to everything they hear.1) ① One reason is the overload of messages we encounter each day. Ⓐ Besides the numerous hours we spend hearing others speak, we may spend several more hours listening to the radio or television. It just isn't possible to avoid having our attention wander at least part of this time. ② Another cause of poor listening is a preoccupation

중심소재: 경청 → 경청을 방해하는 요인
1. 도입부 = 주제문
1) 뒷받침 진술
① 첫번째 이유
  Ⓐ 부연진술
② 두번째 이유
  Ⓑ 부연진술
③ 세번째 이유
  Ⓒ 부연진술

★ 1), 2), 3)은 첫 번째 문장에서 밝힌 주제문에 대한 뒷받침 진술로 주의를 기울이는 사람조차 모든 것을 들을 수 없는 이유를 자세히 설명하는 구체적 진술에 해당한다.

★ 특정 현상의 이유를 밝히는 글임을 알 수 있다.

with personal concerns. ⓑ A romance gone sour or a good grade on a test may take prominence in our mind even as someone is speaking to us. ③ In addition, being surrounded by noise may result in poor listening. ⓒ For example, many voices at a noisy party or the sound of traffic may make it difficult for us to hear everything that is being said.

| 해설

첫 번째 문장에 다음과 같은 내용을 추가하면 주제문으로 설정할 수 있다.

> 청취를 잘하는 사람조차 모든 것을 들을 수 없는데, <u>세 가지 측면에서 그 원인을 파악할 수 있다.</u>

위의 내용에서 밑줄 친 부분, 즉 중심내용(Controlling Idea)을 추가하면 주제문으로 설정할 수 있으며 이를 도식화하면 다음과 같다.

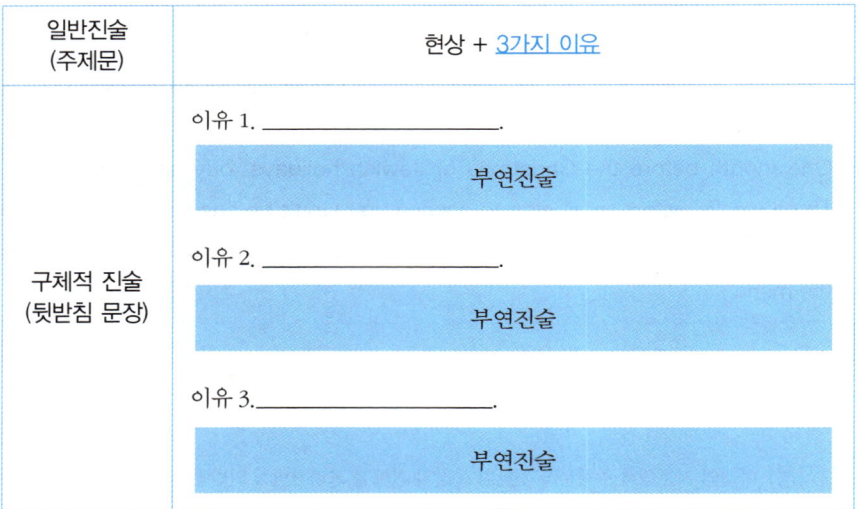

| 해석

아무리 잘 듣는 사람들이라 해도 듣는 모든 것에 신중하게 귀를 기울일 수는 없다. 한 가지 이유는 우리가 매일 마주하는 메시지의 과부하다. 우리가 다른 사람들이 말하는 것을 듣는데 보내는 수많은 시간 외에도 우리는 많은 시간을 라디오나 텔레비전을 들으면서 보낸다. 최소한 이런 시간에는 우리의 주의가 산만해지는 것을 피하는 것이 불가능하다. 잘 들을 수 없는 또 다른 이유는 개인적인 일에 몰두하기 때문이다. 소원해진 애정관계나 시험에서의 좋은 성적 같은 것이 누군가 우리에게 말하고 있을 때조차도 우리 마음을 사로잡고 있을 수 있다. 덧붙여, 소음으로 둘러싸여 있으면 귀 기울이는 것을 제대로 못하게 된다. 예를 들어 시끄러운 파티에서의 많은 목소리나 교통 소음이 우리가 이야기되고 있는 모든 것에 귀 기울이는 것을 어렵게 만든다.

[예시 2]

1. Babies experience anxiety when they see strangers. ① Children aged 2 through 6 show anxiety about things not based in reality such as ghosts. Kids aged 7 through 12 often fear real situations that may happen to them, such as injuries or accidents. 1) As a child grows, fears may disappear. ⓐ For example, a child who couldn't sleep with the light off at age 5 may enjoy a ghost story years later. ⓑ And some fears may extend only to one kind, as in the example of the child who wants to pet a lion at the zoo but wouldn't dream of petting the neighbor's dog.

중심소재: 아이들이 겪는 불안감
1. **도입부**: 중심소재 도출(불안감)
1) 시기에 따른 불안감의 속성
① 2~6: 현실에 바탕을 두지 않는 '유령'과 같은 것에 대해 불안감을 느낌.
② 7~12: 다친다거나 사고가 발생할 것이라는 막연한 불안감(현실에 기반을 둠)
2) 불안감의 제거
① 예시불안
유령에 대한 불안감
3) 불안감의 특수성
특정 대상에게만 적용됨

★주제문으로 글 전체의 중심내용을 포괄하는 일반진술에 해당한다.

★일반진술에서 드러난 중심내용을 자세히 풀어쓴 구체적 진술에 해당한다.

| 해설
본문의 구조는 중괄식으로 다음과 같은 구조를 취한다.

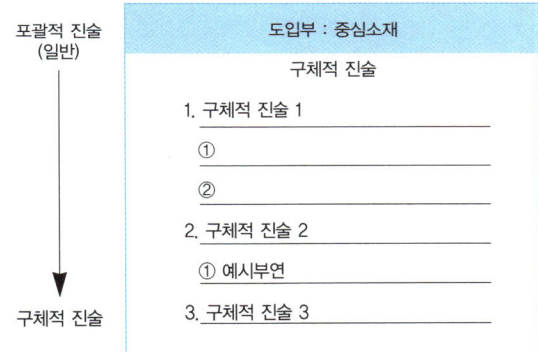

| 해석
아기들은 낯선 사람을 보면 불안감을 경험한다. 어린이들은 2세부터 6세까지 귀신과 같은 실제로는 존재하지 않는 것에 관하여 불안감을 느낀다. 7세부터 12세까지의 아이들은 종종 자신에게 일어날 수도 있는 상황, 예를 들자면 부상이나 사고와 같은 것에 두려움을 느낀다. 어린이는 자라면서 두려움이 사라지기도 한다. 예를 들면, 다섯 살 때에는 불을 끄면 잠들지 못했던 어린이가 다음 해에는 귀신 이야기를 즐기기도 한다. 그리고 어떤 두려움은 한 종류에만 영향을 미치는데, 예를 들어보자면, 동물원에서 사자를 어루만지고 싶어 하는 어린이가 옆집 개를 어루만지는 것은 꿈꾸지도 않는다.

| 참고
일반진술과 구체적 진술은 상대적 개념이다. 일반진술의 내용이 좀 더 포괄적인 개념에서 구체적 진술이 될 수 있고, 구체적 진술의 내용이 범위가 좁혀졌을 때, 다시 일반진술과 구체적 진술로 나뉠 수 있다.

[예시 3]

1. A forest fire in Brazil affects the weather in Moscow by creating huge dust clouds that eventually float over Russia. 1) Every element in an ecosystem depends on every other element, even the so-called non-living elements such as minerals, oxygen, and sunlight. ① Yes, light is an integral element of all life. The sun is food for many of earth's life forms. Physicists speak of photons of light as being interchangeable. When the light from an object hits a person, only some of it bounces off. Most of the photons are absorbed into the person. Its energy becomes that person's energy. 2. This is how incredible interdependence is — everything is constantly becoming everything else.

중심소재: 생태계 → 생태계의 각 요소
1. 도입부: 뒷받침 근거
생태계의 모든 요소는 서로 연관되어 있다는 구체적 사례
1) 주제문
① 뒷받침 예시
2. 결론
주제문 재진술

| 해설
본문의 구성은 다음과 같다.

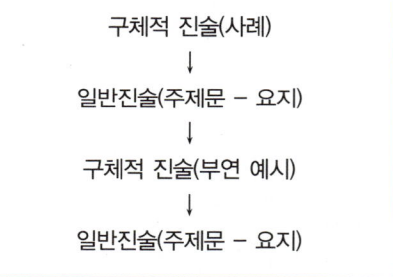

구체적 진술에 해당하는 ①의 내용만을 떼어 다시 '일반진술과 구체적 진술'을 구별하면 다음과 같다.

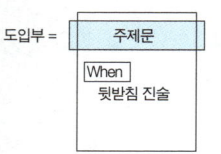

1. Physicists speak of photons of light as being interchangeable. 1) When the light from an object hits a person, only some of it bounces off. Most of the photons are absorbed into the person. Its energy becomes that person's energy.

1. 일반진술
1) 구체적 진술

*구체적 진술을 이끄는 시그널
1. For example / For instance
2. When / If
3. Imagine / Consider / Suppose / Let's think
4. Take(an example of)
5. 시간의 부사(구)
6. 개별적 대상 지칭

글의 요지는 일반진술에서 이끌어낸다는 점을 기억한다.
주제 : The Connectedness of Elements in Nature

| 해석

브라질에서 발생하는 산불은 러시아에서 결국 상공에 떠도는 거대한 먼지 구름을 형성하게 되어 모스크바 날씨에 영향을 미친다. 생태계의 모든 요소는 다른 모든 요소에 의해 영향을 받는데, 무기물, 산소 그리고 태양 빛과 같은 무생물 요소라 불리는 것조차 영향을 받는다. 그렇다. 빛은 모든 생명체에 핵심적인 요소이다. 태양은 지구상의 모든 생명체의 많은 종에게 에너지원이다. 물리학자들은 빛의 광자는 교체가 가능하다고 말한다. 한 물체에서 나오는 빛이 사람에 도달했을 때, 이것의 일부만이 반사된다. 대부분 광자는 그 사람에 흡수된다. 이 흡수된 에너지는 그 사람의 에너지가 된다. 이것이 바로 놀라운 상호의존이다. 모든 것은 끊임없이 다른 것이 되고 있다.

[예시 4]

1. Emotional eaters manifest their problem in lots of different ways. 1) For many people, one of the classic signs of emotional eating is night eating. ① Night eaters are often eating in response to anxiety or to the emotional turmoil they've experienced throughout the day. Boredom and loneliness are also more likely to come to the surface when the rush of the day is done and the night stretches ahead. 2) Sometimes emotional eating is a reaction to a specific situation. ② You had a bad day at work. The kids have been so demanding that you are completely worn out. You and your significant other are fighting. It doesn't matter what the circumstances are; the end result is that 99 times out of 100 you end up on the couch with a bowl of chips or bag of cookies in your hand, telling yourself it's the only way you can relax.

중심소재: Emotional Easters
1. 주제문
1) 뒷받침 진술 1
① 부연진술
2) 뒷받침 진술 2
② 부연진술

★ 포괄적 주제에 해당하는 중심소재이다.

★ 본문에서 구체적으로 다뤄질 중심내용(controlling idea)에 해당한다. 나열의 글 전개방식을 취하는 글임을 파악할 수 있는 힌트(in lots of different ways)가 제시되고 있다.

| 해설

본문은 '주제문 – 뒷받침 진술 – 부연진술'의 깔끔한 구조를 취하고 있다. 일반진술과 구체적 진술은 언제나 상대적 개념으로 본문에서 '뒷받침 진술 – 부연진술'만 따로 떼어내면 '일반진술 – 구체적 진술'에 해당할 수 있다. 본문에 제시된 두 경우를 살펴보면 다음과 같다.

경우 1

1. For many people, one of the classic signs of emotional eating is night eating. 1) Night eaters are often eating in response to anxiety or to the emotional turmoil they've experienced throughout the day. Boredom and loneliness are also more likely to come to the surface when the rush of the day is done and the night stretches ahead.

1. 주제문
1) 뒷받침 진술

경우 2

1. <u>Sometimes emotional eating is a reaction to a specific situation</u>. 1) You had a bad day at work. The kids have been so demanding that you are completely worn out. You and your significant other are fighting. It doesn't matter what the circumstances are; the end result is that 99 times out of 100 you end up on the couch with a bowl of chips or bag of cookies in your hand, telling yourself it's the only way you can relax.

1. 주제문
1) 뒷받침 진술

| 해석

감정적으로 식사하는 사람은 다양한 방식으로 자신의 문제를 드러낸다. 많은 사람의 감정적 식사의 가장 대표적인 징조 중 하나가 바로 밤에 식사하는 것이다. 밤에 식사하는 사람은 종종 낮 동안 경험한 근심(두려움)이나 감정적 혼란 때문에 먹는다. 분주한 하루 일과가 끝나고 밤이 다가왔을 때, 지루함과 외로움이 또한 표면에 드러난다(그러면서 감정적으로 식사하게 된다는 의미). 때로 감정적 식사는 특정 상황에 대한 반응이다. 일터에서 일진이 나빴다. 아이들이 너무 떼를 써 완전히 녹초가 되었다. 당신과 사랑하는 사람이 냉전 중이다. 어떤 상황이든 상관이 없다. 결과는 100번 중 99번(대부분)은 칩으로 가득한 그릇 또는 쿠키 봉지를 손에 들고 소파에 앉아 자기 자신에게 이것이 휴식할 수 있는 유일한 방법이야 라고 말하게 된다.

참고 앞부분의 4·5·6장을 통해서 8장 관련 내용, 응용문제 등을 충분히 다뤘기 때문에 이 장에서는 실전응용 연습문제를 생략했음. ― 저자 注

9 사실·의견·신념·편견의 구별

　글쓴이는 객관적으로 분석한 사실을 바탕으로 얻은 정보에 가치, 감정, 취향 그리고 과거의 경험을 투영시켜 자신의 주장을 전달한다. 그러므로 객관적 정보에 해당하는 사실, 그리고 이것을 바탕으로 글쓴이가 형성하는 의견, 신념 또는 편견을 구별하는 것은 아주 중요하다. 일반적으로 독해에 나오는 문제들이 위의 개념과 관련이 있다. 예를 들어, 요지를 고르는 문제는 신념 또는 편견을 바탕으로 한 특정 견해에 글쓴이가 찬성 또는 반대의 주장을 제시하는 글로 전개될 수 있는데, 이때 글쓴이의 견해가 드러나는 곳이 바로 의견에 해당한다. 내용일치 문제는 사실·의견·신념·편견이라는 4가지 개념을 혼동하게 하여 오답을 유도하기도 한다.

① 사실(Fact)
　사실은 증명할 수 있는 진술을 말한다. 다시 말해 증거를 찾아 사실인지 아닌지를 구별할 수 있다는 말이다. 일반적으로 글쓴이는 수치, 날짜, 증언 등을 통해서 자신의 진술이 사실임을 증명한다. 예를 들자면, '제2차 세계대전은 1945년에 종식되었다.'는 제2차 세계대전과 1945년이란 두 정보를 바탕으로 사실임을 알 수 있다.
　＊ 사실은 옳고 그름을 판단할 수 있다.

② 의견(Opinion)
　의견은 사실을 바탕으로 글쓴이가 전개하는 '판단'이다. 즉, 증거로 제시한 사실을 바탕으로 독자가 이성적으로 이해가 가도록 글쓴이가 제시한 것이다. 예를 들면, '수백만의 사람들이 병원에 간다. 고로 국가는 비용이 들더라도 의료보험을 전국화해야 한다.'
　＊ 객관적 사실을 바탕으로 형성한 글쓴이의 의견은 글의 요지에 해당하므로 아주 중요함.

③ 신념(Belief)
　신념은 문화 또는 개인의 신념, 도덕성 또는 가치관에 근거하여 글쓴이가 제시하는 주장이다.

예를 들어, '사형은 제도화된 법이다.'라는 문장은 '의견'이긴 하지만 객관적인 증거를 바탕으로 한 것이 아니다. 이런 신념의 단점은 일반적인 주장의 논제가 될 수 없다는 점이다. 일반적으로 이런 신념은 같은 생각 또는 신념을 소유한 사람에게 글을 전달할 때 아주 효과적이다.

④ 편견(Prejudice)

편견은 일반적으로 불충분한 또는 검증되지 않은 증거에서 이끌어 낸 불완전한 의견이다. 그러나 신념과는 달리 편견은 옳고 그름이 가능하다. 즉, 객관적 증거를 바탕으로 잘못된 견해임을 증명할 수 있다는 말이다. 고로, 많은 글의 초반에 이런 '편견'을 제시하고 이에 대한 반대 주장을 펼치는 '통념 비판'의 글이 아주 많이 등장하므로 이런 글 전개 방법으로 잘 기억해야 한다. 편견은 '과장'을 통한 경우나, '특정 부분의 사실만을 바탕으로 판단'한 경우가 있다.

[실전응용]

Part 1. 아래의 문장을 Fact와 Opinion으로 구분하시오.

1. Today the temperature is 22 degrees C.
   오늘 날씨는 섭씨 22도이다.

2. Today it is mild to warm.
   오늘 따뜻한 정도로 온화하다.

3. Drink too much alcohol and you get drunk.
   술을 지나치게 많이 마시면 취한다.

4. Alcohol is bad for society.
   술은 사회에 나쁜 영향을 미친다.

5. Drinking alcohol diminishes driving ability.
   술을 마시면 운전 능력을 감소시킨다.

6. Drunk drivers should be locked away.
   취중 운전자는 감금시켜야 한다.

7. Japan condones the harvesting of whales.
   일본은 고래 사냥을 눈감아 준다.

8. Killing whales is bad.
   고래를 죽이는 것은 나쁘다.

9. Wednesday is the longest day of the week.
   수요일은 주중 가장 긴 하루에 해당한다.

10. There have been many proposals recently for a flat income tax.
    최근 정율 소득세에 대한 많은 제안이 있었다.

11. In the United States, you must be at least 21 years of age to drink alcohol.
    미국에선 적어도 21세가 되어야 술을 마실 수 있다.

12. Affirmative action programs have recently been eliminated.
    소수민족해택 프로그램이 최근 제거되었다.

13. Speed limits should remain 55 miles per hour.
    속도제한은 시간 당 55마일로 유지해야 한다.

14. Dress-down days make workers less productive.
    약식 근무일에는 직원들이 오히려 덜 생산적이다.

15. All people who earn more than $100,000 a year should have a flat tax of 25 percent.
    년 수입이 십만 불 이상인 사람들은 모두 25페센트의 고정세를 내야 한다.

16. In 2005, Brazil and FC Barcelona star Ronaldinho was named FIFA World Footballer of The Year.
    2005년 브라질과 바르셀로나 스타 호나우지뉴는 FIFA가 선정하는 올해의 세계 선수로 임명되었다.

17. Wayne Rooney is the best football player in the English Premier League.
    웨인 루니는 영국 프리미엄 리그에서 뛰는 최고의 축구 선수이다.

18. 24 hour pub licensing will ruin our community.
    24시간 술집 허가는 우리 공동체를 파괴할 것이다.

19. 24 hour licensing will stop yobbish behaviour by staggering closing hours.
    24시간 허가는 문 닫는 시간을 유동적이게 함으로 폭력적인 행위를 멈추게 할 것이다.

20. More and more women are deciding to give birth to their children at home. A hospital, after all, is not the best place for a baby to be born.
더욱 더 많은 여성들이 집에서 아이를 낳으려고 결심하고 있다. 결국, 병원은 아이가 태어나기에 최상의 장소는 아니다.

Part 2. 아래 문장은 Fact와 Opinion이 함께 들어간 문장이다. 밑줄 친 부분이 Fact인지 Opinion인지 구별하라.

1. Registration and control of firearms in Canada is 1) not supported by the Canadian public, and 2) will not lead to a decrease in gun-related crime in Canada.
캐나다에서 총기 등록과 관리는 캐나다 국민들이 지지하지 않기에 캐나다 내 총기관련 범죄가 줄어들지 않을 것이다.

2. 1) Indians are the world's biggest bookworms, 2) reading on average 10.7 hours a week, twice as long as Americans, according to a new survey.
인도사람들은 세계 최고의 책벌레로 새로운 한 조사에 따르면 미국인 보다 일주일에 2배에 해당하는 평균 10.7시간을 읽는다고 한다.

3. Area 51 is a military facility approximately 90 miles north of Las Vegas. At the center of the site there sits a large air base. Area 51 is also the site of a U.S. Government UFO coverup.
Area 51은 군사 시설로 라스베가스에서 약 90마일 떨어져 있다. 이 지역의 중심에는 거대한 공군기지가 자리 잡고 있다. Area 51은 또한 미국 정부가 운영하는 UFO 은폐지역이기도 하다.

2) "The government is hiding the remains of alien spacecraft there," says Sarah Mitchell, a long-time resident from the surrounding area.
"정부는 그곳에 있는 외계 비행선의 잔존물을 숨기고 있다"고 주변 지역에서 장기가 거주하고 있는 Sarah Mitchell은 말한다.

4. 1) Others believe that weapons testing done there is causing toxic pollution that could harm people near the site. One such person is Mr. Hayakawa, 2) a member of a civilian intelligence group that monitors covert (secret) government operations.
다른 사람들의 이곳에서 이뤄진 무기 실험이 주변 사람들을 해할 수 있는 유독한 오염을 일으키고 있다고 믿고 있다. Hayakawa씨는 이런 사람 중 한 명으로 그는 정부의 비밀작전을 감시하는 민간정보단체의 구성원이다.

10 요지를 이끄는 시그널 연구

요지는 글쓴이가 궁극적으로 전달하고자 하는 내용으로 주제문에 해당한다. 일반적으로 다음과 같은 표현이 등장하면 글쓴이의 요지가 드러난다.

1. 글쓴이의 주장(의견)을 이끄는 표현

> I think, I believe, I insist, I claim, In my opinion, As for me, For my part, I suggest, I propose

[실전응용] 아래 지문을 분석하고, 글쓴이의 주장을 적으시오.

Right now, there are thousands of incurable patients lying helplessly in bed, suffering pain and misery and wishing they could be allowed to die. But the doctors are afraid to facilitate their deaths for fear of legal or professional repercussions. I propose that doctors be allowed to discontinue treatment or administer lethal doses of painkillers if requested to do so by patients suffering from incurable diseases, or, in the case of comatose patients, by their relatives.	중심소재: 1. 도입부 2. 요지(글쓴이의 주장)

2. 글을 요약하는 표현

> In short, In brief, In a word, In summary, To sum up, That is, In other words, Overall

[실전응용] 아래 지문을 분석하고, 글쓴이의 주장을 적으시오.

Today, the automobile is mostly thought of as a necessity. The car is still a convenience so taken for granted that its absence in our individual lives is almost beyond comprehension. But as a collective entity, the automobile threatens to make us its servant. It requires that we plan our cities or dig them up and rebuild them. Overall, the result is a tie. The car has assumed the confusing status of something we can't live with and can't live without.

중심소재:
1. 도입부

2. 요지

3. 당위성을 나타내는 표현

> Should, Ought to, Must, Have to, Need to, Had better,
> It is important(necessary, natural, essential) that S V

[예시 1]

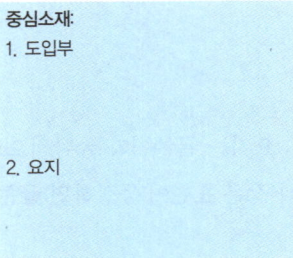

1. For the past seven years, since our former gym was destroyed by fire, students have been deprived of adequate facilities for physical education classes and other activities. 1) We have had to suspend those classes during the winter. Our indoor athletic teams have had to travel long distances to get to practice and to games—this has been inconvenient, expensive and at times even dangerous. School dances have had to be held in hired halls, which is a costly practice. The town Finance Committee assures us we can build a new gym without seriously affecting our tax rate. 2. For those reasons and for the well-being of our children, immediate measures should be taken.

중심소재: 화재로 인한 체육관 부재
1. 도입부: 현상-문제점 지적(주제)
화재로 체육관이 불타면서 학생들은 체육 활동을 위한 시설을 잃었다.
1) 구체적 진술
시설의 부재로 학생들이 겪어야 했던 불편한 사항과 문제점을 구체적으로 언급하고 있다.
2. 결론(요지문)
문제점에 대한 대안이 언급되고 있다.

★ '현상-문제점' 패턴의 글에서 주제와 요지구별

주제도출 ← 도입부 현상-원인파악및 문제점 지적
요지 ← 뒷받침 진술
대안

결론을 이끄는 시그널 (for)을 확인한다.

글쓴이의 주장·견해를 이끄는 시그널을 확인한다.

| 해석

우리가 이용하던 이전 체육관이 화재로 손실된 후 지난 7년 간 학생들은 체육수업과 다른 활동을 위한 적당한 시설을 이용할 수 없었다. 우리는 겨울 동안 그러한 수업을 유보해야만 했다. 실내 운동부들은 연습 장소와 시합 장소로 장거리 이동을 해야만 했는데, 이것은 불편하고 비용이 많이 들었으며, 때로는 위험하기까지 했다. 학교 댄스파티는 따로 섭외한 장소에서 개최해야 했는데, 이것도 비용이 많이 드는 일이다. 시 재정위원회가 세율에 심각한 영향을 주지 않으면서 새로운 체육관을 지을 수 있다고 우리에게 확신을 준다. 위의 여러 이유와 우리 아이들의 행복을 위해 즉각적인 조치가 취해져야 한다.

[예시 2]

1. Clients send a steady stream of clues and messages through their facial expression, body movement, and voice pitch. 1) Counselors **need to** learn how to read these messages without distorting or overinterpreting them in order to establish and maintain relationships with their clients. ① For instance, when Denise says to Jennie, "It seems that it's hard for you to talk about yourself," Jennie says, "No, I don't mind at all." But the real answer is probably in her nonverbal behavior, for she speaks hesitatingly while looking away and frowning. Reading such clues helps Denise understand Jennie better. Our nonverbal behavior has a way of 'leaking' messages about what we really mean. The unplanned nature of nonverbal behavior contributes to this leakage even in the case of highly defensive clients.

중심소재: Nonverbal Clues
1. 도입부
상담을 받는 사람은 얼굴 표정, 몸의 움직임 그리고 목소리 높낮이를 통해서 끊임없이 단서와 메시지를 보낸다.
1) 주제문(요지를 이끄는 need 확인)
상담자는 피상담자와 좋은 관계를 맺고 유지하기 위해서 비언어적 표현을 읽을 수 있어야 한다.
① 뒷받침 문장
예시부연 (For instance)

| 해석

피상담자는 자신의 표정, 몸짓, 그리고 목소리 높낮이를 통해 지속적인 단서와 메시지를 보낸다. 상담자는 피상담자와의 관계를 만들고 유지하기 위해 왜곡하거나 과도하게 해석하지 않고 이 메시지들을 읽는 방법을 배울 필요가 있다. 예를 들어 Denise가 Jennie에게 "당신 자신에 대해 이야기하는 것이 힘들어 보이는군요."라고 말할 때, Jennie는 "아뇨, 전혀 상관없어요."라고 말한다. 그러나 진짜 대답은 아마 그녀의 비언어적인 행동 안에 있을 것인데 왜냐하면 그녀가 먼 곳을 쳐다보며 찡그리는 중에 다급하게 이야기를 하고 있기 때문이다. 그런 단서를 읽어내는 것은 Denise가 Jennie를 더 잘 이해하도록 도와준다. 우리의 비언어적인 행동에는 우리가 정말로 뜻하는 바에 대한 메시지들을 '흘리는' 방식이 있다. 그 비언어적 행동의 예기치 않은 본성이 심지어 매우 방어적인 피상담자의 경우라도 이 누출에 기여하게 된다.

[실전응용 1] 아래 지문을 분석하고, 글쓴이의 주장을 적으시오.

Some universities require students to keep a record of when they met with their supervisor, what was discussed, and what was the agreed next course of action. For advanced research programs, such as a Ph.D., keeping this record up to date is a requirement for progression from one stage of the program to another. Seeing your supervisor regularly is one of the best ways of making sure that your dissertation is of the very highest possible standard. Yet you would be surprised how many students see their supervisor as little as possible. Although your supervisor will probably ask to see you if you have been invisible for a long period, it is normally up to you to arrange such meetings. You should do this as regularly as possible whenever you have something to discuss.

중심소재:
1. 도입부

2. 요지(조언/제안)

[실전응용 2] 아래 지문을 분석하고, 글쓴이의 주장을 적으시오.

A negative response is a most difficult handicap to overcome. When you have said "No," all your pride of personality demands that you remain consistent with yourself. You may later feel that the "No" was hasty; nevertheless, there is your precious pride to consider! Once having said a thing, you feel you must stick to it. When a person says "No" and really means it, he or she is doing far more than saying a word of two letters. Hence it is of the very greatest importance that a person be started in the affirmative direction. The skillful speaker gets, at the outset, a number of "Yes" responses. This sets the psychological process of the listener moving in the affirmative direction.

중심소재:
1. 도입부

2. 요지

[실전응용 3] 아래 지문을 분석하고, 글쓴이의 주장을 적으시오.

Every mother and father wants to raise a child with a strong moral character. We want our children to know good from bad, and right from wrong. We hope they'll learn to behave morally and ethically, and grow up to be honest and considerate. In short, we want our children to develop a conscience—a powerful inner voice that will keep them on the right path. But a conscience does not develop by itself, so the job of building one is ours. It's a process parents

중심소재:
1. 도입부

2. 제안(요지)

need to work on day after day, and year after year. We need to constantly distinguish right from wrong, and to model appropriate behavior. Eventually, our children will fully accept our messages, and they will become the essence of their character.

4. 역접/대조/양보를 나타내는 접속사 및 부사(구)

> But, However, Yet, Still, In fact, In truth, Actually, Although, Now

역접/대조/양보의 접속사 또는 부사(구)가 오는 경우 바로 이어지는 문장이 주제문일 가능성이 높다. 일반적으로 아래와 같은 구조를 취한다.

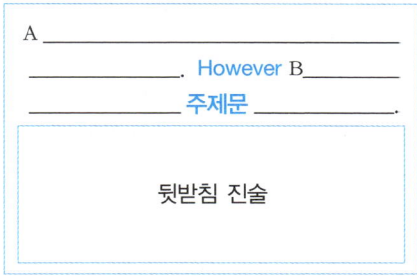

위의 구조와 같이 도입부에서 A에 관한 내용을 전개하다 글의 무게중심이 B로 이동한다. 글에서 다루려는 내용은 B가 된다.

[예시 1]

1. There is no longer much distinction between etiquette and morals; 1) however, manners, which are related to the outer person, must not be confused with morals. ① The failure to distinguish between manners and morals suggests, erroneously, that acceptable social behavior follows effortlessly from personal virtue. All you need is a good heart, and the rest will take care of itself. You don't have to write thank-you letters. To the contrary, it is safer to hope that practicing proper behavior eventually encourages virtuous feeling; that if you write enough thank-you letters, you may actually feel a flicker of gratitude. At the very least, good manners can put a decent cover over ugly feelings.

중심소재: Etiquette and Morals
1. 도입부: 현상
   예절과 도덕의 경계가 무너짐.
1) 주제문
   예절과 도덕은 구별되어야 한다.
① 뒷받침 근거

★ 현상의 문제점을 지적하는 글로 전개되고 있다. 문제점에 대한 글쓴이의 대안이 곧 글의 요지가 된다.

★ 글쓴이의 주장을 이끄는 시그널 'must'를 확인할 수 있다. 주장이 나오면 이에 대한 근거가 뒤따른다는 것을 기억하도록 한다.

| 해석

에티켓과 도덕은 더 이상 구별하지 않는다. 그러나 사회적 자아와 관련된 예의범절을 도덕과 혼동해서는 안 된다. 예절과 도덕을 구별하지 못하게 되면, 개인적인 미덕을 가지고 있는 사람은 저절로 용인될 수 있는 사회적 행동을 하게 된다는 잘못된 결론이 나올 수 있다. (개인적 미덕을 가지고 있는 사람은 어떤 사회적 행동을 해도 괜찮다는 잘못된 결론이 나올 수 있다.) 필요한 것은 선한 마음이면 족하고, 그 밖의 것들은 자연히 해결될 것이라는 식의 생각이다. 예를 들어 감사의 편지를 쓸 필요도 없다는 식이다. 그러나 이와 반대로 예의 바른 행동을 실천하는 것이 결국 미덕을 갖도록 해 줄 것이라고 생각하는 편이 오히려 타당하다. 만약 당신이 충분한 감사의 편지를 쓴다면 당신은 실제로 감사하는 마음이 생기기 시작하는 것을 느낄 수도 있을 것이다. 어쨌든 훌륭한 예절은 추악한 감정마저도 예의 바르게 덮을 수 있다.

[예시 2]

중심소재는 'drug'이다. ★

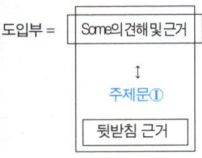

[공간의 배분]
Some의 견해보다 글쓴이 ①의 뒷받침 근거가 지문의 더 많은 공간을 차지하고 있음에 주목한다.

1. **Some people feel** that drugs such as cocaine, heroin, and alcohol help them. 1) They think that these drugs lessen tension and give them a feeling of well-being. 2) Nothing could be further from the truth. 1) Many users develop tolerance to these drugs and over a long period of time increase their dosage. As a result, they can lose sleep and become confused, suspicious, or even anxious. They are not capable of meaningful activity, and their lives revolve around obtaining and taking the drugs.

중심소재: Drug
1. 도입부
　Some의 견해: 마약의 유용성
1) 뒷받침 근거
　마약은 긴장감을 낮추고, 편안함 제공
2. 주제문
　①의 견해: 마약의 부정적 영향력
1) 뒷받침 근거
　마약의 부정적 영향력을 자세히 기술하고 있다.

| 해설

However의 역할을 문장이 대신하고 있다는 점을 파악하는 것이 관건이다.

| 해석

어떤 이는 코카인, 헤로인 그리고 알코올 같은 마약이 도움이 된다고 여긴다. 이들은 이 마약이 긴장을 완화하고 편안함을 준다고 생각한다. 이보다 진실에서 더 먼 사실은 없다(아주 잘못된 주장이다). 많은 사용자가 이 마약에 내성이 커지고 장기간에 걸쳐 (점점) 복용량이 증가한다. 그 결과 이들은 불면증, 혼란스러움, 의심이 생기며 불안해진다. 이들은 의미 있는 활동을 할 수 없으며, 마약을 얻고 복용하는 것 중심으로 삶이 돌아간다.

| 참고

본문과 같이 특정인 또는 단체의 견해로 시작하는 글의 패턴은 다음과 같을 때도 있다.

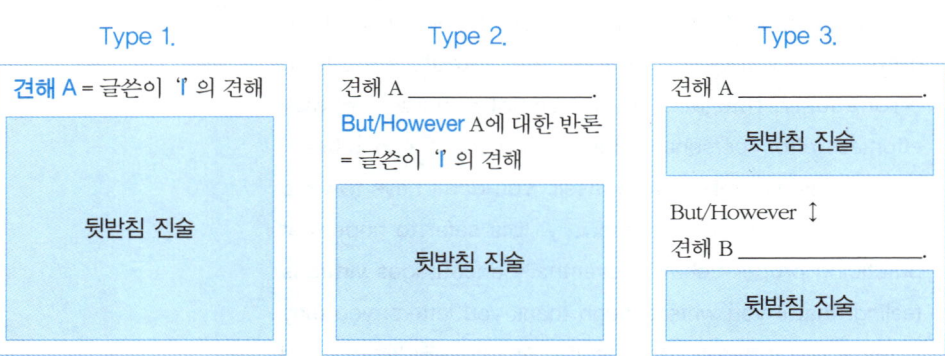

Type 1의 경우 견해 A의 진술 자체가 바로 글쓴이 I의 견해가 된다. 이럴 때 견해 A는 조사·실험·연구·인용 등을 언급하면서 자신의 주장을 간접적으로 전달하는데 이러한 요소는 글의 객관성과 권위의 호소 덕분에 설득력을 높이는 효과를 가져올 수 있다. 이후 구체적 진술에 해당하는 뒷받침 진술이 이어진다. Type 2의 경우 글쓴이의 견해는 바로 견해 A에 대한 반론에 해당한다. 일반적으로 but, however, 문장 단위의 역접 등의 표현을 기점으로 글쓴이의 주장은 뒷부분에 해당한다. 이후 뒷받침 진술이 이어지는 형태로 일반적으로 통념 비판과 같은 양괄식을 주로 취한다. Type 3의 경우 글쓴이는 중립적 태도를 보이면서 대조되는 두 견해를 대등하게 제시하는 형태이다.

[예시 3]

1. **Contrary to popular belief, <u>reading books in poor light does not ruin your eyes</u>.** 1) **When** you read by moonlight or under the covers, you tend to squint to focus on letters. Sometimes, this gives you a headache, makes you tired, or causes pain in the muscles around your eyes and your vision seems less clear. **However, <u>you won't suffer any long-term eye damage</u>.** A good night's rest will help your tired eyes work properly again.

중심소재: Book
통념 비판의 글임을 첫 번째 문장에서 파악할 수 있다. '통념 – but – 반론 – 뒷받침'의 패턴을 잘 따르고 있는지 살펴보도록 한다.
1. 도입부 = 주제문
1) 뒷받침 진술
'However' 이후 글쓴이의 주장의 근거가 드러난다.

★ 통념 비판의 시그널을 확인한다.

★ 구체적 진술을 이끄는 시그널인 'when'을 확인한다.

해석
대중적인 믿음과는 반대로, 어두운 조명에서 책을 읽는 것이 눈을 망치지는 않는다. 달빛에 책을 읽거나 혹은 (담요와 같은) 덮개 아래서 책을 읽으면 글자에 초점을 맞추기 위해 눈을 가늘게 뜨고 보는 경향이 있다. 때때로, 이렇게 하는 것은 두통, 피로, 눈 주변 근육의 통증을 주고 시야가 덜 선명해 보인다. 그러나 어떠한 장기적인 시력 손상을 겪지는 않을 것이다. 하룻밤 푹 자는 것만도 피로한 눈이 다시 적절하게 작동하도록 도와줄 것이다.

참고
빈 ☐ 안에 들어갈 구체적 진술을 이끄는 시그널의 대표적 예는 다음과 같다.
① For example, For instance, Take (an example of)
② Consider, Suppose, Imagine
③ When, if
④ 시간의 부사(구)
⑤ 개별적 대상 지침

도입부 = 주제문

[실전응용 1] 아래 지문을 분석하고, 글의 요지를 적으시오.

You see the world as one big contest, where everyone is competing against everybody else. You feel that there is a set amount of good and bad fortune out there. You believe that there is no way that everyone can have everything. When other people fail, you feel there's a better chance for you to succeed. However, there is not a limited supply of

중심소재:
1. 도입부

resources out there. When one person wins, everyone wins. Every victory one person makes is a breakthrough for all. Whenever an Olympic swimmer sets a new world record, it inspires others to bring out the best within them and go beyond that achievement to set new records of human performance. Whenever a geneticist unlocks new secrets of the DNA molecule, it adds to our knowledge base and enables us to better the human condition. Remember that life is a game where there are multiple winners.

2. 주제문

1) 뒷받침 진술

3. 주제문 재진술

[실전응용 2] 아래 지문을 분석하고, 글의 요지를 적으시오.

According to a psychologist, a business executive spends an hour of his day reading, two hours talking and eight hours listening. Yet in school we spend a large amount of time teaching children how to read, a small amount of time teaching them how to speak, and usually no time at all teaching them how to listen. I do not believe it would be a good thing to make what we teach in school exactly proportional to what we do after school, but I do think it would be wise to give our children some instruction in the process of listening. Listening well is an exercise of attention and those who listen well tend to have good relationships with colleagues.

중심소재:
1. 도입부

2. 주제문

1) 뒷받침 근거

[실전응용 3] 아래 지문을 분석하고, 글의 요지를 적으시오.

A cent is worth so little that we don't usually bother to pick it up on the street. It's difficult to gather between finger and thumb, and the reward seems hardly worth the effort. But, with a little extra effort, these little coins are picked up by goodwill organizations. One person picks up ten coins, ten people pick up 100 coins and so on until they turn into hundreds thousands, even millions of dollars. All this money is being used to help thousands of homeless and hungry people around the world.

중심소재:
1. 도입부

1) 주제문

5. 예시를 나타내는 표현

> For example, For instance, When, If, Suppose, Consider, Take (an example of)

일반적으로 예시를 나타내는 표현 바로 앞 문장이 주제문에 해당하며, 이 경우 예시는 곧 뒷받침 진술이 된다.

```
주제문 _____
       _____. For example_____
   ┌─────────────────────────────┐
   │        뒷받침 문장            │
   └─────────────────────────────┘
```

| 참고

'For example'은 뒷받침 진술뿐 아니라 뒷받침 진술을 보충하는 부연진술의 기능도 있다. 부연진술로 활용되는 예의 구조를 살펴보면 다음과 같다.

```
주제문 _____.
뒷받침 진술 1._____.
뒷받침 진술 2._____.
   ┌─────────────────────────────┐
   │ For example                  │
   │        부연진술               │
   └─────────────────────────────┘
```

'For example'은 뒷받침 진술 2에 대한 부연진술의 역할로 활용되고 있다. 이 경우 'For example' 앞의 진술을 주제문으로 잡을 경우 부분을 전체로 파악하는 일반화 오류를 범하게 된다.

[예시 1]

1. In my opinion, cable companies charge a ridiculous amount of money for their services. 1) For example, the family plan package starts at about $50 per month, has a separate installation fee, and does not even include the movie channels. This discounted price is only good if you are a new customer. Once this initial period is over, the price for

중심소재: 케이블 회사 → 케이블 회사의 요금정책

1. **도입부 = 주제문**
   케이블 회사는 서비스에 비해 지나치게 비싼 요금을 청구한다.

1) **뒷받침 진술**
   예시를 통한 뒷받침 근거를 제시하고 있다.

★ 케이블 회사와 관련해 어떤 내용을 전달하려고 하는가?

★ 예시를 통한 구체적 진술이 전개되고 있다. 바로 앞 문장이 주제문에 해당한다.

91

the same service increases to more than $60 per month. To add different movie channels you have to buy a package for $15 extra. These packages consist of nine to eleven channels. However, only two of the nine are usually worth watching.

| 해설

'For example'을 기준으로 앞쪽에서 글의 요지를 담은 주제문과 이후 이를 뒷받침하는 내용이 전개되는 전형적인 'General → Specific' 유형이다. 주제: 케이블 회사의 과다한 요금정책

| 해석

내 생각에는 케이블 방송사들이 자신들의 서비스에 대해 터무니없이 많은 돈을 부과하는 것 같다. 예를 들면, 가족용 패키지는 월 약 50달러에서 시작하고, 별도의 설치비가 있으며, 심지어는 영화채널들은 포함하지도 않는다. 이런 할인가는 새로운 고객일 때만 유효하다. 일단 최초의 이 기간이 끝나면 동일 서비스에 대한 가격이 월 60달러 이상으로 증가한다. 다른 영화채널을 추가하기 위해서는 추가로 15달러를 더 내고 패키지를 구매해야 한다. 이러한 패키지들은 아홉 개에서 열한 개의 채널들로 구성되어 있다. 하지만 그 아홉 개 중에서도 겨우 두 개만 대체로 볼 만한 가치가 있다.

[예시 2]

포괄적 주제인 중심소재는 ★ 단어 암기이다. 바로 이어지는 중심내용(controlling idea)을 바탕으로 주제의 폭을 조절한다.

본문에서 구체적으로 진 ★ 술된 중심내용(controlling idea)에 해당한다.

1. To memorize a word is easy. Say the word aloud and connect the word to words you already know. 1) For example, the word GARGANTUAN has a similar meaning to the words gigantic, huge, large, etc. You could make a sequence: small, medium, large, very large, GARGANTUAN. List as many things as you can that could be considered GARGANTUAN: Godzilla, the circus fat lady, and so on. Create pictures of the word's meaning that has strong emotions. Think "the GARGANTUAN creature was going to kill me and then eat me!"

중심소재: 단어 → 단어암기
1. 도입부 = 주제문
암기할 단어를 크게 말하고, 이미 알고 있는 단어와 함께 연상한다.
1) 뒷받침 진술
예시를 통해 주제문에서 밝힌 중심내용을 상술하고 있다.

| 해석

단어를 암기하기는 쉽다. 단어를 크게 말하고 이미 알고 있는 단어와 연관시켜라. 예를 들면, GARGANTUAN이란 단어는 gigantic(거인 같은), huge(거대한), large(큰) 등의 단어들과 비슷한 의미를 지니고 있다. small(작은), medium(중간의), large(큰), very large(매우 큰), GARGANTUAN(거대한)의 순서를 만들어 볼 수도 있다. Godzilla, 곡예단의 뚱보 여자 등과 같이 GARGANTUAN이라고 생각되는 것들을 가능한 한 많이 목록으로 작성하라. 강한 느낌이 드는 단어의 의미를 머릿속에 그려보아라. "그 거대한 동물이 나를 죽인 다음 먹으려고 했다!"라고 생각해 보아라.

[실전응용 1] 아래 지문을 분석하고, 글의 요지를 적으시오.

The meaning a speaker intends to communicate may be quite different from the meaning conveyed by the actual words, phrases, and sentences. For example, when a foreigner lays down his fork and says, "Vegetables not thoroughly cooked retain a certain acidity," he is not making a general statement about vegetable cookery but voicing a criticism of American food. We can never, of course, be certain about the intention of a speaker, but we must always be prepared for the fact that what a person is saying is not always exactly what he or she means.

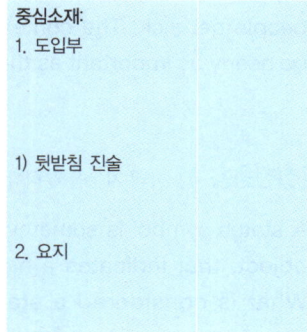

중심소재:
1. 도입부

1) 뒷받침 진술

2. 요지

[실전응용 2] 아래 지문을 분석하고, 글의 요지를 적으시오.

Knowing when something happened is important. Understanding why historic events took place is also important. To do this, historians often turn to geography. Weather patterns, the water supply, and the landscape of a place all affect the lives of the people who live there. For example, to explain why the ancient Egyptians developed a successful civilization, you must look at the geography of Egypt. Egyptian civilization was built on the banks of the Nile River, which flooded each year, depositing soil on its banks. The rich soil could help farmers grow enough crops to feed the people in the cities. That meant everyone did not have to farm, so some people could perform other jobs that helped develop the civilization.

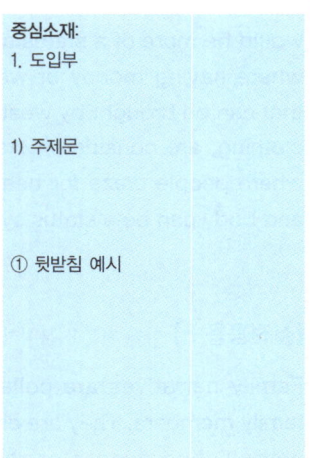

중심소재:
1. 도입부

1) 주제문

① 뒷받침 예시

[실전응용 3] 아래 지문을 분석하고, 글의 요지를 적으시오.

The specific combinations of foods in a cuisine and the ways they are prepared constitute a deep reservoir of accumulated wisdom about diet and health and place. In Latin America, for example, corn is traditionally eaten with beans; each plant is deficient in an essential amino acid that happens to be abundant in the other, so together corn and beans form a balanced diet in the absence of meat. Similarly, corn in Latin America is traditionally ground or soaked with limestone, which makes available a B vitamin in the corn, the absence of which would otherwise lead to a deficiency disease. Very often, when a society adopts a

중심소재:

1. 주제문

1) 뒷받침 진술

new food without the food culture surrounding it, as happened when corn first came to Europe, Africa, and Asia, people get sick. The context in which a food is eaten can be nearly as important as the food itself.

[실전응용 4] 아래 지문을 분석하고, 글의 요지를 적으시오.

A status symbol is something, usually an expensive or rare object, that indicates a high social status for its owner. What is considered a status symbol will differ among countries, based on the states of their economic and technological development, and common status symbols will change over time. Status symbols can indicate the cultural values of a society. Let's take some examples. In a society that cherishes honor or bravery, a battle wound would be more of a status symbol. In a commercial society, where having money or wealth is most important, things that can be brought by wealth, such as cars, houses, or fine clothing, are considered status symbols. And in a society where people craze for beauty, the condition of one's skin and body can be a status symbol.

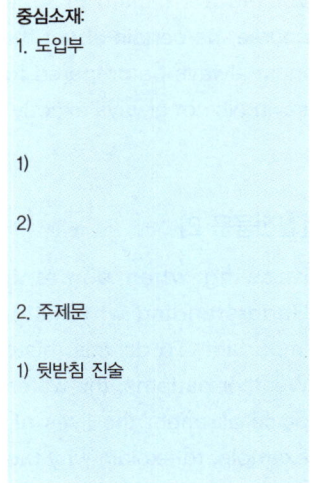

중심소재:
1. 도입부

1)

2)

2. 주제문

1) 뒷받침 진술

[실전응용 5] 아래 지문을 분석하고, 글의 요지를 적으시오.

Family narratives are collections of stories made up by family members. They are either based on real occurrences, embellished events or fantasy materials. Such family storytelling is shown to have numerous advantages. For example, family narratives help children develop values through communicating limits, boundaries and family-endorsed morality. In addition to providing children with a clear sense of right and wrong, family stories are also used to pass along parental insights and knowledge. This process of transmitting knowledge may be critical to positive parent-child relationships, as the absence of family stories has been shown to be related to difficulties among parents to establish a caring or meaningful relationship with their children. They are also cherished as a cause of laughter year after year.

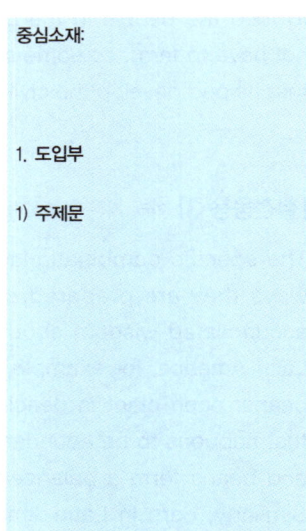

중심소재:

1. 도입부

1) 주제문

[실전응용 6] 아래 지문을 분석하고, 글의 요지를 적으시오.

A "pot-stirrer" is someone who brings up emotional issues that have already been resolved. Pot-stirrers want to feed the emotional fire and keep it burning for the excitement of the conflict. They can be subtle; they often even appear to be the "helpful" friend or "caring" listener. Let's say you've just let go of a minor conflict with your neighbor, when your other neighbor continues to bring up how annoying this person is, encouraging you to hold on to your irritation with the person. The same applies at work. A coworker keeps reminding you that it was you, not Gail, who really deserved the credit for that great idea. Every time he or she says it, it upsets you and opens your wound again.

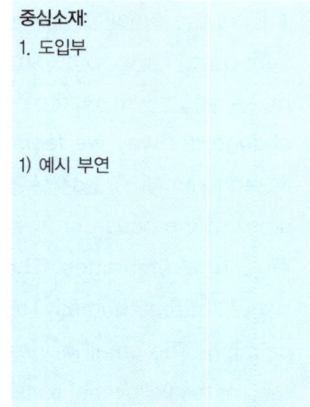

중심소재:
1. 도입부

1) 예시 부연

[실전응용 7] 아래 지문을 분석하고, 글의 요지를 적으시오.

What causes cultures to change? New ideas and inventions often lead people to develop new ways of doing things. For example, the invention of writing systems allowed people to record their thoughts and discoveries and to communicate them to other people. Changes in the environment also cause cultures to change. Over time, the climate in an area can change. Also, natural disasters such as floods and earthquakes can alter the landscape. People must then move or learn to adjust to new living conditions. Another major source of change is contact with other cultures. When people from different cultures meet, they are exposed to the ways of life of each culture. Cultures change from within as well. Factors such as population growth and conflicts between groups within a culture can bring about new ways of doing things.

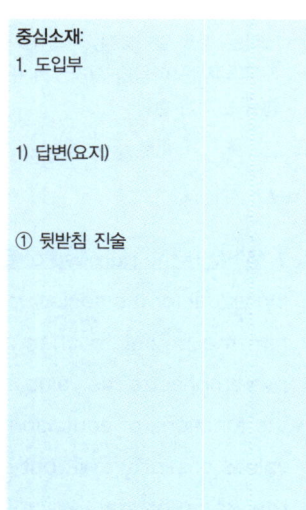

중심소재:
1. 도입부

1) 답변(요지)

① 뒷받침 진술

6. 의문점은 글의 주제에 해당하고, 이에 대한 답변은 글의 요지이다.

글의 도입부 또는 중반부에서 의문점이 제시되는 글은 시험 출제 빈도가 아주 높으므로, 아래 예시와 실전응용을 통해서 숙지해두도록 한다.

[예시 1]

1. Has the smell of something ever made you think of a spring day? Do some smells make you happy? Do others make you feel relaxed? 1) Believe it or not, smells can change the way we feel. Some of our basic emotions are linked to smell. ① For instance, scientists have found that the smell of the ocean or freshly baked cookies can revive very emotional memories. The smell of apples reminds many people of their homes. The smell of trees after a cool rain is calming. The smell of peppermint excites us. The smell of lilies of the valley makes us feel relaxed.

중심소재는 'smell'이다.
중심내용(controlling idea)을 고려하면서 주제의 폭을 설정한다.

뒷받침 문장에서 구체적으로 밝힐 중심내용(controlling idea)이다.

구체적 예시인 'For instance' 앞에 주제문이 제시된다.

도입부 = 의문점 = 주제
→ 주제문
→ 실험을 통한 뒷받침 근거

중심소재: smell
1. 도입부(의문점 = 주제)
감정에 미치는 냄새의 영향
1) 주제문
냄새는 사람의 감정에 영향을 미친다.
① 뒷받침 진술
실험을 통해 발견한 (객관적) 사실을 바탕으로 주제문의 중심내용을 뒷받침하고 있다.

| 해석
어떤 것의 냄새가 당신으로 하여금 봄날을 생각하게 한 적이 있는가? 어떤 냄새를 맡으면 기분이 좋아지는가? 다른 냄새의 경우 긴장이 완화되는가? 믿든 말든, 냄새는 우리의 기분을 바꿀 수 있다. 우리의 기본적인 감정 일부는 냄새와 관련이 있다. 예를 들어, 과학자들은 바다나 갓 구운 과자 냄새는 아주 감정적인 추억들을 되살릴 수 있다는 것을 알아냈다. 사과 냄새는 많은 사람으로 하여금 자신의 집을 생각나게 해 준다. 시원한 비가 내린 다음 나무 냄새는 마음을 가라앉혀 준다. 박하 냄새는 우리를 흥분시키고, 계곡에 핀 백합 냄새는 우리로 하여금 편안함을 느끼게 한다.

[예시 2]

1. What is the purpose of education? 1) It is ① to prepare the individual for the society in which he must live and ② to give him the power to change the society. 2) We should not overemphasize the value of the first part. It should be one of the functions of education to preserve for the society all the values essential to it, but it is more important one to cut out the decayed values which would be harmful to a new society. 2. Thus the school should be the inspiration to social change.

중심소재는 '교육'이며, 이후 중심내용을 바탕으로 주제의 폭을 좁히도록 한다.

'not A but b'와 'should'는 모두 글의 요지를 이끄는 시그널이다.

요지를 이끄는 시그널을 확인한다.

중심소재: Education
1. 도입부(의문점 = 주제)
교육의 목적
1) 교육의 두가지 목적
① 목적 1
② 목적 2
2) but 이유 두번째 목적 강조
2. 주제문(요지)
교육은 사회 변화의 영감이 되어야 한다.

| 해석
교육의 목적은 무엇인가? 이것(교육)은 개인이 살아가는 사회에 대한 준비가 되도록 하고, 사회를 변혁시키는 힘을 제공해 주는 것이다. 우리는 첫 번째 목적의 가치를 지나치게 강조해선 안 된다. 사회에 필수적인 모든 가치를 보존하는 것이 교육의 여러 기능 중 하나이지만, 새로운 사회에 유해한 썩은(시대에 뒤떨어지는) 가치를 잘라내는 것이 더 중요하다. 고로 학교는 사회 변화를 고무시켜야 한다.

| 참고
위 지문은 다음과 같은 두 가지 형태로 글이 진행될 수 있다. 우선 첫 번째 문장에서 주제를 밝히고 있다. 즉, '교육의 목적은 무엇인가?'라고 말한 후 두 가지 목적에 대해 기술되어 있다. 이후 전개될 내용은 다음과 같은 두 가지 방법을 취할 수 있다.

Type 1.	Type 2.
What is the purpose of education? It is ① to prepare the individual for the society in which he must live and ② to give him the power to change the society.	What is the purpose of education? is ① to prepare the individual for the society in which he must live and to give him the power ② to change the society.
①에 대한 구체적 진술 ②에 대한 구체적 진술	①과 ②의 중요도를 다룬 후 한쪽에 더 무게 중심을 두어 강조하는 내용 기술

Type 1은 중립적인 입장에서 '교육의 목적'을 전달하는 설명이고, Type 2는 글쓴이의 견해가 진술되는 논증으로 주제는 '교육의 진정한 목적' 정도로 잡을 수 있다. 아주 미묘한 차이지만, 글의 전개 내용에 따라 주제가 살짝 바뀔 수 있다는 점을 염두에 두자.

[실전응용 1] 아래 지문을 분석하고, 글의 요지를 적으시오.

Why should the government control population planning? Many people say there is no other way because people will continue to have too many children. They will not limit themselves to just one or two children. They have not limited themselves in the past. Why should they limit themselves in the future? Unfortunately, they say, it does not work to leave family planning completely up to individuals. The only choice according to these people, is for the government to play an active role in population planning.

중심소재:
1. 도입부
1) 뒷받침 진술

2. 결론(요지)

[실전응용 2] 아래 지문을 분석하고, 글의 요지를 적으시오.

Some people give up the moment an obstacle is placed in front of them. Some people doggedly continue to pursue a goal even after years of frustration and failure. What is the difference between these two people? Those who feel they are not responsible for choosing their goals and pursuing them tend to believe that results are arbitrary. To them, it does not matter how hard you try or how talented you are. Being successful is all a matter of luck. Those who persevere, however, recognize that they are ultimately responsible not just for pursuing their goals, but for setting them. To them, what you do matters, and giving up for no reasons does not seem very attractive.

중심소재:
1. 도입부

2. 의문점

[실전응용 3] 아래 지문을 분석하고, 글의 요지를 적으시오.

Sea level is rising and we are not sure about the rate of the rise. Another question we are unsure about is: "Where does the extra water come from?" Fifty years or so ago it was thought that a warming phase of climate was responsible for partial melting of the polar ice caps and a consequent addition of mass and volume to the waters of the ocean.

As a result of recent research, models have been proposed which suggest that rather more than half of the sea level rise which has occurred in recent geological time is more likely to be due to the warming of the upper layers of the ocean and a subsequent increase in the volume of the waters. The same models also suggested that slightly less than half of the rise was due to the addition of fresh meltwater from land-based ice in the form of glaciers and the icefields associated with mountainous (Alpine) areas in the mid to sub-polar latitudes.

중심소재:
1. 도입부

1) 의문점

[실전응용 4] 아래 지문을 분석하고, 글의 요지를 적으시오.

A recent study shows that kids who watch a lot of TV are more likely to be overweight than those who do not. Can you guess why? It's because of commercials on TV! The junk food is often advertised in commercials by their favorite cartoon characters. It is so appealing that kids just want to go out and get it right away! Kids who watch a lot of TV and those attractive commercials are also likely to stay only at home and be getting less exercise.

중심소재:
1. 도입부

1) 의문점

7. 명령문은 글쓴이의 충고/조언으로 서론 또는 결론에 주로 위치하여 글쓴이의 주장을 드러낸다.

[실전응용] 아래 지문을 분석하고, 글의 요지를 적으시오.

Any object between you and the person with whom you're talking may interfere with your conversation. That's why many experienced speakers step away from the podium when they lecture; many businesspeople choose not to

중심소재:
1. 도입부
1) 뒷받침 진술

98

speak with customers or employees from behind a desk, but instead come around their desk and sit next to them. If you want to have an unconstrained conversation with someone, get rid of any obstacles between the two of you. Move out from behind your desk, unless maintaining control is more important than exchanging information. At a restaurant, ask the waiter to remove tall flower arrangements, extra glasses, or any other objects that clutter the visual space between you and your tablemate. If you're wearing sunglasses, take them off.

2. 요지

8. 최상급 표현은 언제나 글쓴이가 강조하는 내용이므로 글의 요지를 직/간접적으로 드러낸다.

[실전응용] 아래 지문을 분석하고, 글의 요지를 적으시오.

What should you do if you have trouble sleeping? Taking sleeping pills is dangerous. The best thing is to try to relax and to avoid bad habits. Going to bed and getting up about the same time sets a good and healthy rhythm. Don't drink caffeine drinks in the evening. Smoking and alcohol can also keep you awake. And a heavy meal just before you go to bed may cause sleeping trouble.

중심소재:
1. 도입부

1)

Ⓐ 뒷받침 진술

9. 'Among, (One) of'가 이끄는 문장은 글의 요지가 드러나는 주제문일 가능성이 크다. 글의 초반에 자주 등장하는 것이 일반적이다.

[예시]

1. Of all superstitions, few are as widely believed as the one saying the number thirteen is unlucky. 1) ① Many people are so uncomfortable with thirteen that the number is removed from most airline seating charts. ② Many high-rise office buildings have a twelfth floor and a fourteenth floor—but nothing in between. ③ In France, houses are never numbered thirteen. ④ And the national lottery in Italy doesn't use the number.

중심소재: 불운의 13
1. 주제문
13만큼 불길한 숫자는 없다. 주제: 불길한 숫자 13

1) 뒷받침 진술
① 비행기 좌석 13번
② 고층 빌딩 13층
③ 주소 13번지
④ 로또 숫자 13번
등을 모두 사용하지 않음

★ of의 전치사 구에 이어지는 주절의 내용이 주제문이다.

★ 중심소재는 숫자 '13' 이다.

★ 본문에 다뤄질 중심내용에 해당한다.

★ 인과의 시그널을 확인할 수 있다.

| 해석

모든 미신 가운데, 13이 불운의 수라는 것만큼 널리 믿어지는 것은 없다. 많은 사람이 13이라는 숫자를 너무 싫어해서 13은 여객기 좌석 배치도에도 빠져있다. 많은 고층 건물도 12층과 14층은 있지만, 그 사이에 13층은 없다. 프랑스에서는 집 번호에 13이라는 숫자는 붙이지 않는다. 이탈리아에서도 국가 복권에 그 숫자는 사용하지 않는다.

[실전응용] 아래 지문을 분석하고, 글의 요지를 적으시오.

Among the many physical risks facing astronauts sent to the Moon or Mars, the biggest danger will be the least visible: radiation. This is nuclear particles that arrive at almost light speed from beyond the Solar System. The particles slice through strands of DNA, boosting the risk of cancer and other ailments. A 2001 NASA study found that at least 39 former astronauts suffered cataracts after flying in space, 36 of whom took part in high-radiation missions such as the Apollo landings.

중심소재:
1. 주제문

1) 뒷받침 진술

10. 수사의문문은 글쓴이의 주장을 강조한다.

[실전응용] 아래 지문을 분석하고, 글의 요지를 적으시오.

As a successful entrepreneur, I have always had to meet the challenges, more important than money or business, alone. I have had to decide by myself, and always against tremendous opposition from others. Every great move I have made in life has been ridiculed and opposed by my friends. The greatest winnings I have made, in happiness, in money or content, have been accomplished amid almost universal scorn. But I have reasoned in this way: The average man is not always successful. We meet few who attain their goal, few who are really happy or content. Then why should we let the majority rule in matters affecting our lives?

중심소재:
1. 도입부

1)

2. 요지

11. 비유를 통해 간접적으로 글쓴이의 주장을 드러낸다.

[예시]

1. There were two fathers I knew. 1) Although both of them worked hard, I noticed that ① one dad had a habit of putting his brain to sleep when it came to money matters, and ② the other had a habit of exercising his brain. 2. The long-term result was that one dad grew weaker and the other grew stronger financially. 1) It is not much different from a person who sits on the couch watching television versus someone who goes to the gym to exercise on a regular basis. Proper physical exercise increases your chances for health, and proper mental exercise increases your chances for wealth.

중심소재: 금전
1. 도입부: 두 아버지에 대한 설명이다. 돈에 관한 문제가 발생했을 때
1) 구체적 진술
① 아버지 1
머리를 쓰지 않으려고 한다.
② 아버지 2
적극적으로 머리를 쓴다.
2. 주제문(결과)
아버지 1의 경우 열악한 경제력을 가지는 반면, 아버지 2는 경제적으로 튼튼해졌다.
1) 뒷받침 진술
육체 운동에 비유

★ 두 아버지를 통해 궁극적으로 무엇을 다루는지 파악한다.

★ 금전적 문제에 관한 두 아버지의 특징을 다루고 있음을 파악할 수 있다. 대조의 글임을 쉽게 파악할 수 있는데, 각각의 특징이 무엇인지 정확히 파악하고, 궁극적으로 전달하려는 글의 요지를 파악한다.

도입부 = 두 아버지
↓
대조의 글 전개 예상

| 해설
본문 중반에서 글의 요지가 드러나고, 이후 비유를 통해서 요지를 뒷받침하고 있다.

| 해석
내가 알고 있는 두 명의 아버지가 있었다. 비록 둘 다 열심히 일하지만, 한 아버지는 돈 문제에 관해서는 머리를 쓰지 않는 습관이 있고, 다른 아버지는 머리를 쓰는 습관이 있다는 걸 알게 되었다. 장기적 결과로 보면 한 아버지는 경제적으로 약해졌고, 다른 아버지는 경제적으로 더 강해졌다. 규칙적으로 체육관에 가서 운동하는 사람과 소파에 앉아 TV 보는 사람도 별반 다르지 않다. 적당한 신체적 운동을 하면 건강해질 가능성이 커지듯 적당히 정신적인 운동을 하면 부자가 될 가능성이 커진다.

[실전응용 1] 아래 지문을 분석하고, 글의 요지를 적으시오.

In general, every achievement requires trial and error. As youth, we need not feel ashamed of making mistakes in trying to find or win our place in a social group. It is not easy to learn to fit into a group or to develop a personality that helps us to fit in. It is somewhat like learning to play a game like baseball or basketball. We can hardly expect to learn without making a good many mistakes in the process.

중심소재:

1. 주제문

[실전응용 2] 아래 지문을 분석하고, 글의 요지를 적으시오.

A symphony orchestra can fill a whole building and make it ring with music. But this beautiful sound, which can be joyful or sad, exciting or relaxing, is the result of planning and working together. Just as painters choose different colors for their works of art, composers choose the sounds of different instruments to produce their music. The purpose of a symphony orchestra is not to play section by section. The word "symphony" means "sounding together." This sounding together is what creates the wonderful music we all love.

중심소재:

1. 주제문

1) 뒷받침 진술

[실전응용 3] 아래 지문을 분석하고, 글의 요지를 적으시오.

Money is one of mankind's greatest tools. It is like a refreshing mountain stream. When it spills through the meadow, it turns everything in its path active and green. But once obstructed, the stream and the valley dry up; the flowers wither and die. So, too, with the money we possess. While it flows and circulates freely, it helps many. But when the circulation is halted by accumulating, wasting, or abusing, money becomes a curse. The heart hardens and noble aims become misguided. Wealth doesn't mean a thing if it doesn't translate into opportunities for others.

중심소재:
1. 도입부

1) 뒷받침 이유

2. 주제문

[참고 1] **중심소재 · 주제 · 요지 · 제목 설정의 요령**

주제: **글에서 다루려는 내용**으로 주로 구로 표현

제목: 주제를 그대로 제목으로 사용하는 때도 있고, 주제를 상징적 · 함축적으로 전달하는 구 또는 문장으로 표현

요지(주장): 주제를 통해 궁극적으로 밝히려는 내용으로, 설명의 글이면 요약, 논증의 글이면 글쓴이의 견해로 주로 문장의 형태로 제시

아랫글을 바탕으로 주제, 제목, 요지(주장)를 파악해보자.

도입부	현상 제시 – 문제점 지적	최근 한강이 유난히 더러워졌다.
본문	1) 원인 분석 2) 문제의 심각성	한강 주변 공장의 폐기물이 여과 없이 그대로 한강에 유입되고 있다.
결론	대안	한강 수질 예방을 위해 주변 공장에 대한 폐기물관리법을 강화해야 한다.

우리 주변에 일어나는 사건 중 특히 환경에 초점을 맞춘 글이라고 볼 수 있다. 일반적으로 도입부에서 '내가 쓰는 글은 이런 내용을 다룰 것이다'라는 주제를 통해 글의 방향성을 제시한다. 윗글의 도입부를 보면, 현상이 제시되는데, 이를 통해 '한강의 수질오염'을 다루는 글임을 쉽게 파악할 수 있다. 좀 더 구체적으로 주제를 설정하자면 '한강 수질오염의 실태, 원인' 등으로 잡을 수 있다. 이후 도입부에서 설정한 주제를 본문에서 구체적으로 다룬다. 즉, 한강의 수질오염이 왜

발생하는지에 대한 분석(원인 파악)이 따른 후 글쓴이의 대안이 제시된다. 본문을 좀 더 분석해 보자.

Case 1. 도입부(현상 – 문제점)와 본문(원인 파악)만을 다루는 글이었다면, 다음과 같이 구성된다.

도입부	현상 제시 – 문제점 지적	최근 한강이 유난히 더러워졌다.
본문	1) 원인 분석 2) 문제의 심각성	한강 주변 공장의 폐기물이 여과 없이 그대로 한강에 유입되고 있다.

객관적인 입장에서 현 문제점의 원인과 그 심각성을 고발하는 글이다. 이때 글쓴이가 궁극적으로 전달하려는 사항은 바로 현상의 '원인 파악'이다. 고로 그 원인을 밝히는 내용이 바로 글의 요지가 된다.
1) 주제: 한강 수질오염의 **원인**
2) 요지: **공장의 폐기물** 때문에 한강 수질오염의 상태가 심각하다.

Case 2. 다음과 같이 구성될 경우를 살펴봅시다.

도입부	현상 제시 – 문제점 지적	최근 한강이 유난히 더러워졌다.
본문	1) 원인 분석 2) 문제의 심각성	한강 주변 공장의 폐기물이 여과 없이 그대로 한강에 유입되고 있다.
결론	대안	한강 수질예방을 위해 주변 공장에 대한 폐기물관리법을 강화시켜야 한다.

본문을 통해 글쓴이가 궁극적으로 전달하고자 하는 바는 대안에 해당되는 글쓴이의 제안이다. 도입부에서 문제점이 드러나는 현상을 제시하고, 이에 대한 원인 파악을 통해 자신이 궁극적으로 전달하려는 내용에 근거를 마련하고 있다.

1) 주제 : 한강 수질오염의 원인과 대안
2) 요지 : 폐기물 때문에 한강이 심각하게 오염되어 있기에 이에 대한 **강력한 대처**가 필요하다.
Case 1, 2를 통해서 파악할 수 있는 점은 주제와 요지 모두 본문에서 다뤄진 내용을 바탕으로 중심소재, 중심내용 등을 파악하여 구체적으로 작성했다는 점이다. 주제와 요지는 글 전체를 포함하는 동시에 구체적인 구 또는 문장으로 표현해야 한다.

[주의할 사항]
　Case 1, 2의 주제는 모두 같다. 즉, '무엇을 다루는가?'라는 내용은 동일하다. 요지가 다른 이유는 Case 1은 객관적인 설명의 글이고, Case 2는 글쓴이의 견해가 들어간 글이기 때문이다.

　3) 제목: 제목은 주제를 그대로 사용할 수도 있으나 글의 주제와 요지를 함축적으로 전달하는 내용으로 구성될 때가 많다. 위의 글의 경우, 제목을 주제와 같이 '한강 수질오염의 원인'으로 잡으면 독자의 흥미를 끌기에는 너무 딱딱하거나 밋밋할 수 있다. 본문을 바탕으로 주제를 설정할 때 한 예로 '몸살을 앓고 있는 생명수'라고 할 수 있다. '몸살을 앓고 있는'의 표현은 본문에서 자세히 다루는 '현상의 원인'에 해당하는 내용이 되고, '생명수'는 당연히 '한강'을 상징한다.

[참고 2] 현상의 글의 두 유형
Case 1

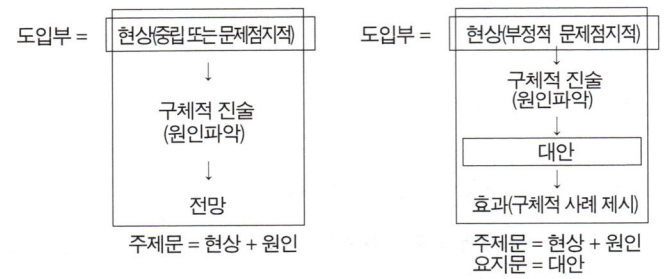

　Case 1의 경우 중립적 또는 긍정적 현상(주로 트렌드)으로 시작하여, 본문의 구체적 진술에서 현상의 원인을 파악하고 글의 마무리에서 전망이 제시되는 반면, Case 2의 경우는 글의 도입부에서 문제점으로 인식되는 부정적 현상이 제시되고, 본문의 구체적 진술에서 원인파악, 대안, 효과의 흐름으로 전개된다. 어느 경우든 주제문은 "현상 + 원인"으로 잡을 수 있으나, Case 2의 경우 현상의 원인 파악을 통해 궁극적으로 전달하려는 요지는 '대안'임을 기억한다.

11 글의 제목

일반적으로 독자를 대상으로 하는 글에는 제목이 있다. 이럴 경우, 독자에게 책을 읽도록 흥미를 유발하기 위한 제목을 설정하는 경우가 많다. 우선, 제목을 설정할 때 일반적으로 반영하는 사항들은 다음과 같다.

> 1. 포괄적인 주제인 중심소재 파악
> 2. 핵심어를 중심으로 중심내용 파악

앞에서 배웠듯이, 주제를 설정할 때는 중심소재를 파악하고 중심내용을 염두에 두면서 주제의 폭을 조절했다. 제목은 주제를 그대로 반영할 수 있는 동시에 주제를 함축적이고, 상징적으로 표현할 수 있다. 문제 풀이의 관점에서 주제와 제목은 다음과 같이 파악할 수 있다

1. 주제를 알면 본문에 전개될 내용을 예측할 수 있다.
2. 주제가 곧 제목이 아닌 경우 본문의 내용을 정확히 파악해야 제목을 고를 수 있다.

주제는 중심소재와 함께 본문에 전개될 구체적 내용을 함축하는 '중심내용(Controlling Idea)'이 반영되어 있기에 글 전개를 예측할 수 있다. 하지만 제목은 함축적이고, 상징적인 표현을 많이 쓰기에 제목만을 보아서는 구체적으로 어떤 대상에 대한 내용을 다루는지 알 수 없는 경우가 많다. 주제는 예측하며 글 읽기에 활용되고, 제목은 본문 내용을 정확히 파악했는지 확인할 수 있는 좋은 기준이 될 수 있다. 주제와 제목 모두 지나치게 포괄적이거나 구체적이지 말아야 한다. 아래의 지문을 보고, 제목을 어떻게 설정할 수 있는지 구체적으로 살펴보자.

[예시 1]

중심소재는 'cockfighting' ★
이다.

중요사건을 이끄는 시간 ★
의 부사 표현에 주의.

중심내용(controlling idea) ★
으로 이후 진술을 통해 구
체적으로 밝히도록 한다.

> 1. Cockfighting is an organized fight between two roosters that are placed in a pit to fight each other. This bloody sport had already been banned in forty-nine states. Louisiana was the only state where cockfighting remained legal because chickens were not defined as animals according to state law.
> 2. Last week we achieved a great success. 1) The state of Louisiana voted to outlaw cockfighting and succeeded in banishing the cruel sport. ① This victory represents a historic achievement for the animal rights movement, which has fought long and hard to ban cockfighting throughout the country.

중심소재: Cockfighting
1. 도입부
투계의 간략한 정의와 현상황('bloodly'라는 표현에서 알 수 있듯이 글쓴이는 투계에 대해 부정적 입장을 취함을 추론할 수 있다): 루이지애나는 여전히 투계를 법적으로 인정 – 이유
2. 주제문
역사적 사건(투계 금지)
1) 구체적 진술
① 역사적 의의

| 해설

본문은 루이지애나 또한 투계를 법으로 금지하게 되어 역사적인 순간을 맞이했다는 내용이다. 아래와 같은 제목을 생각해 보자.

1. 투계
2. 투계의 역사
3. 미국 각 주에서 시행되는 투계
4. 투계에 관한 법적 공방
5. 투계 금지

우선 제목은 본문에서 다루는 중심내용을 전달할 수 있어야 한다. 본문의 중심내용인 'a great success'가 반영된 보기인 5가 정답이다. 보기를 하나씩 구체적으로 살펴보자. 보기 1은 지나치게 광범위한 설정이어서 본문이 구체적으로 어떤 내용을 다룰지 알 수가 없다. 보기 2가 제목이었을 경우, 시간의 글 전개방식에 따라 연도별 특이 사항을 과거에서 현재로 배열하는 글이 될 것이다. 본문과는 거리가 멀다. 보기 3의 경우 미국 각 주에서 시행하는 투계 현황을 주별로 기술하면서 본문의 핵심내용이 부분적으로(특정 주를 중심으로) 제시될 수 있으므로 다소 광범위한 제목 설정이라 할 수 있다. 보기 4의 경우 투계에 관한 법적 공방으로 상반된 두 견해가 제시되면서, 문제 해결에 난항을 겪는 모습이 묘사될 가능성이 크므로 'a great success'를 반영하지 못할 것이다. 보기 5는 중심소재와 함께 글의 중심내용을 가장 잘 반영하고 있다.

| 해석

투계는 서로 싸우도록 경기장에 집어넣는 수탉 두 마리 간의 조작된 싸움이다. 이 살벌한 스포츠는 이미 49개 주(州)에서 금지됐다. 루이지애나는 투계가 합법적으로 남아있었던 유일한 주인데, 그 이유는 주법에 따라 닭이 동물로 규정되지 않았기 때문이다. 지난주에 우리는 큰 성공을 거두었다. 루이지애나 주는 투표를 통해 투계를 불법화하여, 이 잔인한 스포츠를 추방하는 데 성공했다. 이 승리는 동물 권리 운동에서 역사적으로 중요한 성과를 의미하는데, 이 운동은 전국적으로 투계를 금지하기 위해서 오랫동안 열심히 투쟁해 왔다.

[예시 2]

1. No matter how we shake or tap the bottle of ketchup, some of it refuses to come out. In some cases, up to 20 percent of the product is left in the packaging when it is thrown out. This is not only annoying for consumers but also poses difficulties when recycling: The leftovers first have to be removed from the packaging, which is expensive, time-consuming, and uses a great deal of water. 1) A German project by the Fraunhofer Institutes, together with Munich University of Technology and various industrial partners, will put an end to this dilemma. ① <u>Researchers are applying thin films, no more than 20 nanometers thick, to the inside surface of packaging in order to reduce leftover traces</u>.

중심소재: Ketchup
1. **도입부** = 구체적 진술
문제점 지적: 케첩이 항상 남아 재활용을 못할 뿐 아니라 비용·시간 ↑
1) 대안
① 20나노 두께의 얇은 막을 내부에 부착

도입부 =

| 해설
'문제점 지적 – 대안'의 형태에 속하는 글이다. 문제점과 대안을 활용하여 제목을 설정할 수 있다. 문제점을 중심으로 제목을 설정한다면, 'A Dilemma with Leftovers' 정도로 잡을 수 있고, 해결책을 중심으로 제목을 설정한다면 'Good News for Ketchup Lovers'로 잡을 수 있다.

| 해석
케첩 통을 아무리 흔들고 두드린다 해도 어느 정도는 나오지 않는다(병에 항상 남아있다). 어떤 용기는 버릴 때 20% 정도가 남아있다. 이는 소비자에게 짜증 날 뿐 아니라 재활용에도 어려움을 야기한다. 용기에 남아있는 것을 제거해야 하는데, 이는 비용과 시간 그리고 많은 양의 물이 든다. 뮌헨 기술대학 그리고 여러 산업단체와 함께 Fraunhofer 기관에서 실시한 독일의 한 프로젝트 덕분에 이러한 문제점에 종지부를 찍게 되었다. 연구자들은 20나노 두께 정도의 아주 얇은 막을 용기의 내부에 부착해 남은 케첩을 제거할 수 있게 되었다.

[예시 3] 아래의 지문에서 제목을 설정하는 방법을 좀 더 살펴보자.

1. <u>Michelangelo</u> looked at a block of marble and saw a man. Elffers looks at ① <u>a lemon and sees a pig</u>. 1) Growing up in Holland, he was taught to clear his plate; playing with food was forbidden. As an adult, the artist visited Japan, where, he recalls, food was "almost too beautiful, and without humor. Food should be a joy." With his edible produce sculptures, Elffers hopes to share that joy. "If you give people permission to see the pig in the lemon, they will forever see animals in fruit or vegetables," he says. "Americans carve pumpkins but they never use the stem. It's such an

중심소재: 음식
1. **도입부**
조각가 미켈란젤로를 언급한 이유는 무엇인가? 미켈란젤로를 통해서 조각에 관한 글을 쓰려고 하는가?
① **중심소재의 전환**: 건축 → 음식
Elffers라는 사람을 통해서 음식에 대한 어떤 측면을 이야기하려고 하는가?
1) 본격적으로 글이 시작되는 시점이다. 이후 진술(중심내용)을 통해서 주제의 폭을 좁히도록 한다: 어린 시절과 성인의 때를 대조하면서 궁극적으로 어떤 이야기를 풀어내는가?
"음식은 즐거워야 한다 + 먹을 수 있는 농산물 조각품 + 호박 줄기를 이

★ 본문 첫 번째 문장에서 언급된 미켈란젤로는 단순히 비교의 대상이다.
★ 중심소재의 전환

도입부 =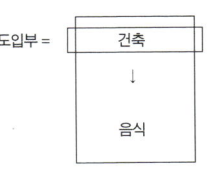

expressive nose!" He urges pumpkin buyers to create their own zoos this Halloween. Elffers says, "Shop with an open mind."

용한 코 + 핼러윈의 호박 동물원" 등의 표현을 통해서 알 수 있듯이 Elffers를 통해 '즐기는 음식'을 강조하고 있다.

| 해설

본문 같은 경우 특정 인물을 통해서 궁극적으로 전달하려는 내용을 이끌어 내야 한다. 음식과 관련된 글이라는 점에서 'Food'가 반드시 반영이 되어야 하고, Elffers를 통해 음식을 통한 즐거움이 글의 중심 내용이므로 핵심어인 'Fun' 등의 단어가 반영되어야 한다. 고로, 'Fun with Food'와 같이 제목을 설정할 수 있다. 이를 조금 응용한다면, 특정 인물을 통해서 음식에 대한 새로운 관점을 드러내는 글이므로 'A New Perspective on Food'와 같이 제목을 삼을 수도 있다.

| 해석

Michelangelo는 대리석 덩어리를 보면서, 인간을 보았다. Elffers는 레몬을 바라보면서 돼지를 본다. 네덜란드에서 자라면서 그는 접시를 깨끗이 비우라고 배웠다. 음식을 가지고 노는 것은 금지였다. 어른이 되어 이 예술가(Elffers)는 일본을 방문했는데, 회상하길 음식은, "너무나 아름다웠고, 그리고 재미없었어요. 음식은 즐거움이어야 합니다." Elffers는 그가 만든 먹을 수 있는 농산물 조각품으로 그 즐거움을 나누기를 희망한다. "만일 당신이 사람들에게 레몬에서 돼지를 보게 해주려고 한다면, 그들은 영원히 과일이나 채소에서 동물들을 볼 겁니다."라고 그는 말한다. "미국인들은 호박을 파내 조각하지만, 그 줄기를 사용하지는 않죠. 그건 정말 표정이 풍부한 코인데 말이죠!" 그는 호박을 사는 사람들에게 이번 핼러윈에 그들 자신의 동물원을 만들어보라고 권유한다. Elffers는 말한다. "열린 마음을 가지고 물건을 사십시오."

[실전응용 1] 다음 글의 제목으로 가장 적절한 것을 고르시오.

You should not watch television and eat at the same time. You just get lost in a program and can't stop eating too much. You'll eat anything — the worst things — when the television is on. You may eat unhealthy food like cookies, snacks, and fast food. It is just like hanging around with the wrong friends in school. You'll do things you wouldn't do if you didn't meet them.

중심소재:
1. 도입부

1) 뒷받침 근거

① Why Healthy Food?
② No TV While Eating
③ Fun with TV Programs
④ TV: Your Lifelong Friend
⑤ Good Friends, Happy Life

[실전응용 2] 본문을 분석하고, 제목을 정하시오.

For their own benefit, companies have various ways of offering lower prices. One way of doing this is a trade discount. It is offered to the shops or businesses that buy goods on a large scale and sell them. There is also a quantity discount, which is offered to individuals who order large quantities of a product. The company gives a price break to these buyers because they help cut the costs of selling, storing, shipping, and billing. Finally, a cash discount is a lower price offered to people who pay in cash.

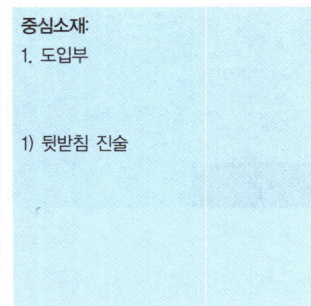

[실전응용 3] 본문을 분석하고, 제목을 정하시오.

Goats like eating weeds. In fact, they prefer weeds to grass. So they are very useful for controlling weeds without using chemicals. The digestive system of the goat is different from that of the sheep or the cow. Weed seeds cannot pass through the goat's body, and so they cannot grow into new weeds. Farmers don't like using chemicals to control weeds because such poisons can kill wild animals or even pets, like dogs. A company in Montana even rents out goats to eat weeds.

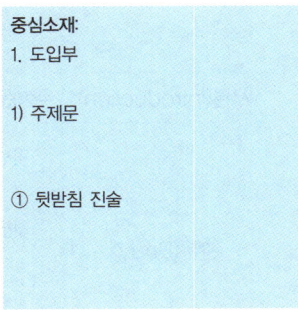

12 글 전개방식

1. 글의 일반적 구조 (Basic Structure of Writing)

서론(Introduction)	주제문(Topic Sentence) = 포괄적 주제(중심소재) + 중심내용(Controlling Ideas)

본문(Body)	뒷받침 진술 1. _____.
	     – 부연진술
	 뒷받침 진술 2. _____.
	     – 부연진술
	 뒷받침 진술 3. _____.
	     – 부연진술

결론(Conclusion)	결론부로 주제문에서 밝힌 글의 요지를 강조

★ 본문에 전개될 구체적 내용에 해당하므로 예측하며 글 읽기에서 반드시 알아야 할 개념이다.

★ 주제문에서 밝힌 중심내용이 구체적으로 전개되는 부분으로 요지를 효율적으로 전달하기 위해 다양한 글 전개방식을 도입한다.

★ 결론(요지)을 이끄는 시그널에 주의한다(제10장 참조).

정형화된 삼단구성이다. 일반적으로 글의 도입부에서 일반진술에 해당하는 주제문을 제시하고, 본문에서 주제문에서 밝힌 중심내용(Controlling Idea)을 구체적으로 전개한다. 결론에서는 요지를 재차 강조하며 글을 마무리한다.

2. 글 전개방식

글의 전개방식은 다음과 같다.

1) Listing(나열)

나열형의 전개방식은 대체로 도입부에서 제시되는 주제문에 "<u>**two, some, various, many + 명사**</u>" 등의 어구를 제시하고 이를 구체적으로 예시, 설명하는 방식을 말한다. 따라서 도입부에서 앞에서 제시된 어구들을 주시하고, 그 의미가 전체 맥락 속(뒷받침 진술)에서 어떻게 구체화하는지를 파악하여야 한다. 또한, 어떤 문제의 속성이나 구체적 의미를 설명하는 개념정의(definition)의 글도 일종의 나열형이다. 나열 순서는 보통 중요도 순서, 빈도 순서, 규모 순서 등이 있어 중요한 것, 빈도가 높은 것, 규모가 큰 것 등에서 시작하여 중요하지 않은 것, 빈도가 낮은 것, 규모가 작은 것 순으로 설명하는 방법도 있고, 이와는 정반대의 순서로 제시하는 방법도 있다.

[예시 1]

1. **A number of problems arose** after the Industrial Revolution. 1) Long hours of work for small wages caused dissatisfaction among workers. 2) <u>In addition</u> to this problem, the physical setup of the factories was grossly inadequate. ① They were dim and poorly ventilated. 3) They <u>also</u> lacked safety devices, which caused thousands of accidents monthly. 4) <u>Finally</u>, child labor was common because parents were forced to send children to work to close the gap between family needs and family income.

1. 도입부 = 주제문
산업혁명은 많은 문제점을 야기했다.
1) **뒷받침 문장 1**
장시간의 노동에도 불구하고 적은 임금
2) **뒷받침 문장 2**
열악한 공장의 외적 환경
① **부연진술**
3) **뒷받침 문장 3**
안전장비 부재
4) **뒷받침 문장 4**
아동 노동 착취

★ 본문에서 다뤄질 중심내용
★ 중심소재
★ 나열의 시그널을 확인한다.
★ 부연진술에 해당하는 문장이다. '주제문 – 뒷받침문장 – 부연진술'을 정확히 구별할 수 있어야 한다.

| 해설
본문의 구조는 다음과 같다.

일반진술 (General Statement) = 주제문	A number of problems arose after the Industrial Revolution.
구체적 진술 (Supporting Sentences) = 뒷받침 문장	1) Long hours of work for small wages (장시간 노동에도 불과하고 적은 임금) 2) Inadequate physical setup of the factories (열악한 공장의 외적 조건) ① 부연진술 3) Lack of safety devices (안전장치의 부재) 4) Child Labor (아동 노동)

| 해석
산업혁명 이후 수없이 많은 문제점이 발생했다. 장기간 일을 함에도 불구하고 적은 임금은 노동자 사이에 불만을 야기했다. 이 문제에 추가로 공장의 외적 환경은 아주 적절하지 못했다. 공장들은 어둡고 통풍이 거의 되지 않았다. 또한 공장에는 안정장치가 없어 이 때문에 매달 수천의 사고가 잇달았다. 마지막으로 아동 노동은 일반화되어 있었는데, 이는 가정의 필요와 수입 사이의 차이를 메우기 위해 어쩔 수 없이 부모가 아이를 일터로 보내야 했기 때문이었다.

[예시 2]

중심내용에 대한 두 가지 가설로 주제를 이끌어 낼 수 있다. 주제: 비만인 사람들이 스트레스를 받을 때 많이 먹는 두 가지 가설

뒷받침 진술에서 자세히 다뤄질 중심내용에 해당한다.

첫 번째 문장에서 밝힌 'Two hypotheses'를 이끄는 시그널(one, different)을 확인한다.

1. **Two hypotheses** may explain why obese people eat more when anxious. 1) ① **One** possibility is that when they were babies, their caregivers interpreted all of their distress signals as requests for food; consequently, as adults, these people have difficulty distinguishing hunger from other feelings, including anxiety. ② A **different** possibility is that some obese persons may respond to an anxiety producing situation by doing the one thing that has brought them comfort all their lives namely, eating. The two hypotheses may apply to different kinds of obese people.

중심소재: 비만 → 비만의 원인
1. 도입부 = 주제문
스트레스와 비만에 관한 두 가지 가설이 있다. ← 주제 설정
1) 뒷받침 진술
① 가설 1
② 가설 2

| 해석
비만인 사람들이 왜 근심·걱정이 있을 때 더 먹는지를 설명하는 두 가지 가설이 있다. 첫 번째 가설은 이들이 아이였을 때, 보호자들이 자신의 투정을 모두 음식을 요구하는 것으로 해석했기 때문이다. 결과적으로 어른이 되어 이들은 근심을 포함한 다른 감정과 배고픔을 구별하는 데 어려움을 겪게 되었다는 것이다. 또 다른 가설은 특정한 비만인은 근심을 만들어 내는 상황을 자신에게 안락을 가져다주는 것을 하면서 반응했는데, 바로 말하자면 먹는 것이다. 이 두 가설은 여러 유형의 비만인 사람에게 적용된다.

[예시 3]

본문에서 전개될 중심내용(controlling idea)에 해당한다.

글에서 밝히고자 하는 주제에 해당한다.

'사람이 당황하는 조건'에 대한 뒷받침 진술이 나열(중요도에 따른)의 글 전개방식에 따라 기술되고 있다.

★중심소재는 'panic'이다.

1. **What conditions** are needed for a **panic**? 1) ① **First and foremost**, the situation must be perceived to be threatening. ② **Next**, the solution to this crisis must be hard to think of. ③ **Third**, the opportunities for successful escape as well as adequate time must be seen as limited. Panics happen when it is difficult for most people to escape.

중심소재: Panic
1. 도입부 = 주제문
의문문은 주제문의 역할을 할 수 있으며, 주제문의 여부와 관련없이 그 자체가 글의 '주제'가 됨을 기억한다.
1) 뒷받침 진술
①, ②, ③을 통해 주제문에서 밝힌 중심내용을 상술하고 있다.

| 해석
당황하기 위해서 어떤 조건이 필요한가? 우선 가장 중요한 것은 그 상황이 위협으로 인식되어야 한다. 다음으로, 위기에 대한 해결책이 떠오르기 쉽지 않아야 한다. 셋째, 적절한 시기뿐 아니라 성공적인 탈출의 기회가 제한적으로 보여야 한다. 사람들이 피하기 어려울 때 공황이 일어난다.

[예시 4]

중심소재는 인터넷 채팅이다. 중심내용을 고려하면서 주제의 폭을 좁히도록 한다.

중심내용(controlling idea)이다.

1. **I think Internet chatting is good for the students**. 1) Internet chatting is fun. ① We can talk about any topic we like. We

중심소재: Internet Chatting
1. 도입부 = 주제문
인터넷 채팅의 유용성

can get lots of useful information from others in the chat rooms. ② We can make new friends with the boys and girls from other countries. ③ Chatting with friends from other countries will improve our English.

1) 뒷받침 문장
① 다양한 주제에 대한 토론과 함께 유용한 정보를 공유할 수 있다.
② 여러 나라의 친구를 사귈 수 있다.
③ 영어 실력 향상

| 해설
나열의 시그널이 전혀 드러나지 않는 글이다. 인터넷 채팅의 유용성에 관한 새로운 정보가 나올 때마다 앞에서 제시된 유용성의 내용에 대한 부연진술인지 새로운 정보인지를 구별해야 한다. 지문이 쉽기 때문에 쉽게 파악이 되지만, '주제문 – 뒷받침 문장 – 부연진술'을 반드시 구별할 수 있어야 한다.

| 해석
나는 인터넷 채팅이 학생에게 유용하다고 생각한다. 인터넷은 재미있다. 우리가 원하는 어떠한 주제에 대해서도 이야기할 수 있다. 우리는 채팅 방의 다른 사람에게서 유용한 정보를 많이 얻을 수 있다. 우리는 다른 나라의 새로운 남녀 친구를 사귈 수 있다. 다른 나라의 친구와 이야기하는 것은 영어 실력을 높여준다.

[예시 5]

1. Computer language can be funny at times. 1) For example, ① we say computers have a "memory." We know they do not really remember or think. But we still say "memory." ② Also, on many computer programs there is a "menu." Of course, we are not talking about restaurants or food. This is a different kind of menu. ③ Another funny example is the "mouse" in some computers. It is hard not to think about a real mouse when you hear the word. But do not worry; there are no little gray animals in the machine.

중심소재: 컴퓨터 언어
1. 도입부 = 주제문
1) 뒷받침 진술
① memory
② menu
③ mouse
* 뒷받침 예시 확인

★ 중심소재는 '컴퓨터 언어'이다. 중심내용을 바탕으로 주제의 폭을 좁히도록 한다.
★ 뒷받침 문장에서 구체적으로 진술된 중심내용(controlling idea)이다.

| 해설
'General → Specific'의 전형적인 형태이며, 'for example, also, another'의 시그널을 확인할 수 있다.

| 해석
컴퓨터 언어는 때때로 재미있다. 예를 들면, 우리는 컴퓨터가 "메모리(기억)"를 가지고 있다고 말한다. 우리는 컴퓨터가 정말로 기억하거나 생각하지 않는다는 것을 알지만, 우리는 여전히 '메모리'라고 말한다. 또한, 컴퓨터 프로그램에는 "메뉴"가 있다. 물론 우리는 식당이나 음식에 대해 이야기하는 것이 아니다. 이것은 다른 메뉴이다. 또 하나 재미있는 것을 예로 들자면 모든 컴퓨터에 딸린 "마우스"이다. 그 낱말을 들으면 쉽게 진짜 쥐가 생각난다. 하지만 걱정하지 마시라. 이 장치에 작은 회색 동물은 없으니 말이다.

중심내용(controlling idea) ★
이다.

중심소재는 'boss' 이다. ★

[예시 6]

1. There are **three important necessaries** in a good boss. 1) ① <u>The most important</u> quality is fairness. If the boss is fair, workers can feel that if they do a good job, their work will be appreciated, and their efforts will be rewarded. ② <u>The second most important</u> quality is leadership. The boss should be an example and a teacher. This allows workers to learn from a boss so that they can increase their job skills and get promoted. ③ <u>The third most important</u> factor is that the boss act with consistency. That way the workers know what to expect each day. They know how they will be treated and what their share of workload will be. I would hire a boss with these qualities for myself.

1. 도입부 = 주제문
훌륭한 사람의 조건
1) 뒷받침 진술
주제문에서 밝힌 중심내용을 중요도에 따라 나열하고 있다.
① fairness
– 부연진술
② leadership
– 부연진술
③ consistency
– 부연진술

| 해설

중요도에 따른 나열의 전개방식을 취하고 있다. 중요도의 순서는 본문과 달리 후반에 더 중요한 사항이 전개되는 경우도 많으므로 함께 기억해 둔다.

| 해석

좋은 상관이 되는 데는 세 가지 중요한 필수사항이 있다. 가장 중요한 자질은 공정성이다. 상관이 공정하면 일하는 사람들은 자기가 잘만하면 칭찬을 받을 것이며 그들의 노력이 보상을 받을 수 있을 것이라 느낀다. 두 번째로 중요한 자질은 지도력이다. 상관은 좋은 예를 보이고 가르치는 사람이 되어야 한다. 이렇게 하면 근로자들이 자신의 직무기술을 증대시키고 승진하기 위하여 상관을 따라 배우게 할 것이다. 세 번째로 중요한 요인은 상관은 일관성을 가지고 행동해야 한다. 그렇게 하면 근로자들은 매일 무엇을 기대해야 할지를 알게 된다. 근로자들은 그들이 어떤 대우를 받을 것이며 그들이 맡은 업무량이 얼마나 될지를 알 수 있다. 나라면 이러한 세 가지 자질을 지닌 상관을 모시고 싶다.

[실전응용 1] 글 전개방식에 주의하면서 본문을 분석하시오.

Smoking is very dangerous and can cause great harm to your body, even endanger your life. When you smoke, your heart beats faster than it needs to and causes your blood pressure to rise, which, eventually, can cause a heart attack or heart disease. In addition, when you smoke, the essential oxygen in your bloodstream is replaced with poisonous carbon monoxide that comes from the tobacco in the cigarette. Finally, many people have fallen asleep while smoking and have set themselves and their homes on fire, endangering their lives.

중심소재:

1. 도입부

1) 뒷받침 진술

[실전응용 2] 글 전개방식에 주의하면서 본문을 분석하시오.

There are at least four things which are more or less under our own control and which are essential to happiness. The first is some moral standard by which to guide our actions. The second is some satisfactory home life in the form of good relations with family or friends. The third is some form of work which justifies our existence to our own country and makes us good citizens. The fourth thing is some degree of leisure and the use of it in some way that makes us happy. To succeed in making a good use of our leisure will not compensate for failure in any one of the other three things to which I have referred, but a reasonable amount of leisure and a good use of it is an important contribution to a happy life.

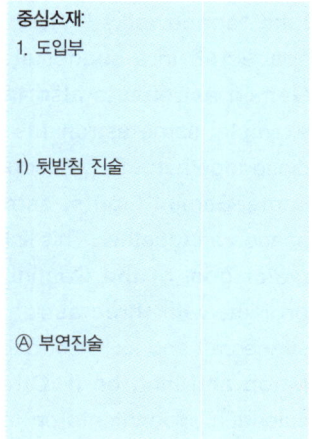

[실전응용 3] 글 전개방식에 주의하면서 본문을 분석하시오.

There are four basic modes of writing. Each mode may take different forms, but has a primary purpose. The first is expository writing, which has a purpose of explaining something or giving directions. Providing directions to your house is an example. The second mode is persuasive writing, which has a purpose of influencing the reader's way of thinking. An advertisement is a an example of persuasive writing. The third mode is descriptive writing, which has a purpose of providing vivid details so that the reader can picture what is being presented. An essay that depicts the glorious Grand Canyon is an example. The fourth mode is narrative writing, which has a purpose of presenting an experience in the form of a story. A personal account of a vacation is an example of narrative writing.

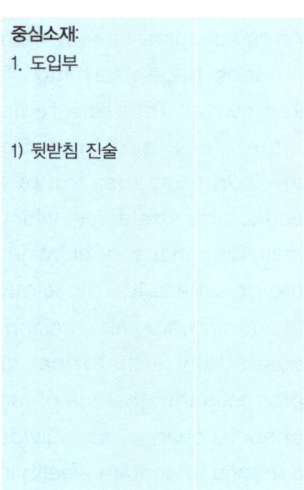

[실전응용 4] 글 전개방식에 주의하면서 본문을 분석하시오.

Each of the U.S. manned space exploration projects had specific major goals. For example, the Mercury project was designed to test whether or not human beings could survive and function in outer space. In addition, the Mercury project tested rockets with the new Mercury space capsule, which could hold one person. As another example, the Gemini project was intended to find out whether two

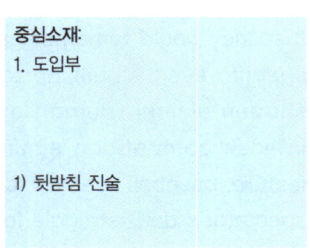

people could work in the weightless environment of space. One way of doing this was by having Gemini astronauts take "spacewalks." That is, they floated outside their spacecraft in a spacesuit, connected to it by a tether. Gemini astronauts also tried out new flying skills. For example, some astronauts flew two spacecraft extremely close together; this procedure was called "rendezvous." On some Gemini flights, astronauts physically linked two spacecraft together. This linking, or "space docking," was a major goal of the Gemini program. Finally, the Apollo project, with three astronauts, had the goal of testing spacecraft and skills so that people could actually fly to the Moon and land on it. Other goals included performing scientific experiments on the lunar surface and collecting rocks for study on Earth.

[실전응용 5] 글 전개방식에 주의하면서 본문을 분석하시오.

Archaeologists have a number of theories to explain why humans began farming. The reasons probably differed somewhat from one region to another. Some theories maintain that population pressure or changes in environment may have forced humans to find new economies strategies, which led to farming. Another theory maintains that a population of humans may have lived in a region where it was relatively easy to domesticate wild plants and animals, making the development of agriculture essentially a historical accident. Still another theory proposes that the rise of farming may have been a function of social change, as individuals began to use agriculture as a means to acquire wealth in the form of food surpluses.

중심소재:
1. 도입부

① 뒷받침 진술

[실전응용 6] 글 전개방식에 주의하면서 본문을 분석하시오.

During a few hours in the ball park, city people saw plays that they could remember afterwards because of the way specific events built up to a memorable moment — the sudden skillful triumph over an adversary. By making intense competition against an opponent its essential feature, baseball seemed to legitimize and appreciate each spectator's daily struggle for success. Watching the rivalry on the diamond introduced standards of competition into

중심소재:
1. 뒷받침 진술
1)

2)

3)

the spectators' lives. The game also reduced their daily tensions because its ups and downs seemed more momentous than their lives.

4)

[실전응용 7] 글 전개방식에 주의하면서 본문을 분석하시오.

What conditions are needed for a panic? First and foremost, the situation must be perceived to be threatening. Next, the solution to this crisis must be hard to think of. Third, the opportunities for successful escape as well as adequate time must be seen as limited. Panics happen when it is difficult for most people to escape.

중심소재:
1. 도입부

1) 뒷받침 진술

2) Cause and Effect (인과)

인과 관계형의 전개 방식은 두 가지 이상의 일이나 사건 사이에 존재하는 원인이나 결과에 중점을 두고 설명하는 방식을 말한다. 원인과 결과가

① 1:1의 대응 관계로 이루어질 때도 있지만,

② 하나의 원인이 여러 가지 결과를 가져올 수도 있고,

③ 여러 가지 원인이 복합적으로 작용해서 하나의 결과를 가져올 수도 있다.

④ 또 여러 가지 원인이 여러 결과를 가져오는 때도 있다. 그러므로 인과 관계형의 글을 읽을 때는 원인과 결과의 관계를 파악하는 것도 중요하지만, 이들 사이에 몇 가지 요소가 존재하는지를 아는 것도 중요하다.

[예시 1]

1. Auto engines, power plants and landfills give off tons of heat trapping gases. These gases, mostly carbon dioxide and methane, tend to build up in the earth's atmosphere. If the buildup becomes too great the heat can no longer escape from the earth's atmosphere. When the heat cannot escape, the result is global warming. ① Global warming in turn **results in** changing weather patterns and higher average temperature.

중심소재: 온난화 현상
1. **온난화 현상**이 발생하는 과정을 자세히 설명하고 있다. 본문 마지막 문장(①)에서는 온난화로 발생하는 결과 (result in)가 언급되고 있다.
* 인과의 글전개 확인

| 해석
자동차, 발전소, 쓰레기 매립지는 열을 흡수하고 가지고 있는 수천 개의 가스를 방출한다. 대부분 이산화탄소와 메탄인 이 가스들은 지구 대기권에 쌓이게 된다. 만일 이렇게 쌓인 가스가 너무 지나치게 많아지면, 열은 더는 지구 대기권에서 빠져나갈 수 없게 된다. 열이 빠져나갈 수 없게 되면, 그 결과 지구 온난화 현상이 일어나는 것이다. 지구 온난화 현상은 결국 기후 패턴의 변화와 평균 기온의 상승이라는 결과를 초래한다.

글의 배경에 해당하는 구체적 현상이 전개되고 있다. ★

인과의 시그널을 확인할 수 있다. ★

중심내용에 해당한다. 본문에서 이에 대한 구체적 진술이 이어질 것을 예상할 수 있다. ★

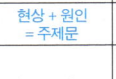

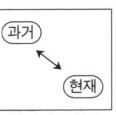

[예시 2]

1. As the impact of globalization spreads to every industry, business people around the world learn to expect tougher competition than they have ever faced before. 1) Back when five or ten rivals could comfortably coexist in a single market, some would offer high-quality products at premium prices while others sold lesser goods for a discount. Today, most consumers and industrial buyers won't even consider low-quality goods, and it's hard to find a company that hasn't joined the quality movement.

중심소재: Globalization
인과의 글 전개방식 확인
1. 도입부 = 주제문
원인: 산업 전반에 세계화의 확대
결과(현상): 그 어느 때보다 치열한 경쟁
1) 뒷받침 진술
과거와 현재를 대조하면서 치열해진 경쟁의 상황을 구체적으로 제시하고 있다.

| 해설
이 글은 세계화의 결과로 발생하는 현상을 언급하고 있다.

| 해석
세계화의 영향이 모든 산업에 퍼져감에 따라, 세계의 사업가들은 예전에 직면했던 것보다 경쟁이 더 심해짐을 알게 된다. 과거 다섯 내지 열 경쟁자가 편안하게 단 하나의 시장에서 공존했을 때, 일부 업체들은 고품질의 제품들을 액면가 이상으로 내놓았고, 다른 업체들은 품질이 낮은 제품들을 할인 판매했다. 오늘날 대부분의 소비자나 산업 구매자들은 질 나쁜 상품은 고려조차 하지 않으며, 품질 향상 운동에 참여하지 않는 기업들도 찾아보기 어렵다.

본문에 등장하는 여러 인과의 시그널을 확인한다. ★

중심소재에 해당한다. ★

[예시 3]

1. World War II ended in 1945. Beginning in 1946, as thousands of American soldiers returned home, the United States birth rate began a dramatic rise. As the number of births increased, the creation of goods and services designed to meet the needs of this growing new population also increased. As advertisers competed to attract this group's attention, the so-called "baby boom generation" became more and more visible. Consequently, it was perceived as more and more powerful—as voters as well as consumers. As a result, this group's emergence has proved to be a major factor in shaping American political, social, cultural, and economic life.

1. 새로운 현상으로 나타난 결과를 인과의 전개방식을 바탕으로 기술하고 있다.
제2차 세계대전이 끝나고 수천의 군인들이 고국으로 귀환 → 출생률 급증(as) → 새로운 인구 층 증가의 수요를 맞추기 위해 생산 증가(결과) → 새로운 층의 관심을 끌기 위해 광고 경쟁으로 이어짐(as) - 이런 과정에서 '베이비붐 세대'가 더욱 두드러짐 → 결과적으로(consequently) 경제적 측면뿐 아니라 정치적으로 큰 영향을 행사하는 단체로 인식됨 → 사회 전반에 영향을 미치는 단체로 평가됨

| 해석
제2차 세계대전이 1945년에 끝났다. 1946년 초 수천 명의 미국인 병사들이 귀향했을 때 미국의 출생률은 엄청난 상승을 하기 시작했다. 출생자 수가 증가했을 때 이 증가하는 새로운 인구의 욕구를 만족하게 하기 위해 의도

된 재화와 용역의 창조도 증가했다. 광고주들이 이 집단의 주의를 끌기 위한 경쟁을 했을 때 소위 베이비 붐 세대는 더욱더 눈에 드러나게 되었다. 그 결과 소비자뿐만 아니라 유권자로서 더욱 더 강력하게 인지되었다. 결과적으로 이 집단의 출현은 미국의 정치, 사회, 문화 그리고 경제적 생활을 형성하는 데 주요한 요소로 판명되었다.

[예시 4]

1. Because toys have become electronic devices, some children today are unable to entertain themselves. 1) ① Gone are the days when children invented their own adventures and used sticks as swords, cookie sheets as armor, and refrigerator box as a fortress to defend. ② The electronic age has delivered children all sorts of gadgets and gizmos that are supposed to be realistic. Some toys even have buttons to push so prerecorded messages can be played to begin scripted adventures that require no imagination. No imagination? No wonder some children today have short attention spans.

1. 도입부 = 주제문
전자 장난감 탓에 오늘날의 아이들은 스스로 즐기지 못한다.

1) 뒷받침 진술
① 과거 – 장난감이 없던 과거에는 스스로 모험을 고안하고, 막대기를 칼로, 종이를 갑옷으로, 냉장고 상자를 요새로 상상하며 즐겼다.
② (하지만) 전자시대가 되면서 온갖 종류의 전자 장난감 등장 → 아이들의 상상력이 없어지고, 심지어 집중력까지 줄어듦(인과를 확인한다).

★ 중심소재는 '전자 장난감'이다.

★ 본문에 구체적으로 다뤄질 중심내용(controlling idea)에 해당한다. 주제: 전자 장난감의 영향력

★ 과거와 현재를 대조하면서 궁극적으로 전달하려는 사항은 무엇인지 생각한다.

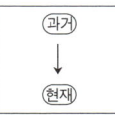
시간의 대조 확인

| 해석
장난감이 이제 전자 장치가 되어 버렸기 때문에, 아이 중 더러는 스스로 놀 수 없게 되었다. 아이들이 스스로 모험을 만들어 내고 막대기로 칼을 삼고, 과자포장지로 갑옷을 만들며, 냉장고 상자를 성채로 생각하며 놀던 시절은 지나갔다. 전자시대는 어린아이들에게 매우 현실적인 것으로 보이는 여러 가지 놀이기구를 제공했다. 어떤 장난감은 단추만 누르면 미리 녹음된 메시지를 들려주고 아이들의 상상력이 전혀 동원되지 않는 모험을 시작하게 된다. 상상력이 전혀 없다? 오늘날 아이들이 집중력을 보이지 못하는 것도 놀랄 일이 아니다.

[예시 5]

1. On September 1, 1914, a twenty nine year-old bird named Martha, the last known passenger pigeon, died in the Cincinnati Zoo. 1) Yet in the nineteenth century, there were so many passenger pigeons in America that no attempt was made to protect them. On the contrary, large scale pigeon shoots were a popular sport. In addition, passenger pigeons were finding it harder and harder to find the wide areas of land they needed to raise their young. 2. By the beginning of the twentieth century, Martha was all that was left from the huge flocks, and with her death, the birds became extinct.

1. 도입부 = 현상(결과)
Martha라는 마지막 passenger pigeon의 죽음

1) 본문(구체적 진술)
'Yet' 이후 도입부에서 전개한 현상과 대조적인 상황을 설명하고 있다 – 19세기에는 이 비둘기를 보호할 필요가 없을 정도로 아주 많은 passenger pigeon 존재 → 대량의 비둘기 사냥이 흥행함(원인 1) + 새끼를 기를 넓은 지역이 없어짐 (원인 2)

2. 결론
20세기 초 Martha만이 유일한 passenger pigeon으로 남았다가 결국 모두 멸종하게 됨.

★ 중심소재는 'Martha'라는 비둘기이다.

★ 마지막 passenger pigeon이 멸종되었다는 현상(결과)으로 시작하는 글이다. 이후 이런 현상의 원인을 파악하는 내용으로 이어질 가능성이 가장 크다.

★ 양괄식의 구조확인

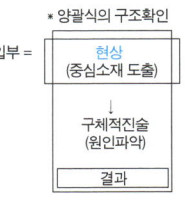

119

| 해설

시간의 흐름에 따라 특정 현상의 결과가 어떤 과정을 통해 발생했는지를 그 원인을 분석하며 기록하고 있다. 글 전개방법은 '인과와 시간' 이다.

| 해석

1914년 9월, 마지막 passenger pigeon으로 알려진 Martha라는 비둘기가 스물아홉 살의 나이로 Cincinnati 동물원에서 죽었다. 19세기까지만 해도 미국에는 passenger pigeon이 많았었기 때문에 이들을 보호하기 위한 어떠한 시도도 이루어지지 않았다. 반대로 대규모의 비둘기 사냥이 인기 있는 스포츠였다. 게다가 passenger pigeon이 새끼를 키울 수 있는 넓은 지역의 땅을 찾는 것이 점점 더 어려워졌다. 20세기가 시작될 무렵, Martha는 무리에서 유일하게 살아남았으며, 이 새의 죽음으로 이 조류는 멸종하게 되었다.

[실전응용 1] 글 전개방식에 주의하면서 아래 지문을 분석하시오.

When people move from one city or country to another, the spread of diseases may result. People often bring in germs which may not have been present there before. These new germs can spread quickly and cause previously unknown diseases. If a germ is completely new to a region, people have no natural protection against it. They become ill more easily and die more often. In turn, newcomers may catch diseases which were not present where they came from. If they go back, they may carry the diseases with them and start an epidemic there, too.

중심소재:
1. 도입부

1) 뒷받침 진술

[실전응용 2] 글 전개방식에 주의하면서 아래 지문을 분석하시오.

In August, the Chilean court took away the exemption right from former dictator Augusto Pinochet. As a result, Pinochet can finally be tried, but the political world of Chile still seems unstable. Now that Pinochet can be sued for human rights abuses during his rule, many Chileans are demanding that the government punish him. The international society also wants justice, and America has even decided to reveal all classified documents on Pinochet. However, punishing Pinochet is not as simple as it looks. This is due to the military in power and Pinochet's parliamentary superpowers. They have already submitted a bill to stop the trial on the grounds that Pinochet is too old and sick.

중심소재:
1. 도입부

1)

2)

[실전응용 3] 글 전개방식에 주의하면서 아래 지문을 분석하시오.

Supposing two foreigners happen to meet and get involved in conversation. Even if both parties are fluent in the same language, differences in interpretations will occur, because of the cultural differences. Each person interprets events through his or her mental filter, and that filter is based on the receiver's experiences, life style, and social tradition to which he or she belongs. As a result, several of the nonverbal forms of communication have different meanings from culture to culture which interfere the conversation to some extent.

중심소재:
1. 도입부

1) 뒷받침 진술

2. 결과(요지)

[실전응용 4] 글 전개방식에 주의하면서 아래 지문을 분석하시오.

Both the advances of science and the horrors of modern history have caused a decrease in religious faith. Scientific insights have explained many of the mysteries once explained only by religion. As a result, for many people, science has become their religion. Moreover, the history of this century has been a recurring nightmare revealing the frightening depths of people's cruelty to one another.

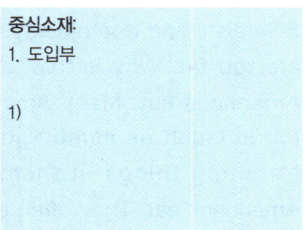

중심소재:
1. 도입부

1)

[실전응용 5] 글 전개방식에 주의하면서 아래 지문을 분석하시오.

To function properly, your brain requires an enormous amount of oxygen: roughly 20% of your body's total supply. But as we age, the blood supply to the brain decreases, which causes oxygen depletion. This leads to loss of concentration and memory. BioGinkgo, derived from the leaves of the ginkgo tree, safely and naturally increases the blood flow to the brain, restoring its oxygen supply. As a result, the brain naturally functions better: things like memory and concentration are all improved. Take BioGinkgo and sharpen your mental sharpness.

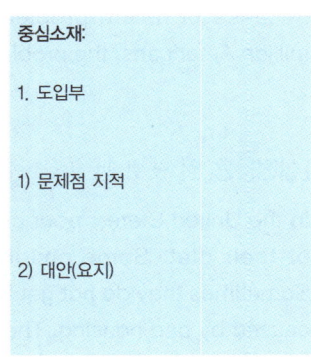

중심소재:

1. 도입부

1) 문제점 지적

2) 대안(요지)

[실전응용 6] 글 전개방식에 주의하면서 아래 지문을 분석하시오.

In recent decades, cities have grown so large that now about 50% of the Earth's population lives in urban areas. There are several reasons for this occurrence. First, the increasing industrialization of the nineteenth century

중심소재:

1. 도입부

resulted in the creation of many factory jobs, which tended to be located in cities. These jobs, with their promise of a better material life, attracted many people from rural areas. Second, there were many schools established to educate the children of the new factory laborers. The promise of a better education persuaded many families to leave farming communities and move to the cities. Finally, as the cities grew, people established places of leisure, entertainment, and culture, such as sports stadiums, theaters, and museums. For many people, these facilities made city life appear more interesting than life on the farm, and therefore drew them away from rural communities.

1) 연결문(이유)
① 뒷받침 진술

[실전응용 7] 글 전개방식에 주의하면서 본문을 분석하시오.

Scientists and doctors say that about 34 million Americans are too fat. Why is this? One cause is the kind of food Americans eat. Many Americans like "fast foods." These foods (such as hamburgers and ice cream) often have fattening things in them. Another cause is the way Americans eat. They often eat little snacks between regular meals. These extra foods add extra fat on the body. A third cause is not enough exercise. Americans like driving everywhere, instead of walking. They often have machines to do a lot of the work. Some Americans are also too heavy because of health problems. But for most of those 34 million Americans, the problem is the American lifestyle.

중심소재:
1. 도입부

1) 연결문

① 뒷받침 진술

[실전응용 8] 글 전개방식에 주의하면서 본문을 분석하시오.

In the United States, poor city children are often ill because of their diet. Some children do not get enough food. Sometimes they do not get healthy food. Poor health is also caused by bad housing. The apartments may not have heat in the winter or fresh air in the summer. Poor health may also be the result of dirty water. Or it may be caused by crowded apartments and crowded schools.

중심소재:
1. 도입부

1)
2)
3)
4)

[실전응용 9] 글 전개방식에 주의하면서 본문을 분석하시오.

Even the Press, that great organ which boasts of its freedom in all democratic countries, is not in reality free at all: it is oppressed under the heel of Advertisements. For a proprietor or editor dare not offend the advertisers by anything he publishes in his paper. If he did, they would withdraw their advertisements and the paper would lose their financial backing. Every child knows that it is the advertisements that pay for a newspaper.

중심소재:
1. 도입부
현상:

1) 원인

[실전응용 10] 글 전개방식에 주의하면서 본문을 분석하시오.

Asthma rates in kids are on the rise. Surprisingly, some experts say it may have to do with our sterile lifestyle and overuse of antibiotics. Exposure to bugs puts the immune system into fighting mode—and that's a good thing. Kids with the pylori bacterium are half as likely to have asthma as those who don't, according to recent research. Since the invention of antibiotics, this bacterium has been on the decline. The discovery could lead to the development of a preventive treatment. Until then, replace antibacterial soaps and cleaning products with normal ones. And when possible, avoid giving your child antibiotics.

중심소재:
1. 도입부
1) 주제문

① 뒷받침 진술

2. 대안과 주의점

3) Comparison and Contrast (비교·대조)

기술 대상의 유사점 또는 차이점에 초점을 두고 글을 전개해 나가는 방식이 비교·대조형인데, 대상의 유사점을 열거하며 서술하는 것을 비교(comparison)형이라고 하고, 기술 대상들의 차이점에 대해 서술하는 것을 대조(contrast)형이라고 한다. 비교·대조형의 글은 읽는 사람에게 친숙할 것이라고 예상되는 것에 근거하여 새로운 것을 설명하는 전개 방식으로, 이 방식은 그 구체적 설명 양식에 따라 크게 두 가지로 나눌 수 있다. 이를테면 A와 B 두 가지 대상을 비교·대조할 때, A의 특징을 서술한 후 이에 상응하는 B의 유사점이나 차이점을 서술하는 형태가 그 첫 번째 형태이고, A와 B의 특징을 하나씩 비교·대조해 나가는 방법이 그 두 번째 형태이다. 첫 번째 방법은 비교·대조할 항목이 그다지 많지 않을 때 자주 사용되며, 두 번째 방법은 대상물 사이에 유사점이나 차이점이 많을 때 주로 사용된다.

중심소재는 경차와 중형 자동차이다.

중심내용(controlling idea)에 해당한다.

대조의 시그널을 확인한다.

도입부 =
| 두 대상 (중심소재) |
| 비유 | 대조 |

[예시 1]

1. Owners of small cars believe that these cars have advantages over large ones. ① A small car is inexpensive to operate because it goes 15 to 18 kilometers on a litter of gasoline. ② The original purchase price of a small car is considerably less than that of the bigger models. ③ And of course small cars are much easier to park.

중심소재: 중형차, 경차
1. 도입부 = 주제문
중형차에 비해 경차가 가지는 장점을 언급하고 있다.
1) 뒷받침 전술
① 장점 1
② 장점 2
③ 장점 3

| 해석
경차를 소유하는 사람은 이 자동차가 중형차에 비해 이점이 있다고 믿는다. 경차는 석유 1리터 당 15에서 18km를 달리기 때문에 운영비가 싸다. 경차의 초기 구매 가격도 상대적으로 중형차 모델에 비해 상당히 싸다. 그리고 물론 경차는 주차하기도 훨씬 쉽다.

중심소재는 'life' 이며, 삶에 대한 대조되는 두 대상의 관점을 파악한다.

대조의 시그널(while+but)을 확인할 수 있다.

[예시 2]

1. The young are inclined to see life, and even youth, as lasting forever; while the middle-aged and elderly become increasingly conscious that they will die and that time places limitations on all their activities. The young believe that they have "all the time in the world," but as one ages, the sense that "time is running out" increases.

삶을 바라보는 관점의 차이가 나이가 들어가면서 달라지는 것을 파악할 수 있다. 대조의 대상으로 젊은이와 노인이 나오는데, 삶에 대한 각각의 관점을 정확히 파악하도록 한다.
주제: 삶에 대한 관점

| 해석
나이가 어린 사람은 삶이 영원히 지속할 것이라 보는 경향이 있는 반면, 중년과 나이가 든 노인은 이들이 곧 죽게 될 것이라는 점과 시간은 이들이 하는 모든 활동을 제약한다고 점차 의식하게 된다. 젊은이는 '세상의 모든 시간을 가진' 것으로 믿으나, 나이가 들면서 '시간이 고갈되어 간다' 라는 인식이 증가하게 된다.

중심내용(controlling idea)에 해당한다.

중심소재: 레몬과 라임

비교의 글 전개방식임을 드러내는 시그널을 확인한다.

[예시 3]

1. Lemons and limes are very similar kinds of fruit. 1) They are both grown in warm places. They both have hard skins and soft insides. People do not usually eat whole lemons and limes. That is because both of these fruits have a very sour taste. They are often used in cooking desserts and main dishes. People make juice from lemons and also from limes. Finally, both fruits have a lot of vitamin C in them.

1. 도입부 = 주제문
1) 뒷받침 진술
주제문에서 밝힌 중심내용을 나열의 글 전체를 통해 뒷받침하고 있다.

| 해석

레몬과 라임은 아주 비슷한 종류의 과일이다. 이 둘은 따뜻한 곳에서 재배된다. 이들 둘 다 딱딱한 껍질이 있고, 내용물은 말랑말랑하다. 사람들은 일반적으로 레몬과 라임 전체를 먹지는 않는다. 이는 신맛이 강하기 때문이다. 종종 음식의 디저트와 주된 음식에 사용되기도 한다. 사람들은 레몬과 라임으로 주스를 만든다. 마지막으로 이 둘은 모두 비타민 C가 많다.

[예시 4]

1. The booming cities of the late nineteenth century had their share of problems: ① crime, fires, garbage, disease. 1) But cities also had their share of pleasures. ① City-dwellers were less isolated than people living in the country. City people were able to get together to share ideas, entertainments, and common creative interests. Because the large populations were necessary to support libraries, theaters, museums, and art galleries, these cultural institutions first developed as part of the trend toward urbanization.

중심소재: 19세기 후반의 도시
1. 도입부
19세기 도시의 문제점(①)을 언급하고 있다.
1) 주제문
But 이후 19세기 말 도시의 '장점'을 언급하고 있다.
① 뒷받침 진술

★ 19세기 급격히 발전하는 도시에 관한 글이다. 이후 전개되는 내용을 바탕으로 주제의 폭을 좁혀야 한다.

★ 'But' 이후 주제가 전환되고 있고, 'But' 이후 주제문 제시라는 전형적인 형태를 취하고 있다.

도입부 = A의 장점
But A의 단점(주제문)
뒷받침 진술

| 해석

19세기 말엽에 급격히 발전한 도시들은 문제점들 — 즉 범죄, 화재, 쓰레기, 질병 — 을 떠안고 있었다. 그러나 도시들 또한 즐길 것들(장점)을 가지고 있었다. 도시 거주자들은 시골에 사는 사람들보다 덜 고립되어 있었다. 도시인들은 사상, 오락, 그리고 공동의 창조적인 관심사들을 공유하기 위해 협력할 수 있었다. 도서관, 극장, 박물관, 미술 전시관들을 후원하기 위해서 많은 인구가 필요했기 때문에, 이러한 문화 단체들은 도시화 경향의 일환으로 먼저 발전하게 되었다.

[예시 5]

During the Renaissance, many people in Europe were becoming prosperous. Nobles and church leaders, who were already members of the wealthiest classes, expanded their fortunes. Newly rich merchants also found themselves with money to spend. Large sums of money were spent on delicacies such as caviar, lavish clothing and jewelry, and elegant estates. Members of the wealthy classes also used their newly increased wealth to support the arts, leading to the achievements for which the Renaissance is best known. Not everyone became wealthy, however. In fact, many members of the peasant class became even poorer than they

중심소재: 본문 'however'를 중심으로 대조를 이루는 두 대상을 설정할 수 있다. 르네상스 시대의 부유한 층의 사람과 가난한 층의 사람이 대조되고 있다.
→ 글의 전반부에 엄청난 부를 누린 '귀족과 교회 지도층'을 비롯하여 신흥 부유 상인, 부유 계층이 소개되고 있는 반면, 'However' 이후 앞에서 언급된 부유층과는 대조적인 가난한 사람들의 어려운 실정을 언급하고 있다. 본문은 문예부흥이란 르네상스와 동시에 드러나는 '빈부의 극심한 격차'를 드러내는 글이다.

★ 'however'를 기점으로 대조되는 내용을 파악한다.

125

were before. As the upper class became more affluent, prices went up and the lower class found it difficult to buy even the necessities. While some were enjoying their upgraded lifestyle, the peasants still found it difficult to obtain basic necessities like food and housing.

| 해석

르네상스 시대에 많은 유럽인은 부유하게 되었다. 이미 최고 부유층이었던 귀족과 교회 지도자들이 그들의 부를 증대시켰다. 신흥 부유 상인들 또한 그들이 써야 할 돈이 많음을 알았다. 많은 돈이 식탁 위의 맛있는 음식, 사치스러운 옷과 보석, 우아한 저택에 쓰였다. 부유 계층의 사람들은 또한 그들이 새로이 축적한 부를 예술작품을 후원하는 데 사용했기 때문에, 그 결과 르네상스라고 가장 잘 알려진 업적이 이루어졌다. 하지만 모든 사람이 부자가 된 것은 아니었다. 사실 많은 소작농은 예전보다 훨씬 더 가난해졌다. 상류층들이 더 부유해짐에 따라, 가격이 상승했고, 하위계층들은 심지어 필수품을 구비하는 것조차도 어려웠다. 어떤 사람들은 향상된 생활을 즐기는 반면, 소작농들은 여전히 음식과 주택과 같은 기본적인 필수품을 얻기 어렵게 되었다.

[예시 6]

대조되는 두 대상을 파악하고, 'But'과 같은 대조의 시그널을 파악한다.

구체적 진술의 시그널

도입부 = 두 대상의 인식 차이
대상 A _____
대상 B _____
① 부연진술

대상 B에 대한 설명이 주된 내용이므로 주제 또한 B를 중심으로 설정한다(공간의 활용에 주의)

1. When we enter a room, 1) we immediately recognize the floor, chairs, furniture, tables, and so forth. But when 2) a robot scans a room, it sees nothing but a vast collection of straight and curved lines, which it converts to pixels. It takes an enormous amount of computing time to make sense out of this jumble of lines. ① A computer sees only a collection of circles, ovals, spirals, straight lines, curly lines, corners, and so on. Spending an enormous amount of computing time, a robot might finally recognize the object as a table. But if you rotate the image, the computer has to start all over again. In other words, robots can see, and in fact they can see much better than humans, but they don't understand what they are seeing.

중심소재: 인간 vs 로봇
대조의 글 전개방식임을 드러내는 시그널로 두 대상의 언급과 함께 'But'이 여러 번 등장한다.
1. 'But'을 기준으로 인간과 로봇의 어떤 차이점을 기술하고 있는가? → 인식(Recognition)의 차이
1) 인간 – 대상을 즉각 인식한다.
2) 로봇 – 대상을 곧은 선과 굴곡으로 파악하고, 이를 화소로 바꾼 후 오랜 처리 시간 후 대상을 인식한다.
① 부연
'But' 이후 오랜 처리 시간 후 다시 이미지를 돌렸을 경우, 컴퓨터는 대상을 인식하는 처리 과정을 모두 다시 시작해야 한다.

| 해설

'인간과 컴퓨터의 인식 차이'를 바탕으로 주로 컴퓨터의 인식방법을 다루고 있다.

| 해석

우리는 방에 들어갈 때, 즉각적으로 바닥, 의자, 가구, 탁자, 기타 등등을 인식한다. 그러나 로봇은 어떤 방을 훑어볼 때 단지 직선과 곡선의 방대한 집합체로만 보며, 그리고 나서 로봇은 그것을 화소로 전환한다. 이런 뒤죽박죽 섞인 선들을 이해하기 위해서는 많은 양의 계산 시간이 필요하다. 컴퓨터는 원, 타원, 나선형, 직선, 곡선, 모퉁이 그리고 기타 등등의 한 집합체로만 보게 된다. 상당한 계산 시간을 보내고 난 후에 로봇은 마침내 그 물체를 탁자로 인식하게 된다. 그러나 만약 당신이 그 이미지를 회전시키면, 컴퓨터는 모든 것을 다시 시작해야 한다.

다시 말해서 로봇은 볼 수 있고 사실 인간보다 훨씬 잘 볼 수 있지만, 자신이 보고 있는 것을 이해하는 것은 아닙니다.

[실전응용 1] 글 전개방식에 주의하면서 아래 지문을 분석하시오.

Two great leaders in American history, Alexander Hamilton and Thomas Jefferson, differed in their view of the American people and the American government. Hamilton distrusted the people and thought they were naturally selfish, unreasonable, and violent. Jefferson, on the other hand, trusted people more and had more faith in their goodness. Hamilton believed in giving the federal government a great deal of power, while Jefferson favored a minimum amount of power in the federal government. Hamilton wanted local government to have very little power, while Jefferson favored strong local government.

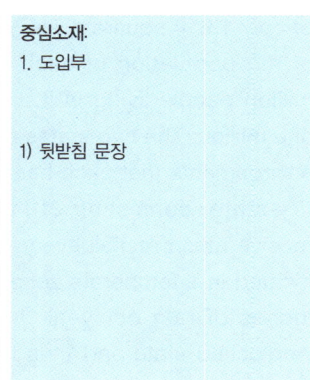

중심소재:
1. 도입부

1) 뒷받침 문장

[실전응용 2] 글 전개방식에 주의하면서 아래 지문을 분석하시오.

While awaiting the birth of a new baby, North American parents typically furnish a room as the infant's sleeping quarters. For decades, child-rearing advice from experts has encouraged the nighttime separation of baby from parent. For example, a study recommends that babies be moved into their own room by three months of age. "By six months a child who regularly sleeps in her parents' room is likely to become dependent on this arrangement," reports the study. Yet parent-infant 'co-sleeping' is the norm for approximately 90 percent of the world's population. Cultures as diverse as the Japanese, the Guatemalan Maya, and the Inuit of Northwestern Canada practice it.

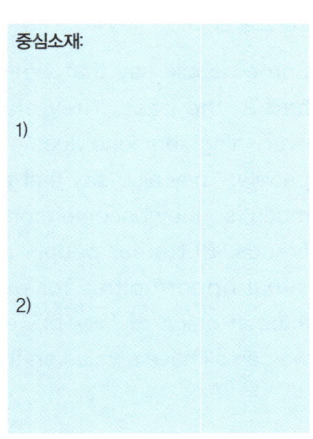

중심소재:

1)

2)

[실전응용 3] 글 전개방식에 주의하면서 아래 지문을 분석하시오.

Some writers think that to impress their readers, they have to use a lot of long words and try to sound "intellectual." This is not so. Most readers prefer to read something that is clear, that they don't have to struggle with. They want the writer to do the work. If they have to spend time figuring out what the writer means, they'll get impatient.

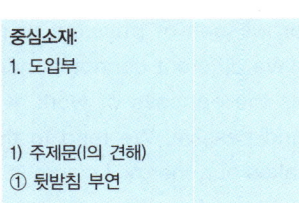

중심소재:
1. 도입부

1) 주제문(I의 견해)
① 뒷받침 부연

[실전응용 4] 글 전개방식에 주의하면서 아래 지문을 분석하시오.

Even though Arizona and Rhode Island are both states of the U.S., they are strikingly different in many ways. For example, the physical size of each state is different. Arizona is large, having an area of 114,000 square miles, whereas Rhode Island is only about a tenth the size, having an area of only 1,214 square miles. Another difference is in the size of the population of each state. Arizona has about four million people living in it, but Rhode Island has less than one million. The two states also differ in the kinds of natural environments that each has. For example, Arizona is a very dry state, consisting of large desert areas that do not receive much rainfall every year. However, Rhode Island is located in a temperate zone and receives an average of 44 inches of rain per year. In addition, while Arizona is a landlocked state and thus has no seashore, Rhode Island lies on the Atlantic Ocean and does have a significant coastline.

중심소재:
1. 도입부

1) 뒷받침 진술

[실전응용 5] 글 전개방식에 주의하면서 아래 지문을 분석하시오.

Some people say that we have less privacy now than we had in the past. They claim it's possible to discover everything someone does on the Internet, and even spy on people. They also say that people can use the Internet too much, so they become more distant from their families and friends. But other people claim that the Internet creates equal opportunities for everyone. They argue that the Internet helps to take power away from the rich, and that we can all have a voice on the Internet.

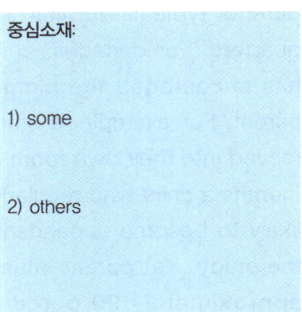

중심소재:

1) some

2) others

[실전응용 6] 글 전개방식에 주의하면서 아래 지문을 분석하시오.

There's an important difference between leisure and recreation. In a general sense, both words suggest processes of physical or mental regeneration. But they have different connotations. Leisure is generally thought of as the opposite of work. It suggests something effortless and passive. We tend to think of work as something that takes our energy. Leisure is what we do to build it up again. Leisure offers a recess, a passive break from the challenges

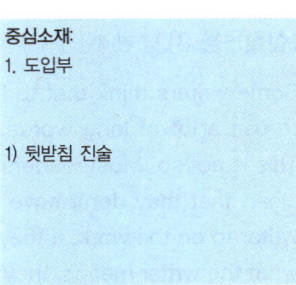

중심소재:
1. 도입부

1) 뒷받침 진술

of the day, a chance to rest and recharge. Recreation carries a more active tone—literally of re-creating ourselves. It suggests activities that require physical or mental effort but which enhance our energies rather than deplete them.

[실전응용 7] 글 전개방식에 주의하면서 아래 지문을 분석하시오.

In all societies, relatives have special names. In every kinship system, some relatives are classed together. That is, they are referred to by the same kinship term. For example, in the kinship language of English, the individual uses the term 'aunt' to refer to both the mother's and father's sisters. In English, the women who marry the brothers of either the father or mother are also called 'aunt.' The English language puts these women together in the same category because their relationship to the individual in terms of intimacy and authority is generally similar. In other cultures, however, where the father's sister and the mother's sister have different rights, obligations, and relationships to the individual, these female relatives are called by different kinship names.

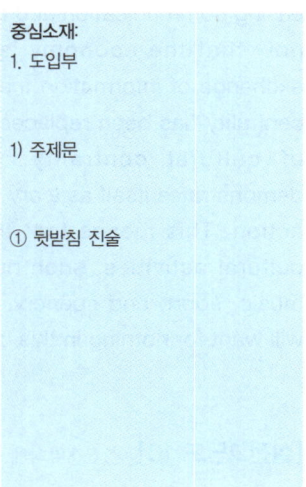

[실전응용 8] 글 전개방식에 주의하면서 아래 지문을 분석하시오.

In Europe, if your industry declines and you lose your job, it is a big blow but not the end of the world. You will still keep your health insurance and public housing, while receiving unemployment benefits, government-subsidized retraining and government help in your job search. In contrast, if you are a worker in the US, you'd better hold on to your current job because losing your job means losing almost everything. Unemployment insurance coverage is smaller than in Europe. There is little public help with retraining and job search. More frighteningly, losing your job means losing your health insurance and your home, as there is little public housing or public subsidies for your rent. As a result, worker resistance to any industrial restructuring that involves job cuts is much greater in the US than in Europe.

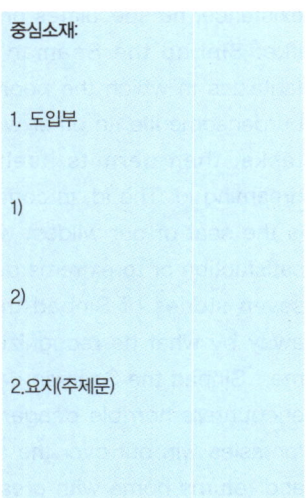

[실전응용 9] 글 전개방식에 주의하면서 아래 지문을 분석하시오.

Now, as always, cities are desperate to create the impression that they lie at the center of something or other. This idea of centrality may be locational, namely that a city lies at the geographical center of England, Europe, and so on. This draws on a well-established notion that geographical centrality makes a place more accessible, easing communication and communication costs. However, now that the economy is characterized more by the exchange of information than by hard goods, geographical centrality has been replaced by attempts to create a sense of cultural centrality. Cultural centrality usually demonstrates itself as a cry that a city is at the center of the action. This means that the city has an abundance of cultural activities, such as restaurants, theater, ballet, music, sport, and scenery. The suggestion is that people will want for nothing in this city.

중심소재:
1. 도입부

1) 구체적 진술

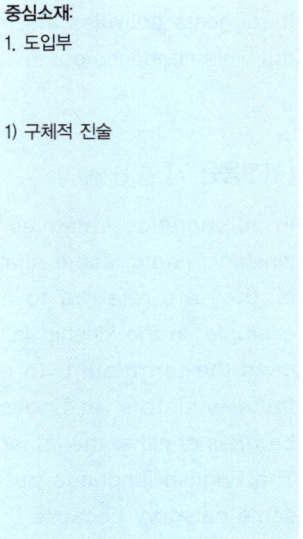

[실전고난도 10] 글 전개방식에 주의하면서 아래 지문을 분석하시오.

Sinbad the Seaman and Sinbad the Porter tells how Sinbad the Porter, who was "carrying a heavy load, became exceedingly weary, the heat and the weight alike oppressing him." Saddened by the hardships of his existence, he speculates on what a rich man's life may be like. Sinbad the Seaman's stories may be viewed as fantasies in which the poor porter engages to escape his burdensome life. In other words, the ego, exhausted by its tasks, then permits itself to be overwhelmed by the dreaming id. The id, in contrast to the reality-oriented ego, is the seat of our wildest wishes, wishes that can lead to satisfaction or to extreme danger. This is given body in the seven stories of Sinbad the Seaman's voyages. Carried away by what he recognizes as the "the bad man within me," Sinbad the Seaman desires fantastic adventures, and encounters horrible dangers. Eventually the wish-fulfilling fantasies win out over the anxious ones, as he is rescued and returns home with great riches to a life of leisure and satisfaction. But each day the requirements of reality must also be met. The id having held sway for a time, the ego reasserts itself and Sinbad the Porter returns to his everyday life of hard labor.

중심소재:
1. 도입부

2.

3.

4.

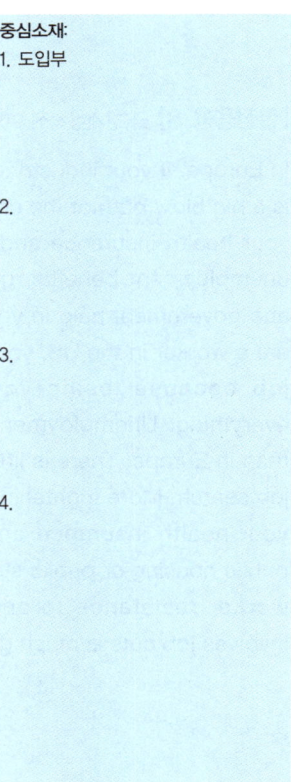

[참고 - 대조의 두 가지 유형과 주제 설정]

유형 1.

```
A _____
But/However A와 상반되는 B의 내용
(= 주제문)

        B의 뒷받침 문장
```

　대조의 글에서 유형 중 글의 내용이 A와 B 중 한쪽으로 치우친 경향을 보인다. 다시 말해, A의 내용보다는 A와 상반되는 B의 내용을 중점으로 다루고 있다. 이런 공간적 비중의 차이가 드러나는 이유는 글쓴이가 A와 상반되는 B의 주장을 전달하는 것이 목적이기 때문이다. 글쓴이의 주장 B가 제시된 후 뒷받침 문장이 전개된다. 주제 및 요지를 고르는 문제가 나오면 당연히 A가 아닌 B의 내용을 바탕으로 풀어야 하며, 일반적으로 주제문은 'But' 뒤에 있다는 점도 기억해야 한다.

유형 2.

```
A _____
  _____
  _____
  _____
  _____
But/However B _____
  _____
  _____
  _____
  _____
```

　두 번째 유형은 위에서 보는 바와 같이 A와 B의 내용이 서로 대등한 분량으로 다뤄짐을 알 수 있다. 이런 유형의 글은 일반적으로 글쓴이가 중립적 입장을 지키며, 특정 대상의 상반된 특징을 드러내고자 할 때 쓰인다. 예를 들자면, '커피의 장단점'의 글 같은 경우이다. 유형 1과 같이 B의 내용만을 바탕으로 답을 고르면 오답이 되므로 주의해야 한다.

[대조의 대표적 두 유형 적용]

지문을 읽은 후 아래 비교 1, 2를 살펴보자.

> Some geographers say that urbanization is a good thing because it relieves pressure on the land and in many countries on the land there are too many people for the work available. Others consider that urbanization is a bad thing because a city depends very much on food being supplied from the surrounding countryside. In countries where there are already very great problems of food supply this massive increase in the size of towns will place a tremendous strain on the surrounding agricultural areas. Moreover, it is generally the young and active members of the population who tend to migrate, leaving the old people, the children, and the infirm to run the farms, which is hardly likely to improve the efficiency of the farms. There is thus a decline in rural industries and food supply.

비교 1.

★ 중심소재다. 중심내용(con-trolling idea)을 바탕으로 주제의 폭을 좁히도록 한다.

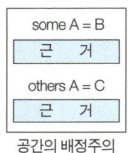

공간의 배정주의

1. Some geographers say that urbanization is a good thing 1) because it relieves pressure on the land and in many countries on the land there are too many people for the work available. 2. Others consider that urbanization is a bad thing 2) because a city depends very much on food being supplied from the surrounding countryside.

중심소재: 도시화
1. 도시화에 대한 'some'의 긍정적 견해
1) 근거 · 이유
2. 도시화에 대한 'others'의 부정적 견해
2) 근거 · 이유

도시화에 관한 장단점을 기술한 글이다. 도시화에 관한 긍정적 측면과 부정적 측면을 각각 비슷한 비중으로 다루고 있다. 주제: Urbanization in Different Perspectives

비교 2.

★ 글의 절반 이상이 도시화의 부정적인 측면을 다루고 있다.

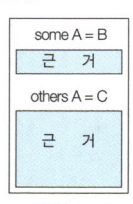

주제문 A = C

1. Some geographers say that urbanization is a good thing 1) because it relieves pressure on the land and in many countries on the land there are too many people for the work available. 2. Others consider that urbanization is a bad thing 2) because ① a city depends very much on food being supplied from the surrounding countryside. In countries where there are already very great problems of food supply this massive increase in the size of towns will place a tremendous strain on the surrounding agricultural areas. ② Moreover, it is generally the young and active members of

중심소재: 도시화
1. 도시화에 대한 'some'의 긍정적 견해
1) 이유 · 근거
2. 도시화에 대한 'others'의 부정적 견해
2) 이유 · 근거
① 도시는 주변 농가에서 제공되는 음식에 아주 크게 의존하고 있기에 도시가 급성장하게 되면 농가에 큰 압박을 가하게 된다.

> the population who tend to migrate, leaving the old people, the children, and the infirm to run the farms, which is hardly likely to improve the efficiency of the farms. There is thus a decline in rural industries and food supply.

② 추가 부연(moreover)
도시화 탓에 젊은 인구 층이 도시로 이동하면서 농가에 노인, 여성, 아이들만 남게 되어 생산력이 낮아지면서 결국 도시에 공급하는 식량에도 문제가 발생한다.

특정 현상에 대한 대조되는 견해를 제시하는 글로 한쪽의 견해로 치우치는 경향을 보인다. 이런 경우, 'some'의 견해가 아닌 'others'의 견해가 바로 글쓴이가 궁극적으로 전달하려는 내용이다. 당연히 이에 할당되는 부분도 많아진다. 이럴 경우 'others'의 견해를 주제(The Problems of Urbanization)로 설정해야 한다. 비교 1, 2의 차이점을 반드시 구별할 수 있도록 한다.

| 해석
일부 지리학자들은 도시화가 좋은 현상이라고 말한다. 왜냐하면, 도시화가 토지에 대한 (인구의) 압력을 덜어주며, 많은 나라에서 농촌의 유효노동력이 너무 많기 때문이다. 또 어떤 사람들은 도시가 근교의 농촌에서 공급되고 있는 식량에 매우 많은 의존을 하고 있기 때문에 나쁘다고 말한다. 이미 식량공급이라는 큰 문제점을 안고 있는 나라의 도시 규모의 이러한 양적인 큰 증가는 주변 농업지역에 큰 부담을 가하게 될 것이다. 더구나 노령층과 어린이들 그리고 허약자들을 농장 경영에 남겨놓은 채 일반적으로 젊은 층과 활동적인 인원들은 일을 찾아 이주해 나가려는 경향이 있기 때문에 농장의 효율성을 증대시키기는 어려울 것 같다. 그러기에 농촌산업과 식량공급은 쇠퇴한다.

4) Order (순서)

글의 전개가 시간 순서나 공간 순서에 따라 이루어지는 전개 방식을 순서형 전개 방식이라고 한다. 넓은 의미에서 보면 순서형 전개 방식은 열거형 전개 방식에 속하지만, 특히 글의 내용이 시간과 공간의 순서에 따라 전개되므로 순서형이라고 한다. 시간 순서에 따른 순서형 전개 방식에서는 먼저 일어난 일이 앞에 전개되고, 나중에 일어난 일이 뒤에 전개되는 것이 일반적이지만 어떤 경우에는 그 역순이 사용되기도 한다. 독해할 때는 시간상의 전후 관계를 정확히 파악하는 것이 중요하다. 한편 공간 순서에 따른 순서형 전개 방식에서는 대체로 넓은 공간에서 시작하여 좁은 공간으로 옮겨지는 것이 보통이지만, 경우에 따라서는 특정한 장소를 먼저 언급하고 난 후 그 배경이 되는 넓은 공간을 이야기하기도 한다. 세부 종류로는 다음과 같다.

① Chronological Order

시간적 흐름에 따른 글 전개 방식의 예를 확인해 보자.

아인슈타인에 관한 글임을 알 수 있다.

시간의 흐름에 따라 한 인물의 생애를 간략하게 정리하는 '전기(Biography)'에 해당하는 글이다.

[예시 1]

1. Albert Einstein was born in 1879 in Ulm, Germany. He graduated from the University of Zurich in Switzerland in 1905. In 1905 he also did some of his most famous work in physics. In 1919 he won the Nobel Prize for Physics. Between 1919 and 1933 he lived in Germany and traveled a lot to talk to other scientists. Then in 1933 he had to leave Germany because of Hitler and the Nazi party. He moved to the United States. From 1933 until his death he lived in Princeton, New Jersey. He died on April 18, 1955.

| 해설
전기의 경우 해당 인물을 중심으로 시기별로 어떤 사건이 발생했는지 정리하도록 한다.

| 해석
알베르트 아인슈타인은 독일의 Ulm이라는 도시에서 1879년에 태어났다. 그는 1905년에 스위스에서 취리히의 대학교를 졸업하였다. 1905년에는 물리학 분야에서 그의 가장 유명한 몇 가지 업적도 남겼다. 1919년에 그는 노벨화학상을 받았다. 1919년 그리고 1933년 사이에 그는 독일에서 살았고 많은 다른 과학자들과 이야기를 나누기 위하여 여행하였다. 그러고 나서 1933년에 그는 히틀러와 나치당 때문에 독일을 떠나야 하였다. 그는 미국으로 이사하였다. 1933년부터 죽기 전까지 그는 프린스턴(뉴저지)에서 살았다. 그는 1955년 4월 8일에 죽었다.

첫 번째 문장에서 주제를 파악할 수 있다.

[예시 2]

It seemed like an ordinary day when she got up that morning, but Lynda was about to embark on the worst day of her life. First, she fell in the bathtub because her mother forgot to rinse out the bath oil. Then she spilled orange juice on the outfit she had spent hours putting together for school pictures. When she changed, she messed up the French braid her mother had put in her hair. As she walked out the door, she dropped all of her school books and her math homework flew away. Once she made it to the car she thought everything would be all right. She was wrong; her father didn't look before he backed out of the driveway and ran into the neighbor's truck. Lynda's side of the car was damaged the most, and she ended up with a broken arm. That night, she cried herself to sleep.

본문에서 구체적으로 전개될 내용인 중심내용(controlling idea)를 파악할 수 있다.

시간의 흐름을 나타내는 시그널을 확인한다.

| 해설
이야기체의 글은 주인공을 중심으로 주변 인물 사이에 발생하는 '사건'을 중심으로 파악하고, 이를 통해 글쓴이가 궁극적으로 이끌어내려는 요지를 파악한다.

| 해석
그날 아침에 일어났을 때 평범한 날처럼 보였으나, Lynda는 생애 최악의 날을 막 시작하려 하였다. 첫 번째로 어머니가 욕조에서 목욕용 오일을 씻겨낸다는 것을 까먹는 바람에 그녀는 욕조에서 넘어졌다. 그리고서 그녀는 학교 사진촬영을 위해 몇 시간 동안이나 준비해서 입은 옷에 오렌지 주스를 쏟았다. 그녀가 옷을 갈아입었을 때 엄마가 그녀의 머리에 얹어준 프랑스풍의 장식을 엉망으로 만들었다. 그녀가 집 밖을 나섰을 때 그녀는 교과서를 모두 떨어뜨렸고, 그녀의 수학 숙제 파일은 날아가 버렸다. 그녀가 차에 갔을 때, 아무 일 없이 이젠 다 괜찮다고 생각했다. 그러나 그것은 틀린 생각이었다. 그녀의 아버지가 차도 밖으로 후진하기 전에 이웃 차를 보지 못해 충돌해 버렸다. Lynda 쪽 차체가 가장 많이 파손되면서 그녀는 결국 팔이 부러졌다. 그날 밤 그녀는 울다 잠이 들었다.

[예시 3]

The Olympic games began as athletic festivals to honor the Greek gods. The most important festival was held in the valley of Olympia to honor Zeus, the king of the gods. It was this festival that became the Olympic games in 776 B.C. These games were ended in A.D. 394 by the Roman Emperor who ruled Greece. No Olympic games were held for more than 1,500 years. Then the modern Olympics began in 1896. Almost 300 male athletes competed in the first modern Olympics. In the games held in 1900, female athletes were allowed to compete. The games have continued every four years since 1896 except during World War II, and they will most likely continue for many years to come.

★ 올림픽 경기에 관한 글임을 파악할 수 있다. 본문의 이후 전개되는 내용을 바탕으로 주제의 폭을 좁히도록 한다.

★ 시간의 글 전개 방식의 시그널을 확인한다.

| 해설
올림픽의 역사를 다루는 글로 시간의 글 전개방식을 확인할 수 있다.

| 해석
올림픽 경기는 그리스의 신을 찬양하는 운동 축제로 시작했다. 가장 중요한 축제는 왕 중의 왕인 제우스신을 찬양하기 위해 올림피아에서 열렸다. 이것이 기원전 776년에 올림픽이 된 축제였다. 이러한 경기는 394년 그리스를 통치한 로마의 황제에 의해서 끝나게 된다. 1500년 이상이나 어떠한 올림픽 경기도 열리지 않았다. 그런 다음, 현대 올림픽은 1896년에 시작했다. 거의 300명의 남자 경기자가 첫 번째 현대 올림픽에서 경쟁했다. 1900년대에 열린 경기에서 여성 경기자 또한 경기에 참여할 수 있게 되었다. 제2차 세계대전을 제외하고 1896년 이래 4년마다 열리고 있으며, 올림픽은 앞으로 오랫동안 계속될 것이다.

[예시 4]

The first sign any of the hikers had of the impending storm was a tall white cloud looming in an otherwise bright blue Sierra sky, far to the north. Late that day, the cloud had grown larger and had moved in closer. By sundown, the sky had turned uniformly gray; the temperature dropped ten degrees. They made camp hurriedly, ate a cold meal, and set up camp as snugly as possible.

★ 중심소재는 '폭풍'이고, 주제는 '곧 다가올 폭풍'이다.

★ 시간의 흐름에 따라 곧 다가올 폭풍을 긴박하게 묘사하는 글이다.

| 해석
등산객들이 곧 다가올 폭풍에 대해 얻은 첫 번째 징조는 크고 흰 구름 기둥이 저 북쪽 멀리 원래 밝고 푸른 시에라 하늘에 드리워진 것이었다. 그날 늦게, 그 구름은 더 크게 번지면서, 더 가까이 이동해왔다. 태양이 질 무렵, 하늘은 모두 회색으로 변했다. 온도는 10도나 떨어졌다. 그들은 급히 텐트를 치고, 차가운 음식을 먹고는 가능한 한 아늑하게 야영했다.

본문에서 구체적으로 기★
술될 중심내용(controlling
idea)이다.

[예시 5]

1. This is the way Frank studies. 1) First, he sits at his desk and thinks about the assignment. Next he decides that he needs a glass of water. After he goes to the kitchen, drinks and returns to his room, he opens his book. Then he starts to read the lesson. His first distraction comes when he begins to think about the party on the weekend. His second distraction comes when he realizes it is time to watch his favorite program on television. Finally he decides he can study his assignment between classes the next day.

중심소재: Frank → Frank의 공부 방법
1. 도입부 = 주제문
첫 번째 문장에서 주제를 파악할 수 있으며, 이후 전개될 내용에 대한 예측이 가능하다: 단계별로 '**프랭크의 공부 방법**'을 설명하고 있다.
1) 뒷받침 진술
'프랭크의 공부 방법'을 시간의 흐름에 따라 단계별로 기술하고 있다.

| 해석
프랭크가 공부하는 방법은 다음과 같다. 우선, 책상에 앉은 후 숙제에 대해서 생각한다. 다음 그는 물 한 잔이 필요하다고 판단한다. 부엌에 가서 물을 마시고 방으로 돌아온 후, 그는 책을 편다. 그런 다음 그 장을 읽기 시작한다. 그의 첫 번째 방해는 이번 주말에 있을 파티에 대해서 생각하기 시작할 때 일어난다. 두 번째 방해는 그가 TV에서 자신이 가장 좋아하는 프로그램을 봐야 할 시간이라는 것을 깨달을 때 일어난다. 마침내 그는 내일 쉬는 시간에 숙제할 수 있다고 결심한다.

[실전응용 1] 글 전개방식에 주의하면서 본문을 분석하시오.

The first American postal service was established in the colony of Massachusetts in 1639. From 1707 until the year before the American Revolution, the General Post Office in London controlled the postal service in America. In 1775, the Continental Congress resolved to have a postal system of its own, and Benjamin Franklin was elected to carry on the work. When Congress authorized a postal service in 1789 under the U.S. Constitution, the nation had 75 local post offices, and the mails were carried over 1875 miles (more than 3,000 km) of postal routes.

The introduction of adhesive stamps in 1847 greatly simplified post office operations. The system of registering letters was first adopted in 1855. In cities, street letterboxes were introduced in 1858 and free mail delivery in 1863 under Postmaster General Montgomery Blair. The Pony Express began mail service between Saint Joseph, Missouri, and San Francisco in 1860. The money order system was put into operation in 1864, and rural free delivery service was established in 1896. The parcel post system came into operation in the U.S. in 1913. The first

중심소재:

1. 도입부

1) 구체적 진술

regular service for airmail was established between New York City and Washington, D.C., in 1918. The Postal Savings System, established by Congress in 1911, was terminated in 1966.

[실전응용 2] 글 전개방식에 주의하면서 본문을 분석하시오.

Susan B. Anthony, a famous American women's rights movement leader, was born in New York in 1820. Susan's father sent Susan to a school for girls, but she had to return when her father's business failed. She started teaching the children in her hometown. But soon she stopped teaching and began to work for women's equal rights. Though many people hated her message, Susan organized groups to get women the right to vote. In 1872, she was arrested for voting in a national election, which was against the law. However, she kept fighting for her belief until she died in 1906. In 1920, the law finally gave women the right to vote.

중심소재:

주제:

② Spatial Order

공간의 흐름에 따른 글 전개방식의 예를 확인해 보자.

[예시 1]

1. The new mall is planned to be user-friendly. 1) The ground floor will contain food shops, fountains, benches, and tables where people can stroll, eat, and chat. The second and third floors will contain the thirty or so shops—the business heart of the mall. The top floor will be open to the sun and sky, with small gardens and fine restaurants, and a 180-degree view of the bay.

1. 도입부 = 주제문
사용자 중심(user-friendly)의 새로 들어선 백화점

1) 뒷받침 문장
각 층의 특징을 묘사하면서 사용자 중심의 백화점임을 설명하고 있다.

★ 글에서 묘사하는 대상(중심소재)이다.

★ 본문에서 구체적으로 기술될 중심소재(controlling idea)이다.

★ 장소에 따른 글 전개방식을 확인한다.

| 해석
이번 새로운 백화점은 사용자가 사용하기 편리하게 설계되었다. 1층은 음식 가게, 폭포, 벤치 그리고 테이블이 있어 사람들이 거닐고, 먹고 이야기를 나눌 수 있다. 2층과 3층은 30개 정도의 가게가 있는데 백화점의 판매 핵심부가 된다. 맨 위층은 태양과 하늘에 노출되어 있는데, 작은 정원과 멋진 레스토랑을 갖추고 있으며, 앞에 위치한 만을 180도 볼 수 있다.

중심내용(controlling idea)★에 해당한다.

시간의 흐름: 독립전쟁 → 전쟁 후 → 유럽에서 돌아옴
장소의 흐름: 미국 → 유럽 → 미국

[예시 2]

1. Clara Barton, who grew up in Massachusetts, organized the American Red Cross. 1) During the Civil War she helped wounded soldiers on the battlefield. After the war she spent some time in Europe. There she learned about the International Red Cross and realized the need of such an organization in the United States.

중심소재: Clara Barton → Clara Barton의 미국 적십자 창설
1. 도입부 = 주제문
적십자 창설(기원)
1) 뒷받침 진술
미국 적십자가 어떻게 생기게 되었는지, 시간과 장소의 흐름에 따라 기술하고 있다.

| 해석
매사추세츠에서 성장한 클라라 바턴은 미국적십자사를 조직했다. 남북전쟁 중에 그녀는 전쟁터에서 부상당한 병사들을 도왔다. 종전 후에는 유럽에서 얼마 동안 지냈다. 거기서 그녀는 국제적십자사에 대해 공부하면서, 미국에서 이 기관이 필요하다는 것을 깨달았다.

[실전응용 1] 글 전개방식에 주의하면서 본문을 분석하시오.

I couldn't believe my eyes when we finally emerged from the storm shelter. Where the barn once stood there was now only a few tufts of hay. The path that led to the house was scattered with branches and debris. The house! The entire roof was gone. The north wall was caved in and we could see right into the house. Well, what was left of it. Tears rolled down my cheeks as I noticed that most of our belongings had been sucked up into the great vacuum and scattered across the countryside. We heard a loud cracking and moaning as the west wall gave way and collapsed, sending up a wave of dust. And yet, there in the middle of the front yard was mother's prized rose bush. It swayed in the breeze as if nothing had happened. Seeing it made me realize how lucky we were to be alive. We stood there in dismay, our arms locked around one another.

주제:

③ Process
단계·과정의 흐름이 두드러지는 예를 확인해 보자.

[예시]

1. Raisins are made from special grapes. When the grapes ripen, they are carefully picked and placed on a tray where they remain for several days to dry in the sun. Next, they are shipped to a packing factory. At the packing factory they are washed and their stems are removed. After they are separated according to size, they are washed and dried again. Finally, the raisins are packaged in readiness for delivery to grocers.

★중심소재는 '건포도'이다. 건포도를 가지고 무슨 이야기를 하는가(주제)?

★단계적으로 건포도를 만드는 과정에서 유통까지 기술하고 있다.

| 해석
건포도는 특별한 포도에서 만들어진다. 포도가 잘 익으면, 이것을 조심스럽게 따서 수일 동안 태양에 건조해 놓을 쟁반에 올려놓는다. 그 다음 이것을 잘 싸서 포장 공장에 보낸다. 포장 공장에서 포도를 잘 씻고 줄기를 제거한다. 크기에 따라 따로 분리한 후, 다시 씻고 건조한다. 마지막으로 건포도를 가게에 배달할 수 있게 포장해서 준비해 둔다.

[실전응용 1] 글 전개방식에 주의하면서 본문을 분석하시오.

The first step in redesigning your closet is take everything out and sort through it. Anything you haven't worn in over a year should be given to charity. Check garments for wear and tear. Take care of anything that needs mending. If it is beyond repair, get rid of it. The second step is to install a closet organizer. Choose one that will hold the different types of garments in your wardrobe. The third step is to put items in the closet so that those you wear most often are easy to access. The final step is to stay organized. Put garments back in their appropriate places so that you will be able to find them.

중심소재:
1. 구체적 진술

1)

2)

3)

4)

[실전응용 2] 글 전개방식에 주의하면서 본문을 분석하시오.

Koreans have a long history of papermaking and have always used native good-quality paper. Korea's oldest paper, called Maji, was made from hemp. Maji is produced using the following steps. First, small pieces of hemp are soaked in water for some time and then cut into tiny pieces. Next, these pieces are turned into a slippery pulp by using a grindstone. After that, it is steamed, cleansed with water, ground again and placed in a tank. This raw material is pressed onto a frame and sun-dried while being whitened. This method of papermaking was most popular during the Three Kingdoms period.

중심소재:
1. 도입부

1) 주제문

① 뒷받침 진술

13 글의 종류

글의 종류에는 설명, 논증, 서사, 묘사가 있다.

1. 설명

어떤 사실이나 사물, 현상, 사건의 내용, 의의, 이유 등을 알기 쉽게 밝히는 진술 방식이다. 정보의 전달을 목적으로 하는 글에 주로 쓰인다. 상황에 따라서는 설득을 위한 의도로 설명하는 때도 있다. 일반적으로 독해 지문의 상당수가 설명문의 형식으로 되어 있다. 대체로 설명에는 주제문이 제시된다. 설명의 방식에는 과정을 분석하고, 분류를 사용할 수도 있으며, 비교와 대조, 원인과 결과, 예증 등을 이용하여, 저자가 독자에게 이해시키고자 하는 바를 효과적으로 전달해 준다. 즉 알지 못하던 사실이나 모호한 것을 분명하고 정확하게 표현하고자 하는 것이다.

[예시 1]

1. **According to ancient lore**, every man is born into the world with two bags suspended from his neck—one in front and one behind, and both are full of faults. But the one in front is full of his neighbor's faults; the one behind, full of his own. 1) **Consequently**, men are blind to their own faults but never lose sight of their neighbor's.

1. 민간전승의 한 이야기를 설명하면서 궁극적으로 드러내는 내용은 무엇인지 생각한다.
1) 글을 요약하는 결론(요지): **인간은 자신의 잘못은 보지 못하고 이웃의 잘못만을 보는 그릇된 본성**을 가지고 있음을 지적하고 있다.

| 해석
옛날 전설에 의하면, 모든 인간은 목의 앞쪽과 뒤쪽에 둘 다 잘못으로 가득 찬 두 개의 가방을 매달고 세상에 태어난다고 한다. 그런데 앞쪽의 것은 이웃의 잘못들로 가득 차 있고, 뒤쪽의 것은 자신의 잘못으로 가득 차 있다고 한다. 따라서 인간은 자신의 잘못은 못 보지만 이웃의 잘못은 절대 놓치지 않게 된다.

[예시 2]

1. Animals **play** probably to learn some of life's serious activities. 2) Adult animals, <u>for example</u>, need to look for food, to fight, to look for a mate, and to get along with other animals of their kind. Young animals can practice these important life activities **by playing**. **Through play**, they can learn how to control their movements, how to interact with their environment, and how to interact with other animals in their group.

중심소재: Animal → 동물의 놀이
1. 도입부 = 주제문
동물은 놀이를 통해 삶의 중요한 활동을 배운다.
1) 뒷받침 진술
예시를 통해 주제문에서 밝힌 중심내용을 뒷받침하고 있다.

| 해설
동물은 놀이를 통해 삶의 중요한 활동을 배운다는 내용을 설명하는 글이다.

| 해석
동물들은 아마도 생활의 중요한 몇몇 활동을 배우기 위해 노는 것 같다. 예를 들어, 다 큰 동물은 음식을 찾고, 싸우며, 배우자를 얻고, 그들과 같은 부류의 다른 동물과 잘 지낼 필요가 있다. 어린 동물은 이러한 삶의 중요한 활동을 놀이를 함으로 연습할 수 있다. 놀이를 통해서, 동물들은 어떻게 그들의 행동을 통제하는지, 어떻게 다른 환경에 적응하는지, 그리고 어떻게 그들의 무리 안에 있는 다른 동물들과 상호작용하는지를 배울 수 있다.

[예시 3]

1) <u>Whether they live in the country or the city, Americans are usually on the move.</u> 1) Americans are following jobs and businesses more readily than ever before, moving by automobile — and later by trailer. Some people are worried about a growing American restlessness, **but** the automobile suits the American temperament. Americans have always been a venturesome, mobile, pioneering people. They like to think that a rolling stone will gather experience, adventure, new and better opportunities.

중심소재: 미국인 → 미국인들의 유용성
1. 도입부 = 주제문
미국인의 유동성
1) 뒷받침 진술
주제문에서 밝힌 중심내용을 뒷받침하고 있다.

도입부 = | 중심소재 파악 |

글의 도입부에서 언제나 중심소재 파악에 주력한다.

| 해석
미국 사람들은 시골에 살든 도시에 살든, 대개 이동한다. 미국인들은 자동차로 그리고 나중에는 트레일러로 이전 어느 때보다 더 기꺼이 직업과 사업을 따라 이동한다. 어떤 사람들은 정착하지 못하는 미국인들이 증가하는 것을 걱정하지만, 자동차는 미국인의 성격에 알맞다. 미국인은 항상 모험적이고, 이동을 좋아하며 개척적인 사람들이다. 그들은 구르는 돌이 경험, 모험, 새롭고 더 나은 기회를 잡을 수 있다고 생각하는 경향이 있다.

[실전응용 1] 글의 종류를 고려하면서, 본문을 분석하시오.

How can you create closeness when the two of you are hundreds of miles apart? How can you make the person you are talking to on the phone feel special when you cannot pat their back or give them a little hug? The answer is simple. Just use your caller' name far more often than you would in person. In fact, shower your conversations with his or her name. Saying a person's name too often in face-to-face conversation sounds manipulative. However, on the phone the effect is dramatically different. If you heard someone say your name, even if you were being pushed around in a big noisy crowd, you would pay attention and listen.

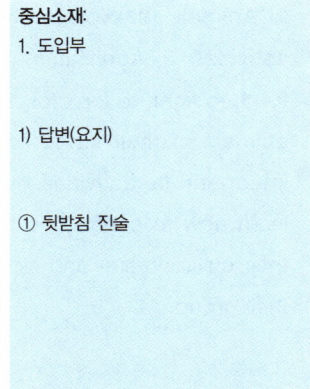

중심소재:
1. 도입부

1) 답변(요지)

① 뒷받침 진술

[실전응용 2] 글의 종류를 고려하면서, 본문을 분석하시오.

In the 1950s, agricultural scientists around the world started a campaign known as the green revolution. It was an attempt to increase available food sources worldwide. The green revolution helped avoid famine in Asia and increased crop yields in many different parts of the world. However, the green revolution had its negative side, too. Fertilizers and pesticides are dangerous chemicals that cause cancer and pollute the environment. Also, the cost of the chemicals and the equipment to harvest more crops was far too expensive for an average peasant farmer. Consequently, owners of small farms received little benefit from the advances in agriculture. In some cases, farmers were forced off the land by larger agricultural businesses.

중심소재:
1. 도입부

[실전응용 3] 글의 종류를 고려하면서, 본문을 분석하시오.

Unlike the modern society, the primitive society has less specialized knowledge to transmit, and since its way of life is enacted before the eyes of all, it has no need to create a separate institution of education such as the school. Instead, the child acquires the heritage of his culture by observing and imitating adults in such activities as rituals, hunts, festivals, cultivation, and harvesting. As a result, there is little or none of that alienation of young from old so marked in modern industrial societies. A further reason for

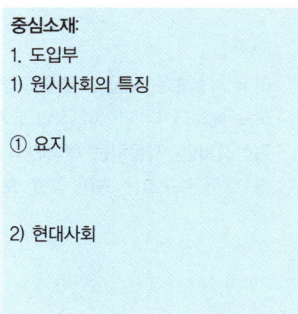

중심소재:
1. 도입부
1) 원시사회의 특징

① 요지

2) 현대사회

this alienation in modern societies is that in his conception of reality the modern adult owes less to his direct experience and more to the experience of his culture than does primitive man. Clearly, his debt to culture will vary with the nature of his education. Hence, the contemporary child must travel much further than the offspring of primitive man to acquire the world view of his elders. He is, therefore, that much more removed from the adults of his society.

[실전응용 4] 글의 종류를 고려하면서, 본문을 분석하시오.

Everywhere in the world, the issue of how to manage urban growth poses the highest stakes, complex policy decisions, and strongly heated conflicts in the public area. The contrast between Western Europe and America is particularly sharp. In Western Europe, steep gasoline taxes, investment policies favoring built-up areas over undeveloped greenfields, continuous investment in public transportation, and other policies have produced relatively compact cities. Cities in Western Europe tend to be economically healthy compared with their suburbs. By contrast, in the United States, cheap gas, massive highway investment, policies that favor construction on the edges of cities, and heavy reliance on property taxes to fund public schools have encouraged much more car-reliant and spread-out urban areas, where eight in ten Americans now live.

중심소재:
1. 도입부

1) 연결문

① 뒷받침 진술

[실전응용 5] 글의 종류를 고려하면서, 본문을 분석하시오.

Most people around the world think family planning should be a personal choice. In other words, they think people should decide how many children to have without any advice or control by the government. Some people feel this way because of religious reasons. Others object to having government or religious leaders involved in family planning and population control. They want the freedom to make their own personal decisions.

중심소재:
1. 도입부

1) 뒷받침 근거

2. 논증

어떤 주장에 대하여 옳고 그름의 이유를 밝히는 논리적 절차, 또는 이를 통해 상대방의 신념이나 태도를 변화시키는 것을 목적으로 하는 진술 방식으로, 설득이 목적인 글에 주로 쓰인다. 논증은 논거를 전제로 하며 결론이 이미 주어진다는 점에서 추론과 다르다. 자신이 주장하는 바가 드러나기 때문에 주제문이 필요한 구조를 취한다. 논증에서는 구체적인 논거로부터 타당한 결론을 이끌어 내는 추론 과정이 있는데, 추론에는 연역적 추론과 귀납적 추론이 있다. 개별적이고 특정한 것으로부터 일반적인 것을 끌어내는 것이 귀납적 방식이고, 그와 반대로 이미 확립된 일반화로부터 개별적이고 구체적인 것을 끌어내는 것을 연역적 방식이라고 한다. 인간의 사고는 귀납과 연역적 사고가 혼재하므로, 자신의 주장을 효과적으로 드러내기 위해서는 이 양자 모두의 효과적인 사용이 중요하다.

[예시 1]

1. I have always taught my children that politeness, learning, and order are good things, and that something good is to be desired and developed for its own sake. 2. But at school they learned, and very quickly, that children earn Nature Trail tickets for running the quarter-mile track during lunch recess. Or Lincoln Dollars for picking up trash on the playground or for helping a young child find the bathroom — deeds that used to be called 'good citizenship.' 1) Why is it necessary to buy the minimal cooperation of children with rewards and treats? ① What disturbs me is the idea that good behavior must be reinforced with incentives. 3. Children must be taught to perform good deeds for their own sake, not in order to receive stickers, stars, and candy bars.

본문은 'But'을 중심으로 글쓴이 'I'가 아이들에게 가르치려는 사항과 학교에서 아이들이 배우는 사항이 상반되는 대조를 이루고 있다. 당연히 글쓴이 'I'의 주장이 글의 요지가 된다.
1. I의 주장: 선한 것을 추구할 때는 그 자체의 선함을 위한 것이 되어야 한다(무언가를 바라고 선한 행위를 해서는 안 된다).
2. 'But' 이후 대조적 관점
School – 학교에서는 보상을 바라고 행위를 하도록 조장함.
1) 문제제기: 글쓴이의 주장이 간접적으로 드러난다.
① 보상을 바라는 행위를 반대
3. 결론: 선한 행위는 그 자체로 추구되어야 한다.

| 해설

글쓴이의 견해가 드러나는 문장에서 이것을 알리는 시그널이 있는 경우가 많다. 본문 마지막 문장을 예로 살펴보자.

> Children must be taught to perform good deeds for their own sake, not in order to receive stickers, stars, and candy bars.

당위성을 나타내는 'must'와 'not A but B'의 강조 구문과 같은 'B, not A'가 보인다. 놓치지 말아야 할 부분이다.

| 해석

나는 항상 나의 아이들에게 공손함, 지식 그리고 질서는 좋은 것이고 선한 것을 추구하고, 그 자체로 계발해야 한다고 가르쳐왔다. 그러나 아이들은 학교에서 점심시간의 휴식 때 마일 트랙을 달려서 1/4 Nature Trail을 획득하는 것을 배웠는데 그것도 빨리 배웠다. 혹은 운동장에서 쓰레기를 줍거나 혹은 어린아이가 화장실을 찾도록 도와주는 훌륭한 시민이라고 불리곤 했던 행동을 하고 Lincoln Dollars를 획득하는 것을 배웠다. 보상과 선물로 아이들의 최소한의 협동을 획득하는 것이 왜 필요할까? 나를 혼란스럽게 하는 것은 좋은 행동이 보상으로 강화될 수 있다는 생각이다. 아이들은 스티커 별 그리고 막대사탕을 받기 위해서가 아니라 그 자체를 위해 좋은 행동을 하도록 가르침을 받아야 한다.

[예시 2]

1. Nowadays, we can enjoy athletic competition of every kind without leaving our homes. 1) It is the fun that comes from cheering on our team and celebrating its skills while complaining about the opposing team's good luck. ① But some individuals sit and watch a football game or tennis match without cheering for anyone or any team. They are not willing to risk the possible disappointment of picking the loser, so they give up the possible joy of picking the winner. They live in the world of neutrality. 2. Don't be one of them. Sure, your team might lose. But then again, your team might win. Either way, your spectator experience will have been a fun one, and you will have avoided being merely a passive observer.

중심소재: 운동경기 → 운동경기 관전
1. 도입부: 운동경기 관점에 관한 글이다.
① 글쓴이의 견해: **경기를 보는 즐거움은 바로 자신의 팀을 응원하는 것에서 나온다.**
2) 'But' 이후 글쓴이의 견해와 상반되는 대상이 언급되고 있다: 자신의 팀이 졌을 때의 실망감 때문에 어느 팀도 응원하지 않는다(글쓴이의 생각에는 바람직하지 못한 현상).

2. 글쓴이의 견해(명령문, But 이후)가 드러난다: 중립적인 입장이 아닌 한 팀을 적극 응원하면서 그 재미를 즐겨라.
* 1)+2) = 주제문

도입부 = 중심소재
주제문(I의 견해)
I와 대조되는 some의 견해
주제문(I의 견해)

| 해석

오늘날 우리는 집을 벗어나지 않고 모든 종류의 운동 경기를 즐길 수 있다. 자신의 팀을 응원하고 그 팀의 기술에 찬사를 보내는 한편, 상대방 팀의 행운에 대해 불평하는 것들에서 생겨나는 것은 바로 즐거움이다. 하지만 일부 사람들은 누구 또는 어떤 팀도 응원하지 않고 축구 경기, 테니스 시합을 앉아서 시청한다. 그들은 패자를 선택해서 일어날 수 있는 실망을 굳이 감행하려 하지 않기에 승자를 선택해서 일어날 수 있는 기쁨을 포기한다. 그들은 중립의 세계에 안주한다. 그런 사람이 되지 않도록 하라. 물론 당신의 팀이 질 수도 있다. 하지만 나중에 다시 이길 수도 있다. 이기든 지든 간에 관람객으로서의 경험은 즐거운 경험이 되어 있을 것이고, 당신은 이제 단순히 수동적인 관찰자에서 벗어나 있을 것이다.

[예시 3]

1. People who run sports camps think of the children first. They do their best to create enjoyable and protective environments in which the children feel comfortable and safe.

중심소재: 스포츠 캠프
1. 도입부

'unfortunately' 라는 부사로 보아 '문제점' 이 제시될 가능성이 크다.

도입부 = 중심소재
　　　　문제점 지적
　　　　　　↓
　　　　대안(요지)

2. **Unfortunately**, 1) some sports coaches in the camps occasionally become over-enthusiastic in their desire to help the children excel. As a result, they put pressure on them to perform at high levels, win at all costs, and keep playing, even when they get hurt. This 'no pain, no gain' approach is extremely stressful, and leads to unnecessary injuries. 3. Parents <u>should</u> therefore take care when they send their children to a sports camp, and <u>should talk with the sports coaches to see if they will respect the children's wishes</u>.

2. 문제점 지적
1) 코치들이 아이들의 최고의 기량을 발휘하도록 하는데, 지나치게 열정적이어서 아이에게 지나친 압력을 가한다.
3. 글쓴이의 주장(대안)
부모는 스포츠 코치가 아이가 바라는 것을 존중해주도록 언급해야 한다. (should 확인)

| 해설
본문은 '자녀에게 알맞은 스포츠 캠프를 선택해 줄 때 부모들은 코치들이 아이들에 대해 잘 돌봐주려는 태도를 지니고 있는지를 확인해야 한다.' 는 글쓴이의 주장이 드러나는 논증의 글이다.

| 해석
스포츠 캠프를 운영하는 사람들은 아이들을 가장 먼저 고려한다. 이들은 아이들이 편안하고 안전한 느낌이 들 수 있는 즐겁고 보호받는 환경을 조성하기 위해 전력을 기울인다. 불행히도 그러한 캠프의 일부 운동 코치들은 아이들이 탁월한 실력을 갖추는 것을 돕기 위해 때로 지나친 의욕을 갖게 된다. 그 결과 그들은 아이들에게 높은 수준의 실력을 발휘하라고, 어떤 희생을 치르더라도 이기라고, 그리고 부상을 당할 때조차도 계속 뛰라고 강요한다. 이러한 '고통 없이는 아무것도 못 얻는다' 는 식의 접근방식은 극단적으로 스트레스를 주어서 불필요한 부상을 초래한다. 그러므로 부모들은 자녀를 스포츠 캠프에 보낼 때 유의해야 하고, 운동 코치들이 자녀가 바라는 것을 존중할 것인지를 확인하기 위해 운동 코치들과 상담해야 한다.

[실전응용 1] 글의 종류를 고려하면서, 본문을 분석하시오.

No great optimism is justified when it comes to cutting medical costs overall. Medicine cannot be made cheap because of the costs of its technology, and by its nature it cannot be anything but a seller's market. But U. S. health care bills do not have to shoot up as rapidly as they are doing now. The big question is whether doctors, hospital administrators, insurers and employers can devise ways to bring the public the benefits of technology at a reasonable price, without a federal whip being held over them.

중심소재:

1. 도입부

1)

2. 요지

[실전응용 2] 글의 종류를 고려하면서, 본문을 분석하시오.

Of all the ways that automobiles damage the urban environment and lower the quality of life in big cities, few are as maddening and unnecessary as car alarms. Alarms

중심소재:

are more than just an annoyance; they are a costly public health problem and a constant irritation to urban civil life. The benefits, meanwhile, are nonexistent. Auto makers, alarm installers, insurers, police, and the biggest experts of all—car thieves—all agree that alarms do nothing to stop theft. What's more, there are now a number of good, inexpensive car security devices available on the market. It's time for us all to reconsider the seriousness of the problem and to do something about it.

1. 도입부

1) 뒷받침 근거

2. 요지

[실전응용 3] 글의 종류를 고려하면서, 본문을 분석하시오.

I believe that a person can find truth in life by focusing on one thing and mastering it. For example, I know a carpenter who has devoted himself to his work for years. He has got great skills and can also tell much about life. Unfortunately, young people graduating from school quickly grow impatient with their unattractive, basic-level jobs. They wonder if their work will lead to anything meaningful, and they ask for different responsibilities—but they may never be satisfied. If our knowledge is broad but shallow, we really know nothing. Yet developing one skill in great depth can show truth in life.

중심소재:
1. 도입부

1) 뒷받침 진술

2. 주제문 재진술

3. 묘사

　특정 대상을 눈에 보여 주듯이 글로써 그려내는, 즉 대상의 감각적 인상을 재현하는 진술 방식으로 서사와 마찬가지로 정서 표현, 정보 전달을 목적으로 하는 글에 두루 쓰인다. 묘사는 대상을 객관적으로 정확하게 재현하는 설명적 묘사와 주관적 인상이나 느낌을 제시하는 문학적 묘사가 있다. 서사의 경우처럼 묘사도 주제문이 필요한 구조가 아니다. 묘사는 그 자체의 의미보다는 필요한 곳에 적용하여 글의 효과를 높이는 데 목적이 있다. 그러므로 명확성과 사실성이 중요하다. 독자는 추상적인 것보다 구체적인 것에, 일반적인 것보다는 개별적인 것에 더 강한 인상을 받는다. 즉 막연히 '탈것'이라기보다, '자동차', '자동차'라기보다 '사장님들이 주로 타는 검은색 세단'이라고 해야 더 분명한 인상을 받을 수 있다. 묘사는 예리한 관찰을 통한 적합한 단어의 선택이 중요하다. 그러기 위해서는 수식어구보다는 단어 자체의 정확한 선택이 중요하며, 이를 보완해주는 비유법이 효과적일 수 있다. 그러므로 직유나 은유나 과장의 방법도 묘사를 나타내는 데 중요한 기여를 하는 것이다.

[실전응용] 글의 종류를 고려하면서, 본문을 분석하시오.

The traveller stepped into the hall of the old castle and looked around. It was a large room with stone walls. Several sleeping dogs lay against the wall on the left. In the middle of the room there was a fire. The smoke rose to a hole in the ceiling, but some of it remained in the room. The windows, high in the wall on the right, were not very large and the great room was rather dark.

중심소재:
1)
2)
3)

4. 서사

서사는 경험하거나 만들어낸 이야기를 기술하는 것으로, 일반적으로 주인공을 중심으로 등장인물 사이에 발생하는 사건이나 행동의 전개 과정을 시간의 경과에 따라 구체적으로 풀어 진술하는 방식이다. 서사에서는 행동(움직임)의 과정, 시간의 흐름, 의미 있는 사건의 연속이 중요한 요소이다. 이 역시 주제문이 필요한 구조는 아니다. 서사 역시 독자의 흥미를 자아내고 글의 효과를 높여 어떤 교훈을 주려는 데 그 목적이 있다. 즉 아무런 의미가 없는 이야기를 쓰는 것이 서사는 아니므로, 흥미를 야기할 만한 내용이나 긴장감을 줄 만한 그러한 요소가 있어야 한다. 그러므로 이러한 서사의 구성에서는 어휘의 사용도 일반적이라기보다는 좀 더 개별적이고 구체화한 언어를 사용하게 된다. 즉 단순히 say보다는 whisper, mutter, yell, cry 등으로 쓰는 것이 더 좋다.

[예시 1]

중심소재는 '스시'이다. ★

1. Recently, after eating a little bit of sushi, I woke up in the middle of the night and told my husband I felt itchy, especially the palms of my hands and the soles of my feet. My skin was red and blotchy, and my throat was terribly sore. ① I'd had mild allergic reactions to seafood before, so I got up, took an antihistamine and tried to go back to sleep, even though I was having a hard time swallowing. ② I never connected the sore throat to the itching and didn't look in the mirror until I woke up the next morning. I was shocked to see that my eyes were puffy and swollen.

중심내용은 간밤에 일어 ★
난 '알레르기 반응'이다.

이야기체의 서사 방식을 취하고 있다. 사건 중심으로 글을 파악하되, 주제문이 반드시 드러나지 않는 경우이므로 글쓴이가 자신의 경험담을 통해 궁극적으로 전달하려는 내용을 잡아내야 한다.
1. 최근 간밤에 발생한 사건: 생선회를 먹고 몸에 알레르기 반응을 보임.
① 심각하게 여기지 않고, 항히스타민을 먹고 다시 잠.
② 다음 날 심각한 알레르기 반응을 보인 자신의 모습을 보고 놀람.

| 해설
무엇에 관한 글인가? 최근 자신에게 발생한 예상치 못한 심각한 '알레르기 반응(Allergic Reactions)'에

관한 글임을 알 수 있다.

| 해석

최근 생선회를 먹고 한밤중에 잠이 깨어, 남편에게 몸이 가려운데 특히 손바닥과 발바닥이 가렵다고 말했다. 피부가 빨개지고, 반점이 생겼다. 그리고 목구멍이 몹시 아팠다. 전에도 해산물을 먹고 약간 알레르기 반응을 보인 적이 있었다. 그래서 일어나 항히스타민제를 복용하고 침을 삼키기도 힘이 들었지만, 다시 잠을 청했다. 나는 목구멍이 아픈 것이 가려움증과 관련이 있다는 것을 생각하지 못하고 다음 날 아침에 일어날 때까지 거울도 들여다보지 않았다. 나는 두 눈이 통통 부어오른 것을 보고 깜짝 놀랐다.

[예시 2]

A fox tumbled into a water tank and could not get out. Along came a thirsty goat. He sang the praises of water. The goat was so thirsty that he went down and drank his fill. Then they began to consider how they were to get up again. The fox said, "Be so kind as to place your forefeet against the wall and hold your horns up. Then I can jump and then pull you up, too." The goat was glad enough to comply. The fox climbed over his shoulders and horns, reached the edge of the tank, and began to make off. The goat complained that he had broken their promise. But he only came back to say, "You have more hairs in your beard than brains in your head. Otherwise you wouldn't have gone down without thinking how you were going to get up."

★ 주제문이 따로 존재하지 않는 이야기체의 우화로 등장인물을 파악하고, 등장인물 사이에 발생하는 사건을 중심으로 글쓴이가 궁극적으로 전달하려는 사항을 파악한다.

★ 우화는 교훈적 내용 전달을 목적으로 하는데, 일반적으로 글의 마지막 부분에 나타나는 경우가 많다.

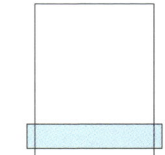

| 해석

여우 하나가 물탱크에 굴러떨어져서 밖으로 나올 수 없었다. 마침 목마른 염소가 지나갔다. 여우는 물을 찬미하는 노래를 불렀다. 이에 염소는 너무 목이 말라서 아래로 내려와 물을 마셨다. 그리고 여우와 염소는 어떻게 하면 밖으로 나갈지 궁리하였다. 여우가 말하길, "제발 부탁인데 앞발을 벽에 기대고 뿔을 위로 올려 봐. 그러면 내가 뛰어 나가서 너를 올려 줄게." 염소는 기꺼이 이 말을 따랐다. 여우는 염소의 어깨와 뿔을 타고 올라가 물탱크 끝으로 빠져나와 도망치기 시작했다. 염소는 여우가 약속을 어겼다고 불평했다. 그러자 여우는 다시 돌아와서 "너는 수염에 털만 있지, 머리에 뇌가 없어. 그렇지 않다면 어떻게 하면 나올지 생각하지도 않고 들어가진 않았겠지."라고 말했다.

[예시 3]

1. My parents and I moved from North Carolina to St. Petersburg, Florida, when I was just about to start my senior year of high school. It was a difficult time to be uprooted; I had lived in North Carolina all my life. 1) **But** I loved the water, so Florida seemed an okay place to live. ① I can't remember how I first chose my special beach at the end of Eighth Avenue. But once I chose my spot, I never switched

1. 주인공이 새로운 장소로 이사를 하게 됨(사건)
1) 'But'을 기준으로 주인공이 평생 North Carolina에서 살다 다른 곳으로 이주했지만, 새로운 장소를 좋아하게 됨 – 바닷가
① 바닷가를 중심으로 아름다운 추억을 그리고 있다.

★ 이야기체로 구성되는 서사의 글은 주로 주인공 중심으로 발생하는 사건에 초점을 맞추어 글을 읽어 나간다. 일반적으로 구체적 사건을 먼저 기술하고, 여기서 글쓴이가 느낀 감정, 반성, (도덕적) 교훈 등을 전달한다.

beaches. Almost daily, I swam and sunned there. I watched the sun set. I thought about life. On weekend nights in college, I hung out at the beach with friends, playing music or just listening to the waves. My bedroom at my parents' house holds no memories for me. My memories of Florida are all a mile away, at Eighth Avenue beach. 2. I live in Boston now and visit my parents in Florida twice a year. Whenever I visit, I spend many hours at my beach, usually under a hot sun, but sometimes at night, when the sand is cool and the sea seems to offer answers it won't share during the day. I go to my beach not only to relax and think, but also to feed off the sea. The waves are gentle, the water soothing. **But** more important to me is the sea's permanence and sheer force. I want to be strong like that.

★ 강조추가의 'But'을 확인한다.

2. 현재는 보스턴에 살지만, 여전히 플로리다를 방문할 때마다 **바닷가**로부터 얻게 된 득을 기술하고 있다: **삶의 휴식을 얻고, 성찰하며, 새로운 힘을 얻는 계기가 됨**

| 해설

본문은 주인공이 새로운 장소로 이사하게 되면서 삶의 큰 전환을 맞는 내용을 기술하고 있다. 새로운 장소에서 발견한 바닷가는 그의 가장 친한 동료이자 삶의 휴식과 성찰 그리고 삶의 재충전의 힘을 제공하는 대상이다. 주제는 중심소재 '바닷가'와 함께 주인공이 이로부터 얻는 긍정적 요소가 반영되어야 한다.

| 해석

부모님과 나는 노스캐롤라이나에서 플로리다의 세인트 피터즈버그로 이사를 하였는데, 거기서 나는 막 고등학교 마지막 학년을 시작하려는 차였다. 이전의 뿌리를 들어내야 했기에 힘든 시간이었다. 나는 내내 노스캐롤라이나에서 살았었다. 그러나 나는 바다를 좋아했기에, 플로리다는 살기 괜찮은 장소처럼 보였다. 내가 나의 특별한 장소로 8번가의 끝에 있는 바닷가를 어떻게 처음 택하게 되었는지 기억은 나지 않는다. 그러나 일단 나의 장소를 선택한 후 나는 바닷가를 바꾸지 않았다. 거의 매일 나는 거기서 수영을 하고 태양을 쬤다. 나는 해가 지는 걸 지켜보았다. 나는 인생에 대해 생각했다. 대학 생활 중 주말 밤이면 나는 친구들과 바닷가에서 놀면서 노래도 부르고, 그냥 파도소리를 듣기도 했다. 나는 부모님 집의 나의 방에 대한 기억이 없다. 플로리다에 대한 나의 기억은 일 마일 떨어진 8번가의 바닷가이다. 나는 현재 보스턴에 살고, 일 년에 두 번 플로리다에 있는 나의 부모님을 방문한다. 방문할 때마다 나는 일반적으로 뜨거운 태양 아래 바닷가에서 많은 시간을 보내지만, 때로 모래가 시원하고, 낮 동안 숨겨둔 해답을 제공하는 것처럼 보이는 밤의 바닷가를 즐긴다. 나는 바닷가에서 휴식과 사색을 즐길 뿐 아니라 바다로부터 (삶의) 영양분을 얻는다. 파도는 부드럽고, 바다는 마음을 가라앉힌다. 그러나 나에게 더욱 중요한 것은 바다의 변하지 않는 영속성과 온전한 강한 힘이다. 나는 그와 같이 강하고 싶다.

[실전응용 1] 글의 종류를 고려하면서, 본문을 분석하시오.

Old Hawk gestured up at the tall, old cottonwood. It was so large that a grown man could not put his arms around it. "This tree," he said, "has stood guard over our family all its life. Strength is what I feel each time I look at it. Yet, there

중심소재:

have been moments when its great strength was also its weakness." "That's hard to believe," Jeremy said. "It's the biggest tree for miles around." Old Hawk pointed at the chokecherry trees in a dry river bed not far away. "Look there," he said, "those chokecherry trees are small and weak in comparison to this cottonwood. But when you were a child, they survived a storm without losing a branch. This old cottonwood, on the other hand, lost several branches. It stood up to the storm, but it could not bend with the wind the way the chokecherry trees could."

[실전응용 2] 글의 종류를 고려하면서, 본문을 분석하시오.

Dan Rice was perhaps the most famous clown of the 19th century. He started his circus career when he bought a half interest in a trained pig. Rice then worked briefly as a strongman before settling on clowning and horse tricks. In 1848, he campaigned for his friend, Zachary Taylor, for president. Rice frequently would invite him to ride on his circus bandwagon during parades. The 1860s were Rice's glory days, the decade when he toured the country for a then amazing salary of $1,000 a week, recognized by his trademark white beard. He got so popular that President Zachary Taylor made him an honorary colonel. And about twenty years after Taylor had died, Rice ran for the Republican nomination for president. Unfortunately, he didn't win.

중심소재:

[실전응용 3] 글의 종류를 고려하면서, 본문을 분석하시오.

The minute white or yellowish eggs laid by the queen hatch in two to six weeks and develop into white larvae. After feeding a few weeks to several months, larvae become pupae, commonly but incorrectly called ant eggs. In some species the pupae are naked, and in others they are covered with cocoons spun from a substance that they secrete at the end of the larval stage. After the pupal state, during which no food is taken, the adults appear. The immature ants are fed, cleaned, and attended by the adult workers. As in all insects with a complete metamorphosis, the ant has attained its full size when it leaves the pupa stage.

중심소재:

14 글의 유형

본 장에서는 시험에 자주 등장하는 일반통념, 실험·조사·연구 그리고 현상의 글을 다루도록 한다.

1. 통념 비판 (Myth-breaking)

통념 비판의 글은 도입부에서 일반인들의 견해가 진술되고, 이후 역접의 'But, However' 등이 나온 후 글쓴이의 반대 주장이 제시되는 유형이다. 다음과 같은 패턴을 보인다.

통념을 나타내는 시그널은 다음과 같다.
People say that S V
= It is said that S V
　Many people say that S V
　Many of us say that S V
　We say that S V
　A is said to be B
등의 표현이 오면 통념 비판의 글일 가능성이 크다.

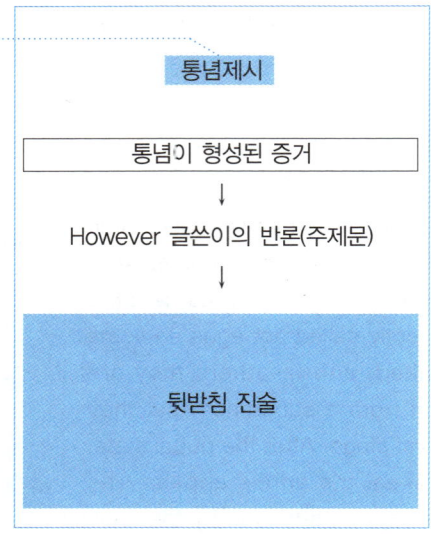

★ 글쓴이의 주장을 뒷받침 하는 내용이 글 전체로 보아 통념의 근거보다 '공간'을 더 차지함에 주목한다.

* 일대 다수의 법칙

"People / We / Mary ↔ I"와 같은 패턴을 따르는 이유는 다수와 대조되는 글쓴이 I의 견해를 진술하면서 자신의 주장을 더욱 두드러지게 하는 효과를 얻을 수 있기 때문이다.

[예시 1]

1. **People argue** that English is already the international language. 1) **But** English <u>must</u> stop being used as the international language. ① Scientists and business people do use English, but there are relatively few people in the world who use English conversationally. Ⓐ According to recent statistics, English is not spoken by more than 3.5 billion of the world's population. To put it a different way, fewer than one out of ten people in the world speak English.

중심소재: English
1. 도입부 = 통념
영어는 이미 국제언어이다.
1) 주제문(논리적 반전: But)
영어는 국제어로 사용되지 말아야 한다(주장을 이끄는 must 확인). ← 이후 주장의 근거가 제시되어야 한다.
① 뒷받침 문장
과학과 무역에서 영어를 사용하지만, 상대적으로 적은 인구가 영어를 사용함
Ⓐ 구체적 수치로 주장을 부연하고 있다.

★ 일반통념의 글임을 파악할 수 있다.
★ 중심소재는 English이다.
★ '통념 – But 주제문 – 뒷받침 문장' 의 패턴을 기억한다.

| 해석
사람들은 영어는 이미 국제어라고 생각한다. 그러나 영어가 국제어로 사용되는 것은 중단되어야 한다. 과학자들과 기업가들이 영어를 사용하지만, 영어를 대화로 사용하는 사람들은 세계에서 상대적으로 적다. 최근의 통계를 보면, 영어 사용자는 세계 인구 중 3억 4천(과거 영국의 단위로 billion이 1억이었다)을 넘지 않는다. 이를 다시 말하면, 세계에서 10명 중 1명보다 적은 인구가 영어를 사용한다는 말이다.

[예시 2]

1. **We think** that everybody would welcome a new invention and honor the inventor. 1) **But** this has not always been true. ① A Frenchman named Thimonnier invented a sewing machine in 1830. This machine made it possible for one tailor to do the work of several, and it also made the work much easier. But instead of welcoming the new invention, the tailors smashed the machine to pieces. They feared it would throw many of them out of work.

1. 도입부 = 통념
모든 이는 새로운 발명품과 그것을 발명한 사람을 높인다.
1) 주제문
But 이후 상반된 글쓴이의 견해: 항상 그렇지는 않다. ← 이후 이에 대한 근거로 뒷받침 문장이 이어진다.
① 뒷받침 문장
역사 속 구체적 인물을 제시하며, 그가 만든 발명품을 사람들이 긍정적으로 받아들이지 않았다는 내용이 이어진다.

★ 통념 비판의 글임을 드러내는 시그널을 확인할 수 있다.
★ 중심소재는 'a new invention' 이다.

| 해설
일반 통념으로 시작한 본문은 첫 문장에서 일반인들은 새로운 발명품과 그것을 발견한 사람을 칭송할 것이라 생각하지만, 사실 그렇지 않은 경우도 있다고 말했다. 고로, 새로운 발명품이 환영을 받지 못한 그런 상황과 그에 대한 이유가 본문의 뒷받침 문장으로 전개될 것을 예측 할 수 있다.

| 해석
우리는 모든 사람이 새로운 발명품을 환영하고 발명자를 존경할 것으로 생각한다. 그러나 항상 그런 것은 아니었다. Thimonnier라는 이름의 한 프랑스 사람이 1830년에 재봉틀을 발명했다. 이 기계는 한 사람의 재봉사가 여러 사람의 일을 할 수 있게 하였고, 일을 훨씬 쉽게 만들었다. 그러나 재봉사들은 이 새로운 발명품을 환영하기보다는 그 기계를 때려 부수어 산산조각으로 만들었다. 그들은 재봉틀이 많은 사람을 일자리로부터 쫓아낼 것으로 우려했다.

[예시 3]

중심소재는 'aspirin'이다. ★

도입부 = 통념
But 주제문
뒷받침 진술
주제문(요지)

1. The king of all painkillers, of course, is aspirin. The US Food and Drug Administration permits aspirin to be sold without prescription, 1) but the drug, contrary to popular belief, can be dangerous and, in sustained doses, potentially lethal. ⓐ Aspirin is self-administered by more people than any other drug in the world. Some people are aspirin poppers, taking ten or more a day. What they don't know is that the smallest dose can cause internal bleeding. 2. Aspirin can do more harm than the pain it is supposed to suppress.

중심소재: Aspirin
1. 도입부 = 통념
처방전 아스피린 구입이 가장 안전한 고통완화제
1) 주제문(But 이후 통념 비판)
아스피린은 일반인의 생각과 달리 아주 위험하다.
ⓐ 뒷받침 진술
아스피린의 무분별 처방 → 10개 이상 처방 → 내출혈
2. 요지 재진술

| 해석
진통제 중의 왕은 물론 아스피린이다. 미국 식품 및 의약품 당국에서는 아스피린을 처방 없이도 판매할 수 있도록 허용하고 있다. 그러나 아스피린은 통념과는 달리 위험성이 있으며, 지속해서 복용하면 잠재적으로 치명적일 수 있다. 아스피린은 세계의 어떤 다른 약보다도 더 많은 사람이 자가 복용하고 있다. 어떤 사람들은 걸핏하면 아스피린을 찾아서 하루에 열 알 이상까지 복용한다. 그들은 아스피린은 조금만 복용해도 내출혈을 일으킬 수 있다는 것을 모르고 있다. 아스피린은 기대할 수 있는 진통 효과보다 더한 해를 끼칠 수 있다.

[예시 4]

통념의 시그널 ★

주제문
개인의 경험담을 통한 뒷받침 진술

1. Many people believe that it is critical to share similar, if not identical, beliefs and values with someone with whom they have a relationship. 1) While this may seem referable, it is far from mandatory. 2) Individuals from extremely diverse backgrounds have learned to overlook their differences and live harmonious, loving lives together. ⓐ I've seen people from opposite ends of the spectrum economically and politically that ended up in happy, lasting marriages. I've seen couples from different ethnic groups merge into harmonious relationships, and I've seen people from different religions come together for a strong, lasting bond. Furthermore, many good friends have little in common except a warm loving feeling of respect and rapport. That's the only essential thing.

1. 도입부 = 통념
비슷한 관심사를 가진 사람끼리 교제를 나눈다.
1) 'But/However' 이후 주제문 제시
ⓐ 주제문
Ⓐ 뒷받침 진술
개인적 경험을 바탕으로 주제문의 중심내용을 뒷받침하고 있다.

| 해석
많은 사람이 그들이 관계를 맺고 있는 사람과 똑같지는 않더라도, 비슷한 신념과 가치관을 공유하는 것이 중요하다고 생각한다. 이것이 바람직할지는 모르지만, 반드시 그러하다는 것과는 거리가 멀다. 아주 다양한 배경을 가진

개인들이 그들의 차이를 너그럽게 보고 조화롭고 사랑하는 삶을 함께 누리는 것을 배웠다. 나는 경제적으로 그리고 정치적으로 반대의 양 끝 지점에 있는 사람들이 행복하고 지속적인 결혼 생활을 하는 것을 보아왔다. 나는 다른 인종 집단 출신의 부부들이 조화로운 관계로 함께 사는 것을 보아왔으며, 서로 다른 종교를 가진 사람들이 강하고 지속적인 유대 관계로 뭉치는 것을 보아왔다. 게다가, 많은 좋은 친구들이 존경과 친밀한 관계의 따뜻한 사랑하는 감정을 제외하고는 공통적인 것이 거의 없다. 이것이 유일한 필수적인 것이다.

[실전응용 1] 글의 유형에 유의하면서 본문을 분석하시오.

When people think of skyscrapers, they think of New York, a city with many high-rise buildings. There is no other city like New York, and this is because of its great buildings that reach up into the sky. It comes as a surprise then to learn that Chicago, not New York, is the home of the skyscraper. The first high-rise building was built in Chicago in 1884, and it was nine stories high. This is not tall compared with today's buildings, but it was the first building over six stories. There were no tall buildings before that because the needed technology didn't exist.

중심소재:
1. 도입부

1) 주제문

① 뒷받침 근거

[실전응용 2] 글의 유형에 유의하면서 본문을 분석하시오.

Many people believe that they will be free of their anger if they express it, and that their tears will release their pain. This belief derives from a nineteenth-century understanding of emotions, and it is no truer than the flat earth. It sees the brain as a steam kettle in which negative feelings build up pressure. But no psychologist has ever succeeded in proving the unburdening effects of the supposed safety valves of tears and anger. On the contrary, over forty years ago, controlled studies showed that fits of anger are more likely to intensify anger, and that tears can drive us still deeper into depression. Our heads do not resemble steam kettles, and our brains involve a much more complicated system than can be accounted for by images taken from nineteenth-century technology.

중심소재:
1. 도입부

1) 주제문

① 뒷받침 근거

[실전응용 3] 글의 유형에 유의하면서 본문을 분석하시오.

Contrary to what many people think, hot deserts are not lifeless wastelands. We can find many living things that survive there in their own ways. For example, the acacia tree sends its roots down over one hundred feet to reach ground water. Many desert animals do not drink water at all. Instead, they get all their water from the foods they eat. Others can go without food and water for many days. A camel, for instance, can go without water for over two weeks, and when it must go without food, it depends on the fat stored in its body.

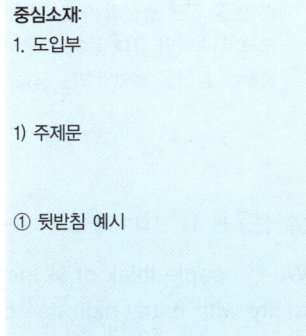

중심소재:
1. 도입부

1) 주제문

① 뒷받침 예시

[실전응용 4] 글의 유형에 유의하면서 본문을 분석하시오.

Contrary to popular assumption, slavery was not usually based on racism, but on one of three other factors. The first was debt. In some cultures, an individual who could not pay a debt could be enslaved by the creditor. The second was crime. Instead of being killed, a murderer or thief might be enslaved by the family of the victim as compensation for their loss. The third was war and conquest. When one group of people conquered another, they often enslaved some of the vanquished.

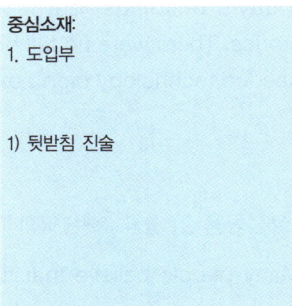

중심소재:
1. 도입부

1) 뒷받침 진술

[실전응용 5] 글의 유형에 유의하면서 본문을 분석하시오.

People worry that spending too much time playing video games isn't good for a child's health. But some doctors have noticed that kids who bring their handheld game players to the hospital seem less worried about being there. These patients also seem to experience less pain when they are concentrating on the games. For example, at the Johns Hopkins Children's Center in Baltimore, young patients are finding hospital visits easier, thanks to a program. The program allows kids to play online sports, racing, and adventure games with each other. It brings together kids who feel they are isolated by their illnesses, and lets them know they are not alone.

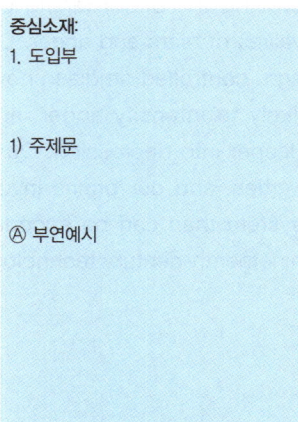

중심소재:
1. 도입부

1) 주제문

Ⓐ 부연예시

156

[실전응용 6] 글의 유형에 유의하면서 본문을 분석하시오.

People are often under stress. Some are taking exams, some are considering moving to another job, and others are worried about deadlines. They believe these stressful situations give them gray hair. However, so far no scientific evidence proves a bad day turns your hair silver. According to medical doctors, your hair turning gray runs in your family. In other words, if your father's hair becomes gray when he is quite young, you are highly likely to be in the same situation. Thus, when you get gray hair, it might be wise to dye your hair rather than to blame those stressful situations.

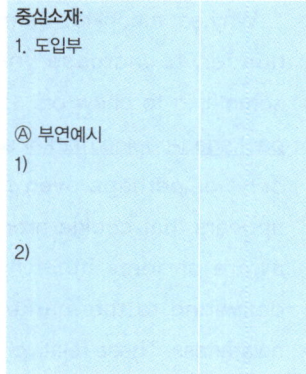

중심소재:
1. 도입부

Ⓐ 부연예시
1)

2)

2. 현상

글의 도입부에서 현상에 대한 기술이 제시되는 지문은 일반적으로 다음과 같은 내용으로 이어지는 경우가 많다.

[문제점(문제 제기)/원인/대안/기원]

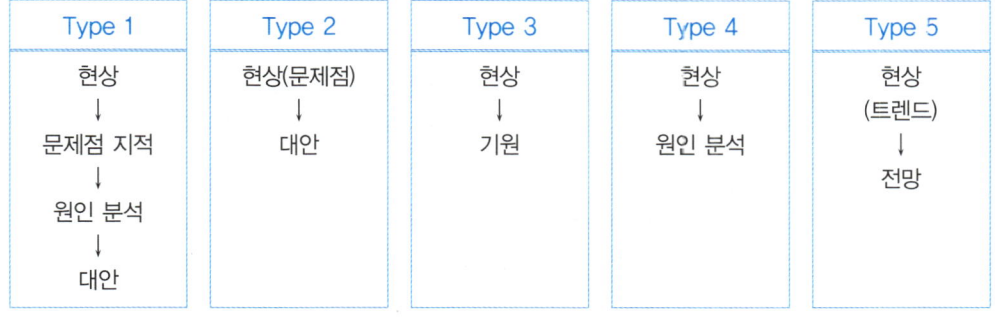

일반적으로 지문 초반부에 현상이 제기는 되는 형태는 최근 시험 출제빈도가 높은 시사와도 연관성이 높다.

* 주제문 설정 요령

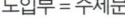
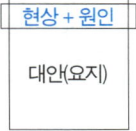

현상의 글의 유형에서 주제문을 글의 도입부에서 제시되는 "현상과 원인"에서 이끌어 낼 수 있으며, 글의 중반 이후에 제시되는 대안은 주제문을 통해 궁극적으로 전달하려는 요지가 된다. 현상의 글을 아래와 같이 정리할 수 있다.

* 주제문 = 현상 + 원인
* 주제 = 현상
* 대안 = 요지

중심소재는 'cookie'이다. ★

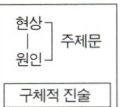

현상 + 원인 = 주제문

[예시 1]

1. Why eat a cookie? Some reasons might be to satisfy your hunger, to increase your sugar level, or just to have something to chew on. 1) However, recent success in the packaged-cookie market suggests that these may not be the only, or perhaps even the most important, reasons. It appears that cookie-producing companies are becoming aware of some other influences and, as a result, are delivering to the market products resulting from their awareness. These relatively new product offerings are usually referred to as 'soft' or 'chewy' cookies, to distinguish them from the more typical crunchy varieties. ① Why all the fuss over their introduction? Apparently much of their appeal has to do with childhood memories of sitting on the back steps devouring those melt-in-your-mouth cookies that were delivered by Mom straight from the oven, while they were still soft. This emotional and sensory appeal of soft cookies is apparently at least as strong as are the physical cravings that the product satisfies.

1. 도입부
사람들이 왜 쿠키를 먹는지 자문하며 글을 시작하고 있다. ← 중심소재 도출

1) 현상
쿠키 시장의 최근에 이룬 성공 – 그 원인은 무엇인가?
쿠키 회사는 전통적인 과자 제조(바삭하고 딱딱한)와 달리 'soft'와 'chewy'의 영향력을 인식하게 됨.

① 원인
'soft' 또는 'chewy'한 쿠키가 갑작스러운 인기를 누리는 이유는? 'soft'와 'chewy'는 어린 시절의 기억을 연상케 함으로 구매를 촉구한다.

| 해설
현상에 대한 원인을 분석하는 대표적인 지문이다.

| 해석
왜 쿠키를 먹을까? 허기를 채우기 위해서라든지, 혈당을 증가시키기 위해서, 혹은 단지 씹어 먹을거리로서 등의 몇 가지 이유를 들 수 있다. 하지만 최근의 포장 쿠키 시장에서의 성공은 이것들이 유일한, 혹은 아마도 심지어 가장 중요한 이유는 아닐지도 모른다는 것을 시사한다. 쿠키 제조 회사들은 다른 특정 영향들을 깨닫고 있으며, 그 결과 그 깨달음에서 기인한 시장 상품을 내어놓는 것처럼 보인다. 이러한 상대적으로 새로운 상품 제공은 대개 부드러운 또는 씹는 맛이 있는 쿠키로 언급되는데, 이는 더욱 전형적인 바삭한 종류와 그것들을 구별하기 위한 것이다. 왜 이 상품의 도입에 떠들썩한 것일까? 분명히 그 매력의 상당 부분은 뒤 계단에 앉아서 오븐에서 엄마가 바로 가져다 준 아직 부드러운, 입에서 녹는 쿠키를 게걸스럽게 먹던 어린 시절의 기억과 관련이 있다. 언뜻 보기에, 부드러운 쿠키에 대한 이런 감정적이고 감각적인 매력은 적어도 그 상품이 만족하게 하는 신체적인 갈망만큼이나 강하다.

[예시 2]

1. During a recent excavation in a very old city, archaeologists found the remains of a water well about four meters deep in a stratum, which dates back to about 9,000 years ago. Since

중심소재: Well
1. 도입부 = 현상
아주 오래된 고대 도시에서 발견된 특이한 현상이 기록되고 있다.

1) 이유

the site is located near a large river, where inhabitants could get drinking water, it was a mystery as to why they needed a well. 1) <u>One possible explanation</u> is that sanitation was already a problem for the inhabitants of the settlement. As the settlement grew and population increased, the river might have been polluted with waste from livestock and people. The well may have been part of an effort to prevent the polluted water from becoming a health hazard to the people of the community. Therefore it may be the oldest example of a well being dug to gain access to a clean water source.

| 해설

본문은 어느 고대 사회에서 발견된 특이한 현상에 대한 원인/이유를 밝히는 글이다. 단순한 구조이지만, 현상으로 시작하는 글은 '현상 – 문제점/원인/기원/대안'의 형태를 취하기에 이런 패턴을 익혀두는 것이 중요하다. 참고로, 최근 중요시되고 있는 시사 문제 대부분이 이런 패턴의 글인 것으로 보아 그 중요도가 점점 높아지고 있는 것 같다.

| 해석

최근 아주 오래된 도시에서 발굴하는 동안에, 고고학자들은 지층 속 4미터 정도의 깊이에서 우물 유적을 발견했는데, 그것은 연대가 9,000년 전까지 거슬러 올라가는 것이었다. 그 지점은 주민이 마실 물을 구할 수 있는 거대한 강과 가까운 곳에 있었으므로, 이는 그들이 왜 우물이 있어야 했는지 미스터리였다. 한 가지 가설은 그곳에 거주하는 주민에게 이미 위생이 문제가 되었다는 것이다. 마을의 규모가 커지고 인구가 증가함에 따라, 가축이나 사람들에게서 나온 쓰레기 탓에 강이 오염되었을지도 모른다. 그 우물은 오염된 물이 지역사회 사람들에게 건강에 대한 위험이 되는 것을 막기 위한 노력의 일부였을 것이다. 그러므로 이는 깨끗한 급수 공급원을 얻기 위해서 우물을 판 가장 오래된 예가 된다.

[예시 3]

1. In the old days, when classical music was pop music, audiences openly approved (or disapproved) of a performance of a piece of music while it was being played. 1) **However**, the popularity of classical music has declined because it got too holy for the audience to express responses. If Beethoven were alive today, he would be surprised to see the audience keeping silent while his works were being played. 2. Fortunately, as orchestras try to get lost audiences back into the concert halls, this stuffy atmosphere is slowly changing. 1) <u>For example</u>, conductors, who have been mute on stage, now speak from the podium sometimes.

1. 도입부
대중음악으로써 고전음악이 성행했던 시대: 연주하는 동안 음악에 대한 평가가 이루어졌다.
1) 'However' 이후 앞에서 언급된 내용과 대조되는 현상이 제시되고 있다 : 고전음악이 너무 거룩해져 관객이 반응이 없어지면서 대중성이 떨어졌다.
2. 최근의 현상(글쓴이가 궁극적으로 전달하려는 내용): 과거 고전음악이 대중음악이었을 때와 같이 대중과 소통을 하려는 노력이 일고 있다.
1) 예시부연(for example)

★중심소재는 '고전음악'이다. 'However'를 기점으로 어떤 점이 대조되고 있는지 파악하도록 한다.

| 해설

과거에 누렸던 대중성을 잃은 고전음악이 다시 대중과 소통하려는 노력을 기울이고 있다는 내용이 본문의 요지이다.

| 해석

옛날 클래식 음악이 대중음악이었던 시절에는 청중들이 곡이 연주되고 있는 동안에 그 음악 공연에 대해 솔직하게 인정했다 (혹은 인정하지 않았다). 그러나 클래식 음악이 너무 성스러워져서 청중이 반응을 표현할 수 없게 되었기 때문에 클래식 음악의 대중성이 쇠퇴하게 되었다. 만약 베토벤이 오늘날 살아 있다면, 그의 곡이 연주되는 동안에 청중들이 조용히 있는 것을 보고 놀랄 것이다. 다행히도 관현악단이 놓쳐버린 청중들을 연주회장으로 되돌리려고 애쓰고 있기 때문에 이런 숨이 막히는 분위기가 변하고 있다. 예를 들어, 지휘자들은 무대에서 말을 하지 않았는데, 지금은 때때로 지휘대에서 말을 한다.

[예시 4]

1. Would a modern music composer be your first choice for a hero? Or would you think of the painter of a contemporary masterpiece? If you are like most people, the answer to both questions is "no." 1) More likely, a sports hero or a movie star would be your first choice. ① It seems that the worlds of contemporary art and music have <u>failed to offer people works that reflect human achievements</u>. People, <u>therefore</u>, have lost interest in modern arts and have turned to sports stars and other popular figures to find their role models.

★ 인과의 글 전개방식을 확인한다.

중심소재: 영웅 → 영웅의 부재
1. 도입부 = 현상(문제점 지적)
현대 음악가들 사이에 영웅의 부재를 지적하고 있다.
1) 대부분 사람들은 스포츠 또는 영화 배우를 선택
① 원인 – 결과
현대 예술과 음악은 인간의 업적을 반영하는 작품을 제대로 제공하지 못했기에 현대 예술에 등을 돌리고 스포츠나 다른 대중적 인물을 자신의 롤 모델로 삼는다.

| 해석

현대 음악 작곡가가 당신이 선망하는 첫 번째 영웅일까? 또는 (영웅으로서) 당대의 명작을 그린 화가를 생각할까? 만일 당신이 대부분 사람들과 같다면, 이 두 가지 질문에 대한 대답은 "아니오."이다. 더 가능성 있는 것은, 스포츠 영웅이나 영화배우가 당신의 첫 번째 선택이 될 것이다. 현대의 미술이나 음악의 세계는 사람들에게 인간의 성취를 반영하는 작품들을 제공하는 데 실패한 것 같다. 그래서 사람들은 현대 예술에 흥미를 잃어버리고 그들의 본보기로 삼을 수 있는 대상을 찾아 스포츠 스타나 다른 인기 있는 인물들에게 돌아서고 있다.

[예시 5]

1. A study uncovered something fascinating about people at a racetrack: Just after placing a bet, they are much more confident of their horse's chances of winning than they are immediately before laying down that bet. Of course, nothing about the horse's chances actually shifts; it's the same horse, on the same track, in the same field; 1) **but** in the

1. 도입부: 관찰의 결과(성향 · 현상)
경마장에서 사람들이 '일단 돈을 거두면 자신이 건 말이 승리할 것에 대한 확신이 이 전보다 훨씬 높아진다. ← 성향 · 현상이 제시되는 경우 일반적으로 이에 대한 원인을 파악하는 글로 전개된다.
1) 현상의 원인 파악: 자신이 한 행위 (승리할 것으로 생각하고 돈을 건 행

minds of those bettors, its prospects for success improve significantly once that ticket is purchased. <u>The reason for the dramatic change has to do with our nearly obsessive desire to be and to appear consistent with what we have already done</u>. Once we have made a choice or taken a stand, we will encounter personal and interpersonal pressures to behave according to that commitment. Those pressures will cause us to respond in ways that make us justify our earlier decision.

위)에 일치하려는 강박적 소망으로 말미암은 것이다.
– 부연진술

| 해설
성향·현상으로 시작하는 글로 인과의 전개방식을 취하고 있다.

| 해석
한 연구는 경마장에 있는 사람들에 관한 아주 재미있는 사실을 발견해 냈다. 즉, 돈을 건 직후에 사람들은 돈을 걸기 직전보다 자신들의 말이 우승할 승산에 대해 훨씬 더 확신을 한다는 것이다. 물론, 말의 승산에 관해서 실제로 변한 건 아무것도 없다. 똑같은 말에, 똑같은 트랙에, 똑같은 경기장이지만, 내기를 건 사람들의 생각에는 일단 (내기하기 위한) 그 표가 구매되면 성공에 대한 기대감이 상당히 커진다. 그러한 극적인 변화에 대한 이유는 우리가 이미 했던 일과 일관성을 가지려 하는 (그리고 그렇게 보이려고 하는) 거의 강박 관념에 가까운 소망과 관련이 있다. 일단 우리가 어떤 선택을 했거나 어떤 태도를 보였으면 우리는 그렇게 마음을 정한 것에 따라 행동하도록 하는 개인적인 그리고 대인 간에 생기는 압박감을 만나게 된다. 그러한 압박감이 우리가 우리의 앞선 결정을 정당화시키는 방식으로 반응하게 하는 원인이 된다.

[예시 6]

1. One custom that is common at weddings in the United States is throwing rice at the bride and groom as they leave the place where the wedding ceremony has just been held. 1) No one knows exactly why people throw rice. One explanation is that the rice assures that the couple will have many children. ① If this is true, then the custom is not always a good one now because a lot of couples do not want many children.

중심소재: 미국의 결혼 풍습
1. 도입부 = 현상
신랑·신부에게 쌀을 던지는 미국의 결혼 관습 묘사
1) 기원 파악
다산의 상징으로 쌀을 던짐
① 부연설명

| 해석
미국 결혼에서 흔한 관습 중 하나는 신부와 신랑이 결혼이 막 열린 장소를 떠날 때 쌀을 던지는 행위이다. 누구도 사람들이 왜 쌀을 던지는지는 모른다. 그 중 한 이론에 의하면 쌀은 이 부부가 많은 자손을 가질 것을 보장해 준다는 것이다. 만약 이것이 사실이라면, 이 관습은 항상 좋은 것이 아닌데 이는 많은 부부가 아이를 원하지 않기 때문이다.

[실전응용 1] 글의 유형에 유의하면서 본문을 분석하시오.

Habitat diversity refers to the variety of places where life exists. Each habitat is the home of numerous species, most of which depend on that habitat. When it disappears, a vast number of species disappear as well. More often, an entire habitat does not completely disappear but instead is reduced gradually until only small patches remain. This has happened to old-growth forests and coastal wetlands in the United States and is now occurring in tropical forests throughout the world. Elimination of all but small patches of habitat is especially damaging because it not only eliminates many local species but also threatens those species that depend on vast acreage for their survival.

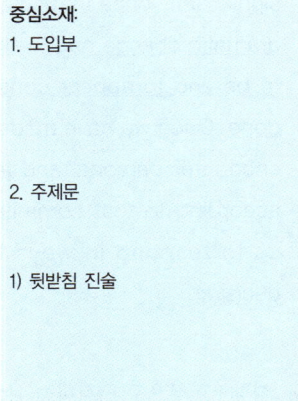

중심소재:
1. 도입부

2. 주제문

1) 뒷받침 진술

[실전응용 2] 글의 유형에 유의하면서 본문을 분석하시오.

Since the end of World War II, industrialization has been increasing very fast throughout the world. This is causing family life to change faster too. Societies are losing their extended families. More married couples want their own homes where they can live with their children. The West has had nuclear families instead of extended families at least since the Industrial Revolution started in England around 1760, when people changed from making things by hand to making them in factories.

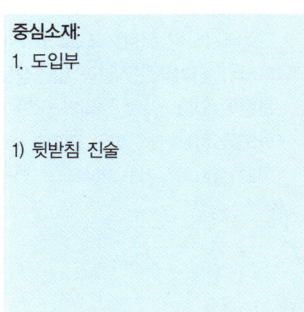

중심소재:
1. 도입부

1) 뒷받침 진술

[실전응용 3] 글의 유형에 유의하면서 본문을 분석하시오.

Most of us buy our food from supermarkets. In fact, many of us don't even get as far as the supermarket but make our choices at the click of a mouse. We have abandoned our relationship with the food we eat and with the people who produce our food. Is it any wonder that our children don't know where food comes from? Is it any wonder that we're tired, overweight, irritable, and low? It is important to be mindful about every single aspect of purchasing food. Try not to race through your shopping. In my hometown, nobody would buy a melon without feeling it and smelling it; and nobody would dream of buying a chicken without knowing which farm it came from and what it ate.

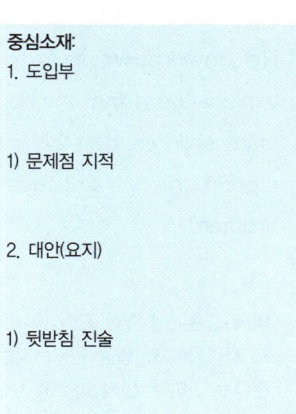

중심소재:
1. 도입부

1) 문제점 지적

2. 대안(요지)

1) 뒷받침 진술

[실전응용 4] 글의 유형에 유의하면서 본문을 분석하시오.

For many generations, scholars and artists tended to concentrate their energy on one particular subject. For Shakespeare, that interest was literature. For Mozart, that interest was musical composition, and for Newton, physics. Visual artists were not expected to understand higher mathematics, nor were philosophers expected to study engineering. However, with the development of the Internet and other sources of instantaneous information, many people strive to gain at least a working knowledge of many different subjects. So-called pancake people no longer concentrate their energies on one area of interest, but instead choose to spread themselves thinly over a large area. As a result, a new generation of pancake people have essentially become the proverbial jacks of all trades, but masters of none.

중심소재:
1. 도입부

1) 과거

① 뒷받침 부연(예시)

2) 현재

② 문제점 지적

[실전응용 5] 글의 유형에 유의하면서 본문을 분석하시오.

The forbidding sands of the Sahara might seem an unusual place for farming. But if you're farming silicon to make solar panels, the conditions in the Sahara are more or less optimal. At least, that's the thinking behind the Sahara Solar Breeder Project. The plan, a joint project proposed by Japanese and Algerian universities, would use the desert's immense supplies of sunlight and sand to "breed" solar power plants and solar panel factories. The idea is to start with a small number of silicon manufacturing plants that will produce the silicon needed to manufacture solar panels. Once those panels are operating, they can be used to power the silicon plants, which in turn produce more silicon and solar panels. The universities envision breeding enough silicon and solar panels by 2050 to supply half the world's energy.

중심소재:
1. 도입부

1) 주제문

3. 실험 · 연구 · 조사

① 기본적으로 '주제문 → 뒷받침 문장'으로 전개되는 두괄식 유형에서 가장 많이 등장한다.

다시 말해, 글쓴이는 자신의 주장을 뒷받침하기 위해 본인 또는 다른 사람의 구체적 실험 또는 연구를 통해 주장에 대한 설득력을 높인다.

② 구체적 실험을 먼저 전개하고 이후 일반화를 이끌어내는 형태.

'실험의 목적 = 글의 주제'이며, '실험의 결과 또는 의의를 통해 글의 요지 및 주장'을 이끌어낼 수 있다.

실험·연구·조사의 글 구조는 다음과 같다.

Type 1.

주제문 제시(일반진술)

실험을 통한 뒷받침 문장
(구체적 진술)

실험의 결론에서 다시 한 번 글쓴이의 요지 확인(일반진술)

Type 2.

실험을 통한 구체적 진술
(구체적 진술)

글쓴이의 요지인 실험의 결과 및 분석 제시(일반진술)

[예시 1]

1. Many years ago, psychologists performed an experiment in which they put a number of people in a room, alone except for a ring toss set. It was one of those children' toys with a short wooden post held upright on the floor and a bunch of round rings. The subjects were left alone to amuse themselves as best they could. As expected, with time to kill, they began trying to toss the rings around the post. 1) What the psychologists <u>discovered</u> was that most of the people moved far enough away from the post so that tossing the rings around it was challenging but not so difficult as to be totally frustrating. ① **In other words,** they deliberately positioned themselves between frustration on the one hand and boredom on the other. <u>The process of alternately producing and relieving tension was what made the activity stimulating.</u>

* 실험의 결과를 이끄는 시그널
① show
② find out
③ suggest
④ reveal
⑤ indicate
⑥ discover

실험이 등장하는 지문이다.

| 실험의 목적: 글에서 밝히려는 사항(주제) |
| 실험의 결과: 요지 |

1. **도입부 = 구체적 진술**
실험의 구체적 내용이 먼저 제시되는 형태이다. (때로 실험 결과가 먼저 제시되고, 이후 구체적 실험이 나오는 형태와 구별해 둘 것)

1) **일반화 = 실험의 결과**(discovered)
고리 기둥과 던지는 거리를 적절히 조절하여 게임의 적절한 수위를 조절함 (너무 어렵지도 너무 쉽지도 않게끔).

① 결론을 다시 풀어쓰면서(in other words) 글쓴이가 궁극적으로 전달하려는 사항이 제시된다: 긴장감을 조절하면서 게임을 자극적으로(재미있게) 유도한다.

| 해설

실험이 등장하는 지문에서 요지를 묻는 문제는 실험의 결과에서 글쓴이가 이끌어낸 결론에 해당한다는 점을 잊지 말자. 실험이 등장하는 지문의 일반적 두 패턴을 보면 다음과 같다.

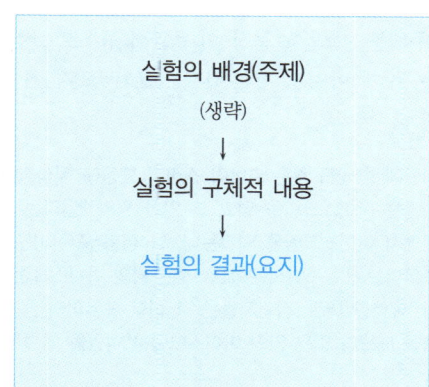

Pattern 1
실험의 결과(요지)
↓
실험의 배경(주제)
↓
구체적 실험 내용
↓
실험의 결과 재 언급(요지)

Pattern 2
실험의 배경(주제)
(생략)
↓
실험의 구체적 내용
↓
실험의 결과(요지)

당연히 실험 결과에서 주제를 이끌어낼 수도 있다.

| 해석

여러 해 전 심리학자들이 한 가지 실험을 하였는데 그 실험에서 그들은 사람들을 고리 던지기 세트 외에는 아무 것도 없는 방에 있게 하였다. 그 기구는 바닥에서 위로 세워진 짧은 나무로 만든 기둥과 여러 개의 고리를 갖춘 아이들의 장난감 중 하나였다. 피실험자들은 최대한 즐겁게 시간을 보내도록 오직 그들만 방안에 남겨졌다. 예상했던 대로 그들은 시간을 죽이기 위해 고리를 기둥을 향해 던지기 시작했다. 심리학자들은 그 사람들 대부분이 기둥을 향해 고리를 던지는 것이 도전적이기는(어렵기는) 하지만 완전히 좌절감을 느끼게 할 만큼 그렇게 어렵지는 않을 정도의 거리를 기둥으로부터 둔다는 사실을 발견하였다. 다시 말하면, 그들은 한편으로는 좌절감과 다른 한편으로는 무료함 사이의 경계에 자신들을 의도적으로 위치시켰다. 긴장을 만들어냈다 해소하는 반복적인 과정이 그 행위를 자극적으로 만들었던 것이다.

[예시 2]

1. Recently, a researcher found that imitation has a direct influence on consumer behavior. 1) In her experiments, participants were asked to eat ice cream and to judge its taste. Each experimental participant ate ice cream in the presence of a confederate, and the confederate was always the first to take a sample of ice cream. The confederate was either instructed to eat a large amount or a very modest amount, but the participants didn't know about it. As predicted, participants followed the behavior of the

중심소재: 소비성향
1. 도입부 = 주제문
실험의 결과로 '모방이 소비자의 행동에 미치는 직접적인 영향'을 언급하고 있다.
1) 뒷받침 진술
실험의 구체적 내용

★ 실험 · 조사 · 연구는 글의 요지에 해당한다.

> confederate. They ate significantly more ice cream when the confederate had taken a large amount relative to when the confederate had taken a small amount.

| 해설

'주제문 – 뒷받침 문장'의 두괄식 구조로 실험을 통해 뒷받침 문장을 제시하는 형태이다. 실험의 목적은 '주제'이며, 실험의 결과는 글의 '요지'에 해당한다.

| 해석

최근에 한 연구원은 모방이 소비자 행동에 직접적인 영향을 미친다는 것을 발견하였다. 그녀의 실험들에서 참가자들은 아이스크림을 먹고 그 맛을 평가해달라는 요청을 받았다. 각 실험 참가자들은 그 실험의 도우미가 있는 곳에서 아이스크림을 먹었는데, 그 실험 도우미는 항상 시식용 아이스크림을 먹는 첫 번째 사람이었다. 그 실험 도우미는 많은 양 혹은 매우 적은 양의 아이스크림을 먹도록 지시받았는데, 참가자들은 그것에 대해 모르고 있었다. 예측한 대로, 참가자들은 그 실험 도우미의 행동을 따랐다. 그들은 실험 도우미가 적은 양의 아이스크림을 먹었을 때보다 많은 양의 아이스크림을 먹었을 때 상당히 더 많은 아이스크림을 먹었다.

[예시 3]

조사의 결과가 바로 등장★한다. 일반적으로 조사의 결과가 요지가 되는 경우가 많으므로 결과를 드러내는 시그널을 주목한다. 시그널에는 'show, find out, reveal, indicate' 등이 있다.

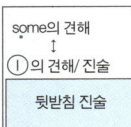

some의 견해
↕
ⓘ의 견해/ 진술
뒷받침 진술

some의 견해가 제시되면 글쓴이가 이에 동조하는지, 반대하는지 또는 중립적인 입장에서 다른 대상(others)의 견해를 제시하는지 살핀다.

시간의 대조를 확인한다.

> 1. New research has shown that Neanderthals cooked and ate grains and plants. 1) American researchers came to that conclusion after they had found cooked grains and plants in the teeth of preserved Neanderthal specimens. ⓘ Ⓐ Their diet was more varied than previously thought. Before, Neanderthals were widely believed to be great meat eaters. Ⓑ Some had believed that they had gone extinct when the Ice Age began because they relied on meat. Now, the new evidence has challenged this theory. Ⓒ Although grains had been found at Neanderthal sites before, it wasn't known whether they were cultivated for food or perhaps for some other reason. 2. The new findings show that the food was actually being consumed as it was found in the mouth of a Neanderthal.

중심소재: Neanderthals

실험이 나오는 지문은 실험을 글의 요지를 파악한다는 관점에서 '실험의 결과'에 주목하여 글을 읽도록 한다.

1. 도입부 = 주제문
네안데르탈인들은 곡식과 식물을 먹었다는 사실(글의 요지)

1) 뒷받침 진술
앞에서 제시한 결론에 대한 증거를 제시하고 있다: 이빨에서 곡물과 채소 발견
ⓘ 기존의 정보와 다른 새로운 사실 발견과 의의
Ⓐ 다양한 종류의 음식 섭취
Ⓑ 육식만을 주로 했기에 빙하기가 되면서 멸종했다고 하는 기존 이론에 이의 제기 ← 네안데르탈인에 대한 새로운 시각의 연구의 필요성 제기

2. 결과(요지)
네안데르탈인이 실제 식량을 위해 재배한 것을 증명

| 해석

새로운 연구 결과에 따르면 네안데르탈인들이 곡물과 채소를 조리해서 먹었다는 사실이 밝혀졌다. 미국 연구자들은 보존된 네안데르탈인 표본의 이빨에서 조리된 곡물과 채소를 발견한 후 그러한 결론에 이르게 되었다. 그들의 음식은 이전에 생각한 것보다 훨씬 다양했다. 전에는 그들이 육식을 아주 좋아한다고 널리 믿어졌다. 어떤 이들은 그들이 고기에 의존했기 때문에 빙하기가 시작되자 멸종했다고 믿기도 했었다. 이제 새로운 증거로 이 이론에 이의가 제기되었다. 네안데르탈인 거주 지역에서 전에도 곡물이 발견되었지만, 식량을 얻기 위해 재배한 것인지 혹은 다른 어떤 이유에서 재배한 것인지는 밝혀지지 않았다. 새로운 발견은 네안데르탈인의 입 안에서 음식이 발견되었으므로 곡식을 실제로 먹었다는 것을 보여준다.

[예시 4]

1. The researchers asked 300 people, half of whom had health problems, a long list of "what if" questions. ① What if they arrived at a party wearing exactly the same clothes as someone else there? What if a waiter spilled a drink on them at a meal out with friends? Would they be able to laugh it off? 1) It was found that people with health problems were 40 percent less likely to see the humor in such situations than healthy people. 2. We know that exercising, not smoking, and eating healthy foods will reduce the risk of diseases. Perhaps regular, hearty laughter **should** be added to the list.

중심소재: 건강상태파악 목록
1. 도입부 = 구체적 진술
조사로 글을 시작하고 있다 → 건강상에 문제가 있는 사람에게 ①과 같은 질문을 조사
1) **뒷받침 근거**(조사에서 발견한 사실)
건강상에 문제가 있는 사람은 건강한 사람과 달리 위의 상황을 웃으며 넘기지 못하는 경우가 많다.
2. **일반진술(요지)**
웃음을 건강상태파악 목록에 넣어야 한다.

| 해설
구체적 조사를 먼저 제시하고, 조사를 통해 발견한 사실을 통해 글쓴이의 주장을 이끌어 내고 있다.

| 해석
연구자들이 300명의 사람에게 긴 목록의 '만일 ~라면?'이라는 질문을 했는데, 그 중의 절반은 건강상의 문제가 있는 사람들이었다. 만일 그들이 파티에 갔는데 그곳의 어느 누군가가 똑같은 옷을 입고 있다면? 친구와 외식을 하러 갔는데 종업원이 그들에게 물을 쏟는다면? 그냥 웃어넘길 수 있겠는가? 건강에 문제가 있는 사람들이 그런 상황에서 웃음을 발견하는 것이 건강한 사람들보다 40% 정도 적다는 연구결과가 나왔다. 우리는 운동과 금연, 건강식품 섭취가 질병의 위험을 낮춘다는 것을 알고 있다. 늘 마음껏 웃는 것도 그 (건강확인) 목록에 덧붙여져야 할 것이다.

[예시 5]

1. There is a famous psychology experiment to help us understand how opinions and judgements can be formed. 1) The general experiment procedure was devised by Dr. Asch in the U.S. What happens is this: A volunteer is asked to join a group for the study of the discrimination of length. And he goes to a room where a number of people and the experimenter are seated. The volunteer doesn't know that the other people in the room are researchers working together with the experimenter. A pair of cards is introduced. On one of them there is a line and on the other, three lines. Of these three, one is clearly longer than the line on the other card, one is shorter and one the same length. Seeing the cards, everyone is in turn asked which of the three lines on

중심소재: 의견과 판단 → 의견과 판단의 형성
실험이 등장하는 지문이다. 실험의 목적·의도는 글쓴이가 글을 통해 다루려는 내용이고, 실험의 결과 또는 결과로부터 발견한 사실은 글의 요지에 해당한다.
1. **도입부 = 일반진술**
'의견과 판단의 형성(주제)'에 관한 글로 실험을 통해 사람들의 의견과 판단이 구체적으로 어떻게 형성하는지 이어질 것을 예상할 수 있다.
1) **구체적 진술**
실험의 구체적 내용

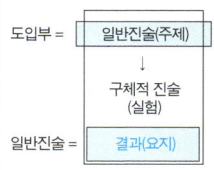

167

the second card is equal to the line on the first. They all pick —as they have been told to pick— the wrong line. Last of all, comes the turn of our volunteer. In many cases the volunteer, faced with the opinion of the group, denies the plain evidence of his senses and picks the same one as others do.
2. This experiment shows even the sane and ordinary people could be made to deny the obvious facts, feeling the pressure to conform. The people around you, "the pressure group" can have a great influence on your judgement and decisions.

결과를 나타내는 시그널★로 'show, reveal, indicate, find out' 등의 표현이 있다.

2. 일반진술(요지)
실험의 결과(show)를 통해 발견한 사실: 정상적인 사람이라도 주변 사람들의 압력이 작용할 때 자신의 바른 판단과 결정을 뒤집는다.

| 해설
글의 제목은 주제가 될 수 있는 동시에 글의 요지를 드러내는 표현 또한 제목 자체로 쓸 수 있다. 본문 같은 경우 한 사람이 판단과 결정을 내릴 때 주변인의 압력을 의식한다는 내용이므로 본문에 제시된 'Pressure to Conform'으로 잡을 수 있다. 주제를 좀 더 구체적으로 드러내는 제목을 설정한다면 'Great Influence of the Pressure to Conform on People's Judgement and Decisions' 이다.

| 해석
의견과 판단이 어떻게 형성되는지 이해하는 데 도움을 주는 유명한 심리학 실험이 있다. 그 일반적인 실험 절차는 미국의 Asch 박사가 고안하였다. 그 절차는 이렇다. 한 자원자가 길이 구별 연구를 위한 그룹에 합류할 것을 요청받는다. 그리고 그는 많은 사람과 실험자가 앉아 있는 방으로 간다. 그 자원자는 방안에 있는 다른 사람들이 실험자와 함께 일하는 연구원이라는 것을 모른다. 한 쌍의 카드가 소개된다. 그 카드 중 한 장에는 하나의 선이 있고, 다른 한 장에는 세 개의 선이 있다. 세 개의 선 중 하나는 다른 카드에 있는 선보다 분명히 길고, 다른 하나는 더 짧으며, 나머지 하나는 길이가 똑같다. 카드를 보면서, 모든 사람은 차례로 두 번째 카드에 있는 세 개의 선 중 어느 선이 첫 번째 카드의 선과 길이가 같은지 질문을 받는다. 그들은 모두—그렇게 고르라고 말을 들었기 때문에—틀린 선을 고른다. 마침내, 자원자의 차례가 온다. 많은 경우에, 그룹의 의견에 직면한 자원자는 그의 감각을 통한 분명한 증거를 부정하고 다른 이들이 고른 것과 똑같은 선을 고른다. 이 실험은 분별 있고 평범한 사람들도 순응해야 한다는 압력을 느낄 때는 명백한 사실을 부정하게 될 수 있다는 것을 보여준다. 우리 주변의 사람들, 즉 "압력 집단"은 우리의 판단과 결정에 큰 영향을 줄 수 있다.

[예시 6]

1. In a study, hundreds of participants were asked to watch a short film and then discuss it with another participant. Half the participants were given an "impression management goal" to appear outgoing, smart, or happy. After the discussions, participants rated themselves and the person they had chatted with across several personality traits. 1) Those with an impression management goal rated their conversation partner significantly lower on the trait they were

1. 도입부 = 구체적 진술
구체적인 연구를 소개하며 글을 시작하고 있다: 단편 영화를 보고 다른 참여자와 논의함. 참가자 중 반은 인상관리 목표(다른 사람에게 활기차거나, 똑똑하거나 행복하다는 인상을 주는 것)를 부여받음

1) 실험의 결과: 자신에게 부여받은 인상(예를 들어 활발함)은 상대방에게 낮은 점수를 부여함.

① 이유: 자신에게 부여받은 인상을 과장하기 때문에 이 특성에 대한 기준

trying to show in themselves, but not on other personality traits. ① This seems to happen because when we focus on exaggerating a particular trait in ourselves, we unconsciously increase the standard for that trait in others — and they usually fall short. 2. So just because someone you're trying to impress does not seem as active, friendly or positive as you are, don't assume that they truly are not. It could just be that what impression you are trying to give to others has changed the game.

을 높게 잡는 경향을 보이게 됨. 그래서 상대방의 이런 특성은 자연스럽게 낮게 평가됨 – 실험의 요지
2. 일반진술(요지)
실험을 통해 궁극적으로 전달하려는 내용으로 '상대방에게 주려는 특정 인상 때문에 상대방의 그런 특성을 낮게 평가 말아야 한다' 가 요지다.

| 해설
실험을 통해서 글쓴이가 궁극적으로 전달하려는 사항을 이끌어 내고 있다. 주의할 점은 실험의 결과에서 이끌어 낸 사실은 글의 요지에 해당하고, 이를 바탕으로 글쓴이가 전달하고자 하는 사실은 글쓴이의 주장이 된다는 점을 구분해야 한다. 본문에서 실험을 통해 글쓴이가 궁극적으로 전달하려고 하는 사항은 '상대방에게 주려는 특정한 인상 때문에 상대방의 그런 특성을 낮게 평가하지 말아야 한다' 는 내용이다.

| 해석
한 연구에서는 수백 명의 참가자가 단편 영화를 본 후 이것을 다른 참가자들과 함께 토론하도록 했다. 참가자 중 절반의 사람들은 스스로 외향적이거나, 똑똑하거나, 행복한 것처럼 보이도록 하는 '인상 관리 목표' 를 부여받았다. 토론이 끝난 후 참가자들은 자기 자신과 그들이 대화를 나눈 사람들의 여러 성격적 특징에 대해 평가했다. 인상 관리 목표를 부여받은 사람들은 자신이 보여주도록 요청된 특성에 대해서는 함께 대화한 사람들에게 상당히 낮은 점수를 부여했다. 그러나 다른 특성들에 대해서는 그렇지 않았다. 이것은 사람들이 자신에 해당하는 어떤 특성을 과장하는 것에 초점을 맞출 때, 우리가 무의식적으로 다른 사람이 가지고 있는 해당 특성에 대한 기준을 상승시켜, 다른 사람들이 대부분 그 기준에 미치지 못하기 때문에 생기는 것으로 보인다. 그러므로 여러분이 인상을 주고 싶어 하는 누군가가 여러분만큼 활기차거나, 친절하거나, 적극적으로 보이지 않는다는 이유만으로 그들이 정말로 그렇지 않다고 가정하지 말아야 한다. 이것은 당신이 다른 사람에게 주고 싶어 하는 인상이 바로 그 게임의 규칙을 바꿀 수 있기 때문이다.

[실전응용 1] 글의 유형에 유의하면서 본문을 분석하시오.

Recent studies have shown that the more lasting effects of hormones ultimately result in the activation of specific genes. For example, when a steroid hormone enters a cell, it binds to a receptor in the cell's cytoplasm. The receptor becomes activated and enters the cell's nucleus, where it binds to specific sites in the deoxyribonucleic acid (DNA), the long molecules that contain individual genes. This activates some genes and inactivates others, altering the cell's activity. Hormones have also been shown to regulate ribonucleic acids (RNA) in protein synthesiss.

중심소재:
1. 도입부

1) 뒷받침 진술

[실전응용 2] 글의 유형에 유의하면서 본문을 분석하시오.

People avoid feedback because they hate being criticized. Psychologists have a lot of theories about why people are so sensitive to hearing about their own imperfections. One is that they associate feedback with the critical comments received in their younger years from parents and teachers. Whatever the cause of our discomfort is, most of us have to train ourselves to seek feedback and listen carefully when we hear it. Without that training, the very threat of critical feedback often leads us to practice destructive, maladaptive behaviors that negatively affect not only our work but the overall health of our organizations.

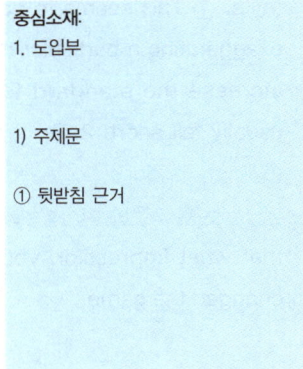

중심소재:
1. 도입부

1) 주제문

① 뒷받침 근거

[실전응용 3] 글의 유형에 유의하면서 본문을 분석하시오.

Flea trainers have observed a predictable and strange habit of fleas while training them. They trained fleas by putting them in a cardboard box with a top on it. The fleas will jump up and hit the top of the cardboard box over and over again. As you watch them jump and hit the lid, something very interesting becomes obvious. The fleas continue to jump, but they are no longer jumping high enough to hit the top. When you take off the lid, the fleas continue to jump, but they will not jump out of the box. They won't jump out because they have conditioned themselves to jump just so high. Many times, people do the same thing. They restrict themselves and never reach their potential, failing to jump higher like the fleas.

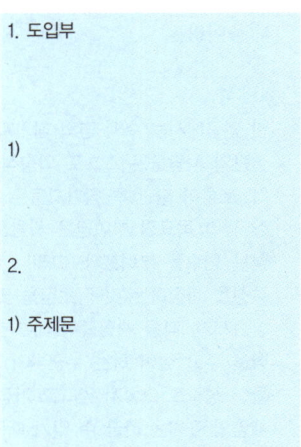

1. 도입부

1)

2.

1) 주제문

[실전응용 4] 글의 유형에 유의하면서 본문을 분석하시오.

Most of us make at least three important decisions in our lives: where to live, what to do, and whom to do it with. We choose our towns, our jobs, and our spouses and friends. Making these decisions is such a natural part of adulthood that it is easy to forget that we are among the first human beings to make them. For most of recorded history, people lived where they were born, did what their parents had done, and associated with those who were doing the same. Social and physical structures were the great dictators that determined how and where people would spend their lives.

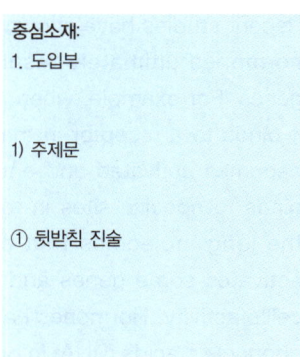

중심소재:
1. 도입부

1) 주제문

① 뒷받침 진술

This left most folks with little to decide for themselves. But the industrial and technological revolutions changed all that, and the resulting explosion of personal liberty created an array of options, alternatives, and decisions that our ancestors never faced.

[실전응용 5] 글의 유형에 유의하면서 본문을 분석하시오.

There is evidence that the usual variety of high blood pressure is, in part, a familial disease. Since families have similar genes as well as similar environment, familial diseases could be due to shared genetic influences, to shared environmental factors, or both. For some years, the role of one environmental factor commonly shared by families, namely dietary salt, has been studied at Brookhaven National Laboratory. The studies suggest that excessive ingestion of salt can lead to high blood pressure in men and animals. Some individuals and some rats, however, consume large amounts of salt without developing high blood pressure. No matter how strictly all environmental factors were controlled in these experiments, some salt-fed animals never developed hypertension, whereas a few rapidly developed very severe hypertension followed by early death. These marked variations were interpreted to result from differences in genetic makeup.

중심소재:
1. 도입부

1) 근거

2.

3. 요지

[실전응용 6] 글의 유형에 유의하면서 본문을 분석하시오.

A team of researchers found out the alarming low death rate of a small village of Roseto and started to investigate it. While investigating, they realized that the secret of Roseto wasn't diet or exercise or genes or location. They looked at how the Rosetans visited one another. They learned about the extended family clans that underlay the town's social structure. They saw how many homes had three generations living under one roof, and how much respect grandparents commanded. They noticed the particular belief in equality of the community, which discouraged the wealthy from boasting about their success and helped the unsuccessful obscure their failures. These findings suggested the Rosetans had created a closely connected and protective social structure.

중심소재:
1. 도입부

1) 뒷받침 진술

2. 요지

[실전응용 7] 글의 유형에 유의하면서 본문을 분석하시오.

Erik Erikson, well-known for his psycho-social development theory, says that the first issue an infant faces right after birth is trust. He emphasizes that trust is the most important factor in the child's developing personality and love, quality not quantity, is the key. According to Erikson, basic trust involves having the courage to let go of the familiar and take a step toward the unknown. Studies suggest that when a healthy trust is formed from the start of life, it leads one to moral, honest, balanced conduct in relations with others.

중심소재:
1. 도입부

1) 뒷받침 진술

[실전응용 8] 글의 유형에 유의하면서 본문을 분석하시오.

White people often avoid mentioning race because they fear even noticing skin color might somehow make them appear racist, but two new studies from psychologists at Tuffs and Harvard universities show that such "strategic color blindness" can backfire. White participants studied a batch of photographs, then tried to deduce, as quickly as possible, which picture a black partner was holding by asking questions about each one in succession. Asking whether the person pictured was black or white would have sped up their performance, yet subjects—adults in one study and children as young as age 10 in the other—rarely mentioned race unless their partner did so first. Black observers who watched the recorded interactions perceived whites who avoided talking about race as more prejudiced than the intrepid few who acknowledged skin color. And blacks who watched silent video clips of the interactions even rated whites who avoided mentioning race as having more unfriendly nonverbal behavior.

중심소재:
1. 도입부

1) 뒷받침 진술

[실전응용 9] 글의 유형에 유의하면서 본문을 분석하시오.

After an event, all one has are memories of it. Because most waits expect a desired outcome, it is the memory of the outcome that dominates, not the intermediate components. If the overall outcome is pleasurable enough, any unpleasantness suffered along the way is minimized. Terence Mitchell and Leigh Thompson call this 'rosy

중심소재:
1. 도입부

1) 주제문

retrospection.' Mitchell and his colleagues studied participants in a 12-day tour of Europe, students going home for Thanksgiving vacation and a three-week bicycle tour across California. In all of these cases, the results were similar. Before an event, people looked forward with positive anticipation. Afterward, they remembered fondly. During? Well, reality seldom lives up to expectations, so plenty of things go wrong. As memory takes over, however, the unpleasantness fades and the good parts remain, perhaps to intensify, and even get amplified beyond reality.

1. 00

[실전응용 10] 글의 유형에 유의하면서 본문을 분석하시오.

University students in several of my seminar classes sat in a circle and each student took turns telling the others his or her name. At the end of the round of introductions, the students were asked to write down the names of as many other students as they could remember. In almost every case, students wrote down the names of students that were seated far away from them. However, surprisingly, they were not able to recall the names of students who were seated close to them. This effect was worst for the students who sat on either side of them. What was the reason for such findings? The student who was next in line for an introduction was clearly on edge and after finishing his or her introduction, he or she was preoccupied with calming his or her nerves. The effect was clearly due to the social anxiety they experienced immediately before and after having to introduce themselves to the entire group.

1. 도입부

1) 결과

① 뒷받침 근거(이유)

PART 2
실전대비
유형별 문제

Test 1　주제를 고르는 문제 • 176
Test 2　요지를 고르는 문제 • 193
Test 3　제목을 고르는 문제 • 202
Test 4　내용일치 · 세부사항 확인 문제 • 216
Test 5　실전 종합문제 • 233

Test 1 주제를 고르는 문제

1. 본문을 분석하고, 주제를 고르시오.

Selfishness is not identical with self-love but with its very opposite. Selfishness is one kind of greediness. Like all greediness, it contains an insatiability, as a consequence of which there is never any real satisfaction. Greed is a bottomless pit which exhausts the person in an endless effort to satisfy the need without ever reaching satisfaction. Close observation shows that while the selfish person is always anxiously concerned with himself, he is never satisfied, is always restless, always driven by the fear of not getting enough, of missing something, of being deprived of something. He is filled with burning envy of anyone who might have more. If we observe still closer, especially the unconscious dynamics, we find that this type of person is basically not fond of himself, but deeply dislikes himself.

① The Attribute of Selfishness
② Self-love and Its Opposition
③ The Unconscious Dynamics
④ Insatiability and Greediness

중심소재:
1. 도입부

1) 뒷받침 진술

2. 요지

2. 본문을 분석하고, 주제를 고르시오.

The Industrial Revolution brought the big machine to the world. It ushered in the Machine Age. What is a machine? It is a big tool to help man to do his work. Man has been called a tool-making animal, and from his earliest days he has made tools and tried to better them. His supremacy over the other animals, many of them more powerful than he was, was established because of his tools. The tool was an extension of his hand; or you may call it a third hand. The machine was the extension of the tool. The tool and the machine raised man above the brute creation. They freed human

중심소재:
1. 도입부

1) 뒷받침 진술

society from the bondage of Nature. With the help of the tool and the machine, man found it easier to produce things. He produced more, and yet had more leisure. And this resulted in the progress of the arts of civilization, and of thought and science.

① Freedom of Nature
② Mechanical Age
③ Industrial Revolution
④ Machine Factory

3. 본문을 분석하고, 주제를 고르시오.

In a famous series of studies, Calhoun(1962) placed rats in cages specifically designed to produce very high densities in certain areas. The animals in these cages exhibited a wide range of abnormal behavior. They fought violently, mated indiscriminately, trampled nests and the young who were in them, and failed to build adequate nests in the first place. Calhoun called this phenomenon of antisocial and disruptive behavior a behavioral sink. Although other work had failed to find these effects on aggressiveness, there is little doubt that under some circumstances high density does cause a breakdown in normal social behavior.

In any case, humans are not rats. We have much more complex social systems, higher levels of congenital functioning, all sorts of rules and laws and customs with which to deal with the environment, and a flexible system of communication with other people. Generalizing from work on other animals to humans is always both difficult and questionable. This is particularly true when complicated social factors and interpersonal relations are involved. Thus, although this work on other animals is suggestive, we must wait for more research on humans to discover how they respond to crowding.

① The danger of generalization
② The impact of crowding on humans
③ The relationship between rats and humans
④ Density and life

4. 본문을 분석하고, 주제를 고르시오.

In ancient times wealth was measured and exchanged tangibly, in things that could be touched: food, tools, and precious metals and stones. Then the barter system was replaced by coins, which still had real value since they were pieces of rare metal. Coins were followed by fiat money, paper notes that have value only because everyone agrees to accept them. Today electronic monetary systems are gradually being introduced that will transform money into even less tangible forms, reducing it to arrays of "bits and bytes," of units of computerized information, whizzing between machines at the speed of light. Already, electronic fund transfer allows money to be instantly sent and received by different banks, companies, and countries through computers and telecommunications devices.

① Current Problems in the Economy
② The History of Exchange System
③ The Development of Paper Currencies
④ International Banking Policies

5. 본문을 분석하고, 주제를 고르시오.

Imagine that we stand on any ordinary seaside pier, and watch the waves rolling in and striking against the iron columns of the pier. Large waves pay very little attention to the columns — they divide right and left and reunite after passing each column, much as a regiment of soldiers would if a tree stood in their road; it is almost as though the columns had not been there. But the short waves and ripples find the columns of the pier a much more formidable obstacle. When the short waves impinge on the columns — they are "scattered." The obstacle provided by the iron columns hardly affects the long waves at all but scatters the short ripples.

We have been watching a sort of working model of the way in which sunlight struggles through the earth's atmosphere. Between us on earth and outer space, the atmosphere interposes innumerable obstacles in the form of air, tiny droplets of water, and small particles of dust. These are represented by the columns of the pier.

The waves of the sea represent the sunlight. We know that sunlight is a blend of lights of many colors — as we can prove for ourselves by passing it through a prism, or even through a jug of water, or as Nature demonstrates to us when she passes it through the raindrops of a summer shower and produces a rainbow. We also know that light consists of waves, and that the different colors of light are produced by waves of different lengths, red light by long waves and blue light by short waves. The mixture of waves which constitutes sunlight has to struggle through the obstacles it meets in the atmosphere, just as the mixture of waves of the seaside has to struggle past the columns of the pier. And these obstacles treat the light waves much as the columns of the pier treat the sea waves. The short waves which constitute blue light are scattered in all directions. Furthermore, the different constituents of sunlight are treated in different ways as they struggle through the earth's atmosphere. A wave of blue light may be scattered by a dust

본문 분석 …▸

particle and turn out of its course. After a time a second dust particle again turns it out of its course, and so on, until it finally enters our eyes by a path as zigzag as that of a flash of lightning.

① Waves and Sunlights
② How the Atmosphere Affects Light Waves
③ Why the Sky Looks Blue
④ The Relationship of Sunlight to Sea Wave

6. 주제를 가장 잘 나타내는 문장을 고르시오.

(A) Stereotypes influence the way we process information. (B) We tend to remember favorable information about outgroups. This, in turn, affects the way we interpret incoming messages from members of in-groups and out-groups. (C) We interpret incoming messages in a way that is consistent with our stereotypes, when we are not mindful. (D) Sorority and fraternity members, for example, know how much money they raise for charity, but nonmembers may not recall this information even after reading it in the student newspaper because it is inconsistent with their stereotypes of fraternities and sororities.

중심소재:
1. 도입부

1) 뒷받침 진술

① (A)   ② (B)   ③ (C)   ④ (D)

7. 빈칸 (A)에 어울리는 주제문을 고르시오.

_____(A)_____. The type most people think of immediately is alcoholism. People who cannot stop drinking until they become intoxicated have an addiction that is usually as much physical as psychological. Another example is an addiction to gambling. Some people are so drawn to the possibility of "striking it rich" that they gamble even their rent and food budget and become penniless in their search for fortune. Another type of addictive behavior is overeating. To compensate for some psychological problems in their lives, some people eat much more than needed to satisfy their hunger. Even though they aren't in the least hungry, they can't resist reaching for one more slice of pizza or piece of cake. Psychiatrists often treat patients with addictive behaviors that are ruining their lives.

중심소재:
1. 도입부

1) 뒷받침 진술

① Alcoholism is hard to stop.
② Addictions are really dangerous.
③ Everybody has some kinds of addictions.
④ There are many different kinds of addictions.

8. 빈칸에 들어갈 주제문으로 가장 적합한 것을 고르시오.

_____. Never anywhere has there been matter without motion, nor can there be. Motion in cosmic space, mechanical motion of smaller masses on the various celestial bodies, the motion of molecules as heat or as electrical or magnetic currents, chemical decomposition and combination, organic life—at each given moment each individual atom of matter in the world is in one or other of these forms of motion, or in several forms at once. All rest, all equilibrium is only relative, and has meaning only in relation to one or other definite form of motion.

① Every matter has several definite forms
② Motion is the mode of existence of matter
③ Motion varies according to the size of matter
④ It is matter which causes the variety of motion

중심소재:
1. 도입부

1) 뒷받침 진술

9. 본문을 분석하고, 주제를 고르시오.

Many people think that only children are lucky because of the material goods and attention they receive. But consider that only children have no privacy. Parents always feel entitled to know everything that's going on in an only child's life. Another drawback of only children is they lack the advantages that children with brothers and sisters have. They can never blame a sibling for something that goes wrong, or ask for a privilege that an older brother or sister was given earlier. In addition, only children miss the companionship of siblings. Not only can they be lonely, but they may have trouble making friends later in life because they never learned to get along with a brother or sister.

① Privileges of Only Children
② Loneliness of Only Children
③ Disadvantages of Only Children
④ Relationship Between Parents and Only Children

중심소재:
1. 도입부

1) 뒷받침 근거

10. 본문을 분석하고, 주제를 고르시오.

There are basically two types of families: nuclear families and extended families. The nuclear family usually consists of two parents and their children. The mother and father form the nucleus, or center, of the nuclear family. The children stay in the nuclear family until they grow up and marry. The extended family is very

중심소재:
1. 도입부
1) 뒷받침 문장

large. There are often many nuclear families in one extended family. An extended family includes children, parents, grandparents, uncles, aunts, and cousins. The members of an extended family are related by blood or by marriage. They are all related, so the members of an extended family are called relatives.

① The Importance of Family Value
② The Importance of Being Relatives
③ The Superiority of The Extended Family
④ The Difference Between the Nuclear Family and the Extended Family

11. 본문을 분석하고, 주제를 고르시오.

With 950 million people, India ranks second to China (1.2 billion) among the most populous countries. But since China launched a draconian birth control program in 1971, India has been closing the gap. Indians have reduced their own fertility but not nearly as much as the Chinese have. If current growth rates continue, India's population will pass China's around the year 2028 at about 1.7 billion. Should that happen, it won't be the fault of the enlightened women of Kerala, a state in southern India. While India as a whole adds almost 20 million people a year, Kerala's population is virtually stable. The reason is no mystery: close to two-thirds of Kerala women practice birth control, compared with about 40% in the entire nation. The difference lies in the emphasis put on health programs. And an educational tradition and matrilineal customs in parts of Kerala help girls and boys get equally good schooling. While one in three Indian women is literate, 90% of those in Kerala can read and write. Higher literacy rates foster family planning. "Unlike our parents, we know that we can do more for our children if we have fewer of them," says Laila Cherian. She has limited herself to three children—one below the national average of four. That kind of restraint will keep Kerala from putting added pressure on world food supplies.

중심소재:
1. 도입부

1) 예외적 현상

① Effects of Female Education on Birth Control
② A Comparison of the Birth Control Policies between China and India
③ High Population Growth Rates in China and India
④ Population Explosion in India
⑤ Learning about Birth Control

12. 본문을 분석하고, 주제를 고르시오.

A married man and woman, who take no greater excursions outside themselves than an occasional turning-on of the radio or an occasional watching together of a movie, are both likely to feel frustrated and confined, and to express these obscurely entertained feelings by an everlasting wrangle. It is notorious that the business or professional man, who has confined his whole interest to his business or profession, is likely not to survive his retirement for very long. Ennui, expressing itself via heart or kidneys or arteries, drops him in his tracks. The physical organism has no reason to go on continuing. In contrast, men devoted to hobbies and similar interests have a way of continuing into great old age, still lively and alert and inquisitive as chipmunks.

① How to Survive the Retirement Long
② Ennui and Health
③ Importance of Hobbies
④ How to Keep Balance between Family and Work
⑤ How to Be as Inquisitive as Chipmunks

중심소재:
1. 도입부

1) 부연 강조

2. 주제문

13. 본문을 분석하고, 주제를 고르시오.

Television's variety becomes a narcotic, not a stimulus. Its serial, kaleidoscopic exposures force us to follow its lead. The viewer is on a perpetual guided tour: 30 minutes at the museum, 30 at the cathedral, 30 for a drink, then back on the bus to the next attraction—except on television, typically, the spans allotted are on the order of minutes or seconds, and the chosen delights are more often car crashes and people killing on another. In short, a lot of television usurps one of the most precious of all human gifts, the ability to focus your attention yourself, rather than just passively surrender it.

① Television and a Guided Tour: Similarities and Differences
② Attractions on Television
③ Pitfalls of Television
④ Kaleidescope and Concentration
⑤ How to Break Free of TV

중심소재:
1. 도입부

1) 뒷받침 근거

2. 요지

14. 본문을 분석하고, 주제를 고르시오.

The high-tech economy is on the ropes and the old economy is coming back with a vengeance. For all the amazing, productivity-

중심소재:

enhancing things the Internet can do, dirty industrial details like the price of oil and the quality of steel still matter. All in all, it's a good time to be in a business where the workers need to scrub their hands at the end of a hard day. The bursting of the high-tech bubble will have consequences for nearly everybody in 2001. Consumers are feeling nervous again and corporations are finding that cash, once so plentiful in a booming stock market, is a scarcer commodity. Economic growth is slowing in many place in the world, with even some hints that a recession is on the way. For the first time in a long while, there's no money to be made just by riding the market momentum. In the economy of 2001, it will be survival of the smartest.

① A Let-down in Consumers' Confidence Rating
② How to Encourage Global Economic Growth
③ A Market Prediction for 2001
④ The Decline of Conventional Economy
⑤ The Productivity-Enhancing Capacity of the Internet

15. 본문을 분석하고, 주제를 고르시오.

One of the most controversial methods of hazardous waste disposal is incineration at sea. Several firms have built sophisticated tanker ships designed to reduce millions of gallons of waste to harmless vapor by burning them. Yet tankers in the United States remain inactive while their owners await governmental approval to operate them. Those who favor incineration over other techniques of waste disposal (such as burying them underground) argue that such tanker ships reduce the need to transport dangerous substances overland. They also point out that the disposal process is carried out in isolated waters, miles away from any population centers. Critics counter that inadequate burning of toxic wastes can produce substances even more deadly, such as certain forms of dioxin. And they say that spills at sea are extremely difficult to clean up, thus increasing the risk of poisoning marine life, upsetting the ecological balance and ultimately harming people.

① Controversy Over the Incineration at Sea
② How to Incinerate Dangerous Substances Safely
③ The Side Effects Caused by Using the Tanker Ships
④ How to Protect Marine Environment by Reducing Wastes

16. 본문을 분석하고, 주제를 고르시오.

When we take the most distant prospect of life, what does it present to us but a chaos of unhappiness, a confused and tumultuous scene of labor and contest, disappointment and defeat? If we view past ages in the reflection of history, what do they offer to our meditation but crimes and calamities? One year is distinguished by a famine, another by an earthquake; kingdoms are made desolate, sometimes by war and sometimes by pestilence; the peace of the world is interrupted at one time by the caprices of a tyrant, at another by the rage of the conqueror. The memory is stored only with vicissitudes of evil; and the happiness, such as it is, of one part of mankind, is found to arise commonly from sanguinary success, from victories which confer upon them the power not so much of improving life by any new enjoyment as of inflicting misery on others and gratifying their own pride by comparative greatness.

중심소재:
1. 도입부

1) 뒷받침 진술

① Reflections on History
② Suffering Humanity
③ A Distant View of Life
④ Fluctuating Failure and Success in Life
⑤ The Price of Victory

17. 본문을 분석하고, 주제를 고르시오.

It is a great nuisance that knowledge cannot be acquired without trouble. It can only be acquired by hard work. It would be fine if we could swallow the powder of profitable information made palatable by the jam of fiction. But the truth is that, so made palatable, we can't be sure that the powder will be profitable. I suggest to you that the knowledge the novelist imparts is biased and thus unreliable, and it is better not to know a thing at all than to know it in a distorted fashion. If readers wish to inform themselves of the pressing problems of the day, they will do better to read, not novels, but the books that specifically deal with them.

중심소재:
1. 도입부

1) 뒷받침 진술

2. 요지(대안)

① Novels: Knowledge Made Palatable
② The Limitations of Novels as a Source of Knowledge
③ The Acquisition of Knowledge
④ Novels: a Distortion of Reality
⑤ Knowledge and Information

18. 본문을 분석하고, 주제를 고르시오.

It is often helpful when thinking about biological processes to consider some apparently similar yet better understood nonbiological process. In the case of visual perception an obvious choice would be color photography. Since in many respects eyes resemble cameras, and percepts photographs, is it not reasonable to assume that perception is a sort of photographic process whereby samples of the external world become spontaneously and accurately reproduced somewhere inside our heads? Unfortunately, the answer must be no. The best that can be said of the photographic analogy is that it points up what perception is not. Beyond this it is superficial and misleading. As an experiment, hungry, thirsty and satiated people are asked to equalize the brightness of pictures depicting food, water and other objects unrelated to hunger or thirst. When the intensities at which they set the pictures are measured it is found that hungry people see pictures relating to food as brighter than the rest (i.e. to equalize the pictures they make the food ones less intense), and thirsty people do likewise with 'drink' pictures. For the satiated group no differences are obtained between the different objects.

① Differences between Perception and Photography
② Biological Processes and Non-biological Processes
③ Perception as a Photographic Process
④ An experimental Research on Perception
⑤ Consciousness and Perception

중심소재:

1. 도입부(전제)

1) 뒷받침 진술

2. 요지(대안)

1) 뒷받침 근거

19. 본문을 분석하고, 주제를 고르시오.

The total impression made by any work of fiction cannot be rightly understood without a sympathetic perception of the artistic aims of the writer. Consciously or unconsciously, he has accepted certain facts, and rejected or suppressed other facts, in order to give unity to the particular aspect of human life which he is depicting. No novelist possesses the impartiality, the indifference, the infinite tolerance of Nature. Nature displays to us, with complete unconcern, the beautiful and the ugly, the pure and the impure, the precious and the trivial. But a writer must select the aspects of Nature and human nature that are demanded by the work in hand. He is forced to select, to combine, to create.

① Unity in Disunity
③ The Novelist's Dilemma
⑤ How to Understand Fiction
② The Tolerance and Impartiality of Nature
④ Nature: the True Novelist

중심소재:

1. 도입부

1) 뒷받침 근거

① 부연 진술

20. 본문을 분석하고, 주제를 고르시오.

In industry, the laser has proven to be a very versatile tool, particularly for cutting and welding. Lasers are now also used in high-speed printing and in the creation of three- dimensional images, called holograms. Laser tracking and ranging systems have been developed, using light signals to measure distance rather than the radio signals of radar. The use of the laser in biological and medical applications is also rapidly expanding, and the laser is already being used with great success in certain surgical procedures. In the field of communications the laser, used in conjunction with fiberoptic networks, is capable of carrying much more information than conventional wires and is setting the stage for the "electronic superhighway" of the near future.

① How Laser was Developed
② The Value of the Laser
③ Too Much Rampant Use of the Laser in Modern Society
④ The Electronic Superhighway and the Laser
⑤ The Extensive Uses of the Laser in Society

21. 본문을 분석하고, 주제를 고르시오.

Back in my early twenties I tried a diet that was limited to just a few healthy foods. Three weeks into it, I had nearly reached my goal of losing eight pounds. But my progress wasn't as sweet as I had expected. One night I abandoned the diet and gorged on every food I'd been missing. Over the next two weeks, I ate more than ever. No surprise that I quickly regained eight pounds, and put on two more. It sounds like the old diet-binge cycle that we've all heard about so often. My brazen act of indulgence was the direct effect of a boring, restrictive diet. "If you tell someone they cannot have, say, a piece of cheesecake, then that is the first thing they want to have," says Dr. Hubbert. "And then when they eat that piece of cheesecake, they say, 'Oh, now I've blown it, so I might as well blow it every day." At Tufts University in Boston, researchers studied 71 healthy men and women aged 20 to 80 years who provided detailed reports of everything they ate for six months. People who routinely ate a variety of nutrient-dense foods such as vegetables, fruits, and whole grains tended to be lean. The researchers found that when people eat a variety of desirable foods, especially vegetables, they eat fewer nutrient-poor, calorie-dense foods such as cookies, candy, and chips. Overall, they consume fewer calories without consciously restricting their intake.

① Importance of a Restrictive Diet
② Dangers of Calorie-Dense Foods
③ Effects of Long-Term Weight Training
④ Advantages of Long-Term Weight Control
⑤ Importance of Eating Nutrient-Dense Foods

22. 본문을 분석하고, 주제를 고르시오.

Psychologists find more inaction, conformity, passivity and reliance on others in the elderly. Yet, desires for mastery and control are likely to remain strong. At the very least, old people are able to continue to make choices and exert control over daily routines. Work of some sort, which imparts a sense of being productive and useful, predicts living to an old age. Research findings suggest that feelings of control actually enhance mental and physical health and promote longevity.

In one series of studies, for instance, psychologists randomly divided nursing home residents from ages 65 to 90 into two groups. Adults in the first group heard a pep talk emphasizing the need to take greater responsibility in caring for themselves and improving the quality of their lives. Members of this high-responsibility group chose a living plant to tend, to symbolize their commitment. The residents in the low-responsibility group were told that the staff would serve them well. Each individual in this group also received a symbolic plant that the nurses would feed and water, just as the nurses planned to take care of them.

What was the result of this experiment? The members of the high responsibility group thrived. They showed significantly more signs of alertness, active participation, and positive feelings than did those in the low responsibility group. The differences lasted long. There was an even more remarkable finding: A sense of control appeared to prolong life, with more patients in the high responsibility group surviving than those in the other group by 15 percent eighteen months later.

1. 도입부

1) 주제문

① 뒷받침 진술

2. 결론(요지)

① Dramatic Changes that Occur through Aging
② Social Responsibility of the Elderly
③ Mental Health Issues of the Elderly
④ Effects of the Sense of Control in Old Age
⑤ Importance of Power Relations among the Aged

23. 본문을 분석하고, 주제를 고르시오.

Copernicus wrote De Revolutionibus Orbium Coelestium, a book explaining his theory of a sun-centered solar system. Copernicus realized that his theory would not be readily accepted and was hesitant to make his ideas public. The Christian religious community placed a great importance on the Earth's role as the center of the heavens. Therefore, he would be contradicting not just the scientific establishment, but also the teaching of the Christian church. Copernicus waited until 1530—twenty-three years—to present his ideas to other scholars. He waited another thirteen years—until just before his death—to have his work published.

중심소재:
1. 도입부

1) 구체적 진술

2. 결과

① How the Theory of Copernicus was Known to the Public
② The Significance of the Sun-centered Solar System
③ The Tension between Science and Religion
④ The Role of Christian Church Regarding the Solar System
⑤ How Copernicus Contributed to the Study of the Solar System

24. 본문을 분석하고, 주제를 고르시오.

One reason that so many people fail is that they lack confidence in themselves. If you think of yourself as being unworthy of great achievement, you will never achieve greatness. If, on the other hand, you know yourself and understand what your abilities are, and if then you determine to accomplish everything of which you are capable, you will certainly stand a much better chance of success. How may one become inspired to realize all his possibilities or to gain confidence in himself? One of the surest ways is for him to associate with persons who have really achieved greatness. It is impossible, however, for most people to come frequently into the actual presence of the great. The next best thing, perhaps, is for him to spend part of his time in reading about great achievers. Biography is a powerful stimulant to action. But these processes will not avail unless one rids himself of a sense of inferiority and determines to do the best that he possibly can. One of our great philosophers expressed the idea in a single sentence when he said that each individual should hitch his wagon to a star.

중심소재:
1. 도입부

1) 의문문

① 답변(요지)

① The Value of Biography
② Worthy Use of Time
③ Outstanding Persons
④ A Sense of Superiority
⑤ Ways of Becoming Successful

25. 본문을 분석하고, 주제를 고르시오.

The profusion of life has a secret: South Georgia is a relatively temperate island in the path of a seasonal swarm of krill borne up by currents from the Antarctic Peninsula—a living river of krill. This river of krill fed the largest herds of fur seals and great whales on Earth in the ages before the sealers and whalers came. Today it is fueling the astonishing resurrection of the Antarctic fur seal, as well as the slow but steady recovery of several whale species.

① Temperature in South Georgia
② Shrinking Number of Krill
③ Resurrecting Fur Seals and Whales
④ Currents and the Weather

26. 본문을 분석하고, 주제를 고르시오.

It has been noticed that traditionally courts have granted divorces on fault grounds: one spouse is deemed to be at fault in causing the divorce. More and more today, however, divorces are being granted on a no-fault basis.

Proponents of no-fault divorce argue that when a marriage fails, it is rarely the case that one marriage partner is completely to blame and the other blameless. A failed marriage is much more often the result of mistakes by both partners.

Another argument in favor of no-fault divorce is that proving fault in court, in a public arena, is a destructive process that only serves to lengthen the divorce process and that dramatically increases the negative feelings present in a divorce. If a couple can reach a decision to divorce without first deciding which partner is to blame, the divorce settlement can be negotiated more easily and equitable and the post-divorce healing process can begin more rapidly.

① What a Divorce is Like
② Traditional Grounds for Divorce
③ The Increase in No-fault Divorces
④ The Various Reasons for Divorces
⑤ Who is at Fault in a Divorce

27. 본문을 분석하고, 주제를 고르시오.

It was necessary for the ancient peoples to grow their own food, since there were no methods of preserving or transporting it. Foods must be preserved from the invasion of bacteria if they are not to be injurious when eaten. In early times it was learned that meat kept longer when temporarily preserved by roasting and smoking, and this was done without any knowledge of bacteria. The Crusaders introduced sugar into Europe from Cyprus, and as a result of this, it was discovered that a heavy syrup made from sugar would preserve fruits and also vegetables and meats. Then it was discovered that foods could be preserved by the use of spices, vinegar and alcohol. You remember from your history that Columbus went before Ferdinand and Isabella of Spain to receive financial aid so that he might find a new route to India to obtain more easily the spices that were in demand at that time for preserving foods. Glass and porcelain were the only containers used in preserving food until 1862, when Thomas Kimmett secured a patent on the use of cans. The canning of foods has increased so greatly that all kinds of foods are being preserved today by this modern method. Modern canning does not change the nutritive values of foods as much as ordinary cooking. The quality of preserved food, whether the preservation is done at home or commercially, depends largely on the selection of the food, the shortness of the interval between harvesting and packing or canning, and the care used in processing or storing.

① Foods of the Ancient Peoples
② Diet and Disease
③ The Transportation of Foods
④ Food Canning
⑤ The Preservation of Foods

28. 본문을 분석하고, 주제를 고르시오.

We are sometimes eager to celebrate the influence of our surroundings. In the living room of a house in the Czech Republic, we see an example of how walls, chairs and floors can combine to create an atmosphere in which the best sides of us are offered the opportunity to flourish. We accept with gratitude the power that a single room can possess.

But sensitivity to architecture also has its more problematic aspects. If one room can alter how we feel, if our happiness can hang on the colour of the walls or the shape of a door, what will happen to us in most of the places we are forced to look at and inhabit? What will we experience in a house with prisonlike windows, stained carpet tiles and plastic curtains? It is to prevent the possibility of permanent anguish that we can be led to shut our eyes to most of what is around us, for we are never far from damp stains and cracked ceilings, shattered cities and rusting dockyards. We can't remain sensitive indefinitely to environments which we don't have the means to alter for the good.

2. 요지(대안)

① What Makes Us Less Sensitive to Architecture
② What Caused the Ugliness of our Physical Surroundings
③ How Architectural Techniques have Changed in Modern Times
④ What Emotions a Beautiful Room of a Czech House can Arouse in Us

29. 본문을 분석하고, 주제를 고르시오.

Children whose parents have foreign accents don't speak with accents. They learn to talk like their peers. Little girls and little boys learn how to have conversations as they learn how to pronounce words from their playmates. Between the ages of five and fifteen, when children are learning to have conversations, they play they learn different ways of having and using conversations. Anthropologists point out that boys and girls socialize differently. Little girls tend to play in small groups or, even more common, in pairs. Their social life usually centers around a best friend, and friendships are made, maintained, and broken by talk—especially secrets. It's hard for newcomers to get into these tight groups, but anyone who is admitted is treated as an equal. Little boys tend to play in larger groups, often outdoors, and they spend more time doing things than talking. It's easy for boys to get into the group, but not everyone is accepted as an equal. Their talk is often competitive talk about who is best at what.

중심소재:
1. 도입부

1) 현상의 이유

2. 또 다른 현상

1) 현상의 이유

① When Do Children Learn to Have Conversations?
② How do Children Learn to Speak Foreign Languages?
③ Why Boys Have More Secrets than Girls?
④ What is a Major Difference between Girls and Boys?

30. 본문을 분석하고, 주제를 고르시오.

George Orwell was the pseudonym of Eric Blair, who was born in India, where his father was a British civil servant. He was sent to private school in England, and won a scholarship to Eton, the foremost "public school" (i.e, private boarding school) in the country. It was at these schools that he first became conscious of

1. 도입부

the difference between his own background and the wealthy background of many of his schoolmates. On leaving school he joined the Imperial Police in Burma (both Burma and India were then still part of the British Empire). His service in Burma from 1922 to 1927 produced a sense of guilt about British colonialism and a feeling that he must make some kind of personal expiation for it. This he would later do with a fiercely anti-colonialist novel, *Burmese Days* (1934). He returned to England determined to be a writer and adopted a pseudonym as one way of escaping from the class position in which his birth and education had placed him.

① Orwell and His Parents
② Orwell and His Jobs
③ Orwell and British Schools
④ Orwell and British Imperialism

Test 2 요지를 고르는 문제

1. Which of the following is the main idea of the passage?

Every winter, especially in cold climates, people sink into the familiar round of illness, with coughing and sore throat being two of the most common symptoms. Sometimes other conditions, such as fever, are also present and people wonder whether they have simply caught a cold or are suffering from the flu. Since the flu can be quite serious, it is wise to be aware of the differences. Coughing, blocked nose, and sore throat are the most common symptoms of colds, and they are often present with the flu as well. Chest pain may also accompany both illnesses, but with the flu it has a tendency to become severe. The symptoms particularly pertaining to the flu, which are rarely, if ever, present with the cold, are headache, high fever, and pains all over the body. Often the flu begins with vague body pains and headache, then quickly gets worse as the victim's body temperature rises. People with the flu may find themselves in bed for several days batting temperatures of 38-39 degrees, and may end up with pneumonia, which is serious. Waking moments may be spent coughing continuously. Though there is presently no cure for the common cold, antibiotics can help fight the flu. And getting a flu shot at the beginning of each season is a particularly good idea.

중심소재:
1. 도입부

1) 문제점 지적

① 주제문

Ⓐ 뒷받침 진술

① There are several cold-weather illnesses.
② It is important to get a flu shot at the beginning of the winter.
③ Temperatures as high as 39 degrees are not uncommon with the flu.
④ Colds and the flu have many similarities but they also have some differences.

2. Which of the following is the main idea of the passage?

As ethnicity became an accepted subject for study in the late 1960s, textbooks were assailed for their failure to portray blacks accurately; within a few years, the textbooks in wide use were carefully screened to eliminate bias against minority groups and women. At the same time, new scholarship about the history of women, blacks, and various ethnic minorities found its way into the textbooks. At first, the multi-cultural content was awkwardly incorporated as little boxes on the side of the main narrative. Then some of the new social historians themselves wrote textbooks, and the main narrative itself began to reflect a broadened historical understanding of race, ethnicity, and class in the American past. Consequently, today's history textbooks routinely incorporate the experiences of women, blacks, American Indians, and various immigrant groups.

중심소재:
1. 도입부

1) 대안(요지)

2.

3. 요지

① Some of the new social historians contributed to raising the quality of the history textbooks.
② The multi-cultural content is not a popular subject for history textbooks.
③ There has been controversy on racial discrimination for more than 40 years.
④ Today the experiences of blacks, and women are described more accurately than before.

3. Which of the following is the main idea of the passage?

There are two ways in which one can own a book. The first is the property right you establish by paying for it, just as you pay for clothes and furniture. But this act of purchase is only the prelude to possession. Full ownership comes only when you have made it a part of yourself, and the best way to make yourself a part of it is by writing in it. An illustration may make the point clear. You buy a beefsteak and transfer it from the butcher's icebox to your own. But you do not own the beefsteak in the most important sense until you consume it and get it into bloodstream. I am arguing that books, too, must be absorbed in your bloodstream to do you any good.

중심소재:
1. 도입부

1) 뒷받침 문장
①

②

① You can own a book simply by paying for it, just as you pay for clothes.
② You can claim your property right after purchasing books.
③ Full ownership of a book comes only when you make it a part of yourself.
④ You have to consume a beefsteak and get it into your bloodstream.

4. Which of the following is the main idea of the passage?

I fully admit that the mischief which a person does to himself may seriously affect, both through their sympathies and their interests, those nearly connected with him and, in a minor degree, society at large. When, by conduct of this sort, a person is led to violate a distinct and assignable obligation to any other person or persons, the case is taken out of the self-regarding class, and becomes amenable to moral disapproval in the proper sense of the term. If, for example, a man, through extravagance, becomes unable to pay his debts, or, having undertaken the moral responsibility of a family, becomes from the same cause incapable of supporting or educating them, he is deservedly criticized, and might be justly punished; but it is for the breach of duty to his family or creditors, not for the extravagance. If the resources which ought to have been devoted to them had been diverted from them for the most prudent investment, the moral culpability would have been the same. Whenever there is a definite damage, or a definite risk of damage, either to an individual or to the public. The case is taken out of the province of liberty, and placed in that of morality or law.

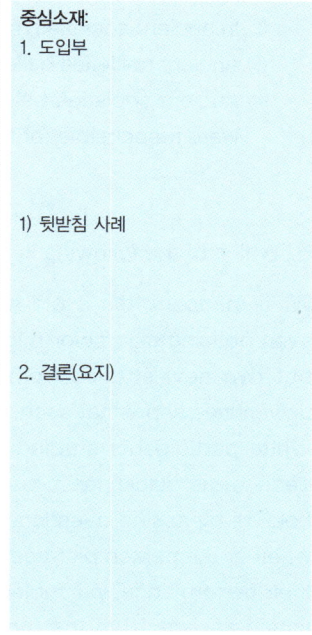

① As a social animal, we should keep in mind the fact that consideration of other people is prior to self-gratification.
② Moral responsibility should be the first principle in the code of social behavior.
③ When pursuing liberty, one should consider moral responsibility.
④ No one can achieve a true sense of freedom without giving up his selfish interests.

5. Which of the following is the main idea of the passage?

Some half a million years ago, ancient societies apparently did not recognize any difference between mental and physical disorders. Abnormal behaviors, from simple headaches to convulsions, were believed to be caused by evil spirits that lived in the victim's body. According to this system of belief—called demonology—those suffering from disease were considered responsible for their misfortune. For example, some Stone Age cave dwellers appear to have treated behavior disorders by a surgical method called trephining. During this procedure, part of the skull was chipped away to make an opening. Once the skull was opened, the evil spirits could escape. It was believed that when the evil spirit left, the person would return to his or her normal state. Surprisingly, several trephined skulls that healed over have been found. This indicates that some patients survived what had to be an extremely crude operation.

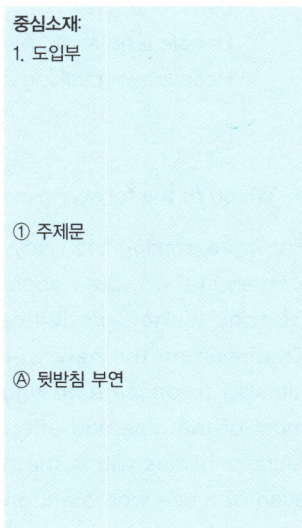

① Stone Age cave dwellers did not differentiate mental disorders from physical illness and treated them with trephining.
② In ancient societies, most patients passed away during the trephining procedure.
③ Ancient societies believed that when the skull was chipped away, the evil spirits could escape.
④ Ancient societies believed that disease was a result of demonic possession and the victims were responsible for their illness.

6. Which of the following is the main idea of the passage?

White people often avoid mentioning race because they fear that even noticing skin color might somehow make them appear racist, but two new studies from psychologists at Tufts and Harvard universities show that such "strategic color-blindness" can backfire. White participants studied a batch of photographs, then tried to deduce, as quickly as possible, which picture a black partner was holding by asking questions about each one in succession. Asking whether the person pictured was black or white would have sped up their performance, yet subjects—adults in one study and children as young as age 10 in the other—rarely mentioned race unless their partner did so first. Black observers who watched the recorded interactions perceived whites who avoided talking about race as more prejudiced than the intrepid few who acknowledged skin color. And blacks who watched silent video clips of the interactions even rated whites who avoided mentioning race as having more unfriendly nonverbal behavior.

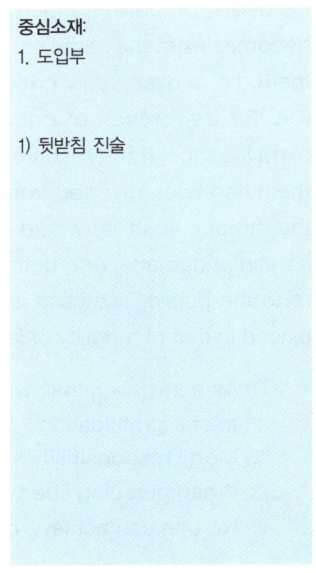

① White people tend to avoid talking about race more frequently than black people.
② According to the two new studies, white people asked whether the person pictured was black or white.
③ People who avoid mentioning race appear more prejudiced.
④ People avoid talking about race because they think that noticing skin color might be unfriendly.

7. Which of the following is the main idea of the passage?

Far more striking than any changes in the kinds of work done by women in the U.S.A. labor force is the shift of wives and mothers from household activities to the world of paid employment. Emphasis on the new work of women, however, should not be allowed to obscure an equally important fact. Today, as always, most of the time and effort of American wives is devoted to their responsibilities within the home and the family circle. This is true even of those who are in the labor force. Since 1890 the demands of paid work have become much lighter. The normal work week has decreased from sixty to forty hours; paid holidays and vacations have become universal; and most of the hard, physical labor that work once required has been eliminated. Because of these developments, many women can work outside the home and still have time and energy left for home and family. Moreover, most working mothers do not assume the burdens of a full schedule of paid work. Among employed mothers of preschool children, four out of five worked only part time or less than half the year in 1956. Among those whose children were in school, three out of five followed the same curtailed work schedule. And even among working wives who had no children at home, only a little more than half were year-round, full-time members of the labor force.

① Even today working women in America take their home and family responsibilities.
② Most women are year-round, full-time members of the labor force.
③ Wives and mothers work in the world of paid employment rather than within the home.
④ Since 1890 the demands of paid work have become lighter.

8. 주제문으로 옳은 것을 고르시오.

(A) A psychology professor introduced the same guest lecturer to two different classes. The first class was told to expect a rather cold, dull, uninteresting person. The second class was told to expect a warm, intelligent, friendly lecturer. (B) The lecturer presented identical information in the same manner to both groups. The first group found his lecture boring and did not ask questions; the second group found him warm and stimulating and asked many questions. (C) This experiment has been replicated successfully many times. (D) The outcome of these experiments suggests that telling someone what to perceive in another person will influence what is experienced.

① (A)　　② (B)　　③ (C)　　④ (D)

9. Which of the following is the main idea of the passage?

Whereas family relationships usually constitute a child's first experience with group life, peer-group interactions soon begin to make their powerful socializing effects felt. From play group to teenage clique, the peer group affords young people many significant learning experiences — how to achieve status in a circle of friends. Peers are equals in a way parents and their children or teachers and their students are not. A parent or teacher sometimes can force young children to obey rules they neither understand nor like, but peers do not have formal authority to do this; thus the true meaning of exchange, cooperation, and equity can be learned more easily in the peer setting. Peer groups increase in importance as the child grows up and reach maximum influence in adolescence, by which time they sometimes dictate much of a young person's behavior both in and out of school.

① Children learn about cooperation in their peer groups.
② Peer groups are powerful influences in children's lives.
③ Parents can force children to do things that a peer group cannot.
④ Parents have greater influences on children than their teachers do.
⑤ Relationships in and out of school provide learning opportunities for children.

10. Which of the following is the main idea of the passage?

The Broken Windows theory was the brainchild of the criminologists James Wilson and George Kelling. They argued that crime is the inevitable result of disorder. If a window is broken and left unrepaired, people walking by will conclude that no one cares and no one is in charge. Soon, more windows will be broken, and the sense of anarchy will spread from the building to the street on which it faces, sending a signal that anything goes. In a city, relatively minor problems like graffiti, public disorder, and aggressive panhandling are all the equivalent of broken windows, invitations to more serious crimes.

What does this suggest? It says that the criminal — far from being someone who acts for fundamental, intrinsic reasons and who live in his own world — is actually someone acutely sensitive to his environment, who is alert to all kinds of cues, and who is prompted to commit crimes based on his perception of the world around him. That is an incredibly radical — and in some sense unbelievable — idea. It says that behavior is a function of social context.

① Most break-ins in the city occur through windows.
② An individual's behavior is deeply influenced by the environment.
③ Minor offenders may become serious criminals in the long run.
④ Criminals are born to disturb the public peace.
⑤ Pedestrians are irresistibly affected by the condition of street-side windows.

11. Which of the following is the main idea of the passage?

Shizuo Torii, a professor at Toho University in Japan, has studied the sense of smell. He studied the effects that odors have on the feelings and behaviors of humans. By measuring the brain waves of people after they smelled a particular odor, Torii found that some odors produced a brain wave pattern that showed the people were calm. Other odors produced a pattern that showed excitement. It was discovered, for example, that lemon and peppermint have an exciting effect; nutmeg and lavender reduce stress; and a mix of rosemary and lemon will improve concentration. Some Japanese corporations are using the results of this research to make the workplace more productive and pleasant.

중심소재:
1. 도입부

1) 실험의 목적

① 결과(요지)

④ 뒷받침 예시

① The smells of lemon and rosemary improve concentration of workers.
② Japanese corporations want to make the workplace more pleasant and efficient.
③ Shizuo Torii is a Japanese professor paid by corporations to improve the workplace environment.
④ A Japanese researcher has discovered that smells affect people's brain waves.
⑤ The sense of smell is not influenced by the brain wave pattern.

12. Which of the following is the main idea of the passage?

Researchers at the University of Michigan are studying the effects of nicotine on the brain. Nicotine is the major drug in cigarettes. Recently they have found that cigarettes give several "benefits" to smokers that may help explain why quitting smoking is so hard. The nicotine in cigarettes seems to help smokers with problems of daily living. It helps them feel calm. Nicotine also caused short-term improvements in concentration, memory, alertness, and feelings of well-being.

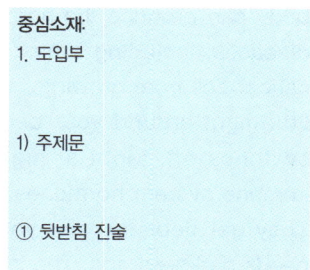

① Researchers at the University of Michigan are studying how to help smokers stop smoking.
② Nicotine improves concentration, memory, and alertness.
③ Some "benefits" of smoking may help explain why smokers have a hard quitting.
④ Researchers at the University of Michigan have developed a new program help people stop smoking.

13. Which of the following is the main idea of the passage?

An important influence on people's ability to cope with stressful situations is the degree of control they feel they can exercise over the situation. Both animals and humans have been found to cope better with painful or threatening stimuli when they feel that they can exercise some degree of control rather than being passive and

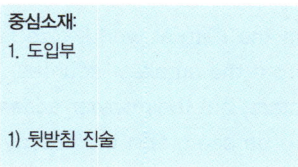

helpless victims. Such a sense of control can help minimize the negative consequences of stress, both psychological and physical In one wellknown experiment, Jay Weiss administered electric shocks to pairs of rats. In each pair, one of the two animals was given a degree of control over the situation; it could reach through a hole in the cage and press a panel that would turn off the shock both for itself and for its partner. Thus, the two rats received exactly the same number of shocks, but one was passive and helpless, and the other was in control. After a continuous 21-hour session, the animals were sacrificed and their stomachs examined for ulcers. Those rats who could exert control had much less ulceration than their helpless partners.

① 부연 진술

① The more control you have over a stressful event, the easier it is to cope with.
② The more you are positive to the situation, the more stressful it is to cope with.
③ The more the rat is negative to the experiment, the easier it is to be endured.
④ The more the rat is stressful to the experience, the easier it is to cope with.

14. Which of the following is the main idea of the passage?

We need darkness to make our immune systems work well. Scientists have now discovered that only when it's really dark your body can produce the hormone called melatonin. Melatonin fights diseases, including breast and prostate cancer. "It turns off the cancer cell from growing," says one scientist. But if there's even a little light around your bed at night, your melatonin production switches off. Light at night, even watching TV turns on other immune system hormones that should be active only in daytime. They get depleted and you're more likely to get a cold. Nature needs darkness, too. The immune systems of animals grow weak if there's artificial light at night.

중심소재:

1. 도입부

1) 뒷받침 근거

① Melatonin is essential to every living things.
② All living things including humans need darkness.
③ We need sleep to keep our immune system active.
④ We have to turn the light off while sleeping at night.

15. Which of the following is the main idea of the passage?

In the natural world, size is deceptive. The greatest power comes from the smallest sources. The largest objects we know of are the stars, but their power arises from the interaction of atoms too small to be seen, and the energy travels to us in waves too intangible to have mass. Human kind had no idea what real power was until a

중심소재:
1. 도입부

1) 뒷받침 진술

half-century ago, when we unlocked the forces of the sub-atomic realm. The same lesson applies to the world of industry: Power lies in the ability to squeeze the most information into the tiniest space and in the ability to make smaller machines that are more efficient.

① In the natural world, size is deceptive.
② The greatest power arises from the interaction of atoms.
③ Human kind unlocked the forces of the sub-atomic realm.
④ The same lesson applies to the world of industry.

16. Which of the following is the main idea of the passage?

Humans are often thought to be insensitive smellers compared with animals, but this is largely because, unlike animals, we stand upright. This means that our noses are limited to perceiving those smells which drift through the air, missing the majority of smells which stick to surfaces. In fact, though, we are extremely sensitive to smells, even if we do not generally realize it.

Strangely, some people find that they can smell, for example, one type of flower but not another, whereas other people are sensitive to the smells of both flowers. This may be because some people do not have the genes necessary to create particular smell receptors in the nose. These receptors are the cells which sense smells and send messages to the brain. However, it has been found that even people who are at first insensitive to a particular smell can suddenly become sensitive to it, if they are exposed to it often enough.

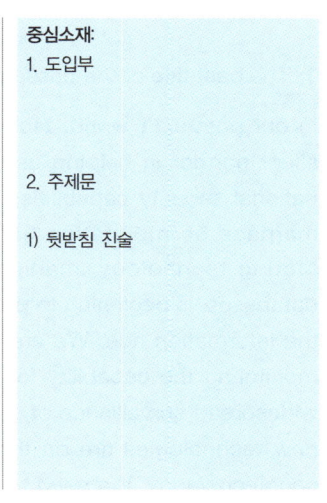

① Humans stand upright.
② Humans can be as sensitive to smells as animals.
③ Some humans have special genes for hearing.
④ Smells stick to surfaces.

17. Which of the following is the main idea of the passage?

The City Transit supervisors have received numerous complaints over the last several weeks about buses on several routes running hot. Drivers are reminded that each route has several checkpoints at which drivers should check the time. If the bus is ahead of schedule, drivers should delay at the checkpoint until it is the proper time to leave. If traffic makes it unsafe for a driver to delay at a particular checkpoint, the driver should proceed at a reasonable speed to the next stop and hold there until the bus is back on schedule.

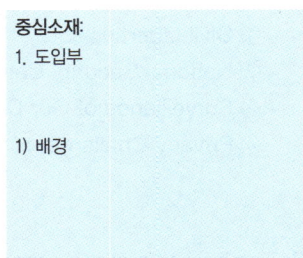

① Drivers should drive at a reasonable speed.
② Drivers should check the time at every stop.
③ Drivers should stop their buses when traffic is congested.
④ Drivers should see that their buses run on schedule.

Test 3 제목을 고르는 문제

1. The best title of the passage is _____.

In our post-9/11 world, technology often has been our crucial but silent partner in helping us to ramp up our law enforcement and national security capabilities. But we also need to do it right. The marriage of information-gathering technology with information-storing technology, manipulated in increasingly sophisticated databases, is beginning to produce the defining privacy challenge of the information age. We are on the verge of a revolution in micro-monitoring the capability for the highly detailed, largely automatic, widespread surveillance of our daily lives. Moreover, other powerful new technologies are on the horizon, like sensor technology and nanotechnology. We need to think about these issues broadly while keeping them from overtaking our civil liberties. Who will have access to those data banks, and under what checks-and-balances? In what cases should law enforcement agencies be able to use this information? There should be a general presumption that Americans can know when their personal information is collected, and to seek, check, and correct any errors.

① Civil Liberties
② National Security Capabilities
③ Surveillance of Our Daily Lives
④ Privacy Challenge of the Information Age

중심소재:
1. 도입부

1)

ⓟ 주제문

Ⓐ 뒷받침 배경

2. 대안

2. The best title of the passage is _____.

Many words have more than one meaning, and occasionally arguers may exploit the ambiguity in language to make a fallacious claim. One way to do this is through the fact that a word has more than

중심소재:

202

one meaning so as to lead to a false conclusion. Equivocation exploits the fact that a word has more than one meaning so as to lead to a false conclusion. Equivocation is often used in deceptive advertising. For example, an advertisement that appeared in several notional publications proclaimed that "Parents can receive FREE college education" for their children. On its face, the bold letters across the top of the ad made a fairly spectacular promise that the average person might find it difficult to ignore. For most people, the word free means something very different to the producers of the ad. To them, free means that parents need to invest a substantial sum of money in their "tax-free open-end mutual funds and unit trust" and pay for a variety of administrative "charges and expenses." The point is that if enough is invested, then the interest produced should be sufficient to send a child to college. Words thus mean different things to different people, and when word choice misdirects the audience's understanding of the argument, then an equivocation has taken place.

① Fallacy of Equivocation
② Deceptive Advertisement
③ How to Become a Smart Consumer
④ How to Eliminate the Ambiguity of Language

1. 도입부

1) 주제문

① 뒷받침 예시

3. 다음 글을 읽고 질문에 답하시오.

During the first few of life, when babies' cells continue to undergo "programming," exposure to certain toxic chemicals can disrupt the delicate process. Bisphenol A (known as BPA), a compound in hard, clear polycarbonate plastics that mimics the effects of estrogen, has raised particular concern because it interferes with hormone levels and cell signaling system. In August, several dozen scientists issued a review of 700 studies on BPA warning that the levels most people are exposed to put them at, elevated risk of getting cancer. Infants, the report said, are most vulnerable to BPA. "Plastic bottles and plated that are boiled or put in the microwave or dishwashers are especially problematic because heating them repeatedly causes high amounts of BPA to leach out," says Retha Newbold, a reproductive biologist at the NIEHS in Triangle Park, N.C. Once small cracks form in the surface, a product should be discarded. She recommends that parents, to be on the safe side, switch to glass bottles of those with disposable plastic liners that don't contain BPA. And they should use microwave-safe pager plates of glass dishes covered with pater towel rather than plastic wrap.

중심소재:
1. 도입부

1) 주제문

① 뒷받침 근거

2. 결론(대안)

문제 1. The best title of the above passage would be _____.

① the Problem with Plastic
② new Reasons to Watch What You Eat
③ the Influence of Chemicals on Human Beings
④ some Factors to Increase Cancers in Babies
⑤ the Side Effects of Modern Kitchenwares

문제 2. The main point of the passage would be _____.

① it is a tough job to raise the baby safely
② the environment is getting more and more contaminated
③ there is no way to escape from the dangers of chemicals
④ humans are working hard to get rid of the pollution
⑤ the chemical BPA is especially bad for babies

4. The best title of the passage is _____.

An interesting fact about adolescents is that their sleep-wake cycle gets delayed by up to two hours. This means they don't become sleepy until later in the night and, subsequently, wake up later in the morning. Children under 13 begin to secrete melatonin — the hormone that makes them sleepy — at around eight or nine o'clock at night. Most teenagers secrete melatonin at around 11pm. So, essentially, any time before this is a no-sleep zone for teens; they physically cannot fall asleep. At the other end of the sleep zone is cortisol, the chemical responsible for waking us up. Cortisol isn't secreted in teenagers until around 8:15 am, and that's usually too late to make it to school on time. So if your teenage son is dreamily vague and rubbing the sleep out of his eyes breakfast, remember this; if his brain had its way, he'd still be tucked up in bed. For parents who are trying to get the household out the door on time each morning, this sleepiness can easily be misconstrued as laziness. Insead of giving angry admonitions or well-meaning motivational lectures, try to realize that your teenager is just battling his or her physiology. It may be better to try to be his brain for a time — do the thinking for him.

중심소재:
1. 도입부

1) 뒷받침 근거

2. 요지

① Aging and Sleep
② Brain and Sleep
③ Sound Sleep and Health
④ The Science of Sleep for Teens
⑤ The Secret of Sleep: Melatonin and Cortisol

5. Which of the following is the best title for the passage?

The quest for manliness is essentially right-wing, cowardly, neurotic, and fueled largely by a fear of women. The youth who is misled into believing in the masculine ideal is conveniently separated from women, and he spends the rest of his life finding women a riddle and a nuisance. Masculinity celebrates the exclusive company of men. That is why it is so grotesque; and that is also why there is no manliness that is absolutely complete—because it denies men the natural friendship of women.

Of course, there is a female version of this male affliction. It begins with mothers encouraging little girls to say, "Do you like my new dress?" In a sense, little girls are traditionally urged to please others with a kind of coquettishness, while boys are enjoined to behave like monkeys towards each other. The nine-year-old coquette proceeds to become womanish in a subtle power game in which she learns to be sexually indispensable, socially decorative, and always alert to a man's needs. Femininity—being ladylike—implies needing a man as witness and seducer.

① The Quest for Manliness
② The Search for Femininity
③ Misguided Sexual Identities
④ Masculine and Feminine Ideals

6. Which of the following is the best title for the passage?

Books are the greatest and the most satisfactory recreation. I mean the use of book for pleasure. Without books, without having acquired the power of reading for pleasure, none of us can be independent, but if we can read we have a sure defence against boredom in solitude. If we have not that defence, we are dependent on the charity of family, friends, or even strangers to save us from boredom. But if we can find delight in reading, even a long railway journey alone ceases to be tedious, and long winter evenings are to ourselves an inexhaustible opportunity for pleasure.

① How to Choose Good Books
② How to Write a Book
③ Books as a Means of Recreation
④ The Relationship between Books and Friends

7. Which of the following is the best title for the passage?

What hunger is in relation to food, zest is in relation to life. The man who enjoys watching football is to that extent superior to the man who does not. The man who enjoys reading is still more superior to the man who does not, since opportunities for reading are more frequent than opportunities for watching football. The more things a man is interested in, the more opportunities of happiness he has, and the less he is at the mercy of fate, since if he loses one thing he can fall back upon another. Life is too short to be interested in every thing, but it is good to be interested in as many things as are necessary to fill our days.

① The Comparison between Food and Life
② The Way to be a Superior Man
③ Having a Good Relationship with Other People
④ The Road to Happiness

8. 제목으로 가장 적절한 것을 고르시오.

I fully admit that the mischief which a person does to himself may seriously affect, both through their sympathies and their interests, those nearly connected with him and, in a minor degree, society at large. When, by conduct of this sort, a person is led to violate a distinct and assignable obligation to any other person or persons, the case is taken out of the self-regarding class, and becomes amenable to moral disapproval in the proper sense of the term. If, for example, a man, through extravagance, becomes unable to pay his debts, or, having undertaken the moral responsibility of a family, becomes from the same cause incapable of supporting or educating them, he is deservedly criticized, and might be justly punished; but it is for the breach of duty to his family or creditors, not for the extravagance. If the resources which ought to have been devoted to them had been diverted from them for the most prudent investment, the moral culpability would have been the same. Whenever there is a definite damage, or a definite risk of damage, either to an individual or to the public, the case is taken out of the province of liberty, and placed in that of morality or law.

① On Liberty
② How to Educate People
③ The Conquest of Happiness
④ The Difference between Private and public Life

9. 제목으로 가장 적절한 것을 고르시오.

In other words, science gives us power which can be used either constructively or destructively. It provides us with means which may facilitate our pursuit of bad ends as well as good. Science itself is not only morally neutral, that is indifferent to the value of the ends for which the means are used; it is also totally unable to give any moral direction. You are quite right, therefore, in suggesting that science must be supplemented by philosophy if the means that science gives us are to be used for worthwhile ends. Many people today think that philosophy is useless as compared with science, because it cannot be applied in the production of things. But philosophical knowledge is useful in a quite different and, in my judgment, superior way. Its utility or application is moral or directive, not technical or productive. Where science furnishes us with means we can use, philosophy directs us to ends we should seek.

중심소재:
첫번째 문단
1. 도입부

1) 주제문

두 번째 문단
2. 통념

1) 주제문

① 뒷받침 진술

① The Morality of Science and Philosophy
② The Constructive and Destructive Power of Science
③ The Utility of Scientific Knowledge
④ Philosophy in a Age of Science

10. 제목으로 가장 적절한 것을 고르시오.

Can anyone compete with Microsoft in the world of software applications? For years now, Bill Gates & Co. have had clear sailing: the Window operating system monopoly has helped make their key products—like Word and Outlook—into unbeatable juggernauts. Meanwhile, innovation in those areas proceeds only at the pace that Microsoft deems appropriate.

The Open Source Application Foundation has a different idea: to promote free software and innovation by creating cool new applications on a bare-bones budget. The not-for-profit OSAF was initially funded with five million dollars from Lotus Development Corp. founder Mitch Kapor. For Kapor, this is a fascinating departure. Twenty years ago, he introduced one of the first killer applications of the PC age, the Lotus 1-2-3 spreadsheet; it was (unabashedly for-profit and was closed source.

But Kapor always had his heart in the counter-culture, and after leaving his company he co-founded the Electronic Frontier Foundation, a cyber-rights organization. Though he has seen success as an investor, he feels strongly about the open-source movement, which posits that in the age of complex software many

중심소재:

1. 도입부

1) 배경

2.

1)

3.

people working for nothing can duplicate or even exceed the efforts of the rake-in-the bucks gang. And because the source code is available to all, anyone can improve the product. The continued success of the Linux-powered operating system and Apache Web servers shows that open source is no hippie-dippy pipe dream, but a serious challenge to the establishment.

① The Future of Bill Gates & Co.
② The Continued Success of the Linux-powered Operating System
③ Microsoft vs. Lotus Development Corp.
④ A Plan to Bring Free Software to Everyone

11. Which of the following is the best title of the passage?

A thousand years ago, when the earth was reassuringly flat and the universe revolved around it, the ordinary person had no last name, let alone any claim to individualism. The self was subordinated to church and king. Then came the Renaissance explosion of scientific discovery and humanist insight and, as both cause and effect, the rise of individual self-consciousness. All at once, it seemed, humanity had replaced God at the center of earthly life. And perhaps more than any great war or invention or feat of navigation, this upheaval marked the beginning of our modern era. There are now 20 times as many people in the world as there were in the year 1000. Most have last names, and many of us have a personal identity or reasonable expectation of acquiring one. This special issue examines the transformation of identity through different lenses and concludes with reflections on how hard it is, in a time of gathering global conformity, to find one's own way.

① Identification of humanity
② Divinity over individualism
③ Importance of the Renaissance in the human history
④ How individual identity was acquired
⑤ Relationship between God and humanism.

12. Which of the following is the best title of the passage?

In Europe, Southeast Asia and all sorts of places inbetween, something remarkable is happening. Alternative-energy-technologies have moved quietly but decisively from experimental curiosity to commercial reality, economically turning sunlight, wind and other renewable resources into useful forms of energy. This achievement opens up an intriguing possibility. Just as the economic miracles of the 20th century were powered by fossil fuels, the 21st century may be marked by an equally dramatic move away from those fuels—and the environmental havoc they have wrought. The result may be nothing less than an energy revolution.

Roughly 100 years have passed since a transition of this magnitude has taken place. Much of the energy system now in place was created by an explosion of invention between 1890 and 1910. During that short period, cities were transformed, as automobiles and electric lights replaced horse-drawn carriages and gas lamps. The old technologies had prevailed for centuries, but they became obsolete in a matter of years. Today we may be at a similar turning point. Thanks to a potent combination of government incentives and private investment, technologies that use synthetic materials, advanced electronics and biotechnology are sweeping through the energy industry. That will foster a new generation of mass-produced machines that efficiently and cleanly provide the energy that enables people to take a hot shower, sip a cold beer or even surf the Internet.

① The Development of Alternative Energy
② The Use of Fossil Fuels
③ The Future of Traditional Industry
④ The Economic Miracle of the 20th Century

13. Which of the following is the best title of the passage?

Forgive and forget. Most of us find the forgetting easier, but maybe we should work on the forgiving part. "Holding on to hurts and nursing grudges wears you down physically and emotionally," says Stanford University psychologist Fred Luskin, author of Forgive for Good. "Forgiving someone can be a powerful antidote."

In a recent study, Charlotte van Oyen Witvliet, assistant professor of psychology at Hope College in Holland, Michigan, and colleagues asked 71 volunteers to remember a past hurt. Tests recorded steep spikes in blood pressure, heart rate and muscle tension—the same responses that occur when people are angry. Research has linked anger and heart disease. When the volunteers were asked to imagine empathizing, even forgiving those who'd wronged them, they remained calm by comparison.

What's more, forgiveness can be learned, insists Luskin, director of the Stanford Forgiveness Project. "We teach people to rewrite their story in their minds, to change from victim to hero. If the hurt is from a spouse's infidelity, we might encourage them to think of themselves not only as a person who was cheated on, but as the person who tried to keep the marriage together."

Two years ago Luskin tested his method on five Northern Irish women whose sons had been murdered. After undergoing a week of forgiveness training, the women's sense of hurt, measured using psychological tests, had fallen by more than half. They were also much less likely to feel depressed and angry. "Forgiving isn't about condoning what happened," says Luskin. "It's about breaking free of the person who wronged us."

The early signs that forgiving improves overall health are promising: A survey of 1,423 adults by the University of Michigan's Institute for Social Research in 2001 found that people who had forgiven someone in their past also reported being in better health than those who hadn't.

However: While 75 percent said they were sure God had forgiven them for past mistakes, only 52 percent had been able to find it in their hearts to forgive others. Forgiveness, it seems, is still divine.

① The Divine Forgiveness
② The Healing Power of Forgiveness
③ From a Victim to a Hero
④ Linking Anger and Heart Disease

14. Which of the following is the best title of the passage?

According to E-Marketer, during the 1999 holiday season some 34 million individuals made at least one purchase online. Web users are often lulled into believing that browsing online is an anonymous process. In reality, the explosion in electronic commerce has been accompanied by increasingly sophisticated information-gathering techniques. Clearly there is nothing inherently unethical in gathering information on customers when appropriate safeguards are put into place to protect them. Since the dawn of commerce, bricks-and-mortar store owners have gathered information on their regular customers. However, what has irrevocably altered this information-gathering process is the growth of sophisticated technology that enables the collection, dissemination, and combination of detailed information on customers at previously unprecedented levels.

① Increase of E-marketing during the holiday season
② Customers' misunderstanding of online process
③ Rapid increase of electronic commerce
④ Complication of information-gathering techniques
⑤ Problems of information collection and release in E-marketing

15. Which of the following is the best title of the passage?

A moment's reflection will make it clear that one cannot live a full, free, influential life in America without argument. No doubt people often argue on insufficient evidence and for insufficient reasons; no doubt they often argue on points about which they should rather be thinking and studying; no doubt they sometimes fancy they are arguing when they are merely wrangling and disputing. But this is only proof that argument is employed badly, that it is misused rather than used skillfully. Argument, at the right moment and for the right purpose and in the right way, is undoubtedly one of the most useful instruments in American life. It is an indispensable means of expressing oneself and impressing others.

① Principles of Argument
② The Usefulness of Argument
③ How to Win Arguments
④ Misuses of Argument
⑤ Need for Evidence in Argument

16. The title of the passage is _____.

Bill Smith and Mike Hugh are examples of men who committed three felonies and are now serving life in prison under California's "Three Strikes" law. However, the men's crimes were not violent. Hugh says it is a waste of money to keep people like him locked up for the rest of their lives. Many people agree with him. A new study by the Justice Policy Institute claims that the ten-year-old Three Strikes law has cost California billions of dollars, but it has not reduced crime. The authors of the study believe that sending people to jail is not a good way to reduce crime, and they think that people who commit nonviolent crimes should not suffer from Three Strikes. Some prosecutors agree that the law is unfair and unreasonable, and that it does not deter crime. The author of the Three Strikes law, Bill Jones, disagrees. According to Jones, Three Strikes has saved California billions of dollars, and crime in the state has gone down by 46 percent. For example, California now has its lowest level of burglaries since 1957. Jones also says there are two million fewer crime victims and 100,000 fewer prisoners than without Three Strikes. He points out that California has not built any new prisons since the law was passed.

① Criminals and Crime Victims
② Violent and Nonviolent Crimes
③ Advantages of the Three Strikes Law
④ Controversy Surrounding the Three Strikes Law
⑤ Disadvantages of the Three Strikes Law

17. The title of the passage is _____.

Violence and homicide are not always the work of criminals and terrorists. In recent times, people around the world have been shocked by widespread examples of horror perpetrated by religious cults claiming to be in the service of God. In 1978 in Guyana, 900 men, women, and children belonging to the People's Temple obediently drank poisoned Kool-Aid to die along with their leader, Jim Jones. In 1994, the bloody remains of 50 followers of the Order of the Temple of the Sun were found in various houses in Switzerland and Canada: they had killed themselves and their children, believing that the end of the world is near.

At first glance it is hard to comprehend how ordinary people can be induced to these acts of murder and suicide under the guise of religion and morality. Most experts suggest that the cause lies at least party in the breakdown of traditional institutions, such as the church and family, which formerly provided a feeling of security and identity to most individuals. New groups arise to fill the void, and these are the so-called cults. Young people in particular, alienated by the competition, stress, and greed they perceive at many levels of modern society, often begin to search for simple alternatives that will provide them with meaning and certainty. The cults generally promise an all-embracing surrogate family and a perfect paradise after death, and that combination seems attractive indeed.

Cult promises paradise but delivers subjugation and exploitation, and even at times, death and violence. Yet it is not fair to say that cults are completely bad. Good and evil are mixed together in many cults, as they are in most fields of human endeavor.

① The Dangerous Attraction of Cults
② The Essence of Cults
③ The History of Cults
④ The Causes of Violence in Cults
⑤ The Influence of Cults on Young People

18. The title of the passage is _____.

Once upon a time, only Santa Claus knew whether you had been good or bad. But jolly supernaturalism has been supplanted by aggressive data processing. Your chances of finding work, getting a mortgage or qualifying for health insurance may be up for grabs, because almost any body with a computer, modem and telephone can surf through cyberspace into the deepest recesses of your private life. A fairly accurate profile of your financial status, tastes and credit history can be gleaned from such disparate things as your ZIP code, Social Security number and records of credit-card usage. But legal access to data is only part of the problem. Another difficulty is unauthorized peeking into personal records, which occurs with alarming regularity because company safeguards are often laughable. A second problem is that wrong and harmful "facts" can creep into the databases. Malicious tipsters can poison a person's record within innuendo, and it takes much effort to correct the mistake.

① Santa Claus knows everything.
② Invasion of Privacy
③ Let's surf through cyberspace.
④ How to Get a Mortgage Loan

19. The title of the passage is _____.

The African country of Ghana owes a lot of its success to a pocketful of seeds brought into the country in 1879 by a young black man named Tetteh Quashie. He had been living and working on an island near Africa for several years. When he decided to go back home to Ghana (then owned by England and called the Gold Coast), he had to smuggle cacao seeds into the country. This was because the island's leaders did not want any other places to grow and sell cacao seeds, which are used to make cocoa. Cocoa is used to make chocolate.

Tetteh Quashie set up a small nursery to grow cacao plants. Then he traveled all around the country, giving seedlings to poor farmers and showing them how to grow the plants. Within thirty years, the Gold Coast became the world's largest producer of cacao. With the money brought in by selling cacao, the Gold Coast was able to buy new and costly things that were now affordable, such as railroads. When the Gold Coast became independent in 1950s and changed its name to Ghana, it was one of the richest countries in Africa—thanks to a pocketful of seeds.

① Planting Cacao Seeds
② From Seeds to Riches
③ The Gold Coast Becomes Independent
④ The World's Largest Cacao Plantation

20. The title of the passage is _____.

People usually build their houses out of the materials that are available to them. In some areas, most people build their homes out of wood. This is true in parts of North America and in Scandinavia. These areas have large forests, so wood is easy to get and inexpensive. In many other areas of Europe, there are few forests left. Stone and brick are cheaper, so most people build their houses of these materials. In tropical regions, houses are sometimes made from plants that grow there. For example, in parts of Africa or Asia, houses may be made out of bamboo. Finally, in the very coldest areas near the Arctic, people make their homes out of blocks of cement.

① Materials Used for Houses　　② The Wooden Houses of Scandinavia
③ Houses in Asia　　④ Man and Environment

21. Which of the following is the best title for the passage?

We are all probably familiar with the fact that the wedding ring, or "circle," symbolizes perfection, perfect unity with no beginning and no end. For some it represents holiness, perfection and peace, as well as the sun, earth and universe. You may even be aware that it was once believed that the third finger of the left hand had a special vein, "vena amoris" or "the vein of love," running directly to the wearer's heart. And it is from this romantic custom that we today have the custom of placing the wedding ring on this finger.

① The Value of Wedding Rings　　② The Old Customs of Wedding
③ The History of Wedding Rings　　④ Some Myths on Wedding Rings

22. Which of the following is the best title for the passage?

On Peru's barren Nazca plain is one of the most perplexing mysteries facing archaeologists today. Enormous shapes have been etched into the ground over a thirty-mile area. Among the many shapes are drawings of spiders and other animals. Some of the figures are so large that they can be recognized only from the air. The drawings were made over one thousand years ago by South American Indians.

The mystery that has continually puzzled so many archaeologists is why the drawings were made. A sciencefiction writer has suggested that the giant drawings may have been landing strips for alien spaceships. Some scientists think the great shapes may have been used as a sort of primitive astronomical observatory. A more practical explanation is that the religious Indians were trying to communicate with their gods through the drawings. One thing everyone does agree upon is that the large drawings need government protection.

214

① Mysterious Shapes in Peru
② Peru's Barren Nazca Plain
③ The Mysterious Archaeologists Cannot Solve
④ Why the Large Drawings in Peru Need Government Protection

23. Which of the following is the best title for the passage?

America's great old form of entertainment was vaudeville. Long before radio, television, or movies, in the late nineteenth century, vaudeville theaters became popular. On their stages, audiences would see shows featuring singers, dancers, comedians, ventriloquists, trained animals, mimics, and magicians. Each performer would entertain the crowd for a few minutes, followed immediately by the next performer. The show was carefully planned to give variety — in fact, an early name for vaudeville theaters was "variety houses." Soon every city of middle or large size, and even some small towns, had a vaudeville theater. Vaudevillians, as the performers were called, were the most prominent stars of the day. Then, in the 1920s and 1930s, two new entertainment forms came along — talking movies and radio. The movies were more spectacular than vaudeville ever could be, and radio became available in the home. Vaudeville couldn't compete with them.

중심소재:
1. 도입부
1) 과거와 현재의 대조

① 과거

② 현재

① The Ups and Downs of Vaudeville
② The Coming of Radio and Movies
③ The Old and New Form Entertainment
④ The Types of Entertainment in Vaudeville

Test 4 내용일치·세부사항 확인 문제

1. According to the passage, which of the following is true?

You should beware of introducing outside files into your computer as these may contain computer viruses. If you introduce an infected disk into your system, you run the risk of having your entire hard drive wiped out. This can also happen if you download something from the web that contains a virus. You should have an anti-virus program running at all times and be careful about what you bring into your computer.

중심소재:
1. 도입부
1) 뒷받침 진술

2. 요지

① All outside files contain computer viruses.
② If you download something from the web you don't need an anti-virus program running.
③ Your entire hard drive can be wiped out by an infected disk.
④ The speaker warns about your computer hard drive.

2. According to the passage, which of the following is true?

Neil and Marie appear to be a young, newly married couple excited to be walking around the sidewalks of New York City as tourists. They stop to take pictures and ask people on the street to take a picture of two of them on their brand new, sleek Ericsson all-in-one phone. Most people they approach listen intently as the couple instruct them how to use the camera features and extol the virtues of the product. The invited photographers leave thinking that they have done a good deed and probably unaware that they have just been subjected to a ten-minute sales presentation. This is the essence of stealth or covert marketing. Marketers have used this kind of marketing for years by placing them in popular television programs or by displaying their soft drinks in sitcoms. More recently, groups of sales people have taken to the streets with a variety of products and a covert message intended to create a

중심소재:
첫번째 문단
1. 도입부

1) 일반진술

두 번째 문단
1. 구체적 진술

216

"buzz" about their product. When people are faced with an overt sales attempt such as a door-to-door salesperson, their defenses go up. They become wary of the seller's "angle" or may not even let the salesperson finish the first sentence of the "pitch." Covert marketing attempts to persuade people to try a new product without their being aware of the persuasive attempt. It gets past a buyer's defense to overt sales.

① Neil and Marie are door-to-door salespersons.
② Covert marketing is more effective than overt sales.
③ Buyers are more defensive when they are subjected to stealth marketing.
④ The invited photographers doing a favor for the couple are hired by Ericsson.

3. 본문과 일치하지 <u>않는</u> 문장을 고르시오.

The quest for manliness is essentially right-wing, cowardly, neurotic, and fueled largely by a fear of women. The youth who is misled into believing in the masculine ideal is conveniently separated from women, and he spends the rest of his life finding women a riddle and a nuisance. Masculinity celebrates the exclusive company of men. That is why it is so grotesque; and that is also why there is no manliness that is absolutely complete—because it denies men the natural friendship of women.

Of course, there is a female version of this male affliction. It begins with mothers encouraging little girls to say, "Do you like my new dress?" In a sense, little girls are traditionally urged to please others with a kind of coquettishness, while boys are enjoined to behave like monkeys towards each other. The nine-year-old coquette proceeds to become womanish in a subtle power game in which she learns to be sexually indispensable, socially decorative, and always alert to a man's needs. Femininity—being ladylike—implies needing a man as witness and seducer.

① The concept of masculinity is exclusive of women.
② Females are trained from childhood to please others.
③ Manliness allows female companionship.
④ Girls learn to be coquettish.

4. According to the passage, which of the following is NOT true?

The evolution of sex ratios has produced, in most plants and animals with separate sexes, approximately equal numbers of males and females. Why should this be so? Two main kinds of answers have been offered. One is couched in terms of advantage to population. It is argued that the sex ratio will evolve so as to maximize the number of meetings between individuals of the opposite sex. This is essentially a "group selection" argument. The other, and in my view correct, type of answer was first put forward by Fisher in 1930. This "genetic" argument starts from the assumption that genes can influence the relative numbers of male and female offspring produced by an individual carrying the genes. That sex ratio will be favored which maximizes the number of descendants an individual will have and hence the number of gene copies transmitted. If the population consisted of equal numbers of males and females, sons and daughters would be equally valuable. Thus a one-to-one sex ratio is the only stable ratio; it is an "evolutionarily stable strategy." Although Fisher wrote before the mathematical theory of games had been developed, his theory incorporates the essential feature of a game—that the best strategy to adopt depends on what others are doing.

중심소재:
1. 도입부

1) 연결문
① 뒷받침 진술

Ⓐ 이유 1

Ⓑ 이유 2

① Group selection argument explains the evolution of sex ratios based on the total number of population.
② The evolution of sex ratios has kept the numbers of males and females at approximately the same level.
③ Fisher sought an explanation of why certain sex ratios exist.
④ The mathematical theory of games has been useful in explaining some biological phenomena.

5. According to the passage, which of the following is correct?

Before adolescence, there is little difference in the rate of depression in boys and girls. But between the ages of 11 and 13 there is a precipitous rise in depression rates for girls. By the age of 15, females are twice as likely to have experienced a major depressive episode as males. This comes at a time in adolescence when roles and expectations change dramatically. The stresses of adolescence include forming an identity, emerging sexuality, separating from parents, and making decisions for the first time, along with other physical, intellectual, and hormonal changes. These stresses are generally different for boys and girls, and may be associated more often with depression in females.

중심소재:
1. 도입부

1) 원인

① Teenage girls undergo depression as they try to cope with stresses of adolescence.
② Prepubescent girls are more susceptible to depression than prepubescent boys.
③ Teenage boys experience higher level of depression than teenage girls.
④ Teenage boys are more susceptible to stresses of adolescence than girls.

6. According to the passage, which of the following is correct?

I was once stopped by a California Highway Patrol officer because I was exceeding the speed limit. He walked up to the car window, looked me straight in the eye, and, with a slightly concerned look, asked me if I knew why he had stopped me. He waited while I performed a few verbal somersaults, and then, with a calm voice, he told me the specific details of my offense. He stuck to the facts and never once made any assumptions about why I had done what I did. He was so good at giving me the bad news that when he finished writing the ticket and said, "Have a nice day," I responded back with a genuinely enthusiastic, "You too, Officer." I later found out that the California Highway Patrol Academy puts officers through a 27 week training course that emphasizes dealing with confrontation and conflict with their customers It works!

① The driver was offended by the police officer.
② The police officer was very impatient with the driver.
③ The driver dared not make any excuses to the police officer.
④ The training course teaches officers to regard citizens as customers.

7. Which of the following statements corresponds to the content of the passage?

But why should we blame the poor machine for the ills that have followed from it? The fault lies with man, who has misused it, and with society, which has not profited by it fully. It seems to be unthinkable that the world, or any country, can go back to the old days before the Industrial Revolution, and it hardly seems desirable or wise that, in order to get rid of some evils, we should throw away the numerous good things that industrialism has brought us. And, in any event, the machine has come and is going to stay. Therefore the problem for us is to retain the good things of industrialism and to get rid of the evil that attaches to it. We must profit by the wealth it produces, but see to it that the wealth is evenly distributed among those who produce it.

① The Industrial Revolution did something to preserve learning and art.
② Democracy dealt with the political aspect of liberty.
③ The Industrial Revolution was a reaction against autocracy and other despotisms.
④ The Industrial Revolution did good and harm.

8. 다음 내용과 일치하지 <u>않는</u> 것을 고르시오.

Thanks to the recent development of agricultural technology, we have various kinds of flowers, vegetables, and fruits all through the seasons, because they are grown in greenhouses all the year round. Most people living in urban areas have gradually lost the sense of season and become indifferent to the seasonal change of nature. Nature was once our friend and we lived in harmony with her, but now, somehow alienated from her to live in a mechanical age, we have come to be less and less attracted by her beauties.

중심소재:
1. 도입부

1) 부정적 결과

① We were once less attracted by the beauties of nature.
② We were once on friendly terms with nature.
③ We are now estranged from nature.
④ We are now less sensitive to the seasonal change of nature.

9. According to the passage, which of the following is <u>NOT</u> true?

The high-tech economy is on the ropes and the old economy is coming back with a vengeance. For all the amazing, productivity-enhancing things the Internet can do, dirty industrial details like the price of oil and the quality of steel still matter. All in all, it's a good time to be in a business where the workers need to scrub their hands at the end of a hard day. The bursting of the high-tech bubble will have consequences for nearly everybody in 2001. Consumers are feeling nervous again and corporations are finding that cash, once so plentiful in a booming stock market, is a scarcer commodity. Economic growth is slowing in many place in the world, with even some hints that a recession is on the way. For the first time in a long while, there's no money to be made just by riding the market momentum. In the economy of 2001, it will be survival of the smartest.

중심소재:
1. 도입부

1) 뒷받침 진술

2. 2001년 경제 전망

① The old economy is making a strong comeback.
② The Internet could increase industrial productivity.
③ The high-tech industry will not suffer a setback of any sorts.
④ It has become more difficult to find investors on the stock market.
⑤ The world economy may slow down in the year 2001.

10. According to the passage, which of the following statements is not true?

Because early man viewed illness as divine punishment and healing as purification, medicine and religion were inextricably linked for centuries. This notion is apparent in the origin of our word "pharmacy," which comes from the Greek, pharmakon, mean "purification through purging."

By 3500 B.C. the Sumerians in the Tigris-Euphrates valley had developed virtually all of our modern methods of administering drugs. They used gargles, inhalations, pills, lotions, ointment, and plasters. The first drug catalog, or pharmacopoeia, was written at that time by an unknown Sumerian physician. Preserve in cuneiform script on a single clay tablet are the names of dozens of drugs to treat ailments that still afflict us today.

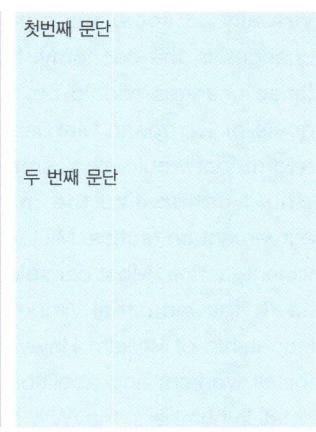

첫번째 문단

두 번째 문단

① Today, we are still suffering from the diseases of the early man.
② In the early age, medicine and religion had some family resemblance for centuries.
③ The first drug catalog was produced by a Sumerian.
④ The modern methods of administering drugs stem from religion only.

11. According to the passage, which of the following statements is true?

After nearly a year of emotional arguments in Congress—but no new federal laws—the national debate over human cloning has shifted to the states. Six states have already banned cloning in one form or another, and this year 38 anticloning measures were introduced in 22 states. The resulting patchwork of laws, people on all sides of the issue say, complicates a nationwide picture already clouded by scientific and ethical questions over whether and how to restrict cloning or to ban it altogether. Like their counterparts in Washington, state legislators say they are concerned about the prospect of cloned babies. They are also divided over the ethics of cloning human embryos for research, which proponents say holds vast promise for treating diseases, and which detractors say raises the specter of "embryo farms." At the same time, they say they are frustrated with Congress, and hopeful that their actions might ultimately force Washington to follow suit.

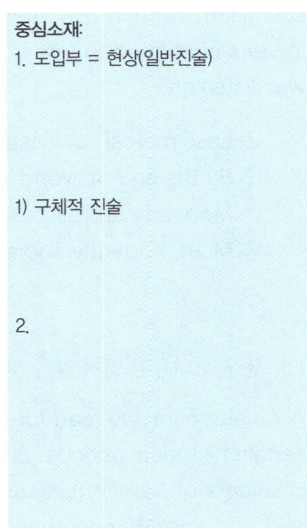

중심소재:
1. 도입부 = 현상(일반진술)

1) 구체적 진술

2.

① Several pieces of new federal laws were legislated during the past year.
② The new laws against cloning will only add to the controversy surrounding it.
③ Twenty-two states have already prohibited cloning altogether.
④ The supporters of cloning promised to treat diseased babies.

12. Which of the following statements is true according to the passage?

Virtually all socialists agreed on the need for basic structural changes in the economy, but they differed widely on how drastic those changes should be. Some endorsed the sweepingly radical goals of European Marxists; others envisioned a more moderate reform that would allow small-scale private enterprise to survive but would nationalize the major industries. There was still less agreement on tactics. Militants within the party favored drastic, even violent, action. Most conspicuous was the radical labor union calling itself "the Industrial Workers of the World(the IWW)." Under the leadership of William Haywood, the IWW advocated a single union for all workers and abolition of the "wage slave" system. Although small in numbers, the IWW struck terror into the hearts of the middle class with their inflammatory rhetoric and their occasional dynamiting of railroad lines and power stations. More moderate socialists advocated a peaceful change through political struggle, and it was they who dominated the party. They emphasized a gradual education of the public to the need for change, and patient efforts within the system to enact it. It soon became clear, however, that the period before World War I was not the first stage of an effective social movement but the last. By the end of the war, socialism was virtually dead as a significant political force. Party leaders continued to talk of the need for change, but hardly anyone was listening.

① Less radical socialists advocated peaceful change.
② By the end of World War II, socialism was greatly weakened in America.
③ Moderate socialists insisted on a single union for all workers.
④ Most moderate socialists supported the drastic measures some socialist groups used.

13. 본문의 내용과 맞지 <u>않는</u> 것을 고르시오.

As students, we read for many reasons. We read to explore life in certain historical periods, cultures, and regions. We read to examine problems of human justice, to explore basic issues of race, class, sex, and age. By encountering many different and conflicting ideas and beliefs, we learn to think critically, to ask intelligent questions, and to form our own opinions.

Educators should not tell us what to think but should teach us how to think. Rather than flatly stating whether a certain book has value, instructors and school officials should encourage us to read extensively and to decide for ourselves. By encouraging lively debates in the classroom, teachers can help us to clarify what we believe and why. Book censorship, by inhibiting a free and open exchange of ideas, squelches the vitality of our classrooms and threatens our freedom to learn.

1) 뒷받침 진술

① Censorship means that some authors would have to go to prison.
② Censorship makes it impossible to have a free exchange of ideas.
③ Censorship means that someone else would have to do our thinking for us.
④ Censorship discourages active discussions in our classrooms.

14. 다음 글을 읽고, 아래 질문에 답하시오.

By the fifteenth century, when the European nations were "discovering" America, the continent had been inhabited by millions of natives who had migrated from Asia before. Most of the tribes had developed some kind of agriculture or fishing while remaining as hunters and retaining nomadic characteristics. They roamed the high western plains, hunted mountain valleys, and farmed along the rivers from coast to coast. There was considerable diversity and there were several hundred different languages among the wide-ranging tribes. Several tribes, such as the Iroquois, were very successful in achieving political unity and extending their influence.

The native peoples were well adapted to their environment, and without the aid of the natives, the first European settlers might not have survived. Many native vegetables, such as maize and potatoes, became important staples. Moreover, native trackers guided expeditions and taught hunters and explorers the ways of the land.

For years, U.S. history began with Columbus, but today the cultures and contributions of the early inhabitants of America are studied and acknowledged. The story of North America begins with the true origin of the continent and its people.

중심소재:
1. 도입부

1) 뒷받침 진술

① 뒷받침 1

② 뒷받침 2

2. 결론

문제 1. The passage implies that _____.

① the Europeans arrived in America well-prepared and ready to survive
② The natives were hostile and refused to offer help to the first European settlers
③ the history of North America begins with the story of the natives
④ North America opens its history with the settlement by the Europeans
⑤ the Europeans found their own way of living independently of the natives

문제 2. According to the passage, which is true?

① North America has a relatively short history.
② North America was uninhabited when the Europeans arrived.
③ It was the natives, not the Europeans, who "discovered" North America.
④ The natives suffered the same difficulties in surviving as the Europeans.
⑤ The cultures of the native people are still not acknowledged in the U.S.

15. Which of the following is stated or implied in the passage?

During the past two decades the rise in the real income of manual laborers has been not only great in absolute terms, but also greater in comparison with that of non-manual workers. The effect of this has been to blur the old division between the working and middle classes, many manual workers' families now acquiring habits, tastes, and, to some extent, attitudes which were formerly regarded as "middle class." Due to considerable upward mobility of the working class, social distinctions based on occupation have become less clear-cut. Whether they exist and what they consist of depend on what part of the country one is looking at, but people today should not assume that a doctor is regarded as several steps on the ladder above a garage keeper, or that the headmaster of the local state school is regarded as a higher being than the skilled worker who now earns not one quarter of his salary, but just as much as he does, if not more.

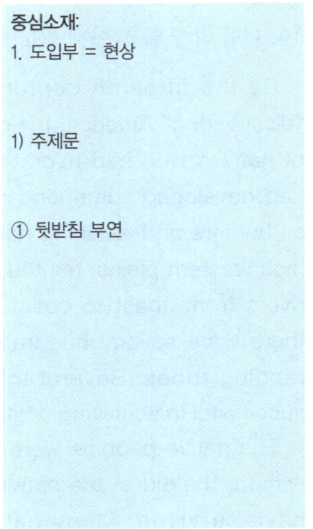

① The things that make up social distinctions are universal.
② Occupations are a clear criterion for determining social status across the country.
③ The rise in manual workers' wages blurred the class distinctions.
④ All societies have hierarchically structured social distinctions.
⑤ Headmasters earn four times as much as some skilled workers.

16. According to the passage, which is NOT true?

The danger of stereotypes lies not in their existence, but in the fact that they become for all people some of the time, and for some people all the time, substitutes for observation. Worse yet, stereotypes get in the way of our judgment, even when we do observe the world. Someone who has formed rigid preconceptions of all Latins as "excitable," or all teenagers as "wild," doesn't alter his point of view when he meets a calm and deliberate Genoses, or a serious-minded high school student. He brushes them aside as

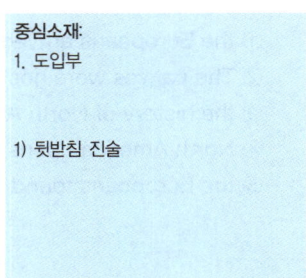

"exceptions that prove the rule." And, of course, if he meets someone true to type, he stands triumphantly vindicated. "They're all like that," he proclaims, having encountered an excited Latin, an ill-behaved adolescent. Thus, stereotyping makes people mentally lazy.

① Stereotyping interferes with our judgment.
② Nobody is free from stereotyping.
③ Stereotyping enhances people's mental efforts.
④ Stereotyping sometimes makes people overgeneralize.
⑤ Stereotyping interferes with our observation.

17. 다음 글을 읽고, 아래 질문에 답하시오.

Early-Victorian costume not only made women look weak and helpless, it made them weak and helpless. The main agent of this debility was the corset, which at the time was thought of not as a mere fashion item but as a medical necessity. Ladies' "frames," it was believed, were extremely delicate; their muscles could not hold them up without assistance. Well-brought-up little girls were laced into juvenile versions of the corset as early as three or four. Gradually their stays were lengthened, stiffened and tightened. By the time they reached late adolescence they were wearing cages of heavy canvas reinforced with steel, and their back muscles had often atrophied to the point where they could not sit or stand for long unsupported. The corset also deformed the internal organs and made it impossible to draw a deep breath. As a result fashionably dressed ladies fainted easily, suffered from digestive complaints, and felt weak and exhausted after any strenuous exertion.

According to the passage, why did people think that women needed corsets?

① Because they had to look beautiful.
② Because they wanted to look weak and helpless.
③ Because they needed to support their delicate bodies.
④ Because they were forced to wear them.
⑤ Because they had stiff backs.

18. 다음 글을 읽고, 아래 문제에 답하시오.

The youngest child in a family often becomes a real charmer, playful or manipulative in his desire to get attention. Such children develop strategies to make their presence felt, either by behaving disagreeably or by finding creative or athletic outlets such as writing, drawing, or sports. The youngest child's parents are often older, more tired, or more relaxed about rules that seemed important with their preceding children. The youngest child, therefore, grows up experiencing fewer family pressures and more independence. The result is a more creative, carefree person, which is why the youngest frequently choose careers in the arts, entertainment, and sales.

중심소재:
1. 도입부

1) 뒷받침 진술

2. 결론

The youngest child in a family _____.

　　① feels more pressures from other family members
　　② hardly chooses jobs such as artists and entertainers
　　③ often behaves in an odd way to get more attention
　　④ depends too heavily upon his preceding sisters or brothers
　　⑤ is usually less important to his parents than older sisters or brothers

19. 다음 글을 읽고, 아래 질문에 답하시오.

But vaccination may have risks of its own. The problem lies with the nature of the chicken-pox virus. After you get it, you always have it in your body. Normally you only suffer from chicken-pox once, but the virus can flare up again later in life, producing shingles, a painful skin rash. The vaccine is a weakened form of virus, and it too may be harbored in the body forever. The debilitated virus could conceivably spring to life years after the vaccination, and no one knows what damage might occur. Another danger is that the vaccine may not confer life-long immunity and will make a person vulnerable to chicken-pox during adulthood, when the disease can be more serious. "It is impossible in the experimental studies preceeding licensing to study a vaccine's effects for 50 years," says Dr Caroline Hall of the American Academy of Pediatrics. "To the best of my knowledge, the varicella vaccine is safe."

중심소재:
1. 도입부

1) 뒷받침 문장

문제 1. According to the author, vaccination for chicken pox _____.

　　① can cause later developments of diseases among chickens
　　② may have its own problem(s)

226

③ is tested and proven safe and effective for the life time
④ may be a cause of some deadly diseases

문제 2. 윗글에 가장 잘 부합하는 것을 고르시오.

① Chicken-pox vaccine can reside in the human body only for a short period of time.
② Adults are immune to chicken-pox.
③ Chicken-pox vaccine does not affect human bodies.
④ Chicken-pox vaccination does not give people a complete protection from chicken-pox.

20. 아래 본문과 일치하지 않는 것은?

Black holes are more difficult to observe than almost any other object in the universe because they emit no visible light. A black hole forms when a large star exhausts the heated gasses (typically hydrogen and helium) that it consumes as fuel during thermonuclear reactions. When this happens, the star becomes very unstable. The forces of gravity cause the dying star to collapse inward upon itself with such intense force that its matter compresses into a single point with a volume of zero and an infinite density. This remarkable point is known as the singularity, because it defies all traditional theories about gravity and the behavior of matter. The singularity is the center of a black hole, but an outer surface called the event horizon surrounds the black hole itself. In fact, the force of gravity is so intense within the event horizon that even ray of light cannot escape. The size of a black hole's event horizon is known as its Schwarzschild radius, after the German astronomer Karl Schwarzschild, who predicted the existence of black holes. Physicists believe that the Schwarzschild radius is proportionally related to the mass of the star that originally collapsed. Thus, theorists claim that a star with a mass ten times greater than that of the Sun would form a black hole with a Schwarzschild radius of 18.6 miles (30km).

중심소재:
1. 도입부

1) 블랙홀의 생성

2) 블랙홀의 특징

① 블랙홀은 별의 핵융합 반응 과정에서 형성된다.
② 블랙홀의 크기를 재는 단위는 독일 천문학자의 이름을 딴 것이다.
③ 소멸하는 별이 블랙홀이 되는 것을 Schwarzschild radius라 부른다.
④ 블랙홀의 크기는 원래 소멸한 별의 크기와 비례한다.

21. 본문과 일치하지 <u>않는</u> 것을 고르시오.

Malaria is neither a virus like polio nor a bacterium like tuberculosis. Rather, it's a parasite that invades red blood cells and has a three-stage life cycle. Infection starts out with a mosquito bite that releases a few of the parasites into the human bloodstream. The invaders travel to the liver where the body's cells hide them from the immune system, allowing them to multiply. Soon afterwards, the parasites burst out of the liver, and attack red blood cells. These, too, eventually burst and release still more parasites, triggering malaria's symptoms.

In the 1950s, malaria was believed to be on the verge of eradication. The introduction of insecticides such as DDT seemed to signal the end of the malaria-carrying mosquito in certain countries.

중심소재:
1. 도입부

1) 단락 주제문

① 뒷받침 진술

2. 현상

① A mosquito bite infects a human body with malaria that attacks the bloodstream.
② Malaria multiplies in the liver, where the body's cells hide it from the immune system.
③ The parasites released into the human blood by a mosquito bite start malaria's symptoms.
④ DDT exterminated the malaria-carrying mosquito in the 1950s.

22. 본문과 일치하지 <u>않는</u> 것을 고르시오.

Employers sometimes terminate employees due to poor job performance, negative attitudes toward work and co-workers, and misconduct such as dishonesty or sexual harassment. Terminating poor performers is a necessary act, because they lower productivity and employee morale. Co-workers resent employees who receive the same pay and benefits as themselves without contributing fairly to the company's work. Employers need to carefully document reasons for terminating employees. According to the Equal Employment Opportunity Commission, almost half of the cases of files against employers involve charges of wrongful dismissal. In recent years, employers have terminated employees through downsizing and outsourcing.

중심소재:
1. 도입부

1) 주제문

① 뒷받침 근거

① Employers terminate employees for different reasons.
② It is not important that employers terminate poor employees.
③ Poor performers lower productivity and employee morale.
④ Downsizing and outsourcing are methods of terminating employees.

23. 본문의 내용과 일치하는 것은?

In the movies, sharks are dangerous predators. They are ready to attack at the first sight of human flesh. But as many experienced shark divers and photographers will tell you, real-life sharks don't generally fit their movie image. Most sharks don't swim around the ocean looking for people to eat. While you can generalize about various species of shark, it's still true that sharks as individuals have very different personalities. Some are relaxed and laid back. They don't become aggressive even when faced with human intruders. Other sharks are extremely territorial. They are quick to be enraged by an outsider entering their watery world. Yet, on the whole, most sharks are more afraid of human beings than not. Despite sharks' aggressive movie image, only a few species are dangerous.

① Unlike their movie image, sharks are very ferocious creatures.
② In summer a few sharks often attack people.
③ Sharks reluctantly shun contact with human beings.
④ Sharks are usually different from their movie image.

24. 본문의 내용과 일치하지 <u>않는</u> 것은?

Until a few short decades ago, the notion that love between a man and a woman would lead to marriage was as alien a concept to the Chinese as the assumption that women had any control over whom they would marry. Marrying, according to the traditional Chinese view, was a family business, not the couple's affair. Having a daughter was considered a "moneylosing proposition," given the lack of return on the investment. After raising a daughter, to marry her off required a dowry and losing her permanently to another family, for once married, the daughter's identity was with her husband's family. A woman was taught from birth that she must prepare herself for lifelong servitude, to serve her parents and elders while at home, her husband and in-laws once married, and her own sons after the death of her husband. The only redeeming hope for a woman was to become a mother-in-law herself so the cycle could go on.

① The thought that love between a man and a woman in old China would lead to marriage was uncommon.
② Marrying, according to the traditional Chinese view, was primarily a family business, not the couple's affair.
③ The only redeeming hope for an old Chinese woman was to become a mother-in-law herself.
④ An old Chinese woman served her parents and elders, but didn't serve his own sons after the death of her husband.

25. Which is true, according to the paragraph?

There is no reason why philosophers should not be also men of letters. But to write well does not come by instinct; it is an art that demands arduous study. The philosopher does not speak only to other philosophers and to undergraduates working for a degree; he speaks also to the men of letters, politicians, and reflective persons, who directly mould the ideas of the coming generation. They, naturally enough, are taken by a philosophy that is striking and not too difficultly assimilated. We all know how the philosophy of Nietzsche has affected some parts of the world, and few would assert that its influence has been other than disastrous. It has prevailed, not by such profundity of thought as it may have, but by a vivid style and an effective form. The philosopher who will not take the trouble to make himself clear shows only that he thinks his thought of no more than academic value.

① Philosophers can never become good men of letters.
② Some philosophers are gifted writers who do not need to practice writing.
③ A charming philosophy is one that is impressive and easily understood.
④ A man's well-written philosophy may be interpreted as his literature.
⑤ However well a philosopher writes, sometimes he may not be clear.

26. 본문의 내용과 <u>거리가 먼</u> 것을 고르시오.

According to anti-consumer and environmental rights organizations, the high consumption lifestyles of affluence cause People to be less happy even though they are acquiring more "things." The major negative effect on the environment is that overconsumption is depleting the world's natural resources, anti-consumer groups argue.

Anti-consumer activist Noam Chomsky, a Massachusetts Institute of Technology professor, points out that the United States has five percent of the world's population, yet consumes forty percent of the world's resources. Chomsky believes that "a lot of that consumption is artificially induced— it doesn't have to do with people's real wants and needs. People would probably be bolter off and happier if they didn't have a lot of those things." Indeed, anti-consumer groups assert that without advertisements by corporations, people would be less likely to overconsume goods.

① Without advertisement by corporations, people would be less likely to overconsume goods.
② High consumption lifestyles of affluence cause People to be less happy.
③ Overconsumption makes people feel fulfilled.
④ Nowadays, people have an insatiable desire to buy more things.

27. 본문과 일치하는 것은?

One of the things which separate humans from other animals is the ability to learn from our predecessors. Our Knowledge increases because we stand on the shoulders of others who have gone before us. Creativity does not occur in a vacuum. It is usually fueled by studying what other scientists have done. For example, when Newton proposed that gravity in the solar system was the same type of force as gravity on the earth, this concept was an extension of the work of Galileo concerning shadows on the moon.

중심소재:
1. 도입부

1) 뒷받침 문장
① 예시 부연

① Galileo was the greatest scientist in the history of the world.
② Our predecessors are always right.
③ It is important to read and build on the work of others.
④ Humans learn something from animals.

28. 본문과 일치하지 않는 것은?

Humans are often thought to be insensitive smellers compared with animals, but this is largely because, unlike animals, we stand upright. This means that our noses are limited to perceiving those smells which drift through the air, missing the majority of smells which stick to surfaces. In fact, though, we are extremely sensitive to smells, even if we do not generally realize it.

Strangely, some people find that they can smell, for example, one type of flower but not another, whereas other people are sensitive to the smells of both flowers. This may be because some people do not have the genes necessary to create particular smell receptors in the nose. These receptors are the cells which sense smells and send messages to the brain. However, it has been found that even people who are at first insensitive to a particular smell can suddenly become sensitive to it, if they are exposed to it often enough.

중심소재:
1. 도입부

2. 주제문

1) 뒷받침 진술

① Humans mainly detect smells in the air, not on surfaces.
② Different people are sensitive to different smells.
③ Smell receptors send messages from the brain to the nose.
④ Humans may be insensitive to a certain smell.

29. 본문과 일치하는 것은?

Only humans speak. No other animal has anything approaching the complexity of language. However, evidence is accumulating that linguistic ability is also a quantitative rather than a qualitative difference between humans and other primates, especially gorillas and chimps. Wild chimps communicate through gestures and calls. Jane Goodall identified twenty-five distinct calls used by Gombe chimps. Each had a distinct meaning and was used only in particular situations. Like people, chimps also communicate through facial expressions, noises, and body movements. Other primates also use calls, which are evoked by environmental stimuli, to communicate messages to other members of the group

중심소재:
1. 도입부

1) 주제문

① 뒷받침 진술

① Only humans have communication systems.
② There is a quantitative difference in linguistic ability between humans and other primates.
③ Gorillas use calls only.
④ Chimps speak to communicate with each other

Test 5 실전 종합문제

[1-3] 다음 글을 읽고, 아래 질문에 답하시오.

In a large, crowded hospital in Zimbabwe, a 30-year-old woman was lying on a stretcher about to be wheeled into the operating theater for minor gynecological surgery when Dr. Bingham happened to walk by. Although she'd never seen the patient before—and knew nothing of her medical history—the doctor had a sudden sense of alarm. "I feel I should check her heart," said Dr. Bingham. She put her stethoscope to the woman's chest, and heard a murmur—abnormal blood flow through the heart, a possible sign of mitral stenosis, a heart condition that can cause serious complications if the person is anesthetized. Bingham alerted the surgeons, who cancelled the operation to further evaluate the patient. Tests confirmed that she did, in fact, have the dangerous condition. An amazed surgeon asked Dr. Bingham why she had suspected the disorder. The family practitioner replied that it was "just a hunch." Experience working in Africa had taught her that mitral stenosis was more common there than in the Untied State. In addition, something about the woman had drawn the doctor to her. Like Dr. Bingham, most of us have had remarkably accurate intuitions that seem to spring from nowhere. We call these mysterious flashes of insight hunches, gut feelings, animal instinct, or even a sixth sense. Some people dismiss them as lucky guesses. But several eminent psychologists acknowledge the power of intuition.

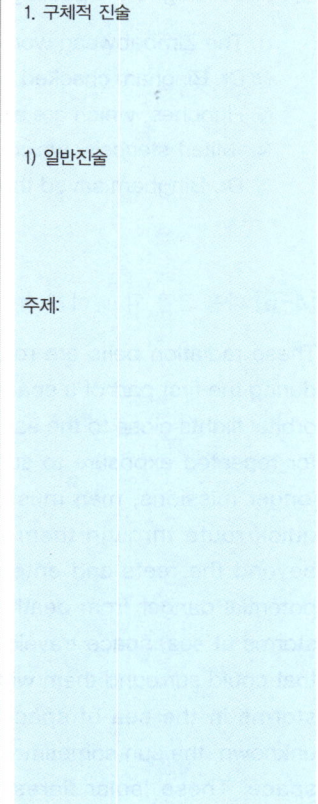

1. 구체적 진술

1) 일반진술

주제:

1. What does the whole passage illustrate?

   ① The poor condition of Zimbabwe's hospitals
   ② Dr. Bingham's lucky guess
   ③ Mitral stenosis in Africa
   ④ The need for caution during operations
   ⑤ The power of intuition

2. Which of the following is true of Dr. Bingham?

   ① She is a gynecologist.
   ② She is a doctor in an American hospital.
   ③ She is a specialist in cardiology.
   ④ She is a family physician.
   ⑤ She is a cognitive psychologist.

3. According to the passage, which of the following is true?

   ① The Zimbabwean woman on the stretcher was portraying a patient in a play.
   ② Dr. Bingham checked on the Zimbabwean woman because she was her regular doctor.
   ③ Hunches, which are also called a sixth sense, are merely lucky guesses.
   ④ Mitarl stenosis, which is a kind of heart disorder, is more common in America than in Africa.
   ⑤ Dr. Bingham saved the Zimbabwean woman thanks to her instinct.

[4-6] 다음 글을 읽고, 아래 질문에 답하시오.

These radiation belts are round the earth area a dangerous barrier during the first part of a space flight. They are like invisible reefs. On orbital flights close to the earth, astronauts must steer clear of them, for repeated exposure to such strong radiation would be fatal. On longer missions, men must either avoid radiation reefs or find a quick route through them. Even after a spaceship has passed beyond the reefs and entered interplanetary space, there is still potential danger from death rays. Just as sailors must prepare for storms at sea, space travelers have to be wary of radiation storms that could surround them with a hail of deadly rays. These radiation storms in the sea of space begin on the sun. For reasons still unknown, the sun sometimes shoots off great masses fiery gas into space. These 'solar flares' do not happen often. There are no advance warnings, _____(a)_____ . At any time the sun can send a radiation storm sweeping into space.

중심소재:
1. 도입부 = 구체적 진술

1)
① 부연 진술

2)
② 부연 진술

3)
③ 부연 진술

4. 이 글의 제목으로 가장 적절한 것을 고르시오.

   ① Death Rays
   ② Space Flight
   ③ Danger in Space
   ④ Radiation Belts

5. 이 글의 내용과 맞지 <u>않는</u> 것을 고르시오.

   ① Space is full of unseen dangers.
   ② The sun often sends radiation storms into space.
   ③ The radiation belts are comparable to invisible reefs.
   ④ Radiation storms surround astronauts with deadly rays.

6. 문맥상 <u>밑줄 친</u> (a)에 넣을 가장 적절한 것을 고르시오.

   ① however
   ② absolutely
   ③ to be sure
   ④ as a matter of fact

[7-9] 다음 글을 읽고, 아래 질문에 답하시오.

Determined to prove the doctors wrong, Rocket began rigorous physiotherapy. If he made his left foot more over and over again, he figured, eventually the undamaged cells of his brain would find a way to tell the foot what to do. After he learned to stand, he strapped his left foot to the pedal of a stationary bike at the gym then started pedalling. On the first day, he lasted only 30 seconds—but he persisted. It was like doing sit-ups for the brain. Twelve years later, after thousands of hours in the gym, Rocket, danced on both feet. His doctors were amazed. "It was dramatic." says Dr Robert Willinsky, the neuroradiologist who saved Rocket's life with the clot-buster. "He's (a) <u>a poster child</u> for sure." It turned out Rocket's hunch was right; It is possible to retrain your brain to make up for the part that's out of order. A generation ago, that idea was dismissed as folly by most medical practitioners. They thought the adult brain was like a machine; It couldn't change or grow; all it could do was break down. But over the past few decades, brian scans such as the PET and functional MRI have allowed scientists to observe this organ in action. Now they can see that the conventional thinking about the brain was wrong.

중심소재:
첫번째 문단
1. 도입부
1) 뒷받침 진술
2. 결론(요지)
두 번째 문단
1. 도입부
1) 주제문

7. The main theme of the passage is _____.

   ① A New Finding about the Brain
   ② Medical Breakthrough by Brain Scanning
   ③ A Miracle in Medical History
   ④ Conflict between Doctors and Patients
   ⑤ A Typical Example of Wrong Diagnosis

8. Rocket proved that _____.

   ① damaged brain can be restored
   ② there is no illness which be cured
   ③ undamaged brain part con work for the damaged one
   ④ he has a special ability to train his brain
   ⑤ brain scanners can be used to observe the brain

9. What does the underlined (a) "a poster child" mean?

   ① a handsome boy   ② still young and healthy
   ③ good at drawing   ④ a good example
   ⑤ stigmatized as a troublemaker

[10-12] 다음 글을 읽고, 아래 질문에 답하시오.

Work—the very word calls up to many of us a picture of sheer boredom; meaningless routines; tiresome activity done only to earn enough money so that existence is possible; something that at least there is a chance to "live." Yes, despite this picture—for which perhaps the biblical depiction of work as "the curse of Adam" has some responsibility—not all work, nor work at all times, is so deadly and dull, so lacking is purpose and value. For work can provide not only an escape from the worry and loneliness that so many suffer but also material for the realization of our human possibilities. It can be an opportunity to develop toward genuine wholeness also.

중심소재:
1. 도입부

1) 주제문

① 뒷받침 근거

10. The best theme of the passage is _____.

   ① Work and the curse of the God   ② The value of work
   ③ How to escape from boredom of work ④ The meaning of work in modern society
   ⑤ Negative effects of daily work

11. According to the passage, which of the following is true?

   ① Religion is a means to overcome the pains of hard work.
   ② Christian belief is partly responsible for viewing work as a kind of suffering.
   ③ Work is simply a necessary evil for human existence.
   ④ Most of work is monotonous and sometimes even soul-destroying.
   ⑤ Work has nothing to do with perfection of the self.

12. Which of the following is NOT an advantage of work?

   ① Escape from daily worries
   ② Fleeing from loneliness
   ③ Realization of human possibilities
   ④ Development of genuine wholeness
   ⑤ Realization of social justice

[13–14] 다음 글을 읽고, 아래 질문에 답하시오.

Suppose we asked you to keep track of all the emotions you experience in the course of a day. (A) You might report that for brief periods you felt happiness, sadness, anger, relief, and so on. (B) There is one emotion, however, that people often report as a kind of background noise for much of their day-to-day experience, and that is stress. Modern industrialized society sets a rapid, hectic pace for living. (C) People often have too many demands placed on their time, are worried about uncertain futures, and have little time for family and fun. (D) A stress-free life would offer no challenge—no difficulties to surmount, no new fields to conquer, and no reasons to sharpen your wits or improve your abilities.

중심소재:
1. 도입부

1)
① 주제문

13. 윗글에서 다음 문장이 들어가기에 가장 적절한 곳은?

   | But would you be better off without stress? |

   ① (A)   ② (B)   ③ (C)   ④ (D)

14. The main idea of the above passage is _____ .

   ① Little stress can be helpful in one's life
   ② Different people struggle to overcome stress in different ways
   ③ People have difficulties coping with emotions, especially stress
   ④ Stress is a negative aspect of emotions to be removed for a better life

15. 다음 글의 요지를 고르시오.

Teaching is supposed to be a professional activity requiring long and complicated training as well as official certification. The act of teaching is looked upon as a flow of knowledge from a higher source to an empty container. The student's role is one of receiving information; the teacher's role is one of sending it. There is a clear distinction assumed between one who is supposed to know (and therefore not capable of being wrong) and another, usually younger person who is supposed not to know. However, teaching need not be the province of a special group of people nor need it be looked upon as a technical skill. Teaching can be more like guiding and assisting than forcing information into a supposedly empty head. If you have a certain skill you should be able to share it with someone. You do not have to get certified to convey what you know to someone else or to help them in their attempt to teach themselves. All of us, from the very youngest children to the oldest members of our cultures should come to realize our own potential as teachers. We can share what we know, however little it might be, with someone who has need of that knowledge or skill.

① It is difficult to be a good teacher.
② Every person has a potential to be a good teacher.
③ Teaching is a professional activity requiring special training.
④ Teaching is the flow of knowledge from a higher source to an empty container.

[16–18] 다음 글을 읽고, 아래 질문에 답하시오.

When journalists hear journalists claim a "larger truth." (가) they really ought to go for their pistols. The New Yorker's Alsstair Reid said the holy words last week; "A reporter might take liberties with the factual circumstances to make the larger truth clear." oh! large, large truth. Apparently Mr. Reid believes that imposing a truth is the same as arriving at one. But his error is more fundamental still in assuming that larger truth is the province of journalism in the first place. The business of journalism is to present facts accurately — Mr. Reid notwithstanding. For one thing, journalism rarely sees the larger truth of a story because reporters are usually chasing quite small elements of information.

16. The underlined (가) means _____.

    ① cry against it
    ② support it enthusiastically
    ③ kill themselves
    ④ surrender themselves
    ⑤ congratulate themselves

17. The author argues that _____.

    ① Journalism must report facts accurately. That's all
    ② Larger truth is more important and valuable than small facts
    ③ To deliver truth, liberties may be taken with facts
    ④ Journalism may impose a truth on the public, if they do not know
    ⑤ Sometimes the public is not smart to find out the larger truth themselves

18. The author's attitude toward the so-called "larger truth" is _____.

    ① positive
    ② enthusiastic
    ③ highly supportive
    ④ indifferent
    ⑤ cynical

[19–20] 다음 글을 읽고, 아래 문제에 답하시오.

The population of the world has increased more in modern times than in all other ages of history combined. World population totaled about 500 million in 1650. It doubled in the period from 1650 ~ 1850. Today the population is more than five billion. Estimates based on research by the United Nations indicate that it will more than double in the next fifty years, reaching ten billion by the year 2050.

중심소재:
1. 도입부
1) 뒷받침 문장

19. By 1850, approximately what was the world population?

    ① 500 million
    ② Five billion
    ③ One billion
    ④ Seven billion

20. According to this passage, by the year 2050 the earth's population should exceed the present figure by _____.

    ① three billion
    ② five billion
    ③ four billion
    ④ seven billion

239

[21-22] 다음 글을 읽고, 아래 질문에 답하시오.

The second point is the more familiar one of the historian's need of imaginative understanding for the minds of the people with whom he is dealing, for the thought behind their acts. Take Burckhardt's censorious remark about the Thirty Years' War: "It is scandalous for a creed, no matter whether it is Catholic or Protestant, to place its salvation above the integrity of the nation." It was extremely difficult for a nineteenth-century liberal historian, brought up to believe that it is right and praiseworthy to kill in defense of one's country, but wicked and wrong-headed to-kill in defense of one's religion, to enter into the state of mind of those who fought the Thirty Years' War. Much of what has been written in English-speaking countries in the last ten years about the Soviet Union, and in the Soviet Union about the English-speaking countries, has been vitiated by this inability to achieve even the most elementary measure of imaginative understanding of what goes on in the mind of the other party, so that the words and actions of the other are always made to appear malign, senseless, or hypocritical. History cannot be written unless the historian can achieve some kind of contact with the mind of those about whom he is writing.

중심소재:
1. 도입부

1) 뒷받침 진술
① 첫번째 예

② 두 번째 예

2. 결론(요지)

21. According to the passage, why do historians need imaginative understanding?

　　① To handle the enemy more effectively
　　② To better understand the mind of the people they meet in their ordinary life
　　③ To elicit more agreements easily
　　④ To get the idea of why people behaved in a certain way

22. Which is true about Burckhardt according to the author?

　　① He failed to understand the mind of the people during the War.
　　② He believed that it was right to kill people in defense of one's religion.
　　③ He thought that it was horrible to kill people in defense of one's country.
　　④ He was a historian who interpreted the War with imaginative understanding.

[23-25] 다음 글을 읽고, 아래 문제에 답하시오.

Historically, women, children, and people of color have been underrepresented in clinical trials. Usually, children are restricted from clinical trials to protect them from the risks of unproven

중심소재:

therapies. (A) Unlike adults, children cannot give informed consent. The rationale for excluding women of childbearing age, particularly women who are pregnant, is to protect their developing and future children from possible long-term side effects of unproven drugs. (B) Unless they participate in clinical trials, the effectiveness and safety of therapies cannot be rigorously established. For example, the trials of the effect of zidovudine (also known as azidothymidine, or AZT) on mother-to-child transmission provided important information that has dramatically reduced perinatal HIV transmission. (C) Without the participation of pregnant women in clinical trials, the effectiveness of antiretroviral therapy in preventing mother-to-child transmission of HIV would not be proven. What is more, there would be no evidence basis for enhanced public health measures and increased funding to prevent mother-to-child transmission. ____(a)____, the increased inclusion of minorities in trials has provided information on the efficacy and adverse effects in these populations. (D) In addition, it is problematic to take away women's decision-making about research participation simply because they are pregnant.

23. Where does the following sentence fit best in the passage?

> But restricting women and children from clinical trials may also be harmful to them in the long run.

① (A)   ② (B)   ③ (C)   ④ (D)

24. Which of the following is most appropriate for (a)?

① Similarly   ② Nevertheless   ③ For example   ④ In conclusion

25. Which of the following is the best title for the passage?

① Side Effects Proven from Clinical Trials
② Race and Gender Issues in Clinical Trials
③ Who Should Participate in the Clinical Trials?
④ How to Prevent Mother-to-Child HIV Transmission

[26–30] 다음 글을 읽고, 아래 질문에 답하시오.

Thomas Kuhn made some controversial claims about the overall direction of scientific change. According to a widely-held view, science progresses towards the truth in a linear fashion, as older incorrect ideas get replaced by newer, correct ones. ㉮_____ This 'cumulative' conception of science is popular among laymen and scientists alike, but Kuhn argued that it is both historically inaccurate and philosophically naive. For example, he noted that Einstein's theory of relativity is in some respects more similar to Aristotelian than Newtonian theory—so the history of mechanics is not simply a linear progression from wrong to right. ㉯_____, Kuhn questioned whether the concept of objective truth actually makes sense at all. The idea that there is a fixed set of facts about the world, independent of any particular paradigms, was of <u>dubious</u> coherence, he believed. Kuhn suggested a radical alternative: the facts about the world are paradigm-relative, and thus change. If this suggestion is right, then it ㉰_____ to ask whether a given theory corresponds to the facts 'as they really are', nor therefore to ask whether it is objectively true.

중심소재:
1. 도입부

1) 통념

2) 주제문

① 뒷받침 진술

26. Which of the following is the most appropriate for the blank ㉮?

① But earlier theories are subjectively better than later ones.
② Later theories are thus objectively better than earlier ones.
③ So both earlier and later theories exist side by side.
④ So later theories are not necessarily better than earlier ones.

27. Choose one that best fits in the blank ㉯?

① On the contrary   ② Nonetheless
③ Ironically   ④ Moreover

28. Choose one that is closest in meaning to the underlined word "dubious."

① questionable   ② trustworthy
③ enduring   ④ intermittent

29. Which of the following is the most appropriate for the blank ㉰?

① holds good   ② is of vital importance
③ makes no sense   ④ makes a great difference

242

30. According to the above passage, which of the following is NOT true?

① Before Kuhn, people generally believed that the history of science is a straightforward progression towards the truth.
② Kuhn doubted whether the concept of objective truth is valid.
③ Kuhn believed that he could find a fixed set of facts about the world outside any particular paradigm.
④ Kuhn thought that Einstein's theory of relativity had something in common with Aristotelian theory.

31. 다음 글에서 말하고자 하는 얼음과 담요의 관계를 가장 잘 설명한 것은?

People are so accustomed to using blankets to make themselves warm that they are surprised to see blankets used to keep ice cold, and to prevent it from melting. Expecting that (A) <u>the same thing will have the same effect</u>, they think that (B) <u>a blanket must make ice warm</u>. But what a blanket always does is to prevent heat passing from one side to the other. Thus (C) <u>it keeps the heat of something from passing into the colder air around</u>, and (D) <u>it keeps the air from passing into some objects</u>.

① (A)　　② (B)　　③ (C)　　④ (D)

[32-34] 다음 글을 읽고, 아래 질문에 답하시오.

The basic principle of broadcasting in our country is that people grant private businesses the ability to make money while using our public airwaves. In exchange for a license, we demand that broadcasters air programs that serve the public interest, and we ask them not to broadcast indecent material at times when children are likely to be watching or listening. The reason we have special rules for radio and television programming is that the broadcast media is a uniquely (A) presence in the lives of all Americans. (ⓐ) When 100 million Americans, including myself, tuned into the Super Bowl, we allowed a broadcast company to enter the privacy of our homes. (ⓑ) We expected the Super Bowl broadcast to be respectful of us and our families. (ⓒ) But what we all got on February 1 was anything but a good guest. Besides the now infamous incident involving Justin Timberlake and Janet Jackson, the half-time show was full of crude and sexually explicit performances. (ⓓ) Throughout the game, we were subjected also to some offensive advertising. It is estimated that one in five American children were watching this year's Super Bowl broadcast.

243

32. Which of the following best fits into (A)?

① pervasive   ② predictive   ③ possessive   ④ persuasive

33. Where does the following sentence fit best in the passage?

> We do not expect to agree with our house guests on everything, but we do expect them to show good judgment and to refrain from saying crude and offensive things, especially when children are in the room.

① ⓐ   ② ⓑ   ③ ⓒ   ④ ⓓ

34. According to the passage, which of the following is true?

① Broadcasters are invited although they infringe upon people's privacy.
② Broadcasting is not so much a public sector as a private business.
③ The writer is attentive to children as a particular audience of aired programs.
④ Justin Timberlake and Janet Jackson were respectful of the families watching the half-time show.

[35–36] 다음 글을 읽고, 아래 질문에 답하시오.

Automakers are loading up vehicles with more sophisticated technology challenging engineers with how to continue the business boom without further (A) safety. They have made a huge bet that hands-free technology would be the answer. But a recent research shows people talking on cell phones are distracted even if their hands remain on the steering wheel. It indicates clear trade-off with hands-free technology. Even though their hands remained on the wheel, study subjects using voice-activated systems take longer to dial—a potentially dangerous distraction. To the extent that hands-free technology gives drivers a false sense of security and prods them to engage in longer phone conversations, it may even exacerbate the safety problem. Despite the safety concerns, customers' desire to stay connected to the outside world is only expected to increase. Consequently, many organizations have called for the prohibition of mobile phone use by drivers while on the road.

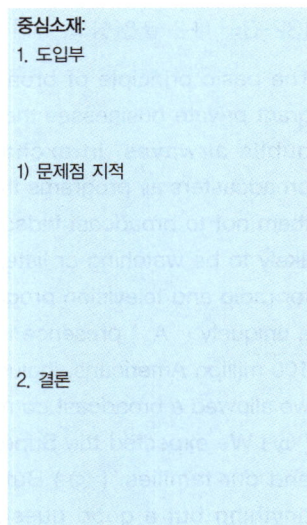

35. Which of the following is most appropriate for (A)?

① leveling   ② considering   ③ compromising   ④ championing

36. According to the passage, which of the following is true?

① The research belies the expectations of the automakers.
② Hands-free technology is an answer to the safe driving issues.
③ There is no need to prohibit drivers from using cell phones while they are driving.
④ Drivers tend to have a shorter phone conversation when they are using hands-free gadgets.

[37-39] 다음 글을 읽고, 아래 질문에 답하시오.

Speaking of anthropological canards, no discussion of language and thought would be complete without the Great Eskimo Vocabulary Hoax. _____ popular belief, the Eskimos do not have more words for snow than do speakers of English. They do not have four hundred words for snow, as it has been claimed in print, or two hundred, or one hundred, or forty-eight, or even nine. One dictionary puts the figure at two. Counting generously, experts can come up with about a dozen, but by such standards English would not be far behind, with *snow, sleet, slush, blizzard, avalanche, hail, hardpack, powder, flurry, dusting*, and a coinage of Boston's WBZ-TV meteorologist Bruce Schwoegler, *snizzling*.

Where did the myth come from? Not from anyone who has actually studied the Yupik and Inuit-Inupiaq families of polysynthetic languages spoken from Siberia to Greenland. The anthropologist Laura Martin has documented how the story grew like an urban legend, exaggerated with each retelling. In 1911 Boas casually mentioned that Eskimos used four unrelated word roots for snow. Whorf embellished the count to seven and implied that there were more. His article was widely reprinted, then cited in textbooks and popular books on language, which led to successively inflated estimates in other textbooks, articles, and newspaper columns of Amazing Facts.

37. Which of the following would be best for the blank?

① Despite
② Contrary to
③ In spite of
④ Due to
⑤ Since

38. The underlined "the myth" means that _____.

① The first word for snow came from the Eskimos
② The English invented many words for snow
③ No one knows the Eskimo word for snow
④ The Eskimos have more words for snow than others
⑤ The English word snow derived from the Eskimo language

39. Who tried to explain the Great Eskimo Vocabulary Hoax?

① Bruce Schwoegler   ② Laura Martin
③ Boas   ④ Whorf ⑤ the Eskimos

[40-42] 다음 글을 읽고, 아래 질문에 답하시오.

Languages seem to be converging to a smaller number, as languages like English seem to eat up regional ones. The three languages used the most by first language speakers today are Mandarin Chinese, English, and Spanish. English is being used more and more as the main language for business, science, and popular culture. Evidence suggests that the dominant languages are (a) <u>squeezing out</u> the local tongues of various regions in the world. Linguists estimate that of the approximately 6,500 languages worldwide, about half are endangered or on the brink of extinction. According to some linguists, the estimated rate of language extinction is one lost in the world every two weeks. If this sounds like the world is losing a species, in a way it is. When a language is lost, meaning no living person can teach another, a world perspective is lost. Some foreign language expressions simply cannot be translated. Colloquial phrases are pleasant to the ear, _____ because they are familiar, but also because they reflect a unique aspect of a culture. Aboriginal languages in Canada and other countries such as Australia have words that reflect a way of life that is connected closely to the Earth. There are fifty different words that mean 'snow' in one Canadian native language, and in the Eastern Arrernte language of Central Australia the word nyimpe translates to 'the smell of rain.'

중심소재:
1. 도입부

1) 뒷받침 진술

2. 대안

40. 밑줄 친 (a) <u>squeezing out</u>과 가장 근접한 의미를 가진 말을 고르시오.

① restricting   ② encouraging
③ coming over   ④ playing

41. 빈칸에 들어갈 적절한 말을 고르시오.

① not
② never
③ not so much
④ not only

42. 윗글의 내용과 <u>다른</u> 것은?

① A dominant language discourages a local tongue.
② Language is important to constitute a world perspective.
③ One language can easily be translated into other languages.
④ A native language in Canada reflects the way of aboriginal life.

READING INNOVATOR

리딩 이노베이터 기본편

외고/자사고 · TOEFL · 편입 · 수능 1등급 · TEPS

어떤 독해 시험이든 그대로 통한다!

똑같은 지문, 똑같은 시간, 하지만 점수는 다르다?
독해의 깊이가 다르기 때문!

영문 독해의 깊이를 더해줄, 최고의 영어 독해 비법서!

JH press
박지성 지음

영어 독해 지문의
종류·유형·전개방식에 따른
영문 독해 패턴 학습

영어 독해 지문의
중심소재와 주제를
한눈에 찾는 연습

킬러 문항도 쉽게 푸는
영어 독해 지문의
통일성과 응집성 훈련

독학 가능한
완벽한 해설
부가 학습 자료 제공

리딩이노베이터
기본편

| 정답 및 해설 |

TABLE OF CONTENTS

⟨Part 1⟩ 실전응용 연습문제 분석 및 해설(원문해석·정답포함) 4

1 주제와 중심소재의 폭 6
2 중심내용 바탕으로 중심소재 범위설정 8
3 중심소재와 중심내용을 드러내는 주제문 14
4 글의 구조와 주제문과의 관계 17
5 주제문과 뒷받침 문장 31
6 부연진술 53
7 통일성과 응집성 57
9 사실·의견·신념·편견의 구별 60
10 요지를 이끄는 시그널 연구 61
11 글의 제목 79
12 글 전개방식 81
13 글의 종류 104
14 글의 유형 113

⟨Part 2⟩ 유형별 문제 분석 및 해설(원문해석·정답포함) 128

Test 1 주제를 고르는 문제 130
Test 2 요지를 고르는 문제 156
Test 3 제목을 고르는 문제 171
Test 4 내용일치·세부사항 확인 문제 193
Test 5 실전 종합문제 226

〈PART 1〉
실전응용 연습문제
분석 및 **해설** (원문해석·정답포함)

1 주제와 중심스재의 폭 • 6
2 중심내용 바탕으로 중심소재 범위설정 • 8
3 중심소재와 중심내용을 드러내는 주제문 • 14
4 글의 구조와 주제문과의 관계 • 17
5 주제문과 뒷받침 문장 • 31
6 부연진술 • 53
7 통일성과 응집성 • 57
9 사실·의견·신념·편견의 구별 • 60
10 요지를 이끄는 시그널 연구 • 61
11 글의 제목 • 79
12 글 전개방식 • 81
13 글의 종류 • 104
14 글의 유형 • 113

참고: 여기에서는 8장「일반진술과 구체적 진술」을 생략했는데, 그 이유는 4·5·6장에서 8장 관련 내용, 실전 응용 문제 등을 충분히 다뤘기 때문이다. — 저자 注

1 주제와 중심소재의 폭

[실전응용 1]

중심소재는 'smoking'이다. 중심내용을 바탕으로 주제의 폭을 설정한다.

본문에서 구체적으로 다뤄질 중심내용(controlling idea)에 해당한다.

구체적 진술을 이끄는 시그널을 확인한다.

1. Smoking is very dangerous and can cause great harm to your body, even endanger your life. 1) When you smoke, your heart beats faster than it needs to and causes your blood pressure to rise, which, eventually, can cause a heart attack or heart disease. In addition, when you smoke, the essential oxygen in your bloodstream is replaced with poisonous carbon monoxide that comes from the tobacco in the cigarette. Finally, many people have fallen asleep while smoking and have set themselves and their homes on fire, endangering their lives.

중심소재: 담배 피우는 행위

1. **도입부 = 주제문** 담배는 몸에 해로운데, 심지어 생명에 지장을 초래할 수도 있다. ← 이후 글쓴이의 견해에 대한 뒷받침 진술이 이어진다(근거 제시).

1) **뒷받침 진술**
① 담배를 피우면, 심장박동 증가 → 심장마비 또는 질환 유발
② In addition – 혈관 속 산소가 해로운 일산화탄소로 전환됨
③ Finally – 담배를 피우다 졸아서 집과 생명 모두 잃어버린 사례

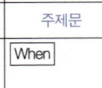

도입부 = 주제문 When

구체적 진술을 이끄는 When → 앞 문장이 일반진술에 해당하는 주제문일 가능성이 높다.

| 해설

첫 번째 문장에서 포괄적 주제에 해당하는 중심소재인 'smoking'을 파악할 수 있다. 나열의 글 전개방식을 취하고 있는 점을 확인한다. 주제: Bad Effects of **Smoking**

| 해석

흡연은 대단히 위험하고, 신체에 커다란 해를 끼칠 수 있으며 심지어 생명을 위태롭게 할 수도 있다. 흡연을 하면, 심장은 필요 이상으로 더 빠르게 뛰고 혈압을 상승시키며, 결국에는 심장마비나 심장질환을 일으킬 수 있다. 게다가, 담배를 피우면, 혈관 속의 몸에 필수적인 산소가 담배의 타바코에서 유발되는 해로운 일산화탄소로 대체된다. 마지막으로 많은 이들이 담배를 피우다 잠이 들어 화상을 입거나 집에 화재를 일으켜 그들의 삶을 위협한다.

[실전응용 2]

1. <u>The owl and the crow</u> prey on each other's weakness. ① At night, owls often make dinner of crows, which cannot see well in the dark. ⓐ During the day, it's a different story. ② Vengeful groups of crows attack and kill sleeping owls, which are resting for another night of hunting.

1. 주제문
1) 뒷받침 진술
① 뒷받침 진술 1
ⓐ 대조되는 대상으로 화제 전환
② 뒷받침 진술 2

★ 중심소재는 '올빼미와 까마귀'이다.

★ 뒷받침 진술에서 구체적으로 다뤄질 중심내용(controlling idea)이다.

도입부 =	중심소재 A, B
	비유 / 대조

글의 도입부에서 두 대상이 제시될 경우 유사점을 다루는 비교의 글인지 또는 차이점을 따르는 대조의 글인지 파악하도록 한다.

| 해설

첫 번째 문장이 주제문이고, 이후 본문 끝까지 이에 대한 뒷받침 진술이 전개되는 유형으로 대조의 글 전개방식을 취하고 있다. 첫 번째 문장에서 글의 중심소재인 올빼미와 까마귀를 파악할 수 있고, 서로의 포식관계를 설명한 글이다. 주제: **올빼미**와 **까마귀**의 포식관계

| 해석

올빼미와 까마귀는 서로의 약점을 이용하여 먹이로 삼는다. 밤에 올빼미들은 종종 어둠 속에서 제대로 볼 수 없는 까마귀들을 저녁으로 삼는다. 그러나 낮에는 상황이 전혀 다르다. 복수심에 불탄 까마귀 떼가 또 다른 밤 사냥을 위해 휴식을 취하고 있는 올빼미들을 공격하여 죽여 버리는 것이다.

2 중심내용 바탕으로 중심소재 범위설정

[실전응용 1]

첫 번째 문장이 주제문에 해당한다. 글의 중심소재는 "computer"이다. 만약 중심소재를 글의 주제로 파악할 경우, **지나치게 포괄적인 주제**에 해당하고, 본문에 다뤄질 내용(Controlling Idea)에 대한 예측이 불가능하다. 첫 번째 문장을 좀 더 자세히 살펴보자.

> These days, it is important to know something about <u>computers</u>.
> There are <u>a number of ways</u> to learn.
>
> 오늘날 컴퓨터에 대해서 아는 것은 중요하다. (컴퓨터를) 배우는 방법에는 다양한 것이 있다.

첫 번째 문장에서 중심소재를 설정하고 바로 이어지는 문장을 통해 구체적 주제 설정이 가능하다. 중심소재는 'computer'이며, Controlling Idea는 "a number of ways"이다. 본문에 대한 예측은 주제의 폭을 구체화했기 때문에 가능한 것임을 기억하도록 한다. 주제: **컴퓨터**를 배우는 다양한 방법

* Controlling Idea(중심내용): 본문에서 다뤄질 중심내용으로 Controlling Idea를 중심으로 본문에 이어질 내용을 예측한다.

| 본문 분석

> These days, 1. it is important to know something about computers. 1) There are a number of ways to learn. ① Ⓐ Some companies have computer classes at work. Ⓑ Also, most universities offer day and night courses in computer science. Ⓒ Another way to learn is from a book. There are many books about computers in book stores and libraries. Ⓓ Or, you can learn from a friend. After a few hours of practice, you too can work with computers. You may not be an expert, but you can have fun!

중심소재: Computer
1. 도입부
컴퓨터에 지식 습득의 중요성
1) 주제문
컴퓨터를 배우는 방법은 다양하다(나열).
① 뒷받침 진술
Ⓐ, Ⓑ, Ⓒ, Ⓓ

★ 나열의 시그널
also, another, or를 확인한다.

| 해설

앞에서 언급한 대로 중심소재는 'computer'이며 Controlling Idea는 "a number of ways"에 해당한다. 주제는 "컴퓨터를 배우는 다양한 방법"이다. 주제를 설정할 때 그 폭을 좁히는 방법의 하나는 바로 Controlling Idea를 활용하는 것이다.

| 해석

오늘날 컴퓨터에 대해 아는 것은 중요하다. 컴퓨터를 배우는 방법에는 많은 것이 있다. 어떤 회사는 직장에서 컴퓨터 강좌를 제공한다. 또 대부분의 대학교는 컴퓨터 과학 강좌를 주야로 제공한다. 컴퓨터를 배울 수 있는 또 다른 방법은 책을 통해서이다. 책방이나 도서관에 컴퓨터에 관한 책이 많이 있다. 또는 친구를 통해서 배울 수 있다. 몇 시간만 연습하면, 당신 또한 컴퓨터를 다룰 수 있다. 전문가는 아니겠지만, (충분히) 컴퓨터를 즐길 수 있다.

[실전응용 2]

첫 번째 문장에서 중심소재와 주제 설정이 가능하다. Controlling Idea를 중심으로 주제의 폭을 좁히도록 한다.

> There are at least four things which are more or less under our own control and which are essential to happiness.
> 행복에 필수적이며 우리가 정확히 통제할 수 있는 적어도 네 가지 것이 있다.

주제문으로 중심소재는 'happiness'이다. 만약 중심소재를 그대로 주제로 설정할 경우, 지나치게 포괄적이어서 본문에 다뤄질 내용에 대한 감을 잡을 수가 없다. Controlling Idea에 해당하는 'four things'를 포함하여 '행복을 위한 네 가지 조건'으로 설정하는 것이 가장 적절하다. Controlling Idea를 바탕으로 전체 글은 다음과 같은 구조를 가질 것을 예상할 수 있다.

controlling idea로 본문에 ★
전개될 구체적 내용에 대
한 예측 가능

controlling idea에 대한 ★
구체적 내용에 해당하는
본문

There are four things ... to happiness.
First, _____.
Second, _____.
Third, _____.
Fourth, _____.

* 문장삽입 문제와의 연관성

도입부 = | 주제문 |
          | Ⓐ____ |
          | ____ |
          | ④ |

Ⓐ의 내용은 뒷받
침 문장 ④에 대한
부연진술임을 확인
한다.

| 본문 분석

1. There are at least **four things** which are more or less under our own control and which are essential to **happiness**. 1) ① The **first** is some moral standard by which to guide our actions. ② The **second** is some satisfactory home life in the form of good relations with family or friends. ③ The **third** is some form of work which justifies our existence to our own country and makes us good citizens. ④ The **fourth** thing is some degree of leisure and the use of it in some way that makes us happy. Ⓐ To succeed in making a good use of our leisure will not compensate for failure in any one of the other three things to which I have referred, but a reasonable amount of leisure and a good use of it is an important contribution to a happy life.

중심소재: 행복
1. 도입부 = 주제문
행복에 필수적이면서 우리가 통제할 수 있는 네 가지 요소가 있다(four things: Controlling Idea).
1) 뒷받침 진술
① 첫 번째: moral standard
② 두 번째: satisfactory home life
③ 세 번째: some form of work
④ 네 번째: leisure
Ⓐ 부연진술

| 해석

행복에 필수적이면서 우리가 정확히 통제할 수 있는 것은 적어도 네 가지가 있다. 첫 번째는 우리 행동의 기준을 제시하는 특정 도덕적 잣대이다. 두 번째는 가족 또는 친구와 좋은 관계를 유지하는 형태의 만족스러운 가정생활이다. 세 번째는 국가에 우리 존재의 정당성을 증명하고 바람직한 시민이 되도록 하는 일이다. 네 번째는 어느 정도의 여가와 이를 우리가 행복해지는 방법으로 활용하는 것이다. 여가를 잘 활용하는 것이 앞에서 내가 언급한 다른 세 가지 것 중 어느 것이라도 실패하는 것을 보상해 주지는 못하지만, 적절한 여가와 이를 잘 활용하는 것은 행복한 삶에 아주 중요한 공헌을 한다.

[실전응용 3]

첫 번째 문장에서 주제문이 드러난다. 주제와 중심내용의 설정이 가능하다.

One way to accomplish teaching morals and values to your kids is to give them on-the-spot lessons in honesty.

글의 중심소재는 '도덕성'과 '가치관'이며, 주제는 '도덕성과 가치관의 교육'이다. 만약 주제를 '도덕성과 가치관'으로 잡을 경우 주제의 폭이 지나치게 광범위하게 되어 글쓴이가 구체적으로 어떤 내용을 다루려는지 예측할 수 없게 된다. 본문에서 전개될 구체적 내용을 알려주는 Controlling Idea는 '**on-the-spot** lessons in honesty'이다.

본문 분석

1. One way to accomplish teaching morals and values to your kids is to give them on-the-spot lessons in honesty. 1) For example, ① your four-year-old has just walked out of the toy store with a car you didn't buy. You notice the car in his hand as you are buckling him into his safety seat. Do not make excuses for your child and laugh it off, saying to yourself, "He's only four—he didn't mean to steal it." That may be true—young children don't completely comprehend the notion of stealing—② **but** if you don't deal with what he did, you are letting him know that it's okay to take something that's not his. Hold your child accountable for his action. Explain to him in a calm manner that you are disappointed in him for taking the toy from the store. Just hearing those words can have a deep effect on your child. Further explain that taking the car was wrong and that he needs to return it to the store manager and apologize immediately.

중심소재: 도덕과 가치 → 도덕과 가치의 학습

1. 도입부 = 주제문
1) 뒷받침 진술
① 네 살짜리 아이가 등장하는 구체적 상황을 설정한 후 '도덕성과 가치관 교육'이라는 주제를 전달하고 있다. Controlling Idea인 'on-the-spot lessons in honesty'의 내용이 강조되는 부분은 ②의 'but' 이후부터 본문 끝까지 이어지고 있다. 본문 마지막 문장의 'immediately'라는 부사는 'on-the-spot'을 직접 드러내는 표현이 된다.

★도입부 =

주제문
뒷받침 진술 For example

본문의 For example은 뒷받침 예시에 해당한다. 이 경우 바로 앞의 문장은 주제문이 됨을 기억한다.

해석

도덕과 가치를 당신의 아이들에게 가르치는 방법의 하나는 솔직하게 그 자리에서 교훈을 주는 것이다. 예를 들어, 당신의 4살 난 아이가 당신이 사지 않은 장난감 차를 가지고 상점에서 나왔다. 당신은 아이의 안전띠를 채워주면서 손에 든 (장난감) 차를 알아챈다. "얘는 네 살밖에 안 됐어. 이걸 훔치려고 한 게 아니야."라고 웃어넘기며 아이를 위한 변명을 하지 마라. 그게 맞을지도 모른다. 어린아이들은 훔치는 것에 대한 개념을 확실히 이해하지 못한다. 그러나 만약 당신이 그가 한 행동에 대해 아무것도 하지 않는다면, 당신은 그에게 자신의 물건이 아닌 것을 가져가도 된다고 알려주는 꼴이 된다. 당신의 아이가 자신의 행동에 대해 책임을 질 수 있도록 해라. 아이에게 상점에서 장난감을 가져온 것에 대해 당신이 실망했다고 차분한 방법으로 설명해라. 그런 말을 듣는 것만으로도 아이에게 깊은 효과를 이끌어 낸다. 나아가 (장난감) 차를 훔치는 것이 옳지 않다는 것과 그가 상점 주인에게 그것을 되돌려 주어야 하며, 즉각적으로 사과해야 한다고 설명해라.

참고

글의 도입부에 'for example'이 나올 경우 바로 앞 문장이 주제문일 가능성이 크다(Case 1). 글의 중반에 등장하는 'but' 이후와 'for example'의 사이의 문장도 주제문이 될 수 있다(Case 2).

Case 1

```
_____주 제 문_____
For example, _____
_____
_____
_____
```

Case 2

```
_____
_____
_____. But _____주 제 문_____
For example, _____
_____
_____
```

★ 'But'을 기준으로 앞에서 전개된 내용과 상반되는 글쓴이의 견해가 진술되고 이에 대한 뒷받침 진술이 따른다.

[실전응용 4]

인구증가에 따른 식량 대책의 필요성
주제문(현상 – 문제점)
구체적 진술   현상 ⓐ   ↕ But   현상 ⓑ
일반진술 : 요약·정리

★ 중심소재는 '인구증가에 따른 식량문제'이고, 제목은 "Two Conflicting Realities Regarding Food Problem"으로 잡을 수 있다.

| 본문 분석

1. If there are more people in the world, then there must be more food for these people. 1) **But** food is already a problem in today's world. ① Ⓐ A third of the world's population is very hungry, because there is not enough food. Ten thousand people die of hunger every day in some parts of the world. Ⓑ **But** in other parts of the world, people become ill or die because they are too fat. 2. Some countries have no food, but others have too much, and throw it away.

중심소재: 식량문제
1. 도입부
인구증가에 따른 식량 증가의 필요성 언급
1) 주제문(현상 – 문제점 지적)
식량문제 대두
① 구체적 진술(Ⓐ ↔ Ⓑ 대조)
식량문제와 관련하여 상반된 현실 제시
Ⓐ 식량문제로 고통받는 지역
↕ But
Ⓑ 식량풍족으로 인한 모순적 문제 대두
2. **일반적 진술(요약·정리)**

| 해석

만약 세상에 사람들이 더 많다면, 이 사람들을 위한 더 많은 음식이 있어야 한다. 하지만 오늘날 식량은 이미 문젯거리이다. 세계 인구 중 1/3은 매우 굶주리고 있다. (이는) 충분한 음식이 없기 때문이다. 매일 이 세계의 어딘가에서 하루에 1만 명의 사람이 굶어 죽어가고 있다. 하지만 다른 곳에서는 사람들이 지나치게 뚱뚱해서 병에 걸리거나 죽는다. 어떤 나라는 음식이 없지만, 어떤 나라는 지나치게 많아, 그것을 내다 버린다(낭비한다).

[실전응용 5]

1) Collecting can open new worlds for children. ① Collecting stamps, for example, shows them cultures or historical events of a country. Plant or animal specimens teach them about the natural world. 2) Collecting also gives children opportunities to learn skills that can be used every day. ② While playing with collections such as dolls, comic books, stickers, and so on, children can organize their treasures by size, shape, or color. 3) This will teach them to see the world from different points of view. ③ Thinking about the relationships among their pieces, they may realize things in the world are connected with each other.

★ 중심소재에 해당한다.

★ 본문에서 구체적으로 진술된 중심내용(controlling idea)이다.

중심소재: 수집

1. 도입부 = 뒷받침 진술
1) **뒷받침 1**
수집의 첫 번째 기능: 아이들에게 새로운 세상을 열어준다.
① 부연진술
예시부연을 통해 수집의 첫 번째 기능 부연
2) **뒷받침 2**
수집의 두 번째 기능: 새로운 일상의 기술을 배울 기회제공
② 부연진술
3) **뒷받침 3**
수집의 세 번째 기능: 다양한 시각에서 세상을 바라보는 눈
③ 부연진술

| 해설

주제문 이후 바로 뒷받침 진술이 이어지는 두괄식 지문의 전형이다. 첫 번째 문장에서 중심소재인 'Collecting'을 파악할 수 있다. 중심소재 자체를 주제로 설정했을 때, 주제의 폭이 지나치게 포괄적일 수 있기에 중심내용을 바탕으로 중심소재의 폭을 좁혀야 한다. 주제 또는 제목: Educational Effects of Collecting

| 해석

수집은 아이들에게 새로운 세상을 열어 줄 수 있다. 예를 들어, 우표 수집은 아이들에게 한 나라의 문화 또는 역사적 사건들을 보여준다. 식물이나 동물의 표본은 아이들에게 자연 세계를 가르쳐준다. 또한, 수집은 아이들에게 일상에서 활용될 기술을 배울 기회를 제공해 준다. 인형이나 만화책, 스티커 등과 같은 수집품들을 가지고 노는 동안에 아이들은 자신들의 보물들을 크기, 모양, 또는 빛깔에 따라 구성할 수 있다. 이를 통해 아이들은 다양한 관점으로 세상을 바라보는 법을 배우게 된다. 아이들은 수집품 사이의 관계에 대해 생각하면서 세상에 존재하는 것들이 서로 관련이 있음을 깨달을 수 있다.

3 중심소재와 중심내용을 드러내는 주제문

* 실전단락 엿보기

도입부 = 통념 A = B↑
But A ≠ B
주제문
뒷받침
진술

[실전연습]

예제 1 |

<u>Camping</u> can be <u>an inexpensive vacation</u>.
A (Topic)　　　　B (Controlling Idea)

주제: 휴가로 즐길 수 있는 저렴한 캠핑을 다루는 글

중심내용: '캠핑은 비싸다' 는 일반인들의 인식과 반대되는 글쓴이의 견해를 드러내고, 뒷받침 문장을 통해 이에 대한 근거를 제시한다. 중심내용은 '저렴한 가격으로 즐기는 휴가' 이다.

★ '캠핑' 은 중심소재인 동시에 좁은 범위의 주제이다. 중심내용을 고려하여 '저렴한 휴가로 즐기는 캠핑' 이 주제로 더 적절하다.

중심내용에 해당한다. ★

주제문	<u>Camping</u> can be <u>an inexpensive vacation</u>.
뒷받침 진술	캠핑을 저렴하게 즐길 수 있다는 글쓴이의 견해를 뒷받침할 내용이 전개된다.

* 실전단락 엿보기

도입부 = 현상(⊖)
주제문
구체적
진술

예제 2 |

<u>Air pollution in Mexico City</u> is <u>the worst in the world for a number of reasons</u>.
　　　　A (Topic)　　　　　　　　B (Controlling Idea)

주제: 멕시코시티의 심각한 공해

중심내용: 멕시코시티가 세계 최악인 여러 이유가 소개된다.

주제문	Air pollution in Mexico City is the worst in the world for a number of reasons.
뒷받침 진술	심각한 공해로 몸살을 앓고 있는 멕시코시티를 소개하고(현상제시), 이후 나열의 글 전개방식을 통해 이유가 나열될 것이다. Reason 1. _____. Reason 2. _____. Reason 3. _____.

★ 중심소재는 공해이며, 주제는 '멕시코시티의 심각한 공해'이다.

★ 중심내용은 '멕시코시티가 최악의 공해도시'인 이유에 해당한다. 특히 'a number of reasons'를 통해 현상의 원인이 나열될 것을 예상할 수 있다.

예제 3 |

There are <u>several enjoyable ways</u> to <u>travel between the US and Korea</u>.
    A (Controlling Idea)   B (Topic)

주제: 미국과 한국을 오가는 여행

중심내용: 미국과 한국을 오가는 즐거운 여행 방법

주제문	There are several enjoyable ways to travel between the US and Korea.
뒷받침 진술	최근 한국과 미국 사이에 오가는 여행객 수의 증가(현상)를 언급하면서 자연스럽게 중심내용을 이끌어 낼 수 있도록 글을 구성한다. Way 1. _____. Way 2. _____. Way 3. _____.

★ 중심내용으로 '다양한 즐거운 여행 방법'이 된다.

★ 핵심어는 '여행'이며 주제는 '한국과 미국을 오가는 여행'이다.

* 실전단락 엿보기

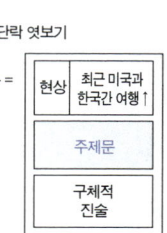

* 실전단락 엿보기

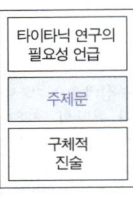

예제 4 |

In order to fully <u>explore the wreck of the Titanic</u>, scientists must <u>address several problems</u>.
　　　　　　　　　 A (Topic)　　　　　　　　　　　　　　 B (Controlling Idea)

주제: 난파된 타이타닉 연구

중심내용: 타이타닉호 연구의 걸림돌을 언급한 후, 이에 대한 해결 방안을 제시한다.

★ 중심소재는 '타이타닉호'이고, 주제는 '난파된 타이타닉호의 연구'이다.

★ 타이타닉호 연구의 걸림돌을 언급한 후 이에 대한 해결책을 제시한다.

주제문	In order to fully explore the wreck of the Titanic, scientists must address several problems.
뒷받침 진술	'문제점 제시 → 해결책'으로 구성한다. 문제점 1 – 해결책 문제점 2 – 해결책 문제점 3 – 해결책

* 실전단락 엿보기

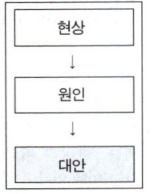

현상 + 원인 = 주제문

예제 5 |

<u>Animals in danger of becoming extinct</u> <u>come from a wide range of countries</u>.
　　　　　　 A(Topic)　　　　　　　　　　　　　　 B(Controlling Idea)

주제: 멸종 위기에 처한 동물

중심내용: 다양한 나라를 언급하며 멸종 위기에 처한 동물을 구체적으로 진술한다. "현상(문제점 지적) — 원인 대안"으로 내용이 전개될 수 있다.

★ 중심소재는 '동물'이고, 주제는 '멸종 위기의 동물'이다.

★ 중심내용 – 멸종 위기의 동물이 특정 지역에서만 국한되어 있지 않고, 전 세계에서 발생하는 보편적 현상임을 지적한다.

서론	Animals in danger of becoming extinct come from a wide range of countries.
본론	여러 나라에서 발생하고 있는 멸종 위기의 동물을 소개한다 (문제점 지적).
결론	대안으로 글쓴이의 견해가 제시된다. 예를 들어, 협력을 통한 해결책 강구가 시급함을 여러 나라에 호소한다.

16

4 글의 구조와 주제문과의 관계

1. 두괄식

[실전응용 1]

1. <u>Primitive man never looked out over the world and saw 'mankind' as a group and felt his common cause with his species</u>. 1) From the beginning he was a provincial who raised ① the barriers high. Whether it was ② a question of choosing a wife or of taking a head, the first and important distinction was between his own human group and those beyond the pale. ③ His own group, with all its ways of behaving, was unique.

중심소재: 원시인 → 원시인의 편협성
1. **도입부** = 주제문
원시인들은 자신이 속한 공동체 외 외부에 관심이 없었으며, 자신이 속한 종과의 대의를 느끼지 못했다.
1) **뒷받침 진술**(근거제시)
① 울타리를 세워 외부와 차단
② 아내 또는 족장을 뽑을 때 자신의 공동체에 속한 사람인지의 여부 확인
③ 자신만의 독특한 생활방식 고수

★ 글의 도입부에서 주제문 설정은 앞으로 전개될 글의 방향성을 제시한다는 점에서 절대 놓쳐서는 안 된다. 첫 번째 문장을 포함한 도입부는 집중해서 읽도록 한다.

★ 나열의 시그널이 보이지 않더라도 뒷받침 진술 내 화제가 바뀌는 부분을 확인할 수 있어야 한다.

| 해설

깔끔한 두괄식 구조를 취하고 있다. 원시인에 관한 어떤 측면을 다루는지(주제)와 이에 대한 뒷받침 진술로 어떤 내용이 나오는지 확인하도록 한다. 주제: 원시인의 편협성

| 해석

원시인은 세상 너머를 본 적이 없었으며, 인류를 한 집단으로 간주하여 그의 종족과 공동의 목적을 느껴 본 적은 결코 없었다. 처음부터 벽을 높게 쌓아 올린 편협한 존재였다. 아내를 고르거나 추장을 뽑는 문제가 되든, 가장 우선시 되고 중요한 구별은 자기 집단 사람이냐 아니면 그런 경계를 넘어선 사람이냐이다. 나름의 집단 행동 방식을 가진 그 자신의 집단은 독특했다(편협한 집단생활로 다른 집단과 구별이 되었다).

[실전응용 2]

세계화에 관한 글로 이로 ★
말미암은 결과에 해당하는
'tougher competition'을
파악하도록 한다.

도입부 = 주제문
┌─────────┐
│ 뒷받침 │ 과거
│ 진술   │ ↕
│   │ 현재
└─────────┘
시간의 대조를 확인
한다.

1. <u>As the impact of globalization spreads to every industry, business people around the world learn to expect tougher competition than they have ever faced before</u>. 1) <u>Back when</u> five or ten rivals could comfortably coexist in a single market, some would offer high-quality products at premium prices while others sold lesser goods for a discount. <u>Today</u>, most consumers and industrial buyers won't even consider low-quality goods, and it's hard to find a company that hasn't joined the quality movement.

중심소재: Globalization
인과의 글 전개방식 확인
1. 도입부 = 주제문
원인: 산업 전반에 세계화의 확대
결과(현상): 그 어느 때보다 치열한 경쟁
1) 뒷받침 진술
과거와 현재를 대조하면서 치열해진 경쟁의 상황을 구체적으로 제시하고 있다.

| 해석
세계화의 영향이 모든 산업에 퍼져감에 따라, 세계의 사업가들은 예전에 직면했던 것보다 더 심한(거친) 경쟁을 예측해야 함을 알게된다. 과거 다섯 내지 열 경쟁자가 안락하게 단일의 시장에서 공존했을 때, 일부 업체들은 고품질의 제품들을 액면가 이상으로 내놓았고, 다른 업체들은 품질이 낮은 제품들을 할인 판매했다. 오늘날 대부분의 소비자나 산업 구매자들은 질 나쁜 상품은 아예 고려조차 하지 않으며, 품질 향상 운동에 참여하지 않는 기업들도 찾아보기 어렵다.

[실전응용 3]

1. <u>Even now, ancient India is still visible and accessible to us in a very direct sense</u>. 1) At the beginning of the twentieth century, some Indian communities still lived as all our primeval ancestors must once have lived, by hunting and gathering. ① The bullock-cart and potter's wheel of many villages today are much the same as those used 4,000 years ago. ② A caste-system whose main lines were set by about 1,000 B.C. still regulates the lives of millions, and even of some Indian Christians and Moslems. ③ Gods and goddesses whose cults can be traced to the Stone Age are still worshipped at village shrines.

중심소재: 고대 인도
1. 도입부 = 주제문
고대 인도는 우리와 아주 가까운 의미에서 볼 수 있고, 접근할 수 있다 – 이후 근거에 대한 뒷받침 문장이 제시될 것을 예측할 수 있다.
1) 뒷받침 진술
인도의 특정 공동체는 여전히 고대 조상의 삶(수렵·채집)을 답습하고 있다.
① 황소가 끄는 차와 물레
② 카스트제도
③ 종교

| 해설
첫 번째 문장에서 주제문이 제시되고, 이후 뒷받침 문장으로 이어지는 전형적인 'General statement → Specific statement' 구조이다.

| 해석
지금도, 고대 인도는 아직 우리에게 매우 직접적인 의미에서 눈에 띄며 접근할 수 있다. 20세기 초 몇몇 인도인 공동체들은 여전히 우리의 원시 선조가 한때 분명히 살았던 방식인 수렵과 채집을 하며 살고 있었다. 오늘날 많

은 마을의 소달구지와 도공용 돌림판은 4천 년 전에 사용된 것과 상당히 비슷하다. 서기 1천 년 경에 (사회) 계층의 주된 선(구별)이 정해진 카스트제도(신분제)는 여전히 수백만 명의 삶을 지배하고 있으며, 심지어 인도 기독교인들과 모슬렘의 삶까지도 규제하고 있다. 그 숭배의 전례가 석기 시대까지 거슬러 올라갈 수도 있는 남신과 여신들도 마을의 신전에서 여전히 경배 되고 있다.

[실전응용 4]

1. The therapeutic value and healing powers of plants were demonstrated to me ① when I was a boy of about ten. 1) I had developed an acute, persistent abdominal pain that did not respond readily to hospital medication. My mother had taken me to the city's central hospital on several occasions, where different drugs were tried on me. In total desperation, she took me to Egya Mensa, a well-known herbalist in my hometown in the western province of Ghana. This man was no stranger to the medical doctors at the hospital. He had earned the reputation of offering excellent help when they were confronted with difficult cases where Western medicine had failed to effect a cure.

중심소재: plants → The Healing Powers of Plants

1. 도입부 = 주제문
① 에서 알 수 있듯이 주인공의 경험담을 바탕으로 뒷받침 진술이 이어질 것을 예상할 수 있다.

1) 뒷받침 진술
'약초의 효능'에 대한 뒷받침 진술이 제시되고 있다.

★ 본문에서 구체적으로 다뤄질 중심내용(controlling idea)에 해당한다.

★ 중심소재는 'plant'이다.

| 해설
개인의 경험담을 바탕으로 뒷받침 문장을 제공하는 대표적인 예이다.

| 해석
내가 약 10세의 소년이었을 때, 약초의 치료 가치와 치유력은 나에게 입증되었다(약초의 치료 가치와 치유력을 경험했다). 나는 병원의 약물치료에 쉽사리 낫지 않았던 계속되는 격렬한 복통에 시달렸다. 어머니는 몇 차례나 나를 도시의 중앙병원으로 데려가셨으며, 그곳에서 여러 가지 약들이 나에게 시험되었다. 큰 절망감에 빠진 어머니는 가나의 서부지역에 있는 내 고향마을의 유명한 본초학자에게 나를 데려가셨다. 이 분은 병원 의사들 사이에서도 유명한 분이셨다. 그는 서구의학이 치료하지 못한 난치병에 걸린 사람들에게 큰 도움을 줌으로써 명성을 얻은 분이셨다.

[실전응용 5]

1. The work of makeup artists ranges from ① highlighting the natural features of a film star to ② changing altogether actors' appearances to fit the characters they portray. 1) ① In the black and white era of filmmaking, movies favored stars such as Katharine Hepburn and Lauren Bacall whose angular faces and prominent cheekbones caught the light and cast

중심소재: 메이크업 아티스트의 역할

1. 도입부 = 주제문
'메이크업 아티스트의 역할'에 관한 글이다. 이후 뒷받침 문장으로 각 역할에 대한 구체적 진술이 뒤따른다.

1) 뒷받침 문장
① 주제문에서 밝힌 '영화배우의 자연적인 얼굴의 특징 부각'에 대한 내용을 두 시대로 나눈 후 각 시대의 구체적 인물을 들어 설명하고 있다.

★ 메이크업 아티스트에 관한 글임을 알 수 있다.

★ 본문에서 구체적으로 진술될 중심내용(controlling idea)에 해당한다.

lovely shadows. **With the advent of color**, the emphasis shifted to the glowing complexion of Marilyn Monroe, Grace Kelly, and Kim Novak. The job of makeup artists, in either case, was to prepare these stars to face the camera by accentuating the telling features. ② **At the same time**, makeup artists have also created totally new faces for actors, making them seem older or younger and, in the case of horror films, turning normal people into vampires, werewolves, mummies, or other monsters.

② 순접 추가의 'at the same time' 확인 – 주제문에서 밝힌 '등장인물에 맞는 전혀 새로운 인물 창조'의 역할에 관한 구체적 진술이 이어지고 있다.

| 해석

메이크업 아티스트의 일은 영화배우의 자연스러운 모습을 드러내 보이는 것부터 배우가 극 중 인물의 성격에 맞게 외모를 모두 바꾸는 일까지 다양하다. 흑백으로 영화를 만들던 시기에는 각진 얼굴 윤곽과 광대뼈가 두드러진 캐서린 헵번이나 로렌 바콜 같은 사람들이 조명을 받아 아름다운 그림자가 드러나게 했다. 컬러 시대가 도래하면서 초점이 마릴린 먼로, 그레이스 켈리 그리고 킴 노백과 같은 사람들의 빛나는 화장 기법으로 옮겨졌다. 흑백이거나 컬러이거나 메이크업 아티스트의 임무는 배우들이 돋보이는 특징을 강조하여 카메라 앞에 서게 하는 것이다. 그와 동시에 메이크업 아티스트는 나이가 더 들어 보이게 하거나 더 젊어 보이게 하는 등 배우에게 전혀 다른 얼굴을 만들어 주었으며 특히, 공포영화는 정상적인 사람을 흡혈귀, 늑대인간, 미라 그리고 여러 괴물로 변장시키기도 한다.

2. 미괄식

[실전응용 1]

1. ① Most of us believe that we can trust in technology to solve our problems. Whatever problem you name, you can also name some hoped-for technological solution. ② Some of us have faith that we shall solve our dependence on fossil fuels by developing new technologies for hydrogen engines, wind energy, or solar energy. ③ Some of us have faith that we shall solve our food problems with genetically modified crops newly or soon to be developed. ④ Those with such faith assume that the new technologies will ultimately succeed, without harmful side effects. 2. However, there is no basis for believing that technology will not cause new and unanticipated problems while solving the problems that it previously produced.

중심소재: Technology

1. 도입부 = 통념

①, ②, ③, ④에서 일반인들의 통념을 비판하는 글임을 알 수 있다. 통념비판의 글은 '일반인의 견해 – However – 글쓴이의 견해(주장)'의 패턴을 따른다. 보통 중괄식 구조를 취하나 본문은 문미에 'However'가 나오는 미괄식 구조를 취하고 있다.

– 일반인의 견해: 현대 기술을 통해 우리가 직면한 모든 문제를 긍정적 방향으로 해결할 수 있다.

2. 주제문

'However' 이후 글쓴이의 주장이 드러난다: 기술이 이전의 문제를 해결하고, 기대하지 못했던 새로운 문제를 야기하지 않을 것이란 믿음은 근거가 없다.

| 해석

대부분 우리는 과학기술이 우리가 직면한 문제를 해결할 수 있다고 신뢰한다. 당신이 어떤 문제를 제기하든 간에, 당신은 또한 희망 즉, 과학 기술적 해결책을 제기할 수 있다. 우리 중 일부는 수소엔진, 풍력에너지, 또는 태양에너지에 대한 새로운 기술을 개발함으로써 우리의 화석연료에 대한 의존을 해결할 것이라는 믿음을 가지고 있다. 우리 중 일부는 새로운 또는 머지않아 개발할 유전자 변형 곡물로 우리의 식량문제를 해결할 것이라고 믿는다. 그러한 믿음을 가진 사람들은 새로운 과학기술이 해로운 부작용 없이 결국 성공할 것이라고 간주한다. 그러나 과학기술이 이전에 초래한 문제를 해결하는 동시에 새롭고 예기치 못한 문제를 야기하지 않을 거라고 믿을 수 있는 근거는 없다.

[실전응용 2]

1. Over the past twenty years, I've asked thousands of people, "Where are you when you get your best ideas?" 1) The most frequent answers are: ① 'resting in bed,' 'walking in nature,' 'listening to music while driving in my car,' and 'relaxing in the bath.' People rarely get their best ideas at work. What is so special about walking in the woods or resting in bed? Solitude and relaxation. 2. Most people have their best ideas when they are relaxed and by themselves. 1) Leonardo da Vinci once wrote, "If you are alone you are completely yourself, but if you are accompanied by a single companion you are half yourself."

중심소재: 아이디어 → 아이디어의 원천
1. **도입부 = 주제문**
의문점(문제 제기)의 유형이다.

의문점(문제 제기) = 주제
답변 = 요지

의문점: 최고의 아이디어는 언제 얻을 수 있는가?
1) 대부분 사람들은 ①의 상황에서 최고의 아이디어를 얻는다.
2. **주제문**
휴식을 취하거나 혼자 있을 때 최상의 아이디어를 얻는다.
1) **뒷받침 진술**
권위 있는 사람의 말을 인용하면서 주제문의 중심내용을 뒷받침하고 있다.

도입부 = 의문점 (주제) / 답변 (요지) / 뒷받침 진술

| 해석

지난 20년에 걸쳐 나는 수천 명의 사람에게 다음과 같이 물었다. "어디에 계실 때 최상의 아이디어가 떠오릅니까?" 가장 흔한 답변은 '침대에 누워 쉬고 있을 때,' '자연 속에서 거닐 때,' '음악을 들으며 차를 몰 때,' 그리고 '목욕을 하며 편히 쉴 때' 등이었다. 사람들은 일하고 있는 동안 최상의 아이디어를 떠올리는 경우는 거의 없다. 숲에서 산책하거나 침대에 누워 쉬는 것이 뭐가 그리도 특별한 것일까? 혼자 있는 것과 휴식이다. 대부분의 사람은 편히 쉬고 혼자 있을 때 최상의 아이디어를 얻는다. 레오나르도 다빈치는 다음과 같은 글을 쓴 적이 있다. "홀로 있으면, 당신은 온전히 당신이 될 수 있지만, 단 한 사람이라도 동행하게 되면 당신은 반쪽이 될 뿐이다."

[실전응용 3]

1. Years ago, I was involved in planning a police operation that was to take place in Lakeland, Florida. As the mission planner was describing the operation order, he seemed to have everything covered. His arms were outstretched over two chairs as he confidently explained the very detailed

중심소재: 자신감과 행동의 관계
1. **도입부**
글쓴이 'I'가 겪은 구체적인 사례를 소개하고 있다.

★구체적 사례로 시작하는 글은 미괄식 구조인 'Specific Statement(구체적 진술) → General Statement(일반진술)'를 취할 수 있으므로 이후 진술의 내용을 바탕으로 어느 시점에서 일반진술로 이어지는지 확인할 수 있어야 한다.

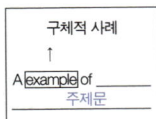

'an example of A' 에서 A는 일반진술에 해당한다. 이는 'an example' 이 구체적 진술에 해당하기 때문임이다.

arrest plan. 1) **Suddenly** someone asked, "Have you contacted the Lakeland ambulance crew?" Instantly the mission planner withdrew his arms and dropped them between his knees, palms together. He went from dominating a large space to being as narrow as possible, all because he had not made the necessary arrangements. He suddenly lost the initiative. 2. This is a striking example of how quickly our behaviors ebb and flow depending on our level of confidence.

1) 반전된 상황을 이끄는 suddenly가 활용되고 있다.

2. 주제문
앞에서 전개한 구체적 사례에서 일반화를 이끌어내고 있다. 글쓴이의 요지가 드러난다. 주제: 자신감의 정도에 따른 행동의 변화

| 해설

구체적인 예에서 일반화를 이끌어내는 'Specific statement → General statement' 의 전형이다. 이런 유형의 글은 글의 초반에 구체적 예가 등장하기에 글의 요지를 찾기가 어려울 수 있다. 이런 경우, 글을 따라 읽어가면서 '글쓴이가 이런 구체적 사례에서 전달하려고 하는 숨은 요지는 무엇인가' 라는 자문을 끊임없이 던져야 한다. 본문은 글의 말미에서 글의 요지가 드러나도록 일반화하고 있지만, 어떤 경우 이런 일반화를 독자가 이끌어 내야 하는 경우(Implicit)가 있으니 주의해야 한다.

| 해석

몇 년 전에 나는 Florida의 Lakeland에서 수행한 경찰작전에 관여한 적이 있었다. 작전 계획자가 작전 순서를 설명할 때 그는 모든 것을 다 준비한 것처럼 보였다. 그가 매우 구체적인 체포 계획을 자신 있게 설명할 때, 그의 양팔은 두 개의 의자 위로 쭉 뻗어져 있었다. "Lakeland의 응급구조대원들과는 연락되었나요?"라고 갑자기 어떤 사람이 물었다. 그 즉시 그 작전 계획자는 그의 양팔을 거두어 두 손바닥을 마주 댄 채 그의 무릎 사이로 떨어뜨렸다. 그는 아주 넓은 공간을 지배하다가 가능한 한 작아졌는데, 이는 그가 필요한 준비를 하지 않았기 때문이었다. 그는 순식간에 주도권을 잃었다. 이것은 자신감의 수준에 따라 우리의 행동이 얼마나 빨리 위축되고, (거침없이) 자유로울 수 있는지를 보여주는 인상적인 예이다.

[실전응용 4]

일반적으로 'some – others' 의 형태는 대조에서 많이 나오지만 다양한 견해를 언급할 때도 사용됨을 확인하자.

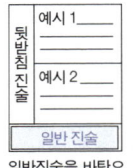

일반진술을 바탕으로 주제/요지를 이끌어낸다.

1. Some people can learn a foreign language just by hearing it, and then trying to speak it. Other people have to read it and write it in order to learn it. So some people use their ears more, and others use their eyes more to learn new things. 1) Take another example. I can't learn how to use a computer just by reading an instruction manual. But many people seem to learn how to use a computer just by reading the manual. 2. In short, people learn things in different ways.

중심소재: 학습방법

1. 도입부 = 구체적 진술
1) 예시 1
외국어 학습에 있어 다양한 방법이 존재함 설명.
2) 예시 2
컴퓨터 학습의 다양성
2. 주제문(요지)
학습방법은 다양하다.

| 해설

본문의 주제 또는 제목을 '외국어 학습방법의 다양성' 이라고 설정하지 않도록 주의한다. 컴퓨터 학습 방법과 같이 또 하나의 예로 외국어 학습 방법이 제시되고 있을 뿐이다.

| 해석

어떤 이는 듣고 따라 말해봄으로써 외국어를 배울 수 있다. 어떤 사람은 외국어를 배우기 위해 읽고 써야 하는 경우가 있다. 그래서 어떤 이들은 새로운 것을 배우기 위해 귀를 더 사용하고, 어떤 이들은 눈을 더 사용한다. 다른 예를 들어보자. 나는 지침서를 읽고서도 컴퓨터 사용법을 배울 수 없다. 그러나 많은 사람들은 단지 그 설명서만 읽고 컴퓨터 사용법을 배우는 것 같다. 간단히 말해, 사람들은 다양한 방식으로 무언가를 배운다.

3. 양괄식

[실전응용 1]

1. In youth I was harshly intolerant. 1) I remember my indignation upon hearing someone made the remark, not an original one, but new to me then, that hypocrisy was the tribute that vice paid to virtue. I thought that one should have the scourge of one's vices. I had ideals of honesty, uprightness, truth: I was impatient not of human weakness, but of cowardice, and I would make no allowances for those who hedged and temporized. 2. It never occurred to me that no one stood in greater need of indulgence than I.

중심소재: 관용

첫 번째 문장에서 주제가 드러나는 'G → S'의 전형이다. 과거의 자신을 돌아보며 관용을 몰랐던 자신에 대해 진술하고 있다. 이후 뒷받침 문장으로 자신의 과거로 돌아가 구체적으로 어떤 측면에서 불관용 했는지를 다룬다.
1. 도입부 = 주제문
1) 뒷받침 문장
2. 글의 주제가 다시 드러나고 있다.

★ 주제문으로 핵심어는 '편협성'이다.

양괄식의 구조를 파악한다.

| 해설

첫 번째 문장을 주제문으로 'General Statement(일반진술) → Specific Statement(구체적 진술) → General Statement(일반진술)'로 진행되는 삼단구성을 취하는 지문이다. 주제를 한 단어로 표현하자면 'Indulgence(관용)'가 된다.

| 해석

젊었을 때 나는 아주 편협했다. 나는 누군가가 위선은 악덕이 덕에 보내는 찬사라는 이전에도 있던 말이지만 나에게는 전혀 새로웠던 말을 하는 것을 듣고는 분노했던 것을 기억한다. 사람은 자신의 악행에 대해 처벌을 받아야 한다고 나는 생각했다. 나는 정직, 강직, 진리라는 이상을 갖고 있었다. 나는 인간의 약점이 아닌 비겁함을 용납하지 않았기에, 애매한 법으로 변명하고 시세에 영합하는 사람들을 전혀 고려해 주려고 하지 않았다. 내가 다른 누구보다도 타인의 관용을 받아야 할 필요성이 더 큰 사람이라는 생각은 절대 들지 않았다.

[실전응용 2]

중심소재는 'sense of sight'이다.

본문에서 구체적으로 진술될 '중심내용(controlling idea)'이다.

서론 (주제문)	Scientists have learned to supplement the <u>sense of sight</u> **in numerous ways**.
본론 (뒷받침 문장)	In front of the tiny pupil of the eye they put, on Mount Palomar, **a great monocle 200 inches in diameter**, and with it see 2000 times farther into the depths of space. Or they look through **a small pair of lenses** arranged as a microscope into a drop of water or blood, and magnify by as much as 2000 diameters the living creatures there, many of which are among man's most dangerous enemies. Or they can bring happenings of long ago and far away as colored motion pictures, **by arranging silver atoms and color-absorbing molecules** to force light waves into the patterns of original reality. Or if we want to see into the center of a steel casting or the chest of an injured child, they send the information on **a beam of penetrating short-wave X rays**, and then convert it back into images we can see on a screen or photograph.
결론	<u>Thus</u> almost every type of electromagnetic radiation yet discovered has been used to <u>extend our sense of sight</u> in some way.

| 해설

본문은 '서론 – 본론 – 결론'을 갖추고 있는 삼단구성의 전형적 형태이며 본문의 글 전개 방법은 나열(Listing)이다. 독해는 단순히 해석의 차원에 머물러서는 안 된다. 글의 구성과 전개방식에 신경을 쓰도록 한다.

| 해석

과학자들은 다양한 방법으로 시각을 보충(눈의 한계를 극복)하는 것을 익혔다. 작은 동공 앞에서 이들은 팔로마 산 위에 지름이 200인치인 엄청나게 큰 외알 안경을 놓고, 이것으로 우주 깊은 2,000배나 먼 곳을 본다. 또는 물방울 또는 혈액 안을 들여다보는 현미경으로 조절된 작은 쌍 렌즈를 통해서 대부분 인간에게 치명적인 생물체를 2,000배의 지름만큼 확대한다. 또는 이들은 은 원자와 색상을 흡수하는 분자를 조합해서 빛 파장을 원래 현실의 형태에 부여하도록 함으로 색이 들어간 영상으로 아주 먼 과거에 발생한 사건을 불러낼 수 있다. 또는 만약 우리가 강철 캐스트(강철을 녹여서 거푸집에 넣어 만든 주물) 또는 다친 아이의 가슴 내부를 보기 원한다면, 이들은 물체를 관통하는 단파 엑스레이 선에 정보를 전송하고, 그런 다음 이것을 화면 또는 사진상으로 우리가 볼 수 있는 이미지로 다시 변환시킨다. 그러므로 지금까지 발견된 거의 모든 전자자기장 방사선은 각자의 특정 방법으로 우리의 시각을 확장시키는 데 사용이 되었다.

4. 중괄식

[실전응용 1]

1. Most common forms of exercise, such as bicycling and swimming, rarely cause serious injury. 1) **But** contact sports, such as football and judo, can cause wear on the joints that can lead to articular disease, or joint problems. 2. <u>The problem for most beginners is overexercise</u>. Many people experience stiffness after the first day of exercise, but this is harmless and does not last long. ① People who are overweight or past middle age or who suffer from heart disease should consult a physician before starting any exercise program.

중심소재: 운동
1. 도입부
자전거와 수영(혼자 하는 운동) 같은 흔한 운동은 심각한 부상을 유발하지 않는다.
1) 역접의 'But' = 근거
축구와 유도와 같은 접촉 운동의 경우 관절염이나 관절 문제를 일으킬 수 있다.
2. 주제문
초보자의 지나친 운동은 무리가 된다.
① 뒷받침 부연
과체중 또는 중년이 넘은 나이 또는 심장질환을 겪는 사람은 운동하기 전에 의사와 논의하는 것이 중요하다.
← 지나친 운동이 심각한 부상을 유발할 수 있기 때문에

★ 운동에 관한 글임을 파악할 수 있다.

★ 주제문이 글의 중반에 나오는 중괄식으로 운동을 할 때 초보자가 가지는 문제점을 지적하면서 주의할 점으로 이어지고 있다.

| 해석
자전거 타기나 수영 같은 가장 일상적인 형태의 운동이 심각한 부상을 유발하는 경우는 드물다. 하지만 축구나 유도 같은 접촉 경기는 관절염이나 관절 관련 문제를 유발할 수 있는 관절 마모를 야기할 수 있다. 대부분 초보자들이 가지는 문제는 과도한 운동이다. 많은 사람이 운동을 시작한 후에 뻣뻣함을 경험하나 이것은 해가 없고 그렇게 오래가지 않는다. 체중 과다나 중년이 지난 사람들과 심장 질병으로 고통을 받는 사람들은 운동 프로그램을 시행하기 전에 반드시 의사의 진찰을 받아야 한다.

도입부 = 중심소재
근거
주제문
뒷받침 부연

[실전응용 2]

1. Every society needs heroes, and every society has them. 1) ① Some heroes shine in the face of great adversity, performing amazing deeds in difficult situations; ② other heroes do their work quietly, unnoticed by most of us, but making a difference in the lives of other people. 2. Whatever their type, <u>heroes are selfless people who perform extraordinary acts</u>. 1) The true mark of heroes lies **not** necessarily in the result of their actions, **but** in what they are willing to do for others and for their chosen causes. Even if they fail, their determination lives on to inspire the rest of us. Their glory lies **not** in their achievements **but** in their sacrifices.

중심소재: 영웅
1. 도입부
영웅의 필요성 언급
1) 구체적 진술
영웅의 종류
① 역경을 이겨낸 눈에 띄는 영웅
② 눈에 띄지 않게 조용히 사람들의 삶을 변화시키는 영웅
2. 주제문
어떤 종류의 영웅이건 이기심을 버리고 타인을 위해 위대한 일을 하는 사람이 진정한 영웅이다.
1) 뒷받침 부연
진정한 영웅의 증표

★ 중심소재는 '영웅'이며, 주제는 '진정한 의미의 영웅'이다.

★ 글의 요지가 글의 중반에 위치하는 중괄식의 유형이다.

| 해설

본문을 통해 다음과 같은 사실을 파악하도록 한다.
1) 결론을 이끄는 signal(whatever)이 나올 경우, 글의 요지가 등장한다.
2) not A but B와 같이 한쪽을 강조하는 표현에는 글쓴이의 견해가 드러나므로 글의 요지가 될 가능성이 크다.
3) 글의 요지를 알면, 주제를 유추할 수 있다.

| 해석

모든 사회는 영웅을 필요로 하며, 영웅을 가지고 있다. 어떤 영웅은 큰 역경과 마주칠 때 빛나며 어려운 상황에서 놀라운 행동을 한다. 다른 영웅은 우리 대부분의 눈에 띄지 않게 조용히 자신의 일을 하지만 다른 사람들의 삶 속에 큰 변화를 이끌어 낸다. 어떤 유형이든, 영웅들은 엄청난 일을 해내는 이타적인 사람들이다. 영웅의 진정한 증표는 반드시 이들의 행위의 결과에 있는 것이 아니라 다른 이와 이들이 선택한 대의를 위해 기꺼이 행함에 있다. 실패한다 하더라도 이들의 결단력은 우리 모두에게 지속해서 살아남아 영감을 준다. 이들의 영광은 이들이 성취한 업적이 아니라 이들의 희생에 있다.

[실전응용 3]

1. The ability to sympathize with others reflects the multiple nature of the human being, his potentialities for many more selves and kinds of experience than any one being could express. 1) <u>This may be one of the things that enable us to seek through literature an enlargement of our experience.</u> ① Although we may see some characters as outside ourselves—that is, we may not identify with them completely—we are nevertheless able to enter into their behavior and their emotions. Thus, the youth may identify with the aged, one gender with the other, and a reader of a particular limited social background with members of a different class or a different period.

중심소재: 문학작품을 통한 공감대 형성능력 배양

1. 도입부
타인과의 공감대를 형성하는 능력은 한 사람이 표현할 수 있는 자아와 경험의 잠재적 능력을 증폭할 수 있다는 것을 반영한다.

1) 주제문
문학작품을 통해 타인과의 공감대 형성능력을 늘려 다양한 자아와 경험을 체험할 수 있다.

① 뒷받침 진술

| 해석

다른 이와 공감할 수 있는 능력은 인간의 다양한 본성 즉, 한 인간이 표현할 수 있는 것보다 더 많은 인간상과 각종 경험을 할 수 있는 잠재력이 있음을 반영한다. 이것은 우리가 문학작품을 통해 우리 경험을 확대할 수 있도록 가능하게 해 주는 것 중 하나가 될 수도 있다. 우리가 몇몇 등장인물들을 우리 자신과 관계없는 존재로 바라볼 수도 있지만 즉, 그들과 완전히 동화될 수 없을 수도 있지만, 그럼에도 우리는 그들의 행동과 감정 속으로 몰입할 수 있다. 그리하여 젊은이들이 노인들과, 하나의 성이 다른 성과, 그리고 한정된 특정 사회적 배경을 지닌 독자가 다른 계층이나 다른 시대의 구성원과 공감을 형성할 수 있을 것이다.

[실전응용 4]

1. A catastrophe is a sudden, often life-threatening calamity or disaster that pushes people to the outer limits of their coping capability. Catastrophes include natural disasters such as earthquakes, tornadoes, fires, floods, and hurricanes as well as wars, torture, automobile accidents, violent physical attacks, and sexual assaults. 1) <u>Catastrophes often continue to affect their victims' mental health long after the event has ended</u>. ① <u>For example</u>, Ⓐ in 1972 a dam burst and flooded the West Virginia mining town of Buffalo Creek, destroying the town. Two years after the disaster, most of the adult survivors continued to show emotional disturbances. Ⓑ Similarly, most of the survivors of concentration camps in World War II (1939-1945) continued to experience nightmares and other symptoms of severe emotional problems long after their release from the camps.

중심소재: Catastrophe
본문 중반에 나오는 'for example'을 확인한다면 좀 더 쉽게 본문을 파악할 수 있다.
1. 도입부
catastrophe(중심소재)'의 간략한 정의와 함께 다양한 종류를 언급하고 있다.
1) 주제문
재해의 정신적 피해(주제)
① 뒷받침 진술
Ⓐ 예 1
Ⓑ 예 2

★ 중심소재

★ 정의를 통한 중심소재 파악. 단순 정의의 글이 아님을 파악한다.

★ 글의 중반부에 주제문이 등장하는 것을 'For example'의 위치를 통해서 알 수 있다. 중괄식의 구조를 취한다.

도입부 = 정의(중심소재)

포괄적 개념의 정의에서 중심내용을 바탕으로 중심소재의 폭이 좁아지는 과정을 이해하도록 한다.

| 해설
도입부에서 간략한 중심소재의 정의를 내린 후, 글에서 궁극적으로 밝히려는 사항이 글의 중반에 나오는 중괄식을 취하고 있다. 주제문 이후 뒷받침 문장으로 구체적인 예를 2가지 제시하고 있다.

| 해석
재앙이란 갑작스러운 재난이거나, 종종 목숨을 위협하는 재난 또는 사람들이 자신의 대처능력의 한계까지 떠미는 참사이다. 재앙은 지진, 태풍, 화재, 홍수 그리고 허리케인과 같은 자연재해뿐만 아니라 전쟁, 고문, 교통사고, 물리적 폭력사고와 성폭력을 포함한다. 재앙은 사건이 끝난 후 오랫동안 그 희생자들의 정신 건강에 지속해서 영향을 끼친다. 예를 들면, 1972년에 댐이 폭발하여 버지니아 서부 Buffalo Creek의 광산마을을 파괴하며, 홍수가 발생했다. 재난이 발생한 2년 뒤, 대부분의 성인 생존자들은 지속적인 정서 장애를 보였다. 마찬가지로, 제2차 대전 강제수용소에 살아난 대부분 생존자들은 수용소에서 풀려난 후에도 오랫동안 지속해서 악몽과 극심한 정서장애를 겪었다.

* 대안이 제시하는 현상의 글

주제문 = 현상(문제점 지적) ↓ 원인

대안(요지)
구체적 부언

구체적 요지가 다를 수 있다는 점을 파악한다.

[실전응용 5]

1. Several students receive poor grades on writing assignments, 1) not because they lack the ability to communicate, but because they can not seem to manage their time when it comes to a large project. They do not know where to begin, and therefore put things off until the last minute. 2) <u>To solve this problem, students need to develop a timeline for completing the project</u>. ① <u>If</u> they divide

중심소재: 저조한 글쓰기 점수
1. 도입부
문제점 지적: 글쓰기 점수↓
1) 원인
버거운 프로젝트를 받았을 때 시간관리 능력 부재로 어디서부터 시작할지 몰라 프로젝트를 미룸
2. 대안(요지)
1) 구체적 부언
구체적 진술을 이끄는 시그널 if를 확인한다.

★ 글쓴이의 견해가 글의 중반부에 나오는 중괄식의 글임을 파악한다.

the assignment into manageable "chunks" or parts and then set a schedule for completing each part, they will be able to finish the entire project before the deadline. Without the pressure of not knowing where to begin, the students will be able to focus on the assignment and communicate their ideas effectively.

① 구체적 부연진술(If)이 이어짐

| 해설
주제문 이후 등장하는 구체적 진술의 시그널로 'for example' 또는 'for instance'가 대표적인데, 이외에도 'if' 또는 'when' 또한 구체적 예를 이끄는 시그널로 활용할 수 있다는 점을 기억한다.

| 해석
여러 학생이 작문 숙제에서 나쁜 점수를 얻었는데, 이는 의사전달 능력이 부족해서가 아니라 큰 프로젝트를 다룰 때, 시간 관리를 못 하기 때문으로 보인다. 이들은 어디서 시작을 해야 할지 모르기에 마지막까지 해야 할 일을 미룬다. 이것을 해결하기 위해 학생들은 프로젝트를 완성할 수 있는 일정표를 만들 필요가 있다. 만약 이들이 숙제를 다룰 수 있는 '덩어리' 또는 부분으로 나눈 후 각 부분을 완성할 수 있는 일정표를 정한다면, 마감 전에 전체 프로젝트를 마칠 수 있게 된다. 어디서 어떻게 시작할 줄 모르는 것에서 오는 압박감 없이 학생들은 숙제에 초점을 맞추어 자신의 생각을 효과적으로 전달할 수 있게 된다.

| 참고
If의 활용

Case 1
도입부 | 주제문
(If)_____
뒷받침 진술

주제문이 중심내용에 대한 뒷받침 예시

Case 2
도입부 | (If)_____
뒷받침 진술
일반진술(주제문)

구체적 진술을 이끄는 If이 후 글의 말미에 주제문이 따르는 형태

Case 3
도입부 | 중심소재
주제문
(If)_____
뒷받침 진술

도입부에서 포괄적 주제인 중심소재가 제시되고 글의 주제문이 따른 후 뒷받침 예시로 If가 이어지는 유형

[실전응용 6]

1. Brave skydivers leap from airplanes at great heights, trusting that training, good equipment, and favorable weather will carry them safely to the ground. 1) Still, skydiving successfully from, say, 9,000 feet involves more than courage and luck; it requires real skill. ① When a skydiver jumps out of a plane, he or she begins to fall, traveling through the air with the parachute tightly packed and no way to control the speed. A good skydiver, however, knows when the time is right to open the parachute. Then it's up to the diver to steer the parachute to a landing point by pulling on lines attached to the parachute.

중심소재: 스카이다이빙
1. 도입부
스카이다이빙 소개
1) 주제문
성공적 스카이다이빙을 위해서 실질적인 기술이 필요하다.
① 뒷받침 진술

★ 첫 번째 문장에서 중심소재 파악은 독해의 가장 기본이 되는 사항이다.

★ 주제문 이후 구체적 진술을 이끄는 'When'을 확인한다.

| 해석
용감한 스카이다이버는 아주 높은 곳의 비행기에서 뛰어내리는데, 이는 훈련, 철저한 장비 그리고 알맞은 날씨가 갖추어지면 이들이 안전하게 땅에 내릴 수 있다고 믿기 때문이다. 그러나 가령 9,000피트 상공에서 성공적으로 스카이다이빙을 하기 위해서는 용기와 행운 이상이 필요하다. 그것은 실질적인 기술을 필요로 한다. 스카이다이버가 비행기에서 밖으로 뛰어내릴 때, 그는 떨어지기 시작하면서, 단단하게 꾸려진 낙하산을 지닌 채 공기를 가르며 이동하지만 속도를 통제할 방법은 전혀 없다. 그러나 훌륭한 스카이다이버는 낙하산을 펼 가장 적절한 시점이 언제인지를 안다. 그때 낙하산에 달린 줄을 잡아당기면서 착륙 지점까지 낙하산을 조종하는 것은 스카이다이버에게 달려있다.

[실전응용 7]

1. Even our most highly educated guesses often go disastrously wrong. 1) Albert Einstein remarked, "There is no chance that nuclear energy will ever be obtainable." 2. Why is predicting the future so difficult? Would it be smart not to try to guess what's coming next? 1) Not predicting the future would be like driving a car without looking through the windshield. 3. We desperately need people who can foretell the future. 1) They help us narrow the infinity of possible futures down to one or, at least, a few. We look at the present and see the present; they see the seeds of the future. They are our advance scouts, going secretly over the border to bring back priceless information to help the world to come.

중심소재: 미래예측
1. 도입부
미래예측의 위험성
1) 예시부연
2. 의문문(주제)
예측의 위험성을 고려했을 때 이를 하지 말아야 하는가?
1) 비유적 표현을 통해 예측의 필요성 강조(뒷받침 근거)
3. 주제문(요지)
미래예측이 가능한 원인이 필요하다.
1) 뒷받침 근거
예측의 유용성과 가능

★ 문제 제기를 통해 글쓴이가 궁극적으로 전달하려는 내용은 무엇인지 파악한다.
* 글의 통일성과 중심소재 설정의 중요성

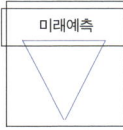

글이 복잡하게 느껴질 수도 있지만 처음부터 끝까지 글의 도입부에서 설정한 '미래예측'에 관한 글이며 글의 전개 과정에서 그 폭이 좁혀질 뿐임을 파악한다.

| 해설

글의 요지를 이끄는 'need'를 확인한다. 특히 본문은 비유적 표현을 통해 글쓴이의 주장을 뒷받침하고 있다. "like driving a car without looking through the windshield + going secretly over the border to bring back priceless information to help the world to come"

| 해석

아주 많은 경험을 통해 나온 추측조차도 종종 비참한 결과를 가져온다. Albert Einstein은 "핵에너지를 얻게 될 가능성은 전혀 없다."라고 말했다. 미래를 예측하는 것은 왜 이리 힘든 것인가? (그렇다면) 앞으로 다가올 일을 추측하려고 하지 않는 것이 현명할까? 미래를 예측하지 않는 것은 자동차 앞유리를 통해 앞을 보지 않고 운전하는 것과 같다. 우리는 미래를 예견해 줄 사람이 절실히 필요하다. 이들은 우리에게 무한히 가능한 미래를 하나, 혹은 적어도 몇 가지로 좁히는 데 도움을 준다(선택의 폭을 좁혀준다). 우리는 현재를 보면서 현재를 보지만 이들은 미래의 씨앗들을 본다. 이들은 다가올 세상을 돕기 위한 귀중한 정보를 가져오기 위해 비밀스럽게 경계선을 넘어가는 우리의 정찰대이다.

5. 주제문과 뒷받침 문장

[실전응용 1]

1. **Many people** do not understand that <u>hypnosis is a natural phenomenon. It is an altered state that we frequently go into and out of.</u> 1) Some natural <u>examples</u> of hypnosis include ① highway hypnosis, where our sense of time and consciousness becomes altered. Have you ever taken a long trip and remembered a town you drove through? ② An illusion about time is a common trait of hypnotic states. Have you ever become so absorbed in a good book or a good movie that two hours rushed by like minutes? Being severely focused on something makes us enter a hypnotic state.

중심소재: 최면
1. 도입부 = 주제문
통념: 최면은 자연적 현상이 아니다.
통념비판(주제문): 최면은 우리가 일상적으로 겪는 자연적 현상이다.
1) 뒷받침 예시
① Highway Hypnosis
② Illision about time

★ 'people say, we say, many of us, some of us, it is said that' 등의 일반인의 견해가 드러나는 표현이 문장 첫머리에 나오면 통념 비판의 글일 가능성이 크다.
'일반통념 – However – 글쓴이의 반대 주장'으로 이어지는 패턴을 기억하도록 한다.

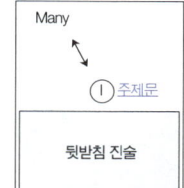

1대 다수의 법칙

| 해설
본문의 구조는 다음과 같다.

일반진술 (주제문)	주제문: Many people do not understand that hypnosis is a natural phenomenon.
구체적 진술 (뒷받침 진술)	① Example 1: Highway Hypnosis – 부연 진술 ② Example 2: Time Illusion – 부연 진술

| 해석
많은 사람이 최면은 자연적인 현상이라는 것을 이해하지 못한다. 그것은 우리가 자주 빠져 들어갔다가 나오는 변

화된 상태이다. 최면의 몇몇 자연적인 예들은 고속도로 최면을 포함하고 있는데, 이 상태에서 우리의 시간감각과 의식이 바뀐다. 장기간의 여행을 하면서 당신이 운전해 지나간 마을을 기억하지 못한 적이 있는가? 시간에 대한 착각은 최면상태의 일반적인 특징이다. 당신은 좋은 책이나 좋은 영화에 매우 몰입하여 두 시간이 몇 분처럼 지나간 적이 있는가? 무언가에 심하게 집중하게 되면 우리는 최면상태로 들어가게 된다.

[실전응용 2]

※ 중심소재 – 한옥의 창문

※ 본문에 다뤄질 중심내용에 해당한다.

1. Windows of *hanok* reflect the traditional view that forms should be created by relying on feelings. 1) The size and the placement of windows in *hanok* are determined ① by the senses, not by mathematical calculation. Ⓐ It is like building things with the eye, not with measuring instruments. There is no standard size or position for windows. ② They are installed where it feels right. Ⓑ This is a natural approach to creation and is based on the aesthetics of feelings. This characteristic of windows of *hanok* shows an example of the abstract beauty in traditional Korean architecture.

중심소재: 한옥의 창문
1. 도입부 = 주제문
주제(Topic): 한옥의 창문에 반영된 전통적 관점
중심내용(Controlling Idea): 형태는 감각에 의존해 창조된다.
1) 뒷받침 진술
① 'by the senses'
Ⓐ 부연 진술
② 'where it feels right'
Ⓑ 부연 진술

| 해석
한옥의 창문은 형태는 느낌에 의존해서 만들어야 한다는 전통적인 견해를 반영한다. 한옥에서의 창문의 크기와 배치는 수학적인 계산에 의해서가 아니라 감각에 의해 결정된다. 측정 도구에 의해서가 아니라 맨눈으로 건물을 짓는 것과 같다. 창문의 크기나 위치에 대한 표준은 없다. 창문은 적절하다고 느껴지는 곳에 설치된다. 이것은 창조에 대한 자연적인 접근법이고 느낌의 미학에 근거한다. 한옥 창문의 이러한 특성은 전통 한국 건축물에 나타나는 추상미의 한 예를 보여준다.

[실전응용 3]

※ 중심소재는 통계. 글의 도입부에서 중심소재 설정은 반드시 잊지 말아야 한다.

도입부 =

주제문
뒷1 ①
뒷2 ②
① 부연
② 부연

1. Statistics can tell us many things. 1) ① They can help us learn more about people and places and what is happening in the world around us. ② We can also use statistics to help us make decisions about the things we do. Ⓐ For example, if you did a survey in your classroom to find out about people's favorite activities, you would be gathering statistics. Ⓑ If you examined these statistics to find out what they were saying, you could then use them to help you decide on the best place to go for a class trip. There are many ways in which we can use statistics to help us every day.

중심소재: 통계
1. 도입부 = 주제문
글 전체의 방향성을 제시해 주는 주제가 드러나는 문장이다: 통계의 유용성
1) 뒷받침 문장
① 뒷받침 문장 1: 사람, 장소 그리고 주변에서 일어나는 일에 관한 새로운 정보를 알려준다.
② 뒷받침 문장 2: 의사결정을 내리는 데 도움을 준다.
Ⓐ ①의 부연 진술
Ⓑ ②의 부연 진술

| 해석

통계를 통해 우리는 많은 것을 알 수 있다. 통계는 사람들과 장소 그리고 주변에서 일어나는 일에 대해 더 많은 것을 알 수 있게 해 준다. 또한, 통계를 이용해서 하는 일에 대한 결정을 내릴 수 있다. 예를 들면, 학급에서 급우들이 가장 좋아하는 활동이 무엇인지를 알아내기 위한 조사를 한다면 통계 자료를 모을 것이다. 이 자료가 뜻하는 바를 알아내기 위해 잘 조사해 보면 학급 견학을 어디로 가는 것이 가장 좋을지 결정하는 데 도움을 받을 수 있다. 일상생활 속에서 우리가 통계를 사용하여 도움을 얻는 방법은 많다.

[실전응용 4]

1. There is healing power in flowers — and in trees, fresh air, and sweet-smelling soil. 1) ① Just walking through a garden or, for that matter, seeing one out your window, can lower blood pressure, reduce stress, and ease pain. ⓐ Get out there and start digging, and the benefits multiply. ② While it may be basic and even old-fashioned, using gardening as a health care tool is blossoming. ⓑ New or remodeled hospitals and nursing homes increasingly come equipped with healing gardens where patients and staff can get away from barren, indoor surroundings. Many also offer patients a chance to get their hands dirty and their minds engaged in caring for plants.

중심소재: Gardening
→ Healing Power of Gardenig
1. 도입부 = 주제문
정원을 가꾸는 일은 치유 효과가 있다.
2. 뒷받침 진술
1) 정원을 거닐면서 얻게 되는 Healing power에 대한 구체적 언급.
ⓐ just walk보단 digging이 더 효과적임.
② 효과(사례)
ⓑ 예시 부연

| 해석

꽃에는 치유력이 있다. 그리고 나무, 신선한 공기 그리고 향기로운 토양에도 역시 치유력이 있다. 단지 정원을 걷는 것 혹은 이야기가 나온 김에 말하자면, 창밖으로 정원을 보는 것만으로도 혈압을 낮추고 스트레스를 줄이고 고통을 완화해줄 수 있다. 저기 밖에 나가서 땅 파기를 시작해 보라. 그 유익은 증대한다. 기본적이고 심지어는 구식일 수 있지만, 건강관리 도구로서 원예를 사용하는 것이 활기를 띠고 있다. 새 병원 혹은 개조된 병원과 요양소들은 점차 환자들과 직원들이 메마른 실내 환경에서 벗어날 수 있는 치유의 정원을 갖추어 나가고 있다. 또한, 많은 곳에서 환자들에게 그들의 손에 흙을 묻히고, 그들의 정신을 식물 돌보는 일에 전념하게 하는 기회를 제공한다.

[실전응용 5]

1. Conventions are the most important source of income for some hotels and motels. 1) In the U.S., for example, it is estimated that some 10 million people attend conventions each year. ① Conventions assure a steady income both from sleeping accommodations and from meeting rooms, which

중심소재: Conventions
1. 도입부 = 주제문
첫 번째 문장 바로 뒤에 이어지는 'for example'은 구체적 진술을 이끄는 뒷받침 문장에 해당한다. 첫 번째 문장이 주제문인 '두괄식 구성'의 전형이다. 주제문: 회의는 호텔과 모텔의 주 수입원이다 ← 이후 구체적 진술(예)을 통해 근거를 제시한다.

are used for conferences and lectures. ② Dining facilities are the source of additional revenue through the sale of food and beverages. ③ Local residents also use the catering services, meeting rooms, and ballrooms for social functions and business meetings.

1) 뒷받침 문장
① + ② 호텔: 숙박숙식을 통한 수입
③ 추가부연: 주민 또한 이로부터 큰 득을 얻는다.

| 해설

첫 번째 문장에서 주제문이 제시되고, 이후 이를 뒷받침하는 구체적 진술이 이어지는 전형적인 'General statement(일반진술) → Specific statement(구체적 진술)'의 두괄식 유형이다. 글쓴이는 언제나 전달하고자 하는 내용에 대한 뒷받침 내용을 반드시 언급한다는 점을 기억하고, 글의 도입부에서 제시되는 내용과 이후 전개되는 내용을 비교하면서 주제문과 뒷받침 문장을 정확히 구별하는 연습을 하도록 한다.

| 해석

회의는 호텔이나 모텔의 가장 중요한 수입의 원천이다. 미국을 예로 들자면, 천만 명의 사람들이 매년 회의를 한다고 평가된다. 회의는 잠을 자는 숙박시설과 회의나 강의를 위한 회의실로 꾸준한 수입을 올리고 있다. 외식 시설은 음식과 음료를 파는 것을 통해 부수적인 수익을 올리는 원천이다. 지역 거주자 또한 사회적 기능과 비즈니스 미팅을 위한 출장 외식업, 회의 장소 그리고 댄스장을 활용한다(활용하여 수입을 올린다).

[실전응용 6]

본문에서 진술될 중심내용(controlling idea)에 해당한다.

1. <u>Aristotle distinguished between essential and accidental properties</u>. 1) ① Essential properties are those without which a thing would not be what it is, and accidental properties are those that determine how a thing is, but not what it is. Ⓐ **For example**, Aristotle thought rationality was essential to being a human being. Socrates' rationality was essential to his being Socrates. ② **On the other hand**, Aristotle thought Socrates' property of being snub-nosed was merely accidental; being snub-nosed was part of how Socrates was, but it wasn't essential to what or who he was. In other words, take away Socrates' rationality, and he's no longer Socrates, but give him plastic surgery, and he's Socrates with a nose job.

중심소재: 근본적 속성/부수적 속성
1. 도입부 = 주제문
근본적 속성과 부수적 속성의 차이점
1) 뒷받침 문장
① 근본적 속성
Ⓐ 예시 부연
② 부수적 속성

| 해석

아리스토텔레스는 본질적 속성과 부차적 속성을 구분했다. 본질적 속성은 그것이 없다면 한 사물이 그것으로서 존재할 수 없을 속성이고, 부차적 속성은 사물의 존재가 아니라 사물의 존재 양태를 결정하는 속성이다. 예를 들어 아리스토텔레스는 인간 존재에 이성은 본질(본질적 속성)이라고 생각했다. 소크라테스가 가진 이성은 소크라테스 자신의 존재의 본질이었다. 반면에 아리스토텔레스는 들창코라는 소크라테스의 속성은 단지 부차적이라고 생각했다. 들창코라는 것은 소크라테스의 존재 양태의 일부분이지만, 그의 존재에 본질적이지는 않았다. 다시 말

해, 소크라테스에게서 이성을 제거하면 그는 더는 소크라테스가 아니다. 하지만 그에게 성형수술을 시키면 그는 (여전히) 코를 성형한 소크라테스이다.

[실전응용 7]

1. <u>Sometimes a person's whole life</u> <u>can be changed in an instant</u>. 1) Elizabeth Blackwell's life changed one afternoon in 1844 when she went to visit a friend who was dying. The dying woman asked her why she did not think of studying medicine, since she was smart and healthy. When she reminded her dying friend that there were no women doctors, the woman sighed and said that if she had been treated by a "lady doctor," she might not be dying. Her sick friend had been so ashamed to mention her internal problems to a man that she hid her pain for too long. When she finally sought treatment, it was too late to save her life. Elizabeth couldn't get the dying woman's suggestion out of her mind. So she decided to devote her life to medicine. In 1849 she became the first woman in the United States to receive a medical degree.

중심소재: 삶의 변화
1. 도입부 = 주제문
1) 뒷받침 진술
한 인물의 구체적 예를 통해 주제문의 중심내용을 뒷받침하고 있다.

★ 중심내용(controlling idea)에 해당한다.

도입부 = 일반진술 / 구체적 진술

· 보편적 적용 = 일반진술
· 개별적 사례 = 구체적 진술

| 해설
첫 번째 문장과 두 번째 문장만을 떼어서 '일반진술'과 '구체적 진술'을 구별하는 방법을 살펴보자.

Sometimes <u>a person</u>'s whole life can be changed in <u>an instant</u>.

첫 번째 문장은 주제문으로 일반진술에 해당한다. 위 문장에서 'a person'과 'an instant'는 본문에서 전달하고자 하는 대상 또는 사건을 모두 포괄하는 부정명사이다.

<u>Elizabeth Blackwell</u>'s life changed one afternoon in 1844 <u>when she went to visit a friend who was dying</u>.

포괄적인 문장에 대한 구체적 진술로 'a person'과 'an instant'에 해당하는 인물과 사건을 구체적으로 언급하고 있다.

| 해석

때로 한 사람의 인생 전체가 한순간에 바뀔 수도 있다. Elizabeth Blackwell의 인생은 1844년 어느 날 오후 그녀가 죽어가는 친구를 방문했을 때에 바뀌었다. 죽어가는 그 여자는 똑똑하고, 건강한 그녀가 왜 의학 공부를 생각하지 않느냐고 물었다. 그녀가 죽어가는 친구에게 여자 의사가 없다는 사실을 일깨워 주었을 때, 그 죽어가는 여자는 한숨을 지으며 자신이 '여성 의사'에게 치료를 받았더라면 죽어가고 있지 않을지도 모른다고 말했다. 그녀의 병든 친구는 자기 신체 내부의 문제에 대해 남성에게 말하는 것이 너무나도 부끄러워서 자신이 느끼는 통증을 너무 오랫동안 숨겼다. 결국, 그녀가 치료하려고 나섰을 때에는, 그녀의 생명을 구하기에 너무 늦었다. Elizabeth는 그 죽어가는 여성이 한 제안을 마음에서 떨쳐버릴 수가 없었다. 그래서 그녀는 의학 분야에 자신의 인생을 바치기로 했다. 1849년에 그녀는 의학 학위를 받은 미국 최초의 여성이 되었다.

[실전응용 8]

1. Signs of growth of Islam in the United States, Canada, and recently in Mexico are evident everywhere. 1) ① Mosques, where Muslims worship, are being built in neighborhoods where once only churches or synagogues stood. ② Women who wear scarves covering their hair according to Islamic customs are now a common sight in many towns and cities. ③ Moreover, Muslim holidays are gaining official recognition in such places as Los Angeles, Toronto, and New York. ④ In addition, an increasing number of employers are accommodating the religious needs of their Muslim workers in the same way they respond to the needs of their Jewish workers.

미국, 캐나다, 멕시코 내 이슬람에 관한 글이다. 중심내용을 바탕으로 중심소재의 폭, 즉 주제의 폭을 좁히도록 한다.

나열의 전개방식을 드러내는 signal에 주목한다.

도입부 = 현상 → 구체적 예시

중심소재: 북미와 남미내 이슬람 → 이슬람의 성장
1. 도입부 = 주제문
현상: 북미 및 남미로 뻗는 이슬람의 성장
1) 뒷받침 문장
나열의 글 방식에 따라 뒷받침 예시 제시.

| 해석

미국, 캐나다, 그리고 최근에는 멕시코에서도 이슬람교가 성장하고 있음을 보여주는 징후가 곳곳에서 뚜렷하게 발견된다. 한 때 교회와 유대교 회당만 있었던 지역에 이슬람교도들이 예배를 드리는 장소인 이슬람 사원들이 세워지고 있다. 이제는 많은 도시에서 이슬람 관습에 따라 머리를 가리기 위해 스카프를 쓰는 여성들을 흔히 볼 수 있다. 더욱이 이슬람 휴일이 로스앤젤레스, 토론토, 뉴욕과 같은 곳에서 공식적 인정을 받고 있다. 게다가, 점점 더 많은 고용주가 유대인 근로자들의 요구에 대해 반응하는 것과 똑같은 방식으로 이슬람 근로자들의 종교적인 요구에 대해 편의를 제공하고 있다.

[실전응용 9]

1. Modern technology has now rendered many learning disabilities virtually obsolete by providing learners with access to alternative ways of getting information and expressing themselves. 1) ① Poor spellers have access to

본문에서 구체적으로 밝혀질 중심내용(controlling idea)이다.

중심소재: 학습장애의 대안으로써 현대 기술
1. 도입부 = 주제문
첫 번째 문장이 주제문이다: 학습 장애를 겪는 사람들이 현대 기술이 제공하는 다양한 대안적 방법으로 정보를 얻고 의사를 표현할 수 있게 되었다.
1) 뒷받침 문장

spell checkers and individuals with illegible handwriting can use a word processor to produce a neat typescript. ② People with dyscalculia benefit from having a pocket calculator handy when a math problem comes up. ③ Similarly, learners with poor memories can tape lectures, discussions, and other verbal exchanges. ④ Individuals with faulty visualization skills can use computer-aided design (CAD) software programs that allow them to manipulate three-dimensional objects on screen.

구체적 대안에 대한 예와 설명(①, ②, ③, ④)이 이어진다.

| 해석

현대 기술은 이제 학습자가 정보를 수집하고 자신을 표현할 수 있는 대안적 방법에 접근할 수 있도록 함으로 여러 학습장애를 실질적으로 과거의 산물로 만들었다. 철자에 약한 사람은 철자 검사기를 사용할 수 있고, 악필을 가진 자는 깔끔한 원고를 만들기 위해 워드프로세서를 사용할 수 있다. 난산증(연산부전증)을 가진 자는 수학문제가 나왔을 때, 포켓용 계산기를 사용해서 손쉽게 혜택을 누릴 수 있다. 마찬가지로 기억력이 안 좋은 학생들은 강의 내용, 토의 내용 및 기타 음성 교환 내용을 테이프에 녹음할 수 있다. 시각화 기술에 문제가 있는 사람은 화면상에 나타나는 3차원 물체를 조작할 수 있도록 해 주는 CAD를 이용할 수 있다.

[실전응용 10]

1. Two hypotheses may explain why obese people eat more when anxious. 1) ① One possibility is that when they were babies, their caregivers interpreted all of their distress signals as requests for food; consequently, as adults, these people have difficulty distinguishing hunger from other feelings, including anxiety. ② A different possibility is that some obese persons may respond to an anxiety producing situation by doing the one thing that has brought them comfort all their lives namely, eating. The two hypotheses may apply to different kinds of obese people.

중심소재: obese people
1. 도입부 = 주제문
사람들이 긴장할 때 더 많이 먹는 현상에 관한 두 가지 가설
1) 뒷받침 문장
① 첫 번째 가설 설명
② 두 번째 가설 설명

★ 두 가지 가설에 관한 내용인데, 본문에서 구체적으로 다룰 중심내용(controlling idea)에 해당한다.

도입부 =
| 현상 |
| 가설 1 _____ |
| 가설 2 _____ |

| 해석

비만인 사람들이 왜 근심·걱정이 있을 때 더 먹는지를 설명하는 두 가지 가설이 있다. 첫 번째 가설은 이들이 아이였을 때, 이들의 보호자들이 아이들의 투정을 모두 음식을 요구하는 것으로 해석했기 때문이다. 결과적으로 어른이 되어 이들은 근심을 포함한 다른 감정과 배고픔을 구별하는 데 어려움을 겪게 되었다는 것이다. 또 다른 가설은 특정한 비만인은 근심을 만들어 내는 상황을 자신에게 안락을 가져다주는 것을 하면서 반응했는데, 바로 말하자면 먹는 것이다. 이 두 가설은 여러 유형의 비만인 사람에게 적용된다

[주제문을 통해 예측하며 글 읽기 연습]

1. 첫 번째 문장이 주제문이고, 두 번째 문장을 이끄는 'For instance' 이후 주제문에 대한 뒷받침 문장으로 구체적 예를 제시하고 있다. 이후 전개될 내용은 병렬구조를 취하면서 북미 각 지역의 자연환경에서 구할 수 있는 서로 다른 재료를 가지고 인디언들이 다양한 가옥의 형태를 발전시켰다는 내용이 전개될 것을 예측할 수 있다. General → Specific의 대표적 형태이다.

도입부 General Statement			주제문 - 예시
Supporting Sentences	문단 1	지역 1	각 지역의 자연적 특성 → 가옥의 재료 → 각 특성에 따른 가옥의 구체적 형태
	문단 2	지역 2	
	문단 3	지역 3	
	문단 4	지역 4	
	문단 5	지역 5	

실제 이어지는 두 문단의 내용은 다음과 같다.

★ 문단의 수에 따라 소주제의 수도 결정된다. 문단이 두 개면 각각의 소주제를 먼저 설정하고, 이후 두 소주제를 포괄하는 전체 주제를 잡도록 한다.

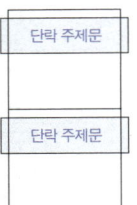

1. <u>The Indians in the Northest Culture lived in wooden lodges</u>. 1) These buildings, built using a wooden frame, were rectangular buildings that each held several families. The frame was then covered with pieces of bark, or boards. The inside of the building had a pit in the middle which had a fire in it to be used for cooking. The families would share the fireplace in the middle. Outside of each wooden lodge was a totem pole, which was considered a very important part of the lodge. Some lodges even had totem poles decorated on the inside beams of their homes, and each lodge had a different totem pole.

2. <u>The indians of the California-intermountain Culture lived in circular homes of arched poles covered with brush and mat</u>. 1) This type of home, also called a wickiup or thatch home, was used for a short time when the indians were hunting.

첫번째 문단
중심소재: 북미 인디언들의 통나무집
1. **도입부 = 주제문**
북미문화의 인디언들은 통나무집에서 살았다 - 지역과 자연적 특성이 드러나면서 가옥의 형태와 간략한 특징이 문장 첫머리에 드러난다.
1) **구체적 진술**
가옥의 구체적 특성이 본문 끝까지 기술되고 있다.

두번째 문단
중심소재: 산악지역에 사는 인디언들의 주거지
2. **주제문**
산으로 둘러싸인 환경에서 사는 인디언들은 잡목과 매트로 덮인 아치형 기둥으로 구성된 원형의 집을 지음 - 지역적 특성과 가옥의 특성이 함께 기술되고 있다.
1) **부연진술** - 기능

| 해석
다수의 다양한 미국 원시 부족들이 북미에 살고 있었다. 그리고 각 부족은 그들 고유의 주거 형태를 지니고 있었으며, 가옥을 만들기 위해서 천연자원을 사용했다. 예를 들면, 숲이나 숲 근처에서 산다면, 가옥에 목재를 사용했다. 이는 다양한 인디언 문화가 서로 다른 가옥 형태를 가지는 이유이다. 북미 문화의 인디언들은 통나무집에서

살았다. 나무 골재를 사용하여 지어진 이 건물들은 각각이 몇 씨족을 이루는 직사각형의 건물들이다. 골격은 나무껍질 조각이나 널빤지로 덮여 있다. 건물의 내부는 중앙에 그 안에 불을 피우는 구덩이가 있는데, 이는 요리를 하기 위해 사용된다. 씨족들은 중앙에 난로를 공유한다. 각각의 통나무집 바깥에는 통나무집에서 매우 중요한 부분으로 간주하는 장승이 있다. 어떤 통나무집은 심지어 그들의 집 안쪽 대들보에 장식된 장승을 가지고 있다. 그리고 각 통나무집은 다른 장승을 가지고 있다.

    캘리포니아 산간지방 문화의 인디언들은 잡목과 거적으로 덮여 아치형의 기둥으로 구성된 원형의 집에 살았다. 막집 혹은 초가집이라 불리는 이런 종류의 집은 인디언들이 사냥하는 도중에 임시로 사용되었다.

2. 이 책의 다른 장에서 좀 더 자세히 다루겠지만, 부사 'now'는 새로운 정보를 이끄는 시그널(signal)이다. 예를 들어, 이전에 밝혀지지 않은 사실을 언급한 후 'now'를 제시하면 이후 앞에서 전개된 내용과 상반된 '새로 발견한 사실'에 대한 기술이 이어진다. 또는 이전과 다른 '현상'을 이끌 때 'now'가 쓰이기도 한다. 본문에서 now는 과학자들이 대하가 어떻게 육식동물을 쫓아내는지에 대한 새로운 사실을 밝혀냈다는 내용이다. 또한 실험/조사 등이 등장하는 지문의 경우 실험에서 밝힌 사항이 바로 글의 요지가 된다. 본문은 도입부에서 글의 주제와 요지를 모두 드러내고 있다. 이후 전개될 내용에서 반드시 빠져서 안 되는 부분은 대하가 구체적으로 어떻게 소리를 이용해 육식동물을 쫓는지에 관한 내용이며, 이를 뒷받침하는 실험의 내용이 따라야 한다.

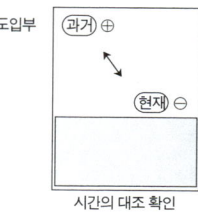

시간의 대조 확인

실제 이어지는 내용 중 한 문단을 살펴보자.

1. Dr. Sheila Patek of Duke University closely investigated the method by which spiny lobsters produce sound. She attached small sensors to the muscles of the spiny lobster's antenna and then recorded the sound the lobster produced using an underwater microphone. Additionally, she examined the physiology of the lobster's sound-producing structures. She found that the lobster slides a soft, fleshy plectrum over a smooth file-like surface located just beneath its eyes. Due to friction, the plectrum repeatedly sticks, then slips, each time producing a burst of sound.

1. 구체적 진술
듀크 대학의 Sheila Patek 박사가 조사한 구체적 내용이 부연되고 있다.

* 일반적으로 실험의 전개방식은 실험의 결과를 먼저 제시하고, 이후 실험의 구체적 내용을 언급하는 두괄식 구성과 실험의 구체적 내용을 먼저 기술하고 이후 실험의 결과를 제시하는 미괄식 구성을 취한다. 당연히 중괄식 및 양괄식의 구성도 취할 수 있다.

* 실험/조사/연구의 양괄식 예

도입부 = 실험의 결과 (일반진술)

실험내용 (구체적 진술)

실험의 결과 · 의의 (일반진술)

| 해석
과학자들은 대하가 포식자들을 막기 위해서 소리를 내는 독특한 방법에 대해서 더 많이 이해하고 있다. 현악기의 방식과 유사한 발성법을 사용하면서 대하는 침입자를 크고 거친 소음을 내어 위협한다. 듀크 대학의 Sheila Patek 박사는 대하가 소리를 내는 방식을 연구했다. 그녀는 대하의 더듬이 근육에 작은 센서를 부착한 후 수중 마이크를 사용하여 대하가 내는 소리를 녹음했다. 추가로 그녀는 대하의 발성구조에 대한 생리학을 연구했다. 그녀는 대하가 부드럽고 살이 오른 피크로 눈 밑에 바로 위치한 부드러운 서류철과 같은 표면 위를 문지르는 것을 발견했다. 마찰 때문에, 피크는 매번 파열음을 내며 반복해서 부딪혀 미끄러진다.

3. 피아제의 인지발달이론에 관한 글이다. 그의 이론을 단계적으로 설명하는 글임을 쉽게 파악할 수 있다. 본문 마지막에 알 수 있듯이 이후 문단에서 병렬구조를 취하면서 각 단계에 대한 구체적 진술이 이어질 것을 예측할 수 있다.

도입부 General Statement		주제문 – 예시	
Supporting Sentences	문단 1	sensorimotor stage	구체적 부연
	문단 2	pre-operational stage	
	문단 3	concrete operational stage	
	문단 4	formal operational stage	

| 해석

어떠한 인지발달이론도 장 피아제가 발표한 인지발달 단계보다 더 큰 영향을 주지는 못했다. 스위스의 심리학자인 피아제는 아이들이 모든 유아에 걸쳐 공통적인 일정한 순서의 네 단계를 겪는다고 주장했다. 피아제는 이 단계들은 각각의 단계에서 얻는 정보의 양에서 차이가 있을 뿐만 아니라 각 단계에서의 지식의 양과 이해의 정도에 있어서도 차이가 있다고 발표했다. 피아제는 한 단계에서 다음 단계로의 이동은 아이가 일정한 성장수준에 다다랐을 때, 그리고 적절한 형태의 경험에 노출되었을 때 발생한다고 주장했다. 경험이 없이는, 아이들이 그들의 최고 인지 능력에 도달하는 것이 불가능하다고 판단되었다. 피아제의 네 단계는 감각운동기, 전조작기, 구체적 조작기 그리고 형식적 조작기로 알려졌다.

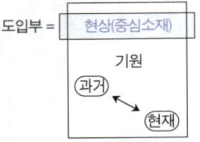

*기원을 밝히는 글에서는 동사의 시제에 주목한다.

기원의 글임을 드러내는 시그널에는 come from, stem from, go back to, trace back to, originate 등이 있다.

4. 주어진 문장이 주제문이라 했으므로, 기원을 밝히는 글일 가능성이 크다. 일반적으로 기원을 밝히는 글은 글쓴이가 관측한 특정 현상으로 이 경우, 이러한 현상이 어떠어떠한 기원에 의해서 발생하였을 것이라는 내용으로 전개되는 경우가 대부분이다. 주제문 이후 뒷받침 문장을 전개할 때 시제는 과거에서 현재로 전개되는 순행의 형태가 일반적이지만 역으로 전개되기도 한다는 점을 기억한다.

전체 본문을 분석해 보자.

1. <u>Art probably began as a form of communication or record-keeping</u>. 1) ① Archaeologists and anthropologists have speculated that the early cave paintings found throughout the world are records of tribal hunts or hunting seasons, because of the proliferation of repeated animal figures. Later, such figures probably took on a symbolic importance. ② Just as you or I might find that pleasant things happened each time we wore a certain shirt, and take to thinking of that shirt as "lucky," so too early people may have associated animals,

중심소재: 예술 → 예술의 기원

1. 도입부 = 주제문
첫 번째 문장에서 '예술의 기원은 '의사소통 또는 정보 기록의 형태로 시작했을 것이다.'라고 추정하고 있다 – 이후 전개될 내용으로 글쓴이가 이렇게 언급한 내용에 대한 뒷받침 문장을 예측할 수 있다.

1) 뒷받침 문장
① 동굴의 동물 그림은 상징적 의미로 사냥 또는 사냥 철임을 알림
② 비유를 통해 특정 사물이 상징적 의미로 사용되고 있음을 설명하고 있다.

plants and people with good and bad luck, seasonal changes like floods or snow, successful hunting and other things important to hunting and gathering lifestyles. ③ So eventually, we see artifacts discovered which show an attempt at more than just record-keeping—carved figures of women, for example, or small animal figurines. ④ Even utilitarian objects like knives and arrowheads begin to show some attempts at craftsmanship in the elaborate way the edges were chipped and feathered to a point. The implication is that early craftsmen became interested not just in the usefulness of an item, but also in its appearance.

③ 구체적 예(for example)를 통해서 인위적 물체가 상징적 의미를 드러냄을 부연하고 있다.
④ 칼과 화살촉 같은 유용한 물체조차 특정한 의미를 전달하는 한 형태였다.
* General → Specific

★ 'for example' 이 주제문에 대한 뒷받침 진술인지 아니면 뒷받침 문장에 대한 부연인지 구별할 수 있어야 한다.

| 해석

예술은 의사소통이나 정보기록의 한 형태로 시작되었다. 고고학자들과 인류학자들은 전 세계에 걸쳐 발견된 과거의 동굴벽화들이 반복되는 동물 형상의 풍부함을 이유로 원시부족의 사냥이나 사냥 기간의 기록이라고 추정해왔다. 나중에 그런 형상들은 아마 상징적인 중요성을 띄게 되었을 것이다. 당신과 내가 우리가 특정한 셔츠를 입을 때 매번 기쁜 일이 생겼다는 것을 알게 되는 것처럼 그리고 우리가 "행운"으로써 그 셔츠를 떠올리는 것처럼, 과거 사람들도 동물들, 식물들 그리고 사람들을 행운과 불운, 홍수와 폭설과 같은 계절의 변화, 성공적인 사냥과 채집의 생활방식에 중요한 다른 것들과 연관 지어왔을지 모른다. 그래서 결국, 우리는 예를 들어, 여성들을 조각한 형상이나 작은 동물들의 형상들과 같은 단지 기록보관 이상의 시도를 보여주는 발견된 유물을 본다. 심지어 칼이나 화살촉과 같은 실용적인 물건들은 끝에 흠집을 내고 한 지점에 깃털을 다는 정교한 방식에서 장인정신의 어떤 시도들을 보여주기 시작한다. 그 의미는 과거의 수공업자들이 단지 물건의 유용성에만 관심이 있었던 것이 아니라 이것의 외관에도 관심이 있었다는 사실을 나타낸다.

5. 미국 시라는 용어가 여러 면에서 모순이라고 밝히고 있다. 이후 이런 주장에 대한 근거/이유를 설득력 있게 뒷받침해주는 내용이 전개되어야 한다. 인과의 글로 전개될 가능성이 높다. 전체 지문을 살펴보자.

1. The term American poetry is in some ways a contradiction. 1) America represents a break with tradition and the invention of a new culture separate from the European past. Poetry, on the other hand, represents tradition itself, a long history of expression carried to America from a European past. American poetry thus embodies a clearly identifiable tension between tradition and innovation, past and future, and old forms and new forms. American poetry remains a hybrid, a literature that tries to separate itself from the tradition of English literature even as it adds to and alters that tradition.

중심소재: 미국의 "시" 용어
1. 도입부 = 주제문
미국 시라는 용어의 모순점(주제)
1) 뒷받침 진술
글쓴이의 주장에 대한 근거/이유가 본문 끝까지 기술되고 있다.

* General → Specific

★ 본문에 구체적으로 기술된 중심내용에 해당한다.

41

| 해석

미국 시라는 용어는 여러모로 모순이다. 미국은 전통의 타파를 상징하고 새로운 문화의 발명은 과거 유럽인들로부터 분리되었다. 반면에 과거 유럽에서부터 미국으로 전해진 시는 표현의 긴 역사인 전통 그 자체를 대표한다. 미국 시는 전통과 혁신 사이에서, 과거와 미래 사이에서, 그리고 기존의 형태와 새로운 형태 사이에서 명확하게 구별되는 긴장을 구체화한다. 미국 시는 심지어 그 전통에 더하고 변화를 주어, 그 자신을 영국 문학의 전통으로부터 분리하려는 문학인, 혼합물의 형태로 남아있다.

6. 멸종은 전혀 새로운 현상이 아니라고 말하면서 수 억 년 동안 진화의 한 과정의 일부분으로 자연스럽게 지속해서 발생한 것이라 말하고 있다. 이후 이를 뒷받침하는 구체적 근거가 제시될 것을 예측할 수 있다. 전체 본문을 살펴보자.

도입부 = 주제문
뒷받침 진술
뒷 1. some
뒷 2. others
뒷 3. sometimes
부연예시 (example)

1. <u>Extinction is not a new phenomenon. For hundreds of millions of years, extinction has been occurring naturally, as part of the evolutionary process.</u> 1) Some cases of extinction have been caused by natural disasters, such as volcanic eruptions. Others have been the result of environmental changes, such as shifts in climate. Sometimes extinction occurs on a very large scale, with hundreds or thousands of species becoming extinct over a relatively short period of time. An <u>example</u> of this is the dinosaurs and their contemporaries, victims of a mass extinction that took place at least 65 million years ago.

중심소재: Extinction
1. 도입부 = 주제문
멸종은 진화의 한 과정으로 자연스럽게 오래전부터 일어난 현상이다.
1) 뒷받침 문장
자연계에서 진화의 일환으로 발생하는 멸종의 다양한 원인(형태)과 구체적 예(example)로 주제문에서 밝힌 중심 내용을 뒷받침하고 있다.

* General → Specific

| 해석

멸종은 새로운 현상이 아니다. 수 억년 동안 멸종은 진화 과정의 일부로써 자연스럽게 발생해왔다. 어떤 멸종은 화산 폭발과 같은 자연재해로부터 기인해왔다. 다른 경우들은 기후의 변화와 같은 환경 변화에 따른 결과이다. 때때로 멸종은 수십만의 종이 상대적으로 짧은 기간에 걸쳐 멸종하며 매우 큰 규모로 발생한다. 이것의 한 예는 최소 6천5백만 년 전에 발생한 엄청난 멸종의 희생자인 공룡들과 그들의 동시대에 살던 동물들이다.

7. 논리적 반전이 이루어지는 'Yet'이 첫 번째 문장에 등장한다. 'Yet'이 이끄는 내용을 보면, '수렵채집을 하던 원시인들도 자신의 자원(동물·식물 등의 먹을 것)과 식량의 양을 늘리기 위한 다양한 세련된 관행을 가지고 있었다'라는 내용이다. 'Yet' 이전에 전개될 내용으로는 과거 원시인은 자연에서 허용된 동물을 사냥하고 식량을 채집했다는 일반적 내용이 전개되고, 'Yet' 이후 전개될 내용은 주제문을 뒷받침하는 내용이 전개될 것을 예측할 수 있다. 글 전체 내용을 살펴보자.

1. Most California Indians lived entirely by hunting and gathering the abundant resources provided by nature. 1) Yet these hunter-gatherers engaged in an array of sophisticated practices to manage their resources and enhance the yield of potential food sources. ① They pruned plants and trees, culled animal and insect populations, and practiced periodic burning of ground cover to replenish the soil.

중심소재: 캘리포니아 인디언
→ 자연에 대한 능동적 주체
1. 도입부
수동적 생활 방식
1) 주제문
논리적 반전을 이끄는 Yet을 중심으로 자연에서 취한 자원을 능동적으로 활용하는 인디언을 소개하고 있다.
① 뒷받침 진술

```
A = B
  ↕ Yet
A ≠ B
```

| 해설
글의 반전을 이끄는 'Yet'을 주목한다.

| 해석
대부분의 캘리포니아 인디언들은 전체적으로 사냥과 자연이 제공하는 풍부한 자원을 채집하며 살았다. 그러나 이 수렵·채집인들은 자원을 관리하고 잠재적인 식량자원의 생산량을 증대시키기 위해서 일련의 정교한 작업에 몰두했다. 이들은 식물들과 나무들을 전지하고 동물들과 곤충 개체 수를 모았으며 토양을 보충하기 위해 지표를 정기적으로 소각했다.

8. 다이아몬드와 흑연의 차이점이 기술되고 있다. 전체 문장을 이끄는 접속사가 논리적 반전을 이루는 'But'인 점을 고려할 때, 이 앞에 기술된 내용은 '다이아몬드와 흑연은 (겉으로 보기에) 이러이러한 점에서 유사하다'의 내용이 기술되고, 제시된 문장 이후에는 다이아몬드가 흑연보다 어떤 측면에서 더 강하고 투명하며, 밀도가 높은 이유가 기술될 가능성이 크다.

1. Both graphite and diamond are made from pure carbon. 1) **But** diamond is extremely hard and transparent. Diamond also is much denser than an equal amount of graphite. ① Graphite and diamond have different crystal structures—that is, the carbon atoms are arranged differently in the two minerals. Graphite contains carbon atoms arranged in flat layers that slide easily over each other. Thus, graphite is soft and slippery. In diamond, **on the other hand**, the atoms are arranged in a strong three-dimensional pattern that prevents the atoms from slipping over each other.

중심소재: Diamond, Graphite
1. 도입부
두 대상의 공통점
1) 주제문(But → 차이점 기술)
다이아몬드의 독특한 속성: Hard, Transparent, denser
① 뒷받침 진술
흑연과 달리 다이아몬드가 주제문에서 밝힌 속성을 가지게 된 이유를 밝히고 있다.

도입부 =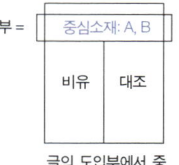

글의 도입부에서 중심소재가 두개인 경우 비교 또는 대조의 글 전개가 될 가능성이 크다.

| 해설
글의 주된 전개방식은 대조이다. 뒷받침 문장에서 근거가 제시되고 있다고 해서 인과로 잡아서는 안 된다. 글의 주제와 요지를 가장 효율적으로 전달하는 도구로 글 전개방식을 선정하기에 이 둘의 관계를 중심으로 글 전개방식을 선정한다.

| 해석

흑연과 다이아몬드는 모두 순수한 탄소로 만들어진다. 그러나 다이아몬드는 너무나 단단하고 투명하다. 다이아몬드는 역시 같은 양의 흑연보다 밀도가 더 높다. 흑연과 다이아몬드는 서로 다른 결정체 구조로 되어 있다. 다시 말해, 탄소 원자가 두 물질에서 다르게 배열되어 있다. 흑연은 서로 쉽게 미끄러지는 평평한 층에 배열된 탄소 원자를 포함한다. 그래서 흑연은 부드럽고 쉽게 미끄러진다. 반면 다이아몬드 안에는 원자들이 서로 미끄러지는 것을 막는 강력한 3차원의 방식으로 배열되어 있다.

9. 제시된 주제문에서 인과의 글임을 드러내는 시그널인 'factor'와 'contribute to'를 확인할 수 있다. 이후 전개될 내용은 '시골에서 도시로 급격한 인구이동'을 일으킨 여러 요소에 관한 구체적 내용이 전개될 것을 예측할 수 있다.

도입부 =
현상 - 원인
- 주제문
뒷받침 진술
(나열)

현상의 글의 경우 주제문은 '현상 + 원인' 임을 파악한다.

1. <u>Several factors contributed to the dramatic population shift from the countryside to urban areas</u>. 1) ① Through the years, Americans greatly improved agricultural methods and equipment. From the 1800's onward, farm work has become more and more efficient, farm production has soared, and fewer and fewer people have been needed to work on the nation's farms. ② <u>At the same time</u>, an industrial boom has created large numbers of new jobs in the nation's urban areas. Ⓐ <u>As a result of</u> these economic changes, a steady flow of people from rural to urban areas has taken place. ③ <u>Also</u>, large numbers of immigrants—many of whom had been farmers in their homelands—found jobs in cities and settled there when they reached the United States. ④ <u>In addition</u>, the variety of job choices and recreational, educational, and cultural opportunities in cities attracted many rural people, especially the young. Large numbers of rural people left home to seek employment and excitement in cities.

중심소재: 인구이동
1. 도입부 = 주제문
현상: 시골에서 도시로 급격한 인구 증가의 다양한 원인을 살피는 글임을 알 수 있다.
1) 뒷받침 진술
① 농업의 발달로 농장 일이 더욱 효율적으로 되면서 일손이 덜 필요하게 됨.

② 순접 추가(at the same time): 산업혁명의 붐으로 도시에 일자리가 늘어남.
Ⓐ 결과적으로 일자리를 찾아 농촌의 인구가 도시로 꾸준하게 이동하게 되었음.
③ 미국으로 건너온 이민자
④ 다양한 직업의 종류, 여가, 문화적 기회 등으로 시골의 젊은이들이 도시로 이동하게 됨.

* 추가적 사항을 제시하는 시그널 확인

| 해설

현상으로 시작하는 글로 주된 글 전개방식은 인과이며, 뒷받침 문장에서 나열이 함께 쓰이고 있다.

| 해석

몇 가지 요소들이 교외에서 도시 지역에 이르기까지의 급격한 인구 변화에 작용했다. 수년간, 미국인들은 농작법과 농기계를 크게 개선했다. 1800년대 이후 계속, 농업은 더욱더 효율적으로 되었고, 농업 생산량은 급증했으며 점점 더 적은 수의 사람들이 국가소유의 농장에 필요하게 되었다. 같은 시기에, 급격한 산업 성장은 도시 지역에 많은 일자리를 창출해냈다. 이러한 경제적인 변화로 농촌에서 도시 지역으로의 사람들의 꾸준한 유입이 발생했다. 또한, 많은 수의 이민자들은 대부분이 고국에서 농부였는데 미국에 도착하면서 도시에서 일자리를 찾고 정착했다. 더욱이, 도시 지역에서 직업 선택과 여가와 교육 그리고 문화적 기회의 다양성은 많은 농촌 사람들을, 특히 젊은이들을 끌어들였다. 많은 수의 농촌 사람들은 도시 지역의 고용과 재미를 찾아 고향을 떠났다.

10. Hognose 뱀의 독특한 특성을 설명하는 글임을 알 수 있다. 이후 이 뱀이 구체적으로 어떤 상황에서 어떻게 죽은 척하는지에 대한 자세히 부연이 전개될 것을 예상할 수 있다.

1. <u>The Hognose Snake is renowned for its "death feigning" behavior</u>. 1) When threatened, it flattens its head and neck and hisses loudly. It may strike, but only with its mouth closed. If it is further harassed, it will flip on its back and convulse for a short period and may defecate and regurgitate its food. It will then remain motionless with its belly up, mouth open, and tongue hanging out. It may play dead for several minutes before cautiously turning over, looking around to see if it is safe before crawling away.

중심소재: 인구이동
1. 도입부 = 주제문
Hognose 뱀의 '죽은 척하기' 행동 (주제)
1) 뒷받침 진술
구체적 상황을 들어 Hognose 뱀이 어떤 식으로 '죽은 척하기' 행동을 하는지 뒷받침 진술이 상술되고 있다.

* General → Specific

도입부 = 주제문
구체적 진술을 이끄는 when에 주목한다.

| 해석
돼지코 뱀은 죽은 척하는 행동으로 유명하다. 위협을 받았을 때, 머리와 목을 납작하게 하고 크게 '쉬-' 하는 소리를 낸다. 입을 다물었다는 것을 제외하면 놀라울지도 모른다. 만약 더 시달리게 되면, 등을 대고 드러누울 것이고 짧은 시간 경련을 일으키며 배설을 하거나, 음식을 토해낼지도 모른다. 배를 드러낸 채로, 입을 벌리고, 혀가 빠져 움직임이 없는 상태를 유지한다. 조심스럽게 돌아 기어가도 괜찮은지 주위를 살펴보기 전에 몇 분간 죽은 체하기도 한다.

11. 특정 인물에 관한 이야기로 1920년대 아프리카계 미국인들의 예술 운동이었던 할렘 르네상스에 가장 중요한 작가이자 사상가라고 소개하고 있다. 주제문으로 '할렘 르네상스에 미친 Langston Hughes의 영향력'을 다루는 글이므로 이후 구체적으로 Langston Hughes의 어떤 측면이 할렘 르네상스에 영향을 미쳤는지 구체적으로 살펴보는 내용이 전개될 것을 예측할 수 있다. 실제 본문을 살펴보자.

1. <u>Langston Hughes was one of the most important writers and thinkers of the Harlem Renaissance, which was the African American artistic movement in the 1920s that celebrated black life and culture</u>. 1) ① Hughes's creative genius was influenced by his life in New York City's Harlem, a primarily African American neighborhood. His literary works helped shape American literature and politics. ② Hughes, like others active in the Harlem Renaissance, had a strong sense of racial pride. Through his poetry, novels, plays, essays, and children's books, he promoted equality, condemned racism and injustice, and celebrated African American culture, humor, and spirituality.

중심소재: 할렘 르네상스의 작가 Langston Hughes
1. 도입부 = 주제문
Langston Hughes가 할렘 르네상스에 미친 중요한 작가이자 사상가이다.
1) 뒷받침 진술
① 뉴욕의 할렘에서 영향을 받은 그의 문학적 창조성은 곧 미국 문학과 정치에 큰 영향력을 미침.
② 다양한 장르를 통해 평등을 높이고, 인종주의와 불의를 비난하면서 아프리카계 미국인들의 문화, 유머 그리고 정신을 찬양했다.

| 해석

Langston Hughes는 할렘 르네상스의 가장 중요한 작가이자 사상가 중 한 사람인데, 이는 1920년대의 흑인의 삶과 문화를 기리는 아프리카계 미국인 예술 운동이다. Hughes의 창조적인 천재성은 기존 아프리카계 미국인의 지역인, 뉴욕의 할렘가의 그의 삶에서 영향을 받았다. 그의 문학 작품들은 미국 문학과 정책들을 형성하는 데 도움을 주었다. 할렘 르네상스의 다른 활동처럼 Hughes는 강한 인종적 자부심을 지니고 있었다. 시와 소설, 연극, 수필 그리고 동화책들을 통하여 그는 평등을 고취하고, 인종차별과 불의를 비난했으며 아프리카계 미국인들의 문화와 유머 그리고 정신을 찬양했다.

12. 두 문단으로 나뉜 지문임을 알 수 있다. 문단별 주제를 설정하고, 이후 전체 지문의 주제를 설정할 수 있어야 한다. 첫 번째 문단의 주제문은 돌고래가 무리를 지어 다니는 사회적 동물이란 내용이고, 두 번째 문단은 돌고래가 다른 돌고래를 돌보는 세 가지의 특징적인 행동을 한다는 것을 과학자들이 관찰을 통해 밝혀냈다는 내용이다. 두 내용 문단의 공통점은 바로 돌고래가 '사회성(Socialization)'을 가지고 있다는 점이다.

문단이 나뉘면 문단의 수★ 만큼 소주제를 설정해야 한다.

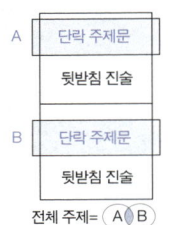

1. Dolphins are social animals that travel in schools varying in size from small herds of 2 to 5 members to immense schools of 1,000 or more. 1) ① A school of bottlenose dolphins typically numbers about 10 to 20 individuals in coastal areas. ② Killer whale groups can range from around 8 to more than 50 animals, and herds of several hundred have been reported. ③ Spotted dolphin schools can include up to 2,500 animals.

2. Scientists have observed dolphins displaying three types of caregiving behaviors: standing by, excitement, and supporting. 1) ① In standing-by behavior, dolphins remain in the vicinity of an injured or ill companion without offering aid. ② In excitement behavior, dolphins swim swiftly in circles around an injured dolphin, responding aggressively toward threats to the injured animal. Ⓐ For instance, they may bite harpoon lines or charge boats that come too close to the animal. ③ In supporting behavior, one or more dolphins will help a sick or injured dolphin by supporting it at the surface to prevent the animal from drowning.

첫번째 문단
중심소재: 돌고래
1. 도입부 = 주제문
돌고래는 무리를 지어사는 사회적 동물이다.
1) 뒷받침 진술
① 예 1
② 예 2
③ 예 3

두번째 문단
중심소재: 돌고래
1. 도입부 = 주제문
돌고래는 주위에 있는 자기 동족을 보살피는 세 가지 행동을 보인다.
1) 뒷받침 진술
① standing by
② excitement
Ⓐ 예시 부연
③ supparting behavior

→ 첫 번째 문단과 두 번째 문단 모두 '돌고래의 사회성'을 언급하고 있다.

| 해설

문단이 두 개로 나뉜 경우 각 문단의 소주제를 설정하고, 이후 각 문단의 공통된 내용을 바탕으로 전체 주제를 설정한다.

분석 Tip -

문단의 수만큼 소주제가 설정되며, 각 문단의 공통분모를 찾아 전체 주제를 설정한다.

| 해석

돌고래들은 2마리에서 5마리의 작은 무리의 규모에서부터 1,000마리 혹은 그 이상의 수많은 무리에 이르기까지 떼 지어 이동하는 사회적 동물이다. 큰 돌고래의 한 무리는 해안지역에서 10마리부터 20마리에 달한다. 범고래 무리는 8마리에서 50마리 이상에 이를 수도 있고 수백의 무리가 보고되기도 했다. 알락돌고래 무리는 2,500마리에 달하기도 한다.

  과학자들은 지지, 열광, 보조의 세 가지 형태로 종족 부양 행위를 보이는 돌고래를 관찰해왔다. 지지 행위에서, 돌고래들은 상처를 입거나 아픈 동료 주위에 도움을 주지 않은 채로 머무른다. 열광 행위에서 돌고래들은 부상당한 돌고래 주위를, 그 부상당한 동물에 위협적인 존재를 향하여 공격적으로 반응하면서, 원형으로 재빠르게 헤엄친다. 예를 들면, 그들은 작살 도구를 물어뜯거나 그 동물에 지나치게 가까이 접근하는 선박을 습격한다. 보호 행위에서, 하나 또는 그 이상의 돌고래들은 아프거나 상처 입은 돌고래가 바다 표면에서 가라앉는 것을 막기 위해 보조하며 돕는다.

13. Louis Sullivan은 미국 최초의 진정한 건축가라고 말하고 있다. Louis Sulivan의 어떤 측면에서 이전의 건축양식과 차이를 보이면서 초기 현대 건축의 특징을 잘 드러내는지 구체적 진술이 따를 것을 예측할 수 있다. 대조의 글이 전개되고 있다. 전체 본문을 살펴보자.

1. <u>Louis Sullivan is widely considered America's first truly modern architect</u>. 1) ① Instead of imitating historic styles, he created original forms and details. Ⓐ Older architectural styles were designed for buildings that were wide, **but** Sullivan was able to create aesthetic unity in buildings that were tall.
② Sullivan's designs often used masonry walls with terra cotta designs. Intertwining vines and leaves combined with crisp geometric shapes. This Sullivanesque style was imitated by other architects, and his later work formed the foundation for the ideas of his student, Frank Lloyd Wright.
③ Louis Sullivan believed that the exterior of an office building should reflect its interior structure and its interior functions. Ⓑ Ornament, where it was used, must be derived from Nature, instead of from classical architecture of the past. The work of Louis Sullivan is often associated with the Art Nouveau movement in architecture.

중심소재: 미국 초기 현대 건축가인 Louis Sullivan
1. 도입부 = 주제문
Louis Sullivan은 진정한 미국 초기 현대 건축가이다.
1) 뒷받침 근거
Louis의 예측적 특징이 나열되고 있다.
① 과거의 단순 모방이 아닌 창조적 형식과 구체성을 띤다.
Ⓐ 부연근거(wide-tall)
② Louis가 추구한 디자인의 특징과 영향력
③ 고전 건축양식과 다른 Sullivan의 특징: 건물 외부는 내부의 구조와 기능적 측면을 반영해야 한다.
Ⓑ 부연
자연에서 가져온 장식품 활용

| 해설

세 문단으로 구성되어 다양한 이야기를 하는 듯하나, 궁극적으로 Louis Sullivan이 미국의 진정한 초기 현대 건축가라는 첫 번째 문장에 대한 근거가 제시되는 글이다. 글의 특징이라면, 주제문에서 알 수 있듯이 이전(고전주의)의 건축양식과 **대조**하면서 Sullivan의 건축양식을 부각시키고 있다.

| 해석

Louis Sullivan은 미국 최초의 현대 건축가로 폭넓게 인정받고 있다. 기존의 양식을 모방하는 대신에, 그는 독창적인 형태와 세부묘사를 창조해냈다. 오래된 건축양식들은 넓은 건축물을 위해 계획되었지만, Sullivan은 높은 건축물에서 미적 통합을 이뤄낼 수 있었다.

Sullivan의 디자인은 적색토로 구성된 석조 벽을 사용했다. 뒤얽힌 덩굴과 나뭇잎을 푸석푸석한 기하학적 지형에 결합했다. 이 Sullivan 식의 양식을 다른 건축가들이 모방하였고, 그의 후기 작업은 그의 학생인 Frank Lloyd Wright 사상의 기초가 되었다.

Louis Sullivan은 사무실 건물의 외부는 그것의 내부 구조와 내부 기능들을 반영해야 한다고 생각했다. 건물이 사용되는 곳에서 장식은 과거의 기존 건축물에서가 아니라 자연으로부터 기인해야만 한다. Louis Sullivan의 작품은 종종 건축에서 아르누보 운동과 관련이 있다.

14. 'differ from'이라는 표현에서 두 대상의 차이점을 기술하는 대조의 글이 됨을 쉽게 파악할 수 있다. 본문에 주로 기술될 내용은 'format, publication schedule, content'라는 면에서 차이점이라고 예상할 수 있다. 전체 본문을 살펴보자.

대조의 시그널인 'differ from, by contrast' 확인한다.

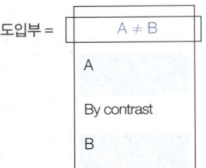

도입부 =

A ≠ B
A
By contrast
B

1. Historically, most periodicals have differed from newspapers in their format, publication schedule, and content. 1) ① Most newspapers deal with the news of the day and are issued on pulp paper with relatively large, unbound pages. By contrast, ② other types of periodicals focus on more specialized material, and when they deal with news they tend to do so in the form of summaries or commentaries. For centuries these periodicals generally have been printed on finer paper than newspapers, with smaller bound pages, and issued at intervals longer than a day (weekly, every two weeks, monthly, quarterly, or even annually).

중심소재: 주간지, 신문
1. 도입부 = 주제문
주간지와 신문의 차이점을 3가지 측면(format, publication schedule, content)에서 기술하는 설명문임을 알 수 있다.
1) 뒷받침 진술
① 신문의 특징
    ↕ by contrast
② 주간지의 특징

| 해설
대조를 드러내는 시그널(signal)을 놓치지 말자.

| 해석
역사적으로 대부분의 정기간행물은 형식과 발행 일정 그리고 내용에서 신문과 차이가 있다. 대부분 신문은 매일의 소식을 다루고, 상대적으로 크고, 제한이 없는 매수의 종이에 발행된다. 대조적으로 다른 정기간행물은 더 전문적인 내용에 초점을 맞추고, 새로운 소식을 다룰 때 요약 혹은 논평의 형태로 그렇게 하는 경향이 있다. 몇 세기 동안 이러한 정기간행물은 일반적으로 신문보다 질이 좋은 종이에 더 작은 범위의 페이지로 인쇄됐고, 하루보다 더 긴 간격으로 발행되었다(주간, 격주간, 월간, 분기 간 또는 년간).

15. 중심소재는 'insect'이다. 어떤 내용을 다루고 있는가? 다른 어느 종류의 동물보다 곤충은 지구 상에 더 많이 존재하고 3억 년 이상 지구에 존재했다는 '현상'을 제시하고 있다. 일반적으로 현상으로 기술되는 글은 다음과 같은 종류로 나눌 수 있다.

논증 – 인과	설명	설명 – 시간	설명
현상 ↓ (문제점) ↓ (원인) ↓ (대안)	현상 ↓ 원인/이유	현상 ↓ 기원(일반적으로 '과거 → 현재')	현상(새로운 트렌드) ↓ 전망

본문은 두 번째에 해당한다. 본문 전체를 살펴보자.

1. A remarkable variety of insects inhabit this planet. More species of insects exist than all other animal species together. Insects have survived on earth for more than 300 million years, and may possess the ability to survive for millions more.
1) There are many reasons why insects are so successful at surviving. ⓐ Their amazing ability to adapt permits them to live in extreme ranges of temperatures and environments. The one place they have not yet been found to any major extent is in the open oceans. Insects can survive on a wide range of natural and artificial foods—paint, pepper, glue, books, grain, cotton, other insects, plants and animals. Because they are small, they can hide in tiny spaces. A strong, hard but flexible shell called an exoskeleton covers their soft organs and is resistant to chemicals, water and physical impact. Their wings give them the option of flying away from dangerous situations or toward food or mates. ⓑ Also, insects have an enormous reproductive capacity: a honey bee queen lays as many as 4,000 eggs a day, and an African termite queen can lay as many as 43,000 eggs a day. ⓒ Another reason for their success is the strategy of

중심소재: Incects
1. 도입부 = 현상
곤충의 다양성과 생존력
1) 주제문
곤충은 다른 어느 동물의 종보다 지구 상에서 더 많은 종이 존재하고, 오래 존속한다.

① 뒷받침 근거(이유)
ⓐ 이유 1: 극한의 상황에서 살아남을 수 있는 놀라운 적응력을 갖추고 있다 – 이후 '놀라운 적응력'에 관한 구체적 부연이 기술될 것을 예측할 수 있다.

ⓑ 이유 2: 놀라운 번식 능력 – 이후 객관적 수치를 언급하면서 뒷받침 진술이 이어질 것이다.

ⓒ 이유 3: 보호색을 이용해 외부의 위험에서 자신을 보호하는 능력을 갖추고 있다 – 이후 이에 관한 구체적 부연이 따를 것을 예측할 수 있다.

★ 중심내용(controlling idea)을 확인한다.

도입부 = | 첫번째 문단
현상 |
| 두번째 문단
주제문 |
뒷받침 진술
이유①_____
이유②_____
이유③_____

*두 문장의 글에서 주제문의 위치

Case 1
도입부 =
주제문 = A + B
A
B

Case 2
도입부 =
단락 주제문(A)
뒷받침 진술
단락 주제문(B)
뒷받침 진술
전체 주제문 = A + B
A◇B

Case 3
도입부 =
중심소재 파악
주제문
뒷받침 진술

Case 4
도입부 =
중심소재 파악
주제문
뒷받침 진술

protective coloration. An insect may be right before our eyes, but nearly invisible because it is cleverly camouflaged like a green leaf, lump of brown soil, gray lichen, a seed or some other natural object. Some insects use bright, bold colors to send warning signals that they taste bad, sting or squirt out poison. Others have wing patterns that look like the eyes of a huge predator, confusing their enemies. Some insects also mimic bitter-tasting insects; hungry foes are fooled into avoiding them.

| 해설
본문은 인과와 나열의 글 전개방식을 취하고 있다. 주된 글 전개방법은 언제나 주제문과 관련하여 생각한다. 고로 주된 글 전개방식은 인과가 된다.

| 해석
  엄청나게 다양한 곤충들이 지구에 산다. 다른 동물 종의 합보다 더 많은 종의 곤충들이 존재한다. 곤충들은 3억 년 이상 동안 지구에서 살아남았다. 그리고 수백만 년을 살아갈 능력을 갖추고 있을지 모른다.
  곤충들이 생존하는 데 있어서 성공적인 많은 이유가 있다. 그들의 적응 능력으로 인해 극한 온도와 환경에서 살아남는다. 상당한 정도까지 그들이 발견되지 않았던 한 장소는 드넓은 바다이다. 곤충들은 폭넓게 — 페인트, 고추, 풀, 책, 곡물, 면, 다른 곤충들, 식물들 그리고 동물들과 같은 — 자연식품이나 인공 식품에서도 살아남는다. 그들은 작아서 작은 공간에도 숨을 수 있다. 강하고 단단하지만, 외골격이라 불리는 유연한 껍질은 그들의 무른 장기들을 덮고 화학물질과 물 그리고 물리적 충격에 저항력이 있다. 그들의 날개는 위험한 상황으로부터 날아 도망가고, 음식물 또는 짝을 향하여 날아갈 수 있는 선택권을 주었다. 또한, 곤충은 엄청난 번식능력을 갖추고 있다. 여왕벌은 하루에 4천 개의 알을 낳고, 아프리카 여왕 말벌은 하루에 4만 3천 개의 알을 낳을 수 있다.
  그들의 성공의 또 다른 이유는 보호색 전략이다. 어떤 동물은 우리의 눈앞에서는 보이지만 이것이 녹색 잎, 갈색 흙덩이, 회색 이끼, 씨앗이나 다른 자연물과 같이 교묘하게 위장되어 거의 보이지 않는다. 어떤 곤충은 그들이 톡 쏘며, 독을 뿜거나, 맛이 없다는 경고를 보내기 위해서 밝고 대담한 색상을 사용한다. 다른 것들은 그들의 적을 교란시키며, 커다란 포식자의 눈과 같이 보이는 날개 무늬를 가지고 있다. 다른 곤충들은 쓴맛의 곤충들의 색을 모방한다. 그래서 배고픈 천적들은 속아 그들을 피하게 된다.

16. 인간과 유인원이란 두 대상을 비교(Comparison)하는 글임을 파악할 수 있다. 'reflective of'를 통해 공통점이 기술된다는 점을 확인할 수 있으며, 두 대상의 비슷한 신체적 특성을 나열을 통해서 전개한다. 전체 본문을 확인해 보자.

비교의 시그널을 확인한★다.

1. Modern humans have a number of physical characteristics **reflective of** an ape ancestry. 1) <u>For instance</u>, people have ① shoulders with a wide range of movement and fingers capable of strong grasping. In apes, these characteristics are highly developed as adaptations for brachiation—swinging from branch to branch in trees. Although humans do not

중심소재: 인간과 유인원
1. 도입부 = 주제문
두 대상의 유사점 기술
1) 뒷받침 예시
① 유사 특징 1
② 유사 특징 2

50

brachiate, the general anatomy from that earlier adaptation remains. ② Both people and apes also have larger brains and greater cognitive abilities than do most other mammals.

★ 비교의 글임을 드러내는 시그널 확인.

| 해설
두 대상의 유사한 특징을 드러내는 signal로 본문에서 **reflective of**와 **both**가 쓰이고 있다. General → Specific의 전형적 두괄식을 취하고 있다.

| 해석
현대인들에게는 많은 유인원 조상이 반영된 신체적 특성이 있다. 예를 들면, 사람들은 넓은 운동 범위를 갖는 어깨와 강한 악력을 가진 손가락이 있다. 원숭이의 경우, 양손으로 나무를 타기 위한 — 나뭇가지에서 다른 가지로 오르락내리락하는 — 적응으로 이러한 특성이 매우 발달했다. 비록 사람들이 나무를 타지는 않지만, 이러한 이전의 적응으로 말미암은 공통된 신체 구조가 남아있다. 사람과 유인원 둘 다 대부분의 다른 포유동물이 가진 것보다 큰 두뇌와 대단한 인지능력을 갖췄다.

17. 대기 중 이산화탄소의 증가와 이에 따른 온실효과 심화라는 두 가지 현상이 제시되고 있다. 하지만 이 글은 이런 현상들의 원인을 밝히는 글이 아님을 알 수 있다. 왜냐하면, 문장 첫머리에 이미 벌써 이러한 현상의 원인이 기술되고 있기 때문이다.

1. 1) The amount of carbon dioxide in the atmosphere has been increasing by 0.4 percent a year because of the use of oil, gas, and coal and the burning of tropical forests. 2) The other gases that contribute to the greenhouse effect are increasing even faster. 2. ① The net effect of these increases may be a worldwide rise in temperature, estimated at from 2C to 6C over the next 100 years. ② Warming of this magnitude would not only alter climates throughout the world, it would also cause sea levels to rise at least 30cm. If this happened, millions of people living in low-lying coastal areas would be affected, as would crop production and natural vegetation.

중심소재: 이산화탄소 → 이산화탄소 증가로 인한 온실효과
1. 도입부
현상(원인): 화석연료 사용과 열대우림 파괴로 인해 대기중 이산화 탄소↑ + 온실효과에 영향을 미치는 다른 가스로↑
1) 결과
온도↑ → 기후 및 해수면↑
① 현상의 심각성(대안의 필요성 강조)
해안에 사는 사람에게 피해를 줄 뿐 아니라 농작물과 식생에 부정적 영향을 미침

| 해설
대기 중의 이산화탄소의 양은 석유와 가스 그리고 석탄과 열대우림의 소각으로 매년 0.4퍼센트씩 증가하고 있다. 온실효과에 영향을 주는 다른 가스들은 심지어 더 급격히 증가하고 있다. 그러한 증가로 인해 발생하는 순수한 영향력은 다가오는 100년간 2~6℃까지 예상되는 전 세계적인 온도 상승이다. 이 정도의 상당한 온도 상승은 전 세계에 걸쳐 기후를 변화시킬 뿐 아니라 해수면을 적어도 30cm까지 오르기 한다. 만약 이러한 현상이 발생한다면, 낮은 해안가에 사는 수백만의 사람들이 식량 생산과 자연 식생과 같은 영향을 받을 수 있다.

18. 글의 방향을 설정하는 중요한 단서는 바로 'Of course ~ not' 이다. 일반적으로 '물론 ~은 아니지만...' 으로 전개되기에, 이후에 'But' 이 전개된다. 다시 첫 번째 문장을 살펴보자.

> People sometimes call the human body a machine—the most wonderful one ever built. Of course, the human body is not a machine.

'사람들은 때로 인간의 몸을 기계로 간주한다... 물론 인간이 기계는 아니다.' 라고 하고 있으므로 이후 '그러나 인간의 몸은 기계적인 측면이 있다' 라는 내용으로 전개되는 것이 논리적이다. 고로 이후 내용은 인간의 기계적 측면의 내용이 다뤄진다. 즉, 인간과 기계의 유사점을 다루는 비교(Comparison)에 해당하는 글이다. 전체 지문을 살펴보자.

1. People sometimes call the human body a machine—the most wonderful one ever built. Of course, the human body is not a machine. But it can be compared to one in many ways.
1) ① Like a machine, the body is made up of many parts. Each part of the body, like each part of a machine, does special jobs. But all the parts work together and so make the body or the machine run smoothly. ② Also like a machine, the body needs energy to work. In such a machine as a car, the energy comes from petrol. In the body, it comes from food and oxygen.

중심소재: 인간의 몸과 기계
1. 도입부 = 주제문
몸과 기계는 유사해 여러가지 측면에서 비교 가능

1) 뒷받침 진술
① 유사점 1
인간의 몸은 기계와 같이 여러 부분으로 구성되어 있고, 서로 유기적으로 협력한다.

② 유사점 2
기계와 같이 인간의 몸도 움직이기 위해 에너지가 필요하다.

| 해석
사람들은 때때로 인간의 몸을 지금껏 만들어진 가장 놀라운 기계라고 부른다. 물론, 인간의 몸은 기계는 아니다. 그러나 다양한 면에서 비교될 수 있다. 기계처럼 몸은 많은 부분으로 구성된다. 기계의 각 부분처럼 몸의 각 부분은 특별한 일을 한다. 그러나 모든 부분이 함께 작용해서 몸이나 기계를 부드럽게 만든다. 역시 기계와 같이, 몸은 일할 수 있는 에너지가 필요하다. 자동차와 같은 기계의 경우, 에너지는 휘발유로부터 얻는다. 신체의 경우, 이것은 음식과 산소로부터 얻는다.

6. 부연진술

[실전응용 1]

1) <u>Drug abusers</u> cause a great deal of damage to themselves. ① They may spend too much on drugs and create money problems for themselves. They may also get into trouble with police, and this can destroy their lives. 2) And drug abusers hurt people around them as well. ② They cause great pain to their family and friends, who have to watch a loved one destroy his or her life. 3) They also damage their communities. ③ <u>For example</u>, many drug abusers end up in jail or in the hospital, and the community must pay for this.

중심소재: Drug
1. 도입부 = 구체적 진술
1) 뒷받침 진술 1
마약 중독자들은 자신에게 큰 피해를 준다.
① 부연 진술
2) 뒷받침 진술 2
마약 중독자는 주위 사람에게 피해를 준다.
② 부연 진술
3) 뒷받침 진술 3
마약 중독자는 공동체에 피해를 준다.
③ 부연 예시(For example)

★ 마약 중독에 관한 글임을 파악할 수 있다.

★ 본문은 전체 주제문을 이끌어 내야 하는 주제가 숨어 있는 'implicit'의 유형이다. 이 부분은 전체 주제의 중심내용(controlling idea)이 아니라 뒷받침 진술의 중심내용이며 이후 구체적 내용은 부연진술에서 다뤄지고 있다. 이후 나머지 뒷받침 문장과 부연진술의 관계도 동일하다.

| 본문 구조

일반진술 (주제문)	마약 중독자는 자신뿐 아니라 주변 사람에게도 큰 피해를 준다. (주제: 마약 중독자의 폐해)	주제문을 독자가 이끌어내는 유형
구체적 진술	뒷받침 문장 1. Drug abusers cause a great deal of damage to themselves. – 부연 진술	
	뒷받침 문장 2. And drug abusers hurt people around them as well. – 부연 진술	
	뒷받침 문장 3. They also damage their communities. – 부연 진술	

| 해석

마약 중독자들은 자기 자신에게 커다란 피해를 끼친다. 이들은 마약을 사는 데 지나치게 많은 돈을 쓰며, 스스로 금전적인 문제를 일으킨다. 이들은 또한 경찰과 문제를 일으키기도 하며, 이 때문에 이들의 삶은 엉망이 되기도 한다. 그리고 마약 중독자들은 이들의 주변 사람들에게도 피해를 줄 수 있다. 이들은 가족과 친구들에게 큰 고통을 안겨 주는데, 이들을 사랑하는 사람이 자신의 삶을 파괴하는 것을 지켜보아야만 한다. 이들은 또한 지역 사회에 피해를 준다. 예를 들면, 많은 마약 중독자들은 결국 교도소나 병원으로 가는데, 지역 사회가 그 비용을 부담해야 한다.

[실전응용 2]

중심소재는 '기억' 이다. ★

1. Psychologists who study memory tell us that our memories have three parts. 1) ① First, there is short-term memory, which holds on to sights, sounds, smells, tastes and tactile experiences for only a minute or so. ② The second type of memory is working memory, which is where we use memory to think. ⓐ We make comparisons, look for causes and effects, predict what will happen in the future. ③ Finally, long-term memory is what we keep for many years. ⓑ It is where we store the words to a song learned in childhood. We need all three kinds of memory to function well in life.

중심소재: 기억 → 기억의 구성
1. 도입부 = 주제문
우리의 기억은 세 부분으로 구성되어 있다.
1) 뒷받침 진술
① Short-term memory
② Working memory
ⓐ 부연 진술
③ Long-term memory
ⓑ 부연 진술

중심내용(controlling idea)★ 에 해당하는 것으로 본문에서 기억의 세 부분에 대해서 다룰 것을 예상할 수 있다. 나열의 시그널을 확인한다.

* 부연진술의 위치 파악

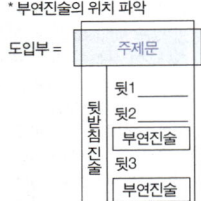

* 주제문/뒷받침 진술/부연진술의 관계

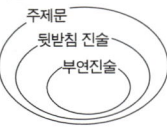

| 해석

기억을 연구하는 심리학자들은 기억에는 세 개의 부분이 있다고 말한다. 첫 번째는 단기 기억이 있는데 이것은 시각, 청각, 후각, 미각, 촉각 경험을 일분 정도단 기억한다. 두 번째 기억의 형태는 작동 기억으로 이것은 생각하기 위해서 사용하는 기억이다. 우리는 비교를 하고, 원인과 결과를 찾고, 미래에 일어날 일을 예측한다. 마지막으로 장기 기억은 우리가 여러 해 동안 유지하는 기억이다. 바로 여기에 우리가 어린 시절 배운 노랫말이 저장된다. 생활을 잘하기 위해서는 우리는 세 가지 기억이 모두 필요하다.

[실전응용 3]

본문에서 구체적으로 다룰 중심내용에 해당한다. ★

1. It is important to use water carefully. Here are some ways you can use less water. 1) First, be sure to turn off faucets tightly. They should not drip in the bathroom or kitchen sink. 2) Second, do not keep the water running for a long time. Turn it off while you are doing something else. ① For example, it should be off while you are shaving or brushing your teeth. It should also be off while you are washing the dishes. 3) Finally, in the summer you should water your garden in the evening. That way you will not lose a lot of water.

물 절약과 관련된 글이다. ★ 중심소재는 물이다.

중심소재: 물 → 물절약
1. 도입부 = 주제문
물을 아껴쓰는 것의 중요성을 언급하면서 "구체적 방법"을 소개하고 있다.
1) 뒷받침 진술
① 방법 1
물을 꼭 잠가라.
② 방법2
물을 오래 쓸데없이 틀어놓지 마라.
ⓐ 예시 부연(For example)
③ 방법 3
저녁에 잔디에 물을 주어라.

| 해석

주의 깊게 물을 사용하는 것은 중요하다. 물을 보다 적게 사용하는 방법이 몇 가지 있다. 첫 번째 수도꼭지를 꼭 잠가라. 수도꼭지의 물이 목욕탕이나 부엌 싱크대에서 흘러나오게 해서는 안 된다. 둘째로 오랫동안 수도꼭지에서 물이 흘러나오게 해서는 안 된다. 당신이 다른 일을 하고 있을 때에는 반드시 잠가라. 예를 들어, 양치질한다거나 면도를 할 때는 수도꼭지를 잠가야 한다. 설거지할 때도 수도꼭지를 감가야 한다. 마지막으로 여름철에는 저녁에 정원에 물을 주어야 한다. 이렇게 하면, 물을 많이 아낄 수 있게 된다.

| 참고

'뒷받침 진술 – 부연진술'의 관계는 '주제문 – 뒷받침 문장'과 같은 구조를 지닌다. 본문의 뒷받침 진술에 해당하는 2)를 자세히 살펴보면 다음과 같다.

1. <u>Second, do not keep the water running for a long time. Turn it off while you are doing something else</u>. 1) **For example**, it should be off while you are shaving or brushing your teeth. It should also be off while you are washing the dishes.	1. 주제문 1) 예시를 통한 **뒷받침 문장** (For example)

[실전응용 4]

1. In 2003, there were already estimated to be several hundred thousand blogs on the Internet, and the number is growing by tens of thousands a month. 1) A blog, <u>however, differs from a traditional web site in several ways</u>. Ⓐ Most importantly, it is updated much more regularly. Many blogs are updated every day, and some are updated **several** times a day. Ⓑ Also, most blogs use special software or web sites which are specifically aimed at bloggers, so you don't need to be a computer expert to create your own blog. ⓐ This means that ordinary people who may find computer difficult to use can easily set up and start writing their own blog.

중심소재: 인터넷의 블로그
1. 도입부(현상)
  1) 주제문
블로그는 전통적인 웹사이트와 여러 측면에서 다르다(대조의 글전개 방식 예상)

① 뒷받침 진술
Ⓐ 훨씬 더 규칙적으로 업데이트 가능
Ⓑ 블로거(blogger)를 위한 특별한 소프트 또는 웹사이트를 운영하는 개인이 블로그를 손쉽게 만들 수 있는 특징
ⓐ 부연 재진술

★ 현상제시 - 중심소재 도출

★ 현상을 이끄는 시그널에는 'recently, during the last 숫자, Now' 등의 부사(구)가 있으며, 동사 표현으로 'have + p.p., be + V-ing, seem' 등이 있다.

★ 본문에서 다뤄질 중심내용(controlling idea)에 해당한다.

| 해석

2003년 인터넷상에는 이미 수십만 개의 블로그가 존재하는 것으로 추산되었으며, 그 수는 한 달에 수만 개씩 증가하고 있다. 하지만 블로그는 몇 가지 측면에서 전통적인 웹 사이트와 다르다. 가장 본질적인 것으로 블로그는 훨씬 더 정기적으로 갱신된다는 점이다. 많은 블로그가 매일 갱신되며, 일부는 하루에도 몇 번씩 갱신된다. 또한, 대부분의 블로그는 특별한 소프트웨어나 특별히 블로그 사용자들을 겨냥한 웹 사이트를 사용한다. 그래서 자신의 블로그를 만들기 위해서 컴퓨터 전문가여야 할 필요가 없다. 이는 컴퓨터 사용을 어려워하는 보통 사람들도 쉽게 자신의 블로그를 만들거나 글쓰기를 시작할 수 있음을 의미한다.

[실전응용 5]

본문에서 구체적으로 다 ★
뤄질 중심내용(controlling
idea)에 해당한다.

도입부 =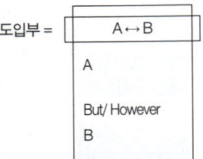

1. In some cases, analysis of texts has shown that men and women tend to have different styles of writing. 1) ① They differ, first of all, in the amount of personal pronouns they use. For instance, women are far more likely than men to use pronouns like "I," "you," and "she." On the other hand, men tend to use words like "a," "the," "that," and "these" more than women do. ② They also are more inclined to use numbers and quantifying words like "more" and "several." ③ In contrast to women, men more readily modify nouns with phrases rather than single words. For example, women will probably write "rose garden" whereas men would write "garden of roses."

중심소재: 남녀의 글쓰기 차이점
1. 도입부 = 주제문
Different Styles of Writing between Men and Women
주제문에서 알 수 있듯이, 주된 글 전개방식은 대조이다. 이후 주제를 뒷받침하는 내용을 '나열/예시'의 글 전개 방식을 함께 쓰고 있다. 일반적으로 주된 글 전개방식을 고를 때는 주제에서 강조하는 부분(남녀의 차이점)을 중심으로 설정한다.
1) 뒷받침 문장

| 해설

대조, 나열, 예시가 모두 들어간 짧지만 알찬 구조를 보이고 있다. '주제문 – 뒷받침 문장 – 부연 진술'이 모두 들어간 대표적인 'General → Specific' 유형이다. 부연진술의 기능을 잘 파악할 수 있는 글이므로 주의해서 살펴본다. 글의 구조는 다음과 같다.

일반진술	Different Styles of Writing between Men and Women
구체적 진술 (뒷받침 문장)	1. First of all: the amount of personal pronouns they use 　— 부연 진술(For instance) 2. Also: numbers and quantifying words they use 3. (In addition): how they modify nouns with phrases 　— 부연 진술(For example)

| 해석

어떤 경우 글을 분석해 보면 남자와 여자가 서로 다른 글쓰기 스타일을 지닌 경향을 보인다. 무엇보다도, 이들이 사용하는 인칭대명사의 양이 다르다. 예를 들면, 여성들이 남성들보다 "I", "you", 그리고 "she"와 같은 대명사를 사용하는 경향이 훨씬 더 많다. 반면, 남성들은 여성들이 사용하는 것보다 "a", "the", "that", 그리고 "these"와 같은 단어를 더 많이 사용하는 경향이 있다. 이들은 또한 "more"나 "several"과 같은 수나 양을 나타내는 단어를 더 많이 사용하는 경향이 있다. 여성들과는 대조적으로, 남성들은 하나의 단어보다는 쉽사리 구로 명사를 수식한다. 예를 들어, 여성들은 아마도 "rose garden"이라고 쓰겠지만, 남성들은 "garden of roses"라고 쓸 것이다.

7 통일성과 응집성

1. 통일성

[실전응용 1]

1. <u>Anger can make you physically sick.</u> 1) The next time you hear someone arguing in a raised voice, try to imagine what is happening in his body. Blood pressure builds up. A weak heart can be stressed to a dangerous point. **Headaches** often follow the buildup of rage. The whole internal system is stressed, ready for an emergency, and the whole digestive process is shut off or slowed down. **Stomachaches, indigestion, and all sorts of trouble with digestive organs** can arise from chronic anger. You can turn red, sweat, tremble, and be very uncomfortable—all because you are angry.

중심소재: Anger
1. 도입부 = 주제문
분노는 신체적 고통을 유발할 수 있다.
→ 하나의 단락은 하나의 주제만을 다루는 통일성을 지켜야 하므로 이후 뒷받침 내용은 모두 '분노는 신체적 고통을 유발'한다는 내용과 관련이 있어야 한다.
1) 뒷받침 진술
앞에서 언급한 '분노로 말미암은 신체적 고통'에 관한 구체적 예로 '두통, 복통, 소화불량'을 언급하면서 하나의 주제에 대한 뒷받침 문장을 제시하고 있다.

★ 주제는 'Anger' 이다.
★ 본문에 다뤄질 중심내용 (controlling idea)에 해당한다.

*통일성

도입부 =

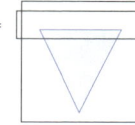

도입부에서 설정한 중심소재의 내용을 처음부터 끝까지 일관성 있게 그 폭을 좁혀 전개되는 흐름을 파악한다.

| 해설
첫 번째 문장이 주제문이고, 이후 뒷받침 문장으로 '신체적 고통을 유발하는 분노'에 관한 글이다. 하나의 주제만을 잘 전달하는 통일성을 잘 갖춘 지문이다. 글 전개상의 특징으로 'A 때문에 B가 일어난다' 는 인과의 글 전개방식이 두드러진다.

| 해석
분노는 신체적으로 당신을 아프게 할 수 있다. 다음에 누군가 격앙된 목소리로 다투는 소리를 듣거든 그의 몸에서 어떤 일이 벌어지고 있는지 상상해보라. 혈압이 올라간다. 약한 심장은 위험할 정도로 스트레스를 받을 수 있다. 분노가 쌓여 종종 두통이 생긴다. 신체 내부 전체가 스트레스를 받고 곧 응급상황에 대비하게 되며 전체 소화 과정이 중단되거나 느려진다. 복통, 소화 불량 그리고 모든 종류의 소화 기관 관련 문제는 만성적인 분노로 생길 수 있다. 당신은 얼굴이 붉어지고, 땀이 나고, 몸이 떨리고, 매우 불편해질 수 있는데 이 모든 것은 당신이 화가 나 있기 때문이다.

일상대화의 의사전달에 ★
관한 글이다.

구체적 진술을 이끄는 시 ★
그널을 파악한다.

본문에서 다뤄질 중심내 ★
용에 해당한다.

도입부 =

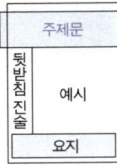

[실전응용 2]

In everyday conversation, 1. <u>there are different ways to say what we want</u>. 1) ① When we are with a group of friends, we can say to them, "Go get me that plate!" or "Shut up!" ② However, when we are invited to other people's house with our parents, we must say, "Could you please pass me that plate, if you don't mind?" and "I'm sorry. I don't mean to interrupt, but I'm not able to hear the speaker." 2. <u>We should use different expressions in different social situations</u>.

중심소재: 의사전달 방법
1. 도입부 = 주제문
상황에 따라 원하는 말을 전달하는 방법은 다양하다.
1) 뒷받침 진술
구체적 예를 통해 뒷받침 문장 제시
①과 ② 동일한 상황에 다른 표현을 쓰는 구체적 예 제시.
2. 결론(요지)
글의 요지를 이끄는 시그널인 'should'를 확인한다.

| 해석
일상의 대화에서 우리가 원하는 것을 말하는 다양한 방법이 있다. 우리가 친구들과 함께 있을 때, 이들에게 "가서 저 접시 좀 갖다 줘!" 또는 "닥쳐!"라고 말할 수 있다. 그러나 우리가 부모와 함께 다른 이의 집에 초대되었을 때, 우리는 "괜찮으시다면, 저 접시 좀 건네주시겠습니까?" 그리고 "미안합니다. 방해하려는 것은 아니지만, 연설하는 사람 말을 잘 들을 수가 없습니다."라고 말해야 한다. 우리는 여러 사회적 문맥에 따라 다양한 표현을 사용해야 한다.

[실전응용 3]

통념비판의 시그널을 확 ★
인한다.

1. **People think** that English is already the international language. 1) <u>But</u> English must stop being used as the international language. ① Scientists and business people do use English, <u>but there are relatively few people in the world who use English conversationally</u>. According to recent statistics, English is not spoken by more than 3.5 billion of the world's population. To put it a different way, <u>fewer than one out of ten people in the world speak English</u>.

중심소재: English
1. 도입부 = 통념
영어는 국제언어이다.
1) 주제문
영어는 국제어로써의 기능이 될 수 없다.
① 뒷받침 진술
상대적으로 적은 사람들이 영어를 사용한다(10명 중 한 명도 안 되는 꼴).
* 통계수치를 통해 근거의 객관성을 높이고 있다.

| 해설
일반 통념으로 시작하는 대표적인 지문이다.

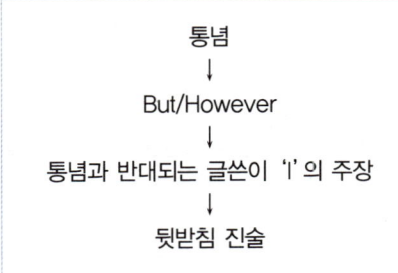

58

'But' 이후 글쓴이의 주장이 드러나고, 이후 객관적 수치를 제시하면서 자신의 주장이 옳음을 뒷받침하고 있다. 본문은 '영어는 국제언어로 사용되지 말아야 한다.'는 하나의 주장과 이에 대한 근거로 이뤄진 통일성을 잘 갖추고 있다.

| 해석
사람들은 영어는 이미 국제어라고 생각한다. 그러나 영어가 국제어로 사용되는 것은 중단되어야 한다. 과학자들과 기업가들이 영어를 사용하지만, 영어를 대화로 사용하는 사람은 세계에서 상대적으로 적다. 최근의 통계를 보면 영어는 3억 4천(과거 영국의 단위는 billion이 1억이었다)의 세계보다 적은 인구가 사용한다. 이를 다시 말하면, 세계에서 10명 중 1명보다 적은 인구가 영어를 사용한다는 말이다.

| 참고
본문에서 사용된 'billion'은 '1억'에 해당한다. 과거 영국에서 'billion'을 1억으로 사용했으나, 현재는 미국과 같이 10억으로 사용하는 경향이 있으므로 수치가 나왔을 때 주의하도록 한다.

9 사실·의견·신념·편견의 구별

[실전응용 1]

Part 1

1. Fact 2. Opinion 3. Fact 4. Opinion 5. Fact 6. Opinion 7. Fact 8. Opinion 9. Opinion 10. Fact 11. Fact 12. Fact 13. Opinion 14. Opinion 15. Opinion 16. Fact 17. Opinion 18. Opinion 19. Opinion 20. Opinion

Part 2

1.
1) 사실에 해당하는 내용이다: Fact
2) 앞으로 어떤 일이 벌어질지 아무도 모르기에 앞의 내용을 바탕으로 의견을 제시한 것이다.
   즉, '사실을 바탕으로 전개한 의견'이기에 Opinion에 해당한다.

2.
1) Opinion
2) Fact

3.
1) Fact
2) Opinion

4.
1) Opinion
2) Fact

10 요지를 이끄는 시그널 연구

1. 글쓴이의 주장(의견)을 이끄는 표현

[실전응용]

1. Right now, there are thousands of incurable patients lying helplessly in bed, suffering pain and misery and wishing they could be allowed to die. 1) But the doctors are afraid to facilitate their deaths for fear of legal or professional repercussions. 2) <u>I propose</u> that doctors be allowed to discontinue treatment or administer lethal doses of painkillers if requested to do so by patients suffering from incurable diseases, or, in the case of comatose patients, by their relatives.

중심소재: 불치병 환자 → 불치병 환자에 대한 안락사
1. **도입부 = 현상**
수천의 환자들이 고통 속에서 죽기를 바라고 있다.
1) 의사의 견해
안락사 신청 기피 - 이유
2. **요지(글쓴이의 주장)**
조건부에 한해 안락사를 허용해야 한다.

★ 불치병을 앓고 있는 환자에 관한 글이다. 글쓴이의 궁극적인 주장이 무엇인지 파악하도록 한다.

| 해설
'현상 – 문제점 제기 – 대안'으로 이어지는 지문이다. 일반적으로 이런 글에서 글쓴이의 주장은 바로 '대안'에 해당하므로 본문 마지막에 등장할 가능성이 크다. 본문에서 글의 요지/주장을 이끄는 시그널 중 하나인 'propose'가 등장하고 있다.

| 해석
현재 무기력하게 침대에 누워 불치병을 앓고 있는 수천의 환자들이 있는데, 이들은 고통과 비참함을 느끼며 죽기를 희망한다. 그러나 의사들은 법적 문제 또는 전문적 반격의 두려움으로 죽음을 재촉하는 것을 꺼린다. 나는 불치병을 앓고 있는 환자나 혼수상태에 있는 환자의 친척이 치료를 중단하고 안락사를 시키려 한다면 의사는 그렇게 해야 한다고 제안하는 바이다.

도입부 =
현상
견해 A _____
↕ 근거
① 견해 _____
뒷받침 진술

문제를 푸는 학습자 입장에선 ① 견해가 가장 중요하다.

2. 글을 요약하는 표현

*주제 설정

도입부 = 중심소재(A)
A의 긍정적 측면
↕
B의 부정적 측면
요지 = A + B

주제 = A의 모순적 특성

[실전응용]

1. Today, the automobile <u>is mostly thought of as</u> a necessity. The car is still a convenience so taken for granted that its absence in our individual lives is almost beyond comprehension. 1) **But** as a collective entity, the automobile threatens to make us its servant. ① It requires that we plan our cities or dig them up and rebuild them. 2. <u>Overall, the result is a tie. The car has assumed the confusing status of something we can't live with and can't live without.</u>

중심소재: 자동차
1. 도입부 = 일반적 관점
1) 자동차에 대한 긍정적 관점
자동차 = 필수품
2) 자동차에 대한 부정적 관점
인간이 차의 종이 되는 현상
① 부연 근거
2. 요지(overall)
자동차는 있을 때는 위험한 대상이지만, 없으면 불편한 그런 모순적 존재이다.

| 해설

요지를 이끄는 시그널(Signal)을 잘 활용해야 한다. 일반통념으로 시작하는 글이지만, 글의 궁극적 요지는 'But' 뒤가 아닌 'Overall' 뒤에 있다. 때로 내용파악이 우선인 경우가 있으니, 단순히 몇 가지 요령으로 풀다간 큰코다친다.

| 해석

오늘날 자동차는 주로 필수품으로 간주된다. 자동차는 너무나 당연한 필수품으로 여겨져서 우리 개인의 삶에서 이의 부재는 거의 생각할 수 없을 정도이다. 그러나 집합적 존재로서 자동차는 우리를 자동차의 하인으로 만들려고 위협한다. 자동차로 인해 우리는 도시를 계획하고, 파내며, 다시 건설한다. 전반적으로 결과는 동점이다(자동차는 장점과 단점이 있다). 자동차는 있어도 살 수 없고 없이도 살 수 없는 애매한 지위를 지녔다.

3. 당위성을 나타내는 표현

[실전응용 1]

1. Some universities require students to keep a record of when they met with their supervisor, what was discussed, and what was the agreed next course of action. 1) For advanced research programs, such as a Ph.D., keeping this record up to date is a requirement for progression from one stage of the program to another. Seeing your supervisor regularly is one of the best ways of making sure that your dissertation is of the very highest possible standard. 2. Yet

중심소재: 지도주임과의 정기적 만남 기록
1. 도입부
지도주임과의 정기적 만남 기록
1) 이러한 사항은 박사학위나 고등과정에서 중요하다는 점과 이유(요지의 근거)
2) 현상 – 문제점 지적
역집의 But 확인
2. 요지(조언/제안)
요지를 이끄는 should 확인:
지도주임과 정기적 만남을 가져야 한다.

you would be surprised how many students see their supervisor as little as possible. Although your supervisor will probably ask to see you if you have been invisible for a long period, it is normally up to you to arrange such meetings. 3. You should do this as regularly as possible whenever you have something to discuss.

| 해설

부정적인 특정 현상에 대한 글쓴이의 조언/제안(대안)이 제시되는 글의 유형이다. 일반적으로 'Yet' 이후에 전개되지만, 본문에서 글쓴이가 파악한 문제점이 'Yet' 이후에 등장하고, 본문 마지막에서 요지를 이끄는 시그널인 'should' 와 함께 주장이 드러난다.

| 해석

몇몇 대학들은 학생이 언제 자신이 지도교수를 만났고, 무엇을 논했으며, 앞으로 하기로 한 다음 단계의 일이 무엇인지에 관한 기록을 해 두도록 요구하고 있다. 박사 과정과 같은 상급 연구 과정의 경우 매일 기록을 남기는 것이 한 단계에서 다음 단계로 나아가는 필수 요건이다. 지도교수를 정기적으로 만나는 것은 자신의 학위 논문이 가능한 최고의 수준이 되도록 하는 최선의 방법 중 하나이다. 그러나 당신은 얼마나 많은 학생이 자신의 지도 교수를 만나지 않으려 하는지에 놀랄 것이다. 비록 당신의 지도교수가 오랫동안 보이지 않아서 만나자고 요청을 하더라도, 그러한 만남을 결정하는 것은 보통 당신에게 달려 있다. 논할 것이 있을 때마다 규칙적으로 이를 행해야 한다.

[실전응용 2]

1. A negative response is a most difficult handicap to overcome. 1) When you have said "No," all your pride of personality demands that you remain consistent with yourself. You may later feel that the "No" was hasty; nevertheless, there is your precious pride to consider! Once having said a thing, you feel you must stick to it. When a person says "No" and really means it, he or she is doing far more than saying a word of two letters. 2. Hence it is of the very greatest importance that a person be started in the affirmative direction. 1) The skillful speaker gets, at the outset, a number of "Yes" responses. This sets the psychological process of the listener moving in the affirmative direction.

중심소재: 대화의 반응
1. 도입부 = 주제문
부정적 반응은 극복하기가 어렵다.
1) 뒷받침 진술(이유)
'No' 라는 말을 하고 나면, 자신이 한 말을 일관성 있게 유지해야 하는 '자존심' 의 문제가 되기 때문

2. 요지
긍정적인 대답으로 시작하는 것이 중요하다.
1) 뒷받침 사례

* 주제문과 요지의 구별

도입부 = | 주제문 |
| 뒷받침 이유 |
| 요지 |
| 뒷받침 사례 |

주제문은 반드시 주제를 포함하고 있지만 요지는 포함될 수도 그렇지 않을 수도 있음을 파악한다.

| 해설

결론을 이끄는 접속사 'Hence' 와 글쓴이의 주장이 드러나는 'It is of importance that S V' 구문을 확인할 수 있다. 바로 이어 글쓴이의 주장이 드러난다.

| 해석

부정적인 반응은 극복하기 몹시 어려운 장애물 중 하나다. 당신이 "아니오(No)"라고 말했을 때 당신의 모든 자존심은 당신이 일관성을 유지하도록 요구한다. 당신은 나중에 "아니오"가 성급했다고 느낄지도 모른다. 그럼에도 당신의 중요한 자존심을 고려해야 한다. 일단 말을 하고 나면, 당신은 그것을 고수해야 한다고 느낀다. 어떤 사람이 "아니오(No)"라고 말하고 진정 그것을 의미할 때 그 사람은 그 두 글자로 된 단어를 말하는 것보다 더 많은 것을 하는 것이다(단순히 'No'라는 단어를 말하는 그 이상의 의미이다). 그러므로 어떤 사람이 긍정적인 방향에서 출발하도록 하는 것이 아주 중요하다. 노련한 화자는 초반부에 "예"라는 반응을 많이 얻어낸다. 이렇게 되면 청자가 긍정적인 방향으로 움직이도록 심리적인 과정이 조성된다.

[실전응용 3]

1. Every mother and father wants to raise a child with a strong moral character. We want our children to know good from bad, and right from wrong. We hope they'll learn to behave morally and ethically, and grow up to be honest and considerate. In short, we want our children to develop a conscience — a powerful inner voice that will keep them on the right path. 1) But a conscience does not develop by itself, 2. so the job of building one is ours. It's a process parents need to work on day after day, and year after year. We need to constantly distinguish right from wrong, and to model appropriate behavior. Eventually, our children will fully accept our messages, and they will become the essence of their character.

중심소재: 도덕적 아이의 양육

1. 도입부
어머니와 부모는 도덕성을 잘 갖춘 아이로 성장하길 바란다.
1) 도덕적 양심의 속성
저절로 생기지 않는다.
2. 제안(요지)
아이에게 매일 옳고 그름을 구별하는 모범이 되는 적절한 행위(모범)을 제시해 줌으로써 윤리교육을 해야 한다.

| 해설

제안은 곧 글쓴이의 주장에 해당한다.

| 해석

모든 부모는 자녀가 도덕성을 잘 갖춘 아이로 양육하기를 바란다. 우리는 자녀가 선과 악, 그리고 옳은 것과 그른 것을 구별하기를 바란다. 우리는 자녀가 도덕적이고 윤리적으로 행동하는 방식을 배워서 정직하고 사려 깊은 사람으로 성장하기를 희망한다. 간단히 말해, 우리는 자녀가 양심, 즉 이들이 올바른 길을 걷게 할 확고한 내적인 목소리를 계발하기를 바란다. 그러나 양심은 저절로 계발되는 것이 아니어서, 양심을 세우는 일은 우리의 몫이 된다. 그 일은 부모가 매일 그리고 매년 염두에 두고 노력할 필요가 있는 과정이다. 우리는 끊임없이 옳은 것과 잘못된 것을 구별하고 적절한 행동을 본보기로 제시할 필요가 있다. 그러면 결국 우리 자녀는 우리가 의도하는 뜻을 완전히 받아들이게 될 것이고, 그러한 뜻은 그들의 성격의 바탕이 될 것이다.

4. 역접/대조/양보를 나타내는 접속사 및 부사(구)

[실전응용 1]

1. You see the world as one big contest, where everyone is competing against everybody else. You feel that there is a set amount of good and bad fortune out there. You believe that there is no way that everyone can have everything. When other people fail, you feel there's a better chance for you to succeed. 2. However, there is not a limited supply of resources out there. When one person wins, everyone wins. Every victory one person makes is a breakthrough for all. 1) Whenever an Olympic swimmer sets a new world record, it inspires others to bring out the best within them and go beyond that achievement to set new records of human performance. Whenever a geneticist unlocks new secrets of the DNA molecule, it adds to our knowledge base and enables us to better the human condition. 3. Remember that life is a game where there are multiple winners.

중심소재: 세상을 바라보는 관점
지문 속에 등장하는 'However'는 글쓴이의 요지가 어디에 등장하는지를 알려주는 단서이다. 이어지는 내용이 글쓴이의 요지가 된다.

1. 도입부
일반인의 관점(통념): 세상은 하나의 거대한 경쟁이다.
1) 뒷받침 근거
제한된 자원으로 인해 상대의 패배가 곧 나의 승리
2. 주제문(However 확인)
경쟁을 통한 승리는 또 다른 승리로 이끄는 발판이기에 결국 모두가 승자라는 주장.
1) 뒷받침 진술

3. 주제문 재진술

★ 통념 비판의 글

도입부 =	통념 A - B
요지 =	But A ≠ B
	뒷받침 진술
요지 =	A ≠ B

| 해설

상반된 두 견해를 보이는 글에서 글쓴이의 요지/주장은 'But/However' 뒤에 있음을 절대 잊어서는 안 된다. 또한, 본문 마지막에서 명령문을 통해 글쓴이의 주장이 다시 한 번 드러난다. 전체적인 글의 구조는 '구체적 진술 – 일반진술 – 구체적 진술 – 일반진술'로 전개되고 있다.

| 해석

당신은 세상을 모든 사람이 다른 모든 이와 경쟁하는 하나의 큰 경기로 간주한다. 당신은 세상 바깥 저쪽에는 정해진 양의 행운과 불운이 있다고 느낀다. 당신은 모든 사람이 모든 것을 다 가질 방법은 없다고 믿는다. 다른 사람이 실패할 때 당신은 당신이 성공할 더 좋은 기회가 왔다고 여긴다. 하지만 저 밖에는 제한된 공급량의 자원만이 있는 것이 아니다. 한 사람이 이길 때 모든 사람이 이긴다. 한 사람이 맺는 모든 승리는 다른 모든 이에게 돌파구이다. 한 명의 올림픽 수영선수가 세계 신기록을 세울 때마다, 이는 다른 사람들로 하여금 그들 속에 있는 최상을 끄집어내어 인간행위의 새로운 기록을 세우기 위한 성취를 달성하도록 고무시킨다. 유전학자가 DNA 분자의 새로운 비밀을 알아낼 때마다 우리의 지식기반을 충실하게 해 주어, 우리가 인간 생활을 더 윤택하게 하게 한다. 인생은 다수 승자가 있는 경기임을 명심하라.

[실전응용 2]

1. According to a psychologist, a business executive spends an hour of his day reading, two hours talking and eight hours listening. 1) Yet in school we spend a large amount of time teaching children how to read, a small amount of time teaching them how to speak, and usually no time at all teaching them how to listen. 1) I do not believe it would be a good thing to make what we teach in school exactly proportional to what we do after school, but I do think it would be wise to give our children some instruction in the process of listening. ① Listening well is an exercise of attention and those who listen well tend to have good relationships with colleagues.

중심소재: 학교교육 커리큘럼
1. 도입부
한 중견 간부의 예를 통해 사회생활에서 'Listening'의 중요성을 언급하고 있다: 본문은 'Listening'을 중심으로 이야기가 전개됨을 예측할 수 있다.
1) 대조(Yet)적 현상 및 문제점 지적: 현재 학교에서 'Reading' 위주의 교육이 이뤄짐
2. 주제문
학교에서 듣기 과정을 제공해야 한다.
1) 뒷받침 근거
경청은 집중력의 행위인 동시에 동료와 좋은 관계를 유지하게 하는 긍정적인 측면도 있다.

| 해설
강조구문인 'not A but B' 에서 'but' 뒤에 글쓴이의 주장이 드러나고 있으며, 'I think' 와 강조 'do' 동사가 활용되고 있다. 글쓴이의 주장은 '학생들에게 남의 말을 경청하는 법을 가르치자' 이다.

| 해석
한 심리학자가 말한 바로는 회사 경영자는 하루에 한 시간을 읽기에, 두 시간을 말하기에, 여덟 시간을 듣기에 쓴다고 한다. 그러나 우리는 학교에서 읽는 방법을 가르치는 데에 많은 시간을 쓰고, 말하는 방법을 가르치는 데에 적은 시간, 듣는 방법을 가르치는 데에는 일반적으로 전혀 시간을 쓰지 않는다. 나는 우리가 학교에서 가르치는 것을 학교를 졸업한 후에 하는 것에 정확히 비례하도록 하는 것이 좋을 것으로 생각하지는 않는다. 하지만 나는 우리 아이들에게 듣기 과정을 교육한다면 현명한 일이 될 것이라고 확신한다. 잘 듣는다는 것은 주의를 기울이는 것이고, 잘 듣는 사람들은 동료와 좋은 관계를 맺는 경향이 있다.

[실전응용 3]

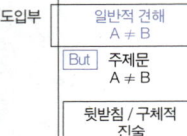
* I = 글쓴이

1. A cent is worth so little that we don't usually bother to pick it up on the street. It's difficult to gather between finger and thumb, and the reward seems hardly worth the effort. 1) ① But, with a little extra effort, these little coins are picked up by goodwill organizations. One person picks up ten coins, ten people pick up 100 coins and so on until they turn into hundreds thousands, even millions of dollars. ② All this money is being used to help thousands of homeless and hungry people around the world.

중심소재: 1 Cent
1. 도입부 = 일반적 견해
1 cent는 가치가 없다 - 부연 근거
1) 주제문(역접의 But)
①+②: 아주 적은 노력으로 합심하여 1센트를 모으면 자선 단체에 의해 집 없고, 배고픈 사람을 돕는 데 쓰일 수 있다.
* 결국 '1센트를 줍는 작은 노력을 필요한 사람에게 큰 도움을 줄 수 있다' 는 내용이다
* 제목
'Many drops make a shower'

| 해석

1센트는 가치가 아주 작아 길에서 떨어져 있어도 굳이 주우려 하지 않는다. 엄지와 손가락으로 잡기도 어렵거니와, 그 보상이란 게 수고만큼의 가치도 안 된다. 그러나 여분의 사소한 노력으로, 이 소액의 동전을 선의의 단체들이 모은다. 한 사람이 열 개의 동전을 줍고, 열 사람이면 백 개의 동전을 줍게 되고 계속해서 그것은 백 달러, 천 달러, 백만 달러가 된다. 이렇게 모든 돈은 전 세계 수천의 집 없고 배고픈 사람들을 돕는 데 사용되고 있다.

5. 예시를 나타내는 표현

[실전응용 1]

1. The meaning a speaker intends to communicate may be quite different from the meaning conveyed by the actual words, phrases, and sentences. 1) For example, when a foreigner lays down his fork and says, "Vegetables not thoroughly cooked retain a certain acidity," he is not making a general statement about vegetable cookery but voicing a criticism of American food. 2. We can **never**, of course, be certain about the intention of a speaker, but we **must** always be prepared for the fact that what a person is saying is not always exactly what he or she means.

글의 요지가 두 번 드러나는 글 'General → Specific → General'로 이어지는 글이다.
중심소재: 의미전달의 왜곡
1. 도입부 = 주제문
화자가 전달하려고 한 의도와 실제 말, 구, 문장으로 전달된 의미와 다를 수 있다.
1) 뒷받침 전술
주제문에서 밝힌 중심내용을 예시로 뒷받침하고 있다.
2. 요지
요지를 이끄는 시그널인 not A but B + must를 확인한다.

* 양괄식 구조
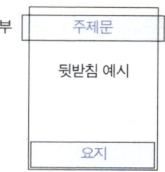

| 해설

'For example' 앞에 주제문이 등장하고, 글쓴이의 궁극적인 주장이 본문 마지막 부분(must)에 드러나는 'General → Specific → General' 구성을 보인다.

| 해석

말하는 사람이 전달하고자 하는 의미가 실제 단어, 어구, 문장들에 의해 전해지는 의미와 전혀 다를 수 있다. 예를 들어, 한 외국인이 포크를 내려놓고 "채소는 철저하게 요리하지 않으면 약간의 신맛을 그대로 지니게 된다."라고 말하면, 그는 채소 요리에 대해 일반적 진술을 한 것이 아니라 미국 음식에 대한 비판의 목소리를 내고 있는 것이다. 물론 우리는 말하는 이의 의도를 결코 확신할 순 없지만, 우리는 어떤 사람이 말하고 있는 것이 항상 정확하게 그가 의도하고 있는 것은 아니라는 사실에 대해 준비를 해야 한다.

★ 주제와 요지의 구별
1. 주제
글을 통해 다루고자하는 내용
2. 요지
주제를 통해 궁극적으로 전달하려는 내용

[실전응용 2]

1. Knowing when something happened is important. Understanding why historic events took place is also important. 1) To do this, historians often turn to geography.

중심소재: 역사적 사건
1. 도입부
역사적 사건 이해와 이유를 알아야 함의 중요성 언급

Weather patterns, the water supply, and the landscape of a place all affect the lives of the people who live there. ① <u>For example</u>, to explain why the ancient Egyptians developed a successful civilization, you must look at the geography of Egypt. Egyptian civilization was built on the banks of the Nile River, which flooded each year, depositing soil on its banks. The rich soil could help farmers grow enough crops to feed the people in the cities. That meant everyone did not have to farm, so some people could perform other jobs that helped develop the civilization.

1) 주제문
역사가는 지리학에 의해 도입부에서 언급한 사항을 실천하고 있다.
① 뒷받침 예시
*주제: 역사연구에서 지리학의 중요성

| 해석
언제 어떤 일이 일어났는지를 아는 것은 중요하다. 역사적인 사건이 왜 발생했는지를 이해하는 것 또한 중요하다. 이런 것을 하기 위해서, 역사학자들은 종종 지리학에 의존한다. 어떤 장소의 날씨 패턴, 물의 공급, 장소의 경치와 같은 모든 것은 그곳에 사는 사람들의 삶에 영향을 미친다. 예를 들어, 고대 이집트인들이 성공적인 문명을 발달시킬 수 있었던 이유를 설명하기 위해서, 우리는 이집트의 지리를 살펴보아야 한다. 이집트 문명은 매년 범람하여 그 강둑에 흙을 퇴적시킨 나일 강의 강둑 위에 건설되었다. 이 풍부한 토양 덕에 농부들은 도시에 사는 사람들을 먹여 살리기에 충분한 농작물을 재배할 수 있었다. 이는 모든 사람이 농사를 지을 필요가 없다는 점과 그래서 일부 사람들이 문명을 발달시키는 데 도움이 되는 다른 일을 수행할 수 있게 되었다는 것을 의미했다.

[실전응용 3]

1. <u>The specific combinations of foods in a cuisine and the ways they are prepared constitute a deep reservoir of accumulated wisdom about diet and health and place</u>. 1) In Latin America, <u>for example</u>, corn is traditionally eaten with beans; each plant is deficient in an essential amino acid that happens to be abundant in the other, so together corn and beans form a balanced diet in the absence of meat. ① Similarly, corn in Latin America is traditionally ground or soaked with limestone, which makes available a B vitamin in the corn, the absence of which would otherwise lead to a deficiency disease. Very often, when a society adopts a new food without the food culture surrounding it, as happened when corn first came to Europe, Africa, and Asia, people get sick. The context in which a food is eaten can be nearly as important as the food itself.

중심소재: 음식
일반적으로 'for example'이 주제문을 뒷받침하는 구체적 예시라는 것을 안다면 바로 앞에 진술된 첫 번째 문장이 주제문임을 알 수 있다.
1. 주제문
음식의 내용과 만드는 독특한 방법은 전통적으로 내려온 식단, 건강 그리고 장소에 의해 결정된다. 즉, **전통 음식 문화는 지역의 재료와 환경적 특성의 소산이다.**
1) 뒷받침 진술
남미의 구체적 예를 통해 주제문에서 밝힌 중심내용을 뒷받침하고 있다.
① 추가 부연(Similarly)

| 해설

'General Statement(일반진술) → Specific Statement(구체적 진술)'의 전형적 두괄식 구조이다.

| 해석

특정 요리법에서 음식을 독특한 방식으로 조합하는 것과 이를 준비하는 방법은 식단, 건강 그리고 장소에 대한 축적된 지혜의 보고를 이룬다. 예를 들면, 라틴아메리카에서는 옥수수는 전통적으로 콩과 함께 섭취했다. 각 식물은 상대에게 풍부한 필수 아미노산이 부족하므로 옥수수와 콩은 함께 고기를 빼고도 균형 잡힌 식사를 형성한다. 이와 비슷하게 라틴아메리카에서 옥수수는 전통적으로 석회암과 함께 갈거나 석회암에 담가 왔는데 이 석회암은 옥수수 내 비타민 B를 섭취할 수 있게 하지만, 이렇게 하지 않으면 비타민 B가 부족하게 되어서 (비타민 B) 결핍성 질환에 걸리게 된다. 아주 흔히 일어나는 일로, 옥수수가 처음 유럽과 아프리카와 아시아에 들어올 때 발생한 바와 같이, 한 사회가 음식과 관련된 문화를 빠뜨린 채 새로운 음식을 받아들이면 사람들이 아프게 된다. 음식이 섭취되는 (주변) 상황은 거의 그 음식 자체 만큼이나 중요하다.

[실전응용 4]

1. A status symbol is something, usually an expensive or rare object, that 1) indicates a high social status for its owner. 2) What is considered a status symbol will differ among countries, based on the states of their economic and technological development, and common status symbols will change over time. 2 Status symbols can indicate the cultural values of a society. ① Let's take some examples. In a society that cherishes honor or bravery, a battle wound would be more of a status symbol. In a commercial society, where having money or wealth is most important, things that can be brought by wealth, such as cars, houses, or fine clothing, are considered status symbols. And in a society where people craze for beauty, the condition of one's skin and body can be a status symbol.

중심소재: Status Symbol
1. 도입부
지위 상징에 대한 일반적 정의로 시작하는 글이다.
1) 지위 상징의 기능 – 지위 상징은 그 사람의 높은 사회적 지위의 지표가 된다.
2) 지위 상징의 특징 – 나라의 경제, 기술 발달의 상황에 따라 지위의 상징이 다양하며, 시간에 따라 변한다(절대적 가치의 기준이 존재하지 않는다).
2. 주제문
지위 상징은 한 사회의 문화 가치를 반영한다.
1) 뒷받침 진술
다양한 예를 통해 주제문에서 밝힌 중심내용을 뒷받침하고 있다.

★ 중심소재는 'status symbol'이다.

★ 예시를 드러내는 'For example' 앞의 문장이 주제문이 되는 경우가 많다는 점을 기억한다.

| 해설

문화적 가치를 드러내는 지위 상징에 관한 글인데, 다음과 같은 중괄식 구조를 지닌다.

구체적 진술	중심소재의 간략한 정의 및 특징
일반진술	주제문
구체적 진술	뒷받침 진술

★ 글의 도입부에서 제시되는 정의를 통해 '중심소재'를 이끌어 내고, 이후 진술을 바탕으로 궁극적으로 다루려는 내용을 파악하도록 한다.

★ 제시된 지문을 통해 궁극적으로 전달하려는 사실이 제시된다.

| 해석

지위 상징은 보통 값비싸고 귀한 대상인데, 그 소유자의 높은 사회적 지위를 나타낸다. 지위 상징이라고 여겨지는 것은 경제적, 기술적 발전 상태에 따라 나라마다 다양할 것이고, 일반적인 지위 상징은 시대에 흘러감에 따라 변화한다. 지위 상징은 한 사회의 문화적 가치를 알려줄 수 있다. 몇 가지 예를 들어보자. 명예와 용기를 소중히 여기는 사회에서는 전투에서 입은 부상이 지위 상징으로 더욱더 높이 여겨질 것이다. 돈이나 부를 얻는 것이 대단히 중요한 상업 사회에서는 자동차, 주택, 또는 고상한 의복 등과 같이 부를 통해 얻어질 수 있는 것들을 지위 상징으로 간주한다. 그리고 사람들이 아름다움을 열렬히 추구하는 사회에서는 피부와 신체의 조건이 지위 상징이 될 수 있다.

[실전응용 5]

중심소재이다.

1. Family narratives are collections of stories made up by family members. They are either based on real occurrences, embellished events or fantasy materials. 1) Such family storytelling is shown to have numerous advantages. ⓐ Ⓐ For example, family narratives help children develop values through communicating limits, boundaries and family-endorsed morality. Ⓑ In addition to providing children with a clear sense of right and wrong, family stories are Ⓒ also used to pass along parental insights and knowledge. This process of transmitting knowledge may be critical to positive parent-child relationships, as the absence of family stories has been shown to be related to difficulties among parents to establish a caring or meaningful relationship with their children. They are also cherished as a cause of laughter year after year.

중심내용(controlling idea)에 해당한다.

*나열의 글전개 방식

도입부 — 중심소재 도출
뒷받침 전술 — 예 1_____ 예 2_____ 예 3_____

우선 글의 초중반부에 ① 'For example'이 있음을 확인한 후 다음의 사항이 적용되는지 살펴본다.
첫째, for example 앞의 진술이 주제문인가?
둘째, 그렇다면, 뒤에 이어지는 내용은 그에 대한 구체적 진술이어야 한다.

1. 도입부: 중심소재 도출
가족이야기에 대한 간략한 정의
1) 주제문
가족이야기의 장점
① 뒷받침 진술
나열의 글 전개방식에 따라 장점을 세 가지 제시하고 있다.

| 해설

'For example' 바로 앞에 전개된 내용이 주제문이며, 이후 전개되는 내용이 뒷받침 문장이다. 가족 이야기의 다양한 장점을 드러내는 글로, 나열을 통해 글을 전개하고 있으며, 시그널(signal)로 'for example, in addition to, also'가 쓰이고 있다.

| 해석

가족 이야기는 가족구성원이 만든 이야기를 모아 놓은 것이다. 이것들은 실제 사건을 토대로 하며 각색한 사건들이나 상상의 소재들이다. 이러한 스토리텔링에는 수많은 이점이 있다는 것이 밝혀져 있다. 예로, 가족 이야기는 자녀가 제한 사항, (넘지 말아야 할) 경계 그리고 가정에서 인정되는 도덕성을 (이야기를 통해) 소통함으로 가치관을 개발하는 데 도움이 된다. 자녀에게 옳고 그름에 대한 분명한 감각을 주는 것 이외에, 가족 이야기는 부모들에게 통찰력과 지식을 전달하는 데 활용된다. 가족 이야기가 없다는 이야기는 부모들이 자신의 자녀와 아끼고 의미있는 관계를 형성하는 데 어려움을 느낀다는 것과 관련이 있기에 지식 전수라는 이런 과정은 긍정적인 부모-자녀관계 형성에 중요하다. 또한, 가족 이야기는 해마다 웃음의 동기로서 소중하게 간직된다.

[실전응용 6]

1. "Pot-stirrer" is someone who brings up emotional issues that have already been resolved. Pot-stirrers want to feed the emotional fire and keep it burning for the excitement of the conflict. They can be subtle; they often even appear to be the "helpful" friend or "caring" listener. 1) ① <u>Let's say</u> you've just let go of a minor conflict with your neighbor, when your other neighbor continues to bring up how annoying this person is, encouraging you to hold on to your irritation with the person. ② <u>The same applies at work</u>. A coworker keeps reminding you that it was you, not Gail, who really deserved the credit for that great idea. Every time he or she says it, it upsets you and opens your wound again.

중심소재: Pot-stirrer
1. 도입부
'Pot-stirrer'에 대한 정의

1) 예시 부연
① 예시 1
② 예시 2

★ 중심소재는 'pot-stirrer' 이다.

★ 예시를 이끄는 시그널을 확인한다.

* 정의의 글의 유형
유형 1.
도입부 — 정의(중심소재 파악)
대상의 다양한 측면에서 설명

유형 2.
도입부 — 정의(중심소재 파악)
대상의 폭을 좁혀 하나의 측면만을 다룸

| 해설
본문은 'pot-stirrer'가 어떤 역할을 하는 사람인지 구체적 상황을 통해 뒷받침하는 'General → Specific'의 전형적인 형태이다.

| 해석
pot-stirrer는 이미 해결된 감정적인 문제를 화제에 올리는 사람이다. pot-stirrer들은 갈등을 즐기기 위해 감정적인 불을 돋우어 그것이 계속 타오르기를 원한다. 이들은 알아보기 어려울 수도 있다. 이들은 심지어 도움이 되는 친구나 남의 말을 "기꺼이" 들어줄 사람으로 종종 보이기도 한다. 당신이 이웃과의 사소한 갈등을 이제 막 잊어 털어 버렸을 때, 다른 이웃이 그 사람에 대한 화를 계속 품고 있을 것을 당신에게 부추기면서 그 사람이 얼마나 짜증 나는 사람인지를 계속해서 화제에 올린다고 해보자. 직장에서도 동일하게 적용된다. 한 동료가 그 훌륭한 아이디어에 대해 정말 공로를 인정받아야 할 사람이 Gail이 아니라 당신이라고 계속해서 당신에게 상기시킨다. 그 혹은 그녀가 그런 말을 할 때마다, 이것으로 당신은 화가 나게 되며, 당신의 아물었던 상처는 다시 덧나게 된다.

[실전응용 7]

1. <u>What causes cultures to change?</u> <u>New ideas and inventions often lead people to develop new ways of doing things</u>. 1) <u>For example</u>, the invention of writing systems allowed people to record their thoughts and discoveries and to communicate them to other people. Changes in the environment **also** cause cultures to change. Over time, the climate in an area can change. **Also**, natural disasters such as floods and earthquakes can alter the landscape. People must then move or learn to adjust to new living conditions. **Another** major source of change is contact with other

중심소재: 문화-문화변화
1. 도입부
의문문(=주제): 문화변화의 요인은?
1) 답변(=요지)
새로운 사상과 발명이 문화의 변화를 이끈다.
① 뒷받침 진술
나열의 글 전개방식에 따라 주제문의 중심내용을 다양한 예를 통해 뒷받침하고 있다.

★ 의문점으로 시작하는 지문은 이에 대한 답변이 곧 요지가 될 수 있다.

* 의문점(주제) + 답변(요지)
도입부 — 의문점 + 답변 = 주제문

뒷받침 진술

주제문 = 의문점 + 답변

71

cultures. When people from different cultures meet, they are exposed to the ways of life of each culture. Cultures change from within **as well**. Factors such as population growth and conflicts between groups within a culture can bring about new ways of doing things.

| 해석

문화 변화의 원동력은 무엇인가? 새로운 아이디어와 발명품은 종종 사람들이 새로운 방식으로 일하는 방법을 개발하도록 이끈다. 예를 들어, 글자 체계의 발명으로 사람들은 자신이 생각하고 발견한 것을 기록하고 이것들을(자신의 생각과 발견한 것)을 다른 사람에게 전달할 수 있게 되었다. 환경의 변화 또한 문화를 바꾸는 원인이 된다. 시간이 흐르면서, 한 지역의 문화는 변할 수 있다. 또한, 홍수나 지진과 같은 자연재해도 환경을 변화시킨다. 그렇게 되면, 사람들은 새로운 주거환경으로 이동하거나 적응하는 방법을 익혀야 한다. 변화의 주요 원인 중 또 다른 하나는 다른 문화와의 접촉이다. 서로 다른 문화권의 사람들이 만났을 때, 이들은 각자의 문화에 따른 생활방식에 노출된다. 문화는 내부에서도 변한다. 인구증가와 한 문화 내 여러 단체 간의 충돌과 같은 요소도 삶의 새로운 방식을 이끈다.

6. 의문점은 글의 주제에 해당하고, 이에 대한 답변은 글의 요지이다.

[실전응용 1]

* 양괄식 구조

주제문(의문문)

뒷받침 근거
(답변)

결론: 주제문 재진술

1. Why should the government control population planning? 1) Many people say there is no other way because people will continue to have too many children. They will not limit themselves to just one or two children. They have not limited themselves in the past. Why should they limit themselves in the future? Unfortunately, they say, it does not work to leave family planning completely up to individuals. 2. The only choice according to these people, is for the government to play an active role in population planning.

중심소재: 인구통제
1. 도입부 = 주제
정부의 인구통제 개입여부
1) 뒷받침 진술
의문문을 통해 밝힌 글쓴이의 견해를 글의 말미에 제시하기 전에 근거를 통해서 뒷받침 내용이 전개되고 있다.

2. 결론(요지)
정부는 인구계획에 적극적인 역할을 해야 한다.

| 해설

중심소재는 "인구계획 통제"이며, 중심내용은 "정부를 통해 인구계획 통제가 이뤄져야 한다."이다. 이어지는 내용이 이에 대한 답변으로 중심내용을 뒷받침하는 내용이 전개되고 있다. 글쓴이는 객관적 입장에서 "Many people"의 견해를 진술하고 있으며, 주제는 "가족계획에 대한 정부통제"이다.

| 해석

왜 정부가 인구계획을 통제해야 하는가? 많은 사람들은 사람들이 지속적으로 지나치게 많은 아이들을 가지려 하기에 다른 방법이 없다고 말한다. 이들은 스스로 단지 한 명 또는 두 명으로 제한하지 않는다. 이들은 과거에 스스로 제안하지 않았다. 이들이 왜 스스로 미래에는 제한하겠는가? 불행히도, 이들은 가족계획을 개인에게 전적으로 맡겨서는 효과가 없다고 말한다. 이 사람들에 따르면, (이를 해결할 수 있는) 유일한 방법은 정부가 인구계획에 적극적인 역할을 하는 것이다.

[실전응용 2]

1. 1) Some people give up the moment an obstacle is placed in front of them. 2) Some people doggedly continue to pursue a goal even after years of frustration and failure. 2. What is the difference between these two people? 1) Those who feel they are not responsible for choosing their goals and pursuing them tend to believe that results are arbitrary. To them, it does not matter how hard you try or how talented you are. Being successful is all a matter of luck. Those who persevere, 2) **however**, recognize that they are ultimately responsible not just for pursuing their goals, but for setting them. To them, what you do matters, and giving up for no reasons does not seem very attractive.

중심소재: 장애물에 대한 상반된 반응을 보이는 두 사람
1. 도입부
두 종류의 사람
1) 첫번째 종류의 사람: 장애물이 나타나면 쉽게 포기
2) 두번째 종류의 사람: 좌절과 실패에도 계속 시도
2. 의문점(=주제문)
이들의 차이점은 무엇인가?
1) 첫번째: 운명론적 관점
2) 두번째: 목표설정과 실천은 본인에게 달렸다.

★ 대조의 글 전개방식이 두 드러진다. 'some ↔ some'과 'however'에서 확인할 수 있다.

★ 문제 제기에 대한 답변이 곧 글에서 밝히려는 요지가 된다.

도입부 | 두 대상 A, B
대조의 글 전개

| 해석
어떤 사람들은 자신 앞에 장애물이 놓인 순간 포기한다. 어떤 사람들은 심지어 수년간의 좌절과 실패 후에도 집요하게 목표를 추구해 나간다. 이러한 두 종류의 사람들 사이의 차이점은 무엇인가? 목표를 선택하고 추구하는 데 있어서 책임감을 느끼지 않는 사람들은 일의 결과는 임의적이라고 믿는 경향이 있다. 그 사람들에게는 당신이 얼마나 노력하는지, 얼마나 재능이 있는지는 중요하지 않다. 성공한다는 것은 전부 운에 달린 문제이다. 그러나 인내심 있는 사람들은 자신의 목표를 추구하는 것뿐 아니라, 목표를 설정하는 것에도 궁극적으로 책임이 있다는 것을 알고 있다. 그들에게는 당신이 하는 행동이 중요한 것이고, 아무 이유 없이 포기하는 것은 바람직해 보이지 않는다.

[실전응용 3]

1. Sea level is rising and we are not sure about the rate of the rise. 1) Another question we are unsure about is: "Where does the extra water come from?" ① Ⓐ Fifty years or so ago it was thought that a warming phase of climate was responsible for partial melting of the polar ice caps and a consequent addition of mass and volume to the waters of the ocean.
Ⓑ As a result of recent research, models have been proposed which suggest that rather more than half of the sea level rise which has occurred in recent geological time is more likely to be ⓐ due to the warming of the upper layers of the ocean and a subsequent increase in the volume of the waters. The same models also suggested that slightly less than half of the rise was ⓑ due to the addition of fresh meltwater from land-based ice in the form of glaciers and the icefields associated with mountainous (Alpine) areas in the mid to sub-polar latitudes.

중심소재: 해수면 상승
1. 도입부 = 현상
해수면 상승
1) 의문점(주제)
추가적인 물이 어디서 온 것인가
① 답변(요지)
Ⓐ 기존의 이론
Ⓑ 새로운 가설
ⓐ 가설 1
ⓑ 가설 2
* 인과의 글전개방식 주목

도입부 | 현상
원인
가설 1. _____
가설 2. _____
주제문 = 현상 + 원인

| 해설

'현상 → 원인'의 패턴을 따르는 인과의 글이다.

| 해석

해수면은 상승하고 있는데, 우리는 그 상승률을 예상할 수 없다. 우리가 확신할 수 없는 또 다른 의문점은 "여분의 해수는 어디서 발생하는가?"이다. 50년 혹은 좀 더 이전에 기후 온난화 양상은 극지방 빙하의 부분적인 용해와 해수의 부피와 질량의 지속적인 증가의 원인이라고 생각했다.

최근 연구결과로, 최근 지질연대에 발생한 절반 이상의 해수면 상승은 바다의 상층부의 온난화와 해수 부피의 지속적인 증가 때문일 가능성이 더 크다는 사실을 드러내는 모형이 제시되었다. 그와 같은 모형을 통해 절반에 약간 못 미치는 정도의 해수면 상승은 빙하와 극지방 중부의 산악지대와 연관된 설원 형태의 육지빙하로 발생한 맑은 해빙수가 더해졌기 때문이라 주장한다.

[실전응용 4]

도입부 | 현상
       | 원인
       | 주제문 = 현상 + 원인

1. <u>A recent study</u> shows that kids who watch a lot of TV are more likely to be overweight than those who do not. 1) <u>Can you guess why?</u> ⓐ It's because of commercials on TV! The junk food is often advertised in commercials by their favorite cartoon characters. It is so appealing that kids just want to go out and get it right away! ⓑ Kids who watch a lot of TV and those attractive commercials are also likely to stay only at home and be getting less exercise.

중심소재: 아이의 TV 시청
1. 도입부
조사를 통한 현상 제시:
TV를 많이 보는 아이는 비만 가능성이 크다.
1) 의문점(주제)
왜 그럴까?
ⓐ 답변(요지)
Ⓐ 원인 1
Ⓑ 원인 2

| 해석

최근의 한 연구는 TV를 많이 보는 아이들이 그렇지 않은 아이보다 좀 더 과체중인 경향이 있다는 점을 보여주고 있다. 왜 그런지 추측할 수 있는가? 이는 TV의 광고로 인한 것이다. 정크푸드는 종종 아이들이 가장 좋아하는 만화주인공에 의해 광고된다. 이는 매우 유혹적이어서 아이들은 그것을 가서 바로 사고 싶어 한다! 또한, TV와 이런 매혹적인 광고를 많이 보는 아이들은 집에 있으면서 운동을 덜 하는 경향이 있다.

7. 명령문은 글쓴이의 충고/조언으로 서론 또는 결론에 주로 위치하여 글쓴이의 주장을 드러낸다.

[실전응용]

1. <u>Any object between you and the person with whom you're talking may interfere with your conversation</u>. 1) That's why many experienced speakers step away from the podium when they lecture; many businesspeople choose not to speak

중심소재: 대화를 방해하는 요소
1. 도입부 = 주제문
화자와 청자 사이의 물건은 대화를 방해한다.
1) 뒷받침 진술

with customers or employees from behind a desk, but instead come around their desk and sit next to them. 2. If you want to have an unconstrained conversation with someone, get rid of any obstacles between the two of you. Move out from behind your desk, unless maintaining control is more important than exchanging information. At a restaurant, ask the waiter to remove tall flower arrangements, extra glasses, or any other objects that clutter the visual space between you and your tablemate. If you're wearing sunglasses, take them off.

2. 요지
다양한 상황에서 구체적으로 어떤 행동을 취해야 하는지 명령문을 통해 조언하고 있다.

* 양괄식 구조

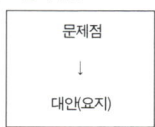

* 문제점 - 대안의 유형

* 주제와 요지의 구별
주제는 제시된 지문이 "무엇에 관한 글"인지를 파악하는 것이고, 요지는 주제를 통해 "궁극적으로 전달하려는 내용"을 말한다.

| 해설
본문 중반 이후에 구체적 상황을 들며, 명령문을 통해 글쓴이의 주장이 드러나고 있다. 주제: Remove Obstacles for Effective Communication

| 해석
당신과 대화를 나누고 있는 사람 사이에 놓인 물건은 어떤 것이든 대화를 방해할 수 있다. 이런 이유에서 노련한 연설가들은 강의할 때, 강단으로부터 몇 발자국 떨어져 서 있다. 많은 사업가는 고객이나 노동자들과 책상 뒤에서 이야기하지 않고, 그 대신에 책상 근처로 와서 그들 곁에 앉는 것을 선택한다. 만일 당신이 누군가와 자유로운 대화를 하고 싶다면, 당신들 두 사이에 어떤 장애(물)도 두지 마라. 지속적인 통제가 정보 교환보다 더 중요하지 않다면, 당신의 책상 뒤로부터 빠져나와라. 식당에서, 당신과 당신 식사 동료 사이의 가시적 공간을 혼란스럽게 하는 높이가 큰 꽃장식, 여분의 유리잔이나 장애물은 어떤 것이든 옮겨 달라고 웨이터에게 청하라. 만일 당신이 선글라스를 쓰고 있다면, 벗도록 하라.

8. 최상급 표현은 언제나 글쓴이가 강조하는 내용이므로 글의 요지를 직/간접적으로 드러낸다.

[실전응용]

1. What should you do if you have trouble sleeping? 1) Taking sleeping pills is dangerous. ① The best thing is to try to relax and to avoid bad habits. Ⓐ Going to bed and getting up about the same time sets a good and healthy rhythm. Don't drink caffeine drinks in the evening. Smoking and alcohol can also keep you awake. And a heavy meal just before you go to bed may cause sleeping trouble.

중심소재: sleeping
1. 도입부
'수면문제'에 관한 글임을 파악(주제 선정)
1) 수면제의 위험성
① 주제문(글쓴이의 견해)
긴장을 풀고, 나쁜습관을 피할 것을 권장
Ⓐ 뒷받침 진술
주제문의 중심내용에서 밝힌 사항을 구체적 예와 함께 뒷받침하고 있다.

★ 최상급과 강조 표현은 글의 요지를 이끈다.

★ 본문에 구체적으로 기술될 중심내용

| 해설
최상급이 이끄는 문장은 글쓴이의 주장이 직접 드러나는 곳이므로 놓치지 말아야 한다.

| 해석

수면 장애를 겪고 있다면 어떻게 해야 할 것인가? 수면제 복용은 위험하다. 가장 좋은 방법은 긴장을 풀고 좋지 않은 습관들을 피하는 것이다. 거의 같은 시간에 잠자리에 들고 일어나면 바람직하고 건강한 삶의 리듬을 형성할 수 있다. 저녁에는 카페인이 든 음료를 마시지 마라. 흡연과 알코올 역시 당신을 깨어 있게 한다. 그리고 잠자리에 들기 바로 직전에 음식을 많이 먹는 것은 수면 장애를 유발할 수 있다.

9. 'Among, (One) of'가 이끄는 문장은 글의 요지가 드러나는 주제문일 가능성이 크다. 글의 초반에 자주 등장하는 것이 일반적이다.

[실전응용]

우주 조종사가 직면한 물리적 위험에 관한 글이다. 글의 중심내용(controlling idea)을 바탕으로 주제의 폭을 좁히도록 한다.

글의 도입부에서 'Among'이 제시되면 주부의 내용이 곧 주제문이 될 가능성이 크다.

중심내용(controlling idea)이다.

*Among, of의 기능

도입부	Among Ns, ⓝ_____
	이후 전개되는 내용은 ⓝ에 초점이 맞춰지고, 그 폭을 더욱 좁혀 이야기 한다.

글의 도입부에서 Among 또는 (one) of가 나올 경우 다양한 소재(Ns)에서 하나의 소재로 그 폭을 좁히는 기능을 한다.

1. <u>Among the many physical risks facing astronauts sent to the Moon or Mars, the biggest danger will be the least visible: radiation.</u> 1) This is nuclear particles that arrive at almost light speed from beyond the Solar System. The particles slice through strands of DNA, boosting the risk of cancer and other ailments. ① A 2001 NASA study found that at least 39 former astronauts suffered cataracts after flying in space, 36 of whom took part in high-radiation missions such as the Apollo landings.

중심소재: 방사능

1. 주제문
우주에서 비행사들이 직면하게 되는 위험 즉, radiation을 다루는 글이다. 주제는 '우주 조종사에게 미치는 방사선의 위험성'이다.

1) 뒷받침 진술
방사선의 간략한 특징을 설명하면서 어떤 과정을 통해 구체적으로 우주 조종사에게 피해를 미치는지 설명하고 있다.
① 권위 있는 기관의 구체적 수치를 통해 부연하고 있다 – 객관성 확보

| 해석

달이나 화성에 파견된 우주비행사들이 직면하는 많은 신체적인 위험 중에서, 가장 큰 위험은 눈에 거의 보이지 않는 방사능이다. 이것은 태양계를 넘어서 광속에 가까운 속도로 도달하는 미립자들이다. 이 미립자들은 DNA 가닥들을 뚫고 들어가서 암이나 다른 질병들에 걸릴 위험을 증가시킨다. 2001년 나사의 연구 결과, 적어도 39명의 전직 우주비행사들이 우주에서 비행한 후 백내장으로 고통을 겪었고, 그들 중 36명은 아폴로 착륙과 같은 높은 수준의 방사능 관련 임무에 참여했다고 한다.

10. 수사의문문은 글쓴이의 주장을 강조한다.

[실전응용]

개인의 경험담을 통해 궁극적으로 전달하려는 사항이 무엇인지 파악하도록 한다.

1. <u>As a successful entrepreneur, I have always had to meet the challenges, more important than money or business, alone.</u> 1) I have had to decide by myself, and always against

1. 도입부
성공한 사업가로서 개인의 경험담을 언급하는데, 돈 또는 사업 자체보다 더 중요한 도전에 직면했다고 시작하고 있다. ← 이후 진술에서 'challenge'에 대한 구체적 진술이 이어질 것을 예측할 수 있다.

tremendous opposition from others. Every great move I have made in life has been ridiculed and opposed by my friends. The greatest winnings I have made, in happiness, in money or content, have been accomplished amid almost universal scorn. 2) But ① I have reasoned in this way: The average man is not always successful. We meet few who attain their goal, few who are really happy or content. 2. Then why should we let the majority rule in matters affecting our lives?

1) challenge = 결단은 홀로 내려야 하며, 많은 이들의 엄청난 반대에 부딪힘 – 같은 맥락의 내용이 이어진다.
2) 논리적 반전 'But' 바로 뒤 글쓴이가 내린 결론이 언급되는 부분을 확인한다(①).
일반인들(앞에서 언급한 나를 비난한 사람들)은 거의 성공하지 못했다. 즉, 다른 이의 말을 듣고 홀로 결정하지 않는 일반인들은 대부분 자신의 목적을 성취하지 못하고, 만족하지 않는다.
2. 요지
② 수사의문문을 통해 글쓴이의 주장을 이끌어 낼 수 있다: 인생에 큰 영향을 미치는 일에 있어 다수에게 나의 결정을 맡겨야 하는가? = **중요한 결정은 스스로 내려야 한다.**

★ 결론을 맺는 표현이 나오는 부분에 글의 요지가 담겨 있다.

| 해설
'But' 이후에 글쓴이의 주장이 전개되는 동시에 본문 마지막의 수사의문문(설의법)에서 글쓴이의 주장을 확인할 수 있다.

| 해석
성공한 기업가인 나는 항상 돈이나 사업보다 중요한 도전들에 홀로 맞서야 했다. 나는 스스로 결정해야 했고 항상 다른 사람들의 엄청난 반대에 부딪혀야 했다. 내가 이룩한 인생의 모든 위대한 행보를 친구들은 비웃었고 반대했다. 내가 성취한 가장 위대한 업적들은 그것이 행복이건 돈이나 물질적인 것이건 거의 모두의 조롱 속에서 이루어졌다. 그러나 나는 이렇게 생각하게 되었다. 평범한 사람이 늘 성공할 수는 없다. 우리는 자신의 목표를 성취한 사람은 별로 본 적이 없고 진정으로 행복하고 만족해하는 사람도 별로 보지 못했다. 그렇다면 왜 우리의 삶에 영향을 미치는 일을 대다수의 그들이 지배하도록 해야 하는가?

11. 비유를 통해 간접적으로 글쓴이의 주장을 드러낸다.

[실전응용 1]

1. In general, every achievement requires trial and error. As youth, we need not feel ashamed of making mistakes in trying to find or win our place in a social group. It is not easy to learn to fit into a group or to develop a personality that helps us to fit in. ① It is somewhat like learning to play a game like baseball or basketball. We can hardly expect to learn without making a good many mistakes in the process.

중심소재: 시행착오
1. 도입부
첫 번째 문장에서 글의 중심소재와 함께 주제를 이끌어 낼 수 있다.
주제: 시행착오의 중요성
이후 전개되는 내용에서 키워드가 반복적으로 제시되는 점과 ①과 같이 비유를 통해 자신의 주장을 뒷받침하고 있다.

★ 비유를 통해 글쓴이의 주장을 간접적으로 드러낸다.

| 해석
일반적으로, 모든 성취는 시행착오를 요구한다. 젊을 때는 우리가 사회 집단에서 자신의 자리를 찾거나 차지하려고 노력하면서 실수를 범하는 것을 부끄러워할 필요가 없다. 특정 집단에 잘 어울리는 것을 배우거나, 우리가 잘 어울릴 수 있도록 도와주는 성격을 개발한다는 것은 쉬운 일이 아니다. 이는 야구나 농구와 같은 게임을 배우는 것과 다소 비슷하다. 우리가 그 과정에서 상당히 많은 실수를 범하지 않고 배운다는 것은 거의 기대할 수 없다.

[실전응용 2]

1. A symphony orchestra can fill a whole building and make it ring with music. 1) But this beautiful sound, which can be joyful or sad, exciting or relaxing, is the result of planning and working together. 1) Just as painters choose different colors for their works of art, composers choose the sounds of different instruments to produce their music. The purpose of a symphony orchestra is not to play section by section. The word "symphony" means "sounding together." 2. This sounding together is what creates the wonderful music we all love.

비유를 통해 글쓴이의 주장을 간접적으로 드러낸다.

도입부 — 중심소재 도출
주제문
비유를 통한 뒷받침 진술
주제문

중심소재: 오케스트라
1. **도입부**
오케스트라 연주에 관한 글
1) **주제문**
오케스트라의 아름다운 소리는 계획과 조화의 결과이다.
① **뒷받침 진술**
비유와 구체적 진술을 통한 뒷받침 내용이 전개된다.
2. **결론(요지)**
주제문의 중심내용 재진술

| 해석
교향악단은 음악으로 건물 전체를 꽉 채워 울리게 할 수 있다. 그러나 즐겁거나 슬플 수도, 흥분시키거나 안도시킬 수도 있는 이런 아름다운 소리는 계획과 공동작업의 결과이다. 화가가 자기 미술 작품을 위해서 다양한 색을 선택하는 것처럼 작곡가들은 음악을 만들기 위해 여러 가지 악기 소리를 선택한다. 교향악단의 목적은 한 악절 한 악절을 연주하는 것이 아니다. '교향곡'이란 단어는 '함께 소리를 내는 것'을 의미한다. 이렇게 함께 울리는 소리가, 우리 모두가 좋아하는 훌륭한 음악을 창조해 낸다.

[실전응용 3]

1. Money is one of mankind's greatest tools. 1) It is like a refreshing mountain stream. When it spills through the meadow, it turns everything in its path active and green. But once obstructed, the stream and the valley dry up; the flowers wither and die. So, too, with the money we possess. 2. While it flows and circulates freely, it helps many. But when the circulation is halted by accumulating, wasting, or abusing, money becomes a curse. The heart hardens and noble aims become misguided. Wealth doesn't mean a thing if it doesn't translate into opportunities for others.

글의 주된 수사법은 비유이다.
중심소재는 'money'이다.

중심소재: Money
1. **도입부**
위대한 도구로써 돈을 언급하고 있다.
1) **뒷받침 비유**
돈을 산의 계곡물에 비유하면서 두 대조적 상황을 언급
2. **주제문**
원활한 통화순환의 중요성
1) **뒷받침 부연(비유확인)**

| 해석
돈이란 인간이 소유한 가장 유용한 도구 중 하나이다. 그것은 생기를 돋우는 산의 계곡물과 같다. 그것이 초원을 가로질러 흘러갈 때, 길가의 모든 것을 활기찬 초록색으로 만든다. 하지만 일단 차단되면, 계곡물과 계곡은 완전히 메마르고 꽃들은 시들어 죽는다. 우리가 소유한 돈도 마찬가지이다. 그것이 자유롭게 흐르고 순환할 때는 많은 이들을 도와준다. 하지만 그 순환이 축적과 남용, 오용으로 막히게 되면, 돈은 저주스러운 것이 된다. 마음은 얼어붙고 고결한 목표는 길을 잃는다. 부유함이란 다른 이들을 위한 기회로 변모하지 않는다면 아무 의미도 없다.

11 글의 제목

[실전응용 1] ②

1. You should not watch television and eat at the same time. 1) You just get lost in a program and can't stop ① eating too much. You'll eat anything—the worst things—when the television is on. You may ② eat unhealthy food like cookies, snacks, and fast food. It is just like hanging around with the wrong friends in school. You'll do things you wouldn't do if you didn't meet them.

중심소재: TV
1. 도입부 = 주제문
TV를 보면서 음식을 먹으면 안된다.
1) 뒷받침 근거
① 과식
② 건강에 해로운 음식 섭취

★ 요지를 이끄는 시그널을 파악한다.

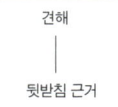

| 해설
인과의 전개방식으로 글쓴이의 주장이 첫 번째 문장에 드러나는 두괄식의 형태를 취하고 있다.

| 해석
당신은 TV를 보며 동시에 식사해서는 안 된다. 당신은 TV 프로그램에 정신이 팔려 먹기를 멈출 수 없게 된다. 당신은 TV가 켜진 동안 아무거나, 다시 말해 최악의 것을 먹게 될 수 있다. 당신은 쿠키나 스낵류, 그리고 패스트푸드와 같이 건강에 해로운 음식들을 먹을 수도 있다. 이는 학교에서 나쁜 친구들과 어울리는 것과 같다. 당신이 그 친구들을 만나지 않는다면 하지 않을 것들을 하게 된다.

[실전응용 2]

1. For their own benefit, companies have various ways of offering lower prices. 1) ① One way of doing this is a trade discount. Ⓐ It is offered to the shops or businesses that buy goods on a large scale and sell them. ② There is also a quantity discount, which is offered to individuals who order large quantities of a product. Ⓑ The company gives a price break to these buyers because they help cut the costs of selling, storing, shipping, and billing. ③ Finally, a cash discount is a lower price offered to people who pay in cash.

중심소재: 회사의 할인 정책
1. 도입부 = 주제문
이윤을 위해 기업이 제공하는 '가격 할인 방법'(나열의 글 전개)
1) 뒷받침 진술
① 도매할인
Ⓐ 부연진술
② 수량할인
Ⓑ 부연진술
③ 현금할인

★ 본문에 구체적으로 기술될 중심내용에 해당된다.

* 부연진술의 위치

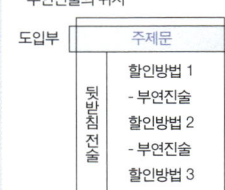

79

| 해설

제목: Types of Discount Pricing

| 해석

각자의 수익을 위해서, 기업들은 낮은 가격을 제공하는 다양한 방식을 취하고 있다. 이러한 방식 중 하나가 도매 할인이다. 도매할인은 대규모로 상품을 사들여 그것들을 파는 도매상이나 도매업자에게 제공된다. 수량할인도 있는데, 이것은 상품의 대량주문을 하는 개인에게 제공된다. 기업은 이들이 판매와 저장, 선적, 그리고 과금비용을 줄여주기 때문에 이러한 구매자들에게 가격할인을 제공한다. 마지막으로 현금할인은 현금으로 내는 사람들에게 제공되는 가격할인이다.

[실전응용 3]

1. Goats like eating weeds. In fact, they prefer weeds to grass. 1) So they are very useful for controlling weeds without using chemicals. ① The digestive system of the goat is different from that of the sheep or the cow. Weed seeds cannot pass through the goat's body, and so they cannot grow into new weeds. Ⓐ Farmers don't like using chemicals to control weeds because such poisons can kill wild animals or even pets, like dogs. A company in Montana even rents out goats to eat weeds.

도입부 — 중심소재 파악
주제문
뒷받침 진술
부연사례

중심소재: Goat
1. 도입부
잡초를 좋아하는 염소의 식성
1) 주제문
염소의 이런 식성은 '잡초 제거'에 유용하다.
① 뒷받침 진술
Ⓐ 염소의 어떤 측면 때문에 잡초 제거에 유용한지를 설명하고 있다. ← 단순히 염소의 소화기관에 대한 설명이 아니라는 점을 파악한다.
ⓐ 뒷받침 부연
잡초 제거 적용 사례를 설명하고 있다.

| 해설

본문은 염소의 식성을 활용하여 잡초를 통제할 수 있는 새로운 방법을 소개하는 설명(expository writing)의 글이다. 주제: Controlling Weeds through Goats / 제목: An "Animal" Way to Control Weeds.

| 해석

염소는 잡초를 먹는 것을 좋아한다. 실제로, 염소는 잔디보다 잡초를 더 좋아한다. 그래서 염소는 화학비료의 사용 없이 잡초를 제거하는 데 매우 유용하다. 염소의 소화기관은 양이나 소의 소화기관과는 차이가 있다. 잡초의 씨는 염소의 신체를 통과할 수가 없어, 새로운 잡초로 자라날 수가 없다. 농부들은 (화학비료의) 독성이 야생동물이나 심지어 개와 같은 애완동물도 죽일 수 있기 때문에 잡초를 제거하는 데 화학비료를 사용하는 것을 선호하지 않는다. 몬태나의 한 회사는 잡초를 먹는 염소를 대여해주기도 한다.

12 글 전개방식

1) Listing(나열)

[실전응용 1]

1. <u>Smoking is very dangerous and can cause great harm to your body, even endanger your life</u>. 1) ① **When** you smoke, your heart beats faster than it needs to and causes your blood pressure to rise, which, eventually, can cause a heart attack or heart disease. ② <u>In addition</u>, when you smoke, the essential oxygen in your bloodstream is replaced with poisonous carbon monoxide that comes from the tobacco in the cigarette. ③ <u>Finally</u>, many people have fallen asleep while smoking and have set themselves and their homes on fire, endangering their lives.

중심소재: 담배 피우는 행위
1. 도입부 = 주제문
담배는 몸에 유해한데, 심지어 생명에 지장을 초래할 수도 있다. ← 이후 글쓴이의 견해에 대한 뒷받침 진술이 이어진다(근거 제시).
1) 뒷받침 진술
① 담배를 피우면, 심장박동 증가 → 심장마비 또는 질환 유발
② In addition – 혈관 속 산소가 유해한 일산화탄소로 전환됨
③ Finally – 담배를 피우다 졸아서 집과 생명 모두 잃어버린 사례

★ 주제문으로 주제와 중심 내용을 이끌어 낼 수 있다.

★ 구체적 진술을 이끄는 시그널 when 확인.

★ 나열의 시그널을 확인한다.

| 해설
나열의 글 전개방식을 취하고 있는 점을 확인한다.

| 해석
흡연은 매우 위험하여, 당신의 몸에 중대한 해를 끼칠 수 있고, 심지어 당신의 생명까지도 위협할 수 있다. 우리가 흡연할 때, 우리의 심장은 필요 이상으로 빨리 뛰어 고혈압을 유발하는데, 이것은 결국 심장마비나 심장질환을 초래할 수 있다. 또한, 당신이 흡연할 때, 혈류 속의 필수적인 산소가 담배의 타바코 성분으로부터 발생하는 독성 일산화탄소로 대체된다. 마지막으로, 많은 사람이 담배를 피우다 잠이 들어, 그들의 생명을 위험에 빠뜨리며 그들 자신과 그들의 가정을 불태우기도 한다.

[실전응용 2]

뒷받침 진술에서 구체적으로 전개될 중심내용(controlling idea)이 된다.

중심소재는 'happiness'이고, 주제는 중심내용을 고려하여 '행복의 네 가지 조건'으로 잡을 수 있다.

나열의 시그널을 확인한다.

*부연진술의 위치 확인

도입부 = 주제문

뒷받침 진술
뒷1 ___
뒷2 ___
뒷3 ___
뒷4 ___
부연진술

1. There are at least four things which are more or less under our own control and which are essential to happiness. 1) ① The first is some moral standard by which to guide our actions. ② The second is some satisfactory home life in the form of good relations with family or friends. ③ The third is some form of work which justifies our existence to our own country and makes us good citizens. ④ The fourth thing is some degree of leisure and the use of it in some way that makes us happy. Ⓐ To succeed in making a good use of our leisure will not compensate for failure in any one of the other three things to which I have referred, but a reasonable amount of leisure and a good use of it is an important contribution to a happy life.

중심소재: 행복
1. 도입부 = 주제문
행복에 필수적이면서 우리가 통제할 수 있는 네 가지 요소가 있다(four things: Controlling Idea).
1) 뒷받침 진술
① 첫 번째: moral standard
② 두 번째: satisfactory home life
③ 세 번째: some form of work
④ 네 번째: leisure
Ⓐ 부연 진술

| 해석

행복에 필수적이며 어느 정도 우리가 통제할 수 있는 것들에는 최소한 네 가지가 있다. 첫째는 우리의 행동을 규율하는 도덕적 기준이다. 둘째는 가족이나 친구들과의 바람직한 관계의 형태인 만족스러운 가정생활이다. 셋째는 자신의 국가에 존재를 정당화하여, 선량한 시민으로 만들어 주는 일정한 형태의 직업이다. 넷째는 어느 정도의 여가와 우리를 행복하게 하는 방향으로의 여가 활용이다. 여가를 잘 활용하는 데 성공하는 것만으로 내가 앞서 언급했던 다른 세 가지 중 어느 하나의 실패를 벌충할 수는 없을 것이나, 상당한 양의 여가와 여가의 유익한 활용은 행복한 삶에 있어 중요한 요소이다.

[실전응용 3]

중심내용(controlling idea)에 해당한다.

중심소재는 'writing'이다.

각 뒷받침 문장의 부연진술인 예시를 확인할 수 있다.

1. There are four basic modes of writing. Each mode may take different forms, but has a primary purpose. 1) ① The first is expository writing, which has a purpose of explaining something or giving directions. Ⓐ Providing directions to your house is an example. ② The second mode is persuasive writing, which has a purpose of influencing the reader's way of thinking. Ⓑ An advertisement is a an example of persuasive writing. ③ The third mode is descriptive writing, which has a purpose of providing vivid details so that the reader can picture what is being presented. Ⓒ An essay that depicts the glorious Grand Canyon is an example. ④ The fourth mode is narrative writing, which has a purpose of presenting an experience in the form of a story. Ⓓ A personal account of a vacation is an example of narrative writing.

중심소재: 글쓰기 → 글쓰기의 4가지 종류
1. 도입부 = 주제문
글의 네 가지 종류가 있다.
1) 뒷받침 진술
① 첫 번째 종류: 설명
Ⓐ 예시 부연
② 두 번째 종류: 논증
Ⓑ 예시 부연
③ 세 번째 종류: 묘사
Ⓒ 예시 부연
④ 네 번째 종류: 서사
Ⓓ 예시 부연

| 해석

글쓰기에는 네 가지 기본 방식이 있다. 각각의 방식은 다른 형태를 취하지만 하나의 주요한 목적을 가진다. 첫째는 설명문으로, 어떤 것을 설명하거나 지시하는 목적을 가진다. 당신의 집을 찾아가는 방향을 제시하는 것이 이러한 예이다. 두 번째 방법은 논설문이며 이것은 독자의 생각하는 방식에 영향을 주는 데 목적이 있다. 광고는 논설의 대표적인 사례이다. 세 번째 방법은 묘사로, 이것은 생생한 부연설명을 제공하여 독자가 표현된 것들을 떠올릴 수 있도록 하는 데 목적이 있다. 장엄한 그랜드 캐니언을 묘사하는 수필이 그 예이다. 네 번째 방식은 서사로, 이것은 이야기 형태로 경험을 나타낼 목적으로 쓰인다. 한 개인의 휴가 경험을 설명하는 것이 서사의 한 예이다.

[실전응용 4]

1. Each of the U.S. manned space exploration projects had specific major goals. 1) ① For example, the Mercury project was designed to test whether or not human beings could survive and function in outer space. ⓐ In addition, the Mercury project tested rockets with the new Mercury space capsule, which could hold one person. ② As another example, the Gemini project was intended to find out whether two people could work in the weightless environment of space. ⓑ One way of doing this was by having Gemini astronauts take "spacewalks." That is, they floated outside their spacecraft in a spacesuit, connected to it by a tether. Gemini astronauts also tried out new flying skills. For example, some astronauts flew two spacecraft extremely close together; this procedure was called "rendezvous." On some Gemini flights, astronauts physically linked two spacecraft together. This linking, or "space docking," was a major goal of the Gemini program. ③ Finally, the Apollo project, with three astronauts, had the goal of testing spacecraft and skills so that people could actually fly to the Moon and land on it. ⓒ Other goals included performing scientific experiments on the lunar surface and collecting rocks for study on Earth.

중심소재: 유인 우주 탐사 계획

1. 도입부 = 주제문
뒷받침 문장이 제시되는 본문에서 어떤 종류의 우주탐사 프로젝트가 있는지 소개하면서 나름의 독특한 목적이 기술된다.

1) 뒷받침 진술
주제문에서 밝힌 중심내용을 뒷받침하는 구체적 예를 나열의 글 전개방식을 활용하여 기술하고 있다.

① 예시 1
ⓐ 부연진술
② 예시 2
ⓑ 구체적 방법 및 추가 목적 예시 부연
③ 예시 3
ⓒ 추가 목적

*연결사에도 순서가 있음을 알아둔다.
For example → As another example → Finally

★ 미국의 유인 우주탐사 프로젝트에 관한 글이다. 구체적으로 어떤 내용을 다루는지(중심내용) 파악한 후 주제를 설정하도록 한다(주제의 폭을 좁히는 과정).

★ 본문에서 전개될 중심내용(controlling idea)이다.

★ 접속사에도 순서가 있음을 알아 둔다.

| 해석
미국의 유인 우주탐사 계획은 각각 특정한 주요 목표가 있다. 예를 들면, 머큐리 프로젝트는 사람이 생존하여 우주공간에서 활동할 수 있는지를 시험하도록 기획되었다. 또한, 머큐리 프로젝트는 한 사람만 탑승할 수 있는 새로운 수성 우주 캡슐이 장착된 로켓을 시험했다. 또 다른 예로, 제미니 프로젝트는 두 사람이 우주의 무중력 상태에서 일할 수 있는지를 알기 위함이었다. 프로젝트를 진행하는 이유 중 하나는 제미니 우주비행사가 "우주 유영"을 할 수 있게 하기 위해서이다. 다시 말해, 우주비행사들이 안전 선으로 연결되어 우주복을 입고 우주선 밖에서 떠 있었다. 제미니 우주비행사들은 또한 새로운 비행기술을 시도해볼 수 있었다. 예를 들면, 일부 우주비행사들이 아주 가깝게 붙어있는 두 우주선을 떠다녔다. 이 과정을 "랑데부(만남)"라고 부른다. 어떤 제미니 비행에서는 비

행사들이 물리적으로 두 우주선을 연결하기도 했다. 이러한 연결, 혹은 "우주 도킹"이 제미니 프로젝트의 주요 목표이다. 마지막으로 3명의 우주인과 함께한 아폴로 프로젝트는 우주선과 기술들을 연구하여 사람들이 사실상 달로 날아가 착륙할 수 있었다. 다른 목표로는 달 표면에서의 과학 실험 수행과 지구 연구를 위한 암석 수집이 있다.

[실전응용 5]

1. Archaeologists have a number of theories to explain why humans began farming. 1) The reasons probably differed somewhat from one region to another. ① Ⓐ Some theories maintain that population pressure or changes in environment may have forced humans to find new economies strategies, which led to farming. Ⓑ Another theory maintains that a population of humans may have lived in a region where it was relatively easy to domesticate wild plants and animals, making the development of agriculture essentially a historical accident. Ⓒ Still another theory proposes that the rise of farming may have been a function of social change, as individuals began to use agriculture as a means to acquire wealth in the form of food surpluses.

나열의 시그널인 'some ★ – another – still another' 를 확인한다.

중심소재: Farming
1. 도입부 = 주제문
인간이 농업을 시작한 이유에 관한 다양한 이론
1) 연결문
① 뒷받침 진술
Ⓐ 이론 1
Ⓑ 이론 2
Ⓒ 이론 3

| 해설
나열을 나타내는 시그널(signal)을 확인한다.

| 해석
고고학자들은 왜 인류가 농경을 시작했는지를 설명하기 위한 많은 이론을 갖고 있다. 이유는 지역마다 다소 차이가 있을 수 있다. 어떤 이론은 인구밀도나 환경의 변화가 인류로 하여금 새로운 경제 전략을 찾도록 한 것이 농경으로 이끌었다고 주장한다. 또 다른 이론은 인류의 인구가 야생 식물과 동물들을 길들이기 쉬운 한 지역에 살다가, 필연적으로 역사적 사건인 농업을 발달시켰을 것으로 주장한다. 또 다른 이론은 농경의 시작이 개인들로 하여금 농업을 나머지 생산물의 형태로 부를 축적하는 수단으로서 농사를 짓게 하여 사회적 변화의 기능을 수행했을 것이라 주장한다.

[실전응용 6]

중심소재는 '야구' 이다. ★

1. 1) During a few hours in the ball park, city people saw plays that they could remember afterwards because of the way specific events built up to a memorable moment —the sudden skillful triumph over an adversary. 2) By making intense competition against an opponent its essential feature,

중심소재: 야구
1. 뒷받침 진술
1) 야구의 이점 1 – 야구를 구경하는 사람들에게 잊지 못할 멋진 경기를 남겨준다.
2) 야구의 이점 2 – 성공을 위한 일상의 경쟁(투쟁)은 정당한 것이다.

baseball seemed <u>to legitimize and appreciate each spectator's daily struggle for success</u>. 3) Watching the rivalry on the diamond introduced <u>standards of competition into the spectators' lives</u>. 4) The game also <u>reduced their daily tensions</u> because its ups and downs seemed more momentous than their lives.

3) 야구의 이점 3 – 일상의 투쟁에 야구와 같은 규칙의 필요성 상기

4) 야구의 이점 4 – 일상의 긴장감 완화

* 주제문이 생략된 형태

도입부 | 주제문
뒷1._____
뒷2._____
뒷3._____
뒷4._____

구체적 진술에 해당하는 뒷받침 문장에서 일반진술에 해당하는 주제문을 이끌어 낸다.

| 해설

전체적으로 나열의 글 전개방식을 취하는 글이다. 주제문이 드러나지 않고, 뒷받침 진술만 드러나는 'Implicit'의 유형이므로 뒷받침 진술을 바탕으로 주제문을 이끌어내야 한다.

| 해석

시민은 야구장에서 몇 시간 동안 경기를 관람하였는데, 원정팀을 누른 (홈팀의) 멋진 역전승같이 기념될 만한 특별한 사건 덕분에 훗날 그 경기를 두고두고 기억할 수 있었다. 야구는 그 본래의 특징이 상대 팀과 격렬하게 경쟁하는 것이므로, 관중(시민)이 성공하기 위해 매일 치열한 싸움(생존경쟁)하는 것을 정당화시켜주고 인정해주는 것처럼 보였다. 관중이 다이아몬드 구장에서 벌어지는 (양 팀 간의) 경쟁을 지켜보는 것은 곧 경쟁의 기준을 자신들의 삶에도 도입하는 것이었다. 경기가 엎치락뒤치락하는 것이 그들의 실제 삶보다 더 중대하게 보였기 때문에 (야구) 경기는 또한 그들 삶에 긴장감을 덜어주었다.

[실전응용 7]

1. **What conditions are needed** for a panic? 1) <u>First and foremost</u>, the situation must be perceived to be threatening. <u>Next</u>, the solution to this crisis must be hard to think of. <u>Third</u>, the opportunities for successful escape as well as adequate time must be seen as limited. Panics happen when it is difficult for most people to escape.

중심소재: Panic → Panic의 조건
1. 도입부 = 주제문
공황의 조건
1) 뒷받침 진술
① 조건 1
② 조건 2
③ 조건 3

* 의문점 = 주제 or 주제문
답변 = 요지

★ 본문에서 구체적으로 밝힌 중심내용(controlling idea)이다.

★ 중심소재는 panic이며 이를 바탕으로 무슨 이야기를 전개하는가? 사람이 당황할 수 있는 조건을 따지는 글이다.

| 해설

의문점으로 시작하는 글은 그 자체가 글의 주제가 될 가능성이 크고 이에 대한 답변이 바로 글쓴이가 궁극적으로 밝히려는 사항임을 기억하도록 한다. 시그널로 'first and foremost, next, third'를 확인할 수 있다.

| 해석

사람이 당황하기 위해서 어떤 조건이 필요한가? 우선 가장 중요한 것은 그 상황이 위협으로 인식되어야 한다. 다음으로, 위기에 대한 해결책이 떠오르기 쉽지 않아야 한다. 셋째, 적절한 시기뿐 아니라 성공적인 탈출의 기회가 제한적으로 보여야 한다. 사람들이 피하기 어려울 때 공황이 일어난다.

85

2) Cause and Effect (인과)

[실전응용 1]

구체적 상황·현상을 이끄는 시그널로 본문에서 제시되는 'When' 외에도 'If'가 종종 쓰인다.

인과의 시그널을 확인한다.

구체적 상황 설정

1. When people move from one city or country to another, the spread of diseases may result. 1) People often bring in germs which may not have been present there before. These new germs can spread quickly and cause previously unknown diseases. If a germ is completely new to a region, people have no natural protection against it. They become ill more easily and die more often. 2) In turn, newcomers may catch diseases which were not present where they came from. If they go back, they may carry the diseases with them and start an epidemic there, too.

중심소재: 질병의 확산
1. 도입부 = 주제문
현상: 인구 이동에 따른 질병확산
1) 뒷받침 진술
① 경우1
여행자가 출신 지역의 질병을 새로운 지역에 옮기는 경우
② 경우 2
여행자가 새로운 질병을 출신 지역으로 가져가는 경우

| 해석
사람들이 한 도시 또는 나라에서 다른 곳으로 이동할 때, 질병의 확산이 초래된다. 사람들은 종종 그곳에는 기존에 없었던 병균을 옮기기도 한다. 이러한 새로운 병균은 빠르게 퍼져 기존에 알려지지 않은 질병을 일으킨다. 만약 병균이 그 지역에서는 전혀 새로운 것이라면, 사람들은 그 병균에 대한 자연적인 면역체계를 전혀 가지고 있지 않다. 그들은 더 쉽게 병들게 되고, 더 자주 죽음에 이르게 된다. 반대로, 그 지역에 새로 이사 온 사람들은 그들이 전에 살던 곳에서는 존재하지 않던 질병에 걸릴 것이다. 만일 그들이 돌아간다면, 자신들과 함께 병을 옮길 것이고, 그곳에서 또한 전염병이 시작될 것이다.

[실전응용 2]

인과의 시그널을 확인하도록 한다.

구체적진술을 이끄는 시그널을 확인한다.

1. In August, the Chilean court took away the exemption right from former dictator Augusto Pinochet. 1) As a result, Pinochet can finally be tried, 2) but the political world of Chile still seems unstable. ① Now that Pinochet can be sued for human rights abuses during his rule, many Chileans are demanding that the government punish him. ② The international society also wants justice, and America has even decided to reveal all classified documents on Pinochet. ③ However, punishing Pinochet is not as simple as it looks. This is due to the military in power and Pinochet's parliamentary superpowers. They have already submitted a bill to stop the trial on the grounds that Pinochet is too old and sick.

중심소재: 칠레의 독재자 피노체트에 관한 법적공방
1. 도입부
칠레 법원은 전 칠레의 독재자 피노체트에게서 면책특권을 박탈
1) 결과(as a result) – 드디어 피노체트를 심판할 수 있게 되었음
2) 'but' 이후 글의 반전
칠레의 정치 세계는 여전히 불안해 보인다는 점을 언급하고 이후 본문 말미에서 피노체트를 처벌하기 쉽지 않은 이유를 설명하고 있다.
① 피노체트는 인권 남용으로 많은 칠레인이 그의 처벌을 요구하고, ② 국제사회 또한 정의를 원한다.
③ '그러나' 군사력과 피노체트가 가진 의회의 지지 세력이 그가 노쇠한 병든 노인이라는 점에서 재판을 멈추게 할 의안을 제기한 상태이다.

| 해설

글의 도입부 내용과 달리 'but' 이후 피노체트에 대한 정의실현이 쉽지 않을 것이라는 내용을 구체적인 원인을 들면서 설명하고 있다.

| 해석

8월, 칠레 법원은 전 정권의 독재자 아우구스토 피노체트로부터 면책특권을 박탈했다. 그 결과, 피노체트는 기소될 수 있었지만, 칠레의 정계는 불안정해 보인다. 지금은 피노체트가 재임 기간의 인권 남용으로 기소될 수 있기 때문에, 많은 칠레인이 정부가 그를 벌하기를 요구하고 있다. 국제 사회 역시 정의를 원하고, 심지어 미국은 피노체트에 관한 기밀문서 전부를 공개하기로 했다. 그러나 피노체트를 처벌하는 것은 보기보다 간단하지 않다. 이것은 강력한 군부 세력과 의회의 피노체트 지지 세력 때문이다. 그들은 이미 피노체트가 너무 늙고 병들었다는 이유로 재판을 중지해야 한다는 법안을 제출했다.

[실전응용 3]

1. **Supposing** two foreigners happen to meet and get involved in conversation. Even if both parties are fluent in the same language, differences in interpretations will occur <u>because of</u> the <u>cultural differences</u>. ① Each person interprets events through his or her mental filter, and that filter is based on the receiver's experiences, life style, and social tradition to which he or she belongs. 2. <u>As a result</u>, several of the nonverbal forms of communication have different meanings from culture to culture which interfere the conversation to some extent.

중심소재: 문화차로 인한 소통장애
1. 도입부 = 주제문
현상-원인: 문화의 차이로 인해 같은 언어를 사용하는 사람간에도 해석의 불일치가 발생한다.
1) 뒷받침 진술

2. 결과(=요지)
다양한 비언어적 형태의 의사소통으로 인해 문화사이에 의미의 불일치가 발생한다.

★ 구체적 상황(현상)을 설정하여 글쓴이가 지적하려는 문제점을 제시하고 있다.

★ 중심소재는 'cultural differences'와 'intercultural communication'이다.

* 양괄식 구조확인

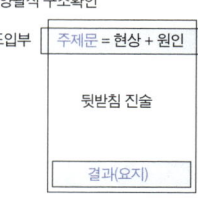

| 해석

두 외국인이 우연히 만나 대화하게 되었다고 가정해보자. 비록 양쪽 다 같은 언어에 유창할지라도, 문화의 차이 때문에 해석에서 차이점이 발생한다. 각자는 자신의 정신적 여과기를 통해서 사건을 해석하고, 그 여과기는 정보를 받아들이는 사람의 경험과 생활방식 그리고 그가 속한 사회적 전통에 기인한다. 그 결과, 몇몇 비언어적인 형태의 의사소통은 문화마다 어느 정도 대화를 방해하는 다른 의미를 지닌다.

[실전응용 4]

1. Both ① the advances of science and ② the horrors of modern history have <u>caused</u> a decrease in religious faith. 1) ① Scientific insights have explained many of the mysteries once explained only by religion. <u>As a result</u>, for many people, science has become their religion. ② Moreover, the history of this century has been a recurring nightmare revealing the frightening depths of people's cruelty to one another.

중심소재: 신앙인감소(현상)
1. 도입부 = 주제문
1) 뒷받침 진술
첫 번째 문장의 ①, ②에 대한 구체적 진술을 뒷받침 진술에서 확인할 수 있다.

★ 인과의 시그널을 확인한다.

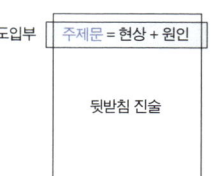

| 해설

두괄식의 구조를 취하는 인과의 글이다.

| 해석

과학의 발전과 현대 역사의 무시무시한 사건들 모두 종교적 믿음을 위축시켰다. 과학적 통찰력은 한때 종교에 의해서만 설명되던 많은 불가사의를 설명해냈다. 그 결과, 많은 사람에게 과학이 그들의 종교가 되어버렸다. 게다가, 현대의 역사는 서로에 대한 사람들의 무시무시한 잔인함의 깊이를 드러내는 반복되는 악몽이었다.

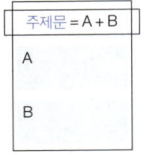

[실전응용 5]

1. To function properly, your brain requires an enormous amount of oxygen: roughly 20% of your body's total supply. 1) But as we age, the blood supply to the brain decreases, which causes oxygen depletion. This leads to loss of concentration and memory. 2) BioGinkgo, derived from the leaves of the ginkgo tree, safely and naturally ① increases the blood flow to the brain, restoring its oxygen supply. ② As a result, the brain naturally functions better: things like memory and concentration are all improved. Take BioGinkgo and sharpen your mental sharpness.

중심소재: 뇌 → 뇌의 퇴화
글 전체에 두드러지는 인과의 표현을 확인한다.
1. 도입부
몸 전체 산소 공급량 중 뇌는 약 20%를 필요로 함
1) 문제점 지적
나이가 들면서 뇌로 가는 피가 줄어듦 → 뇌에 산소 공급이 줄어듦 → 집중력과 기억력 감퇴(인과의 표현인 'cause'와 'lead to'를 확인한다.
2) 대안(요지)
은행나무에서 추출한 'BioGinko'라는 제품 소개 – 앞에서 언급한 문제점 해결
① ← 인과의 표현 'as a result' 확인
② 효과
효과를 언급한 후 마지막 문장에서 물건을 사도록 홍보하고 있다.

| 해석

여러분의 뇌가 제대로 기능을 발휘하기 위해서는 엄청난 양의 산소, 즉 몸 전체 공급량의 약 20%가 필요하다. 그러나 나이가 들어감에 따라, 뇌로 공급되는 혈액은 줄어들어 산소 부족을 초래하게 된다. 이러한 산소부족은 집중력과 기억력의 감퇴를 가져온다. 은행나무 잎에서 추출한 BioGinkgo는 안전하고 자연스럽게 뇌로 가는 혈류를 증가시켜서 뇌의 산소 비축량을 회복하게 해준다. 그 결과, 뇌는 자연스럽게 더 잘 기능하게 되고, 기억력과 집중력 등이 모두 개선된다. BioGinkgo를 먹으면 당신의 정신력이 향상된다.

[실전응용 6]

1. In recent decades, cities have grown so large that now about 50% of the Earth's population lives in urban areas. 2. There are several reasons for this occurrence. First, the increasing industrialization of the nineteenth century resulted in the creation of many factory jobs, which tended to be located in cities. These jobs, with their promise of a better material life, attracted many people from rural areas. Second, there were many schools established to educate the children of the new factory laborers. The promise of a better

중심소재: 도시의 성장 → 도시의 성장에 따른 인구증가
1. 도입부 = 주제문
도시의 성장에 따른 인구집중
1) 연결문(이유)
① 뒷받침 진술
나열의 글 전개를 바탕으로 현상의 이유를 상술하고 있다.

education persuaded many families to leave farming communities and move to the cities. **Finally**, as the cities grew, people established places of leisure, entertainment, and culture, such as sports stadiums, theaters, and museums. For many people, these facilities made city life appear more interesting than life on the farm, and therefore drew them away from rural communities.

| 해설

결과에 해당하는 본문의 구조는 다음과 같다.

연결문?

연결문이란 주로 글의 도입부에 위치하여 다음에 어떤 내용이 이어질지를 알려주는 문장을 말한다. 예를 들어 본문의 경우 첫번째 문장에서 '도시성장에 따른 인구 집중'이란 주제문을 던진 후 뒷받침 진술로 원인을 파악하는 내용이 뒤따르는데 "이러한 현상에는 다양한 이유가 있다"는 연결문을 제시함으로 본문에 구체적으로 전개될 내용을 예측할 수 있는 도움 역할을 하고 있다. 그런 의미에서 연결문을 bridging sentence라 부른다.
단, 본서에서는 문제풀이의 용이성을 위해 주제문과 연결문을 함께 주제문으로 간주한다.

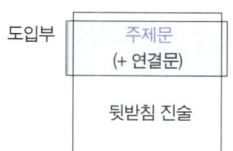

| 해석

최근 몇 년간, 도시는 크게 성장하여 지금은 지구 인구의 50퍼센트가 도시 지역에 살고 있다. 이런 현상에는 몇 가지 이유가 있다. 첫째, 고도화되던 19세기 산업화는 많은 공장의 일자리를 창출해 냈고, 이 공장들은 도시 지역에 있게 되었다. 더욱 풍요로운 삶을 약속하며 이러한 일자리는 시골 지역에서 많은 사람을 불러들였다. 둘째, 새로운 공장 노동자들의 자녀를 교육하기 위해서 설립된 많은 학교가 생겨났다. 더 나은 교육의 보장은 많은 가족이 농업 사회를 떠나 도시로 이동하게 하였다. 결국, 도시가 비대해짐에 따라, 사람들은 운동장, 영화관, 박물관 등의 여가와 오락 그리고 문화를 위한 시설들을 지었다. 많은 사람에게, 이런 공장들은 도시의 삶을 농장에서의 삶보다 더 흥미롭게 보이게 하였고 결국 농촌 사회에서 그들을 불러들이게 되었다.

[실전응용 7]

1. Scientists and doctors say that about 34 million Americans are too fat. 1) Why is this? Ⓐ <u>One cause</u> is the kind of food Americans eat. Many Americans like "fast foods." These foods (such as hamburgers and ice cream) often have fattening things in them. Ⓑ <u>Another</u> cause is the way Americans eat. They often eat little snacks between regular meals. These extra foods add extra fat on the body. Ⓒ A <u>third</u> cause is not enough exercise. Americans like driving

중심소재: 비만
1. 도입부 = 주제문
현상: 많은 미국인들이 비만이다.
1) 연결문
그 이유는?
① 뒷받침 진술
Ⓐ 원인 1: 패스트푸드
Ⓑ 원인 2: 식습관
Ⓒ 원인 3: 운동부족
Ⓓ 원인 4: 생활습관
* Ⓓ는 앞의 원인을 모두 포괄하는 것으로도 볼 수 있다.

★ 본문에서 밝힐 중심내용 (controlling idea)이다.

도입부 — 주제문(현상) (+ 연결문)
뒷받침 진술 (원인 Ⓐ, Ⓑ, Ⓒ, Ⓓ)

everywhere, instead of walking. They often have machines to do a lot of the work. Some Americans are also too heavy because of health problems. ⒟ **But** for most of those 34 million Americans, the problem is the American lifestyle.

| 해석
과학자들과 의사들은 약 3천4백만 명의 미국인이 비만이라고 말한다. 왜 그럴까? 첫 번째 원인은 미국인들이 먹는 음식의 종류이다. 많은 미국인은 "패스트푸드"를 좋아한다. 햄버거나 아이스크림과 같은 이러한 음식에는 종종 살을 찌우는 성분들이 포함되어 있다. 다른 원인은 미국인들이 음식을 먹는 방식이다. 미국인들은 종종 끼니 사이에 약간의 간식을 먹는다. 이런 여분의 음식들이 체내에 초과 지방을 늘린다. 세 번째 원인은 불충분한 운동이다. 미국인들은 어디든 걷기보다는 운전하는 것을 좋아한다. 그들은 종종 많은 일을 기계를 통해 처리한다. 일부 미국인들 중에는 건강 문제 때문에 과체중인 사람도 있다. 그러나 대부분의 3천4백만 명의 미국인들에게 문제는 미국의 생활양식이다.

[실전응용 8]

1) In the United States, poor city children are often ill **because of** their diet. Some children do not get enough food. Sometimes they do not get healthy food. 2) Poor health **is also caused by** bad housing. The apartments may not have heat in the winter or fresh air in the summer. 3) Poor health may also **be the result of** dirty water. 4) Or it may **be caused by** crowded apartments and crowded schools.

중심소재: 가난한 도시 아이들(의 건강)
1. 도입부 = 현상
미국 내 가난한 도시 아이들의 건강이 나쁜 이유를 밝히고 있다.
1) 식단 문제
2) 주거 환경
3) 물
4) 열악한 공공시설

| 해석
미국에서, 가난한 도시의 아이들은 음식 때문에 자주 아프다. 어떤 아이들은 충분한 음식을 먹지 못한다. 때때로 아이들은 청결한 음식물을 먹지 못한다. 건강 문제는 열악한 주거 환경에서 기인하기도 한다. 공동주택은 겨울에 난방되지 않거나, 여름철에 통풍되지 않을 수 있다. 건강 문제는 또한 오염된 물의 결과로 나타나기도 한다. 또는 밀집된 공동주택과 학교가 원인일 수 있다.

[실전응용 9]

1. **Even** the Press, that great organ which boasts of its freedom in all democratic countries, is **not in reality** free at all: it is oppressed under the heel of **Advertisements**. 1) For a proprietor or editor dare not offend the advertisers by anything he publishes in his paper. If he did, they would withdraw their advertisements and the paper would lose their financial backing. Every child knows that it is the advertisements that pay for a newspaper.

중심소재: 언론 → 광고가 언론에 미치는 영향
1. 도입부 = 주제문
현상: 민주주의 사회에서 가장 자유를 누린다는 언론조차 실제로 자유롭지 못하다.
1) 원인: 광고 때문에 언론은 자유롭지 못하다. 신문사의 금전적 지원이 대부분 광고에서 나오기 때문이다.

| 해설

인과적 글 전개방식의 대표적 유형인 '현상 – 원인'이다. 첫 번째 문장에서 'Even, in reality' 등의 표현이 등장하면 글의 요지와 관련된 중요한 내용을 전달하므로 절대 놓쳐서는 안 된다.

| 해석

어느 민주주의 국가에서나 자유를 자랑하는 언론은 사실상 그리 자유롭지만은 않다. 모든 언론매체는 '광고'의 지배 아래 억압당한다. 소유주도 편집장도 감히 광고주의 기분을 상하게 하는 것은 어떤 것도 자기 신문에 싣지 못하니까 말이다. 만약 그런 상황이 벌어진다면 광고주는 재빨리 광고문들을 철회하고 그 신문사는 점차 재정 후원이 줄어들 것이다. 꼬마 아이들도 광고가 신문사에 돈을 준다는 것을 알 정도로 당연한 사실이다.

[실전응용 10]

1. Asthma rates in kids are on the rise. 1) Surprisingly, some experts say it may have to do with our Ⓐ sterile lifestyle and Ⓑ overuse of antibiotics. Ⓐ ① Exposure to bugs puts the immune system into fighting mode—and that's a good thing. ② Kids with the pylori bacterium are half as likely to have asthma as those who don't, according to recent research. Ⓑ Since the invention of antibiotics, this bacterium has been on the decline. The discovery could lead to the development of a preventive treatment. 2. Until then, replace antibacterial soaps and cleaning products with normal ones. And when possible, avoid giving your child antibiotics.

중심소재: 천식
1. 도입부 = 현상(문제점 지적)
1) 주제문
청결한 생활방식(Ⓐ)과 항생제 과다복용(Ⓑ)
① 뒷받침 진술
Ⓐ 병원균 노출 → 면역체계
Ⓑ 항생제의 개발 → pylori 박테리아↓, 천식발생↑
2. 대안과 주의점

| 해설

'문제점이 드러나는 현상 – 분석 – 원인 – 대안'으로 이어지는, '현상'으로 시작하는 지문의 유형이다. 본문과 오른쪽 해설 부분을 잘 파악하도록 한다. 글쓴이의 궁극적인 주장은 대안에 드러난다: 항균 제품 사용을 줄여서 면역력을 향상시켜라.

| 해석

천식을 앓고 있는 아동의 수가 갑작스레 증가하고 있다. 놀랍게도, 많은 전문의는 소독하는 생활 방식과 항생제 과용 때문이라고 주장하고 있기도 하다. 벌레를 접하면 우리의 몸은 저절로 전투 태세로 전환된다 — 그것은 좋은 것이다. Pylori 세균을 가지고 있는 아이들이 천식을 앓게 될 확률은 보통 아이보다 50%씩이나 높다. 하지만 최근 나온 여러 종류의 항생제 덕으로 이러한 세균은 보기 드물어졌다. 이렇게 중요한 발견들은 미래에 예방치료로 큰 도움이 될 것이다. 그때까지, 강한 항균 비누와 세제를 보통 상품들로 바꿔 쓰고, 아이들이 항생제를 복용하는 일은 가능한 한 없도록 한다.

3) Comparison and Contrast (비교 · 대조)

[실전응용 1]

주제문으로 '국민과 정부에 관한 두 위대한 지도자의 상반된 관점'을 다루는 글임을 파악할 수 있다.

중심내용(controlling idea)에 해당한다.

대조의 시그널을 확인한다.

1. Two great leaders in American history, Alexander Hamilton and Thomas Jefferson, differed in their view of the ① American people and ② the American government. 1) ① Ⓐ Hamilton distrusted the people and thought they were naturally selfish, unreasonable, and violent. Ⓑ Jefferson, on the other hand, trusted people more and had more faith in their goodness. ② Ⓐ Hamilton believed in giving the federal government a great deal of power, while Ⓑ Jefferson favored a minimum amount of power in the federal government. Ⓐ Hamilton wanted local government to have very little power, while Ⓑ Jefferson favored strong local government.

중심소재: 위대한 두 지도자
1. 도입부 = 주제문
해밀턴과 제퍼슨은 국민과 정부에 대해 서로 다른 시각을 보였다.
1) 뒷받침 문장
① 국민에 대한...
Ⓐ 해밀턴의 관점
Ⓑ 제퍼슨의 관점
② 정부에 대한...
Ⓐ 해밀턴의 관점
Ⓑ 제퍼슨의 관점

| 해석
미국 역사상 두 명의 위대한 지도자, 알렉산더 해밀턴과 토머스 제퍼슨은 미국인과 미국 정부에 대해 서로 견해가 달랐다. 해밀턴은 사람들을 믿지 않았으며 사람들은 본래 이기적이고, 비합리적이며 폭력적이라고 생각했다. 반면에 제퍼슨은 사람들을 더 믿었으며 그들이 선하다는 데 더 많은 믿음을 가졌다. 해밀턴은 연방정부에 막대한 권력을 부여할 생각이었으나, 반면 제퍼슨은 연방정부에 최소한의 권력을 부여하고자 하였다. 해밀턴은 지방정부가 적은 권한을 갖기를 원한 반면, 제퍼슨은 강력한 지방정부를 선호했다.

| 참고
대조 + 나열로 전개된 글은 주로 다음과 같은 두 가지 구조를 취한다.

Type 1.

주제문	A와 B는 다르다
뒷받침 문장	A _____ _____ _____ .
	But/However/While
	B _____ _____ _____ .

Type 2.

주제문	A와 B는 다르다
뒷받침 문장	A _____ But B _____ .
	A _____ While B _____ .
	A _____ Whereas B _____ .
	A _____ However B _____ .

위 본문은 Type 2에 해당하는 내용으로 Subtopic을 병렬 구조로 배열한 후 두 대상의 차이점을 토픽별로 기술하는 형태이다.

[실전응용 2]

1) While awaiting the birth of a new baby, North American parents typically furnish a room as the infant's sleeping quarters. For decades, child-rearing advice from experts has encouraged the night time separation of baby from parent. For example, a study recommends that babies be moved into their own room by three months of age. "By six months a child who regularly sleeps in her parents' room is likely to become dependent on this arrangement," reports the study. 2) Yet parent-infant 'co-sleeping' is the norm for approximately 90 percent of the world's population. Cultures as diverse as the Japanese, the Guatemalan Maya, and the Inuit of Northwestern Canada practice it.

어린아이를 재우는 관행에 관한 글이다. 북미와 다른 지역이 구체적으로 어떻게 다른지 파악하도록 한다.
1) 북미 – 아이가 태어나기 전 아이만의 방을 준비한 후 부모와 아이는 각방을 쓰는 관행을 보여주고 있다. 이후 부연진술로 이러한 관행은 아이에게 독립심을 길러주기에 권장되었다는 내용을 언급하고 있다(일반적 관행으로 퍼지게 된 계기).
2) 북미와 대조되는 대상을 제시하기 전 'Yet'으로 화제 전환을 알리고 있다.
북미를 제외한 대부분의 나라는 아이와 부모가 함께 잠을 잔다.
(Co-sleeping)

★ 대조의 시그널인 'Yet'을 기준으로 북미와 이외 나라 아이들의 잠자리 관행의 차이점을 설명하고 있다.

| 해석

신생아의 탄생을 기다리는 동안, 북미 지역 부모들은 일반적으로 유아의 침실을 만들어 준다. 수년 동안, 전문가들로부터의 자녀 양육에 대한 조언은 밤에는 부모로부터 아이를 떼어 놓도록 권장해 왔다. 예를 들어, 한 연구는 아기들을 3개월이 될 때까지 자신의 방으로 옮겨야 한다고 권한다. "6개월까지 부모의 방에서 자는 아이는 이러한 환경에 더 의존하게 된다"고 연구는 보고했다. 그러나 부모와 아기가 '함께 자는 것'은 세계 인구의 약 90퍼센트에게 일반적이다. 일본인과 과테말라인, 마야인 그리고 캐나다 북서부의 이누이트 족에 이르기까지 다양한 문화에서 이렇게 한다.

[실전응용 3]

1. Some writers think that to impress their readers, they have to use a lot of long words and try to sound "intellectual." 1) This is not so. Most readers prefer to read something that is clear, that they don't have to struggle with. They want the writer to do the work. ① If they have to spend time figuring out what the writer means, they'll get impatient.

중심소재: 글쓰기
1. 도입부
some의 견해: 장황한 글쓰기를 통해 '지적'으로 보이려 한다.

1) 주제문(I의 견해)
① 뒷받침 부연

★ 특정인의 견해로 다음의 세 경우를 생각하도록 한다.
1. 특정인의 견해가 곧 글쓴이의 견해
2. 특정인의 견해에 반대하면서 글쓴이의 견해 전개
3. 두 대상의 상반된 견해를 중립적 입장에서 객관적으로 전개

★ 문장으로 역접의 표현을 전달하고 있다.

| 해석

어떤 작가들은 그들의 독자들이 감동하게끔 장황한 어휘를 사용하여 '박식하게' 들리도록 해야만 한다고 생각한다. 이는 사실이 아니다. 대부분의 독자는 고심해서 읽을 필요가 없는 명료한 글을 읽고 싶어한다. 독자들은 작가들이 그 작업을 해주기를 원한다. 만약 작가가 의도하는 바를 알아차리는 데 시간을 낭비해야 한다면, 그들은 답답해할 것이다.

| 참고 1

'some'으로 시작하는 글은 일반적으로 'some — others'의 대조를 이루는 지문이 많다. 본문 초반부에서 'Some'으로 시작하는 글을 대할 때는 이후 'some'과 대조를 이루는 또는 그와 상반된 주장을 하는 대조적인 대상이 등장하는지 확인하는 습관을 길러야 한다. 본문에서 'some writers'의 주장과 대

도입부	some의 견해
	↕
	I의 견해
	뒷받침 진술

조를 이루는 대상은 바로 글쓴이로, 역접의 역할을 하는 'That is not so' 를 기점으로 이후 글쓴이의 주장이 드러난다. 이 점을 고려하여 본문을 분석하도록 한다.

| 참고 2

역접의 접속사를 대신하는 문장에 주의하자. 대조의 글에서 등장하는 역접의 접속사 또는 부사 이외에 동일한 역할을 하는 문장이 있다. 본문에서는 'That is not so' 가 그 역할을 하고 있다. 이 외에 'That is not true.' 또는 'That is not the case.' 가 있다.

[실전응용 4]

★ 중심소재에 해당한다. 두 나라와 관련하여 어떤 내용을 전개하는가?

★ 중심내용(controlling idea)에 해당한다.

★ 본문에 예시가 두 번 등장하는데, 첫 번째 예시는 뒷받침 문장에 해당하고, 두 번째 예시는 부연에 해당.

* 위치에 따른 예시의 의미

도입부	
	주제문
	For example
	뒷받침 예시
	For example
	부연 예시

★ 대조를 드러내는 시그널에 주의한다.

1. Even though Arizona and Rhode Island are both states of the U.S., they are strikingly different in many ways. 1) For example, ① the physical size of each state is different. Arizona is large, having an area of 114,000 square miles, whereas Rhode Island is only about a tenth the size, having an area of only 1,214 square miles. Another difference is in ② the size of the population of each state. Arizona has about four million people living in it, but Rhode Island has less than one million. The two states also differ in ③ the kinds of natural environments that each has. For example, Arizona is a very dry state, consisting of large desert areas that do not receive much rainfall every year. However, Rhode Island is located in a temperate zone and receives an average of 44 inches of rain per year. In addition, ④ while Arizona is a landlocked state and thus has no seashore, Rhode Island lies on the Atlantic Ocean and does have a significant coastline.

중심소재: 아리조나, 로드 아일랜드
1. 도입부 = 주제문
1) 뒷받침 진술
예시(for example)를 시작으로 두 주의 차이점을 ① (크기), ② (인구), ③ (자연환경), ④ (해안의 유무)의 측면에서 상술하고 있다.

| 해석

애리조나와 로드아일랜드가 둘 다 미국의 주이지만, 그 둘은 놀랍게도 많은 면에서 다르다. 예를 들면, 각 주의 지리적인 크기가 다르다. 애리조나는 114,000제곱마일에 달하며 거대한 반면, 로드아일랜드는 기껏해야 1,214제곱마일로 약 1/10밖에 안 된다. 다른 점은 각 주의 인구수이다. 애리조나는 약 4백만의 인구가 그곳에 살고 있지만, 로드아일랜드는 백만도 안 된다. 두 주는 또한 각자가 가진 자연환경에도 차이가 있다. 예를 들어, 애리조나는 매년 많은 강수가 내리지 않은 사막지역을 포함하는 상당히 건조한 지역이다. 그러나 로드아일랜드는 온대 기후 지역에 있어 평균 매년 44인치의 강수량을 가진다. 또한, 애리조나가 내륙 지방인 주여서 해안가가 전혀 없는 반면, 로드아일랜드는 대서양에 있어 주요한 해안선을 끼고 있다.

| 참고

대조의 글의 기본 전제는 대조하고자 하는 대상 또는 특징이 반드시 두 개가 있어야 한다는 점이다. 고로 대조되는 두 대상을 먼저 찾는 것이 선행해야 할 작업이다. 또한, 두 대상의 상반된 특징을 다루는 경우 본문에서 차이점을 드러내는 접속사뿐 아니라 동사 또는 형용사 등이 자주 등장한다. 그 예로 'different, opposite, differ from' 등이 있다.

[실전응용 5]

1) <u>Some</u> people say that ① we have less privacy now than we had in the past. They claim it's possible to discover everything someone does on the Internet, and even spy on people. ② They also say that people can use the Internet too much, so they become more distant from their families and friends. 2) <u>But</u> other people claim that ① the Internet creates equal opportunities for everyone. They argue that the Internet helps to take power away from the rich, and that we can all have a voice on the Internet.

중심소재: Internet
'But'을 기준으로 인터넷에 대한 'Some people'의 견해와 'Other people'의 견해가 대조되는 글이다.
1) some – 인터넷에 대한 부정적 견해
① 인터넷으로 사생활 침해가 심해졌다.
② 인터넷에서 보내는 시간이 지나치게 많아 가족과 친구 관계에 소홀해졌다.
2) 대조의 'But' 확인
other – 인터넷의 긍정적 견해
① 모든 사람에게 평등한 기회 제공으로 모든 사람이 자신의 목소리를 낼 수 있다.

★ 'But'을 기점으로 'some – other'의 대조 확인.

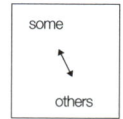

★ 중심소재는 '인터넷'이 고, 주제는 '인터넷에 대한 상반된 관점'이다.

해설

본문은 'But'을 기점으로 '인터넷의 장단점'을 서술하는 글이다. 본문을 읽고, 주제를 독자가 이끌어 내야 하는 유형(implicit)이다. 일반적으로 특정 대상의 장단점을 중립적인 입장에서 대조적으로 서술 하는 글은 두 대상의 상반된 주장을 할애하는 지면도 거의 비슷하게 주어진다. 문단의 구조를 보면 다음과 같다.

일반진술	The Internet has advantages and disadvantages.	숨은 주제(Implicit)
구체적 진술	단점: Less privacy on the Internet Less time with family and friends	하나의 대상의 대조되는 특성을 기술하고 있다.
	↕ But	
	장점: Creating equal opportunities for everyone	

해석

어떤 사람들은 오늘날 우리가 과거에 누렸던 것보다 사생활을 보호받지 못한다고 말한다. 그들은 누군가 인터넷에서 하는 모든 것들을 알아내고, 심지어 사람들을 감시하는 것이 가능하다고 주장한다. 그들은 또한 사람들이 인터넷을 지나치게 사용함에 따라, 그들이 가족이나 친구들과 더 멀어지게 된다고 말한다. 그러나 인터넷이 모든 사람에게 평등한 기회를 만들어 낸다고 주장하는 사람들도 있다. 그들은 인터넷이 부자들로부터 권리를 찾아올 수 있게 해주고, 인터넷에서는 발언권을 가질 수 있다고 말한다.

[실전응용 6]

1. There's <u>an important difference</u> between leisure and recreation. In a general sense, both words suggest processes of physical or mental regeneration. <u>But</u> they have <u>different</u> connotations. 1) Leisure is generally thought of as the opposite of work. It suggests something effortless and passive. We tend to think of work as something that takes

중심소재: 여가와 오락 → 차이점
1. 도입부 = 주제문
여가와 오락의 차이점(대조의 글전개 확인)
1) 뒷받침 진술

★ 중심내용(controlling idea) 이다.

★ 중심소재는 '여가'와 '레크리에이션'이다.

our energy. Leisure is what we do to build it up again. Leisure offers a recess, a passive break from the challenges of the day, a chance to rest and recharge. Recreation carries a more active tone — literally of re-creating ourselves. It suggests activities that require physical or mental effort but which enhance our energies rather than deplete them.

| 해석

여가와 오락 사이에는 중요한 차이점이 존재한다. 일반적인 관점에서, 두 단어는 신체적이거나 정신적인 재충전의 과정을 의미한다. 그러나 이 둘은 다른 의미를 내포한다. 여가는 일반적으로 일의 반대말로 간주한다. 여가는 힘이 들지 않고 소극적인 어떤 것을 의미한다. 우리는 일을 우리의 에너지를 소비하는 것으로 간주하려 한다. 여가는 우리가 다시금 기운을 추스를 수 있도록 하는 것이다. 여가는 휴식과, 낮 동안의 일과에서 벗어날 수 있는 수동적인 쉼, 그리고 쉬어 재충전할 기회를 제공한다. 오락은 말 그대로 우리 자신을 재창조하는 좀 더 활동적인 의미이다. 오락은 신체적이거나 정신적인 노력을 요구하나, 소모라기보다는 에너지를 보충하는 활동이다.

[실전응용 7]

도입부 — 중심소재 파악
주제문
뒷받침 예시

1. In all societies, relatives have special names. 1) In every kinship system, <u>some relatives are classed together</u>. That is, they are referred to by the same kinship term. ① Ⓐ <u>For example</u>, in the kinship language of English, the individual uses the term 'aunt' to refer to both the mother's and father's sisters. In English, the women who marry the brothers of either the father or mother are also called 'aunt.' The English language puts these women together in the same category because their relationship to the individual in terms of intimacy and authority is generally similar. Ⓑ In other cultures, however, where the father's sister and <u>the mother's sister have different rights, obligations, and relationships to the individual, these female relatives are called by different kinship names</u>.

중심소재: 친족호칭
1. 도입부
모든 사회에 존재하는 친족 호칭
1) 주제문
① 뒷받침 진술
Ⓐ 친밀감과 비슷한 권위를 드러내는 의미로 동일한 명칭으로 부르는 영국의 예
Ⓑ 다른 문화권의 경우
다양한 권리, 의무, 관계를 드러내기 위해 친척을 다르게 호칭함

| 해설

주로 대조의 전개방식에 예시가 함께 드러나 글로 '문화에 따라 친족 호칭이 다르다'는 내용을 다루고 있다.

| 해석

모든 사회에는, 친척에 대한 특정한 명칭이 있다. 모든 친족 제도에서, 일부 친척들은 함께 분류된다. 다시 말해, 그들은 같은 친족명칭으로 불리게 된다. 예를 들면, 영어권 친족 내에서, 개인은 어머니의 여자 형제나 아버지의 여자 형제 둘 다 이르는 말로 'aunt'라는 말을 사용한다. 영국에서는, 아버지 또는 어머니의 남자 형제와 결혼한 여성을 역시 'aunt'라고 부른다. 영어는 이들의 관계가 일반적으로 촌수와 항렬이 비슷해서, 이 여성들을 같은

범주로 묶는다. 그러나 다른 문화의 경우, 아버지의 여자 형제와 어머니의 여자 형제가 서로 다른 권리와 의무, 그리고 개인에 대한 관계가 달라서, 이러한 여성 친척들은 다른 친족명칭으로 불린다.

[실전응용 8]

1. 1) In Europe, if your industry declines and you lose your job, it is a big blow but not the end of the world. You will still keep your health insurance and public housing, while receiving unemployment benefits, government-subsidized retraining and government help in your job search. 2) In contrast, if you are a worker in the US, you'd better hold on to your current job because losing your job means losing almost everything. Unemployment insurance coverage is smaller than in Europe. There is little public help with retraining and job search. More frighteningly, losing your job means losing your health insurance and your home, as there is little public housing or public subsidies for your rent. 2. As a result, worker resistance to any industrial restructuring that involves job cuts is much greater in the US than in Europe.

중심소재: 미국과 유럽에서 실업의 의미 차이
경기 상황이 안 좋아 직장을 잃었을 때 발생하는 상황을 유럽과 미국 대조적으로 설명하고 있다.
1. 도입부 = 구체적 진술
1) 유럽에서 직장을 잃었을 때 – 건강보험 및 정부로부터의 다양한 보조를 받음.

2) 대조적으로 미국은 직장을 잃으면 'losing almost everything' 이라고 하면서 유럽과 극명한 대조를 보인다.
① 앞에서 언급한 상황 때문에 발생하는 결과를 언급하고 있다.

2. 요지(주제문)
구조조정에 대한 저항은 미국이 유럽보다 크다.

★ 대조를 기점으로 유럽과 미국의 어떤 차이점을 기술하는지 파악한다.

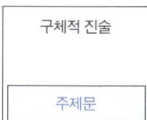

★ 글의 요지가 말미에 드러나는 미괄식 구조로 글 중반부를 기점으로 주제를 파악할 수 있고, 이를 통해 궁극적으로 전달하려는 요지가 마지막에 제시된다.

| 해석
유럽에서는, 만일 당신의 산업이 쇠퇴하여 일자리를 잃게 된다면, 이는 엄청난 타격이겠지만, 세상의 종말이 오는 것은 아니다. 당신은 실업수당과 정부보조의 직업교육, 그리고 구직을 위한 정부보조를 받으면서, 여전히 건강보험과 공공주택을 보유할 것이다. 반대로, 만일 당신이 미국의 노동자라면, 실직이 곧 모든 상실을 의미하기 때문에, 당신은 현재 직업에 계속 종사하는 편이 더 나을 것이다. 실업수당의 적용범위는 유럽보다 제한적이다. 직업교육과 구직을 위한 공공서비스도 거의 없다. 더 두려운 점은, 월세를 위한 정부보조금이나 공공주택이 거의 없으므로, 실직은 곧 건강보험과 주택의 상실을 의미한다. 그 결과, 직원 삭감을 포함한 어떠한 산업 구조조정에 대한 근로자들의 저항은 유럽에서보다 미국에서 훨씬 심하다.

[실전응용 9]

1. Now, as always, cities are desperate to create the impression that they lie at the center of something or other. 1) ① This idea of centrality may be locational, namely that a city lies at the geographical center of England, Europe, and so on. This draws on a well-established notion that geographical centrality makes a place more accessible, easing communication and communication costs. 2) However, now

중심소재: 도심의 구심성
1. 도입부: 도시의 성격
도시의 구심성(주제)
1) 구체적 진술
① 도시 구심성의 전통적 관점
지리적 중심지의 개념으로 특정지역의 접근성이 좋아 의사소통이 쉽고, 비용 절감의 효과
② 현대도시 구심성의 특징
지리적 측면의 구심성이 문화 구심성

★ 도시의 구심성에 관한 글이며, 이후 이에 대한 구체적 진술이 이어질 것을 예상할 수 있다. 중심내용을 바탕으로 주제의 폭을 더 좁히면서 글의 요지를 이끌어 내도록 한다.

that the economy is characterized more by the exchange of information than by hard goods, geographical centrality has been replaced by attempts to create a sense of cultural centrality. Ⓐ Cultural centrality usually demonstrates itself as a cry that a city is at the center of the action. ⓐ This means that the city has an abundance of cultural activities, such as restaurants, theater, ballet, music, sport, and scenery. The suggestion is that people will want for nothing in this city.

의 성격으로 바뀜
Ⓐ 문화구심성의 특징
ⓐ 예시부연

이후 새로운 현상인 문화 구심성에 대한 구체적 진술(특징)을 알 수 있으며, 본문을 통해서 궁극적으로 밝히려는 사항이 된다.

| 해설
글의 도입부에서 중심소재와 'however'를 기점으로 대조되는 개념을 파악하도록 한다.

| 해석
언제나 그렇듯 지금 도시들은 무언가의 중심에 놓여 있다는 인상을 만들어내기 위해 애를 쓴다. 이런 구심성에 대한 생각은 위치에 관한 것인데, 말하자면 어떤 도시가 영국이나 유럽이나 기타 등등의 지리적인 중심에 놓여 있다는 것을 의미한다. 이로부터 지리적인 구심성이 특정 장소에 대한 접근성을 좀 더 쉽게 해 통신과 통신비용을 완화해 줄 것이라는 잘 확립된 개념을 이끌어 낼 수 있다. 하지만 이제 경제가 만질 수 있는 상품보다는 정보의 교환으로 더 특징 지워지기에 지리적인 구심성은 문화적인 구심성의 개념을 만들어 내려는 시도로 대체되었다. 문화적 구심성은 일반적으로 어떤 도시가 활동의 중심에 있다는 표어로 나타난다. 이것은 그 도시가 식당, 극장, 발레, 음악, 스포츠, 그리고 경관과 같은 문화적인 기능이 풍부하다는 것을 의미한다. 이는 사람들이 이 도시에서는 부족함이 없음을 드러낸다.

[실전 고난도 10]

소설 속 이야기를 다룬다. 구체적으로 어떤 내용이 전개되는지 살펴본다.

Sinbad the Porter와 Sinbad the Seaman이라는 상충하는 두 자아를 제시하고 있다. 각각의 특성을 정확히 파악하도록 한다.

대조의 시그널로 'in contrast to'와 'But'을 확인할 수 있다.

1. *Sinbad the Seaman and Sinbad the Porter* tells how ① **Sinbad the Porter**, who was "carrying a heavy load, became exceedingly weary, the heat and the weight alike oppressing him." Saddened by the hardships of his existence, he speculates on what a rich man's life may be like. ② **Sinbad the Seaman**'s stories may be viewed as fantasies in which the poor porter engages to escape his burdensome life. 2. In other words, ① the ego, exhausted by its tasks, then permits itself to be overwhelmed by the dreaming id. ② The id, in contrast to the reality-oriented ego, is the seat of our wildest wishes, wishes that can lead to satisfaction or to extreme danger. 3. This is given body in the seven stories of Sinbad the Seaman's voyages. Carried away by what he recognizes as the "the bad man within me," Sinbad the Seaman desires fantastic adventures, and encounters horrible dangers. 4.

중심소재: 두 자아
1. 도입부
소설에 등장하는 한 인물의 '상충한 자아'를 묘사하고 있다.
① Sinbad the Porter – 고통을 짊어진 인간의 모습
② Sinbad the Seaman – 고통을 짊어진 'Sinbad the Porter'가 자신의 삶을 탈출한 환상의 인물

2. Sinbad the Porter와 Sinbad the Seaman은 각각 Id와 Ego를 상징함.
① Ego – 현실 자아, 즉 고통을 짊어진 모습
② Id – 현실을 벗어나려는 꿈 꾸는 자아
 Id의 추구 – Satisfaction or Extreme danger

3. 이러한 Id와 Ego가 바로 Sinbad the Seaman의 항해 이야기에 구체적으로 드러남 – 이후 구체적 내용을 전개하며 부연 진술

4. 암울한 현실 속 자아 Ego와 그것

Eventually the wish-fulfilling fantasies win out over the anxious ones, as he is rescued and returns home with great riches to a life of leisure and satisfaction. But each day the requirements of reality must also be met. The id having held sway for a time, the ego reasserts itself and Sinbad the Porter returns to his everyday life of hard labor.

을 벗어나려는 Id의 투쟁에서 결국 현실 속 자아 Ego를 벗어날 수 없다는 내용으로 마무리하고 있다.

| 해설

본문은 현실에 속박되어 힘든 노동의 삶을 사는 'Ego'와 그러한 삶의 무게를 벗어나 꿈을 갈망하는 'Id'를 'Sinbad the Seaman'과 'Sinbad the Porter'라는 상충하는 두 자아로 제시하고 있다. 'Sinbad'라는 공통된 표현에서 알 수 있듯이, 이 둘은 한 인물의 상충한 자아이다. 글 전개방법은 **비교/대조**라는 것을 쉽게 알 수 있다.

| 해석

'선원 신드바드와 짐꾼 신드바드' 이야기는 무거운 짐을 나르던 짐꾼 신드바드가 더위와 무게의 이중고에 시달리며 어떻게 극도로 허약해졌는지를 보여준다. 힘든 생활로 우울해진 그는 부자의 삶은 어떠할지에 대해 동경하게 된다. 선원 신드바드의 이야기는 가난한 짐꾼이 그의 곤궁한 삶을 탈출한다는 점에서 공상처럼 보일 수 있다. 다시 말해서, 자신의 일로 지친 자아가 자신을 꿈을 꾸는 본능적 충동인 이드에 압도되도록 한다. 현실적인 자아와는 반대로 이드는 만족이나 극의 위험으로 이끌 수 있는 욕구인 우리의 거친 욕망에 자리한다. 이것은 일곱 편의 선원 신드바드의 모험 이야기 속에 구체화되어 있다. 그가 내 안에 악한 사람으로 인식하는 것에 휩쓸려, 선원 신드바드는 환상적인 모험을 욕망하고, 끔찍한 위험에 직면한다. 결국, 그가 구출되어, 엄청난 부와 함께 여가와 성취의 삶으로 고향에 돌아오면서, 욕망을 따랐던 공상이 근심하던 욕망을 이겨내게 된다. 그러나 매일매일 현실적인 요건들 또한 충족되어야만 한다. 본능적 충동이 잠시 지배한 뒤, 자아는 다시 제 목소리를 내게 되고 짐꾼 신드바드는 그의 힘든 노동의 일상으로 돌아오게 된다.

4) Order (순서)

① Chronological Order

[실전응용 1]

1. The first American postal service was established in the colony of Massachusetts in 1639. From 1707 until the year before the American Revolution, the General Post Office in London controlled the postal service in America. In 1775, the Continental Congress resolved to have a postal system of its

본문의 가장 큰 특징은 시간의 흐름에 따라 기술된다는 점이다. 연도별로 어떤 내용이 구체적으로 언급되는지를 파악하면서 전체 주제를 설정하도록 한다. 특정 인물에 관한 글이면 '전기'에 해당하고, 특정 사물·대상에 관한 글이면 '발달 과정, 기원, 역사' 등이 언급될 가능성이 크다.

own, and Benjamin Franklin was elected to carry on the work. When Congress authorized a postal service in 1789 under the U.S. Constitution, the nation had 75 local post offices, and the mails were carried over 1875 miles (more than 3000 km) of postal routes.

1) The introduction of adhesive stamps in 1847 greatly simplified post office operations. The system of registering letters was first adopted in 1855. In cities, street letterboxes were introduced in 1858 and free mail delivery in 1863 under Postmaster General Montgomery Blair. The Pony Express began mail service between Saint Joseph, Missouri, and San Francisco in 1860. The money order system was put into operation in 1864, and rural free delivery service was established in 1896. The parcel post system came into operation in the U.S. in 1913. The first regular service for airmail was established between New York City and Washington, D.C., in 1918. The Postal Savings System, established by Congress in 1911, was terminated in 1966.

'미국 우편제도'에 대한 글임을 첫 번째 문장에서 알 수 있다. 첫 번째 문장이 주제문이 아니라 하더라도 **주제를 드러내는 중심소재**를 설정할 수 있다는 점에서 집중해서 읽어야 한다.
중심소재: 미국의 우편제도

1. 도입부
미국의 우편제도 발달 중 우편제도를 도입한 초창기에 관한 이야기로 '영국으로부터의 독립'을 주로 다루고 있다.

1) 구체적 진술
두 번째 문단에서 미국 우편제도 발달 중 중요한 사건/일이 발생한 연도를 중심으로 본문 끝까지 기술되고 있다.

| 해설

시간의 흐름에 따른 글 전개방식을 취하는 글은 Signal이 아주 분명하다. 아래 사항을 반드시 암기해 두자.

> 인물을 중심으로 기술 = 전기
> 사물, 대상, 현상, 사건 = 기원, 발달 과정, 역사

| 해석

　최초의 미국 우편 제도는 1639년 매사추세츠 식민지에 수립되었다. 1707년부터 미국 독립전쟁 전까지 런던의 중앙 우체국이 미국의 우편 제도를 총괄하고 있었다. 1775년, 대륙회의는 독자적인 우편 제도를 갖도록 결정했고, 벤자민 프랭클린이 이 일을 수행하는 데 선출되었다. 1789년 미국 헌법에 근거하여 의회는 우편 정책을 공포하여, 미국은 75개의 지역 우체국이 생겨났고, 우편물은 1,875마일(3000킬로미터 이상) 이상의 송달 경로를 통해 배달되었다.
　1847년 접착제 우표의 등장은 우체국 운영을 크게 단순화시켰다. 우편 등록 정책은 1855년에 처음 채택되었다. 1858년 도시에 길거리 우체통이 생겨나 1863년 저널 몽고메리 블레어 국장에 의해서 무료 배달이 시작되었다. 포니 익스프레스는 1860년 세인트 조셉 주와 미주리 주 그리고 샌프란시스코 사이에서 우편배달을 시작했다. 1864년 송금 시스템이 시작되었고, 1896년에는 농촌지역 무료배달 서비스가 시작되었다. 소포 우편 업무는 미국에서 1913년에 시행되었다. 뉴욕과 워싱턴 D.C를 오가는 최초의 정기 항공우편 서비스가 1918년 시작되었다. 1911년 의회가 추진한 우편 적립 시스템은 1966년에 종료되었다.

[실전응용 2]

1. Susan B. Anthony, a famous American women's rights movement leader, was born in New York in 1820. Susan's father sent Susan to a school for girls, but she had to return when her father's business failed. She started teaching the children in her hometown. But soon she stopped teaching and began to work for women's equal rights. Though many people hated her message, Susan organized groups to get women the right to vote. In 1872, she was arrested for voting in a national election, which was against the law. However, she kept fighting for her belief until she died in 1906. In 1920, the law finally gave women the right to vote.

중심소재: Susan B. Anthony의 여성 인권운동

본문은 미국 여성인권운동을 위해 전 생애를 바친 Susan B. Anthony의 삶에 관한 간략한 전기이다. 태어난 시점부터 삶을 마감할 때까지 여성 인권운동 향상과 관련된 굵직한 사건을 시간의 글 전개방식에 따라 기술하고 있다.

주제: A Life Fighting for Women's Rights

| 해석
미국의 유명한 여성인권운동 지도자인 Susan B. Anthony는 1820년에 New York에서 태어났다. 그녀의 아버지는 Susan을 여학교에 보냈으나, 사업이 실패하자 그녀는 집으로 돌아와야 했다. 그녀는 고향에서 아이들을 가르치는 일을 시작했다. 하지만 곧 가르치는 일을 그만두고 여성 평등권을 의해 일하기 시작했다. 비록 많은 이들이 그녀가 전하는 메시지를 싫어했지만, Susan은 여성이 투표권을 얻을 수 있도록 단체를 조직하였다. 1872년에 그녀는 전국적으로 치른 선거에서 법에 저촉되는 투표를 하여 체포되었다. 하지만 1906년에 세상을 떠날 때까지 그녀는 자신의 신념을 위해 지속해서 노력했다. 마침내 1920년에 여성은 법적으로 투표권을 인정받게 되었다.

② Spatial Order

[실전응용 1]

I couldn't believe my eyes when we finally emerged from the storm shelter. Where the barn once stood there was now only a few tufts of hay. The path that led to the house was scattered with branches and debris. The house! The entire roof was gone. The north wall was caved in and we could see right into the house. Well, what was left of it. Tears rolled down my cheeks as I noticed that most of our belongings had been sucked up into the great vacuum and scattered across the countryside. We heard a loud cracking and moaning as the west wall gave way and collapsed, sending

이 글은 폭풍으로 피폐해진 집과 주변 환경을 묘사하고 있다. 글 전개방법을 보면, 폭풍 대피소에서부터 마구간, 집, 집의 지붕, 북쪽 벽, 주변 환경, 다시 서쪽 벽 그리고 앞마당 한가운데 등으로 공간적 이동에 따른 묘사가 이루어지고 있다.

주제: 폭풍의 피해

★ 장소의 이동에 따른 폭풍의 피해를 묘사하고 있다. 장소의 시그널을 확인하도록 한다.

up a wave of dust. And yet, there in the middle of the front yard was mother's prized rose bush. It swayed in the breeze as if nothing had happened. Seeing it made me realize how lucky we were to be alive. We stood there in dismay, our arms locked around one another.

| 해석
우리가 마침내 태풍 피난처에서 빠져나왔을 때, 나는 내 두 눈을 믿을 수 없었다. 전에 헛간이 있던 곳에는 지금 약간의 건초더미만 있을 뿐이었다. 집으로 가는 길은 나뭇가지와 파편들로 흐트러져 있었다. 우리 집! 지붕 전체가 날아갔다. 북쪽 담장은 함몰되었고 집안이 훤히 들여다보였다. 아무것도 남아있지 않았다. 우리가 가진 대부분이 엄청난 진공 속으로 빨려 들어갔고, 온 시골 마을이 산산조각이 난 것을 보고 있자니, 눈물이 뺨을 타고 흘렀다. 서쪽 담장이 무너져 먼지가 일면서 우리는 커다란 굉음과 흐느낌을 들었다. 그러나 앞마당 한가운데에는 엄마의 소중한 장미 덤불이 여전히 자리하고 있었다. 이것들은 아무 일도 없었던 것처럼 바람에 흔들리고 있었다. 이것들을 보며 나는 우리가 살아있다는 사실이 얼마나 행운인지 느낄 수 있었다. 우리는 절망감에 빠져 거기에 서 있으면서 서로 얼싸안았다.

③ Process

[실전응용 1]

단계적 과정을 나타내는 시그널을 확인한다.

1.1) The first step in redesigning your closet is take everything out and sort through it. Anything you haven't worn in over a year should be given to charity. Check garments for wear and tear. Take care of anything that needs mending. If it is beyond repair, get rid of it. 2) The second step is to install a closet organizer. Choose one that will hold the different types of garments in your wardrobe. 3) The third step is to put items in the closet so that those you wear most often are easy to access. 4) The final step is to stay organized. Put garments back in their appropriate places so that you will be able to find them.

중심소재는 'closet' 이고 중심내용(controlling idea)은 '옷장 재정비' 이다.

설명과 논증이라 해서 반드시 지문에 주제문이 제시되는 것은 아니다.

중심소재: 옷장 → 옷장정리
옷장을 재정비하는 구체적 단계를 첫 번째 문장부터 제시하고 있다. 즉, **주제문을 이끌어 내야 하는 'implicit' 의 유형**이다.
1. 구체적 진술
1) 단계 1
2) 단계 2
3) 단계 3
4) 단계 4

| 해설
벽장을 잘 정리하는 방법을 체계적인 단계를 밟아 설명하고 있다. 주제: Steps to Redesign Your Closet

| 해석
옷장을 다시 배치하는 첫 번째 단계는 옷을 전부 꺼내어 분류하는 것이다. 당신이 일 년 내내 입지 않았던 모든 옷가지는 기부하는 것이 좋다. 낡아 헌 옷을 골라내라. 수선이 필요한 옷들은 잘 정리해두어라. 만일 수선이 어렵

다면, 버려라. 두 번째 단계는 옷장 칸막이를 설치하는 것이다. 옷장에 다양한 종류의 옷을 담을 수 있는 것을 골라라. 세 번째 단계는 당신이 가장 잘 입는 옷들을 찾기 쉽게 옷장 속에 넣어두는 것이다. 마지막 단계는 정리된 채로 잘 유지하는 것이다. 당신이 쉽게 찾을 수 있도록 옷가지를 원래 자리에 정리해라.

[실전응용 2]

1. Koreans have a long history of papermaking and have always used native good-quality paper. Korea's oldest paper, called Maji, was made from hemp. 1) Maji is produced using the following steps. ① First, small pieces of hemp are soaked in water for some time and then cut into tiny pieces. Next, these pieces are turned into a slippery pulp by using a grindstone. After that, it is steamed, cleansed with water, ground again and placed in a tank. This raw material is pressed onto a frame and sun-dried while being whitened. This method of papermaking was most popular during the Three Kingdoms period.

중심소재: 마지 → 마지 제작과정
1. 도입부
한국의 오랜역사와 양질의 마지
1) 주제문
마지의 제조과정(주제)
① 뒷받침 진술
마지 제조과정을 단계별로 상술하고 있다.

★ 중심소재를 확인한다.

★ 본문에서 구체적으로 전개될 중심내용(controlling idea)에 해당한다.

| 해석
한국 사람들은 오랜 제지의 역사를 가지고 있으며 항상 고유의 질이 좋은 종이를 사용해왔다. '마지'라고 불리는 한국의 가장 오래된 종이는 대마로 만들어졌다. 마지는 다음의 과정을 통해서 만들어진다. 첫째, 대마의 작은 조각들을 일정 시간 동안 물에 가라앉힌 후 잘게 조각내어 자른다. 다음, 이 조각들이 맷돌로 갈려 미끈한 펄프로 만들어진다. 그 후에, 김을 쐬고 물로 씻어내 다시 갈아서 큰 통에 담아 둔다. 이 원료를 틀에 눌러 붙여 표백하는 동안 일광 건조한다. 이러한 제지술은 삼국시대 때 가장 유행하였다.

13 글의 종류

1. 설명

[실전응용 1]

도입부
- 주제문 = 의문문
- 답변 = 요지
- 뒷받침 진술

1. How can you create closeness when the two of you are hundreds of miles apart? How can you make the person you are talking to on the phone feel special when you cannot pat their back or give them a little hug? 1) <u>The answer is simple. Just use your caller' name far more often than you would in person</u>. ① In fact, shower your conversations with his or her name. Saying a person's name too often in face-to-face conversation sounds manipulative. **However**, <u>on the phone the effect is dramatically different</u>. If you heard someone say your name, even if you were being pushed around in a big noisy crowd, you would pay attention and listen.

중심소재: 전화상 친밀감
의문문으로 시작하는 글이다.

| 의 문 문: 주제 |
| 답　　변: 요지 |

1. 도입부 = 주제
전화상에서 친밀감을 형성하는 방법?
1) 답변(요지)
직접 마주칠 때보다 상대방의 이름을 더욱 자주 불러라!
① 뒷받침 진술
'however' 이후 글쓴이의 주장을 뒷받침하는 내용이 등장한다.

| 해석
당신들 두 명이 수백 마일 떨어져 있다면, 어떻게 친밀감을 만들어 낼 수 있을까? 당신이 그들의 등을 토닥이거나 보듬어 줄 수 없을 때, 어떻게 당신이 통화하고 있는 사람이 특별하다고 느끼게 할 수 있을까? 대답은 간단하다. 직접 대면할 때보다 훨씬 더 자주 상대의 이름을 불러주어라. 실제로 당신의 대화 속에 그들의 이름을 퍼부어라. 직접 마주한 대화상에서 너무 자주 상대의 이름을 말하는 것은 인위적으로 들린다. 하지만 통화에서는 그 효과가 극적으로 다르게 나타난다. 만일 당신이 누군가가 당신의 이름을 말하는 것을 듣게 되면, 시끌벅적한 인파 속에서 치이고 있다고 해도, 집중해서 듣게 될 것이다.

[실전응용 2]

1. In the 1950s, agricultural scientists around the world started a campaign known as the green revolution. ① It was an attempt to increase available food sources worldwide. ② The green revolution helped avoid famine in Asia and increased crop yields in many different parts of the world. 1) **However**, the green revolution had its negative side, too. ① Fertilizers and pesticides are dangerous chemicals that cause cancer and pollute the environment. ② Also, the cost of the chemicals and the equipment to harvest more crops was far too expensive for an average peasant farmer. Consequently, owners of small farms received little benefit from the advances in agriculture. In some cases, farmers were forced off the land by larger agricultural businesses.

중심소재: 녹색혁명
1. 도입부
녹색혁명 목적(①)과 유용성(②)
1) 녹색혁명의 부정적 영향력
① 부정적 측면 1
② 부정적 측면 2

도입부 = 주제문 = A + B
A의 긍정적 측면

However
A의 부정적 측면

| 해설
'However'를 기준으로 글쓴이는 중립적 입장에서 녹색혁명에 대한 긍정적인 면과 부정적인 면을 다루고 있다.

| 해석
1950년대, 세계의 농업과학자들은 녹색혁명으로 알려진 운동을 시작했다. 이 운동은 세계에 이용 가능한 식품원료를 늘리려는 시도이다. 녹색혁명은 아시아 지역의 기근을 막아주고 세계 여러 지역의 작물 생산량을 늘리고 있다. 그러나 녹색혁명은 부정적인 측면 또한 가지고 있다. 비료와 살충제는 암을 유발하고 환경을 오염시키는 독성 화학물질이다. 또한, 화학물질과 농작물을 추수하기 위한 장비의 가격이 일반 농부에게 지나치게 비싸다. 결과적으로, 작은 농장의 소유자들은 농업 분야의 발전으로 말미암은 실익이 거의 없다. 어떤 경우에는, 농부들이 대규모의 농사업체 때문에 농토를 떠나기도 한다.

[실전응용 3]

1. **Unlike** the modern society, 1) the primitive society has less specialized knowledge to transmit, and since its way of life is enacted before the eyes of all, it has no need to create a separate institution of education such as the school. ① **Instead**, the child acquires the heritage of his culture by observing and imitating adults in such activities as rituals, hunts, festivals, cultivation, and harvesting. **As a result**, there is little or none of that alienation of young from old so marked in modern industrial societies. 2) A further reason for this alienation in modern societies is that in his conception of

중심소재: 원시/현대 사회
1. 도입부(중심소재 도출)
1) 원시사회의 특징
원인: 전수지식이 적고, 모든 사람 앞에서 삶의 방식이 실현됨
결과: 학교와 같은 독립된 교육기관이 필요없음.

① 요지(as a result)
아이들은 어른들의 행위를 직접보면서 문화전통을 습득하기에 현대사회와 달리 어른과 아이 사이에 소외가 발생하지 않음
2) 현대사회

★ 대조의 글 전개를 확인하고 두 대상의 특징을 대조할 때 한 대상의 속성을 통해 다른 대상의 반대속성을 예측하도록 한다.

*대조활용
Unlike A, B _____

A의 속성은 B의 속성을 바탕으로 상반된 내용임을 파악할 수 있다.

* 문제점-원인

현상-문제점
(현대사회)
|
원인
|
대안
(원시사회)

전반적으로 현대 사회의 문제점을 지적하면서 그 대안을 원시사회에서 찾고 있다.

reality the modern adult owes less to his direct experience and more to the experience of his culture than does primitive man. Clearly, his debt to culture will vary with the nature of his education. ② **Hence**, the contemporary child must travel much further than the offspring of primitive man to acquire the world view of his elders. He is, therefore, that much more removed from the adults of his society.

원인 제시 후 다시 요지 재언급 (②)

| 해설

본문은 "가까운 환경으로부터 학습하는 원시시대 아이와 달리 현대의 아이는 교육기관에서 학습을 하는데 이는 연장자로부터의 소외를 낳는다."는 내용을 근거와 함께 설명하는 글이다. 주제: Educational Alienation of Child from Adult Society.

| 해석

현대사회와는 다르게, 원시사회는 대물림할 전문화된 지식이 적고, 원시사회의 생활방식은 모든 사람의 눈앞에서 행해지기 때문에, 학교 같은 독립된 교육기관을 만들 필요가 없다. 대신에, 아이들은 제사나 사냥, 축제, 경작 그리고 추수와 같은 활동을 하는 어른들을 관찰하고 모방함으로써 그의 문화유산을 체득할 수 있다. 그 결과, 현대 산업사회에서는 매우 두드러진 어른들과 아이들 간의 소외가 거의 없거나 존재하지 않는다. 현대사회에서 이러한 소외의 다른 이유로 현실에 대한 개념에서 현대 어른은 원시의 어른보다 자신의 직접적인 경험에 덜 의존하며 문화적 경험에 더 많이 의존하고 있기 때문이다. 분명히, 문화에 대한 그의 의존은 교육의 성격에 따라 다양할 것이다. 그러므로 현대의 아이들은 어른들의 세계관을 체득하기 위해서 원시인의 자녀보다 훨씬 더 많이 여행해야만 한다. 그렇게 함으로써, 그는 그 사회의 어른들로부터 더욱 분리되는 것이다.

* 대조의 글전개

도입부 — 주제문 (+연결문)

뒷받침 전술 — 서유럽
↕ by contrast
미국

[실전응용 4]

1. Everywhere in the world, the issue of how to manage urban growth poses the highest stakes, complex policy decisions, and strongly heated conflicts in the public area. 1) <u>The contrast between Western Europe and America is particularly sharp.</u> ① ⓐ In Western Europe, steep gasoline taxes, investment policies favoring built-up areas over undeveloped greenfields, continuous investment in public transportation, and other policies have produced relatively compact cities. Cities in Western Europe tend to be economically healthy compared with their suburbs. ⓑ **By contrast**, in the United States, cheap gas, massive highway investment, policies that favor construction on the edges of cities, and heavy reliance on property taxes to fund public schools have encouraged much more car-reliant and spread-out urban areas, where eight in ten Americans now live.

중심소재: 도시성장관리

1. 도입부 = 주제문
도시성장 관리의 성격에 따라 공공분야에서 정책결정과 과열된 갈등등을 유발한다.

1) 연결문
이러한 특징은 서유럽과 미국 사이에 뚜렷한 차이점을 드러낸다.

① 뒷받침 진술
ⓐ 서유럽
by contrast
ⓑ 미국

| 해석

세계 모든 곳에서, 도시지역의 성장을 관리하는 문제는 공공분야에서 높은 위험 부담과 복잡한 정책 결정 그리고 격렬히 과열되는 갈등을 내포한다. 서유럽과 미국의 차이는 특히 더 명확하다. 서유럽에서는 유류세와, 비개발 녹지보다는 도시지역을 선호하는 투자 정책, 대중교통 분야의 지속적인 투자, 그리고 다른 정책들이 상대적으로 조밀한 도시를 만들게 되었다. 서유럽의 도시들은 교외지역과 비교했을 때 경제적으로 건실한 편이다. 대조적으로 미국에서는 값싼 휘발유, 대규모의 고속도로 투자, 도시 외곽 건설을 선호하는 정책, 그리고 공립학교를 지원하기 위한 과도한 재산세 의존 덕분에 훨씬 많이 차량을 이용하게 되고 도시 지역도 확장되었는데, 현재 미국인 10명 중 8명이 이곳에서 살고 있다.

[실전응용 5]

1. Most people around the world think family planning should be a personal choice. Ⓐ **In other words,** they think people should decide how many children to have without any advice or control by the government. 1) ① Some people feel this way because of religious reasons. ② Others object to having government or religious leaders involved in family planning and population control. They want the freedom to make their own personal decisions.

중심소재: Family Planning
1. 도입부
통념: 가족계획은 개인의 선택이다.
Ⓐ 부연재진술
1) 뒷받침 근거
① 종교적 이유
② 개인적 의사 결정의 자유

★중심소재는 'family planning'이다.

* Most people로 시작하는 글 경우 1.

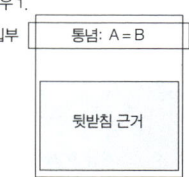

경우 2.

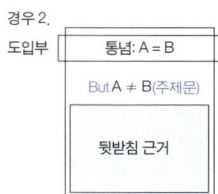

경우 3.

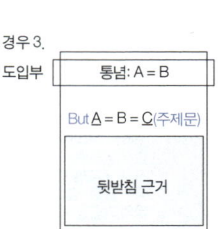

* 주로 2, 3이 활용됨

| 해설

설명의 글로 특정 대상에 대한 견해가 진술되고 있다. 글쓴이는 객관적 입장에서 정부 개입에 의한 가족계획을 반대하는 "most people"의 견해와 근거/이유를 제시하고 있다.

| 해석

세계의 대부분 사람들은 가족계획이 개인적인 선택이어야 한다고 생각한다. 다시 말해, 그들은 사람들이 정부에 의한 어떤 조언이나, 통제 없이 얼마나 많은 아이를 낳을 것인지를 결정해야만 한다고 생각한다. 어떤 사람들은 종교적인 이유로 이렇게 느낀다. 다른 사람들은 가족계획과 인구정책에 정부나 종교지도자가 관여하는 것에 반대한다. 그들은 그들 자신의 개인적인 결정을 내릴 수 있는 자유를 원한다.

2. 논증

[실전응용 1]

1. 1) No great optimism is justified when it comes to cutting medical costs overall. Medicine cannot be made cheap because of the costs of its technology, and by its nature it

중심소재: 의료비용
1. 도입부
1) 비용적 측면에서 의료비용의 특징 기술비용과 판매자 중심의 시장특징으

cannot be anything but a seller's market. ① **But** U. S. health care bills do not have to shoot up as rapidly as they are doing now. 2. The big question is <u>whether doctors, hospital administrators, insurers and employers can devise ways to bring the public the benefits of technology at a reasonable price</u>, without a federal whip being held over them.

로 가격이 쌀 수 없다
글쓴이가 인정하는 부분
① 현상 – 문제점 지적
현재 의료 보험비가 지나치게 높다.
2. 요지(대안촉구)
의료사업과 관계된 단체는 대중이 값 싼 방법으로 으로기술의 혜택을 누릴 수 있도록 해야 한다.

| 해석

전반적인 의료비용 삭감에 대한 어떠한 낙관적인 견해도 정당화되지 않고 있다. 약품은 기술비용 때문에 저가에 생산될 수 없으며, 본질적으로 판매자가 유리한 시장이 될 수밖에 없다. 그러나 미국의 건강보험료는 지금처럼 그렇게 급속도로 올라서는 안 된다. 커다란 의문은 의사들과 병원 경영진, 보험업자와 고용주들이 그들을 쥐고 있는 연방정부의 통제 없이 합리적인 가격에 과학기술의 혜택을 대중들에게 가져올 방법을 고안할 수 있는지의 여부이다.

[실전응용 2]

중심소재를 이끄는 시그★
널 확인.
1. of Ns, N
2. Among Ns, N

* 미괄식 구조 확인

도입부	문제점 지적
	뒷받침 근거 ①, ②, ③
	요지

* 주제와 요지 구별

도입부	주제= What is the text about?
	요지= The point is ...

주제란 무엇에 관한 글 인지를 묻는 말이고 요 지란 주제를 통해서 궁 극적으로 전달하려는 글의 의중을 말한다.

1. <u>Of</u> all the ways that automobiles damage the urban environment and lower the quality of life in big cities, few are as maddening and unnecessary as car alarms. 1) ① Alarms are more than just an annoyance; they are a costly public health problem and a constant irritation to urban civil life. ② The benefits, meanwhile, are nonexistent. Auto makers, alarm installers, insurers, police, and the biggest experts of all — car thieves — all agree that alarms do nothing to stop theft. ③ What's more, there are now a number of good, inexpensive car security devices available on the market. 2. <u>It's time for</u> us all <u>to</u> reconsider the seriousness of the problem and to do something about it.

중심소재: 자동차의 경보장치
1. 도입부
문제점 지적: 경보장치
1) 뒷받침 근거
① 짜증날 뿐 아니라 건강 문제 야기
② 도둑 예방에 전혀 효과가 없음
③ 자동차 경보장치 외 다른 보안장치 가 많음
2. 요지
문제의 심각성을 고려하여, 적극적 대 안의 필요성 강조.

| 해석

자동차가 도시환경에 악영향을 끼치고 대도시에서 삶의 질을 떨어뜨리는 모든 방식 중에서, 차량 경보기만큼 짜 증 나고 쓸데없는 것은 없다. 경보기는 단순한 짜증 그 이상이다. 경보기는 값비싼 공중 보건 문제이고 도시 시민 의 생활에 계속되는 염증이다. 반면 아무런 이득도 없다. 자동차 제조업자와 경보기 설치인, 보험업자, 경찰 그리 고 최고의 전문가인 차량 절도범들 모두가 경보기로는 차량 절도를 막는 데 아무런 소용이 없다는 데 동의한다. 더욱이, 현재 시장에서 구매할 수 있는 많은 값싸고 질 좋은 차량 경비 장치들이 있다. 이제 우리는 이 문제의 심 각성에 대해 재고해보고 조처해야 할 때이다.

[실전응용 3]

1. I believe that a person can find truth in life by focusing on one thing and mastering it. 1) For example, I know a carpenter who has devoted himself to his work for years. He has got great skills and can also tell much about life. Unfortunately, young people graduating from school quickly grow impatient with their unattractive, basic-level jobs. They wonder if their work will lead to anything meaningful, and they ask for different responsibilities—but they may never be satisfied. If our knowledge is broad but shallow, we really know nothing. ① Yet developing one skill in great depth can show truth in life.

★ 본문에 기술될 중심내용에 해당한다.
* 양괄식과 대조의 글전개 확인

| 도입부 | 주제문 |
| 뒷받침 진술 |
| 장인 ↕ 대조 젊은 사랑 |
| 주제문 |

중심소재: 삶의 참된 의미 찾는 방법
1. 도입부 = 주제문
한가지에 초점을 맞추고 그것에 달인이 되는 것이 인생의 참된 의미를 찾는 방법이다.
1) 뒷받침 진술
주제문에서 밝힌 중심내용을 구체적 예시를 통해 뒷받침하고 있다.(대조되는 두 대상 파악)
2. 주제문 재진술

| 해석
나는 인간이란 한 가지에 집중하여 달인이 됨으로써 인생의 진리를 찾을 수 있다고 믿는다. 예를 들면, 나는 오랜 세월 동안 자기 일에 모든 것을 바친 목수 한 분을 알고 있다. 그는 뛰어난 기술을 습득하였고 인생에 관하여 많은 것을 이야기할 수도 있다. 불행하게도, 대학을 졸업한 젊은 사람들은 재미없고 기초적인 수준의 일에는 금방 싫증을 느낀다. 그들은 자기의 일이 의미 있는 어떤 것이 될지 의심하고, 다른 책무를 요구한다. 그러나 그들은 절대 만족하지 않을지도 모른다. 우리의 지식의 폭은 넓지만 그 깊이가 얕다면, 아무것도 모르고 있는 것이나 마찬가지다. 하지만 한 가지 기술을 깊이 있게 발전시켜 나간다면, 인생의 진리를 발견할 수가 있다.

3. 묘사

[실전응용]

The traveller stepped into the hall of the old castle and looked around. It was a large room with stone walls. Several sleeping dogs lay against the wall on the left. In the middle of the room there was a fire. The smoke rose to a hole in the ceiling, but some of it remained in the room. The windows, high in the wall on the right, were not very large and the great room was rather dark.

중심소재: The old castle
장소의 이동에 따라 특정 대상을 묘사하고 있다. 본문에서는 다음과 같은 방향성이 드러난다.
1) 바깥쪽(성 밖) → 안쪽으로(성 안쪽)
2) 큰 공간 → 작은 공간(castle → hall)
3) 좌측 → 중앙 → 천장 → 우측

| 해설
특정 대상을 **묘사**하는 글로 시간/공간의 전개방식을 활용함을 알 수 있다.

| 해석

그 여행객은 오래된 성의 홀 안으로 들어서 주변을 둘러보았다. 석조 벽으로 된 커다란 방이 있었다. 잠든 몇 마리의 개가 왼쪽 벽면을 등지고 누워있었다. 방의 가운데에는 난로가 있었다. 연기는 천정의 배기구로 피어올랐지만, 일부 연기는 방안에 남아있었다. 오른쪽 벽 위쪽에 창문들은 그렇게 크지 않았고 가장 큰 방은 다소 어두웠다.

4. 서사

[실전응용 1]

* 서사는 일반적으로 두괄식의 구조를 지닌다.

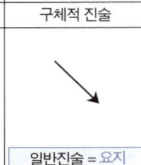

Old Hawk gestured up at the tall, old cottonwood. It was so large that a grown man could not put his arms around it. "This tree," he said, "has stood guard over our family all its life. Strength is what I feel each time I look at it. Yet, there have been moments when its great strength was also its weakness." "That's hard to believe," Jeremy said. 1. "It's the biggest tree for miles around." Old Hawk pointed at the chokecherry trees in a dry river bed not far away. "Look there," he said, "those chokecherry trees are small and weak in comparison to this cottonwood. 2. But when you were a child, they survived a storm without losing a branch. This old cottonwood, on the other hand, lost several branches. It stood up to the storm, but it could not bend with the wind the way the chokecherry trees could."

중심소재: Old Hank

본문은 주인공이 등장하고, 일종의 이야기가 전개되는 서사체이다. 서사체는 주인공을 중심으로 특정한 사건이 전개되는지 주목하고, 이 사건이 주인공에 미친 영향력(주로 교훈적인 내용)이 무엇인지를 파악하면서 주제를 이끌어 내는 경우가 많음을 기억한다.

본문은 'Old Hawk'라는 인물을 통해서 거대한 사시나무와 관련된 이야기를 전달하고 있다. 이 나무를 통해서 궁극적으로 Old Hawk가 드러내려는 사항이 바로 글쓴이가 전달하려는 요지가 된다.

1과 2에서 전달된 내용으로 보아, '강점이 오히려 폭풍 앞에서는 단점이 되어 버릴 수 있다'는 내용을 전달하고 있다.

| 해석

Old Hawk는 키가 키고, 오래된 미루나무를 가리켰다. 그 나무는 너무 커서 성인도 두 팔로 안을 수 없었다. "이 나무는" 그가 말했다, "평생 우리 가족을 지켜줬지. 내가 나무를 볼 때마다, 나는 기운을 느낄 수 있어. 그러나 이 엄청난 힘이 약점이 되는 때도 있지." "믿기 어렵겠지만" 제레미가 말했다. "이 나무는 수 마일 주변에서 가장 큰 나무지." Old Hawk가 멀지 않은 곳에 강바닥이 메말라 드러난 곳에 있는 벚나무를 가리켰다. "저길 봐." 그가 말했다, "저 벚나무들은 이 미루나무에 비해서 작고 약하지만, 네가 어릴 적에, 저 나무들은 가지 하나 꺾이지 않고 폭풍 속에 살아남았단다. 반면, 이 미루나무는 가지 몇 개가 부러지기도 했지. 이 나무는 폭풍에 용감히 맞서기는 했지만, 미루나무처럼 바람이 부는 대로 휘어질 수 없었단다."

[실전응용 2]

Dan Rice was perhaps the most famous clown of the 19th century. He started his circus career when he bought a half interest in a trained pig. Rice then worked briefly as a strongman before settling on clowning and horse tricks. In 1848, he campaigned for his friend, Zachary Taylor, for president. Rice frequently would invite him to ride on his circus bandwagon during parades. The 1860s were Rice's glory days, the decade when he toured the country for a then amazing salary of $1,000 a week, recognized by his trademark white beard. He got so popular that President Zachary Taylor made him an honorary colonel. And about twenty years after Taylor had died, Rice ran for the Republican nomination for president. Unfortunately, he didn't win.

중심소재: Dan Rice
광대이자 정치인이었던 Dan Rice에 관한 짤막한 일대기를 그리고 있다. 본문에서 이야기를 전개할 때 시간의 흐름에 따라 중요한 사건이 일어난 연도 또는 시대를 기록해 주고 있음을 발견할 수 있다.

| 해설

시간의 흐름에 따른 글 전개방식이다. 이런 글은 대부분 내용 일치에 해당하는 문제로 많이 출제된다. 각 연도에 구체적으로 어떤 일이 발생했는지에 주목하여 글을 정리하며 읽어야 내용 일치 문제를 풀 때, 시간을 줄일 수 있다.

| 해석

Dan Rice는 아마 19세기의 가장 유명한 광대라고 할 수 있다. 서커스를 직업으로 시작했을 때, 그는 훈련된 돼지의 소유권 절반을 샀다. 그 후 광대 짓과 말 조련을 하기 전, Rice는 차력사로 잠깐 일했다. 1848년, 그는 친구인 Zachary Taylor를 위해 대통령 선거운동을 했다. Rice는 행진하는 동안 그의 서커스 음악대에 올라타도록 종종 그를 초대했었다. 1860년대는 Rice의 전성기로 당시 주당 1,000달러라는 어마어마한 수익을 올리며 전국을 순회했던 시기다. 그가 인기가 높아지자 Zachary Taylor는 그를 명예대령으로 임명했다. 그리고 Taylor가 죽은 20년 뒤, Rice는 대통령 선거를 위한 공화당의 공천을 받기 위해 출마했으나, 당선되진 못했다.

[비교] 시간의 글 전개 방식을 활용한 설명의 글

The minute white or yellowish eggs laid by the queen hatch in two to six weeks and develop into white larvae. After feeding a few weeks to several months, larvae become pupae, commonly but incorrectly called ant eggs. In some species the pupae are naked, and in others they are covered with cocoons spun from a substance that they secrete at the end of the larval stage. After the pupal state, during which no

중심소재: 개미
번데기에서 성충으로 변하는 개미의 성장을 다루는 글로, 시간의 흐름에 따라 차례로 잘 기록이 되어 있다. 본문에서 시간의 흐름을 나타내는 표현에 주목한다.

주제: Development of Ants

food is taken, the adults appear. The immature ants are fed, cleaned, and attended by the adult workers. As in all insects with a complete metamorphosis, the ant has attained its full size when it leaves the pupa stage.

| 해석

여왕개미가 낳은 작고 희거나 노르스름한 알들은 2주에서 6주가 지나 부화해 흰 유충으로 자라난다. 몇 주에서 몇 달간 먹이를 먹은 후, 유충은 우리가 개미 알로 잘못 알고 있는 번데기가 된다. 어떤 종의 번데기는 벌거숭이이지만, 다른 종 중에서는 유충의 마지막 때 분비했던 물질로 실을 짜 만든 고치로 덮여 있다. 어떤 영양분도 섭취하지 않는 번데기 단계 이후에, 성충이 탄생한다. 다 자란 개미들이 어린 개미들을 먹이고, 씻기며 돌본다. 완벽한 형태를 갖춘 여타 모든 곤충들처럼, 개미는 번데기 상태를 벗어나야 완전한 크기를 갖게 된다.

14 글의 유형

1. 통념 비판 (Myth-breaking)

[실전응용 1]

1. When people think of skyscrapers, **they think** of New York, a city with many high-rise buildings. 1) There is no other city like New York, and this is because of its great buildings that reach up into the sky. 1) **It comes as a surprise** then to learn that Chicago, not New York, is the home of the skyscraper. ① The first high-rise building was built in Chicago in 1884 and it was nine stories high. This is not tall compared with today's buildings, but it was the first building over six stories. There were no tall buildings before that because the needed technology didn't exist.

중심소재: 고층빌딩
1. 도입부
통념: 고층건물의 역사는 뉴욕이다.
Ⓐ 근거
고층건물이 몰려있는 곳이기 때문
1) 주제문
시카고가 고층건물의 본고장이다.
① 뒷받침 근거
역사적 사실을 바탕으로 뒷받침 진술을 제시하고 있다.

★ 중심소재는 skyscraper이다.

★ 통념으로 시작하는 글임을 파악할 수 있다.

도입부	통념: A = B
	But 주제문 (A ≠ B)
	뒷받침 진술

| 해설
'일반통념(잘못된 정보) – However – 바른 정보'의 패턴을 따르고 있다.

| 해석
사람들이 마천루를 떠올릴 때, 그들은 많은 우뚝 솟은 건물의 뉴욕을 생각한다. 뉴욕과 같은 도시는 어디에도 없고, 이는 하늘로 솟아오른 거대한 건물들 때문이다. 그런데 마천루의 발생지가 뉴욕이 아니라 시카고라는 사실을 아는 것은 놀라움을 일으킨다. 최초의 고층건물은 1884년 시카고에 지어졌고, 이 건물은 9층짜리였다. 오늘날의 건물에 비해서 크지 않았지만, 6층을 넘는 최초의 건물이었다. 필요한 과학기술이 존재하지 않았기 때문에, 그 이전에는 높은 건물이 어디에도 없었다.

[실전응용 2]

일반통념으로 시작하는 글임을 파악할 수 있다.

중심소재는 anger이다.

1. **Many people believe** that they will be free of their anger if they express it, and that their tears will release their pain. 1) This belief derives from a nineteenth-century understanding of emotions, 1) <u>and it is no truer than the flat earth</u>. 1) It sees the brain as a steam kettle in which negative feelings build up pressure. But no psychologist has ever succeeded in proving the unburdening effects of the supposed safety valves of tears and anger. 2) **On the contrary**, over forty years ago, ① controlled studies showed that <u>fits of anger are more likely to intensify anger, and that tears can drive us still deeper into depression</u>. Our heads do not resemble steam kettles, and our brains involve a much more complicated system than can be accounted for by images taken from nineteenth-century technology.

중심소재: 화의 표출
1. 도입부
통념: 화를 표출하면 화가 누그러지고, 눈물을 흘리면 고통이 완화된다.
Ⓐ 뒷받침 근거
1) 주제문(+ ①)
화의 표출은 화를 더 악화시키고, 더 깊은 우울증에 빠지게 만든다.
① 뒷받침 근거
실험을 통한 근거 제시

실험/조사/연구에서 결과의 요지를 이끌며 결과의 시그널에는 show, suggest, indicate, reveal, find out 등이 있다.

| 해설
통념비판(Myth Breaking)의 유형으로 역접의 접속사 뒤 글쓴이의 주장, 그리고 실험을 통한 근거 확보의 깔끔한 구조를 보이고 있다. 본문의 경우 역접의 접속사 대신 문장이 이를 대신하고 있음을 확인한다.

| 해석
많은 사람이 만일 그들이 분노를 표현하게 되면, 분노로부터 자유로워질 것이고, 그들의 눈물이 고통을 누그러뜨릴 것으로 생각한다. 이러한 믿음은 19세기 감정의 이해에서 기인하였고, 이는 지구가 평평하다고 믿는 것만큼 사실이 아니다. 이러한 믿음은 두뇌를 부정적인 감정들이 압력을 높여가는 증기 주전자로 간주한다. 그러나 어떤 심리학자도 눈물과 분노의 안전밸브의 부담 경감 효과를 증명하는 데 성공하지는 못했다. 반대로, 40년이 넘도록 수행된 연구결과는 분노의 표출이 훨씬 더 화를 돋우고, 눈물은 우리를 훨씬 더 깊은 우울함으로 몰아간다는 사실을 보여준다. 우리의 두뇌는 증기 주전자를 닮지 않았고 19세기 과학기술로 측정할 수 있는 영상으로 계산될 수 있는 것보다 훨씬 더 복잡한 체계로 이루어진다.

통념 비판의 시그널을 확인한다.

주제문으로 글의 주제와 중심내용을 모두 파악할 수 있다.

* 예시의 성격
경우 1. 뒷받침 예시

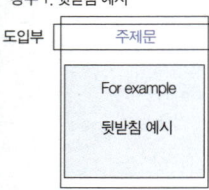

경우 2. 부연예시

[실전응용 3]

1. **Contrary to what many people think,** <u>hot deserts are not lifeless wastelands</u>. 1) We can find many living things that survive there in their own ways. ① <u>For example</u>, the acacia tree sends its roots down over one hundred feet to reach ground water. Many desert animals do not drink water at all. Instead, they get all their water from the foods they eat. Others can go without food and water for many days. A camel, <u>for instance</u>, can go without water for over two

중심소재: 사막
1. 도입부
통념: 사막은 생명체가 없다.
1) 주제문
사막에는 많은 생명체가 살고 있다.
① 뒷받침 예시

weeks, and when it must go without food, it depends on the fat stored in its body.

| 해석

많은 사람이 생각하는 것과 반대로, 열대 사막은 생명체가 없는 황무지가 아니다. 우리는 자신만의 방식으로 사막에서 살아가는 생명체를 발견할 수 있다. 예를 들면, 아카시아 나무는 지하수를 얻기 위해 백 피트 이상 뿌리를 뻗는다. 사막의 많은 동물은 물을 전혀 마시지 않는다. 대신, 그들은 먹는 음식에서 수분을 섭취한다. 다른 동물들도 물이나 음식 없이 며칠을 견딜 수 있다. 예를 들어, 낙타는 2주 이상 둘 없이 살 수 있으며, 식량 없이 지내야 할 때는 몸에 저장된 지방에 의존한다.

[실전응용 4]

1. **Contrary to popular assumption,** slavery was not usually based on racism, but on one of three other factors. 1) ① The first was debt. In some cultures, an individual who could not pay a debt could be enslaved by the creditor. ② The second was crime. Instead of being killed, a murderer or thief might be enslaved by the family of the victim as compensation for their loss. ③ The third was war and conquest. When one group of people conquered another, they often enslaved some of the vanquished.

중심소재: 노예제도
1. 도입부 = 주제문
노예제도는 주로 인종차별로만 일어나는 것이 아니다.

1) 뒷받침 진술
① 첫 번째 이유 – 빚
② 두 번째 이유 – 범죄
③ 세 번째 이유 – 전쟁과 정복

★ 중심소재는 'slavery' 다.

★ 본문에서 구체적으로 진술될 중심내용(controlling idea)이다.

★ 통념비판의 글임을 파악한다.

| 해석

일반적인 가정과 달리, 노예제도는 항상 인종주의에 기초한 것이 아니라 세 가지 다른 요소 중 하나에 기초한다. 첫 번째는 빚(채무)이다. 어떤 문화에서는, 빚을 갚을 수 없는 개인은 채권자에 의해 노예가 될 수 있었다. 두 번째는 범죄이다. 살인자 또는 도둑은 사형을 당하는 대신 피해자 가족에 의해 그들의 손실에 대한 보상으로 노예가 되기도 했다. 세 번째는 전쟁과 정복이다. 한 집단의 사람들이 다른 집단의 사람들을 정복하면, 그들은 정복당한 사람들의 일부를 노예로 삼았다.

| 참고

강조 용법은 글쓴이가 전달하려는 내용을 말 그대로 강조하기 위해 사용하는 구문이다.
1) It A that 강조 용법
2) Not A but B: B의 내용 강조하면서 A의 내용에 반대한다.
3) Not only A but also B: A의 내용에 추가로 강조하고자 하는 내용이 B에 전개된다. 이후 전개되는 내용은 B의 내용에 대한 뒷받침 문장이다.
4) A rather than B: B를 반대하고 A를 강조한다.

[실전응용 5]

주제는 '오락'이다. 중심 내용을 바탕으로 주제의 폭을 좁히도록 한다.

1. People worry that spending too much time playing video games isn't good for a child's health. 1) But some doctors have noticed that kids who bring their handheld game players to the hospital seem ① less worried about being there. These patients also seem to ② experience less pain when they are concentrating on the games. Ⓐ For example, at the Johns Hopkins Children's Center in Baltimore, young patients are finding hospital visits easier, thanks to a program. The program allows kids to play online sports, racing, and adventure games with each other. It brings together kids who feel they are isolated by their illnesses, and lets them know they are not alone.

중심소재: 미디어 게임
1. 도입부
통념: 비디오 게임은 아이의 건강에 좋지 않다.
1) 주제문(But 이후 주제문)
① 치료에 대한 근심이 덜 하고,
② 치료 중 고통을 덜 느낌
Ⓐ 부연예시
병원에서 비디오 게임을 하는 것의 좋은 영향을 구체적 예를 통해서 요지를 뒷받침하고 있다.

| 해석
사람들은 비디오게임을 하며 많은 시간을 보내는 것이 아이들의 건강에 좋지 않다고 걱정한다. 하지만 일부 의사들은 아이들이 병원에 자신들의 휴대용 게임기를 가져왔을 때 병원에 있는 것에 대해 덜 걱정하는 것을 발견하였다. 게임기를 가져온 환자들은 또한 게임에 집중할 때 고통을 덜 경험하는 것처럼 보인다. 예를 들면, 볼티모어의 존 홉킨스 아동병원에서는 특정 프로그램의 덕으로 어린 환자들이 병원 방문에 대해 부담을 덜 느끼는 것을 발견하였다. 이 프로그램은 어린 환자들이 온라인 스포츠, 경주 그리고 모험 게임 등을 병원에 있는 다른 어린 환자들과 함께할 수 있도록 해주고 있다. 이 프로그램은 질병으로 인해 고립된 아이들이 서로 만나게 해주어, 이들이 혼자가 아님을 알게 해준다.

[실전응용 6]

스트레스에 관한 글임을 첫 번째 문장에서 파악할 수 있다. 이후 글의 흐름에 따라가면서 중심내용을 파악하고, 이를 바탕으로 주제의 폭을 조절하도록 한다.

통념 비판의 글은 'However' 이후 글쓴이의 주장이 드러나고, 이후 뒷받침 진술이 이어지는 패턴임을 기억한다.

*1대다수의 법칙
일반인의 견해는 ①가 궁극적으로 비판하는 대상일 가능성이 높다.

1. People are often under stress. Ⓐ Some are taking exams, some are considering moving to another job, and others are worried about deadlines. 1) They believe these stressful situations give them gray hair. However, so far no scientific evidence proves a bad day turns your hair silver. 2) According to medical doctors, your hair turning gray runs in your family. ① In other words, if your father's hair becomes gray when he is quite young, you are highly likely to be in the same situation. Thus, when you get gray hair, it might be wise to dye your hair rather than to blame those stressful situations.

중심소재: Stress
1. 도입부
일상 속에서 접하는 스트레스
Ⓐ 부연예시
1) 일반인들의 견해(통념)
스트레스를 받으면 머리가 센다.
↕ However
2) 주제문
머리가 세는 것은 유전적 요소에 해당한다.
① 뒷받침 근거

| 해석

사람들은 종종 스트레스를 받는다. 어떤 이는 시험을 치르고, 어떤 이는 이직을 고려하며, 또 어떤 이는 마감 시간을 맞추느라 근심한다. 이들은 이런 긴장을 유발하는 상황 탓에 머리카락이 센다고 믿는다. 하지만 지금까지 기분이 좋지 않은 날로 인해 머리카락이 센다는 과학적인 증거는 전혀 없다. 의학박사에 따르면, 가족력 때문에 머리카락이 센다고 한다. 다시 말하자면, 만약 당신의 아버지가 꽤 젊었을 때 흰머리가 많다면 당신도 같은 상황에 부닥칠 가능성이 매우 높다는 말이다. 따라서 당신에게 흰머리가 생긴다면 긴장을 유발하는 상황들을 비난하는 것보다 머리를 염색하는 것이 더 현명하다.

2. 현상

[실전응용 1]

1. Habitat diversity refers to the variety of places where life exists. 1) Each habitat is the home of numerous species, most of which depend on that habitat. When it disappears, a vast number of species disappear as well. 2) More often, an entire habitat does not completely disappear but instead is reduced gradually until only small patches remain. 2. This has happened to old-growth forests and coastal wetlands in the United States and is now occurring in tropical forests throughout the world. 1) Elimination of all but small patches of habitat is especially damaging because it not only eliminates many local species but also threatens those species that depend on vast acreage for their survival.

중심소재: 서식지

1. 도입부 = 서식지의 다양성의 정의
서식지의 다양성의 정의
1) 서식지의 다양성의 중요성
2) 서식지의 다양성의 특징 – 일반적으로 서식지 전체가 없어지는 것이 아니라 부분적으로 사라짐(자연적 현상)
2. 주제문
미국뿐 아니라 전 세계적으로 서식지인 숲과 해안 습지대가 사라지고 있다.
1) 뒷받침 진술
서식지 파괴의 심각성을 통해 대책 마련의 시급성을 강조하고 있다.

★ 글 절반이 배경에 해당하는 내용이다.

★ 중심 소재는 'habitat diversity'이다.

도입부 | 도입부 = 배경
| 주제문 = 현상
| 뒷받침 진술

| 해설
서식지의 다양성이 무너지면서 생태계가 큰 위험에 빠졌음을 고발하는 글이다.

| 해석
서식지의 다양성은 생물이 존재하는 장소의 다양성을 의미한다. 각각의 서식지는 많은 종의 거주지이며, 대부분은 서식지에 의존해 살아간다. 서식지가 사라지게 되면, 많은 수의 생물 종 또한 사라진다. 대개, 하나의 서식지 전체가 완전히 사라지는 않지만, 대신에 점차적으로 줄어들어 결국 작은 부분만이 남게 된다. 이것은 미국의 오랜 기간 성장해온 산림과 연안 습지대에서 발생하고 있으며 세계 전역의 결대우림에서도 발생하고 있다. 작은 일부 지역을 제외한 습지대의 파괴는 토종 생물체를 없앨 뿐만 아니라 생존을 위해 넓은 서식지에 의존하는 많은 종도 위협하기 때문에 특히 더 위험하다.

[실전응용 2]

도입부 — 주제문 = 현상 + 원인
뒷받침 진술

1. Since the end of World War II, industrialization has been increasing very fast throughout the world. 1) This is causing family life to change faster too. ① Societies are losing their extended families. More married couples want their own homes where they can live with their children. The West has had nuclear families instead of extended families at least since the Industrial Revolution started in England around 1760, when people changed from making things by hand to making them in factories.

중심소재: 인터넷 가족구조
1. 도입부 = 주제문
산업화의 가격화로 인해 가족 구조에 큰 변화가 일어나고 있다.

1) 뒷받침 진술
산업혁명으로 가내수공업에서 공장에서 대량으로 물건을 만드는 것으로 바뀌면서 '대가족 → 핵가족'으로 변화

| 해석
제2차 세계대전 종식 이후, 전 세계에 걸쳐 산업화가 급격히 진행되었다. 이것은 가족생활에도 변화를 낳았다. 사회는 대가족을 잃어갔다. 더 많은 혼인 부부들은 그들이 자녀와 함께 살 수 있는 그들만의 집을 원한다. 서구사회는 적어도, 사람들이 손으로 물건을 제작하는 것에서부터 공장에서 상품을 생산하게 된 1760년 영국에서 산업혁명이 일어난 이후에, 대가족 대신 핵가족을 이루게 되었다.

[실전응용 3]

요지를 이끄는 시그널을 확인한다.★

1. Most of us buy our food from supermarkets. In fact, many of us don't even get as far as the supermarket but make our choices at the click of a mouse. 1) We have abandoned our relationship with the food we eat and with the people who produce our food. Is it any wonder that our children don't know where food comes from? Is it any wonder that we're tired, overweight, irritable, and low? 2. It is important to be mindful about every single aspect of purchasing food. Try not to race through your shopping. 1) In my hometown, nobody would buy a melon without feeling it and smelling it; and nobody would dream of buying a chicken without knowing which farm it came from and what it ate.

중심소재: 식품 구매
1. 도입부 = 현상
인터넷을 통한 식품구매

1) 문제점 지적
생산자와 소비자 사이의 관계가 무너짐 → 자신이 먹는 음식에 대한 정보 무지 + tired, overweight, irritable, and low

2. 대안(요지)
음식을 구매할 때 서두르지 말고, 모든 측면을 고려해야 한다.

1) 뒷받침 진술
개인의 경험담을 통해 요지에 대한 뒷받침 진술을 제시하고 있다.

| 해석
우리는 대부분 슈퍼마켓에서 식품을 구매한다. 사실, 우리 중 다수는 슈퍼마켓에 가지도 않고, 마우스 클릭으로 선택한다. 우리는 우리가 먹는 음식과의 관계와 식품을 생산하는 사람들과의 관계를 소홀히 해왔다. 우리 아이들이 음식이 어디서 오는지 알지 못한다는 사실이 놀라울 게 있는가? 우리가 지쳐있고, 과체중에 쉽게 짜증 내며 위축되어 있다는 사실이 놀라울 게 있는가? 구매한 식품 각각의 성향에 대해 주의를 기울이는 것이 중요하다. 서둘러 쇼핑하지 마라. 내 고향에서는 어떤 누구도 멜론을 만지거나 향을 맡아보지도 않고는 구매하지 않으며, 어떤 누구도 어느 농가의 닭이며, 무엇을 먹이는지도 모른 채 닭을 사려는 생각조차 하지 않는다.

[실전응용 4]

1. 1) For many generations, scholars and artists tended to concentrate their energy on one particular subject. 1) For Shakespeare, that interest was literature. For Mozart, that interest was musical composition, and for Newton, physics. Visual artists were not expected to understand higher mathematics, nor were philosophers expected to study engineering. 2) **However**, with the development of the Internet and other sources of instantaneous information, many people strive to gain at least a working knowledge of many different subjects. ② So-called pancake people no longer concentrate their energies on one area of interest, but instead choose to spread themselves thinly over a large area. 1) **As a result**, a new generation of pancake people have essentially become the proverbial jacks of all trades, but masters of none.

중심소재: 지식추구의 방법
1. 도입부
1) 과거: 특정과목에 자신의 모든 열정을 쏟음
① 뒷받침 부연(예시)
2) 현재: 다양한 분야의 지식을 얻으려하는 Pancake 현상
② 문제점 지적
다방면에 관심을 두나 어느 한 분야도 정복하지 못함

★ 'However' 이후 글쓴이의 요지가 드러나는 대표적 지문이다. 인터넷과 같은 즉흥적 정보를 얻을 수 있는 소스 때문에 과거와 현재의 차이점이 발생하고 있다. 본문에서 과거와 달리 현재에 발생하는 새로운 현상과 그 문제점을 찾아야 한다.

* 과거와 현재의 대조

과거
⊕
↓
현재
⊖

* 현상-원인의 패턴

현상
↓
원인

| 해설

However를 기점으로 대조적 상황이 전개되고 있다. 본문은 과거와 달리 인터넷과 같은 소스 덕분에 다방면에 대한 지식 습득은 늘어나지만, 정작 어느 하나를 제대로 알지 못하는 현상을 비판하는 글이다. 'However' 이후 글쓴이가 궁극적으로 다루려는 내용이 등장한다.

| 해석

많은 세대 동안, 학자들과 예술가들은 특정 분야에 그들의 열정을 쏟아 부었다. 셰익스피어에게, 그러한 흥미는 문학이었다. 모차르트에게, 그러한 흥미는 작곡이었고 뉴턴에게는 물리학이었다. 시각 예술가들이 고등 수학을 이해할 것이라 기대하지 않았고, 철학자들이 공학을 연구할 것이라 기대하지도 않았다. 그러나 인터넷과 다른 즉각적인 정보의 발달로, 많은 사람이 다른 분야에서 적어도 실용적인 지식 정보를 얻으려 하고 있다. 이른바 팬케이크형 인간은 더는 하나의 관심 영역에만 열정을 쏟지 않으며, 대신에 전반적인 분야에 얇지만 폭넓은 관심을 둔다. 그 결과, 팬케이크형 인간의 새로운 세대는 근본적으로 속담 내용처럼 많은 재주를 지녔으나 제대로 하는 것이 아무것도 없는 사람이 되었다.

[실전응용 5]

1. The forbidding sands of the Sahara might **seem** an unusual place for farming. 1) **But** if you're farming silicon to make solar panels, the conditions in the Sahara are more or less optimal. At least, that's the thinking behind the Sahara Solar Breeder Project. ① The plan, a joint project proposed by Japanese and Algerian universities, would use the desert's

중심소재: 사하라 사막
the Sahara Solar Breeder Project
1. 도입부
겉보기 현상: 사하라 사막은 농경에 적합하지 않은 듯하다.
1) 주제문
사하라 사막을 실리콘을 이용한 태양 패널 생산에는 최적

★ 상태를 나타내는 동사는 '현상'의 시그널로 쓰인다. 현상을 나타내는 동사 이후 'But'이 나오면, 일반적으로 앞에서 진술된 내용과 반대되는 내용이 이어진다.

119

* seem/look의 일반적 글 전개 단락구조

도입부
겉보기 현상 A looks B
But / in reality
A ≠ B

뒷받침 진술

immense supplies of sunlight and sand to "breed" solar power plants and solar panel factories. The idea is to start with a small number of silicon manufacturing plants that will produce the silicon needed to manufacture solar panels. Once those panels are operating, they can be used to power the silicon plants, which in turn produce more silicon and solar panels. The universities envision breeding enough silicon and solar panels by 2050 to supply half the world's energy.

(=Sahara Solar Breeder Project)
① 프로젝트에 대한 구체적 진술

| 해설
주제는 'A Plan Turns Desert into Energy Farm' 이다.

| 해석
금단의 사하라 사막은 농업에는 적합하지 않은 지역처럼 보인다. 그러나 만일 당신이 태양 전지판을 만들기 위해 실리콘을 생산한다면, 사하라는 어느 정도 최적의 조건이다. 이는 적어도 Sahara Solar Breeder Project의 배경이 되는 생각이다. 일본과 알제리 대학이 제안한 합동 프로젝트인 이 계획은 사막 지방의 엄청난 태양 빛 공급과 모래를 태양력 발전소와 태양 전지판 공장을 "육성하는 데" 사용할 것이다. 이러한 생각은 태양 전지판을 제작하는 데 필요한 실리콘을 생산할 소수의 실리콘 제조공장으로부터 시작된다. 이러한 지판이 일단 작동하게 되면, 이것들은 실리콘 공장의 전력을 공급하는 데 사용될 수 있고, 차례로 더 많은 실리콘과 태양 전지판을 생산하게 된다. 이 대학들은 2050년까지 전 세계 에너지의 절반을 공급하기 위해 충분한 실리콘과 태양 전지판을 생산할 것으로 내다보고 있다.

3. 실험 · 연구 · 조사

실험이 등장하는 지문이다. 실험의 목적은 글의 주제, 실험의 결과는 글의 요지가 될 수 있다는 점을 기억한다. 일반적 단락구조는 다음과 같다.

도입부
실험의 결과(요지)

실험의 구체적 내용

실험의 결과를 나타내는 동사에는 'show, find out, reveal, indicate, observe' 등이 있다.

예시를 이끄는 'for example' 앞 문장이 주제문이다.

[실전응용 1]

1. <u>Recent studies have shown that the more lasting effects of hormones ultimately result in the activation of specific genes.</u> **For example**, when a steroid hormone enters a cell, it binds to a receptor in the cell's cytoplasm. The receptor becomes activated and enters the cell's nucleus, where it binds to specific sites in the deoxyribonucleic acid (DNA), the long molecules that contain individual genes. This activates some genes and inactivates others, altering the cell's activity. Hormones have also been shown to regulate ribonucleic acids (RNA) in protein synthesis.

중심소재: 호르몬

1. **도입부** = 주제문
첫 번째 문장 바로 뒤에 이어지는 뒷받침 진술을 이끄는 'For example' 로 보아 첫 번째 문장은 주제문일 가능성이 크다.
호르몬의 영향력으로 특정 유전자가 활동하게 된다.
(주제: 호르몬의 영향력)

1) **뒷받침 진술**
'For example' 구체적 예시를 통한 뒷받침 진술 → 호르몬이 어떤 방식으로 특정 유전자를 활동시키는지 자세히 기술하고 있다.

| 해설

도입부에서 'For example'이 나올 경우 대개 바로 앞 문장이 주제문일 가능성이 크다. 앞뒤 문맥을 확인하면서 일반진술과 구체적 진술을 구별한다.

| 해석

최근 실시한 연구는 호르몬의 더 오래 지속되는 영향력이 결국 특정 유전자의 활성화를 초래한다고 밝혔다. 예를 들어, 스테로이드 호르몬이 세포 속으로 침투했을 때, 이것은 세포질의 수용체와 결합한다. 수용체는 활성화되어 세포핵으로 침투해, 그곳에서 개인의 유전자를 포함한 긴 입자인 DNA 속 특정 장소와 결합하게 된다. 이것은 세포의 능력을 변화시켜 어떤 유전자는 활성화하게 하고, 어떤 것은 둔화시킨다. 호르몬은 또한 단백질 혼합물의 RNA를 통제하는 것으로 밝혀졌다.

[실전응용 2]

1. People avoid feedback because they hate being criticized. Ⓐ Psychologists have a lot of theories about why people are so sensitive to hearing about their own imperfections. One is that they associate feedback with the critical comments received in their younger years from parents and teachers. 1) Whatever the cause of our discomfort is, most of us have to train ourselves to seek feedback and listen carefully when we hear it. ① Without that training, the very threat of critical feedback often leads us to practice destructive, maladaptive behaviors that negatively affect not only our work but the overall health of our organizations.

중심소재: Feedback
Feedback에 대한 반응
1. 도입부
일반적 성향: 피드백을 기피한다.
Ⓐ 배경
1) 주제문
피드백을 구하고 주의 깊게 듣도록 노력해야 한다.
① 뒷받침 근거
이런 훈련을 하지 않을 때 발생하는 부정적인 영향력에 대한 부연이 이어진다 ← 다시 말해 이런 부정적인 영향력을 피하기 위해 앞에 언급한 글쓴이의 주장인 스스로 피드백을 받는 훈련과 경청의 중요성을 강조하는 내용으로 볼 수 있다.

| 해석

사람들은 비판받는 것을 싫어하기 때문에, 피드백을 꺼린다. 심리학자들은 사람들이 그들의 결점에 관한 이야기를 듣는 것에 예민하게 반응하는 이유에 대해 많은 이론을 내놓았다. 그 중 하나는 그들이 피드백을 어린 시절 부모님과 선생님들로부터 받았던 비판적인 논평과 관련짓기 때문이다. 우리가 불쾌한 이유가 무엇이든 간에, 우리 대부분은 피드백을 구하고, 이것을 들을 때 경청하기 위해서 스스로 훈련해야만 한다. 이러한 훈련 과정이 없다면, 비판적인 피드백이란 바로 그 위협이 우리가 우리의 일뿐만 아니라 우리가 속한 조직의 전반적인 건강에 부정적인 영향을 끼치도록 파괴적이고 부적응적 행동을 하도록 이끈다.

[실전응용 3]

1. Flea trainers have observed a predictable and strange habit of fleas while training them. 1) They trained fleas by putting them in a cardboard box with a top on it. The fleas will jump up and hit the top of the cardboard box over and

중심소재: 벼룩
1. 도입부 = 실험
벼룩 실험을 하다 발견한 'a predictable and strange habit of fleas'를 언급하고 있다. 이후 'habit'에 대한 구체적 진술이 이어진다.

★ 본문에서 구체적으로 다뤄질 'controlling idea'에 해당한다.

over again. As you watch them jump and hit the lid, something very interesting becomes obvious. The fleas continue to jump, but they are no longer jumping high enough to hit the top. When you take off the lid, the fleas continue to jump, but they will not jump out of the box. ① They won't jump out because they have conditioned themselves to jump just so high. 2. Many times, people do the same thing. 1) They restrict themselves and never reach their potential, failing to jump higher like the fleas.

| 해석

벼룩 트레이너들은 벼룩을 훈련하는 동안 벼룩의 예측 가능하고 희한한 습관을 발견했다. 그들은 뚜껑이 있는 종이 상자 안에 벼룩을 넣어 훈련시켰다. 벼룩은 뛰어올라 계속해서 종이 상자 뚜껑에 부딪힌다. 벼룩이 뛰어올라 뚜껑에 부딪힘에 따라 흥미로운 점이 눈에 띌 것이다. 벼룩은 계속해서 뛰어오르나, 뚜껑에 닿을 만큼 높이 뛰어오르지는 않는다. 뚜껑을 제거했을 때, 벼룩은 계속해서 뛰어오르지만, 상자 밖으로 빠져나오지 않는다. 벼룩은 스스로 그 높이에 길들어서, 빠져나오지 못한다. 여러 차례에 걸쳐, 사람도 이와 같은 행동을 보인다. 그들은 스스로 억제하며, 벼룩처럼 높이 뛰는 데 실패하여 그들의 잠재력에 결코 닿을 수 없게 되는 것이다.

[실전응용 4]

1. Most of us make at least three important decisions in our lives: where to live, what to do, and whom to do it with. We choose our towns, our jobs, and our spouses and friends. 1) Making these decisions is such a natural part of adulthood that it is easy to forget that we are among the first human beings to make them. ① For most of recorded history, people lived where they were born, did what their parents had done, and associated with those who were doing the same. Social and physical structures were the great dictators that determined how and where people would spend their lives. This left most folks with little to decide for themselves. **But** the industrial and technological revolutions changed all that, and the resulting explosion of personal liberty created an array of options, alternatives, and decisions that our ancestors never faced.

| 해설

본문 대조와 인과의 글 전개방식을 따르면서 '과거와 달리 산업과 기술혁명으로 인간에게 중요한 3가지 결정 즉, 장소, 직업, 함께 할 사람에 관한 결정을 인간 스스로 내리게 되었다' 는 내용을 전달하고 있다.

| 해석

우리 대부분은 삶에 있어서 어디에 살지, 무엇을 할지, 누구와 살지, 최소한 세 가지 중요한 결정을 한다. 우리는 우리의 마을과 직업, 그리고 배우자와 친구들을 선택한다. 이러한 선택을 하는 것은 성인기의 자연스러운 부분이기 때문에 우리가 그러한 결정을 하는 최초의 인간 중 한 명이라는 사실을 잊기 쉽다. 대부분의 역사 동안, 사람들은 그들이 태어난 곳에 살았고, 그들의 부모가 하던 일을 했으며, 같은 일을 하는 사람들과 어울렸다. 사회, 물리적인 구조는 사람들이 그들의 일생을 어떻게 그리고 어디서 보낼지를 결정하는 강력한 독재자였다. 이것은 대부분의 민중에게 자신을 위해 결정할 수 있는 여지를 남기지 않았다. 그러나 산업과 과학기술의 혁명은 모든 것을 바꾸어 놓았고, 그 결과 나타난 개인의 자유에 대한 열망은 우리 조상은 결코 마주할 수 없었던 일련의 선택과 대안, 그리고 결정들을 만들어냈다.

[실전응용 5]

1. There is evidence that the usual variety of high blood pressure is, in part, a familial disease. 1) Since families have similar genes as well as similar environment, familial diseases could be due to shared genetic influences, to shared environmental factors, or both. 2. For some years, 1) the role of one environmental factor commonly shared by families, namely dietary salt, has been studied at Brookhaven National Laboratory. ① The studies suggest that excessive ingestion of salt can lead to high blood pressure in men and animals. Some individuals and some rats, **however**, consume large amounts of salt without developing high blood pressure. 3. No matter how strictly all environmental factors were controlled in these experiments, some salt-fed animals never developed hypertension, whereas a few rapidly developed very severe hypertension followed by early death. 3. These marked variations were interpreted to result from differences in genetic makeup.

중심소재: High blood pressure
1. **도입부**
통념: 고혈압의 원인은 부분적으로 가족성 질병이다.
1) 근거
비슷한 환경 + 유전자
2. 실험을 통한 통념의 사실여부 확인
1) 실험의 내용(소금섭취)
① 환경적 요인에 대한 연구결과
however를 기점으로 소금 섭취가 고혈압에 미치는 요소가 일관성이 없음이 밝혀짐.
3. 요지(실험 결과의 의의)
고혈압은 유전적 요인이 강하다.

★ 중심소재는 '고혈압' 이다.

★ 일반적으로 'however' 이후 중요 내용이 전개된다.

★ 실험이 등장하는 지문에서 실험의 결과는 곧 글의 요지가 된다.

| 해석

고혈압의 일반적인 종류는 부분적으로 집안 내력의 유전병이라는 증거가 있다. 가족들은 비슷한 유전자뿐만 아니라 비슷한 환경 또한 가지고 있어, 유전병은 공유된 유전적 요소와 환경적 요소 때문일 수 있다. 몇 년 동안, 대개 가족에 의해 공유되는 어떤 환경적인 요인인 염분의 역할이 브룩헤이븐 국립 실험실에서 연구되었다. 연구결과는 과도한 염분의 섭취가 사람과 동물에게 고혈압을 유발하게 할 수 있다는 사실을 보여준다. 그러나 일부 실험 대상자들과 실험용 쥐는 많은 양의 염분을 섭취했음에도 고혈압이 생기지 않았다. 모든 환경적인 요소가 이 실험에서 엄격히 통제되었음에도 불구하고, 어떤 염분 섭취 동물들은 고혈압이 전혀 나타나지 않은 반면, 어떤

동물들에게는 조기 사망에 이르게 하는 극심한 고혈압이 발생했다. 이러한 현저한 차이는 유전자 구성의 차이에 따른 결과로 해석되었다.

[실전응용 6]

※ 본문에서 구체적으로 전개될 중심내용에 해당한다.

1. A team of researchers found out <u>the alarming low death rate of a small village of Roseto</u> and started to investigate it.

※ 조사를 통해 밝혀낸 사실을 통해 "현상" 제시를 제시하고 있다.

1) While investigating, they realized that the secret of Roseto wasn't diet or exercise or genes or location. ① They looked at how the Rosetans visited one another. They learned about the extended family clans that underlay the town's social structure. They saw how many homes had three generations living under one roof, and how much respect grandparents commanded. ② They noticed the particular belief in equality of the community, which discouraged the wealthy from boasting about their success and helped the unsuccessful obscure their failures.

※ 실험·연구·조사의 결과는 바로 요지에 해당한다.

2. <u>These findings suggested the Rosetans had created a closely connected and protective social structure.</u>

중심소재: Roseto 마을 → Roseto 마을의 낮은 사망율
1. 도입부 = 현상
로제토라는 한 마을의 사망율이 현저히 낮다.
1) 뒷받침 진술(이유)
① 이유 1 – 대가족 중심의 사회로 어른들이 존경받는 사회
② 이유 2 – 공동체 모두가 평등하다는 믿음으로 성공한 사람은 자신의 성공을 떠벌리지 않고, 실패한 사람은 공동체에서 보호해 준다.

2. 요지(조사의 결과)
로제토 마을이 장수마을인 이유는 바로 서로 밀접하게 연결되고, 보호하는 사회구조 때문이다.

| 해설
본문은 로제토의 장수비결은 사회구조와 관련이 큼을 설명함으로 "Social structure and Death Rate"로 잡을 수 있다.

| 해석
한 연구팀이 작은 마을인 로제토의 낮은 사망률에 놀랐고, 조사에 들어갔다. 연구가 진행되는 동안, 그들은 로제토의 비밀은 음식이나 운동, 유전자 혹은 지역적인 특성이 아닌 것을 알 수 있었다. 그들은 로제토 사람들이 서로 어떻게 방문하는지를 관찰했다. 그들은 마을의 사회적 구조에 밑바탕을 이루는 대가족에 대해 알 수 있었다. 연구원들은 많은 가정에서 한 지붕 아래 3대가 모여 살며, 조부모가 얼마나 많은 권위를 갖는지 알 수 있었다. 부자들이 그들의 성공에 자만하지 못하게 하며 성공하지 못한 사람들에게는 그들의 실패를 가려줄 수 있는, 공동체의 평등에 대한 특별한 믿음에 대해 알게 되었다. 이러한 발견은 로제토 사람들이 서로 밀접하게 관련되어 보호받을 수 있는 사회 구조를 형성해왔음을 보여주었다.

[실전응용 7]

※ 주제는 에릭 에릭슨의 '심리발달이론' 이다.

Erik Erikson, well-known for <u>his psycho-social development theory</u>, says that 1. <u>the first issue an infant faces right after birth is trust. He emphasizes that trust is the most important factor in the child's developing personality</u> and love, quality not quantity, is the key.

※ 구체적 부연을 이끄는 시그널 확인한다.

1) According to Erikson, basic trust involves having the courage to let go of the familiar and take a step toward the unknown. Studies suggest that when a

중심소재: 에릭 에릭슨의 심리사회 발달
1. 도입부 = 주제문
에릭 에릭슨의 심리사회 발달에서 생후 아이가 직면하는 가장 중요한 문제는 다름 아닌 '믿음(중심소재)'이라는 주장. → 에릭 에릭슨의 이론을 통해 유아 성격 형성에서 '신뢰의 중요성'을 이야기함.
1) 뒷받침 진술
아이의 성격 형성에서 왜 신뢰가 중요한지를 에릭슨의 말과 연구를 통해 밝히고 있다(인과).

healthy trust is formed from the start of life, it leads one to moral, honest, balanced conduct in relations with others.

| 해설

최상급 및 'emphasize'와 같은 강조동사가 쓰인 문장은 글쓴이가 전달하고자 하는 강조의 내용이 들어가 있기에, 주제문과 직간접적으로 연관된다.
* 연구에서 밝히는 사항 = 글쓴이의 요지/주장

| 해석

심리사회 발달이론으로 유명한 Erik Erikson은 출생 이후 아이가 처음 직면하는 문제는 신뢰라고 말한다. 그는 신뢰가 아이들의 인격 형성에 가장 중요한 요소이며, 사랑의 양이 아닌, 사랑의 질이 중요한 열쇠라고 강조한다. Erikson에 따르면, 기본적인 신뢰는 친숙한 것을 버리고 낯선 것으로 다가가는 용기 또한 포함한다. 많은 연구가 인생의 시작에서부터 건강한 신뢰가 형성되었을 때, 이러한 신뢰가 다른 사람과의 관계에서 사람을 도덕적이고 정직하며, 균형 잡힌 행동으로 이끈다는 사실을 보여준다.

[실전응용 8]

1. White people often avoid mentioning race because they fear even noticing skin color might somehow make them appear racist, **but** two new studies from psychologists at Tuffs and Harvard universities **show** that such "strategic color blindness" can backfire. 1) White participants studied a batch of photographs, then tried to deduce, as quickly as possible, which picture a black partner was holding by asking questions about each one in succession. Asking whether the person pictured was black or white would have sped up their performance, yet subjects—adults in one study and children as young as age 10 in the other—rarely mentioned race unless their partner did so first. Black observers who watched the recorded interactions perceived whites who avoided talking about race as more prejudiced than the intrepid few who acknowledged skin color. And blacks who watched silent video clips of the interactions even rated whites who avoided mentioning race as having more unfriendly nonverbal behavior.

중심소재: 인종차별 Strategic Color Blindness
1. 도입부 = 주제문
실험의 결과: 전략적으로 인종을 언급하지 않는 행위(Strategic Color Blindness)는 오히려 역효과가 있다.
1) 뒷받침 진술
실험을 통해 주제문에서 밝힌 중심내용을 뒷받침하고 있다.

★ 'but' 이후 글쓴이의 주장이 제시된다.

★ 요지를 드러내는 주제문으로 실험의 구체적 내용이 이어진다.

★ 실험의 결과를 이끄는 시그널 - show, indicate, suggest, find out, reveal

| 해설

백인들이 알고 있는 '현상'이 잘못된 것임을 증명하는 글이다. 'but' 이후 글쓴이의 주장이 나오고 이를 구체적 실험을 통해 뒷받침하고 있다.

| 해석

백인들은 피부색에 대한 인식만으로도 그들이 다소 인종주의자로 보일까 염려하여 종종 인종에 대해 언급하기를 거리끼지만, Tuffs 대학교와 Harvard 대학교의 심리학자들의 두 가지 연구는 그러한 "전략적인 인종인식회피"가 역으로 작용한다는 점을 보여준다. 백인 실험참가자들은 사진 한 묶음을 자세히 살펴본 후, 연달아 나오는 각각의 사진에 대하여 질문을 함으로써 어떤 사진을 흑인 상대방이 쥐고 있는지를 가능한 한 빨리 추론해야 했다. 사진에 찍힌 사람이 흑인인지 백인인지를 묻는 것이 그들의 실험을 수월하게 할 수 있으나, 한 실험에는 성인들, 그리고 다른 실험에는 10살짜리 아이들인 실험참여자들은 그들의 상대가 먼저 하지 않으면, 좀처럼 인종을 언급하지 않았다. 녹화된 실험참가자의 대화를 지켜본 흑인 관찰자는 인종에 대해서 말하기를 거리낀 백인들이 피부색을 인정한 용감한 몇몇보다 훨씬 더 편견에 사로잡혀있다고 느꼈다. 그리고 대화를 무성녹음 한 비디오 영상을 본 흑인들은 심지어 인종에 대해 언급하기를 거리낀 백인들을 더 불쾌한 비언어적 행위로 간주하기까지 했다.

[실전응용 9]

1. After an event, all one has are memories of it. 1) Because most waits expect a desired outcome, it is the memory of the outcome that dominates, not the intermediate components. Ⓐ If the overall outcome is pleasurable enough, any unpleasantness suffered along the way is minimized. ① Terence Mitchell and Leigh Thompson call this 'rosy retrospection.' Mitchell and his colleagues studied participants in a 12-day tour of Europe, students going home for Thanksgiving vacation and a three-week bicycle tour across California. In all of these cases, the results were similar. Before an event, people looked forward with positive anticipation. Afterward, they remembered fondly. During? Well, reality seldom lives up to expectations, so plenty of things go wrong. As memory takes over, however, the unpleasantness fades and the good parts remain, perhaps to intensify, and even get amplified beyond reality.

★ 실험을 통해 글의 요지를 전달하는 글이다. 실험의 명칭이 곧 글의 주제가 될 수 있다는 점을 기억한다.

중심소재: 기억 기억의 성향

1. **도입부**(중심소재 도출)
기억에 관한 글임을 파악할 수 있다.

1) **주제문**
대부분 사람은 바람직한 결과만을 기대하기에, 중간에 발생한 요소는 기억하지 못한다.

Ⓐ **부연**
마지막 결과가 좋으면, 그 과정에서 겪은 안 좋은 기억은 최소화된다.

① **뒷받침 진술**
실험을 통해 요지를 뒷받침하고 있다.

| 해석

어떤 사건이 일어난 후에, 사람이 가지는 전부는 그것에 대한 기억이다. 대부분의 기다림은 원하는 결과를 기대하므로, 영향력이 있는 것은 중간의 구성 요소가 아니라 결과에 대한 기억이다. 만약 전반적인 결과가 충분히 만족스럽다면, 중간에 겪었던 어떠한 불쾌함도 최소화된다. Terence Mitchell과 Leigh Thompson은 이것을 '장밋빛 회상'이라고 부른다. Mitchell과 그의 동료는 12일간의 유럽여행 참가자들과 추수감사절 휴가로 집에 가는 학생들, 그리고 캘리포니아를 가로지르는 3주간의 자전거 여행을 대상으로 연구했다. 이 모든 경우에서, 결과는 비슷했다. 사건이 일어나기 전에, 사람들은 긍정적인 기대로 미래를 바라보았다. 나중에, 그들은 애틋하게 기억을 했다. 도중에는? 음, 현실은 좀처럼 기대에 부응하지 않으며, 너무 많은 것들이 어긋난다. 그러나 기억이 자리 잡게 되면, 그 불쾌함은 사라지고 좋은 부분만 남으며, 그것은 아마도 더욱 심화하여, 심지어는 현실을 넘어 과장되기도 할 것이다.

[실전응용 10]

1. University students in several of my seminar classes sat in a circle and each student took turns telling the others his or her name. At the end of the round of introductions, the students were asked to write down the names of as many other students as they could remember. In almost every case, students wrote down the names of students that were seated far away from them. 2. However, surprisingly, they were not able to recall the names of students who were seated close to them. This effect was worst for the students who sat on either side of them. 1) What was the reason for such findings? ① The student who was next in line for an introduction was clearly on edge and after finishing his or her introduction, he or she was preoccupied with calming his or her nerves. The effect was clearly due to the social anxiety they experienced immediately before and after having to introduce themselves to the entire group.

실험이 등장하는 글이다.

* 실험의 목적: 글의 주제/제목
* 실험의 결과: 글의 요지(요지에서 주제/제목 도출)

1. **도입부** = 구체적 진술
실험의 구체적 내용
1) 결과
자신의 주변에 앉은 사람에 대한 기억밖에 없다.
① **뒷받침 근거(이유)**
자기소개하기 전과 후에는 긴장된 감정 탓에 주변에 관한 관심을 둘 여지가 없다. 즉, 실험을 통해서 밝히고자 하는 내용은 '긴장감이 기억력에 영향을 미친다.'이다.

* **주제문** = 결과 + 이유

* 실험을 통해 현상을 제시하는 유형

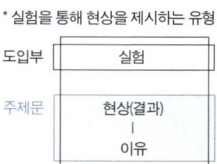

| 해설

실험이 등장하는 글은 반드시 다음 두 사항을 항상 머릿속에 염두에 두고 있어야 한다.
1) 실험의 목적이 무엇인가? (= 주제/제목)
2) 실험의 결과는 무엇인가? (= 요지 및 주제 도출)

| 해석

나의 몇몇 세미나 수업에서 대학생들은 둥글게 둘러앉았고, 각각의 학생들은 돌아가며 자신들의 이름을 말했다. 소개가 한 번 돌아간 후에 그 학생들은 그들이 기억할 수 있는 한 많은 다른 학생들의 이름을 적으라고 요청을 받았다. 거의 모든 경우에 학생들은 그들로부터 멀리 떨어져 앉은 학생들의 이름을 기억했다. 그러나 놀랍게도, 그들은 자신과 가까이에 앉은 학생들의 이름을 기억할 수가 없었다. 이런 결과는 그들의 양쪽에 앉은 학생들에게는 가장 심했다. 이러한 조사 결과가 나온 이유는 무엇인가? 소개할 다음 차례의 학생은 분명 초조했고, 소개를 끝낸 후에, 자신의 초조함을 가라앉히는 데 사로잡혀 있었다. 이러한 결과는 전체에게 자신을 소개하기 직전과 직후에 그들이 경험했던 사교적 불안감 때문이었다.

⟨PART 2⟩
유형별 문제
분석 및 **해설**(원문해석·정답포함

Test 1   주제를 고르는 문제 • 130
Test 2   요지를 고르는 문제 • 156
Test 3   제목을 고르는 문제 • 171
Test 4   내용일치·세부사항 확인 문제 • 193
Test 5   실전 종합문제 • 226

Test 1 주제를 고르는 문제

1. ①

중심소재를 설정하고, 중심내용을 바탕으로 글의 주제를 설정한다.

본문에서 구체적으로 진술될 중심내용이다.

*양괄식 구조확인

도입부 = 주제문
뒷받침 진술
요지

1. Selfishness is not identical with self-love but with its very opposite. 1) Selfishness is one kind of greediness. Like all greediness, it contains an insatiability, as a consequence of which there is never any real satisfaction. Greed is a bottomless pit which exhausts the person in an endless effort to satisfy the need without ever reaching satisfaction. Close observation shows that while the selfish person is always anxiously concerned with himself, he is never satisfied, is always restless, always driven by the fear of not getting enough, of missing something, of being deprived of something. He is filled with burning envy of anyone who might have more. 2. If we observe still closer, especially the unconscious dynamics, we find that this type of person is basically not fond of himself, but deeply dislikes himself.

중심소재: selfishness
1. 도입부 = 주제문
이기심은 자기 사랑이 아니라 그 반대 (자기파괴)이다.
1) 뒷받침 진술
2. 요지
주제문 재진술

2. 글의 말미에서 다시 한 번 글쓴이가 첫 번째 주제문에서 주장한 내용을 강조하면서 글을 마무리 짓고 있다.

| 해설

글의 도입부를 읽으면서, '이 글은 무엇(이기심)을 가지고, 무슨 내용(그것의 특성 및 정의)을 다루는 것인가?' 라는 질문을 던지면서 읽으면 자연스럽게 주제를 잡을 수 있다. 글의 중심소재인 'selfishness' 가 반영되지 않은 보기는 제거하도록 한다.

| 해석

이기심이란 자기애가 아닌 그 반대의 뜻과 같다. 이기심은 바로 일종의 탐욕이다. 모든 탐욕과 마찬가지로, 그것은 만족을 모른다는 의미이며, 그 결과로서, 어떠한 진정한 만족도 없다. 탐욕은 전혀 만족하지 못하고 욕구를 충족시키려고 끝없이 노력하다가 지치게 하는 끝(바닥) 없는 함정이다. 자세히 관찰하면, 이기적인 사람은 늘 자신에게 관심을 두고 노심초사하지만, 결코 만족하지 못하며, 항상 불안해하고, 항상 충분히 갖지 못했다거나 뭔가를 잃어버렸다는 또는 무엇인가를 빼앗겼다는 두려움에 사로잡혀 있음을 알 수 있다. 그는 늘 누군가가 자신보다 더 많이 가질지도 모른다는 불타는 질투심으로 가득 차 있다. 더 자세히 관찰하면, 특히 그 무의식의 역학을 살펴보면, 이런 사람은 근본적으로 자신을 사랑하는 것이 아니고, 자신을 심히 증오하고 있음을 알게 된다.

2. ②

| 해설

본문은 '산업혁명'을 다루는 내용이 아니다. 본문은 '기계화 시대'에 관한 내용을 다루면서 구체적으로 기계화 시대를 이끈 '도구와 기계'를 살펴보고 있다. 전체적으로 인과의 글 전개방법이 쓰이고 있음을 잡아낸다.

| 해석

산업혁명은 커다란 기계를 세상에 이끌어 냈다. 그것은 기계시대를 예고한 것이다. 기계란 무엇인가? 그것은 인간이 일하는 데 도움이 되는 큰 도구이다. 인간은 도구를 만드는 동물이라 불리어 왔으며, 태고 때부터 도구를 만들고, 그 도구들을 개량하려고 노력해 왔다. 인간이 자신보다 힘이 센 많은 다른 동물들을 위압하고 우위를 확립할 수 있었던 것은 도구 때문이었다. 도구는 인간의 손의 연장이며, 또는 제3의 손이라 부를 수도 있을 것이다. 기계는 도구의 연장이었다. 도구와 기계는 인간을 짐승보다 높은 위치로 끌어 올렸다. 그들은 인간 사회를 자연의 속박에서 해방시킨 것이다. 도구와 기계의 도움으로, 인간은 물건을 쉽게 만들 수 있음을 알게 됐다. 인간은 더 많은 것을 만들면서, 더 많은 여가를 가지게 되었다. 그리고 이것은 문화 예술과 사상과 과학의 진보로 이어졌다.

3. ②

1. In a famous series of studies, Calhoun(1962) placed rats in cages specifically designed to produce very high densities in certain areas. The animals in these cages exhibited a wide range of abnormal behavior. They fought violently, mated indiscriminately, trampled nests and the young who were in them, and failed to build adequate nests in the first place. Calhoun called this phenomenon of antisocial and disruptive behavior a behavioral sink. 1) Although other work had failed to find these effects on aggressiveness, there is little doubt that <u>under some circumstances high density does cause a breakdown in normal social behavior.</u>

2. In any case, humans are not rats. We have much more complex social systems, higher levels of congenital functioning, all sorts of rules and laws and customs with which to deal with the environment, and a flexible system of communication with other people. ① Generalizing from work on other animals to humans is always both difficult and questionable. This is particularly true when complicated social factors and interpersonal relations are involved. 3. Thus, although this work on other animals is suggestive, we must wait for more research on humans to discover how they respond to crowding.

첫 번째 단락
1. 도입부
실험의 내용: 밀집된 환경아래 쥐의 행동 관찰
1) 단락 주제문
밀집된 환경에선 사회행위의 붕괴 초래

두 번째 단락
2. 쥐의 사회적 행위를 인간에게 적용하기에는 무리가 있다(①)고 주장을 하면서, (쥐와는 현격한 차이를 보이는) 인간 사회의 복잡한 사회적 요소와 인간과의 관계를 언급하고 있다.

3. 글의 요지
밀집된 환경이 인간에게 어떤 영향을 미칠지에 관한 더 많은 연구가 필요하다.

| 해설

문단이 나뉘어 있을 때는 각 문단의 소주제를 파악하는 동시에 문단 간의 관계를 파악해야 한다. 첫 번째 문단은 '밀집된 환경 속에서 쥐가 취한 이상 행동'을 바탕으로 '특정 환경에서 인간의 사회적 행동에 이상이 생길 수 있다'는 결론을 낸 'a behavioral sink'를 소개하고 있다. 글쓴이는 두 번째 문단을 통해 앞에서 쥐를 통해 이끌어 낸 '밀집된 환경이 인간에 미치는 영향'에 관한 신빙성을 재검토하라고 요구하고 있다. 다시 말해, 인간 집단은 우선 근본적으로 쥐의 집단과 다르므로, 쥐의 실험을 인간에게 적용할 수 없다고 하면서, 마지막 문장에서 글쓴이는 궁극적으로 전달하려는 메시지를 드러낸다.

> 주제: 특정 상황(밀집된 상황)이 인간에 미치는 영향
> 주장: 쥐의 실험을 통해 이끌어낸 결론은 인간에게 그대로 적용할 수 없기에, 특정 상황이 인간에 미치는 영향에 대한 더 많은 연구가 필요하다.

| 해석

일련의 유명한 연구를 통해 Calhoun(1962)은 공간의 밀도를 매우 높이도록 특별히 고안된 우리 속에 쥐들을 집어넣었다. 우리 속에서 쥐들은 여러 가지 이상한 행동을 보였다. 그 쥐들은 격렬하게 싸웠고 무차별적으로 짝짓기했으며 둥지와 그 안에 있는 새끼들을 짓밟았다. 그리고 무엇보다 적절한 둥지를 만들지 못했다. Calhoun은 이러한 반사회적이고 파괴적인 행위의 현상을 "behavioral sink"라고 불렀다. 비록 다른 연구에서 공격성에 미치는 이러한 영향들을 알아내지는 못했지만, 어떤 상황에서 (인구의) 고밀도가 정상적인 사회적 행동의 붕괴를 야기한다는 사실에는 의문의 여지가 없었다.

하지만 인간은 쥐가 아니다. 우리는 더욱더 복잡한 사회 제도와 높은 수준의 선천적인 기능, 환경을 다루는 모든 종류의 규칙과 법률과 관습, 그리고 다른 사람과의 융통성 있는 의사소통 제도를 두고 있다. 다른 동물에 대한 연구를 인간들에게 일반화하는 것은 항상 어렵고 의문스러울 것이다. 복잡한 사회 요인과 개인 상호 간의 관계가 포함되었을 때 이것은 특히 맞는 말이다. 그러므로 비록 다른 동물에 대한 이 연구가 암시하는 바가 있기는 하지만 인간이 혼잡함에 대해 어떻게 반응하는가를 밝히기 위해서 우리는 인간에 대한 더 많은 연구가 진행되기를 기다려야 한다.

4. ②

시간의 흐름에 따라 단계 ★
적으로 화폐가 어떤 식으
로 발달했는지를 다루고
있다. 시그널을 확인하도
록 한다.

* 비교
"과거-현재"의 일반적 패턴-대조

과거 (⊕)
|
현재 (⊖)

1. In ancient times wealth was measured and exchanged tangibly, in things that could be touched: food, tools, and precious metals and stones. Then the barter system was replaced by coins, which still had real value since they were pieces of rare metal. Coins were followed by fiat money, paper notes that have value only because everyone agrees to accept them.

2. Today electronic monetary systems are gradually being introduced that will transform money into even less tangible forms, reducing it to arrays of "bits and bytes," of units of computerized information, whizzing between machines at the speed of light. Already, electronic fund transfer allows money to be instantly sent and received by different banks, companies, and countries through computers and telecommunications devices.

중심소재: 화폐

1. 'Barter System → Coins → Money and Paper notes'로 발달하는 과정을 아주 간략히 다루고 있다.

2. 오늘날 전자 금융제도의 도입을 설명하면서 그 특징을 자세히 부연하고 있다.

| 해설

글의 전개방법은 '시간적 순서'에 따라 특정 현상의 발달 과정을 다루면서 특히, 현대의 제도에 대한 구체적 부연이 뒤따르는 형태이다. 주의할 것은 많은 글이 위와 같은 구조를 취할 경우, 대조의 느낌이 드는 것이 일반적이기에 혼동해선 안 된다. 전체 글의 주제는 '화폐 교환의 역사'라고 볼 수 있는데, 가장 큰 비중을 두어 다루는 것은 전자 화폐 제도이다. 보기 ③의 The Development of Paper Currencies를 주제로 설정하면 종이 화폐만을 다루기 때문에 주제의 범위가 지나치게 협소해진다.

| 해석

옛날에 부(富)는 만져서 알 수 있는 것으로 측정되고 교환되었다. 즉, 식량, 연장, 귀금속이나 보석 같이 만져질 수 있는 것이었다. 그 후 물물 교환은 동전으로 대체되었는데, 동전은 귀금속 조각이었으므로 여전히 실질적인 가치를 가지고 있었다. 동전에 뒤이어 인가받은 화폐인 지폐가 뒤따랐는데, 그것은 모든 사람이 그것을 받겠다고 동의했을 때만 가치가 있었다.

오늘날 돈을 더욱더 만질 수 없는 형태로 바꾸어 놓은 전자 화폐 제도가 점차 도입되고 있다. 그것은 기계 사이에 빛의 속도로 윙윙거리는 (전달되는) 전산화된 정보의 단위로서 돈을 비트와 바이트의 배열로 변형시켜 놓았다. 이미 전자 화폐의 전송은 컴퓨터와 원격 통신 기계를 통해 돈을 여러 은행과 회사 그리고 국가 간에 즉시 보내고 받는 것을 가능하게 하고 있다.

5. ②

1. Imagine that we stand on any ordinary seaside pier, and watch the waves rolling in and striking against the iron columns of the pier. **Large waves** pay very little attention to the columns—they divide right and left and reunite after passing each column, much as a regiment of soldiers would if a tree stood in their road; it is almost as though the columns had not been there. **But the short waves** and ripples find the columns of the pier a much more formidable obstacle. When the short waves impinge on the columns—they are "scattered." The obstacle provided by the iron columns hardly affects the long waves at all but scatters the short ripples. 소주제: How the Iron Columns Affect Waves?   ★ 대조의 글 전개방식을 확인할 수 있다.

2. We have been watching a sort of working model of the way in which sunlight struggles through the earth's atmosphere. Between us on earth and outer space, the atmosphere interposes innumerable obstacles in the form of air, tiny droplets of water, and small particles of dust. These are represented by the columns of the pier. 소주제: Obstacles Inhibiting Sunlight in the Air   ★ 단락별 주제를 반드시 설정하도록 한다.

3. The waves of the sea represent the sunlight. ① We know that sunlight is a blend of lights of many colors—as we can prove for ourselves by passing it through a prism, or even through a jug of water, or as Nature demonstrates to us when she passes it through the raindrops of a summer shower and produces a rainbow. ② We also know that light consists of waves, and that the different colors of light are produced by waves of different lengths, red light by long waves and blue light by short waves. ③ The mixture of waves which constitutes sunlight has to struggle through the obstacles it meets in the atmosphere, just as the mixture of waves of the seaside has to struggle past the columns of the pier. And these obstacles treat the light waves much as the columns of the pier

treat the sea waves. The short waves which constitute blue light are scattered in all directions. Furthermore, the different constituents of sunlight are treated in different ways as they struggle through the earth's atmosphere. A wave of blue light may be scattered by a dust particle and turn out of its course. After a time a second dust particle again turns it out of its course, and so on, until it finally enters our eyes by a path as zigzag as that of a flash of lightning.

| 해설

여러 문단으로 나누어져 있다. 단락별 주제와 함께 각 단락 간의 관계를 파악한 후 주제를 잡아내야 한다.

1. 첫 번째 문단은 '부두의 철각 기둥에 부서지는 파도'를 다루는데, 구체적으로 '큰 파도'와 '작은 파도'를 대조하면서 철각 기둥에 부딪혔을 때 일어나는 상황을 묘사하고 있다. 결과적으로 '큰 파도는 부두의 철각 기둥에 영향을 받지 않지만, 작은 파도는 큰 영향을 받는다.'가 요지이다. 주제: How the Iron Columns Affect Waves?

2. 두 번째 문단의 주제는 무엇인가? 문단 2의 주제: 'Obstacles Inhibiting Sunlight in the Air'를 이야기하고 있다.

3. 문단 3에서는 첫 문단에서 언급한 '부두의 철각 기둥이 파도에 미치는 영향'의 내용을 비유로 하여 두 번째 문단에서 다룬 내용을 더욱 자세히 설명하고 있다. 우선 빛의 구성 요소에 관해 다루면서, 빛이 ① 색깔이 있으며, 추가로 ② 파장으로 구성된다는 사실을 설명하고 있다. 이 사실을 바탕으로 파도가 철각 기둥이란 장애물을 만나듯 빛도 대기의 여러 장애(문단 2에서 나옴)를 만난다(③)고 진술하고 있다. 이후 첫 번째 문단에서 기술한 것과 같이, 짧은 파장(blue light)을 가진 빛은 대기에 존재하는 장애물에 영향을 많이 받아 'scattered' 된다고 말하고 있다. 전체적으로 긴 지문이지만, 글쓴이는 '파도와 철각 기둥'과의 관계를 비유적으로 제시한 후 궁극적으로 '지구에 들어오는 태양 빛과 대기 속 저항'의 관계를 밝히려 한 것이다.

| 해석

우리가 어떤 평범한 해변의 부두에 서서 넘실거리는 파도가 부두의 철각 기둥에 부딪히는 것을 보고 있다고 상상해 보라. 큰 파도는 기둥에 거의 구애받지 않는다. 즉, 파도는 나무 한 그루가 연대 병력이 지나가는 길에 서 있을 때 연대 병력의 군인들이 그러하듯이 오른쪽 왼쪽으로 나누어지고, 기둥을 지나 다시 모인다. 이는 기둥들이 거기에 없는 것과 마찬가지이다. 그러나 낮은 파도와 잔물결에는 부두의 기둥들이 훨씬 더 만만찮은 걸림돌이 된다. 낮은 파도가 기둥에 부딪힐 때마다 파도는 산산이 흩어진다. 철각 기둥이라는 장애물은 높은 파도에는 거의 영향을 주지 못하지만 낮은 파도는 산산이 부서진다.

우리는 햇빛이 지구의 대기권을 헤치며 나아가는 모습을 보여 주는 일종의 실제 모델을 보아 왔다. 지상의 우리와 우주 사이에 대기는 공기, 작은 물방울, 작은 먼지 입자 형태로 수많은 장애물로 차있다. 이러한 것들은 부두의 기둥과 같은 것이다.

바다의 파도를 햇빛으로 생각해 보자. 우리는 햇빛이 많은 색깔의 빛으로 혼합되어 있다는 것을 안다. 우리는 스스로 햇빛을 프리즘 또는 물주전자에 통과시켜 보아도 이를 입증할 수 있으며, 혹은 자연이 햇빛을 여름날 소나기의 물방울 사이를 통과시켜 무지개를 만들어 낼 때에도 이러한 사실을 알 수 있다. 우리는 또한 빛이 파장으로 이루어져 있고, 각기 다른 색깔의 빛은 다른 길이의 파장에 의해, 즉 붉은 빛은 긴 파장에 의해 그리고 푸른빛은 짧은 파장에 의해 생성된다는 것을 알고 있다. 마치 해변의 뒤섞인 파도들이 부두의 기둥을 헤치며, 나아가야 하듯이 햇빛을 구성하고 있는 혼합된 파장들은 대기 중에서 만나는 장애물을 헤치며 나아가야 한다. 그리고 부두의 기둥들이 바다의 파도를 다루는 것과 같이 이러한 장애물들은 빛의 파장을 다룬다. 푸른빛을 구성하는 짧은 파장들은 사방으로 흩어지게 된다. 더욱이 햇빛을 구성하는 다른 구성 요소들은 지구의 대기를 뚫고 나아갈 때 각기 다른 방식으로 나타난다. 푸른빛의 파장은 먼지 입자에 의해 흩어져 진로를 벗어날 수 있다. 조금 지나면 두 번째 먼지 입자가 다시 푸른빛의 파장을 진로에서 벗어나게 하고, 이러한 일이 계속 반복되어 마침내 우리의 눈에는 그 파장이 번개로 지그재그형의 진로를 그리며 나타나게 된다.

6. ①

1. Stereotypes influence the way we process information. 1) We tend to remember favorable information about out-groups. This, in turn, affects the way we interpret incoming messages from members of in-groups and out-groups. We interpret incoming messages in a way that is consistent with our stereotypes, when we are not mindful. ① Sorority and fraternity members, for example, know how much money they raise for charity, but nonmembers may not recall this information even after reading it in the student newspaper because it is inconsistent with their stereotypes of fraternities and sororities.

중심소재: 정보처리
1. 도입부 = 주제문
고정관념이 정보처리에 미치는 영향을 다루는 글이다. 이후 이에 대한 구체적 진술이 이어진다.
1) 뒷받침 진술
① 예시 부연(for example)

도입부 = 주제문 / 뒷받침 진술 / 부연예시

| 해석
고정관념은 우리가 정보를 처리하는 방식에 영향을 미친다. 우리는 외집단에 대해 선호하는 정보만 기억하려는 경향이 있다. 이것 또한 우리가 내집단과 외집단의 구성원으로부터 얻는 메시지를 해석하는 방식에도 영향을 준다. 주의를 기울이지 않으면, 우리는 고정관념과 같은 방식으로 입력된 메시지를 해석한다. 예를 들어 여학생 클럽과 남학생 클럽 회원들은 그들이 자선기금으로 얼마를 모았는가를 알고 있지만, 비회원들은 학생 신문에서 그것을 읽었다고 하더라도 이 정보를 기억해내지 못할 것이다. 왜냐하면, 그것은 남학생 클럽과 여학생 클럽에 대한 고정관념과 일치하지 않기 때문이다.

7. ④

There are many different kinds of addictions. 1) ① The type most people think of immediately is alcoholism. Ⓐ People who cannot stop drinking until they become intoxicated have an addiction that is usually as much physical as psychological. ② Another example is an addiction to gambling. Ⓑ Some people are so drawn to the possibility of "striking it rich" that they gamble even their rent and food budget and become penniless in their search for fortune. ③ Another type of addictive behavior is overeating. Ⓒ To compensate for some psychological problems in their lives, some people eat much more than needed to satisfy their hunger. Even though they aren't in the least hungry, they can't resist reaching for one

중심소재: Addiction
1. 도입부 = 주제문
다양한 종류의 중독
1) 뒷받침 진술
① Alcoholism
Ⓐ 부연진술
② Gambling
Ⓑ 부연진술
③ Overeating
Ⓒ 부연진술

more slice of pizza or piece of cake. Psychiatrists often treat patients with addictive behaviors that are ruining their lives.

| 해설

위 오른쪽 설명과 같이, 본문은 뒷받침 문장으로 다양한 종류의 중독 행위를 기술하고 있으므로, 첫 번째 문장이 주제문에 해당한다. '일반진술 → 구체적 진술' 을 나열을 통해 전개하고 있다.

| 해석

중독에는 여러 종류가 있다. 대부분 사람들이 즉시 떠올리는 것은 알코올 중독이다. 취할 때까지 술 마시는 것을 멈출 수 없는 사람들은 보통 심리적인 것만큼 육체적인 중독성을 갖고 있다. 또 다른 예로, 도박 중독이 있다. 어떤 사람들은 '한방에 부자가 되는' 가능성에 너무 집착해서 그들의 집세와 생활비까지 도박에 걸고 행운을 추구하다 무일푼이 된다. 또 다른 중독 행동은 과식이다. 삶에서 어떤 심리적인 문제에 대하여 보상받기 위해 일부 사람들은 허기를 채우는 데 필요한 이상을 먹는다. 전혀 배가 고프지 않더라도 피자나 케이크를 한 조각 더 먹으려는 것에 저항할 수 없다. 정신 의학자들은 종종 자신의 인생을 파멸시키는 중독성의 태도를 지닌 환자들을 치료한다.

8. ②

주제 또는 요지를 설정할 ★ 때 중심소재인 'motion' 이 반영되어야 한다.

<u>Motion is the mode of existence of matter.</u> **Never** anywhere has there been matter **without** motion, **nor** can there be. Motion in cosmic space, mechanical motion of smaller masses on the various celestial bodies, the motion of molecules as heat or as electrical or magnetic currents, chemical decomposition and combination, organic life — at each given moment each individual atom of matter in the world is in one or other of these forms of motion, or in several forms at once. All rest, all equilibrium is only relative, and has meaning only in relation to one or other definite form of motion.

중심소재: 사물의 운동
1. 도입부 = 주제문
운동은 물질의 생존양식이다(= 운동하지 않는 물질은 없다(①)).
1) 뒷받침 진술
모든 물체는 어떠한 형태로든 운동하고 있음을 설명하고 있다.

| 해석

운동은 물질의 존재 양식이다. 어떠한 곳에서도 운동 없는 물질은 존재하지 않으며, 그럴 수도 없다. 우주공간에서의 운동, 다양한 천체 위의 작은 덩어리들의 기계적 운동, 열로서나, 전기 혹은 자기의 흐름으로서의 분자들의 운동, 화학적 분해 혹은 결합, 유기체의 생명 운동 등 각각 주어진 순간에 세상에 있는 물질의 원자 각각은 이러한 운동 형태 중 하나에 있거나 한 번에 여러 다른 형태의 운동 중에 있기도 하다. 모든 안정과 균형은 단지 상대적이며, 하나 혹은 다른 명확한 형태의 운동과 관련해서만 의미가 있다.

9. ③

통념비판의 글은 '통념 - ★ 'But' - 글쓴이의 주장 - 근거' 의 패턴을 따른다는 점을 기억한다.

1. <u>Many people think</u> that only children are lucky because of the material goods and attention they receive. 1) **But** consider that ① only children have no privacy. Parents

중심소재: 외동아들/ 딸
1. 도입부 = 통념
외동아이에 대한 일반인의 견해: 물질과 관심을 모두 받기에 <u>lucky</u>

always feel entitled to know everything that's going on in an only child's life. ② Another drawback of only children is they lack the advantages that children with brothers and sisters have. They can never blame a sibling for something that goes wrong, or ask for a privilege that an older brother or sister was given earlier. ③ In addition, only children miss the companionship of siblings. Not only can they be lonely, but they may have trouble making friends later in life because they never learned to get along with a brother or sister.

1) 뒷받침 근거
① No privacy
② 형제의 부재로 인해 얻을 수 있는 장점을 누릴 수 없다.
③ 형제간의 우애를 배우지 못함

★ 나열의 시그널을 확인한다.

| 해석

많은 사람은 외동 아이들이 그들이 받는 물질과 관심 때문에 운이 좋다고 생각한다. 그러나 외동 아이들은 사생활이 없다는 점을 고려해 보라. 부모들은 항상 유일한 자식의 생활에 일어나는 모든 일을 알 권리가 있다고 생각한다. 또 다른 외동 아이들의 단점은 그들이 형제자매가 있는 아이들이 보는 이득을 가질 수 없다는 것이다. 외동 아이들은 절대로 잘못된 어떤 일에 대해서 형제나 자매의 탓을 할 수 없으며, 형이나 언니에게 먼저 주어졌던 특권을 요구할 수도 없다. 게다가, 외동 아이는 동기 간의 우애를 갖지 못한다. 그들은 외로울 수 있을 뿐만 아니라, 삶에 있어서 나중에 친구를 사귀는 데 어려움을 겪을지도 모르는데, 이는 그들이 형제 혹은 자매들과 잘 지내는 법을 배우지 못했기 때문이다.

---

10. ④

1. There are basically two types of families: nuclear families and extended families. 1) ① The nuclear family usually consists of two parents and their children. The mother and father form the nucleus, or center, of the nuclear family. The children stay in the nuclear family until they grow up and marry. ② The extended family is very large. There are often many nuclear families in one extended family. An extended family includes children, parents, grandparents, uncles, aunts, and cousins. The members of an extended family are related by blood or by marriage. They are all related, so the members of an extended family are called relatives.

중심소재: 두 종류의 가족
1. 도입부 = 주제문
1) 뒷받침 문장
①, ②로 나눠 '소가족과 대가족'을 각각 소개하고 대조적 특징을 부연진술하고 있다.

★ 중심소재는 가족이며, 'two types of families'를 중심내용이자 주제로 설정할 수 있다.

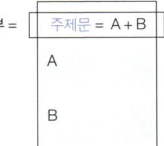

| 해설

전형적인 두괄식 글에 대조를 사용하여 글을 전개하고 있다. 주제는 핵가족과 대가족을 동등한 무게로 다루고 있으므로 주제는 이 둘의 차이점으로 잡아야 한다.

| 해석

가족에는 기본적으로 두 종류가 있는데, 핵가족과 대가족이 그것이다. 핵가족은 보통 두 명의 부모와 자녀로 구성된다. 어머니와 아버지는 핵가족의 핵, 즉 중심을 형성한다. 자녀는 성장해서 결혼할 때까지 핵가족 안에 머무른다. 대가족은 규모가 매우 크다. 한 대가족 안에는 종종 많은 핵가족이 존재한다. 대가족은 자녀, 부모들, 조부

모들, 삼촌, 고모, 그리고 사촌을 포함한다. 대가족의 구성원들은 혈연이나 혼인으로 맺어진다. 그들은 모두 관계되어(related) 있으며, 따라서 대가족의 구성원들은 친척(relatives)이라 불린다.

11. ①

도입부 = 예외적 현상
              ㅣ
           원인(대안)
              ㅣ
             배경

1. With 950 million people, India ranks second to China (1.2 billion) among the most populous countries. But since China launched a draconian birth control program in 1971, India has been closing the gap. Indians have reduced their own fertility but not nearly as much as the Chinese have. If current growth rates continue, India's population will pass China's around the year 2028 at about 1.7 billion. Should that happen, it won't be the fault of the enlightened women of Kerala, a state in southern India. 1) While India as a whole adds almost 20 million people a year, Kerala's population is virtually stable. The reason is no mystery: close to two-thirds of Kerala women practice birth control, compared with about 40% in the entire nation. ① The difference lies in the emphasis put on health programs. Ⓐ And an educational tradition and matrilineal customs in parts of Kerala help girls and boys get equally good schooling. ⓐ While one in three Indian women is literate, 90% of those in Kerala can read and write. Higher literacy rates foster family planning. "Unlike our parents, we know that we can do more for our children if we have fewer of them," says Laila Cherian. She has limited herself to three children—one below the national average of four. That kind of restraint will keep Kerala from putting added pressure on world food supplies.

중심소재: 인도의 인구 증가
→ Kerala의 출산 통계
1. 도입부 = 현상
인도의 인구 증가(중국의 인구와 비교하고 있지만 궁극적으로는 인구의 급격한 인구 증가의 문제점을 지적하고 있다.)
1) 예외적 현상
Kerala의 인구는 안정적이다.
① 원인(문제점으로 지적된 현상의 대안)
건강 교육 프로그램
Ⓐ 배경
교육적 전통과 모계중심의 관습으로 남자뿐아니라 여자도 교육을 받음
ⓐ 부연

| 해설
본문의 골격은 '현상 → 원인' 규명으로 이어지는 '인과'의 글쓰기 방법을 취하고 있다. 즉, 주제 또는 제목을 고르는 문제는 이러한 인과의 내용을 가장 잘 반영하는 것이 답이 된다.

| 해석
9억 5천만 명의 인구를 가진 인도는 12억 명의 중국에 이어 인구가 많은 나라 가운데 2위이다. 그러나 중국이 1971년에 엄격한 산아제한 정책을 시작한 이후로 인도는 그 격차를 좁히고 있다. 인도인들도 출산율을 감소시켜 왔지만, 중국인들이 해 왔던 것에는 미치지 못했다. 만일 현재의 성장률이 지속된다면 인도의 인구는 2028년경에는 17억 명이 되어 중국을 능가하게 될 것이다. 만일 그런 일이 일어난다 하더라도, 인도 남부에 있는 주(州)인 케랄라(Kerala)의 개화된 여성들 잘못은 아닐 것이다. 인도는 전국적으로 매년 2천만 명의 인구가 늘어나는 반면

에 케랄라의 인구는 사실상 안정적이다. 그 이유는 전혀 놀라울 것이 없다. 전국적으로는 약 40%인 것에 비해, 케랄라의 여성들은 2/3 가까이 피임을 하고 있다. 이러한 차이는 보건 프로그램에 중점을 둔 것에 있다. 또 케랄라 지방의 교육적인 전통과 모계중심주의 관습이 소년과 소녀를 동등하게 양질의 학교 교육을 받을 수 있게 해준다. 인도 여성의 1/3이 글을 읽고 쓸 수 있지만 케랄라 여성들은 90%가 글을 읽고 쓸 수 있다. 식자율의 증가는 가족계획을 가능하게 한다. '우리 부모와는 달리, 우리는 아이들을 조금 가지면 아이들에게 더 많은 것을 해줄 수 있다는 것을 알고 있다.' 라고 라일라 체리언은 말한다. 그녀는 아이들을 3명으로 제한했다. 이것은 전국 평균인 4명보다 1명이 적은 것이다. 이런 종류의 출산 억제는 케랄라가 세계 식량 공급에 부담을 가하는 것을 막아줄 것이다.

12. ③

1. A married man and woman, who take no greater excursions outside themselves than an occasional turning-on of the radio or an occasional watching together of a movie, are both likely to ① <u>feel frustrated and confined, and to express these obscurely entertained feelings by an everlasting wrangle</u>. 1) It is notorious that the business or professional man, who has confined his whole interest to his business or profession, is likely not to survive his retirement for very long. ② Ennui, expressing itself via heart or kidneys or arteries, drops him in his tracks. The physical organism has no reason to go on continuing. 2. **In contrast**, men devoted to <u>hobbies and similar interests</u> have a way of continuing into great old age, still lively and alert and inquisitive as chipmunks.

중심소재: 결혼한 남녀 생활

1. **도입부 = 문제점 지적**
딱히 취미가 없는 결혼한 부부는 ①과 같은 현상을 느낀다.

1) **부연 강조** – 특히 일에만 집착하는 남자는 은퇴를 잘 이겨내지 못하고 ②와 같은 현상을 겪게 된다.

2. **주제문(대안)**
취미나 비슷한 관심사를 가진 사람은 활기찬 노년을 보낼 수 있다. (취미의 중요성을 파악할 수 있는 대목이다.)

★ 'In contrast'를 기점으로 대조되는 두 대상이 드러난다. 두 대상 중 글쓴이가 제시하는 바람직한 상(象)을 통해서 요지를 이끌어 내도록 한다.

도입부 = 문제점 지적
↓
대안

| 해설

비록 글쓴이의 주장이 글 마지막에 드러나는 미괄식을 취하고 있지만, 글의 첫 번째 문장에서 설정한 상황을 통해 주제/요지를 어느 정도 이끌어 낼 수 있다. 즉, 다양한 오락거리(취미)의 부재로 발생하는 문제점을 지적하면서, 이후 궁극적으로 '다양한 취미'를 가지는 것의 중요성을 강조할 것임을 예측할 수 있다.

| 해석

가끔 라디오를 켜거나 영화를 보는 것 외에는 바깥으로 소풍을 가는 것조차 하지 않는 기혼 남녀는 좌절감을 느끼거나 갇혀있다는 느낌을 받기 쉬우며, 눈에 띄지 않게 간직하고 있는 이러한 감정들을 끊임없는 말다툼을 통해 표현할 것이다. 자신의 일이나 직업에만 온통 관심을 쏟은 사업가나 전문가는 은퇴할 때까지 장수하지 못하는 것으로 널리 알려졌다. 권태는 심장, 신장, 혹은 동맥을 통해 자연히 드러나며, 결국 사람을 인생의 행로에서 뒤처지게끔 한다. 신체 조직이 존속할만한 동기를 갖지 못하기 때문이다. 반면에 취미나 혹은 유사한 관심거리에 몰두하는 사람은 여전히 생기 있고 깨어 있으며, 또한 다람쥐처럼 호기심 많은 채, 나이를 아주 많이 먹을 때까지 존속할 길을 가지고 있는 셈이다.

13. ③

1. Television's variety becomes a narcotic, not a stimulus. Its serial, kaleidoscopic exposures force us to follow its lead. 1) The viewer is on a perpetual guided tour: 30 minutes at the museum, 30 at the cathedral, 30 for a drink, then back on the bus to the next attraction—except on television, typically, the spans allotted are on the order of minutes or seconds, and the chosen delights are more often car crashes and people killing on another. 2. In short, a lot of television usurps one of the most precious of all human gifts, the ability to focus your attention yourself, rather than just passively surrender it.

중심소재: TV의 다양성
1. 도입부 = 문제점 지적
TV의 다양성을 부정적으로 묘사(A narcotic)하면서 TV의 다양성으로 인해 시청자는 수동적인 자세를 취함을 지적하고 있다.
1) 뒷받침 근거
관광가이드에 수동적으로 이끌리는 관광객을 TV 시청자에 비유 – 짧은 시간에 여러 채널을 돌리면서, '충돌, 살인'에 관한 내용을 접하게 된다.
2. 요지
TV로 인해 시청자는 정작 중요한 자신을 돌보지 않게 된다.

| 해석
텔레비전의 다양성은 일종의 흥분제가 아니라 마취약이 된다. 그것을 연속적으로 또 계속 이리저리 틀며 시청하다 보면 우리는 텔레비전이 이끄는 대로 끌려가지 않을 수 없다. 시청자는 계속 (가이드에 의해) 끌려다니는 관광을 하게 된다. 즉 박물관에서 30분, 대성당에서 30분, 음료수를 마시는 데 30분을 보낸 후 그리고는 다시 버스에 올라 다음 관광 명소로 가는데, 텔레비전에서는 대체로 프로그램에 할당된 시간 [프로그램을 선택하여보는 시간]은 몇 분 또는 몇 초[재미가 없어 딴 데로 돌려버리면 몇 초]에 불과하며, 또 좋아서 선택하는 장면들은 자주 일어나는 자동차 충돌과 사람들끼리 서로 죽이는 장면들이라는 점을 제외하고는 관광과 같다. 한마디로 말해, 많은 텔레비전은 모든 인간에게 주어진 가장 소중한 재능 중의 하나인, 즉 단지 수동적으로 관심이 끌리는 대로 따라가기보다는 관심을 자기 자신에게 집중시킬 수 있는 능력을 빼앗아 버린다.

14. ③

1. The high-tech economy is on the ropes and the old economy is coming back with a vengeance. 1) For all the amazing, productivity-enhancing things the Internet can do, dirty industrial details like the price of oil and the quality of steel still matter. 1) All in all, **it's a good time to** be in a business where the workers need to scrub their hands at the end of a hard day. 1. The bursting of the high-tech bubble will have consequences for nearly everybody in 2001. 1) ① Consumers are feeling nervous again and corporations are finding that cash, once so plentiful in a booming stock market, is a scarcer commodity.　② Economic growth is slowing in many place in the world, with even some hints that a recession is on the way. ③ For the first time in a long while, there's no money to be made just by riding the market momentum. 2. In the economy of 2001, it will be survival of the smartest.

* 내용상 두문단으로 나눔
중심소재: 구식 경제, 첨단 기술 경제
첫번째 문단
1. 도입부 = 단락 주제문
첨단과학은 위기에 빠지고, 오히려 구식 경제가 되살아 날 것이다.
1) 뒷받침 근거
석유와 철강산업과 같은 구식경제가 여전히 중요하다.
2. 결론(요지)
구식 경제의 일을 다시 잡을 시기다.
두번째 문단
1. 단락 주제문
고첨단 산업의 거품이 터지면서 2001년은 잔혹한 결과를 맞이 할 것이다. (부정적 전망)
1) 뒷받침 근거
①, ②, ③의 세 가지 측면에서 부정적 전망에 대한 뒷받침 근거를 제시하고 있다.
2. 결론
2001년 경제는 똑똑한 자만 살아남는 적자생존이 될 것이다.

| 해설

위 본문 분석을 보면 알겠지만, '2001년도 비관적 경제예측'을 설명하고 있다.

| 해석

첨단기술경제는 곤경에 처했고 구식경제가 복수하러 되돌아오고 있다. 인터넷이 할 수 있는, 생산력을 늘리는 놀라운 일들에도 불구하고, 석유 가격이나 철강의 품질 같은 하찮은 세부사항은 여전히 중요하다. 대체로 힘든 하루일이 끝났을 때 노동자들이 손을 씻는 사업을 하기가 좋을 때이다. 첨단기술 거품의 폭발은 2001년의 거의 모든 사람에게 중요하게 될 것이다. 소비자들은 불안감을 느끼고 회사들은 일찍이 주식시장이 호황일 때 그렇게도 풍부하던 현금이 구하기 어려운 상품이 되고 있다는 것을 알아가고 있다. 경기후퇴가 진행 중이라는 징후와 함께 경제성장이 세계 곳곳에서 둔화하고 있다. 오랜만에 처음으로 시장의 힘에 의존해서 돈을 만들 수 없게 되었다. 2001년의 경제에서는, 가장 똑똑한 사람들만이 생존할 것이다.

15. ①

1. One of the most controversial methods of hazardous waste disposal is incineration at sea. Several firms have built sophisticated tanker ships designed to reduce millions of gallons of waste to harmless vapor by burning them. Yet tankers in the United States remain inactive while their owners await governmental approval to operate them. 1) ① Those who favor incineration over other techniques of waste disposal (such as burying them underground) argue that such tanker ships reduce the need to transport dangerous substances overland. They also point out that the disposal process is carried out in isolated waters, miles away from any population centers. ② Critics counter that inadequate burning of toxic wastes can produce substances even more deadly, such as certain forms of dioxin. And they say that spills at sea are extremely difficult to clean up, thus increasing the risk of poisoning marine life, upsetting the ecological balance and ultimately harming people.

중심소재: 바다 소각

1. **도입부**(중심소재 파악)
논란이 되고 있는 바다소각

1) **현상**
여러 회사가 소각할 용도의 탱크 배를 지어놓은 상태인데 정부 승인을 놓고 탱크 배가 비활성화인 **상태**

① **배경**
ⓐ 찬성- 뒷받침 근거
ⓑ 반대- 뒷받침 근거

도입부 = | 현상 |
배경 | ⓐ 찬성 근거 |
| ⓑ 반대 근거 |

* 글쓴이는 **중립적인 입장**에서 글을 쓰고 있음을 파악한다.

| 해설

본문의 초반부에 현재 비활성화 상태로 놓여있는 소각 탱크를 비롯한 논란에 휩싸인 '바다 소각'에 대한 전반적인 소개를 하고, 이후 찬반의 의견을 객관적 입장에서 설명하고 있다. 주제: '바다 소각에 대한 논쟁'으로 잡을 수 있다.

| 해석

해로운 쓰레기를 처리하는 방법 중 가장 격렬한 논쟁을 벌이고 있는 것 중 하나는 쓰레기를 바다에서 소각하는 것이다. 수백만 갤런의 쓰레기를 소각해서 무해 증기로 만들도록 설계된 정교한 유조선을 여러 기업이 건조하였다. 그러나 미국에 있는 쓰레기 소각용 유조선은 소유자들이 그것을 운영하는 것에 대해 정부의 승인을 기다리는

동안 사용되지 못하고 있다. (쓰레기를 지하에 묻어버리는 것과 같은) 다른 쓰레기 처리 기술보다는 소각하는 방법에 지지를 보내는 사람들은, 그러한 유조선이 위험한 물질을 육로로 운송할 필요를 줄이는 역할을 한다고 주장한다. 또한, 그들은 처리 과정이 인구 밀집지역에서 멀리 떨어진 고립된 바다에서 이행된다고 지적한다. 이 방법을 비판하는 사람들은, 유독성 쓰레기를 부적절하게 태움으로 인해서 다이옥신과 같은 훨씬 더 치명적인 물질을 만들어낼 수 있다면서 맞서고 있다. 또한, 그들은 바다에 엎질러진 물질을 정화하기란 매우 어렵고, 따라서 이것은 바다의 생명체를 독살할 위험성을 증가시키고, 생태 균형을 깨뜨리며, 결국 사람들에게 해를 입히게 된다고 말하고 있다.

16. ②

1. When we take the most distant prospect of life, what does it present to us but a chaos of unhappiness, a confused and tumultuous scene of labor and contest, disappointment and defeat? 1) If we view past ages in the reflection of history, what do they offer to our meditation but crimes and calamities? One year is distinguished by ① a famine, another by ② an earthquake; ③ kingdoms are made desolate, sometimes by ④ war and sometimes by pestilence; the peace of the world is interrupted at one time by ⑤ the caprices of a tyrant, at another by ⑥ the rage of the conqueror. ⑦ The memory is stored only with vicissitudes of evil; and ⑧ the happiness, such as it is, of one part of mankind, is found to arise commonly from sanguinary success, from victories which confer upon them the power not so much of improving life by any new enjoyment as of inflicting misery on others and gratifying their own pride by comparative greatness.

중심소재: 인생에 대한 관점
1. 도입부 = 주제문
인생의 종국은 'a chaos of unhappiness, a confused and tumultuous scene of labor and contest, disappointment and defeat'라고 아주 부정적인 관점을 드러내고 있다.

1) 뒷받침 진술
과거를 둘러봐도 ①, ②, ③, ④, ⑤, ⑥, ⑦, ⑧에 나열된 것과 같이 고통받는 부정적인 관점을 드러내고 있다.
내용을 정리하자면, '고통으로 점철된 인간의 역사와 동일한 미래의 인류'를 설명하고 있다.

주제: 고통받는 인류

| 해설
의문문은 일반적으로 '문제 제기' 형태로 제시되며, 이를 통해 주제를 이끌어 낼 수 있다. '수사의문문'의 경우는 글쓴이의 주장이 직접 드러나는 경우가 많다. 본문에선 의문문이 수사의문문의 형태로 쓰인 것인데, 만약 이후 전개되는 내용이 첫 번째 문장에서 드러난 관점과 같은 맥락에서 진행되면 '주제문'인 동시에 '주제'를 빼낼 수 있는 핵심적인 역할을 한다. 본문의 내용을 조금 살펴보자면, 과거와 미래에 드러난 인류는 언제나 고통 속에 갇힌 불행한 존재이며, 행복이 있다 하더라도 그것은 피비린내 나는 싸움에서 승리해서 얻은 것(⑧)일 뿐이라고 말하고 있다.

| 해석
우리가 삶의 먼 미래를 내다볼 때, 우리에게 불행의 혼돈, 일과 경쟁에서 혼란스럽고 시끄러운 장면, 실망과 패배 외에 무엇이 나타나는가? 만약 우리가 역사를 비추어 과거 시대를 바라볼 때, 범죄와 재앙 외에 우리의 상념에 무엇이 떠오르는가? 한 해는 기근으로, 다른 해는 지진으로 특정 지을 수 있다. 왕국은 때로는 전쟁으로, 때로는

전염병으로 황폐해진다. 세계의 평화는 한때 폭군의 변덕으로, 또 다른 때는 정복자의 분노로 중단된다. 단지 악의 교체로만 기억된다. 그리고 행복이란 인류의 한 부분으로서, 유혈이 낭자한 성공으로부터 흔히 일어나며, 어떤 새로운 기쁨으로 삶을 개선하기보다는 오히려 다른 사람들에게 불행을 주고, (남과의) 비교에 의한 위대함으로 그들 자신의 오만함을 만족하게 하며 권력을 부여하는 승리로부터 일어난다.

17. ②

1. It is a great nuisance that knowledge cannot be acquired without trouble. It can only be acquired by hard work. 1) It would be fine if we could swallow the powder of profitable information made palatable by the jam of fiction. But the truth is that, so made palatable, we can't be sure that the powder will be profitable. 2. I suggest to you that the knowledge the novelist imparts is biased and thus unreliable, and it is better not to know a thing at all than to know it in a distorted fashion. If readers wish to inform themselves of the pressing problems of the day, they will do better to read, not novels, but the books that specifically deal with them.

중심소재: 지식 → 지식습득 → 소설을 통한 지식습득

1. **도입부(전제)**
지식습득의 속성: 노력을 통해서만 가능
1) **뒷받침 진술**(비유)
소설이란 잼을 입맛에 맞게 제공하는 정보는 유익한지 확신할 수 없다.(노력을 통한 지식이 아니기에)
2. **요지(대안)**
소설의 지식은 외곡된 지식이기에 문제를 명확히 다루는 책을 읽는 것이 낫다.

* 주제: 믿을 수 있는 정보의 원천으로써 소설이 가지는 한계점

도입부 = 중심소재 파악
|
문제점 지적
|
대안(요지)

★ 요지를 이끄는 시그널을 확인한다.

| 해석
지식이 수고 없이 습득될 수 없다는 것은 아주 성가신 일이다. 지식은 오직 힘든 과정에 의해서만 습득될 수 있다. 만약 소설이라는 잼에 의해 입맛에 맞게 만들어진 유익한 정보라는 분말을 빨아들인다면 괜찮을 수도 있다. 그러나 사실이 그렇게 입맛에 맞게 만들어졌다면, 우리는 그 분말이 유익한 것인지 확신할 수 없다. 내가 · 당신들에게 제안하는 바는 소설가가 나누어주는 지식이 편향되어 신뢰할 수 없기에, 차라리 왜곡된 형태로 알기보다는 전혀 모르는 게 낫다는 점이다. 만약 독자들이 현대의 긴급한 문제들에 관해 알고 싶다면, 그들은 소설이 아니라 그 문제들을 명확하게 다루는 책을 읽는 것이 나을 것이다.

18. ①

1. It is often helpful when thinking about biological processes to consider some apparently similar yet better understood nonbiological process. 1) In the case of visual perception an obvious choice would be color photography. Since in many respects eyes resemble cameras, and percepts photographs, is it not reasonable to assume that perception is a sort of photographic process whereby samples of the external world become spontaneously and accurately reproduced somewhere inside our heads? 2. Unfortunately, the answer must be no. 1) ① The best that can be said of the

중심소재: 시각인식의 과정이해
1. **도입부(전제)**
비생물학적 과정의 이해를 바탕으로 생물학적 과정을 이해하는 것은 도움이 된다.
1) **일반적 견해**
첫번째 문장의 전제를 바탕으로 시각적 인식의 과정을 사진기술과 비교하여 이해할 수 있다.
① **뒷받침 근거**(일반적 견해에 대한 뒷받침 내용)
2. **주제문(요지)**
사진기술을 바탕으로 시각적 인식 과정을 이해할 수 없다.

143

photographic analogy is that it points up what perception is not. Beyond this it is superficial and misleading. ⓐ As an experiment, hungry, thirsty and satiated people are asked to equalize the brightness of pictures depicting food, water and other objects unrelated to hunger or thirst. When the intensities at which they set the pictures are measured it is found that hungry people see pictures relating to food as brighter than the rest (i.e. to equalize the pictures they make the food ones less intense), and thirsty people do likewise with 'drink' pictures. For the satiated group no differences are obtained between the different objects.

1) 뒷받침 근거(글의 요지에 대한 뒷받침 내용)
① 한계점과 문제점 지적
ⓐ 뒷받침 부연
실험을 통해 문제점 지적

| 해설

'일반통념 제시 – 'But(However)' 이후 일반통념을 반대하는 글쓴이의 주장 – 뒷받침 문장(구체적 예)'으로 이어지는 글이다. 이 글은 일반통념 제시 후 'But' 대신 'Unfortunately'를 쓰는 시점이 글의 중반에 나오다 보니 앞쪽에서 글쓴이의 의도를 정확히 파악하기 쉽지 않은 글이다. 주제는 일반인들이 생각하는 '시각적 인식과 사진술은 유사하다'라는 통념에 반대하는 글이므로 '인식과 사진술의 불일치'로 잡을 수 있다.

| 해석

생물학적 과정에 대해 생각할 때, 분명히 그와 유사하지만 더욱더 이해하기 쉬운 비 생물학적 과정을 고려하는 것이 종종 도움이 된다. 시각적 지각 작용은 분명히 컬러 사진술을 택하게 될 것이다. 여러 가지 점에서 눈은 카메라와 유사하고 또한 지각된 것은 사진과 유사하므로 지각이란 그것에 의해 외부세계의 샘플이 우리의 머릿속 어딘가에서 저절로 그리고 정확히 재생되는 일종의 사진 촬영 과정이라고 가정하는 것이 옳지 않을까? 불행히도, 답은 그렇지 않다는 것이다. 사진과의 비유에 대해 말할 수 있는 최선은 이것이 무엇이 지각이 아닌지를 설명해준다는 것뿐이다. 이것을 넘어서게 되면 그것(사진술과의 비교)은 피상적이고, 사실을 오도하는 것이 된다. 하나의 실험으로서, 배고픈 사람과 갈증 난 사람과 포만감에 찬 사람들로 하여금 음식과 물, 그리고 배고픔이나 갈증과는 관계없는 물체를 찍은 사진들의 밝기를 똑같게 만들어보도록 했다. 그들이 사진들에 설정한 조명도가 측정되었을 때, 배고픈 사람들은 음식에 관련된 사진들을 나머지 사진들보다 더 밝게 보는 것으로 드러났다(다시 말해 사진들의 밝기를 같게 하려고 그들은 음식을 찍은 사진을 덜 밝게 만든다). 그리고 갈증이 나는 사람들은 음료수의 사진에 대해 그와 마찬가지로 한다. 먹는 것에 싫증 난 사람들에게서는 서로 다른 물체 사이에 어떤 차이도 없었다.

19. ⑤

1. <u>The total impression made by any work of fiction **cannot** be rightly understood **without** a sympathetic perception of the artistic aims of the writer.</u> 1) Consciously or unconsciously, he has accepted certain facts, and rejected or suppressed other facts, in order to give unity to the particular aspect of human life which he is depicting. ① No

중심소재: 소설작품 → 소설작품의 이해
1. 도입부 = 주제문
소설 작품이 전달하는 온전한 인상은 그 작가의 예술적 목적과 동일한 인식을 할 때만 이해할 수 있다.
1) 뒷받침 근거
소설가는 자신의 묘사하는 인간사의 독특한 특성에 통일성을 주기 위해 특

novelist possesses the impartiality, the indifference, the infinite tolerance of Nature. Nature displays to us, with complete unconcern, the beautiful and the ugly, the pure and the impure, the precious and the trivial. But a writer must select the aspects of Nature and human nature that are demanded by the work in hand. He is forced to select, to combine, to create.

정 사실을 선별하기 때문이다.
① 부연진술
본문 끝까지 같은 맥락에서 부연 진술이 전개되고 있다.

| 해설
본문을 다시 정리하자면, 소설가는 인간사의 특정한 모습을 전달하기 위해 자신의 예술적 목적에 맞는 특정 사실을 받아들이는 동시에 다른 사실은 무시한다. 고로 독자는 소설을 읽을 때 특정 의도를 가진 작가의 의도(목적)와 공감(sympathetic perception)을 해야 한다. 이 글은 '소설을 어떻게 이해할 것인가?'에 대한 답변의 글로 볼 수 있다. 본문 전체를 철저히 분석하여 자신의 것으로 만든다.

| 해석
어떤 소설 작품에 의해서 받는 전체적인 인상은 그 작가의 예술적 목표를 공감하지 못하고서는 제대로 이해할 수 없다. 의식적으로든 또는 무의식적으로든, 작가는 어떤 사실을 받아들이고 또 어떤 사실은 거부하거나 억누르는데, 그것이 그가 묘사하고 있는 삶의 특정한 측면에 통일성을 주기 위해서이다. 그 어떤 소설가도 자연이 가진 공평함, 초연함, 무한한 관용을 소유할 수 없다. 자연은 아주 태연하게 아름다운 것과 추한 것, 순수한 것과 순수하지 못한 것, 귀한 것과 하찮은 것 등을 우리에게 보여준다. 그러나 작가는 그가 쓰고 있는 작품이 요구하는 자연과 인간 본성의 측면들을 선택해야 한다. 그는 선택하고, 결합하고, 창조해야만 하는 것이다.

20. ⑤

1.1) In industry, the laser has proven to be a very versatile tool, particularly for cutting and welding. 2) Lasers are now also used in high-speed printing and in the creation of three-dimensional images, called holograms. 3) Laser tracking and ranging systems have been developed, using light signals to measure distance rather than the radio signals of radar. 4) The use of the laser in biological and medical applications is also rapidly expanding, and the laser is already being used with great success in certain surgical procedures. 5) In the field of communications the laser, used in conjunction with fiber-optic networks, is capable of carrying much more information than conventional wires and is setting the stage for the "electronic superhighway" of the near future.

중심소재: 레이저
1. 구체적 진술
1) 산업 분야에서 커팅과 웰딩의 도구
2) 인쇄와 홀로그램
3) 거리 측정 도구
4) 의술
5) 정보통신
생략된 주제문: 사회의 다양한 분야에서 유용하게 활용되고 있는 레이저

주제: 다양한 사회에 활용되는 레이저의 유용성

★ 중심소재는 'laser'이며, 주제문을 도출해야 하는 'implicit' 유형이다.

주제문
뒷받침 문장
Ⓐ _____
Ⓑ _____
Ⓒ _____
Ⓓ _____
주제문

★ 나열의 시그널을 확인한다.

| 해설

첫 번째 문장 앞에 다음과 같은 주제문을 설정해 놓을 수 있다. '레이저는 사회에서 다양한 용도로 사용되고 있다.' 이후 뒷받침 문장으로 본문이 위치하면 두괄식의 깔끔한 글이 된다.

| 해석

산업 분야에서 레이저는 매우 다양한 용도로 쓰일 수 있는 도구임이 입증되었는데, 특히 절단과 용접 분야에서 그러했다. 레이저는 오늘날 고속 인쇄와 홀로그램이라고 불리는 3차원 영상의 창조에도 사용되고 있다. 레이저 추적과 조준 시스템도 개발되었는데, 이것은 거리를 측정하기 위해 레이더의 무선 신호가 아닌 광신호를 사용하고 있다. 생물학적, 의학적 용도에서의 레이저 사용도 급속히 늘어나서, 레이저는 이미 특정 수술 과정에서는 큰 성공을 거두고 있다. 통신 분야에서는 레이저가 광섬유통신망과 연계되어 이용됨으로써 기존의 통신선보다 더 많은 정보를 전달할 수 있으며, 가까운 미래의 전자 초고속 통신의 초석을 쌓고 있다.

21. ⑤

* 대안의 패턴

문제점
|
대안

* 실험의 패턴

실험의 결과
= 요지

본문의 경우 실험의 결과에 해당하는 사항이 대안이다.

1. Back in my early twenties I tried a diet that was limited to just a few healthy foods. Three weeks into it, I had nearly reached my goal of losing eight pounds. But my progress wasn't as sweet as I had expected. One night I abandoned the diet and gorged on every food I'd been missing. Over the next two weeks, I ate more than ever. No surprise that I quickly regained eight pounds, and put on two more. It sounds like the old diet-binge cycle that we've all heard about so often. My brazen act of indulgence was the direct effect of a boring, restrictive diet. "If you tell someone they cannot have, say, a piece of cheesecake, then that is the first thing they want to have," says Dr. Hubbert. "And then when they eat that piece of cheesecake, they say, 'Oh, now I've blown it, so I might as well blow it every day.'" 1) At Tufts University in Boston, researchers studied 71 healthy men and women aged 20 to 80 years who provided detailed reports of everything they ate for six months. People who routinely ate a variety of nutrient-dense foods such as vegetables, fruits, and whole grains tended to be lean. The researchers found that when people eat a variety of desirable foods, especially vegetables, they eat fewer nutrient-poor, calorie-dense foods such as cookies, candy, and chips. Overall, they consume fewer calories without consciously restricting their intake.

중심소재: Diet

1. **도입부**: 문제점지적

주인공의 구체적 경험을 토대로 "제한적 다이어트"의 부작용 언급

1) 대안(요지)

대안으로 구체적 실험을 통해 '영양가 높은 다양한 음식을 통한 다이어트'의 효율성을 강조하고 있다.

| 해설

'특정 다이어트의 문제점 지적 – 효율적 대안을 실험을 통해 증명하면서 제시' 한, '문제점 – 대안' 의 아주 단순한 글 전개 방법이지만 '대조' 를 이용하는 동시에 실험을 통한 객관성을 높이면서 자신의 주장을 효과적으로 드러내고 있다. 주제를 고르는 문제인데, 글쓴이의 주장인 '영양분이 높은 다양한 음식을 통한 다이어트' 를 주제로 잡을 수 있다.

| 해석

옛날에 20대 초반이었을 때, 나는 건강에 좋은 몇 가지 음식만 먹는 다이어트를 시도했었다. 시작한 지 3주 정도 후에 나는 8파운드를 감량하려는 목표에 거의 도달했다. 그러나 그 과정은 내가 예상했던 것만큼 즐겁지는 않았다. 어느 날 밤에 나는 다이어트를 포기하고 먹고 싶었던 모든 음식을 실컷 먹었다. 그 후 2주 동안 나는 그 어느 때보다 더 많이 먹었다. 당연히 나는 8파운드가 다시 쪘고 게다가 2파운드가 더 쪘다. 이는 우리가 너무 자주 들어온 '다이어트–과식' 주기처럼 들린다. 나의 제멋대로의 뻔뻔한 행동은 지루하면서 제한적인 다이어트의 직접적인 결과였다. "만약 당신이 어떤 사람에게, 이를테면, 치즈 케이크를 먹지 말라고 말하면, 그러면 그것을 가장 먼저 먹고 싶어 한다. 그리고 그들은 치즈 케이크를 먹을 때 이렇게 말한다. '아, 치즈 케이크를 먹어버렸네. 이왕 이렇게 된 거, 차라리 매일 먹는 것이 더 낫겠다.' 라고 허버트 박사는 말하고 있다. 보스턴의 터프츠 대학(Tufts University)에서 연구진들은 자신이 6개월간 먹은 모든 것에 대한 자세한 보고를 한 20세에서 80세에 이르는 71명의 건강한 남성과 여성을 연구했다. 일상적으로 채소, 과일, 전곡과 같은 다양한 영양가 높은 음식을 섭취했던 사람들이 마른 경향이 있었다. 연구진은 자신이 원하는 다양한 음식을, 특히, 채소를 사람들이 먹을 때 그들은 쿠키, 사탕, 과자와 같은 영양가 낮고 열량이 높은 음식을 덜 먹는다는 것을 발견했다. 전반적으로 그들은 의식적으로 자신들의 섭취를 제한하지 않으면서 열량을 더 적게 섭취한다.

22. ④

1. Psychologists find more inaction, conformity, passivity, and reliance on others in the elderly. Yet, desires for mastery and control are likely to remain strong. At the very least, old people are able to continue to make choices and exert control over daily routines. 1) <u>Work of some sort, which imparts a sense of being productive and useful, predicts living to an old age. Research findings suggest that feelings of control actually enhance mental and physical health and promote longevity.</u>

① In one series of studies, for instance, psychologists randomly divided nursing home residents from ages 65 to 90 into two groups. Adults in the first group heard a pep talk emphasizing the need to take greater responsibility in caring for themselves and improving the quality of their lives. Members of this high-responsibility group chose a living plant to tend, to symbolize their commitment. The residents in the low-responsibility group were told that the staff would

1. 도입부
노인들의 성향: 신체적 활동은 줄고, 수동적 삶의 태도를 보이나, 지배와 통제의 욕망은 강하다.

1) 주제문
통제감은 정신 육체 건강과 비례관계 (실험의 결과)

① 뒷받침 진술

2. 결론(요지)
주제문에서 밝힌 내용 재진술(실험의 결과)

serve them well. Each individual in this group also received a symbolic plant that the nurses would feed and water, just as the nurses planned to take care of them.

What was the result of this experiment? The members of the high responsibility group thrived. They showed significantly more signs of alertness, active participation, and positive feelings than did those in the low-responsibility group. 2. The differences lasted long. There was an even more remarkable finding: A sense of control appeared to prolong life, with more patients in the high responsibility group surviving than those in the other group by 15 percent eighteen months later.

| 해설

구체적 실험이 언급되는 글에서 주제는 실험 바로 앞에서 찾거나 실험을 통해 밝혀내려는 결과에서 이끌어 낼 수 있다. 위 지문은 첫 번째 문단에서 이미 주제와 요지를 밝히고 있으며, 이후 구체적 실험을 통해서도 다시 한 번 주제 및 요지를 밝히고 있다. 이 글은 '통제감이 노인에 미치는 영향, 즉 그 필요성'을 밝히는 글이다.

| 해석

　심리학자들은 노인들에게서 더 많은 게으름, 순종, 수동성, 다른 사람들에 대한 의존을 발견한다. 그러나 지배와 관리에 대한 욕망은 강하게 남아있는 것 같다. 적어도 노인들은 계속해서 선택을 하고 일상생활에 대해 관리를 할 수 있다. 생산적이고 유용하다는 느낌이 드는 어떤 종류의 일은 장수를 예측한다. 연구결과는 생활을 제대로 관리하고 있다는 느낌이 정신 건강과 육체 건강을 고취하고 장수를 촉진한다고 암시한다.

　예를 들면 일련의 연구들에서 심리학자들은 65세에서 90세에 이르는 요양원 거주자들을 무작위로 두 집단으로 나누었다. 첫 번째 집단의 노인들은 자기 자신들을 돌보고 그들의 삶의 질을 향상하게 하는 데 있어서 더 큰 책임감의 필요성을 강조하는 격려의 말을 들었다. 이러한 책임감이 높은 집단의 사람들은 그들의 책임을 상징하는 것으로 그들이 돌볼 식물을 골랐다. 책임감이 낮은 집단에 속한 거주자들은 직원들이 그들을 잘 보살필 것이라는 말을 들었다. 이 집단의 사람들 또한 간호사들이 그들을 돌보는 것처럼 간호사들이 기르고 물을 줄 상징적인 식물을 받았다.

　이 실험의 결과는 무엇이었는가? 책임감이 높은 집단의 사람들은 성장했다. 그들은 책임감이 낮은 집단에 있는 사람들보다 상당히 더 많은 조심성, 능동적인 참여, 그리고 긍정적인 감정의 표시를 보여주었다. 그 차이들은 오래 갔다. 훨씬 더 주목할 만한 발견이 있었다. 책임감이 높은 집단의 환자들이 다른 집단의 환자들보다 18개월 후 15%만큼 더 많이 생존해 있었기 때문에 관리 의식이 수명을 연장함을 보였다.

23. ①

Copernicus wrote De Revolutionibus Orbium Coelestium, a book explaining his theory of a sun-centered solar system. 1) ① Copernicus realized that his theory would not be readily accepted and was hesitant to make his ideas public. ② The

중심소재: 지동설을 주장한 코페르니쿠스가 쓴 책 → 책의 출판

1. 도입부(중심소재 도출)
지동설을 주장한 코페르니쿠스의 책

Christian religious community placed a great importance on the Earth's role as the center of the heavens. ③ **Therefore**, he would be contradicting not just the scientific establishment, but also the teaching of the Christian church. 2) Copernicus waited until 1530—twenty-three years—to present his ideas to other scholars. He waited another thirteen years—until just before his death—to have his work published.

1) 구체적 진술(배경/원인)
①에 대한 원인이 ②에 기술되어 있고, 그 때문에 발생하는 결과가 ③에 기술되어 있다.
2. 결과
구체적 진술에서 밝힌 배경으로 인해 코페르니쿠스가 책 출판을 기피하게 되었다.

| 해설
본문은 크게 '인과'의 글 전개방법을 쓰면서, 코페르니쿠스가 왜 자신의 이론을 책으로 출판하는 것을 미뤘는지에 관해 설명하고 있다. 보기 ①이 가장 적절한 주제이다.

| 해석
코페르니쿠스는 태양을 중심으로 한 태양계에 관한 그의 이론을 설명한 책, 『천구의 회전에 관하여』(De revolutionibus Orbium Coelestium)를 썼다. 코페르니쿠스는 그의 이론이 쉽게 받아들여지지 않을 것으로 생각하고 그의 이론을 간행하는 것을 망설였다. 기독교의 종교적 사회에서는 하늘 중심으로서의 지구의 역할을 매우 중요시했다. 그러므로 그는 기존의 과학적 이론뿐만 아니라 기독교 교회의 가르침을 부정하게 되는 것이었다. 코페르니쿠스는 1530년까지 23년을 기다렸다가, 그의 이론을 다른 학자들에게 발표했다. 그는 죽기 바로 전까지 13년을 더 기다려 그의 논문을 출판했다.

24. ⑤

1. One reason that so many people fail is that they lack confidence in themselves. If you think of yourself as being unworthy of great achievement, you will never achieve greatness. If, on the other hand, you know yourself and understand what your abilities are, and if then you determine to accomplish everything of which you are capable, you will certainly stand a much better chance of success. 1) <u>How may one become inspired to realize all his possibilities or to gain confidence in himself?</u> ① Ⓐ One of the surest ways is for him to associate with persons who have really achieved greatness. It is impossible, however, for most people to come frequently into the actual presence of the great. Ⓑ The next best thing, perhaps, is for him to spend part of his time in reading about great achievers. Biography is a powerful stimulant to action. Ⓒ **But** these processes will not avail unless one rids himself of a sense of inferiority and determines

중심소재: 성공과 실패
1. 도입부
'on the other hand'를 기준으로 성공과 실패의 원인을 기술하고 있다.

1) 의문문
(주제도출)
① 답변(요지)
Ⓐ 위대한 업적을 성취한 사람과의 접촉 – 대부분 사람들에게 거의 불가능함을 언급한 후 두 번째 답변으로 넘어감
Ⓑ 크게 성공한 사람들의 전기를 읽을 것을 권장
Ⓒ 강조의 But 확인 – 성공은 '열등감'을 극복하고 자신감을 가져야 성취할 수 있다.

*주제: 성공의 열쇠

to do the best that he possibly can. One of our great philosophers expressed the idea in a single sentence when he said that each individual should hitch his wagon to a star.

| 해석

많은 사람이 실패하는 이유는 스스로 자신감이 없기 때문이다. 당신 스스로 자신이 크게 성공할 가치가 없다고 생각한다면, 당신은 결코 큰 것을 이룰 수 없을 것이다. 만약, 반대로, 당신이 당신 자신을 알고 당신의 능력이 무엇인지를 알고 당신이 할 수 있는 것을 결정한다면 당신은 분명히 성공할 기회를 훨씬 더 얻을 것이다. 사람은 어떻게 그의 모든 가능성을 인식하게 되거나 스스로 자신감을 얻을 수 있을까? 가장 확실한 방법의 하나는 이미 크게 성공한 사람과 교제하는 것이다. 그러나 대부분 사람들은 훌륭한 사람과 실제로 대면하는 것이 불가능하다. 그 다음으로 가장 좋은 방법은 아마도 크게 성공한 사람들에 관한 책을 읽는 데에 시간을 쓰는 것일 것이다. 자서전은 행동하는 데에 강력한 자극이 된다. 그러나 이러한 과정은 스스로 열등감에서 벗어나 할 수 있을 만한 것에 전력을 기울일 결심을 하지 않는 한 효율적이지 못하다. 위대한 철학자 중의 한 사람은 이러한 생각을 한 문장으로 표현하였는데 사람들은 각자의 대망을 품어야 한다고 했다.

25. ③

1. The profusion of life has a secret: South Georgia is a relatively temperate island in the path of a seasonal swarm of krill borne up by currents from the Antarctic Peninsula—a living river of krill. 1) This river of krill fed the largest herds of fur seals and great whales on Earth in the ages before the sealers and whalers came. 2) Today it is fueling the astonishing resurrection of the Antarctic fur seal, as well as the slow but steady recovery of several whale species.

중심소재: South Georgia의 고래와 물개
1. 도입부
현상의 배경: South Georgia의 크릴이 많이 서식할 수 있는 온화한 기후 및 지리적 특성 기술
1) 현상(요지)
다시 한 번 남극에서 고래와 물개가 번성하고 있다는 내용을 전하고 있다.

현상의 시그널 확인: ★
today, be + V -ing

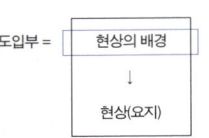

일반적 패턴은 "현상 → 원인" 이나 본문의 경우 "원인 → 현상" 으로 전개되고 있다.

| 해석

생명체들의 풍성함에는 비밀이 있다(수많은 생명체들이 존재하는 데에는 다 이유가 있다). South Georgia는 크릴새우들의 생명의 강인 남극 반도에서 나오는 해류에 의해 주기적으로 크릴새우 떼가 들어오는 길목에 있는 상대적으로 온화한 기후를 가지고 있는 섬이다. 이 크릴새우들의 강은 물개 사냥꾼과 고래 사냥꾼이 들어오기 이전 시대에는 지구 상에서 가장 많은 물개와 고래들에게 먹이를 공급했다. 오늘날, 이는 몇몇 고래 종의 느리지만 꾸준한 개체 수 회복뿐만 아니라 남극 물개의 놀랄만한 증가의 원동력이 되고 있다.

26. ③

1. It has been noticed that ㉠ traditionally courts have granted divorces on fault grounds: one spouse is deemed to be at fault in causing the divorce. More and more ㉡ today, however, divorces are being granted on a no-fault basis.

중심소재: 이혼 → 이혼의 사유
1. 도입부
이혼의 이유에 대한 과거와 현재의 대조적 관점이 드러난다.
㉠ 법원이 인정하는 전통적 이혼 이유: 한쪽이 이혼의 원인을 제공하는 실수를 바탕으로 이혼 허용(과실 이혼)

1) Proponents of no-fault divorce argue that when a marriage fails, it is rarely the case that one marriage partner is completely to blame and the other blameless. A failed marriage is much more often the result of mistakes by both partners.

Ⓐ Another argument in favor of no-fault divorce is that proving fault in court, in a public arena, is a destructive process that only serves to lengthen the divorce process and that dramatically increases the negative feelings present in a divorce. Ⓐ If a couple can reach a decision to divorce without first deciding which partner is to blame, the divorce settlement can be negotiated more easily and equitable and the post-divorce healing process can begin more rapidly.

ⓒ 현대적 관점: 특별한 잘못이 없는 데 이혼을 인정
1) 현대적 관점의 이혼 인정에 대해 찬성하는 쪽: 이혼은 일반적으로 한쪽의 전적인 잘못에 의해 이루어지는 경우는 아주 드물며, 단순한 실수 그 이상의 결과이다.
① 찬성하는 사람들의 또 다른 주장: 법원에서의 이혼 처리는 이혼 과정을 장기화하고, 나쁜 감정만을 극대화한다.
Ⓐ 구체적 예를 통해 과실에 기초하지 않는 이혼 합의의 긍정적인 측면을 부각하고 있다.

* 시간의 일반적 대조

| 과거 ⊖ |
| 현재 ⊕ |

* 본문 단락구조

| 이혼사유(A) |
| A에 대한 전통적 관점 |
| ↕ |
| A에 대한 현대적 관점 |
| 뒷받침 근거 |

공간활용을 볼 때 주로 A에 대한 현대적 관점을 다루는 글임을 파악할 수 있다.

| 해설
과실에 기초하지 않은 이혼을 주로 다루는 글이다.

| 해석
전통적으로 법정은 과실에 기초한 이혼을 인정하고 있다고 알려졌다. 이혼 소송을 제기하는 데 있어서 한 사람의 배우자는 잘못이 있다고 여겨져야 한다는 것이다. 그러나 점점 더 오늘날 결혼 당사자인 쌍방이 책임이 없는 경우에도 이혼이 인정되고 있다.

쌍방이 책임이 없는 이혼을 지지하는 사람들은 결혼이 실패했을 때 한쪽 배우자가 전적으로 책임이 있고 다른 배우자는 과실이 없는 경우는 드문 일이라고 주장한다. 결혼생활의 실패는 보통 두 당사자가 잘못된 결과이다.

쌍방이 책임이 없는 이혼을 지지하는 또 다른 주장에 따르면 공개적인 장소인 법정에서 (서로의) 잘못을 입증하는 것은 이혼 절차를 연장하기만 하고 또 이혼 중에 드러나는 부정적인 감정만 더 증가시키는 파괴적인 과정이라는 것이다. 만약 부부가 배우자 중 누가 책임이 있는지를 먼저 따지지 않고 이혼 결정을 내릴 수 있다면 이혼 합의가 더 수월하게 이뤄질 수 있고, 공정해질 수 있으며, 이혼 후의 치유 과정도 더 빨리 시작될 수 있다.

27. ⑤

1. It was necessary for the ancient peoples to grow their own food, since there were no methods of preserving or transporting it. 1) Foods must be preserved from the invasion of bacteria if they are not to be injurious when eaten. In early times it was learned that meat kept longer when temporarily preserved by roasting and smoking, and this was done without any knowledge of bacteria. 2) The Crusaders introduced sugar into Europe from Cyprus, and as a result of this, it was discovered that a heavy syrup made from sugar

중심소재: 식량보존
1. 도입부
고대 사람들은 식량을 직접 재배할 필요성이 있었음 – 보존 또는 운송할 방법이 없었기 때문.
1) 음식 보존의 필요성 언급
인류 초기에 보존과 관련된 지식의 습득 – 고기를 구워서 일시적으로 보존의 효과(그 당시 박테리아의 개념은 없었음).
2) 십자군 원정에 의해 유럽으로 설탕이 들어오면서 과일, 채소, 고기의 보관이 쉬워짐.

★ 시간의 전개방식을 드러내는 시그널을 확인한다.

would preserve fruits and also vegetables and meats. 3) Then it was discovered that foods could be preserved by the use of spices, vinegar and alcohol. ① You remember from your history that Columbus went before Ferdinand and Isabella of Spain to receive financial aid so that he might find a new route to India to obtain more easily the spices that were in demand at that time for preserving foods. 4) Glass and porcelain were the only containers used in preserving food until 1862, when Thomas Kimmett secured a patent on the use of cans. The canning of foods has increased so greatly that all kinds of foods are being preserved today by this modern method. ① Modern canning does not change the nutritive values of foods as much as ordinary cooking. 5) The quality of preserved food, whether the preservation is done at home or commercially, depends largely on the selection of the food, the shortness of the interval between harvesting and packing or canning, and the care used in processing or storing.

3) 양념, 식초 그리고 알코올로 보관할 수 있다는 것을 발견.
① 구체적 역사적 사례
4) 캔의 발견으로 현대적 개념의 보존이 시작됨.
① 캔의 놀라운 보존력이란 장점을 설명하고 있다.
5) 보존 음식의 질이 여러 가지 변수에 의해서 달라질 수 있다는 설명으로 마무리하고 있다.

| 해설

글 전개 방법은 'Order'를 따르고 있다. 즉, 시간의 추이에 따라 '음식 보존의 발달 과정 또는 역사'를 주로 다루고 있다.

| 해석

고대인들에게 그들 자신의 식량을 재배하는 것은 꼭 필요한 일이었다. 당시에는 음식을 보존하거나 수송할만한 수단이 없었기 때문이다. 그들(고대인)이 음식을 먹을 때 해롭지 않으려면 미생물의 침입으로부터 꼭 보존되어야 한다. 옛날에는 굽고 훈제하는 방식을 통해 일시적으로 고기를 더 오래 보관할 수 있다는 것이 학습되었다. 이것은 미생물에 대한 어떤 지식도 없이 행해졌다. 십자군은 사이프러스에서 유럽으로 설탕을 전했고, 이 결과로, 설탕에서 만들어낸 진한 시럽이 과일뿐만 아니라 채소와 고기를 보존해 준다는 것이 밝혀졌다. 이때 쯤 향신료, 식초와 주정을 이용해서 음식을 보존하는 법도 밝혀지게 되었다. 스페인의 페르디난드 국왕과 이사벨 여왕 시대 이전에 콜럼버스가 재정 지원을 얻기 위해 음식 보존을 위한 수요가 많았던 향신료를 좀 더 편하게 얻으려고 새로운 항로를 찾으려 한 역사를 기억해보라. 유리와 자기(도자기)는 토마스 키밋이 캔을 이용한 특허를 확보하게 된 1862년까지 음식을 보존하기 위한 유일한 용기였다. 음식 통조림 제조는 엄청나게 성장해서 이 현대적인 방법을 이용하여 모든 종류의 음식이 보존되게 되었다. 요즘의 통조림 제조는 보통의 요리만큼 음식의 영양 가치를 변하게 하지 않는다. 보존 음식의 질은 (집에서 혹은 회사 어느 쪽에서 보존이 행해지더라도) 음식의 선택, 수확과 포장이나 통조림 제조를 하는 과정의 단축, 공정이나 재고에서 조심스럽게 다루어지는 것에 많은 영향을 받는다.

28. ①

1. <u>We are sometimes eager to celebrate the influence of our surroundings</u>. 1) In the living room of a house in the Czech Republic, we see an example of how walls, chairs and floors can combine to create an atmosphere in which the best sides of us are offered the opportunity to flourish. We accept with gratitude the power that a single room can possess.

2. But <u>sensitivity to architecture also has its more problematic aspects</u>. 1) If one room can alter how we feel, if our happiness can hang on the colour of the walls or the shape of a door, what will happen to us in most of the places we are forced to look at and inhabit? What will we experience in a house with prisonlike windows, stained carpet tiles and plastic curtains? 3. It is to prevent the possibility of permanent anguish **that** we can be led to <u>shut our eyes</u> to most of what is around us, for we are never far from damp stains and cracked ceilings, shattered cities and rusting dockyards. We can't remain sensitive indefinitely to environments which we don't have the means to alter for the good.

중심소재: 환경에 대한 반응
첫번째 문단
1. 도입부 = 단락 주제문
주변 환경의 영향을 찬양하는 모습을 그리고 있다.
1) 뒷받침 예시

두 번째 문단
2. 단락 주제문
외적 건축물에 너무 민감한 것은 더 큰 문제점이 있다(즉, 너무 민감해선 안 된다).
1) 뒷받침 진술
3. 대안(요지)
주변 환경에 지나치게 반응하지 않는 방법으로 눈을 감아버릴 것을 말하고 있다.

★ 일반인 주어라는 점에서 글쓴이가 이들의 성향의 문제점을 지적하는 글로 갈 가능성이 크다.

★ 'it ~ that' 강조 구문으로 글의 요지가 드러나는 부분이다.

| 해설
문제에서 요구하는 것은 이 글에서 주로 다루고 있는 내용이다. 본문은 '우리가 주위에 너무 민감하게 반응해서는 안 되기에 주변의 부정적인 것에 눈을 감아버리라'고 말하고 있다.

| 해석
　우리는 때때로 주변 환경의 영향을 매우 찬양하고 싶어 한다. 체코 공화국의 주택 거실에서 우리는 벽과 의자와 바닥이 서로 어우러져 우리의 가장 나은 면들이 번영할 기회를 주는 분위기를 만들어낼 수 있는 예를 보게 된다. 우리는 단 하나의 방이 가지는 힘을 감사히 인정한다.
　그러나 건축에 대한 민감성은 더욱 문제가 되는 측면들도 또한 갖고 있다. 만약 하나의 방이 우리의 감정을 바꿀 수 있다면 또 우리의 행복이 벽의 색깔이나 문의 모양에 좌우된다면 우리가 바라보고 살아갈 수밖에 없는 대부분 장소에서는 우리에게 어떤 일이 일어나겠는가? 감옥처럼 보이는 창문과 얼룩진 카펫 타일과 플라스틱 커튼이 있는 집에서 우리는 무엇을 경험하겠는가? 우리 주변의 대부분의 것에 눈을 감게 됨으로 영원한 고뇌의 가능성을 막을 수 있는데, 이는 우리가 축축한 얼룩, 금이 간 천장, 부서진 도시 그리고 녹슨 조선소와 결코 멀어질 수 없기 때문이다.

29. ④

언어행위와 관련된 글이다. 일반적으로 '현상'으로 시작하는 글은
1) 현상 - 원인 파악
2) 현상 - 문제점 지적(원인 파악) - 대안
3) 현상 - 기원
등의 글로 진행되는데, 본문은 첫 번째에 해당한다.

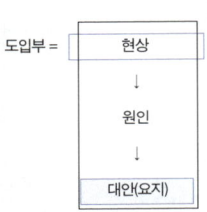

(주제문 = 현상+ 원인)
위 단락과 같이 '현상 원인'의 전개에 대한이 따를 경우 주제문과 요지문을 구별할 수 있어야 한다. 주제문은 요지를 담고 있는 경우도 있지만 일반적으로 "무엇에 관한 글인지?" 에 대한 주제의 정보를 전달하며 이를 통해 궁극적으로 전달하려는 사항이 요지에 해당한다.

1. Children whose parents have foreign accents don't speak with accents. They learn to talk like their peers. 1) Little girls and little boys learn how to have conversations as they learn how to pronounce words from their playmates. 2. Between the ages of five and fifteen, when children are learning to have conversations, they play they learn different ways of having and using conversations. Anthropologists point out that boys and girls socialize differently. 1) Little girls tend to play in small groups or, even more common, in pairs. Their social life usually centers around a best friend, and friendships are made, maintained, and broken by talk—especially "secrets." It's hard for newcomers to get into these tight groups, but anyone who is admitted is treated as an equal. Little boys tend to play in larger groups, often outdoors, and they spend more time doing things than talking. It's easy for boys to get into the group, but not everyone is accepted as an equal. Their talk is often competitive talk about who is best at what.

중심소재: 언어습득

1. 도입부 = 현상
부모의 외국 액센트에도 불구하고 아이들은 액센트가 전혀 없이 친구들 같이 말한다.

1) 현상의 이유
아이들은 부모가 아닌 자기 또래와 놀면서 언어를 배움

2. 또 다른 현상
5~15세 사이 남녀 언어 행위에 차이가 발생

1) 현상의 이유
남녀 간 언어 행위의 차이가 발생한 원인을 기술하고 있다.

| 해석

부모가 외국어 억양을 가진 아이들이라 할지라도 말에 그 억양을 넣어 이야기하지는 않는다. 아이들은 그들의 친구들처럼 말하는 법을 배운다. 어린 소녀와 소년은 그들의 소꿉친구로부터 단어를 발음하는 방법을 배우면서 대화하는 방법도 배우게 된다. 대화하는 법을 배우는 다섯 살에서 열다섯 살 사이의 아이들은 대부분 같은 성별의 친구들과 논다. 그러므로 그들이 서로 다른 대화 방식을 배우는 것은 당연하다. 인류학자들은 소년과 소녀가 서로 다르게 사회화된다는 점을 지적한다. 어린 소녀들은 작은 집단으로, 또는 더 흔하게는 짝지어 노는 경향이 있다. 그들의 사회생활은 보통 가장 친한 친구 주변에 집중되어 있고, 우정은 말, 특히 '비밀'에 의해서 만들어지고 유지되며 깨어진다. 새로 온 아이가 이 빈틈없는 집단에 들어가는 것은 어려운 일이지만, 일단 받아들여진 사람은 누구라도 동등하게 취급된다. 어린 소년들은 더 커다란 집단을 지어 대개 밖에서 노는 경향이 있으며, 이야기 보다는 무엇인가를 하면서 시간을 보낸다. 소년들이 그룹에 들어가는 것은 쉬운 일이지만, 그들 모두가 동등하게 인정받는 것은 아니다. 그들의 이야기는 누가 어떤 것에 최고인지에 대한 경쟁과 관련된 말이 대부분이다.

30. ④

1. George Orwell was the pseudonym of Eric Blair, who was born in India, where his father was a British civil servant. He was sent to private school in England, and won a scholarship to Eton, the foremost "public school" (i.e., private boarding

1. 도입부
조지 오웰의 어린 시절에 관한 이야기가 전개된다.

① 강조 구문인 'It ~ that S V'를 통해 글쓴이는 오웰이 느낀 '문제 인식'을 드러낸다: 자신과 부자 학급친구와

school) in the country. ① **It** was at these schools **that** he first became conscious of the difference between his own background and the wealthy background of many of his schoolmates. 2. On leaving school he joined the Imperial Police in Burma (both Burma and India were then still part of the British Empire). His service in Burma from 1922 to 1927 produced ② a sense of guilt about British colonialism and a feeling that he must make some kind of personal expiation for it. This he would later do with a fiercely anti-colonialist novel, *Burmese Days* (1934). ③ He returned to England determined to be a writer and adopted a pseudonym as one way of escaping from the class position in which his birth and education had placed him.

의 차이점
2. 졸업 이후 왕실 경호대에 들어간 후 전환기를 맞이함: ② 영국의 제국주의에 대한 죄책감과 이것에 대한 개인적 속죄의 필요성 → 반식민지주의를 드러낸 *Burmese Days*(1934)를 쓴 계기
③ 조지 오웰이란 이름을 쓰게 된 이유가 드러난다.

| 해설

무엇에 관한 글인가? 우선 '조지 오웰'에 관한 글이란 것을 첫 번째 문장에서 알 수 있으며, 이후 내용을 바탕으로 그의 삶에서 큰 전환기를 제공하는 원인이 바로 '식민지주의'라는 것을 알 수 있다. '식민지주의'에 대한 죄책감과 사죄를 위해 쓴 책이 바로 'Burmese Days(1934)'라고 했다. 윗글의 주제로 '조지오웰과 식민지주의'라는 보기 ④가 가장 적절하다.

| 해석

조지 오웰은 에릭 블레어의 필명이다. 그는 인도에서 태어났고 거기서 그의 아버지는 공무원이었다. 그는 영국의 사립학교, 국가 최초의 '사립학교(다시 말해, 사립 기숙학교)'에 보내졌고 장학금을 받았다. 그가 자신의 배경과 그의 많은 학교친구의 부유한 배경 차이를 처음 의식하게 된 것은 바로 이런 학교들에서였다. 학교를 졸업하자마자 그는 버마(지금의 미얀마)에서 제국 경찰이 되었다(버마와 인도는 그 당시 대영제국의 식민지였다). 버마에서 1922~1927년까지 경찰 생활을 하면서 영국 식민지 정책에 대한 죄의식을 느꼈고, 그것에 대하여 어떠한 개인적인 속죄를 해야겠다고 생각했다. 이 때문에 그는 훗날 치열한 반식민주의 소설, [버마의 낮]을 펴냈다. 그는 영국으로 돌아와서 작가가 되기로 하고 그의 출생과 교육 배경으로 말미암은 사회적 계급에서 벗어나는 하나의 방법으로서 필명을 사용했다.

Test 2 요지를 고르는 문제

1. ④

1. Every winter, especially in cold climates, people sink into the familiar round of illness, with coughing and sore throat being two of the most common symptoms. Sometimes other conditions, such as fever, are also present and 1) people wonder whether they have simply caught a cold or are suffering from the flu. ① Since the flu can be quite serious, it is wise to be aware of the differences. Ⓐ Coughing, blocked nose, and sore throat are the most common symptoms of colds, and they are often present with the flu as well. Chest pain may also accompany both illnesses, but with the flu it has a tendency to become severe. The symptoms particularly pertaining to the flu, which are rarely, if ever, present with the cold, are headache, high fever, and pains all over the body. Often the flu begins with vague body pains and headache, then quickly gets worse as the victim's body temperature rises. People with the flu may find themselves in bed for several days batting temperatures of 38-39 degrees, and may end up with pneumonia, which is serious. Waking moments may be spent coughing continuously. 2. Though there is presently no cure for the common cold, antibiotics can help fight the flu. And getting a flu shot at the beginning of each season is a particularly good idea.

요지를 이끄는 시그널 확인 ★

중심내용(controlling idea) ★
에 해당한다.

도입부 = 현상
주제문
뒷받침 진술
대안

중심소재: 감기와 독감
1. 도입부 = 현상
겨울이 되면 사람들이 기침과 목이 간질간질한 증상을 겪는다.

1) 문제점 지적
독감과 감기 구별이 쉽지 않다.

① 주제문
독감과 감기를 구별해야 한다.

Ⓐ 뒷받침 진술
본문 끝까지 독감과 감기의 차이점을 기술하고 있다.

2. 대안

| 해석

겨울이면, 특히 추운 기후에서라면 사람들은 주로 기침과 목이 아픈 두 가지 증상을 보이며 한바탕 병으로 앓아눕곤 한다. 때로는 발열 등과 같은 다른 증상들도 동반하기 때문에 사람들은 자기가 그냥 감기에 걸린 것인지 아니면 독감에 걸린 것인지 의아해 한다. 독감은 꽤 심각할 수 있기 때문에 감기와 독감의 차이를 알고 있는 것이 현명하다. 기침, 코 막힘, 그리고 목이 아픈 것이 감기의 가장 일반적인 증상이지만, 독감에도 같은 증상이 생기는 경우가 많다. 가슴 통증도 두 경우 모두 동반할 수 있지만, 두통, 고열 그리고 몸살은 감기의 경우 있다 하더라도 흔하지 않으며, 특히나 독감과 관련이 있다. 보통 독감 초기에는 약한 몸살과 두통이 있지만 금세 악화되어서 환자의 체온이 올라간다. 독감에 걸리면 38, 39도의 열이 나면서 며칠씩 앓아눕게 되고 결국 폐렴으로 이어져 심각할 수도 있다. 깨어 있는 동안 계속 기침을 하게 될 수도 있다. 비록 보통 감기의 치료법은 현재 없지만, 독감은 항생제로 치료할 수 있다. 매년 겨울이 시작될 때마다 독감 주사를 맞는 것도 매우 좋은 생각이다.

2. ④

1. As ethnicity became an accepted subject for study in the late 1960s, textbooks were assailed for their failure to portray blacks accurately; 1) within a few years, the textbooks in wide use were carefully screened to eliminate bias against minority groups and women. At the same time, new scholarship about the history of women, blacks, and various ethnic minorities found its way into the textbooks. 2. At first, the multi-cultural content was awkwardly incorporated as little boxes on the side of the main narrative. Then some of the new social historians themselves wrote textbooks, and the main narrative itself began to reflect a broadened historical understanding of race, ethnicity, and class in the American past. 3. Consequently, today's history textbooks routinely incorporate the experiences of women, blacks, American Indians, and various immigrant groups.

중심소재: 소수민족을 배제한 편향된 교과서

1. 도입부 = 문제점 지적
교과서에서 흑인이 제대로 묘사되어 있지 않다.

1) 대안(요지)
여성, 흑인, 다양한 소수민족의 역사 또한 새 교과서에 반영되었다.

★ 두 번째 문단에 두드러지는 시간의 글 전개방식을 확인한다.

2. 위에서 글쓴이가 밝힌 새로운 조치가 발생하게 된 경위(배경)를 상술하고 있다.

★ 글의 요지를 이끄는 시그널을 확인한다.

3. 요지
오늘날 역사 교과서는 과거에 소외되었던 대상을 반영하고 있다.

문제점 지적
↓
대안(요지)
↓
배경
(시간의 글 전개)
↓
요지

| 해석

인종이 1960년대 말에 연구의 공인된 주제가 되면서 교과서는 흑인들을 정확히 그리지 못한 것 때문에 공격을 받았다. 몇 년 사이에, 널리 사용되는 교과서들을 면밀하게 가려내어 소수 단체나 여성에 대한 편견이 있는 내용은 삭제 조치되었다. 동시에, 여성, 흑인, 그리고 여러 소수민족의 역사에 대한 새로운 학식(적 내용)이 교과서에서 그 길을 찾아가고 있다(반영되고 있다). 처음에, 다문화적인 내용이 주요한 이야기 측면의 작은 상자의 내용으로 다소 어색하게 포함되었다. 그리고 나서 새로운 사회역사학자 중 일부가 교과서를 썼고 주요 이야기 자체는 인종, 민족성 그리고 미국의 과거 속에서의 계급을 폭넓게 역사적으로 이해하는 것을 반영하기 시작했다. 결과적으로, 오늘날의 역사 교과서는 관례로 여성, 흑인, 미국 인디언 그리고 여러 이주민의 경험을 포함한다.

중심소재는 책(book)이며, ★
중심내용은 'two ways to
own a book'이다. 이중 글
쓴이가 제안하는 방법에
주목하도록 한다.

조건 강조로 글의 요지가 ★
드러나는 부분이다.

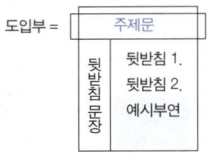

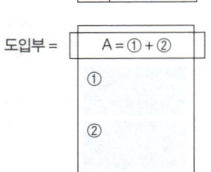

3. ③

1. There are two ways in which one can own a book. 1) ① The first the property right you establish by paying for it, just as you pay for clothes and furniture. But this act of purchase is only the prelude to possession. ② Full ownership comes only when you have made it a part of yourself, and the best way to make yourself a part of it is by writing in it. ④ An illustration may make the point clear. You buy a beefsteak and transfer it from the butcher's icebox to your own. But you do not own the beefsteak in the most important sense until you consume it and get it into bloodstream. I am arguing that books, too, must be absorbed in your bloodstream to do you any good.

중심소재: 책
1. 도입부 = 주제문
책을 소유하는 두 가지 방법(Two Ways to Own a Book)
1) 뒷받침 문장
① 방법 1
돈을 주고 소유권 획득 – 'But' 이후 진정한 소유가 아니라 말함.
② 방법 2 (요지)
자신의 것으로 소화하는 것이 진정한 책의 소유로, 최상의 방책은 글을 쓰는 것이다.
④ 구체적인 예(illustration)를 통해 자신의 주장을 뒷받침함.

| 해석
책을 소유하는 데는 두 가지 방법이 있다. 첫 번째는 마치 당신이 옷이나 가구값을 내는 것처럼 책값을 냄으로써 당신이 얻게 되는 재산권이다. 그러나 이러한 구매 행위는 소유에 대한 전주곡에 불과하다. 완전한 소유는 당신이 그것을 당신의 일부로 만들었을 때 나타나는 것이다. 그리고 당신 자신을 그 일부로 만드는 최고의 방법은 그것을 써보는 것이다. 한 예를 통해서 요점을 명확하게 전달할 수 있다. 당신은 비프스테이크를 사서 정육점 주인의 얼음 상자에서 당신의 얼음 상자로 옮기는 것이다. 그러나 당신이 그것을 소비하고 당신의 혈류 속으로 넣을 때까지는 가장 중요한 의미로는 비프스테이크를 소유하지 않은 것이다. 나는 책도 역시 당신에게 유익하게 되기 위해서는 혈류 속으로 흡수되어야만 한다는 것을 주장하는 바이다.

4. ③

1. I fully admit that the mischief which a person does to himself may seriously affect, both through their sympathies and their interests, those nearly connected with him and, in a minor degree, society at large. When, by conduct of this sort, a person is led to violate a distinct and assignable obligation to any other person or persons, the case is taken out of the self-regarding class, and becomes amenable to moral disapproval in the proper sense of the term. 1) If, for example, a man, through extravagance, becomes unable to pay his debts, or, having undertaken the moral responsibility of a family, becomes from the same cause incapable of supporting or educating them, he is deservedly criticized, and might be justly punished; ① but it is for the breach of

중심소재: 도덕적 불이행
1. 도입부 = 주제문
개인의 실수로 다른 이에 대한 의무를 어기는 경우 이는 "개인적 차원을 떠나 타인에 대한 도덕적 책임감을 불이행 하는 것이다."
1) 뒷받침 사례
주제문에서 밝힌 중심내용을 구체적 사례를 통해 뒷받침하고 있다.
① 사치를 통해 가족에 대한 의무를 다하지 못하는 경우 뿐 아니라, 신중한 투자 또한 결과적으로 낭비되었을 경우 동일한 도덕적 책임감의 불이행에 해당한다.

* 양괄식 구조

158

duty to his family or creditors, not for the extravagance. If the resources which ought to have been devoted to them had been diverted from them for the most prudent investment, the moral culpability would have been the same. 2. Whenever there is a definite damage, or a definite risk of damage, either to an individual or to the public, (B)the case is taken out of the province of liberty, and placed in that of morality or law.

2. 결론(요지)
개인의 자유의지에 따른 행동의 결과는 개인의 차원을 넘어 타인에 대한 도덕적 점주에 놓인다. (즉, 한 사람의 자유로운 행동을 할 때는, 타인에 대한 도덕적 책임감을 고려해야 한다는 의미)

| 해설
본문은 궁극적으로 '개인의 자유라는 명목 아래 자신 또는 다른 사람을 해치는 것은 도덕률에 어긋난 것이다' 라고 주장하고 있다.

| 해석
나는 한 사람이 자신에게 행한 해악은 그와 가깝게 연관된 사람에게 그들이 동정과 관심을 보임으로써 (오히려) 그들에게 심각한 영향을 미치는 동시에 경미하게는 사회 전반에 영향을 미칠 수 있다는 점은 전적으로 인정한다. 이러한 종류의 행위를 통해서 한 사람이 다른 사람 또는 사람들에게 지니는 독특하고, 정해진 의무를 어기게 된다면, 이런 경우는 이기적인 부류에서 취해진 것이며, 적절한 의미에서 도덕적 반감을 받을 여지(amenable)가 있게 된다. 예를 들어, 만약 사치를 통해서 한 남자가 자신의 빚을 갚지 못하게 되거나 또는 한 가정의 도덕적 책임을 가지지만, 같은 원인에서 가족을 부양하지 못하거나 교육을 제공하지 못한다면 그는 당연히 비판받아 마땅하며, 공정하게 벌을 받아야 한다. 하지만 이는 사치에 의한 것이 아니라 가족 또는 채권자에 대한 의무를 어김으로 발생하는 것이다. 만약 자신에게만 부여되었어야만 하는 자원이 가장 신중한 투자를 위해 딴 곳으로 돌려졌다면, 도덕적 문책은 동일하게 적용되었을 것이다. 명확한 피해가 존재하거나 또는 명확한 피해의 위험성이 있을 경우 그것이 개인에게든 대중에든 이러한 경우(결과)는 자유의 영역에서 나온 것이며, 이는 도덕 또는 법의 범주에 놓이게 된다.

5. ④

1. Some half a million years ago, ancient societies apparently did not recognize any difference between mental and physical disorders. 1) Abnormal behaviors, from simple headaches to convulsions, were believed to be caused by evil spirits that lived in the victim's body. ① According to this system of belief — called dermatology — those suffering from disease were considered responsible for their misfortune. Ⓐ For example, some Stone Age cave dwellers appear to have treated behavior disorders by a surgical method called trephining. During this procedure, part of the skull was chipped away to make an opening. Once the skull was opened, the evil spirits could escape. It was believed that

중심소재: 고대 질병의 원인
1. 도입부
고대 사회에서는 육체적 질병과 정신적 질병을 구별하지 않았다.
1) 원인: 두통부터 경련에 이르는 이상 행동은 모두 환자의 몸에 사는 '악령'이 원인이라 보았다.
① 주제문
병을 앓고 있는 자는 자신의 병에 대해 자신의 책임이 있다고 간주함.
Ⓐ 뒷받침 부연(For example)
앞에서 제시된 원인을 바탕으로 고대 사회 중 특히 '석기 시대'의 구체적 예를 제시하고 있다.

도입부
주제문
For example 뒷받침 사례

when the evil spirit left, the person would return to his or her normal state. Surprisingly, several trephined skulls that healed over have been found. This indicates that some patients survived what had to be an extremely crude operation.

| 해석

약 50만 년 전 고대사회는 정신 이상과 신체 이상의 차이점을 명백히 구별하지 못했다. 단순한 두통에서부터 발작에 이르는 비정상적 행위는 희생자의 몸 속에 사는 악한 영에 의해 발생한다고 여겼다. 귀신론이란 믿음 체계에 따르면, 병으로 말미암은 불운은 병으로 고통받는 사람 자신의 책임으로 여겨졌다. 예를 들어, 일부 석기시대 동굴 거주민들은 관상톱 수술법이라 불리는 외과 수술 방식을 통해 이상행동을 치료한 것으로 보인다. 이 수술 과정에서 두개골에 구멍을 내기 위해 두개골의 일부를 떼어냈다. 두개골에 구멍이 나면, 악령이 빠져나갈 수 있을 것이다. 악령이 빠져나가면, 환자는 정상 상태로 돌아올 것으로 여겨졌다. 놀랍게도, 관상톱 수술법 이후에 차차 회복되던 두개골 몇몇이 발견되기도 했다. 이는 일부 환자들이 분명히 극히 원시적인 수술에도 불구하고 살아남았음을 드러낸다.

6. ③

1. White people often avoid mentioning race because they fear even noticing skin color might somehow make them appear racist, **but** two new studies from psychologists at Tuffs and Harvard universities show that such "strategic color-blindness" can backfire. 1) White participants studied a batch of photographs, then tried to deduce, as quickly as possible, which picture a black partner was holding by asking questions about each one in succession. Asking whether the person pictured was black or white would have sped up their performance, yet subjects—adults in one study and children as young as age 10 in the other—rarely mentioned race unless their partner did so first. Black observers who watched the recorded interactions perceived whites who avoided talking about race as more prejudiced than the intrepid few who acknowledged skin color. And blacks who watched silent video clips of the interactions even rated whites who avoided mentioning race as having more unfriendly nonverbal behavior.

'but' 이후 글쓴이의 주장★이 제시된다.

요지를 드러내는 주제문★으로 실험의 구체적 내용이 이어진다.

중심소재: 인종차별 Strategic Color Blindness
1. 도입부 = 주제문
실험의 결과: 전략적으로 인종을 언급하지 않는 행위(Strategic Color Blindness)는 오히려 역효과가 있다.
1) 뒷받침 진술
실험을 통해 주제문에서 밝힌 중심내용을 뒷받침하고 있다.

| 해석

백인들은 피부색에 대한 인식만으로도 그들이 다소 인종주의자로 보일까 염려하여 종종 인종에 대해 언급하기를 꺼리지만, Tuffs 대학교와 Harvard 대학교의 심리학자들의 두 가지 연구는 그러한 "전략적인 인종인식회피"가 역으로 작용한다는 점을 보여준다. 백인 실험참가자들은 사진 한 묶음을 자세히 살펴본 후, 연달아 나오는 각각의 사진에 대하여 질문을 함으로써 어떤 사진을 흑인 상대방이 쥐고 있는지를 가능한 한 빨리 추론해야 했다. 사진에 찍힌 사람이 흑인인지 백인인지를 묻는 것이 그들의 실험을 수월하게 할 수 있으나, 한 실험에는 성인들, 그리고 다른 실험에는 10살짜리 아이들인 실험 참여자들은 그들의 상대가 먼저 하지 않으면, 좀처럼 인종을 언급하지 않았다. 녹화된 실험 참가자의 대화를 지켜본 흑인 관찰자는 인종에 대해서 말하기를 꺼린 백인들이 피부색을 인정한 용감한 몇몇보다 훨씬 더 편견에 사로잡혀있다고 느꼈다. 그리고 대화를 무성녹음 한 비디오 영상을 본 흑인들은 심지어 인종에 대해 언급하기를 꺼린 백인들을 더 불쾌한 비언어적 행위로 간주하기까지 했다.

7. ①

1. Far more striking than any changes in the kinds of work done by women in the U.S.A. labor force is the shift of wives and mothers from household activities to the world of paid employment. 1) Emphasis on the new work of women, **however**, should not be allowed to obscure an equally important fact. ⓐ Today, as always, most of the time and effort of American wives is devoted to their responsibilities within the home and the family circle. This is true even of those who are in the labor force. Ⓐ ⓐ Since 1890 the demands of paid work have become much lighter. The normal work week has decreased from sixty to forty hours; paid holidays and vacations have become universal; and most of the hard, physical labor that work once required has been eliminated. Because of these developments, many women can work outside the home and still have time and energy left for home and family. ⓑ Moreover, most working mothers do not assume the burdens of a full schedule of paid work. Among employed mothers of preschool children, four out of five worked only part time or less than half the year in 1956. Among those whose children were in school, three out of five followed the same curtailed work schedule. And even among working wives who had no children at home, only a little more than half were year-round, full-time members of the labor force.

중심소재: 여성의 사회진출
1. 도입부 =현상
여성의 사회진출
1) 'however'로 글의 내용이 전환되는데, 앞에서 다룬 여성의 사회진출과 동시에 혼동해서 안 될 사항을 주장하고 있다.

① 주제문
오늘날 여성은 언제나 그랬듯 가정 내 책임감에 헌신하고 있다

Ⓐ 뒷받침 진술
ⓐ 1890년 이래 일의 수요가 적어서 일감의 감소, 유급 휴가의 증가, 주당 일거리 감소, 힘든 육체노동의 감소
ⓑ 많은 여성이 대부분 시간제
→ 이러한 이유에서 대부분 미국 여성은 '가정 내 책임감을 수행하는 데 헌신하고 있다.'고 말하고 있다.

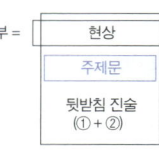

도입부 =

현상

주제문

뒷받침 진술
①+②

| 해석

미국 노동력 중 여성들로 이루어진 종류의 일 중에서 가장 두드러진 변화는 주부들과 어머니들이 가정 활동에서 유급 고용직으로 이동한 것이다. 그러나 여성들의 새로운 직장에 대해 (지나치게) 강조함으로써 마찬가지로 또 하나의 중요한 사실을 모호하게 해서는 안 된다. 언제나 그렇듯 오늘날에도 미국 주부들은 대부분 시간과 노력을 가정과 가족 내에서의 책임을 다하는 데 바친다. 이것은 직업을 가진(노동력에 편입된) 주부들에게조차도 그러하다. 1890년 이후로 유급 직장에 대한 수요는 훨씬 줄어들고 있다. 정상적인 1주 노동시간은 60시간에서 40시간으로 줄었으며, 유급 휴일과 휴가도 보편화하고 있다. 그리고 한때 작업에서 요구되었던, 힘든 육체적 노동도 거의 없어지고 있다. 이러한 발전 때문에 많은 여성은 집 밖에서 일하면서 여전히 가정과 가족을 위한 시간과 에너지를 가질 수 있게 되었다. 더욱이 대부분의 일하는 어머니들은 유급 직장의 꽉 짜인 일정의 부담을 떠맡지는 않는다. 1956년 취학 전 아동을 둔 직장을 가진 어머니 중에서 다섯 중 네 명은 시간제만으로 또는 1년 중 절반 이하의 시간만 일했다. 아이들이 학교에 다니는 어머니들 다섯 중 세 사람은 똑같이 단축된 작업 일정을 따랐다. 그리고 가정에 아이가 없는 전업주부 중에서도 절반 조금 넘는 사람들만이 1년 내내 전 시간을 근무하는 사람들이었다.

8. ④

* 실험의 단락구조

1. 도입부 = 결과(요지)
실험의 구체적 내용
결과(요지)

2. 도입부 = 실험의 구체적 내용
결과(요지)

1. A psychology professor introduced the same guest lecturer to two different classes. The first class was told to expect a rather cold, dull, uninteresting person. The second class was told to expect a warm, intelligent, friendly lecturer. The lecturer presented identical information in the same manner to both groups. The first group found his lecture boring and did not ask questions; the second group found him warm and stimulating and asked many questions. This experiment has been replicated successfully many times. 1) **The outcome of these experiments suggests that** telling someone what to perceive in another person will influence what is experienced.

1. 도입부(실험)
한 심리학자의 구체적인 실험을 소개하고 있다.

★ 실험의 결과는 곧 글의 요지가 될 수 있다는 점을 기억한다.

★ 실험의 결과를 이끄는 시그널: suggest, reveal, find out, indicate, show

1) 결과(요지)
실험을 통해 궁극적으로 밝히려는 사항이 드러난다.

| 해석

한 심리학 교수는 다른 두 교실의 학생들에게 똑같은 객원 강사를 소개했다. 한 교실의 학생들에게는 차갑고 지루하고 재미없는 강사를 기대하도록 말해두었고, 다른 교실의 학생들에게는 따뜻하고 지적이며 친근감 있는 강사를 기대하도록 말해두었다. 그 강사는 두 집단의 학생들에게 똑같은 태도로 같은 정보를 제공하였다. 첫 번째 집단은 그의 강의가 지루하다고 생각했으며 질문도 하지 않았다. 그러나 두 번째 집단은 그가 따뜻하고 활기찬 사람이라 생각했고 질문도 많이 했다. 이 실험은 여러 번 성공적으로 되풀이되었다. 이 실험들의 결과는 어떤 다른 사람에게서 인지하게 될 바를 누군가에게 미리 말해주는 것은 그 사람이 경험하게 되는 것에 영향을 준다는 것을 시사한다.

9. ②

1. Whereas family relationships usually constitute a child's first experience with group life, <u>peer-group interactions soon begin to make their powerful socializing effects felt</u>. From play group to teenage clique, the peer group affords young people many significant learning experiences — how to achieve status in a circle of friends. 1) Peers are equals in a way parents and their children or teachers and their students are not. A parent or teacher sometimes can force young children to obey rules they neither understand nor like, but peers do not have formal authority to do this; thus the true meaning of exchange, cooperation, and equity can be learned more easily in the peer setting. 2. Peer groups increase in importance as the child grows up and reach maximum influence in adolescence, by which time they sometimes dictate much of a young person's behavior both in and out of school.

중심소재: 또래집단의 영향
1. 도입부 = 주제문
'peer-group interactions'를 통해 아이들은 중요한 학습 경험 즉, 친구들 사이에 자신의 위치를 성취하는 사회성을 배운다.
1) 뒷받침 진술
또래 집단과 대조되는 '아이와 부모' 또는 '아이와 선생'은 아이가 일반적으로 권위에 따른 아주 형식적인 관계이나, 또래 집단은 'the true meaning of exchange, cooperation, and equity' 등을 쉽게 학습하게 된다.

2. 결론
'또래 집단은 아이들이 청소년기로 넘어가면서 더욱 큰 영향력을 미친다'는 글의 요지를 재차 언급하고 있다.

★ 중심내용(controlling idea)에 해당한다.

★ 대조의 글 전개방식을 확인할 수 있다. 대조되는 두 대상의 관계에 어떤 차이점이 있는지 정확히 파악하도록 한다.

* 양괄식의 전형적 구조
1. 도입부 = 주제문
   실험의 구체적 내용
   결과(요지)

| 해설

위 본문의 주제는 아이에게 큰 영향력을 주는 '또래 집단(peer group)'에 관한 이야기를 하고 있다. '요지'를 고르라는 문제이다. 부분적인 내용을 요지로 잡아선 안 된다. 보기의 내용이 옳다고 답이 되는 것이 아니다. 글쓴이가 궁극적으로 전달하려는 내용을 본문의 내용을 바탕으로 이끌어내도록 한다. 보기를 보면서 자세히 살펴보자.

① Children learn about cooperation in their peer groups.
→ 아이들은 또래 집단 내에서 협동을 배운다. 맞는 내용이다. 하지만 부분적인 내용을 요지로 잡아선 안 된다.

② **Peer groups are powerful influences in children's lives.**

③ Parents can force children to do things that a peer group cannot.
→ 마찬가지로 본문에 언급되어 있지만, 부분적인 내용이다.

④ Parents have greater influences on children than their teachers do.
→ 구체적 언급이 없는 가장 거리가 먼 오답이다.

⑤ Relationships in and out of school provide learning opportunities for children.
→ 본문을 통해 충분히 이끌어 낼 수 있는 내용이긴 하나 글쓴이의 요지가 아니다.

보기 ②가 글쓴이의 요지에 해당한다.

| 해석

일반적으로 가족관계가 아이들에게 집단생활에 대한 최초의 경험이 되지만, 얼마 안 있어 곧 또래 집단의 상호작용이 사회화에 강력한 영향들을 미치는 것이 느껴지기 시작한다. 놀이 집단에서부터 십 대 집단에 이르기까지 또래 집단은 아이들에게 친구들 사이에서 어떻게 지위를 얻는가와 같은 중요한 많은 학습 경험들을 제공한다. 또래는 부모와 자식 또는 교사와 학생들의 관계와는 다르게 평등하다. 부모나 교사는 때때로 어린아이들이 이해하지

못하거나 좋아하지 않는 규칙에 복종하도록 강요할 수 있지만, 또래는 이런 것을 할 공식적인 권위가 없다. 그래서 상호교류, 협동, 평등의 진정한 의미는 또래 집단 환경에서 더 쉽게 학습될 수 있다. 또래 집단은 아이들이 성장해감에 따라 점점 더 중요해져서 청소년기에 영향력이 최고에 달한다. 청소년기가 되면 이미 또래 집단이 때때로 학교 안팎에서 아이들의 많은 행동에 영향을 준다.

10. ②

구체적 예시를 이끄는 'If'를 확인하고, 개념정의 글에서는 이해를 돕기 위해 예시가 활용된 기억한다.

1. The Broken Windows theory was the brainchild of the criminologists James Wilson and George Kelling. 1) They argued that crime is the inevitable result of disorder. ① If a window is broken and left unrepaired, people walking by will conclude that no one cares and no one is in charge. Soon, more windows will be broken, and the sense of anarchy will spread from the building to the street on which it faces, sending a signal that anything goes here. In a city, relatively minor problems like graffiti, public disorder, and aggressive panhandling are all the equivalent of broken windows, invitations to more serious crimes.

의문문의 답변은 글의 요지에 해당한다.

2. What does this suggest? It says that the criminal—far from being someone who acts for fundamental, intrinsic reasons and who live in his own world—is actually someone acutely sensitive to his environment, who is alert to all kinds of cues, and who is prompted to commit crimes based on his perception of the world around him. That is an incredibly radical—and in some sense unbelievable—idea. It says that behavior is a function of social context.

중심소재: 깨진창문 이론
1. 도입부 = 중심소재 도출
James Wilson과 George Kelling이 주장한 'Broken Windows' 이론에 관한 글임을 첫 번째 문장에서 알 수 있다.
1) 'Broken Windows' 이론이 무엇인지를 밝히고 있다: '범죄는 무질서의 불가피한 결과이다.' 즉, 무질서한 환경의 결과가 바로 범죄를 발생시킨다고 말하고 있다.
① 구체적 부연
깨진 창문(나쁜 환경) → 더 많은 창문이 깨짐(더 많은 범죄가 일어남) + 작은 범죄 → 더 큰 범죄로 이어짐(인과)

2. 요지
'Broken Windows' 이론의 궁극적인 의미를 제시하고 있다: **범죄 행위는 사회적 환경의 작용이다.**

| 해석
'깨진 창문' 이론은 범죄학자인 제임스 윌슨(James Wilson)과 조지 켈링(George Kelling)의 창작물이었다. 그들은 범죄는 혼란의 불가피한 결과라고 말했다. 창문이 깨져서 수리되지 않은 채로 방치되면 지나가는 사람들은 어느 누구도 관심을 보이지 않고, 책임자가 없다고 결론을 내릴 것이다. 곧 더 많은 창문이 깨질 것이고 무질서 의식이 건물로부터 그 건물이 마주하고 있는 거리로까지 퍼져서 여기서는 무슨 짓이든 해도 된다는 신호를 보내게 될 것이다. 도시에서는 낙서, 공공질서 위반, 공격적인 구걸과 같은 비교적 사소한 문제들이 모두 깨진 창문에 해당하는 것으로, 더 심각한 범죄를 초래한다.
이것이 무엇을 암시하는가? 그것은 범죄자란 근본적이고 본질적인 이유에 따라 행동하고 자신의 세계 안에서 사는 사람이 아니라, 실제로는 자신의 환경에 매우 민감하고 모든 종류의 신호들에 주의하고 주변 세계의 인지에 근거해 범죄를 저지르게 되는 사람이라는 것을 말한다. 그것은 대단히 급진적이고 어떤 의미에서는 믿기 어려운 생각이다. 이는 행동이 사회적 상황의 한 기능이라고 말하고 있다.

11. ④

1. Shizuo Torii, a professor at Toho University in Japan, has studied the sense of smell. 1) He studied the effects that odors have on the feelings and behaviors of humans. ① By measuring the brain waves of people after they smelled a particular odor, Torii found that some odors produced a brain wave pattern that showed the people were calm. Other odors produced a pattern that showed excitement. Ⓐ It was discovered, for example, that lemon and peppermint have an exciting effect; nutmeg and lavender reduce stress; and a mix of rosemary and lemon will improve concentration. ⓐ Some Japanese corporations are using the results of this research to make the workplace more productive and pleasant.

중심소재: sense of smell
1. 도입부(실험)
후각에 대한 실험
1) 실험의 목적(주제)
냄새가 인간의 감정과 행동에 미치는 영향
① 결과(요지)
냄새는 사람의 감정을 드러내는 뇌파를 만들어 낸다.
Ⓐ 뒷받침 예시
ⓐ 적용 사례 부연

★ 결과를 이끄는 시그널 확인

① show
② findout
③ suggest
④ reveal
⑤ indicate
⑥ discover

| 해설

보기의 내용을 하나씩 자세히 살펴보자.

① The smells of lemon and rosemary improve concentration of workers.
→ 본문에 언급된 실험 결과의 예이다.

② Japanese corporations want to make the workplace more pleasant and efficient.
→ 응용 사례이다.

③ Shizuo Torii is a Japanese professor paid by corporations to improve the workplace environment.
→ 틀린 내용이 아니라 알 수 없으며, 요지와는 거리가 멀다.

④ A Japanese researcher has discovered that smells affect people's brain waves.
→ 본문에서 궁극적으로 전달하려는 내용이다.

⑤ The sense of smell is not influenced by the brain wave pattern.
→ 글의 요지와 정반대의 내용이다.

요지 문제를 풀 때 주의할 것은 본문에서 기술된 내용과 비교했을 때 보기가 참인지 거짓인지를 판단하는 것이 아니다. 부분적인 내용을 담고 있는 보기는 참/거짓의 유구와 관련 없이 요지가 될 수 없다. 본문을 통해 궁극적으로 전달하려는 내용을 담고 있어야 답이 된다.

| 해석

일본 토호 대학교수인 쉬주오 토리(Shizuo Torii)는 후각을 연구해왔다. 그는 인간의 감정과 행동에 미치는 냄새의 효과를 연구했다. 특정한 냄새를 맡은 사람들의 뇌파를 측정함으로써, 토리는 몇몇 냄새가 사람이 차분해졌다는 것을 보여주는 뇌파를 발생시킨다는 사실을 발견했다. 다른 냄새의 경우 흥분 상태를 보여주는 뇌파를 발생시켰다. 예를 들어, 레몬과 박하는 흥분시키는 효과를 지니고 있다는 사실이 발견되었다. 그리고 육두구와 라벤더는 스트레스를 감소시킨다. 로즈메리와 레몬의 혼합물은 집중력을 높인다. 일부 일본 기업들에서는 이 연구 결과들을 이용하여 더욱 생산적이고 즐거운 일터를 만들고 있다.

12. ③

1. Researchers at the University of Michigan are studying the effects of nicotine on the brain. Nicotine is the major drug in cigarettes. 1) Recently they have found that cigarettes give several "benefits" to smokers that may help explain why quitting smoking is so hard. ① Ⓐ The nicotine in cigarettes seems to help smokers with problems of daily living. It helps them feel calm. Ⓑ Nicotine also caused short-term improvements in concentration, memory, alertness, and feelings of well-being.

실험의 결과는 곧 글의 요지가 될 수 있다.

*실험의 지문

목적 = 주제

결과 = 요지
(주제, 제목 도출)

중심소재: 니코틴

1. **도입부 = 연구의 목적(주제)**
'니코틴이 뇌에 미치는 영향'에 대해 알아보는 연구이다.

1) **주제문**
글의 요지인 실험의 결과가 드러나는 곳: 담배가 주는 여러 '이득'으로 인해 담배를 끊는 것이 힘이 든다.

① 뒷받침 진술
Ⓐ 삶의 문제에 직면한 흡연자에게 안정을 줌.
Ⓑ 단기 집중력, 기억력, 주의력 및 평온함 등의 향상.

| 해석
미시간 대학의 과학자들은 니코틴이 뇌에 미치는 영향에 대해서 연구 중이다. 니코틴은 담배 안에 함유된 주된 약물이다. 최근에 이들은 담배가 흡연자들에게 몇 가지 '이익'을 준다는 사실을 발견했는데, 그것은 담배를 끊는 것이 왜 그토록 어려운지를 설명하는 데 도움이 될 수도 있다는 것이다. 담배 속의 니코틴은 흡연자들이 일상생활에서 일어나는 문제를 해결하는 데 도움을 주는 것처럼 보인다. 흡연자들이 차분하게 느낄 수 있도록 도와주기 때문이다. 니코틴은 또한 집중력, 기억력, 주의력과 행복한 느낌을 단기간 동안 향상하게 한다.

13. ①

1. An important influence on people's ability to cope with stressful situations is the degree of control they feel they can exercise over the situation. 1) Both animals and humans have been found to cope better with painful or threatening stimuli when they feel that they can exercise some degree of control rather than being passive and helpless victims. Such a sense of control can help minimize the negative consequences of stress, both psychological and physical. ① In one well-known experiment, Jay Weiss administered electric shocks to pairs of rats. In each pair, one of the two animals was given a degree of control over the situation; it could reach through a hole in the cage and press a panel that would turn off the shock both for itself and for its partner. Thus, the two rats received exactly the same number of shocks, but one was passive and helpless, and the other was in control. After a continuous 21-hour session, the animals were sacrificed and their stomachs examined for ulcers. Those rats who could exert control had much less ulceration than their helpless partners.

도입부 = 주제문

뒷받침 진술

부연진술(실험)

중심소재: 스트레스 대처 능력

1. **도입부 = 주제문**
스트레스를 다루는 능력 – 자신이 처한 상황에 대한 통제력

1) 뒷받침 진술
스트레스에 대해 어느 정도 통제력을 행사할 때 인간과 동물 모두 스트레스를 더 잘 견딘다는 실험 결과를 먼저 드러내고 있다.

① 부연진술
실험의 구체적 내용을 부연하며, 요지를 다시 전달하고 있다.

| 해석

스트레스를 유발하는 상황에 대처하는 사람들의 능력에 미치는 중요한 영향은 그들이 그 상황에 대해 행할 수 있다고 생각하는 통제의 정도이다. 동물과 인간이 모두 수동적이고 무력한 희생자이기보다는 어느 정도의 통제를 할 수 있다고 생각할 때 고통스럽고 위협적인 자극에 더 잘 대처하는 것으로 밝혀졌다. 그러한 통제 의식이 심리적(정신적), 신체적 스트레스의 부정적인 결과를 최소화하는 데 도움을 줄 수 있다. 한 유명한 실험에서, 제이 웨이스(Jay Weiss)는 여러 쌍의 쥐에게 전기 충격을 가했다. 각 쌍의 쥐에서 둘 중 하나는 그 상황에 대한 어느 정도의 통제를 하게 해주었는데 그것은 그 쥐가 우리 안의 구멍을 통해 나아가 계기판을 눌러 자신과 파트너를 위해 전기 충격을 끌 수 있도록 해주었던 것이다. 그래서 그 두 마리 쥐가 똑같은 수의 자극을 받았지만 한 쥐는 수동적이고 무기력했고, 다른 쥐는 통제를 할 수 있었다. 21시간의 계속되는 실험 후에 그 두 동물은 희생되었고 그들의 위의 궤양 정도가 조사되었다. 통제를 할 수 있는 쥐들이 무기력한 쥐들보다 훨씬 궤양의 정도가 덜했다.

14. ②

1. We need darkness to make our immune systems work well. 1) Scientists have now discovered that ① only when it's really dark your body can produce the hormone called melatonin. Ⓐ Melatonin fights diseases, including breast and prostate cancer. "It turns off the cancer cell from growing," says one scientist. ② But if there's even a little light around your bed at night, your melatonin production switches off. Ⓑ Light at night, even watching TV turns on other immune system hormones that should be active only in daytime. They get depleted and you're more likely to get a cold. Nature needs darkness, too. The immune systems of animals grow weak if there's artificial light at night.

중심소재: 면역체계 → 어둠이 면역체계에 미치는 영향(어둠과 면역체계의 관계)

1. 도입부 = 주제문
면역체계가 효과적으로 작용하기 위해서는 '어둠'이 필요하다.

1) 뒷받침 근거
① 최근 과학자들의 발견 – 어두울 때 바로 몸은 멜라토닌을 생산함.
Ⓐ 멜라토닌의 기능: 병균에 저항
② 빛이 없는 대조적 상황을 전개하면서 빛이 조금만 있어도 멜라토닌이 발생하지 않는다고 말하고 있다.
Ⓑ 예시부연

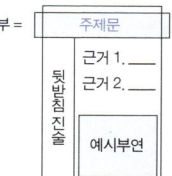

| 해설

본문은 면역체계에서 반드시 필요한 멜라토닌의 발생을 위한 조건으로 '어둠'을 이야기하고 있다. 즉, 면역체계에서의 '어둠의 중요성'을 다루는 글임을 알 수 있다. 보기의 내용을 본문 내용과 비교하면서 답을 이끌어 내 보자.

① Melatonin is essential to every living things.
  → 멜라토닌의 중요성을 이야기하는 글이 아니라 '어둠의 역할'에 중점을 둔 글이다.
② <u>All living things including humans need darkness</u>
③ We need sleep to keep our immune system active.
  → 어둠과 관련하여 '잠'이란 표현을 썼지만, 본문에서 핵심적으로 다루는 내용인 '어둠'이란 표현이 없다.
④ We have to turn the light off while sleeping at night.
  → 단순히 잠잘 때 불을 꺼야 한다는 이야기를 하려는 글이 아니다. 글의 요지를 전달하지 못하고 있다.

| 해석

우리의 면역 체계가 잘 작동되게 하려면 어둠이 필요하다. 과학자들은 우리가 실제 어둠 속에 있을 때에만 우리의 몸에서 멜라토닌(melatonin)이라고 부르는 호르몬을 만들어낼 수 있다는 것을 발견했다. 멜라토닌은 유방암, 전립선암을 비롯한 질병들과 맞서 싸운다. 어떤 과학자는 "그것이 암세포가 자라는 것을 막는다."고 했다. 그러나 만약 밤에 침대 주변에 작은 빛이라도 있으면, 멜라토닌 생산은 멈추게 된다. 밤중에 빛이 있으면, 심지어 TV를 시청하는 것조차도 낮에만 활동해야 하는 다른 면역 체계 호르몬을 활동하게 한다. 이 경우, 호르몬들이 고갈되어, 감기에 더 잘 걸리게 될 것이다. 자연도 마찬가지로 어둠이 필요하다. 만약 밤에 인공적인 빛이 있다면, 동물의 면역 시스템은 약해지게 된다.

15. ①

중심내용(controlling idea)★ 이다.

도입부 =

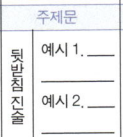

1. In the natural world, size is deceptive. 1) The greatest power comes from the smallest sources. ① The largest objects we know of are the stars, but their power arises from the interaction of atoms too small to be seen, and the energy travels to us in waves too intangible to have mass. Human kind had no idea what real power was until a half-century ago, when we unlocked the farces of the sub-atomic realm. ② The same lesson applies to the world of industry: Power lies in the ability to squeeze the most information into the tiniest space and in the ability to make smaller machines that are more efficient.

중심소재: 자연의 속성(크기)
1. 도입부 = 주제문
크기는 기만적이다.
1) 뒷받침 진술
① 예시 1
힘은 보이지 않고 만질 수 없는 작은 것들인 원자의 상호작용 때문에 발생한다.
② 예시 2
앞에서 적용된 원리를 '산업계'에도 적용하고 있음: 엄청난 정보를 담을 수 있는 작은 기계가 바로 'Power' 이다.

| 해석

자연계에서는 크기란 믿을 게 못 된다. 가장 강력한 힘은 가장 작은 근원에서 나온다. 우리가 알고 있는 가장 큰 물체는 항성이다. 하지만 항성의 힘은 너무 적어서 눈에 보이지 않는 원자들 간의 상호작용에서 발생하며, 그 에너지는 너무나도 미미해서 질량도 없는 파동의 형태로 우리에게까지 도달한다. 원자가 가진 힘을 처음으로 밝혀냈던 50년 전까지만 해도, 인간은 그 진정한 힘이 무엇인지 알지 못했다. 같은 교훈이 산업 분야에도 적용되고 있다. 즉, 산업 분야에서 힘이란 가장 작은 공간에 최대한의 정보를 집어넣고, 보다 효율적이면서도 크기는 더 작은 기계를 만들어내는 능력을 의미하게 된 것이다.

16. ②

통념으로 시작하는 글이다.★
이후 'But' 또는 'However' 가 등장하는지 파악한다.

'in fact' 는 'But' 과 같이★ 역접의 역할을 한다.

1. Humans are often thought to be insensitive smellers compared with animals, 1) but this is largely because, unlike animals, we stand upright. ① This means that our noses are limited to perceiving those smells which drift through the air, missing the majority of smells which stick to surfaces. 2. In fact, though, we are extremely sensitive to smells, even if we

중심소재: 인간과 동물의 후각
1. 도입부 = 통념
인간은 동물보다 후각이 덜 발달됐다고 여겨짐.
1) 원인: 직립보행
① 부연진술
2. 주제문
인간도 특정 냄새에 대해 후각이 아주 발달하여 있다.

168

do not generally realize it.

1) ① **Strangely**, some people find that they can smell, **for example**, one type of flower but not another, whereas other people are sensitive to the smells of both flowers. Ⓐ This may be because some people do not have the genes necessary to create particular smell receptors in the nose. These receptors are the cells which sense smells and send messages to the brain. ② **However**, it has been found that even people who are at first insensitive to a particular smell can suddenly become sensitive to it, if they are exposed to it often enough.

1) 뒷받침 진술
① 인간은 사람에 따라 후각이 민감하게 반응하는 대상이 다를 뿐이다.
Ⓐ 이유/근거 제시
② 'However' 이후 잘 인식하지 못했던 냄새라도 오래 노출되면 민감하게 됨.

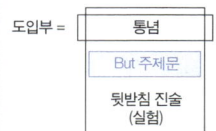

* 실험을 통한 뒷받침 근거

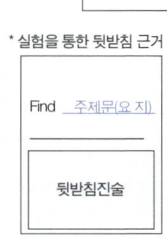

| 해석
인간은 동물과 비교해볼 때 냄새 맡는 것에 둔감하다고 흔히 생각된다. 그러나 이것은 동물과는 다르게 우리가 똑바로 서 있기 때문이다. 이것은 우리의 코가 공기 중에 떠다니는 냄새를 지각하는 데 제한되어 있고 지면에 머물러 있는 대부분 냄새는 놓쳐버린다는 것을 의미한다. 그러나 우리가 일반적으로 깨닫지 못하고 있지만 사실 우리는 지극히 냄새에 민감하다.
예를 들어, 이상하게도 몇몇 사람들은 그들이 어떤 종류의 꽃향기는 맡지만 다른 종류의 꽃향기는 맡지 못한다는 것을 발견한다. 반면, 다른 사람들은 두 종류의 꽃향기에 모두 민감하다. 이것은 어떤 사람들이 코에 특별한 냄새 수용기를 만드는 데 필요한 유전자를 가지고 있지 않기 때문일 수도 있다. 이런 수용기는 냄새를 감지하고 뇌에 메시지를 보내는 세포이다. 그러나 처음엔 어떤 특정한 냄새에 둔감한 사람들일지라도 그들이 그것에 충분히 자주 노출된다면, 갑자기 그것에 민감해진다는 것이 밝혀졌다.

| 참고
In fact의 기능은 다음과 같다.
1. 방금 한 말에 대해 자세한 내용을 덧붙일 때 쓰인다.
   예) I used to live in France; in fact, not far from where you're going.
       전 예전에 프랑스에 살았어요. 사실은 당신이 가려고 하는 곳에서 멀지 않은 곳이에요.
2. 방금 한 말에 반대되는 내용을 강조할 때 쓰인다.
   예) I thought the work would be difficult. In actual fact, it's very easy.
       나는 그 일이 어려울 거로 생각했어. 실제로는 아주 쉬워.

17. ④

1) The City Transit supervisors have received numerous complaints over the last several weeks about buses on several routes running hot. 1) Drivers are reminded that each route has several checkpoints at which drivers should check the time. If the bus is ahead of schedule, drivers should delay at the checkpoint until it is the proper time to

중심소재: 버스 운행 문제
1. 도입부 = 현상
최근에 발생한 **현상**이 제시되면서 번잡한 경로를 달리는 버스에 대한 여러 불평이 언급되고 있다.
1) **배경**(문제점에 대한 대안)

주제 = 현상(문제점)
          |
요지 = 배경

leave. If traffic makes it unsafe for a driver to delay at a particular checkpoint, the driver should proceed at a reasonable speed to the next stop and hold there until the bus is back on schedule.

| 해설

요지 또는 주장을 고르는 문제이다. 일반적으로 "문제점- 대안"의 흐름으로 전개되는 글을 다음과 같은 사항에 유의한다.
1) 문제점 – 글의 주제 도출
2) 대안 – 요지(버스는 시간표에 맞추어 운행해야 한다.)

| 해석

City Transit(도시교통)의 관리자는 지난 몇 주간 사람들이 많이 이용하는 몇몇 노선의 버스에 관한 수많은 항의를 받았다. 운전자들은 각각의 노선마다 그들이 시간을 확인해야 하는 여러 곳의 체크 지점이 있다는 사실을 알고 있다. 만약 버스가 예정된 일정보다 빠르다면, 운전자들은 출발해야 하는 적절한 시간까지 체크 지점에서 지체하여야 한다. 만약 교통의 흐름 때문에 특정한 체크 지점에서 지체하는 것이 안전하지 않다면, 운전자는 적절한 속도로 다음 정류장까지 주행하여 그곳에서 다시 시간표를 맞출 때까지 대기하여야 한다.

주제, 요지, 제목의 구별

주제는 주로 구(phrase) 또는 절(cause)의 형태를 취하며, "무엇에 관한 글인가?"를 묻는 문제이고, 요지는 문장을 형태를 취하면서, 주제를 통해서 궁극적으로 전달하고자 하는 사항이 무엇인지를 파악하는 것이다. 제목은 구, 절, 문장의 형태를 취하는데, 일반적으로 글에서 궁극적으로 전달하고자 하는 사항을 반영한다. 제목은 독자의 환기를 유발하는 함축적인 구의 표현과 함께 글의 요지를 반영한 속담, 격언 등도 활용될 수 있다. 주제와 제목의 관계를 보면, 주제를 그대로 제목으로 설정할 순 있지만, 제목을 주제로 설정하는 것은 오류가 발생할 수 있다. 예를 들어, 아래와 같은 글을 작성했다고 하자.

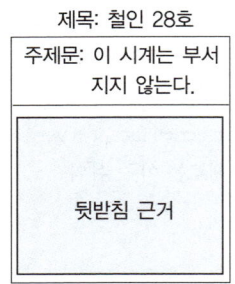

제목: 철인 28호
주제문: 이 시계는 부서지지 않는다.
뒷받침 근거

주제문을 보면, 중심소재인 "시계"를 가지고 "부서지지 않는" 속성을 강조하는 글로 "부서지지 않는 시계"로 주제를 잡을 수 있다. 만약, 제목을 설정한다면 주제와 같이 "부서지지 않는 시계"로 잡을 수 있겠으나, 독자의 흥미를 유발해야 한다는 점을 감안할 때 주제 자체를 제목을 삼을 경우 "밋밋한 감"이 있으므로, "철인 28호"라고 지었다 하자. 이 경우 "부서지지 않는"이란 튼튼한 속성의 대명사로 "철인 28호"를 설정한 것이다. 독자는 "철인 28호"를 보고, 무슨 이야기의 글인지 호기심을 가질 것이고, 궁극적으로 시계의 "튼튼한" 속성을 향수를 불러일으키는 옛 만화 캐릭터의 속성과 연관시켰음을 파악할 수 있다. 주제와 제목의 관계를 보면, 주제는 제목으로 설정할 수 있지만 제목은 그대로 주제로 설정하지 못하는 경우가 있다는 점을 유의해야 한다. 앞에서 설펴본, "철인 28호"의 제목을 글의 주제라고 했을 경우 제시된 글의 중심소재가 "철인 28호"가 되기에 본문의 내용은 말 그대로 "철인 28호"에 관한 글이 된다.

Test 3 제목을 고르는 문제

1. ④

1. In our post-9/11 world, technology often has been our crucial but silent partner in helping us to ramp up our law enforcement and national security capabilities. 1) **But** we **also** need to do it right. ① The marriage of information-gathering technology with information-storing technology, manipulated in increasingly sophisticated databases, is beginning to produce the defining privacy challenge of the information age. Ⓐ We are on the verge of a revolution in micro-monitoring the capability for the highly detailed, largely automatic, widespread surveillance of our daily lives. Moreover, other powerful new technologies are on the horizon, like sensor technology and nanotechnology. 2. We need to think about these issues broadly while keeping them from overtaking our civil liberties. Who will have access to those data banks, and under what checks-and-balances? In what cases should law enforcement agencies be able to use this information? There should be a general presumption that Americans can know when their personal information is collected, and to seek, check, and correct any errors.

중심소재: 정보기술

1. **도입부 = 현상**
9/11 이후 법의 집행과 보안 능력을 높이는 데 첨단 기술이 일조하고 있다.

1) 'But'을 통해 글의 분위기를 반전하여, 'we also need to do it right'에서도 알 수 있듯이 문제점이 있음을 드러낸다.

① **주제문**
정소수집과 저장 기술이 결합되면서 사생활 침해 현상이 대두되었다.

Ⓐ **뒷받침 배경**

2. **대안(요지)**

단락구조

도입부 = 현상
주제문 (문제점 지적)
뒷받침 배경
대안(요지)

★ 글쓴이의 요지와 관련된 내용을 전개할 때 'need to'와 같은 '주장을 드러내는 조동사'가 쓰임을 주지한다.

| 해설
p414 참조
"주제, 제목, 요지, 구별"

| 해석

9.11 테러 사건 후의 세상에서 기술은 법 집행과 국가 안보 능력을 높이는 데 도움을 주는 소리 없는 중요한 동반자였다. 그러나 우리는 이를 제대로 해야 할 필요도 있다. 정보 수집 기술과 정보 저장 기술의 결합이 점점 더 정교한 데이터베이스 속에서 조작되면서 정보화 시대의 특징인 중대한 사생활 문제를 낳기 시작하고 있다. 우리는 매우 자세하게 거의 자동으로 폭넓게 우리의 일상생활을 미세하게 감시하는 능력면에서 혁명의 문턱에 서 있다. 더욱이 센서기술과 나노기술과 같은 다른 강력한 새로운 기술들이 등장하고 있다. 우리는 이러한 기술이 시민의 자유보다 더 중요시되지 않도록 막으면서 이러한 문제들을 넓게 생각해야 할 필요가 있다. 누가 그리고 어떤 견제와 균형 하에서 그러한 데이터뱅크에 접근할 수 있는지, 어떤 경우에 법 집행 기관이 이러한 정보를 이용할 수 있는지 등등의 문제이다. 미국 국민은 자신의 개인 정보가 수집될 때 이를 알고 모든 오류를 찾고, 확인하고, 바로 잡을 수 있다는 일반적인 전제가 있어야 한다.

2. ①

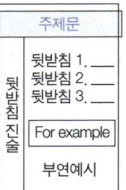

1. Many words have more than one meaning, and occasionally arguers may exploit the ambiguity in language to make a fallacious claim. One way to do this is through the fact that a word has more than one meaning so as to lead to a false conclusion. 1) <u>Equivocation exploits the fact that a word has more than one meaning so as to lead to a false conclusion.</u> ① Equivocation is often used in deceptive advertising. <u>**For example,**</u> an advertisement that appeared in several notional publications proclaimed that "Parents can receive FREE college education" for their children. On its face, the bold letters across the top of the ad made a fairly spectacular promise that the average person might find it difficult to ignore. For most people, the word free means something very different to the producers of the ad. To them, free means that parents need to invest a substantial sum of money in their "tax-free open-end mutual funds and unit trust" and pay for a variety of administrative "charges and expenses." The point is that if enough is invested, then the interest produced should be sufficient to send a child to college. Words thus mean different things to different people, and when word choice misdirects the audience's understanding of the argument, then an equivocation has taken place.

중심소재: Equivocation
(모호함의 오류)

1. 도입부
상대를 교묘히 설득하는 언어의 이중성에 관한 글이다.

1) 주제문
언어의 이중성을 활용한 "모호함의 오류" 소개

① 뒷받침 예시

주제: Fallacy of Equivocation

| 해석

많은 단어는 하나 이상의 의미가 있어서 때로는 주장을 하는 사람들이 애매한 표현을 이용하여 잘못된 주장을 할 수가 있다. 그러한 한 가지 방법이 모호한 동음이의어의 사용을 통한 것이다. 모호함의 오류는 잘못된 결론에 이르기 위해 하나의 단어가 하나 이상의 의미가 있다는 사실을 활용한다. 모호함은 흔히 허위광고에서 사용된다. 예를 들어 여러 전국적인 출판물에 실렸던 어떤 광고가 부모들은 자녀에게 대학 교육을 거저 하게 하는 혜택을 받을 수 있다고 밝혔다. 겉으로 보면 광고 맨 위에 가로로 적힌 굵은 글씨는 보통 사람이라면 무시하기 어렵다고 여길만한 아주 깜짝 놀랄 약속이었다. 대부분 사람들에게 거저라는 말은 부담이나 비용 또는 의무가 없다는 것을 의미한다. 그러나 그 광고의 제작자들에게 거저라는 말은 사뭇 다른 의미가 있다. 그들에게 거저라는 말의 의미는 그들이 제공하는 비과세 개방형 뮤추얼 펀드와 신탁 계좌에 부모들이 상당한 금액의 돈을 투자하고 여러 가지 관리 부담과 비용을 내야 한다는 것이다. 즉 만일 충분한 돈을 투자하게 되면 그에 따른 이자가 자녀를 대학에 보낼 수 있을 만큼 충분하리라는 것이다. 그래서 단어는 사람에 따라 의미가 달라지며, 단어 선택이 듣는 사람에게 상대방의 말을 오해하게 할 때 모호함이 발생한 것이다.

3. ①, ⑤

1. During the first few of life, when babies' cells continue to undergo "programming," exposure to certain toxic chemicals can disrupt the delicate process. Bisphenol A (known as BPA), a compound in hard, clear polycarbonate plastics that mimics the effects of estrogen, has raised particular concern 1) because it interferes with hormone levels and cell signaling system. ① In August, several dozen scientists issued a review of 700 studies on BPA warning that the levels most people are exposed to put them at, elevated risk of getting cancer. Infants, the report said, are most vulnerable to BPA. Ⓐ "Plastic bottles and plated that are boiled or put in the microwave or dishwashers are especially problematic because heating them repeatedly causes high amounts of BPA to leach out," says Retha Newbold, a reproductive biologist at the NIEHS in Triangle Park, N.C. Once small cracks form in the surface, a product should be discarded. 2. She recommends that parents, to be on the safe side, switch to glass bottles or those with disposable plastic liners that don't contain BPA. And they should use microwave-safe pager plates or glass dishes covered with pater towel rather than plastic wrap.

중심소재: Bisphenol A(BPA)

1. 도입부
특정 화학 물질이 아기에게 유해함을 설명하고 있다.

1) 주제문
BPA는 호르몬 수치와 세포 신호체계를 교란시킨다.

① 뒷받침 근거

Ⓐ 발생배경

2. 결론(대안)

*요지: '플라스틱 속의 BPA는 아이에게 유해하다'

★ 주제 및 제목을 설정할 때 'BPA' 또는 '플라스틱 속의 유해 화합물'을 언급해야 한다.

도입부 = Toxic Chemicals
↓
bPA(중심소재의 폭↓)
↓
주제문: BPA의 유해성
↓
뒷받침근거
↓
결론: 대안

| 해석

아기들의 세포가 계속해서 "프로그래밍"을 경험하는 생후 몇 년 동안에 어떤 유독성 화학물질에 노출되는 것은 그 섬세한 과정을 파괴할 수 있다. 에스트로겐의 효과와 유사한 단단하고 투명한 복합탄소 플라스틱에 들어있는

173

화합물인 비스페놀 A(BPA라고 알려진)는 호르몬 수치와 세포 신호 체계를 교란하기 때문에 특별한 우려를 불러 일으켰다. 8월에 수십 명의 과학자가 대부분 사람들의 BPA 노출 수준이 암에 걸릴 위험을 증가시킬 정도라고 경고하면서 BPA에 관한 700개 연구의 검토보고서를 발표하였다. 그 보고서는 유아들이 BPA에 가장 피해를 보기 쉽다고 말했다. "끓이거나 전자레인지, 식기 세척기에 넣는 플라스틱병과 접시는 반복 가열함으로 다량의 BPA가 스며 나오기 때문에 특히 문제가 많다."고 노스캐롤라이나 주 트라이앵글 파크의 미국 국립환경보건원(NIEHS)의 재생 생물학자인 레타 뉴볼드는 전한다. 일단 작은 금이 표면에 생기면 그 제품은 쓸 수가 없다. 그녀는 안전을 위해 부모들이 유리병이나 BPA가 없는 일회용 내벽이 있는 병으로 바꿀 것을 권장한다. 그리고 플라스틱 랩보다는 종이 수건으로 덮인 전자레인지용 종이 접시나 유리 접시를 사용해야 한다고 했다.

4. ④

청소년에 관한 어떤 흥미로운 글인지 파악하도록 한다.

* **요지의 파악**
청소년의 수면과 기상 사이클에 관한 객관적 정보 전달의 글인지 아니면 이를 바탕으로 궁극적으로 글쓴이가 전달하려는 사항이 있는지 파악하도록 한다.

주제와 요지의 구별 및 일반적 위치

도입부 = | 주제문(주제 파악) |
| 뒷받침 근거 |
| 요지 |

주제: 청소년 수면과 기상 사이클
요지: ②

1. An interesting fact about adolescents is that their sleep-wake cycle gets delayed by up to two hours. This means they don't become sleepy until later in the night and, subsequently, wake up later in the morning. 1) Children under 13 begin to secrete melatonin — the hormone that makes them sleepy — at around eight or nine o'clock at night. Most teenagers secrete melatonin at around 11 pm. So, essentially, any time before this is a no-sleep zone for teens; they physically cannot fall asleep. ① At the other end of the sleep zone is cortisol, the chemical responsible for waking us up. Cortisol isn't secreted in teenagers until around 8:15 am, and that's usually too late to make it to school on time. 2. So if your teenage son is dreamily vague and rubbing the sleep out of his eyes breakfast, remember this; if his brain had its way, he'd still be tucked up in bed. For parents who are trying to get the household out the door on time each morning, this sleepiness can easily be misconstrued as laziness. ② Insead of giving angry admonitions or well-meaning motivational lectures, try to realize that your teenager is just battling his or her physiology. It may be better to try to be his brain for a time — do the thinking for him.

중심소재: 수면-기상 사이클

1. 도입부 = 주제문
청소년의 수면과 기상 사이클: 청소년들은 밤에 늦게까지 잠이 오지 않기에 아침에 결과적으로 늦게 일어난다.

1) 뒷받침 근거
청소년은 잠이 오게 하는 멜라토닌이 밤늦게 생산되고, 잠을 깨게 하는 코르티솔(①)은 아침 8시 15분까지 생산되지 않는다(그래서 늦게 자고 늦게 일어나게 된다는 의미).

2. 요지
청소년의 수면과 기상의 생리현상에 바탕을 두기에 아침에 부모가 아이를 깨워 학교에 보낼 때, 아이가 일어나지 않으려고 하면, 다그치거나 야단을 치기보다는 아직 아이는 스스로 자신의 신체현상과 싸우고 있음(②)을 인식하도록 한다.

| 해석
청소년들에 대한 흥미로운 사실은 그들의 잠자고 깨는 주기가 두 시간까지도 지연된다는 것이다. 이것은 그들이 밤늦게까지 졸리지 않는다는 것과 그에 따라서 아침에 더 늦게 깬다는 것을 의미한다. 13세 이하의 어린이들은 졸리게 하는 호르몬인 멜라토닌을 대략 밤 8시~9시에 분비하기 시작한다. 대부분의 십 대들은 멜라토닌을 오후 11시경에 분비한다. 그래서 본질적으로 이 시간 전의 어떤 시간도 십 대들에게는 잠이 없는 시간대 즉 그들이 육체적으로 잠을 잘 수가 없는 시간인 것이다. 수면 시간대의 반대편 끝에는 우리를 깨어나게 하는 코르티솔이 있다. 십 대들에게 있어 코르티솔은 오전 8시 15분까지는 분비되지 않는데 보통 그 시간이면 너무 늦어서 제시간에

학교에 도착할 수 없다. 그래서 만일 당신의 십 대 자녀가 꿈을 꾸듯 몽롱하고 아침 식사 중에 잠을 떨치기 위해 눈을 비빈다면 이 점을 명심하라. 만약 그의 두뇌가 하라는 대로 한다면 그는 아직도 침대 속에 파묻혀 있을 것이라는 점이다. 매일 아침 가족을 제시간에 문밖으로 내보내려고 노력하는 부모들에게 이러한 졸림은 쉽게 게으름으로 오해될 수 있다. 분노에 찬 훈계나 선의의 동기 부여를 위한 강의를 하기보다는 당신의 십 대 자녀가 단순히 그/그녀의 생리 현상과 싸우고 있다는 사실을 이해하기 위해 노력하라. 잠깐 그의 두뇌가 되어 보려고 즉 그를 대신해 생각해 보려고 노력하는 것이 좋을 수 있다.

5. ③

1. <u>The quest for manliness</u> is essentially right-wing, cowardly, neurotic, and fueled largely by a fear of women. ① The youth who is misled into believing in the masculine ideal is conveniently separated from women, and he spends the rest of his life finding women a riddle and a nuisance. ② Masculinity celebrates the exclusive company of men. That is why it is so grotesque; and ③ that is also why there is no manliness that is absolutely complete — because it denies men the natural friendship of women.

2. <u>Of course, there is a female version of this male affliction</u>. 1) It begins with mothers encouraging little girls to say, "Do you like my new dress?" In a sense, little girls are traditionally urged to please others with a kind of coquettishness, while boys are enjoined to behave like monkeys towards each other. The nine-year-old coquette proceeds to become womanish in a subtle power game in which she learns to be sexually indispensable, socially decorative, and always alert to a man's needs. <u>Femininity — being ladylike — implies needing a man as witness and seducer.</u>

첫번째 문단
1. 도입부 = 주제문
남성미 추구는 여러 가지 이유로 왜곡된 것이라고 말하고 나서 ①, ②에서 '왜곡된 남성미 추구로 일어나는 부작용'에 관한 구체적 진술이 이어진다. ③은 ②의 근거이다.
1) 뒷받침 진술
* 소주제: Distorted Quest for Manliness

두번째 문단
1. 도입부(주제 도출)
여성 형태의 왜곡된 병폐 = Feminity
1) 뒷받침 진술
여성(어머니)에 의해서 조장된 이런 'Femininity'는 남성 없이 실현될 수 없는 '의존적 존재'로 만드는 부작용을 드러내고 있다.

| 해설
본문이 두 개로 나뉠 경우, 주제 또는 제목을 찾기는 그리 쉽지 않다. 우선 각 문단의 소주제를 찾은 후 이 두 주제를 포괄할 수 있는 주제 또는 제목을 설정해야 한다.
문단 1의 주제: Distorted Quest for Manliness
문단 2의 주제: 여성 형태의 왜곡된 병폐 = Feminity
고로, 주제는 'Misguided Sexual Identities' 이다.

| 해석
남자다움을 추구하는 것은 본질적으로 보수적이고, 소심하며, 신경증적이며 그리고 주로 여성들에 대한 두려움 때문에 생긴다. 남자다움이라는 이상을 믿도록 잘못 인도된 젊은이는 쉽사리 여성들과 분리되어, 죽는 날까지 여성을 알 수 없는 존재 또는 성가신 존재로 알며 살게 된다. 남자다움은 남자들로 구성된 배타적인 집단을 찬양한

다. 이것이 남자다움이 아주 우스꽝스러운 까닭이다. 그리고 이러한 이유 때문에 또한 절대적으로 완전한 남자다움도 없는데, 왜냐하면, 이것은 남성들로 하여금 여성과의 자연스러운 우정을 받아들이지 못하게 하기 때문이다. 물론 이러한 남성의 고민거리와 같은 것이 여성에게도 있다. 그것은 어머니가 어린 딸에게 "제가 입은 새 옷이 마음에 드세요?"라고 말하도록 부추김으로써 시작된다. 어떤 면에서 보자면, 어린 소녀들은 전통적으로 일종의 애교를 통해 서로 즐겁게 해 주도록 강요받지만, 반면 소년들은 서로 장난꾸러기처럼 행동해도 된다. 아홉 살 된 애교 있는 소녀는 미묘한 힘 싸움에서 여성스러워지기 시작하고 그 속에서 그녀는 성적으로 꼭 필요한 존재가 되고, 사회적으로는 장식과 같은 존재가 되며, 항상 남성의 욕구를 경계하라고 배운다. 여성적, 즉 여성스럽게 된다는 것은 (자신을) 눈여겨보아 줄 사람이자 유혹하는 사람으로서의 남성이 필요하다는 의미를 내포하고 있다.

중심내용(controlling idea)★에 해당한다.

중심소재는 'book' 이다.★

6. ③

1. Books are the greatest and the most satisfactory recreation. I mean the use of book for pleasure. 1) Without books, without having acquired the power of reading for pleasure, none of us can be independent, but if we can read we have a sure defence against boredom in solitude. If we have not that defence, we are dependent on the charity of family, friends, or even strangers to save us from boredom. But if we can find delight in reading, even a long railway journey alone ceases to be tedious, and long winter evenings are to ourselves an inexhaustible opportunity for pleasure.

중심소재: book
1. 도입부 = 주제문
즐거움의 수단으로서의 책
1) 뒷받침 문장
이후 책이 있는 상황과 없는 상황을 대조적으로 드러내면서 세상의 다른 것과 달리 책만이 갖는 즐거움의 특징을 부각하게 하며 주제문을 뒷받침하고 있다.

| 해석
책은 가장 훌륭하고, 가장 만족스러운 오락이다. 내 말의 뜻은 즐거움으로 책을 이용한다는 것이다. 책이 없으면, 또한 즐거움을 위해 독서가 가지고 있는 힘을 얻지 못했다면, 우리 중 누구도 남에게 의존할 수밖에 없지만, 만일 우리가 책을 읽을 수 있다면, 혼자 있을 때 지루함을 이겨내는 확실한 방어 수단을 갖게 되는 셈이다. 만일, 우리가 그 같은 방어 수단을 갖지 못한다면, 우리는 우리 자신을 지루함으로부터 구해 달라고 가족, 친구, 또는 심지어 낯선 사람들의 동정심에까지 의존하게 된다. 그러나 우리가 독서에서 기쁨을 찾을 수 있다면, 혼자서 하는 먼 기차 여행도 지루하지 않게 될 것이며, 기나긴 겨울 저녁도 우리에게는 즐거움을 만끽할 무한한 기회이다.

7. ④

1. What hunger is in relation to food, zest is in relation to life. 1) The man who enjoys watching football is to that extent superior to the man who does not. The man who enjoys reading is still more superior to the man who does not, ① since opportunities for reading are more frequent than opportunities for watching football. 2. The more things a man

중심소재: 삶 → 삶의 열정과 행복
1. 도입부
삶의 열정(행복)
1) 구체적 진술
축구를 보는 자와 책을 읽는 자를 비교하면서 더 많은 (간접) 경험이 가능한 책 읽는 자가 더 우월함을 설명하고 있다.
① 근거
축구를 하는 것보다 책을 읽을 기회가 더 많기 때문

요지를 이끄는 시그널을★ 확인한다.
1. the more ~ the more
2. A but B

is interested in, the more opportunities of happiness he has, and the less he is at the mercy of fate, since if he loses one thing he can fall back upon another. Life is too short to be interested in everything, **but** it is good to be interested in as many things as are necessary to fill our days.

2. 요지
열정을 가지고 **많은 것에 흥미를 느끼**는 사람은 **행복해질 가능성이 크다**. 즉, 행복을 위해서는 많은 것에 흥미를 느낄 것을 제안하고 있다.

| 해석
배고픔과 음식과의 관계는 열정과 삶의 관계와 같다. 축구를 즐겨 시청하는 사람은 그렇지 않은 사람보다 그만큼 낫다. 독서를 즐기는 사람은 독서를 하지 않는 사람보다 더더욱 낫다. 왜냐하면, 책을 읽을 기회는 축구를 시청할 기회보다 더 자주 있기 때문이다. 우리가 더 많은 것에 관심을 두면 둘수록, 우리는 행복을 누릴 기회를 그만큼 더 얻게 되며, 또한 운명의 지배를 덜 받게 된다. 왜냐하면, 설령 한 가지를 잃더라도 또 다른 것에 의지할 수 있기 때문이다. 삶이란 너무 짧아서 모든 것에 관심을 둘 수 없지만, 우리의 삶을 채우는 데 있어 없어서는 안 될 가능한 한 많은 것들에 관심을 두는 것이 좋다.

8. ①

1. I fully admit that the mischief which a person does to himself may seriously affect, both through their sympathies and their interests, those nearly connected with him and, in a minor degree, society at large. When, by conduct of this sort, a person is led to violate a distinct and assignable obligation to any other person or persons, the case is taken out of the self-regarding class, and becomes amenable to moral disapproval in the proper sense of the term. 1) If, for example, a man, through extravagance, becomes unable to pay his debts, or, having undertaken the moral responsibility of a family, becomes from the same cause incapable of supporting or educating them, he is deservedly criticized, and might be justly punished; 2) **but** it is for the breach of duty to his family or creditors, not for the extravagance. ① If the resources which ought to have been devoted to them had been diverted from them for the most prudent investment, the moral culpability would have been the same. 2. Whenever there is a definite damage, or a definite risk of damage, either to an individual or to the public, the case is taken out of the province of liberty, and placed in that of morality or law.

중심소재: 도덕적 불이행
1. 도입부 = 주제문
개인의 실수로 다른 이에 대한 의무를 어기는 경우 이는 "개인적 차원을 떠나 타인에 대한 도덕적 책임감을 불이행 하는 것이다"

1) 뒷받침 사례
주제문에서 밝힌 중심내용을 구체적 사례를 통해 뒷받침하고 있다.
① 사치를 통해 가족에 대한 의무를 다하지 못하는 경우 뿐 아니라, 신중한 투자 또한 결과적으로 낭비되었을 경우 동일한 도덕적 책임감의 불이행에 해당한다.

2. 결론(요지)
개인의 자유의지에 따른 행동의 결과는 개인의 차원을 넘어 타인에 대한 도덕적 점주에 놓인다. (즉, 한 사람의 자유로운 행동을 할 때는, 타인에 대한 도덕적 책임감을 고려해야 한다는 의미)

* 양괄식 구조

주제문
⇅
뒷받침 사례
⇅
요지문

| 해설

본문 마지막 부분에서 글의 요지가 드러난다. 자유에 대한 글쓴이의 견해를 드러내는 글이므로 보기 ①이 정답이다.

| 해석

나는 한 사람이 자신에게 행한 해악은 그와 가까이 연관된 사람에게 그들이 동정과 관심을 보임으로써 (오히려) 그들에게 심각한 영향을 미치는 동시에 경미하게는 사회 전반에 영향을 미칠 수 있다는 점은 전적으로 인정한다. 이러한 종류의 행위를 통해서 한 사람이 다른 사람 또는 사람들에게 지니는 독특하고, 정해진 의무를 어기게 된다면, 이런 경우는 이기적인 부류에서 취해진 것이며, 적절한 의미에서 도덕적 반감을 받을 여지(amenable)가 있게 된다. 예를 들어, 만약 사치를 통해서 한 남자가 자신의 빚을 갚지 못하게 되거나 또는 한 가정의 도덕적 책임을 가지지만, 같은 원인에서 가족을 부양하지 못하거나 교육을 제공하지 못한다면 그는 당연히 비판받아 마땅하며, 공정하게 벌을 받아야 한다. 하지만 이는 사치에 의한 것이 아니라 가족 또는 채권자에 대한 의무를 어김으로 발생하는 것이다. 만약 자신에게만 부여되었어야만 하는 자원이 가장 신중한 투자를 위해 딴 곳으로 돌려졌다면, 도덕적 문책은 동일하게 적용되었을 것이다. 명확한 피해가 존재하거나, 또는 명확한 피해의 위험성이 있을 경우 그것이 개인에게든 대중에든 이러한 경우(결과)는 자유의 영역에서 나온 것이며, 이는 도덕 또는 법의 범주에 놓이게 된다.

9. ④

내용파악의 용의성을 위해 두문단으로 구분하도록 한다.

1. In other words, science gives us power which can be used either constructively or destructively. It provides us with means which may facilitate our pursuit of bad ends as well as good. Science itself is not only morally neutral, that is indifferent to the value of the ends for which the means are used; it is also totally unable to give any moral direction. 1) You are quite right, therefore, in suggesting that science must be supplemented by philosophy if the means that science gives us are to be used for worthwhile ends. **2.** Many people today think that philosophy is useless as compared with science, because it cannot be applied in the production of things. 1) But philosophical knowledge is useful in a quite different and, in my judgment, superior way. ① Its utility or application is moral or directive, not technical or productive. Where science furnishes us with means we can use, philosophy directs us to ends we should seek.

두 번째 문단은 '일반통념 – But – 글쓴이의 주장 - 뒷받침 진술'의 패턴을 따르고 있다.

*첫번째 문단

도입부 = 문제제기
뒷받침 근거
주제문(대안)

*두번째 문단

도입부 = 통념
But 주제문
뒷받침 진술

중심소재: 과학
첫번째 문단
1. 도입부 = 문제 제기(근거)
과학 자체는 도덕적으로 중립적이나 건설적 또는 파괴적으로 활용 될 수 있다.
1) 주제문(대안)
과학은 도덕적 잣대를 제공하는 철학으로 보충되어야 한다.

두번째 문단
2. 통념
철학은 유용성이 없기에 무가치하다.
1) 주제문
철학은(과학보다) 더 고차원적인 의미에서 유용하다.
① 뒷받침 진술

| 해설

주의할 것은 과학을 없애고, 철학으로 대체하자는 내용이 아니라 과학은 도덕적 잣대를 제공하는 철학에 보충되어야 한다는 점이다.

| 해석

바꾸어 말하면, 과학은 우리에게 건설적이거나 파괴적으로 사용될 수 있는 힘을 부여한다. 과학은 우리에게 나쁜

목적뿐만 아니라 선한 목적도 유용하게 할 수 있는 수단을 제공한다. 과학 그 자체는 도덕적으로 중립적일 뿐만 아니라, 말하자면, 목적을 위해 사용되는 수단은 그 목적의 가치와는 무관한 것이다. 또한 완전히 어떤 도덕적 방향을 제시해 주지도 못한다. 따라서 과학이 우리에게 주는 수단이 가치 있는 목적을 위해 사용되려면 철학으로 과학이 보충되어야만 한다고 말하는 것은 당연하다. 많은 사람이 오늘날 철학이 과학과 비교해서 무용하다고 생각한다. 왜냐하면, 그것은 물건을 생산할 때 적용될 수 없기 때문이다. 그러나 철학적 지식은 내가 생각하기에, 꽤 다양하고 훌륭한 면에서 유용하다. 철학의 유용성 혹은 응용은 도덕적 혹은 도덕 지향적이다. 기술적이거나 생산적인 것은 아니다. 과학이 우리에게 우리가 사용할 수 있는 수단을 제공하는 곳에서, 철학은 우리에게 우리가 추구하는 목적에 방향을 제시한다.

10. ④

1. Can anyone compete with Microsoft in the world of software applications? For years now, Bill Gates & Co. have had clear sailing: the Window operating system monopoly has helped make their key products—like Word and Outlook—into unbeatable juggernauts. 1) Meanwhile, innovation in those areas proceeds only at the pace that Microsoft deems appropriate.

2. The Open Source Application Foundation has a different idea: to promote free software and innovation by creating cool new applications on a bare-bones budget. 1) The not-for-profit OSAF was initially funded with five million dollars from Lotus Development Corp. founder Mitch Kapor. For Kapor, this is a fascinating departure. Twenty years ago, he introduced one of the first killer applications of the PC age, the Lotus 1-2-3 spreadsheet; it was unabashedly for-profit and was closed source.

3. **But** Kapor always had his heart in the counter-culture, and after leaving his company he co-founded the Electronic Frontier Foundation, a cyber-rights organization. Though he has seen success as an investor, he feels strongly about the open-source movement, which posits that ① in the age of complex software many people working for nothing can duplicate or even exceed the efforts of the rake-in-the-bucks gang. And because the source code is available to all, anyone can improve the product. The continued success of the Linux-powered operating system and Apache Web servers shows that open source is no hippie-dippy pipe dream, ② but a serious challenge to the establishment.

중심소재: 소프트웨어의 세계초강자 Microsoft

1. 도입부 = 문제 제기
마이크로소프트사와 경쟁할 자가 있겠느냐는 질문의 의도는 지금까지는 그런 강력한 상대가 없었지만, 현재 그에 필적한 대상이 출현했다는 것을 암시하고 있다.

1) 배경 – Bill Gates & Co.의 소프트웨어 응용프로그램 독점으로 인해 이 분야의 혁신은 마이크로소프트사의 적절성 판단 여하에 달려 있다.

2. 막강한 힘을 가진 기존의 마이크로소프트사와는 대조적인 단체인 OSAF를 언급하면서, '무료 소프트웨어와 혁신'을 소개하고 있다.

1) 이 단체는 Lotus Development Corp.의 창시자인 Mitch Kapor의 금전적 후원을 받는다고 언급하면서, 그에 대한 부연진술이 이어진다(Kapor도 20년 전에는 영리만을 목적으로 하는 Lotus 1-2-3 확장 문서를 개발했으며, 배타적 소스로 제한함).

3. 'But'을 기점으로 Kapor가 점차 'open-source' 운동에 강한 매력을 느낀다는 점을 언급하면서, 이후 오픈 소스의 가능성(①)을 언급한 후, 기존의 체제(마이크로소프트사)에 큰 위협(②)이 될 것이라며 글을 마무리하고 있다.

| 해설

다소 복잡한 내용이 전개되는 것처럼 보이나, 첫 번째 문단에서 '마이크로소프트사의 소프트웨어 응용프로그램의 독점'을 다루면서 그로 말미암은 부작용이 언급되고 있다. 마이크로소프트사를 'juggernaut'이란 부정적인 어감의 거대한 조직으로 묘사하고 있다. 이후 두 번째 문단에서 비영리단체인 "OSAF"와 "Kapor"를 언급하면서 기존에 체제에 위협을 줄 새로운 혁신으로 'Open Source'를 다루고 있다. 즉, 윗글은 'Open Source'를 중심으로 기술되고 있다.

| 해석

소프트웨어 프로그램 세계에서 마이크로소프트사와 경쟁할 수 있는 곳이 있을까? 최근 몇 년간 빌 게이츠 법인은 순항하고 있다. 윈도우즈 운영 시스템의 독점 덕택에 워드와 아웃룩과 같은 자사의 주요 상품은 그 누구도 대적할 수 없는 무적이 되었다. 이러는 동안에는 이 분야에서 일어나는 혁신은 마이크로소프트사가 적절하다고 여기는 속도로만 진행된다.

Open Source Applications Foundation은 무료 소프트웨어를 활성화하고 제한된 예산으로 새롭고 신선한 프로그램을 개발함으로써 혁신을 조장하려는 다른 생각을 하고 있다. 비영리 단체인 OSAF는 로터스 개발 회사의 창립자인 Mitch Kapor로부터 5백만 달러의 자금을 받아 시작하게 되었다. 케이퍼에게 이것은 아주 흥미로운 시작이었다. 20년 전에 그는 PC의 첫 번째 유용한 소프트웨어 프로그램 중의 하나인 Lotus 1-2-3 스프레드시트를 도입했는데 그것은 판매용으로 소스가 공개되지 않았다.

하지만 케이퍼는 언제나 대항문화를 지향했고 회사를 떠난 후에 Electronic Frontier 재단을 공동 설립하였다. 그가 투자자로 성공한 것처럼 보였음에도 오픈 소스 운동을 강하게 지지하였는데, 그 운동은 복잡한 소프트웨어 시대에 아무것도 바라지 않고 일하는 많은 사람이 돈을 갈퀴로 긁어모으는 사람들의 성과와 맞먹을 수도 있고 심지어 능가할 수 있다는 사실을 가정한다. 그리고 모든 사람이 소스 코드를 사용할 수 있기 때문에 누구나 상품을 개발할 수 있다. 리눅스 운영 체제와 아파치 웹 서버의 계속되는 성공은 오픈 소스가 바보 같은 몽상이 아니라 기존 체제에 대한 진지한 도전이란 사실을 보여준다.

11. ④

* 시간의 대조 확인

도입부 = | 중세 ⊖ |
         | ↕ |
         | 근대 ⊕ |

1. A thousand years ago, when the earth was reassuringly flat and the universe revolved around it, the ordinary person had no last name, let alone any claim to individualism. The self was subordinated to church and king. 1) Then came the Renaissance explosion of scientific discovery and humanist insight and, as both cause and effect, the rise of individual self-consciousness. ① All at once, it seemed, humanity had replaced God at the center of earthly life. And perhaps more than any great war or invention or feat of navigation, this upheaval marked the beginning of our modern era. There are now 20 times as many people in the world as there were in the year 1000. Most have last names, and many of us have a personal identity or reasonable expectation of acquiring one. 2) This special issue examines the transformation of identity through different lenses and concludes with reflections on how hard it is, in a time of gathering global conformity, to find one's own way.

중심소재: 개인주의와 정체성 발달

1. 도입부
천년전 중세: 개인주의는 고사하고 개인의 정체성이 없던 시대

1) 주제문(근대)
과학과 인문주의가 발달하면서 자의식을 중시 여기는 사회로 발전했다(인과).

① 뒷받침 진술
신 중심의 사회에서 인간 중심의 사회로 발달, 인간의 이성을 바탕으로 한 과학의 발달, 인구 증가 등으로 인간이 역사의 중심이 되면서 **모든 사람이 성과 개인의 정체성을 달성하게 됨.**

2. 책에 실린 글의 서론임을 알 수 있다.

| 해설

중세와 근대라는 시대적 대조를 파악하고, 중세에서 근대로 넘어오던서 이전에 없었던 새로운 근대적 개념에 형성되는 사항을 파악해야 한다. 제목을 고르는 문제이다. 주제를 가장 잘 반영하는 제목을 골라야 한다. 본문은 중세에서 근대로 넘어가면서 중세에 개인이 누리지 못했던 자기 정체성(개인주의)이 근대로 넘어오면서 '르네상스, 과학혁명, 인본주의' 등이 발달하면서 자기 정체성을 강조하는 개인주의가 발달하는 내용을 다루고 있다. 보기 ④가 제목으로 가장 적절하다.

| 해석

지구는 분명 평평하고 우주가 지구의 주위를 돌고 있다고 믿던 1천 년 전, 평범한 사람들은 개인의 독자성을 요구할 권리는 말할 것도 없고, 성(姓)조차 가지고 있지 않았다. 자아는 교회와 왕에 종속되어 있었다. 그 후 르네상스 시대가 되어 과학적인 발견과 인본주의적 통찰력이 폭발하듯 생겨났고, 또한 그것의 원인과 결과로서 개인의 자의식(自意識)이 생겨났다. 갑자기, 인간이 지상의 삶의 중심에서 하느님을 대신하는 듯 보였다. 그리고 아마 그 어떤 커다란 전쟁이나 발명 또는 항해의 위업보다도 이 격변이 근대의 시즈이 되었을 것이다. 지금 세계는 서기 1000년 당시보다 스무 배나 많은 사람이 있다. 대부분의 사람이 성(姓)을 가지고 있으며, 우리 중 많은 사람이 신분증명서나 마땅히 그것을 가지게 될 것이라는 기대를 하고 있다. 이번 특별 호에서는 다양한 시각을 통해 (개인의) 주체성이 변천하는 모습을 살펴보고, 전 세계적인 획일성을 조장하는 시대에서 자신만의 길을 찾는 것이 얼마나 힘든지를 깊이 생각해보는 것으로 결론을 맺는다.

12. ①

1. In Europe, Southeast Asia and all sorts of places inbetween, something remarkable is happening. Alternative-energy-technologies have moved quietly but decisively from experimental curiosity to commercial reality, economically turning sunlight, wind and other renewable resources into useful forms of energy. This achievement opens up an intriguing possibility. Just as the economic miracles of the 20th century were powered by fossil fuels, the 21st century may be marked by an equally dramatic move away from those fuels—and the environmental havoc they have wrought. 1) The result may be nothing less than an energy revolution.

2. Roughly 100 years have passed since a transition of this magnitude has taken place. Much of the energy system now in place was created by an explosion of invention between 1890 and 1910. During that short period, cities were transformed, as automobiles and electric lights replaced horse-drawn carriages and gas lamps. The old technologies had prevailed for centuries, but they became obsolete in a matter of years. Today we may be at a similar turning point.

첫번째 문단

1. 도입부 = 현상
대체에너지 연구가 전 세계에서 일어나고 있다는 점과 상업적 가능성을 언급하고 있다. 대체에너지 연구에 관한 지문이다.

1) 첫 번째 문단 마지막에서 20세기에 화석연료 덕분에 경제 기적을 이룬 것과 마찬가지로 곧 대체에너지 덕분에 21세기에 실현될 현상을 에너지 혁명이라 말하고 있다.

- 첫 번째 문단은 21세기 경제 기적을 이룰 '대체에너지 개발'을 다루고 있다.

2. 두 번째 문단

과거 에너지 역사(배경)를 언급하면서, 마차와 기름 램프가 자동차와 전깃불로 교체된 것과 마찬가지로 오늘날에는 정부의 보조와 개인 기업의 투자로 대체에너지가 에너지 산업을 휩쓸 것이라고 말하고 있다.

- 두 번째 문단에서도 여전히 '대체에너지 발달'에 관한 내용을 다루고 있다.

★현상을 드러내는 시그널 확인
have + p.p
be + V-ing

Thanks to a potent combination of government incentives and private investment, technologies that use synthetic materials, advanced electronics and biotechnology are sweeping through the energy industry. That will foster a new generation of mass-produced machines that efficiently and cleanly provide the energy that enables people to take a hot shower, sip a cold beer or even surf the Internet.

| 해설

단락이 두 개로 나뉜 지문은 단락별 소주제를 설정하고 두 단락을 종합할 수 있는 주제 또는 제목을 골라야 한다. 본문에 나온 두 단락 모두 '대체에너지 발달'을 다루고 있다.

| 해석

유럽, 동남아시아 그리고 그 사이 모든 지역에서 주목할 만한 일이 일어나고 있다. 경제적으로 햇빛, 바람 그리고 다른 재생 가능한 자원들을 유용한 에너지 형태로 전환하면서, 대체에너지 기술은 조용하지만, 분명히 실험적 호기심에서 상업적 현실로 옮겨왔다. 이러한 결과는 흥미로운 가능성을 열어 주고 있다. 20세기 경제 기적이 화석 연료들에 의해 촉진된 것처럼, 마찬가지로 21세기는 그러한 연료들—그리고 그것들이 가져온 환경 파괴—로부터의 극적인 탈출로 발전될 것이다. 그 결과는 다름 아닌 바로 에너지 혁명이 될 것이다.

이러한 거대한 변화가 일어난 지 대략 100년이 흘렀다. 현재 자리 잡고 있는 많은 에너지 시스템은 1890년에서 1910년 사이에 폭발적으로 이뤄진 발명으로 만들어졌다. 그러한 짧은 기간에, 자동차와 전깃불이 마차와 가스 램프를 대체한 것처럼 도시는 변했다. 낡은 기술들은 수 세기를 지배하였지만, 수년 안에 진부한 것이 되었다. 오늘날 우리는 비슷한 전환점에 있는지도 모른다. 정부의 장려금에 개별 투자가 더해진 덕분에 합성 물질, 진보된 전자 공학과 생물 공학을 이용하는 기술이 에너지 산업을 휩쓸고 있다. 그것은 사람들이 뜨거운 물로 샤워하고, 차가운 맥주를 마시거나 심지어 인터넷을 검색하게 해주는 에너지를 효과적이고 솜씨 있게 제공해 줄 대량 생산 기계의 새로운 시대를 만들어 낼 것이다.

13. ②

명령문은 글쓴이가 궁극★적으로 전달하려는 요지를 전달하는 문장이다.

1. **Forgive and forget.** Most of us find the forgetting easier, but maybe we **should** work on the forgiving part. 1) "Holding on to hurts and nursing grudges wears you down physically and emotionally," says Stanford University psychologist Fred Luskin, author of Forgive for Good. 2) "Forgiving someone can be a powerful antidote."

2. In a recent study, Charlotte van Oyen Witvliet, assistant professor of psychology at Hope College in Holland, Michigan, and colleagues asked 71 volunteers to remember a past hurt. Tests recorded steep spikes in blood pressure, heart rate and muscle tension—the same responses that occur when people are angry. ① Research has linked anger

중심소재: 용서
첫번째 문단
1. 도입부 = 요지
"용서에 힘써라"라고 말하고 있다.
1) 뒷받침 근거
용서하지 않고 악의를 지닐 때 발생하는 역작용을 설명하고 있다.
2. 주제문(요지)
용서는 해독제의 효과가 있다.
두번째 문단
1. 뒷받침 진술
실험을 통해 글쓴이의 주장을 뒷받침하고 있다. ①와 ②의 상반된 결과를 통해 '용서의 긍정적 기능'을 강조하고 있다.

and heart disease. When the volunteers were asked to imagine ② empathizing, even forgiving those who'd wronged them, they remained calm by comparison.

3. 1) **What's more**, forgiveness can be learned, insists Luskin, director of the Stanford Forgiveness Project. ① "We teach people to rewrite their story in their minds, to change from victim to hero. If the hurt is from a spouse's infidelity, we might encourage them to think of themselves not only as a person who was cheated on, but as the person who tried to keep the marriage together."

4. Two years ago Luskin tested his method on five Northern Irish women whose sons had been murdered. After undergoing a week of forgiveness training, the women's sense of hurt, measured using psychological tests, had fallen by more than half. They were also much less likely to feel depressed and angry. "Forgiving isn't about condoning what happened," says Luskin. "It's about breaking free of the person who wronged us."

5. The early signs that forgiving improves overall health are promising: A survey of 1,423 adults by the University of Michigan's Institute for Social Research in 2001 found that people who had forgiven someone in their past also reported being in better health than those who hadn't.

6. However: While 75 percent said they were sure God had forgiven them for past mistakes, only 52 percent had been able to find it in their hearts to forgive others. Forgiveness, it seems, is still divine.

세번째 문단
1) 용서의 속성
용서는 학습가능
① 구체적 진술
권위자의 말을 통해 용서의 학습 가능성을 부연하고 있다.

네번째 문단: 용서의 순기능
실험을 통해 용서의 놀라운 순기능을 설명하고 있다.

다섯번째 문단
'용서와 건강의 긍정적 관계'를 실험을 통해 다시 밝히고 있다.

여섯번째 문단: 결론
용서가 쉽지 않지만, 궁극적으로 앞서 언급한 용서의 순기능을 바탕으로 용서는 고귀한 것이며 'we should work on the forgiving part'라고 주장하고 있다.

| 해설

첫 번째 문단의 'Forgive and forget' 과 'Forgiving someone can be a powerful antidote' 라는 글쓴이의 견해에서 알 수 있듯이, 노력을 통한 용서의 학습 가능성과 치유력을 주장하고, 실험을 통해서 이를 증명하고 있다. 만약 글의 도입부에서 주제를 빼내지 못했다 하더라도 실험을 통한 구체적 진술에서 글쓴이의 견해를 빼낼 수 있다. 실험의 목적에서 글의 주제/제목, 실험의 결과에서 주제/제목/요지(특히, 요지)를 빼낼 수 있다는 점 또한 기억해 둔다.

| 해석

용서해라. 그리고 잊어라. 우리 대다수는 망각하는 일이 더 쉽다는 것을 알지만 아마도 우리는 용서하는 쪽에 주력해야만 할 것이다. "상처에 매달리거나 분노를 키우는 것은 당신을 육체적으로나 정서적으로 지치게 한다." 라고 Forgive for Good의 저자이자 스탠퍼드 대학의 심리학자 프레드 러스킨은 말하였다. "어떤 이를 용서하는 것은 강력한 해독제가 될 수 있다."

최근 한 연구에서, 네덜란드의 호프 대학 심리학 조교수인 샬럿 반 오엔 위블릿과 동료들은 71명의 지원자에게 과거의 상처를 기억하도록 했다. 테스트 결과 혈압, 심장 박동수, 근육의 긴장도에서 급격한 상승이 있었다. 이것은 사람들이 화가 났을 때 일어나는 반응들과 같다. 조사는 분노와 심장 질환을 관련지었다. 지원자들에게 그들에게 잘못을 저지른 사람들의 처지를 이해해보고 더 나아가 그들을 용서하도록 요구했을 때, 이들은 비교적 침착한 상태를 유지할 수 있었다.

게다가, 스탠퍼드의 용서 프로젝트 책임자인 러스킨은 용서가 학습될 수 있다고 주장한다. "우리는 사람들이 마음속에 있는 그들의 이야기를 희생자에서 영웅으로 바꾸어 다시 쓸 수 있게 가르칩니다. 상처가 배우자의 부정 때문인 것이라면 우리는 그들이 자기 자신을 단지 배신당한 사람으로만 생각하는 게 아니라 결혼을 지키려 노력했던 사람으로 생각할 수 있도록 격려합니다."

2년 전 러스킨은 그의 방법을 아들이 살해된 다섯 명의 북아일랜드 여성에게 시험해 보았다. 용서 훈련이 한 주 진행되고 난 후 그 여성들의 상처는 심리학적 테스트로 진단해본 결과 반 이상 줄었다. 그들은 또한 낙담하거나 분노하는 감정이 많이 줄었다. "용서는 이미 일어난 일을 용서하는 것이 아닙니다. 용서는 우리에게 잘못한 사람으로부터 자유롭게 되는 것입니다."라고 러스킨은 말했다.

용서가 전반적 건강을 증진한다고 하는 초기 징후들은 일리가 있다. 2001년 미시간 대학 부설 사회 조사 기관이 1,423명의 성인을 조사한 결과 과거에 누군가를 용서했던 사람들이 그렇지 않은 사람들보다 건강 상태가 더 양호하다는 사실이 밝혀졌다.

그렇지만 75%의 사람들이 그들의 지난 잘못들을 하나님이 용서하셨을 거라고 확신하는 반면, 52%의 사람만이 진심으로 다른 이들을 용서했다고 하였다. 용서는 아직도 신의 것으로 보인다.

14. ⑤

도입부 = | 현상
통념(일반인의 견해)
↕ (In reality)
주제문

뒷받침진술

1. According to E-Marketer, during the 1999 holiday season some 34 million individuals made at least one purchase online. 1) Web users are often lulled into believing that browsing online is an anonymous process. ① **In reality**, the explosion in electronic commerce has been accompanied by increasingly sophisticated information-gathering techniques. Ⓐ Clearly there is nothing inherently unethical in gathering information on customers when appropriate safeguards are put into place to protect them. Since the dawn of commerce, bricks-and-mortar store owners have gathered information on their regular customers. Ⓑ **However**, what has irrevocably altered this information-gathering process is the growth of sophisticated technology that enables the collection, dissemination, and combination of detailed information on customers at previously unprecedented levels.

중심소재: 온라인 쇼핑

1. 도입부 = 현상
온라인 쇼핑에 관한 이야기로, 상당한 시장으로 성장한 전자 시장을 언급하고 있다.

1) 통념
일반인들은 온라인이 익명을 바탕으로 한 활동이라 생각한다.

① 주제문 (역접의 In reality)확인
전자상거래와 정보수집의 결합

Ⓐ 뒷받침 진술
However를 기준으로 개인 정보유출의 문제점 지적

| 해석
E-marketer에 따르면, 1999년 휴가 기간에 약 3,400만 명이 온라인으로 적어도 한 번은 물품을 샀다고 한다. 인터넷 사용자들은 종종 온라인상에서의 웹서핑이 익명으로 이루어진다고 믿고서 안심하고 있다. 실제로, 전자상거래의 폭발적인 증가로 인해 정보 수집 기술도 점차 복잡해졌다. 소비자들을 보호하기 위해 적절한 보호 장치가

마련되어 있다면 그들에 대한 정보를 수집하는 데 있어 원래 비윤리적인 것은 분명 없을 것이다. 상거래가 시작된 이래로 실제로 매장이 존재하는(오프라인의) 상점 주인은 단골손님들에 대한 정보를 수집해왔다. 그러나 이 정보 수집 과정을 돌이킬 수 없을 만큼 달라지게 만든 것은 전에 없던 수준으로 소비자에 대한 상세한 정보를 수집하여 퍼뜨리고 결합할 수 있도록 해주는 정교한 기술의 발전이다.

15. ②

1. <u>A moment's reflection will make it clear that one **cannot** live a full, free, influential life in America **without** argument</u>. 1) **No doubt** people often argue on insufficient evidence and for insufficient reasons; no doubt they often argue on points about which they should rather be thinking and studying; no doubt they sometimes fancy they are arguing when they are merely wrangling and disputing. **But** this is only proof that argument is employed badly, that it is misused rather than used skillfully. ① <u>Argument, at the right moment and for the right purpose and in the right way, is undoubtedly one of the most useful instruments in American life</u>. It is an indispensable means of expressing oneself and impressing others.

중심소재: 논쟁 → 논쟁의 중요성

1. 도입부 = 주제문
미국인의 삶에 있어 '논쟁의 중요성'을 언급하고 있다.

1) 뒷받침 진술
'But' 이후 앞에서 말한 논쟁이 때론 '불충분한 증거에 기초하기도 하고, 깊은 생각이나 연구 없이 다투기 위한 논쟁을 벌이긴 하지만 이것은 단지 **논쟁을 잘못 사용한 예**일 뿐이라고 주장하면서 주제문의 중심내용을 재차 언급하고 있다(①).

3) 글쓴이의 주장이 다시 드러난다.

★ 'cannot ~ without'의 강조구문을 확인할 수 있다. 글의 요지를 이끄는 시그널이므로 강조구문은 집중에서 읽도록 한다.

도입부 =
| 주제문 |
| 뒷받침 진술 |
| 요지 |

| 해설
어떤 글을 막론하고, 첫 번째 문장의 중요성과 'But' 이후 글쓴이의 주장과 직간접적으로 관련된 내용이 전개됨을 잊지 말아야 한다.

| 해석
아주 짧은 순간이라도 생각해 보면 논쟁 없이는 미국에서 완전하고, 자유롭고, 영향력 있는 삶을 살 수 없다는 게 명확할 것이다. 확실히 사람들은 종종 불충분한 증거와 부당한 이유로 논쟁한다. 그들은 종종 더 생각하고 연구해야만 하는 사항에 대해 논쟁한다. 단지 말다툼이나 토의를 할 때도 논쟁한다고 때때로 생각하는 게 확실하다. 그러나 이것은 논쟁이 단지 잘못 쓰였고 능숙하게 사용했다기보다는 오용되었다는 증거일 뿐이다. 적시에 옳은 목적을 위한 정당한 방법의 논쟁은 의심할 여지 없이 미국인의 생활에서 가장 쓸모 있는 도구 중 하나이다. 자신을 표현하고 남에게 깊은 인상을 주는 필요불가결한 수단이다.

16. ④

1. Bill Smith and Mike Hugh are examples of men who committed three felonies and are now serving life in prison under California's "Three Strikes" law. 1) **However**, the men's crimes were not violent. Hugh says it is a waste of money to keep people like him locked up for the rest of their lives.

중심소재: Three Strikes law

1. 도입부 = 중심소재 도출
종신형에 해당하는 Three strikes law의 사례 제시

1) 찬반의 견해
① 반대 입장
'However' 이후 'Three Strikes

도입부 =	현상 (Three strikes law)
	반대입장
	찬성입장

글쓴이 ①는 중립적 입장에서 특정 현상에 대한 찬반의 견해를 제시하고 있다.

Many people agree with him. ① A new study by the Justice Policy Institute claims that the ten-year-old Three Strikes law has cost California billions of dollars, but it has not reduced crime. The authors of the study believe that sending people to jail is not a good way to reduce crime, and they think that people who commit nonviolent crimes should not suffer from Three Strikes. Some prosecutors agree that the law is unfair and unreasonable, and that it does not deter crime. ② The author of the Three Strikes law, Bill Jones, disagrees. According to Jones, Three Strikes has saved California billions of dollars, and crime in the state has gone down by 46 percent. Ⓑ For example, California now has its lowest level of burglaries since 1957. Jones also says there are two million fewer crime victims and 100,000 fewer prisoners than without Three Strikes. He points out that California has not built any new prisons since the law was passed.

law'는 돈 낭비라고 비난하고 있다.
Ⓐ 뒷받침 부연예시

② 찬성 입장
'Three Strikes law'에 동의하는 내용을 구체적 인물을 통해 전개하고 있다: 'Three Strikes law' 덕분에 실질적으로 비용절감과 범죄율 감소가 있었다.
Ⓑ 뒷받침 부연 예시

| 해설
글쓴이는 'Three Strikes law'에 대한 찬반을 객관적 입장에서 동등한 무게로 다루고 있다.

| 해석
빌 스미스(Bill Smith)와 마이크 휴(Mike Hugh)는 3번의 중죄를 저지르고 지금 캘리포니아의 'Three Strikes' 법 아래서 종신형을 복역 중인 사람들의 대표적인 예이다. 그러나 그들의 범죄는 폭력적이지는 않았다. 휴는 자신과 같은 사람들을 남은 인생 동안 가두어놓는 것은 돈 낭비라고 말한다. 많은 사람이 그의 의견에 동의한다. 사법 정책 연구소(the Justice Policy Institute)에 의한 한 새로운 연구는 10년이 된 Three Strikes 법이 캘리포니아 주로 하여금 수십억 달러의 비용을 쓰게 했지만, 범죄를 줄이지는 못했다고 주장한다. 연구의 집필자들은 사람들을 감옥에 보내는 것이 범죄를 줄이는 좋은 방법은 아니라고 믿으며, 비폭력적인 범죄를 저지르는 사람들은 Three Strikes 법의 적용을 받지 말아야 한다고 생각한다. 몇몇 검사들 또한 그 법은 불공정하고, 불합리하며 범죄를 막지 못한다는 데 동의한다. Three Strikes 법의 창시자인 빌 존스(Bill Jones)는 동의하지 않는다. 존스가 발표한 바로는 Three strikes는 캘리포니아 주로 하여금 수십억 달러를 절약하게 해왔고 캘리포니아 주의 범죄는 46%만큼 감소했다. 예를 들면 캘리포니아 주는 현재 1957년 이래로 가장 낮은 강도 범죄 수치를 나타내고 있다. 또한, Three Strikes 법이 없을 때보다 2백만 명의 범죄 피해자와 십만 명의 죄수가 줄었다고 존스는 말한다. 캘리포니아 주는 그 법이 통과된 이후로 어떠한 새로운 감옥도 건설하지 않았다고 그는 지적하고 있다.

17. ①

1. Violence and homicide are not always the work of criminals and terrorists. In recent times, people around the world have been shocked by widespread examples of horror perpetrated by religious cults claiming to be in the service of

첫 번째 문단

1. 도입부 = 현상
신에 대한 예배를 목적으로 행해지는 종교 집단의 '폭력과 살해'를 구체적인 예를 통해 설명하고 있다.

God. In 1978 in Guyana, 900 men, women, and children belonging to the People's Temple obediently drank poisoned Kool-Aid to die along with their leader, Jim Jones. In 1994, the bloody remains of 50 followers of the Order of the Temple of the Sun were found in various houses in Switzerland and Canada: they had killed themselves and their children, believing that the end of the world is near.

2. At first glance it is hard to comprehend how ordinary people can be induced to these acts of murder and suicide under the guise of religion and morality. Most experts suggest that **the cause** lies at least partly in ① <u>the breakdown of traditional institutions</u>, such as the church and family, which formerly provided a feeling of security and identity to most individuals. New groups arise to fill the void, and these are the so-called cults. Young people in particular, ② alienated by the competition, stress, and greed they perceive at many levels of modern society, often begin to search for simple alternatives that will provide them with meaning and certainty. ③ The cults generally promise an all-embracing surrogate family and a perfect paradise after death, and that combination seems attractive indeed.

3. Cult promises paradise but delivers subjugation and exploitation, and even at times, death and violence. Yet it is not fair to say that cults are completely bad. Good and evil are mixed together in many cults, as they are in most fields of human endeavor.

도입부 = 현상
원인 원인 1. ___
원인 2. ___
원인 3. ___

두 번째 문단
2. 현상의 **원인**을 파악
① 전통 기관의 붕괴 – lack of security and identity
② 특히 젊은 세대의 경우 현대 사회에서 겪는 '경쟁, 스트레스 그리고 욕심' 탓에 대안으로 'cults'를 찾는다.
③ 젊은이들이 이들 종교 집단에 의지하는 이유를 들고 있다.

세 번째 문단
3. Cults의 문제점을 언급하는 동시에 전적으로 악하기만 한 것은 아니라고 말하고 있다.

| 해설

본문은 현대 사회의 문제로 많은 사람 특히, 젊은이들이 'cults'에 눈을 돌리는데 이러한 집단이 가지는 위험성을 이야기하고 있다. 제목으로 '사이비 종교 집단에 가입하게 되는 이유(매력적 이유), 문제점'을 모두 드러내는 보기 ①이 가장 적절하다.

| 해석

폭력과 살인은 반드시 범죄자와 테러리스트만이 하는 일이 아니다. 최근에 전 세계 사람들이 사이비 종교 집단이 저지른, 널리 유포된 공포 사례에 경악을 금치 못했는데 그 종교 집단은 이를 신에 대한 예배 의식이라고 주장했다. 1978년 Guyana에서 인민 사원 소속 남자, 여자, 어린애들이 독약이 든 Kool-Aid를 고분고분 마시고 지도자인 Jim Jones를 따라 자살했다. 1994년, 태양 신전 종교단 신봉자 50명의 피투성이 유해가 캐나다와 스위스의 여러 가옥에서 발견되었다. 그들은 세상의 종말이 다가오고 있다고 믿었기 때문에 자녀와 더불어 자살했다.

어떻게 정상적인 사람들이 종교와 도덕의 이름으로 살인과 자살이라는 행위로 유인당하는지 처음에는 이해하기 어렵다. 과거에 개인에게 안정감과 정체성을 제공했던 교회와 가족 같은 전통적 제도의 붕괴가 적어도 부분적인 이유가 된다고 전문가들은 생각한다. 새로운 집단이 빈자리를 채우기 위해 생겨나고 이것들이 소위 cult(사이비 집단)라 불린다. 현대사회의 여러 방면에서 느끼는 탐욕과 스트레스와 경쟁으로부터 소외당한 젊은이들이 특히 (삶의) 의미와 확신을 부여하는 단순한 대안을 찾기 시작한다.

광신자 집단은 모든 것을 포옹하는 대리 가족과 사후의 완벽한 낙원 등을 일반적으로 약속하는데 이런 결합은 참으로 매력적으로 보인다. 광신자 집단은 낙원을 약속하지만, 복종과 착취, 때때로 죽음과 폭력을 말한다. 그러나 그들이 전적으로 악하다고 말하는 것은 정당치 못하다. 인간적 노력의 모든 일이 그렇듯이 많은 광신자 집단에도 선과 악이 섞여 있다.

18. ②

*시간의 대조
| 과거 |
| ↕ |
| 현재 |

1. 1) Once upon a time, only Santa Claus knew whether you had been good or bad. ② **But** jolly supernaturalism has been supplanted by aggressive data processing. Ⓐ Your chances of finding work, getting a mortgage or qualifying for health insurance may be up for grabs, because almost any body with a computer, modem and telephone can surf through cyberspace into the deepest recesses of your private life. A fairly accurate profile of your financial status, tastes and credit history can be gleaned from such disparate things as your ZIP code, Social Security number and records of credit-card usage. 2) **But** legal access to data is only part of the problem. Another difficulty is ② unauthorized peeking into personal records, which occurs with alarming regularity because company safeguards are often laughable. A second problem is that ③ wrong and harmful "facts" can creep into the databases. Malicious tipsters can poison a person's record within innuendo, and it takes much effort to correct the mistake.

본문에 등장하는 첫 번째 ★
But은 대조이고, 두 번째는 추가 강조의 기능이다.

중심소재: 인터넷을 통한 개인 정보 유출
1. 도입부(현상)
1) 과거와 현재의 특정 현상과 대조하면서 문제점 지적
① 과거
가상의 초자연적 존재만이 다른 이의 정보를 알 수 있었다(다른 이의 정보를 안다는 것은 가상의 일이지 현실이 아니었음을 나타냄).
② 현재(문제점 지적)
'But' 이러한 초자연적인 현상이 'aggressive data processing(= 인터넷)'으로 대체되면서 현실이 되었다.
Ⓐ 개인의 정보가 다양한 사이버 경로를 통해 새어나가고 있음을 기술하고 있다.

2) 문제의 심각성
'But' 이후 추가로 좀 더 심각한 문제를 언급하고 있다.
① unauthorized peeking into personal records
② 잘못되고 유해한 정보가 개인의 데이터베이스에 침입할 위험성

| 해설
제목을 찾는 문제는 주제 및 글쓴이의 요지를 적절하게 반영한 구체적이면서도 때로는 함축적인 답이 제시된다. 위 문제는 본문에서 언급된 '과거와 달리 현재는 인터넷을 통한 개인 정보의 침범이 손쉽게 이뤄진다.' 는 위험성을 고발하는 글이므로 보기 ②가 가장 적절하다.

| 해석
옛날에는 산타클로스만이 당신이 선했는지 악했는지 알았다. 그러나 유쾌한 초자연력(산타클로스)을 공격적인 정보 처리가 대신하게 되었다. 당신이 직장을 찾고, 담보를 얻고 혹은 건강보험의 자격을 갖추었는지 여부를 누구나 알아볼 수 있다. 왜냐하면, 컴퓨터, 모뎀, 그리고 전화(인터넷 기능)가 있는 사람이면 거의 누구나 사이버 공간을 통해 당신의 사생활 가장 깊숙한 곳까지도 넘나들 수 있기 때문이다. 상당히 정확한 당신의 재정 상태, 기호(嗜好)와 신용거래 등의 내용이 당신의 우편번호, 사회보장 번호와 신용카드 사용 기록과 같이 별 연관이 없는 것

들로부터 수집될 수 있다. 그러나 데이터의 합법적인 입수는 문제의 일부분에 불과하다. 또 다른 문제는 개인적인 자료에 대해 아무 권한 없이 훔쳐보는 것인데, 이것은 회사의 안전장치가 종종 어처구니없을 정도로 허술해서 놀랄 만큼 자주 일어난다. 두 번째 문제는 그릇되고 해로운 "사실들"이 데이터베이스에 들어갈 수 있다는 것이다. 악덕 정보 제공자들은 넌지시 빗대어 한 개인의 이력에 해를 끼칠 수 있으며, 그 실수를 바로잡는 데에는 많은 노력이 필요하다.

19. ②

1. The African country of Ghana owes a lot of its success to a pocketful of seeds brought into the country in 1879 by a young black man named Tetteh Quashie. 1) He **had been** living and working on an island near Africa for several years. When he decided to go back home to Ghana (then owned by England and called the Gold Coast), he had to smuggle cacao seeds into the country. This was because the island's leaders did not want any other places to grow and sell cacao seeds, which are used to make cocoa. Cocoa is used to make chocolate.

2. Tetteh Quashie set up a small nursery to grow cacao plants. Then he traveled all around the country, giving seedlings to poor farmers and showing them how to grow the plants. Within thirty years, the Gold Coast became the world's largest producer of cacao. With the money brought in by selling cacao, the Gold Coast was able to buy new and costly things that were now affordable, such as railroads. When the Gold Coast became independent in 1950s and changed its name to Ghana, it was one of the richest countries in Africa—thanks to a pocketful of seeds.

중심소재: Seed

첫번째 단락

1. 도입부 = 주제문
아프리카의 현재 성공은 과거 한 흑인 청년이 가지고 들어온 씨앗에서 비롯된 것이라 말하고 있다.

1) 뒷받침 문장
'had been'에서 알 수 있듯이, 주제문에서 밝힌 내용을 구체적으로 진술하기 위해 과거로 거슬러 올라간다 – 첫 번째 단락 끝까지 이 흑인 청년이 어떻게 (Smuggling) 카카오 씨앗을 아프리카에 가지고 오게 되었는가에 관한 경위를 설명하고 있다.

두번째 단락

2. 두 번째 단락에서는 아프리카로 가지고 들어온 씨앗으로 아프리카가 어떻게 성공하게 되었는지 상술하고 있다.

글의 요지: 한 청년이 가지고 들어온 카카오 씨앗이 현재의 아프리카 성공의 원동력이었다.

★ 중심소재는 'seed'이다.

★ 시간의 글 전개방식을 확인한다.

| 해설

윗글은 '일반진술 – 구체적 진술'의 아주 단순한 구조를 취하는 글이다. 첫 번째 문장에서 주제문을 제시해 주고, 이후 이것을 뒷받침해주는 구체적인 내용이 진술되고 있다. 일반진술이 생략된 경우 구체적 내용을 읽으면서 '이야기를 통해 궁극적으로 전달하려는 내용은 무엇인가?'라는 물음을 지속해서 던져야 한다.

| 해석

아프리카에 있는 나라인 가나가 성공할 수 있었던 것은 1879년 테떼 쿠아쉬(Tetteh Quashie)라는 흑인 청년이 한 줌의 씨앗을 나라에 들여온 덕택이다. 그는 수년간 아프리카 근처의 섬에서 살고 일해 왔었다. 그가 고향인 가나로 돌아가기로 결심했을 때 (그때 가나는 영국의 소유였고 골드 코스트라고 불렸다), 그는 카카오 씨앗을 몰래 갖고 들어왔다. 왜냐하면, 그 섬의 지도자들은 코코아를 만들 때 사용되는 카카오 씨앗이 다른 장소에서 재배되거나 팔리기를 원하지 않았기 때문이다. 코코아는 초콜릿을 만들 때 사용된다.

테떼 쿠아쉬는 작은 모상을 만들어 카카오나무를 재배했다. 그는 온 나라를 돌아다니며 가난한 농부들에게 묘목을 나눠 주고 그 식물을 기르는 방법을 가르쳐 주었다. 30년도 안 되어서 골드 코스트는 세계에서 가장 큰 카카오 생산지가 되었다. 카카오를 팔아서 벌어들인 돈으로 골드 코스트는 철도와 같이 새롭고 돈이 많이 드는 것들을 이제 살 수 있는 여유가 생겼다. 골드 코스트가 1950년대에 독립하고 그 이름을 가나로 바꿨을 때 가나는 한 줌의 씨앗 덕분으로 아프리카에서 가장 부유한 나라 중 하나가 되었다.

도입부 = 주제문
뒷받침 진술
뒷1. _____
뒷2. _____
뒷3. _____
부연진술
뒷4. _____

20. ①

1. People usually build their houses out of the materials that are available to them. 1) ① In some areas, most people build their homes out of wood. This is true in parts of North America and in Scandinavia. These areas have large forests, so wood is easy to get and inexpensive. ② In many other areas of Europe, there are few forests left. Stone and brick are cheaper, so most people build their houses of these materials. ③ In tropical regions, houses are sometimes made from plants that grow there. Ⓐ For example, in parts of Africa or Asia, houses may be made out of bamboo. ④ Finally, in the very coldest areas near the Arctic, people make their homes out of blocks of cement.

중심소재: 집짓기 → 지역에 나는 집짓기 재료
1. 도입부 = 주제문
사람들은 주변에서 이용할 수 있는 자재로 집을 짓는다.
1) 뒷받침 문장
① 숲이 많은 지역에서는 나무로 집을 짓는다.
② 유럽과 같은 다른 지역에서는 돌과 벽돌로 집을 짓는다.
③ 열대지방에서는 식물로 집을 짓는다.
Ⓐ 예시부연
④ 추운 지방에서는 시멘트로 집을 짓는다.

| 해석

사람들은 대개 그들에게 이용 가능한 재료로 집을 짓는다. 어떤 지역에서는 대부분 사람이 나무로 집을 짓는다. 이것은 북아메리카 일부와 스칸디나비아에 해당한다. 이런 지역에는 숲이 많다. 그래서 나무는 구하기 쉽고 가격도 싸다. 유럽의 다른 많은 지역에서는 숲이 거의 남아 있지 않다. 돌과 벽돌이 더 싸서 대부분 사람들은 이런 재료로 집을 짓는다. 열대지방에서 집은 때때로 거기서 자라나는 식물을 이용해서 만든다. 예를 들어, 아프리카와 아시아 지역에서 집은 대나무로 만든다. 마지막으로 북극 가까이에 있는 매우 추운 지역에서, 사람들은 시멘트 블록으로 집을 만든다.

21. ③

중심소재는 'wedding ring' ★ 이다.

1. We are all probably familiar with the fact that the wedding ring, or "circle," symbolizes perfection, perfect unity with no beginning and no end. 1) For some it represents holiness, perfection and peace, as well as the sun, earth and universe. 2. You may even be aware that it was once believed that the third finger of the left hand had a special vein, "vena amoris" or "the vein of love," running directly to the wearer's heart.

중심소재: 결혼 반지
1. 도입부
결혼 반지의 일반적 의미
– 처음과 끝이 없는 완벽을 상징한다.
1) 결혼 반지의 다른 의미
태양, 지구 그리고 우주 및 거룩함, 완벽 그리고 평화를 의미한다.
2. 오늘날 결혼 반지를 왼쪽 세 번째 손가락에 끼게 된 기원을 밝히고 있다.

And it is from this romantic custom that we today have the custom of placing the wedding ring on this finger.

| 해설

글의 도입부에서 중심소재인 결혼 반지를 언급하면서, 그 의미를 간략히 밝힌 후 중반 이후부터 끝까지 결혼 반지를 세 번째 손가락에 끼게 된 기원을 밝히고 있다.

| 해석

결혼반지나 '원(반지를 상징)'이 완벽, 다시 말해 시작이나 끝이 없는 완전한 통일성을 상징한다는 사실은 우리가 모두 잘 알고 있을 것이다. 몇몇 사람들에게 이는 태양, 지구, 우주뿐 아니라, 신성함, 완전함, 평화를 의미한다. 사람들이 왼손 세 번째 손가락에 심장으로 직접 흐르는 '베나 아모리스' 또는 '사랑의 정맥'이라고 하는 특별한 정맥이 있다고 믿었다는 것조차 알고 있을 것이다. 오늘날 결혼 반지를 이 손가락에 끼우는 관습을 가지게 된 것도 바로 이 로맨틱한 관습에서 유래한 것이다.

22. ①

1. On Peru's barren Nazca plain is one of the most perplexing mysteries facing archaeologists today. Enormous shapes have been etched into the ground over a thirty-mile area. Among the many shapes are drawings of spiders and other animals. Some of the figures are so large that they can be recognized only from the air. The drawings were made over one thousand years ago by South American Indians.

2. 1) The mystery that has continually puzzled so many archaeologists is why the drawings were made. ① A sciencefiction writer has suggested that the giant drawings may have been landing strips for alien spaceships. ② Some scientists think the great shapes may have been used as a sort of primitive astronomical observatory. ③ A more practical explanation is that the religious Indians were trying to communicate with their gods through the drawings. One thing everyone does agree upon is that the large drawings need government protection.

중심소재: 나스카 평야의 미스터리 모양

★중심소재의 폭을 좁히는 시그널

첫번째 문단
1. 도입부 = 현상
현대의 고고학자들에게 미스터리인 페루의 불모지 '나스카 평야의 미스터리 모양'을 다루는 글이다 – 거미와 다른 동물의 거대한 모양

두번째 문단
2. 원인
1) 첫 번째 문단에서 언급한 거대한 모양이 만들어진 **원인**에 관한 내용이다.
① 첫 번째 추측
– 외계 생물체의 증거
② 두 번째 추측
– 고대 천문 관측을 위해 사용되었음
③ 가장 설득력 있는 세 번째 추측
– 신과의 접촉을 위한 도구

| 해석

  오늘날 고고학자들이 직면한 가장 난감한 미스터리 중 하나는 페루의 메마른 나스카 평원에 있다. 거대한 형태들이 30마일이 넘는 지면에 선명하게 새겨져 있다. 여러 모양 중에는 거미와 다른 동물들의 그림도 있다. 그 그림 중 몇 개는 대단히 커서 공중에서만 알아볼 수 있다. 그 그림들은 남아메리카 인디언들에 의해 천 년 전에 그려졌다.

  아주 많은 고고학자에게 계속 풀리지 않고 있는 미스터리는 왜 그 그림들이 그려졌느냐는 것이다. 한 공상과학

소설 작가는 그 거대한 그림들은 외계의 우주선을 위한 활주로였을지도 모른다고 말했다. 어떤 과학자들은 큰 그림들이 일종의 원시 천문대 같은 것으로 사용되었을지도 모른다고 생각한다. 더 현실적인 설명으로 종교심이 강한 인디언들이 그림을 통해 그들의 신과 소통하려고 했다는 것이다. 모든 사람이 동의하는 한 가지 견해는 이 큰 그림들은 정부의 보호가 필요하다는 점이다.

23. ①

시간의 대조를 확인한다. ★

도입부 — 중심소재
　　　　과거
　　　　　↕
　　　　현재

1. America's great old form of entertainment was vaudeville. 1) Long before radio, television, or movies, in the late nineteenth century, vaudeville theaters became popular. On their stages, audiences would see shows featuring singers, dancers, comedians, ventriloquists, trained animals, mimics, and magicians. Each performer would entertain the crowd for a few minutes, followed immediately by the next performer. The show was carefully planned to give variety—in fact, an early name for vaudeville theaters was "variety houses." Soon every city of middle or large size, and even some small towns, had a vaudeville theater. Vaudevillians, as the performers were called, were the most prominent stars of the day. 2) Then, in the 1920s and 1930s, two new entertainment forms came along—talking movies and radio. The movies were more spectacular than vaudeville ever could be, and radio became available in the home. Vaudeville couldn't compete with them.

중심소재: 보드빌
1. 도입부 = 중심소재 도출
1) 과거와 현재의 대조
① 과거
19세기 말 절정을 맞는 보드빌을 기술하고 있다.
② 현재
영화와 라디오가 등장하면서 사양길을 걷게 된 보드빌이 기술되고 있다.

| 해설
특정 대상의 두 가지 상반된 현상이 대조되는 시대를 기술하고 있다.

| 해석
미국에서 아주 오래된 오락 형식은 보드빌이었다. 19세기 후반 라디오, 텔레비전, 영화가 나오기 훨씬 전에 보드빌 극장은 인기를 얻게 되었다. 무대에서 관객들은 가수, 무용가, 희극인, 복화술사, 훈련받은 동물, 광대, 마술사들이 출연하는 쇼를 보곤 했다. 각 연기자는 몇 분 동안 관객을 즐겁게 해주고 다음 연기자들이 바로 나왔다. 사실상 그 연극은 다양함을 주기 위해 면밀히 계획되었으며 보드빌 극장의 초기 이름은 "버라이어티 하우스"였다. 곧 중간 크기의 도시나 대도시에, 그리고 일부 소도시에도 보드빌 극장이 생겼다. 연기자들은 보드빌 배우로 불렸으며 그 당시 그 배우들은 가장 유명한 스타였다. 그러다가 1920년대와 30년대 두 가지 새로운 오락 형식이 생겨났는데 유성영화와 라디오였다. 영화들은 이제껏 보드빌에서 보아왔던 것보다 더 화려했고 라디오는 집에서 들을 수 있었다. 보드빌은 그것들(영화, 라디오)과는 경쟁할 수 없게 되었다.

Test 4 내용 일치

1. ③

1. You should beware of introducing outside files into your computer as these may contain computer viruses. 1) If you introduce ① an infected disk into your system, you run the risk of having your entire hard drive wiped out. ② This can also happen if you download something from the web that contains a virus. 2. You should have an anti-virus program running at all times and be careful about what you bring into your computer.

중심소재: 컴퓨터 바이러스
1. 도입부 = 주제문
1) 뒷받침 진술
바이러스가 들어오는 경로를 두 가지로 나눠 살펴보고 있다. (①과 ②)
2. 요지
글쓴이가 궁극적으로 전달하려는 제안의 메시지로 마무리하고 있다 (should).

★ 구체적 진술을 이끄는 'If'를 확인한다.

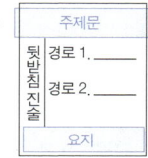

| 해설

'주제문 – 뒷받침 문장 – 결론'의 아주 단순하지만 깔끔한 구조로 다시 한 번 전체 글의 구조를 확인한다. 틀린 것을 고르는 문제의 보기는 '일반화', '과장법', '극단적 표현의 사용(특히 강조 부사)', '수치와 관련된 사항', '다의어의 표현', 본문에 표현되지 않은 사항에 대한 '배경 지식 유도', '논리적 비약' 등을 이용하여 오류 문장을 이끌어 낸다. 보기의 구성을 살펴보자.

① All outside files contain computer viruses.
 → 부분적인 사항을 모든 상황에 적용하고 있지 않은가?
② If you download something from the web you don't need an anti-virus program running.
 → 본문 마지막에 나오는 글쓴이의 제안과 정반대의 내용이다. 뜻밖에 글쓴이의 주장과 반대되는 내용을 보기로 많이 구성한다.
③ Your entire hard drive can be wiped out by an infected disk.
 → 본문에 명확히 명시되어 있다.
④ The speaker warns about your computer hard drive.
 → 주제와 관련된 사항이다. 본문은 하드드라이브가 아니라 '외부 바이러스'와 관련된 사항이다.

| 해석

외부의 파일을 당신의 컴퓨터로 가지고 올 때에는 조심해야 하는데 이는 이것에 컴퓨터 바이러스가 있을 수 있기 때문이다. 만약 당신의 컴퓨터에 감염된 디스크를 가지고 올 경우, 하드 전체가 날아가는 위험성이 생긴다. 또한, 바이러스가 포함된 사이트에서 뭔가를 내려받으면 컴퓨터에 감염이 발생할 수 있다. 항상 바이러스 퇴치 프로그램을 작동시키고, 컴퓨터에 불러오는 것에 주의해야 한다.

2. ②

구체적 진술에서 일반진 술로 전개되는 패턴을 이해한다.

주제도출 ← 일반진술
구체적 진술

1. Neil and Marie appear to be a young, newly married couple excited to be walking around the sidewalks of New York City as tourists. They stop to take pictures and ask people on the street to take a picture of two of them on their brand new, sleek Ericsson all-in-one phone. Most people they approach listen intently as the couple instruct them how to use the camera features and extol the virtues of the product. The invited photographers leave thinking that they have done a good deed and probably unaware that they have just been subjected to a ten-minute sales presentation. 1) This is the essence of stealth or covert marketing.

2. Marketers have used this kind of marketing for years ① by placing them in popular television programs or by displaying their soft drinks in sitcoms. ② More recently, groups of sales people have taken to the streets with a variety of products and a covert message intended to create a "buzz" about their product. ⓐ When people are faced with an overt sales attempt such as a door-to-door salesperson, their defenses go up. They become wary of the seller's "angle" or may not even let the salesperson finish the first sentence of the "pitch." ⓑ Covert marketing attempts to persuade people to try a new product without their being aware of the persuasive attempt. It gets past a buyer's defense to overt sales.

중심소재: Covert Makketing
첫번째 문단
1. 도입부 = 구체적 진술
닐과 마리라는 인물을 등장시켜 구체적 사례를 전개한다. 다채로운 기능을 탑재한 신형 휴대전화를 건네주면서 사진을 찍어 달라고 요청한다.
1) 일반진술
앞에서 제시한 구체적인 사례를 통해 글쓴이가 소개하고자 하는 주제를 이끌어 낸다. 주제: stealth or covert marketing

비교·대조의 글 전개방식을 확인한다. 하나의 대상의 특징을 강조하고자 할 때 이와 대조되는 대상을 도입한다.

* 두번째 문단
도입부 ─ 구체적 진술
    과거 Overt
    특징
    현재 Convert
    특징

두번째 문단
1. 구체적 진술
첫번째 문단의 1)에서 밝힌 주제인 'Covert Marketing'에 대한 상술
1) Overt와 Covert를 대조하여 Covert의 장점(모듈성)을 강조하고 있다.
① Overt Marketing
ⓐ 비효율적 Marketing
② Covert Marketing
ⓑ 효율적 상품홍보 방법 부연

| 해설
본문 옆의 설명을 보면 알겠지만, 글쓴이는 구체적 사례를 설명하면서 자연스럽게 주제('covert marketing')를 이끌어 내고 있다. 이후, 'Covert Marketing'에 대한 부연진술과 함께 장점을 언급하며, 궁극적으로 글쓴이는 'Covert Marketing'이 과거의 'Door-to-door marketing strategy(= Overt Marketing)'보다 훨씬 효과적임을 주장하고 있다. 문제로 돌아가, '옳은 것을 고르시오.'라는 문제는 보기 중 하나만 참인 경우인데 보통 '글쓴이의 주장 또는 관련 내용'이 답일 가능성이 크다. 본 공략법의 맨 처음에 언급한 것과 같이 주제와 요지를 찾는 능력은 다른 문제를 푸는 가장 기본이 됨을 잊지 말아야 한다. 어떤 지문이 나와도(주제 또는 요지를 묻는 문제가 아니라 하더라도) 주제와 요지를 찾는 연습은 꾸준히 해야 한다.

| 해석
닐과 마리는 관광객으로서 뉴욕의 거리를 즐겁게 거닐고 있는 젊은 신혼부부처럼 보인다. 이들은 걸음을 멈추고 사진을 찍다가 길을 걷는 사람들에게 자기들 사진을 찍어달라고 하면서 가지고 있던 에릭슨사의 멋진 신상품 일체형 휴대전화를 건넨다. 이들이 접근하는 사람들 대부분 이 부부가 휴대전화의 카메라 기능을 사용하는 법을 가

르쳐주고 제품의 장점을 칭찬할 때 주의 깊게 듣게 된다. 사진을 찍어준 사람들은 자리를 떠나면서 자기가 좋은 일을 했다고 생각하지만 아마 자신이 방금 10분짜리 판매를 위한 제품 설명을 듣게 된 것을 인식하지 못할 것이다. 이것이 바로 은밀한 스텔스 마케팅의 핵심이다.

이러한 마케팅은 이미 수년 동안 사용된 것으로 인기 TV 프로그램 속에 제품을 갖다 놓거나 시트콤 속에서 자기 회사의 음료수를 드러내는 등의 방법을 이용해 왔다. 최근에는 판매 직원들이 다양한 제품과 자사의 제품에 대한 "소문"을 일으킬 수 있도록 의도된 은밀한 메시지를 가지고 거리로 나선다. 사람들은 방문 판매와 같이 노골적인 판매를 접했을 때는 방어 행동이 증가한다. 이럴 때 사람들은 판매원의 낚싯대 책략을 경계하거나 심지어 판매원이 낚싯대를 던지는 첫 문장을 끝내지도 못하게 한다. 은밀한 마케팅은 설득의 의도를 들키지 않은 채 사람들을 설득해서 신제품을 사용해 보게 한다. 이를 통해 노골적인 판매에 대한 구매자의 방어를 피해 간다.

3. ③

1. <u>The quest for manliness</u> is essentially right-wing, cowardly, neurotic, and fueled largely by a fear of women. ① The youth who is misled into believing in the masculine ideal is conveniently separated from women, and he spends the rest of his life finding women a riddle and a nuisance. ② Masculinity celebrates the exclusive company of men. That is why it is so grotesque; and ③ that is also why there is no manliness that is absolutely complete—because it denies men the natural friendship of women.

2. <u>Of course, there is a female version of this male affliction.</u> 1) It begins with mothers encouraging little girls to say, "Do you like my new dress?" In a sense, little girls are traditionally urged to please others with a kind of coquettishness, while boys are enjoined to behave like monkeys towards each other. The nine-year-old coquette proceeds to become womanish in a subtle power game in which she learns to be sexually indispensable, socially decorative, and always alert to a man's needs. <u>Femininity—being ladylike—implies needing a man as witness and seducer.</u>

첫번째 문단
1. 도입부 = 주제문
남성미 추구는 여러 가지 이유로 왜곡된 것이라고 말하고 나서 ①, ②에서 '왜곡된 남성미 추구로 일어나는 부작용에 관한 구체적 진술'이 이어진다. ③은 ②의 근거이다.
1) 뒷받침 진술
* 소주제: Distorted Quest for Manliness

두번째 문단
1. 도입부(주제 도출)
여성 형태의 왜곡된 병폐 = Feminity
1) 뒷받침 진술
여성(어머니)에 의해서 조장된 이런 'Femininity'는 남성 없이 실현될 수 없는 '의존적 존재'로 만드는 부작용을 드러내고 있다.

| 해설

내용일치 문제 중 '옳지 않은 문제를 고르시오.'라는 문제는 보기 중 하나만 틀린 내용이고 나머지는 본문과 일치하는 문제이기에 본문을 읽기 전 문제를 읽은 후 본문의 내용을 어느 정도 예측하는 도구로 활용할 수 있다.

① The concept of masculinity is exclusive of women.
→ 남성미라는 것은 여성을 배제한 개념이다. (남성과 여성의 통합을 배제함.)
② Females are trained from childhood to please others.

→ 여성은 어렸을 적부터 다른 이를 기쁘게 하도록 훈련을 받는다. (자신의 정체성을 다른 이를 기쁘게 하는 것에서 얻음)

③ Manliness allows female companionship.
→ 남성미는 여성과의 교제를 허용한다. ← 보기 ①과 대조를 이룸.

④ Girls learn to be coquettish.
→ 여자는 (남을 즐겁게 해주는) 교태를 부리도록 훈련을 받는다. 보기 ②와 같음. 결론적으로 보기의 내용으로 '왜곡된 남성형'과 '왜곡된 여성형'이 본문에 언급될 것이라는 점을 알 수 있다. 또한, 문항 간의 관계를 통해 보기를 줄일 수도 있는데, ①와 ③이 대조를 이루기에, 둘 중 하나가 답이란 것을 알 수 있다. 또한, 보기 ②와 ④는 같기에 절대 답이 될 수 없다.

| 해석

남자다움을 추구하는 것은 본질적으로 보수적이고, 소심하며, 신경증적이며 그리고 이것은 주로 여성들에 대한 두려움 때문에 생긴다. 남자다움이라는 이상을 믿도록 잘못 인도된 젊은이는 쉽사리 여성들과 분리되어, 죽는 날까지 여성을 알 수 없는 존재 또는 성가신 존재로 알며 살게 된다. 남자다움은 남자들로 구성된 배타적인 집단을 찬양한다. 이것이 남자다움이 아주 우스꽝스러운 까닭이다. 그리고 이러한 이유 때문에 또한 절대적으로 완전한 남자다움도 없는데, 왜냐하면 이것은 남성으로 하여금 여성과의 자연스러운 우정을 받아들이지 못하게 하기 때문이다.

물론 이러한 남성의 고민거리와 같은 것이 여성에게도 있다. 그것은 어머니가 어린 딸에게 "제가 입은 새 옷이 마음에 드세요?"라고 말하도록 부추김으로써 시작된다. 어떤 면에서 보자면 어린 소녀들은 전통적으로 일종의 애교를 통해 서로 즐겁게 해 주도록 강요받지만, 반면 소년들은 서로 장난꾸러기처럼 행동해도 된다. 아홉 살 된 애교 있는 소녀는 미묘한 힘 싸움에서 여성스러워지기 시작하고 그 속에서 그녀는 성적으로 꼭 필요한 존재가 되고, 사회적으로는 장식과 같은 존재가 되며, 항상 남성의 욕구를 경계하라고 배운다. 여성적, 즉 여성스럽게 된다는 것은 (자신을) 눈여겨보아 줄 사람이자 유혹하는 사람으로서의 남성이 필요하다는 의미를 내포하고 있다.

4. ④

의문점은 곧 글에서 밝히고자 하는 주제에 해당한다.★

도입부 | 주제문(현상)
요인 1.____
요인 2.____

1. The evolution of sex ratios has produced, in most plants and animals with separate sexes, approximately equal numbers of males and females. 1) <u>Why should this be so?</u> ⓐ Two main kinds of answers have been offered. Ⓐ One is couched in terms of advantage to population. It is argued that the sex ratio will evolve so as to maximize the number of meetings between individuals of the opposite sex. This is essentially a "group selection" argument. Ⓑ The other, and in my view correct, type of answer was first put forward by Fisher in 1930. This "genetic" argument starts from the assumption that genes can influence the relative numbers of male and female offspring produced by an individual carrying the genes. That sex ratio will be favored which maximizes the number of descendants an individual will have and hence the number of gene copies transmitted. If the population

중심소재: Evolution of sex Ratios
1. 도입부 = 주제문
현상: 성은 남녀 개체수가 비슷하도록 진화되었다.
1) 연결문(주제도출)
① 뒷받침 진술
남녀 성비율이 같은 이유
Ⓐ 이유 1
Group selection Argument
Ⓑ 이유 2
Genetic Argument
글쓴이는 두 요인 중에서 두 번째 요인이 옳다고 보는 관점을 지녔다.

consisted of equal numbers of males and females, sons and daughters would be equally valuable. Thus a one-to-one sex ratio is the only stable ratio; it is an "evolutionarily stable strategy." Although Fisher wrote before the mathematical theory of games had been developed, his theory incorporates the essential feature of a game—that the best strategy to adopt depends on what others are doing.

| 해설

옳지 않은 내용을 찾는 문제이다. 다시 말해 보기 세 개는 옳다는 뜻이다. 문제를 먼저 읽고 대강의 내용을 파악한 후 지문을 보기 권한다.

① Group selection argument explains the evolution of sex ratios based on the total number of population.
→ 'Group selection argument'에 관한 내용이 나오면 '전체 인구수를 바탕으로 성 비율의 진화'를 설명하는지 확인한다.

② The evolution of sex ratios has kept the numbers of males and females at approximately the same level.
성 비율의 진화로 남녀 성 비율이 거의 비슷한 수준이 되었는지 확인한다.

③ Fisher sought an explanation of why certain sex ratios exist.
Fisher가 특정 성 비율의 존재를 설명하려고 했는지 확인한다.

④ The mathematical theory of games has been useful in explaining some biological phenomena.
수학적 게임이론은 특정 생물학적 현상을 설명하는 데 유용하다고 했는데, 본문에 명시되어 있는지 확인한다. 보기 ④의 경우 본문에 'before the mathematical theory of games had been developed'라고 말하고 있으므로 옳지 못하다.

도입부	현상 → 문제 제기 (Why should this be so?)
본론	원인 1. _____. 원인 2. _____.

| 해석

성비의 진화를 통해 서로 다른 성을 보유한 식물과 동물 중 대부분에서 대략 같은 수의 암컷과 수컷이 태어난다. 왜 이렇게 되는 것일까? 주요한 답 두 가지가 제시되었다. 하나의 답은 개처군에 유리하기 위함이라는 관점에서 표현된다. 성비는 다른 성을 지닌 개별 개체 간의 만남 횟수를 최대화하기 위해 진화했다는 주장이다. 이는 본질에서는 "집단선택"론을 말한다. 나의 견해와 일치하는 또 다른 형태의 답변은 1930년 최초 Fisher에 의해 제시되었다. 이 '유전' 관점의 주장은 유전자는 유전자를 보유하고 있는 개별 개체에 의해 태어나는 수컷과 암컷 후손의 대략적인 수에 영향을 미친다는 가정에서 출발한다. 즉 한 개체가 가지게 될 후손의 수를 최대화하고 따라서 후손에게 전해지는 유전자 사본의 수를 최대화하는 성비가 선호될 것이다. 만약 개체군이 같은 수의 수컷과 암컷으로 구성된다면, 그 개체군의 아들과 딸은 동등하게 귀중한 존재이다. 이와 같은 1:1 성비는 유일하게 안정적인 성비이고, 이는 "진화적으로 안정된 전략"이 된다. 비록 Fisher는 수학적 게임이론이 발전되기 전에 자신의 이론을 작성했지만, 그의 이론은 게임이론이 말하는 게임의 필수 요소를 포괄한다. 즉, 채택할 수 있는 최상의 전략은 상대방이 하는 행동에 달려있다는 것이다.

5. ①

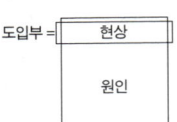

현상의 원인을 밝히는 인과의 글임을 파악한다.

도입부 = 현상
         원인

주제문 = 현상 + 원인

1. Before adolescence, there is little difference in the rate of depression in boys and girls. But between the ages of 11 and 13 there is a precipitous rise in depression rates for girls. <u>By the age of 15, females are twice as likely to have experienced a major depressive episode as males</u>. 1) This comes at a time in adolescence when roles and expectations change dramatically. ① The stresses of adolescence include forming an identity, emerging sexuality, separating from parents, and making decisions for the first time, along with other physical, intellectual, and hormonal changes. These stresses are generally different for boys and girls, and may be associated more often with depression in females.

중심소재: 우울증 → 남녀간 우울증 증상의 차이

1. 도입부 = 현상
'But'을 중심으로 남자아이와 여자아이의 특정한 **현상**의 변화를 다루고 있다. 즉, '남자와 여자아이는 11세 이전에는 우울증을 겪는 비율에 변화가 없지만, 약 15세가 되면 여자아이가 두배 더 우울증을 겪는다.

1) 원인
사춘기 때 찾아오는 스트레스(①)로 남자와 여자는 차이점을 보이며, 특히 여자의 우울증과 더욱 관련이 있는 것으로 보인다.

| 해설

옳은 진술을 묻는 '내용 일치' 문제이다. 보기 4개 중 하나만이 옳은 진술이다. 이럴 때는 일반적으로 본문에서 글쓴이가 하는 주장이나 궁극적으로 전달하려는 요지 또는 그와 관련된 내용이 답일 경우가 많다. 보기 ①이 답인데 내용을 보면,

> Teenage girls undergo depression as they try to cope with stresses of adolescence.

글에서 궁극적으로 밝히고자 하는 내용이 모두 들어간 'Topic Sentence' 이다.

| 해석

사춘기 전에는 남학생들과 여학생들 간에 우울한 정도의 차이가 거의 없다. 그러나 11세부터 13세 사이에 여학생들에게 우울증이 급격히 증가한다. 15세가 되면 이미 여학생들이 남학생들보다 우울한 일을 겪었을 가능성이 두 배 정도 높다. 이는 (성) 역할과 (주변의) 기대가 급격히 변하는 청소년 시기에 발생한다. 사춘기의 스트레스에는 다른 여러 신체적 변화, 지적 변화, 호르몬 변화와 함께 정체성의 형성, 성징의 출현, 부모로부터의 독립, 최초의 의사결정 등이 포함된다. 이러한 스트레스들은 일반적으로 남학생이냐, 여학생이냐에 따라 다르며 여학생들이 우울증과 더 많은 연관이 있는 것으로 보인다.

| 참고

옳은 것을 묻는 문제는 일반적으로 글의 주제, 주장 또는 요지가 되거나 관련된 내용이 답일 가능성이 크다. 다시 한 번 주제, 요지를 글에서 이끌어내는 능력이 얼마나 중요한지를 알 수 있다.

6. ④

1) I was once stopped by a California Highway Patrol officer because I was exceeding the speed limit. He walked up to the car window, looked me straight in the eye, and, with a

1. 도입부 = 구체적 사례
① 캘리포니아 고속도로 순찰원은 발생한 '사실'만을 고수하는 모습을 인상 깊게 그리고 있다.

slightly concerned look, asked me if I knew why he had stopped me. He waited while I performed a few verbal somersaults, and then, with a calm voice, he told me the specific details of my offense. ① <u>He stuck to the facts and never once made any assumptions about why I had done what I did.</u> He was so good at giving me the bad news that when he finished writing the ticket and said, "Have a nice day," I responded back with a genuinely enthusiastic, "You too, Officer." 2) I later found out that <u>the California Highway Patrol Academy puts officers through a 27 week training course that emphasizes dealing with confrontation and conflict with their customers — It works</u>!

1) 일반진술(요지 도출)
글쓴이가 위의 구체적 사실을 통해 궁극적으로 이야기하려는 내용이 등장한다.

* 두번째 문단

| 도입부 | 구체적 진술 |
| 요지도출 | 일반진술 |

| 해설
'Specific statement(구체적 진술) → General statement(일반진술)'로 진행되는 전형적 형태이다. 일반적으로 구체적 사실로 시작하는 글을 접할 때, 주의할 점은 '이 구체적 사건을 통해서 글쓴이가 궁극적으로 전달하려는 내용은 무엇인가?'를 항상 고려해야 한다. 내용 일치의 문제가 모두 '본문의 요지가 답이다.'라고 말할 수 없지만, 그럴 확률이 높기에 본문의 주제와 요지를 파악하는 능력은 아주 중요하다.

| 해석
나는 한때 캘리포니아 고속도로 경찰관에게 과속으로 정차 당한 적이 있었다. 그는 차창으로 다가와 내 눈을 똑바로 보더니 약간 걱정스러운 표정으로 왜 멈추게 했는지 아느냐고 물었다 그는 내가 몇 마디 말로 처벌을 모면하려 애쓰는 동안 기다려주더니 침착한 목소리로 나의 구체적인 범법 사항들을 말했다. 그는 사실에만 입각하여 내가 왜 그렇게 했는지에 대한 추측은 하지 않았다. 그가 나쁜 소식(과속했다는)을 너무나도 친절하게 전달했기 때문에 나에게 딱지를 끊어주고 나서 "즐거운 하루 되세요."라고 인사를 했을 때 나도 "경찰관 아저씨도요"라고 진정으로 답례했다. 나는 캘리포니아 고속도로 경찰학교에서는 경찰관들을 고객(운전자)들과의 대립과 갈등에 대한 대처를 강조하는 27주 과정의 훈련에 참여시킨다는 것을 나중에 알았다. 정말 효과 만점의 훈련이다.

7. ④

1. But why should we blame the poor machine for the ills that have followed from it? <u>The fault lies with man, who has misused it, and with society, which has not profited by it fully.</u> 1) It seems to be unthinkable that the world, or any country, can go back to the old days before the Industrial Revolution, and it hardly seems desirable or wise that, in order to get rid of some evils, we should throw away the numerous good things that industrialism has brought us. And, in any event,

중심소재: 산업혁명의 문제점

1. 도입부 = 주제문
산업혁명으로 발생한 문제점은 인간의 탓이다.

1) 뒷받침 진술
산업혁명의 문제점이 인간으로 인해 발생했다고 해서 산업혁명 이전의 시대로 돌아가거나 산업혁명이 가져다 준 이기를 모두 버릴 순 없다.

199

* 주제와 요지의 구별

도입부 = 주제문 (주제 도출) / 뒷받침 진술 / 결론: 요지

주제는 제시된 단락이 무엇에 관한 글인지를 파악하는 것이고, 요지는 주제를 통해 궁극적으로 전달하고자 하는 내용이다.

the machine has come and is going to stay. 2. **Therefore** the problem for us is to retain the good things of industrialism and to get rid of the evil that attaches to it. We must profit by the wealth it produces, but see to it that the wealth is evenly distributed among those who produce it.

2. 결론(요지)
산업주의의 좋은 점은 취하고 나쁜 점은 버린다.

| 해설

내용 일치를 묻는 문제로 옳은 것을 고르는 문제이다. 일반적으로 글쓴이의 주장 또는 관련 내용이 답일 가능성이 크다. 주장이 드러나는 문장을 잘 파악하도록 하자. 본문에 등장하는 'Therefore, must, should' 등은 글쓴이의 주장이 직/간접적으로 드러나는 곳이므로 집중해서 읽는다. 옳은 것을 묻는 문제이다. 글쓴이의 주장과 관련하여 보기 ④가 가장 적합하다.

④ The Industrial Revolution did good and harm.
  → 고로, 좋은 것은 취하고 나쁜 것은 버리도록 하자!

| 해석

그러나 왜 우리는 아무 잘못 없는 불쌍한 기계가 재난을 가져온다고 비난해야 하는가? 잘못은 인간에게 있다. 기계를 잘못 사용했기 때문이다. 또 잘못은 사회에도 있다. 그것으로 충분히 이익을 얻지 못했기 때문이다. 세계의 어떤 나라든 산업 혁명 이전의 옛날로 되돌아갈 수 있다는 것은 도저히 있을 법하지도 않고, 몇 가지 악을 제거하기 위해 산업화가 우리에게 가져다준 수많은 좋은 것들을 버려야 한다는 것은 바람직하지도 현명하지도 않다. 그리고 어떠한 경우에도 기계는 세상에 등장했고 계속 남아있을 것이다. 그러므로 우리에게 문제는 산업화의 좋은 면을 계속 유지하고, 그것(산업화)과 연관된 악을 제거하는 것이다. 우리는 산업화가 생산해내는 부(富)로 혜택을 누려야 하고, 반드시 부(富)는 그것을 생산해 내는 사람들에게 공평하게 분배되도록 노력해야 한다.

8. ①

도입부 = 현상 – 원인
부정적 결과
① _____
② _____
③ _____

1. Thanks to the recent development of agricultural technology, we have various kinds of flowers, vegetables, and fruits all through the seasons, because they are grown in greenhouses all the year round. 1) ① Most people living in urban areas have gradually lost the sense of season and become indifferent to the seasonal change of nature. Nature was once our friend and we lived in harmony with her, but now, ② somehow alienated from her to live in a mechanical age, ③ we have come to be less and less attracted by her beauties.

중심소재: 농업 기술 발달의 여파

1. **도입부 = 현상 – 원인**
'농업 기술의 발달'로 인해 계절과 관계없이 과일, 채소 등을 먹을 수 있다.

1) **부정적 결과**
① 대부분의 도시 사람들은 계절 변화에 무감각해졌다.
② 자연과 소원해졌다.
③ 자연의 아름다움을 즐기지 못한다.

| 해설

전체 글 전개 방법은 인과(Cause and Effect)이다. 원인과 결과를 정확히 구분하면 주제 및 글쓴이가 궁극적으로 전달하려는 메시지를 쉽게 파악할 수 있다. 내용 일치의 문제 중 틀린 것을 고르는 문제이다. 본문을 읽기 전 본문에 대한 많은 정보를 얻을 수 있으므로, 보기를 먼저 읽는 것도 하나의 전략이 된다.

① We were once less attracted by the beauties of nature.
   과거에 인간은 자연의 아름다움에 매료되었다. (지금은 아니다.)
   → 본문에서 'gradually' 라는 표현을 쓰면서 자연의 아름다움을 점차 인식하지 못한다고 했지, 현재 전혀 인식하지 못하는 것은 아니다. 부분적 사실을 전체로 확대하는 오류를 조심해야 한다.
② We were once on friendly terms with nature.
   → 인간은 한때 자연과 좋은 관계를 유지했다.
③ We are now estranged from nature.
   → 인간은 현재 자연과 거리감이 생겼다.
④ We are now less sensitive to the seasonal change of nature.
   → 인간은 현재 자연의 변화에 덜 민감하다.

| 해석

최근 농업 기술의 발달로 우리는 사계절 내내 다양한 종류의 꽃, 채소, 그리고 과일들을 얻게 되었는데, 이는 이러한 것들이 일 년 내내 온실에서 재배되기 때문이다. 도시 지역에 사는 대부분 사람들은 차츰 계절 감각을 잃어가고 있으며, 자연의 계절적인 변화에도 무관심해지고 있다. 자연은 한때 우리의 친구였으며 우리는 자연과 조화를 이루며 살았으나, 오늘날 기계화된 시대에 살다 보니 우리는 어떤 이유에서인지 자연과 사이가 벌어지게 되어 자연의 아름다움에 차츰 무관심하게 되었다.

9. ③

1. The high-tech economy is on the ropes and the old economy is coming back with a vengeance. 1) For all the amazing, productivity-enhancing things the Internet can do, dirty industrial details like the price of oil and the quality of steel still matter. ① All in all, it's a good time to be in a business where the workers need to scrub their hands at the end of a hard day. ② The bursting of the high-tech bubble will have consequences for nearly everybody in 2001. 2.Consumers are feeling nervous again and corporations are finding that cash, once so plentiful in a booming stock market, is a scarcer commodity. Economic growth is slowing in many place in the world, with even some hints that a recession is on the way. For the first time in a long while, there's no money to be made just by riding the market momentum. In the economy of 2001, it will be survival of the smartest.

중심소재: 구식경제 vs 신경제
1. 도입부 = 주제문
첨단 경제는 위험에 빠지고 구식경제가 다시 돌아올 것이다.
1) 뒷받침 진술
① 석유산업 또는 철강사업과 같은 손에 때를 묻히는 일이 시기에 적절하다고 말하고 있다(구식 경제).
② 고 첨단경제의 거품이 곧 터져 참혹한 결과를 가져올 것이라 보고 있다.
2. 2001년 경제 전망
③ 소비자들도 시장에 돈이 돌지 않을 것이라는 전망에 긴장하고 있다는 내용과 함께 경제성장 둔화와 불경기의 징조 그리고 시장의 역동성 저하 등을 언급하면서 마지막 문장에서 2001년도 경제를 '적자생존'으로 묘사하고 있다.

| 해설

틀린 것을 고르는 문제이다. 보기 하나를 제외하곤 모두 본문에 언급되어 있어야 한다는 사항을 이용한다. 즉, 문제의 보기를 먼저 읽고, 본문의 내용을 미리 짐작할 수 있는데, 이는 일반적으로 본문에 어렵게 표현된 문장을 보기에서는 쉬운 문장으로 바꾸어 제시하는 경우가 대부분이기 때문이다. 보기를 통해 글에서 이야기하는 내용을 최대한 알아보고, 보기 간의 내용이 일치하지 않는 것이 있는지 파악한다.

① The old economy is making a strong comeback.
  → 구식경제의 강세에 대한 언급이 있는지 확인
② The Internet could increase industrial productivity.
  → 인터넷은 산업 생산량을 높일 수 있다는 점 확인
③ The high-tech industry will not suffer a setback of any sorts.
  → 첨단 산업은 어떤 종류의 방해에도 영향을 받는지 아닌지 확인
④ It has become more difficult to find investors on the stock market.
  → 주식 시장에 투자자가 없을 정도로 시장이 불황인지 확인
⑤ The world economy may slow down in the year 2001.
  → 2001년도 세계경제 침체 확인

보기 중 ④와 ⑤는 2001년도 시장을 비관적으로 보는 반면, 보기 ③의 경우 첨단 산업을 아주 긍정적으로 파악하고 있다. 즉, 본문에서 2001년도 경제 불황 중 첨단시장은 예외적인 분야인지 확인할 필요가 있다. 보기에서 "극단적" 표현이 들어간 것은 답이 아닐 가능성이 크기에 보기 ③을 주의할 필요가 있다. 보기 ②도 만만치 않다. 본문에서 'For all ~'의 양보 구문이 등장하는데, 이런 특수한 표현을 이용하면 보기를 구성한다는 점도 잊어선 안 된다.

| 해석

첨단기술경제는 곤경에 처했고 구식경제가 복수하러 되돌아보고 있다. 인터넷이 할 수 있는, 생산력을 늘리는 놀라운 일들에도 불구하고, 석유 가격이나 철강의 품질 같은 하찮은 세부사항이 훨씬 중요하다. 대체로 힘든 하루 일이 끝났을 때 노동자들이 손을 씻는 사업을 하기가 좋을 때이다. 첨단기술 거품의 폭발은 2001년의 거의 모든 사람에게 중요성이 있게 될 것이다. 소비자들은 불안감을 느끼고 회사들은 일찍이 주식시장이 활황일 때 그렇게도 풍부하던 현금이 구하기 어려운 상품이 되고 있다는 것을 알고 있다. 경기후퇴가 진행 중이라는 징후와 함께 경제성장이 세계 곳곳에서 둔화되고 있다. 오랜만에 처음으로 시장의 힘에 의존해서 돈을 만들 수 없게 되었다. 2001년의 경제에서는, 가장 똑똑한 사람들만이 생존할 것이다.

10. ④

첫 번째 문단은 '의학과 종교의 관련성'을 다루고 있다.

1. Because early man viewed illness as divine punishment and healing as purification, medicine and religion were inextricably linked for centuries. This notion is apparent in the origin of our word "pharmacy," which comes from the Greek, pharmakon, mean "purification through purging."

1. 첫 번째 문단
첫 번째 문단은 '의학과 종교의 밀접한 관계'를 다루는 내용으로 그 근거를 'pharmacy'의 어원에서 찾고 있다.

두 번째 문단은 '현대 약 처방의 기원'을 다루고 있다.

2. By 3500 B.C. the Sumerians in the Tigris-Euphrates valley had developed virtually all of our modern methods of

2. 두 번째 문단
두 번째 문단에서는 현대 약 처방이 수메르 사람에 의해서 대부분 발명되었다는 이야기를 하고 있다.

administering drugs. They used gargles, inhalations, pills, lotions, ointment, and plasters. The first drug catalog, or pharmacopoeia, was written at that time by an unknown Sumerian physician. Preserve in cuneiform script on a single clay tablet are the names of dozens of drugs to treat ailments that still afflict us today.

| 해설

옳지 않은 것을 고르는 내용 일치 문제이다. 보기를 먼저 읽고 본문에 접근하는 것이 유리하다. 보기를 통해 글에서 이야기하는 내용을 최대한 알아보고, 보기 간의 내용이 일치하지 않는 것이 있는지 파악한다.

① Today, we are still suffering from the diseases of the early man.
→ 인류 초기에도 현재의 질병으로 고생했는지 파악(두 번째 단락에서 '현재의 약 처방은 수메르인이 개발한 것이다'에서 유추 가능).

② In the early age, medicine and religion had some family resemblance for centuries.
→ 의학과 종교의 관련성에 대한 언급(첫 번째 단락에서 언급되고 있다.)

③ The first drug catalog was produced by a Sumerian.
→ 초기 약 처방 목록이 수메르 사람의 것인지 파악(두 번째 단락에 언급되어 있다.)

④ The modern methods of administering drugs stem from religion only.
→ 'only'라는 극단적 표현을 쓰고 있다. 본문에 'only' 또는 같은 정도를 나타내는 부사가 쓰이지 않는 한 답일 가능성이 크다(본문에서는 의학과 종교가 밀접하게 관련이 있다고만 언급하고 있다).

| 해석

일찍이 사람들은 병을 신이 내린 형벌로, 치유를 정화로 보았기 때문에 약학과 종교는 오랜 세월 동안 긴밀한 연관이 있었다. 이 개념은 pharmacy라는 용어의 기원에서 분명하게 드러나는데, 이 단어는 '정결하게 하여 정화함'을 의미하는 그리스어 pharmakon에서 비롯되었다.

기원전 3500년경에, 티그리스-유프라테스 계곡에 거주하는 수메르인들은 실질적으로 모든 현대에 쓰이는 약 투여 방법을 개발하였다. 그들은 양치질, 흡입, 알약, 로션, 연고, 고약을 사용했다. 최초의 약품 목록 또는 조제서는 당시 이름 모를 한 수메르인 의사에 의해 쓰였다. 오늘날까지도 여전히 우리를 괴롭히는 병들을 치료하는 많은 약의 이름들이 하나의 진흙 판에 설형문자로 쓰인 처방전에 보존되어 있다.

11. ②

1. After nearly a year of emotional arguments in Congress — but no new federal laws — the national debate over human cloning has shifted to the states. Six states have already banned cloning in one form or another, and this year 38 anti-cloning measures were introduced in 22 states. The resulting patchwork of laws, people on all sides of the issue say, complicates a nationwide picture already clouded by

중심소재: Human clonig

1. 도입부 = 현상(일반진술)
인간복제에 대한 전국적 토론 → 국회에서 진전 상황 없음 → 특정 주로 논의가 전이됨 → 여섯 주는 이미 인간 복제를 금지했으며, 이번 연도에 22개 주에서 반 복제 관련 조치 도입. 국회의 임시변통 법안으로 복제 금지에 관한 사안이 더욱 난항을 겪고 있다.

scientific and ethical questions over whether and how to restrict cloning or to ban it altogether. Like their counterparts in Washington, ① state legislators say they are concerned about the prospect of cloned babies. ② They are also divided over the ethics of cloning human embryos for research, which proponents say holds vast promise for treating diseases, and which detractors say raises the specter of "embryo farms." 2. At the same time, they say they are frustrated with Congress, and hopeful that their actions might ultimately force Washington to follow suit.

1) 구체적 진술
① 주 의원 – 복제 아이의 장래 우려
② 인간 배아 연구에 대한 윤리성 양분: 질병 치료에 대한 가망성 vs 배아 농장의 악몽
2. 추가로 연방정부에 대한 주 의원들의 실망과 더불어 정부가 이들의 조치를 따라주기를 희망하는 모습을 보이며 마무리하고 있다.

| 해설
본문은 논란의 정도가 더욱 짙어가는 '인간복제 문제'를 다루고 있다. 보기가 어떤 식으로 구성되어 오답을 유도하는지 살펴보자.

① Several pieces of new federal laws were legislated during the past year.
→ 본문 초반에 dash를 이용한 부연설명에 'no new federal laws' 라는 표현과 정반대되는 내용을 오답으로 만들었다. 본문에서 콤마, 대시, 세미콜론 등에 따르는 부연진술을 잘 읽어야 한다.

② The new laws against cloning will only add to the controversy surrounding it.
→ 본문에서 'The resulting patchwork of laws~' 로 시작하는 문장에 정확히 언급되어 있다.

③ Twenty-two states have already prohibited cloning altogether.
→ 이미 금지한 주는 본문에서 8개 주이고, 반 인간 복제에 관한 조치가 취해진 곳이 22개 주다. 본문에서 수치와 함께 언급된 사항을 각별히 주의해 체크해 두어야 한다.

④ The supporters of cloning promised to treat diseased babies.
→ 본문의 'proponents' 라는 단어를 'supporters' 로 바꾸어 표현했으며, 질병이 있는 아이를 구체적으로 언급한 후 질병 치료를 약속했다고 말하고 있는데, 본문에 구체적인 질병이 있는 아이에 대한 언급이 없으며, 주창자들이 말하는 'promise' 는 질병 치료의 '가망성' 이란 의미에서 사용한 단어이지 '약속하다' 의 구체적 행위를 말하는 동사로 쓰이지 않았다. 동의어의 활용과 다의어를 가진 단어를 이용해 혼동을 주고 있다.

| 해석
새로운 연방 법률을 내놓지 못한 채, 연방의회에서 거의 1년간 감정적 대립을 겪은 후, 인간복제에 관한 전국적인 논쟁은 각 주로 옮겨졌다. 여섯 주는 이런저런 형태로 이미 복제를 금지하였고 올해 38가지의 복제 반대 조치가 22개 주에 도입되었다. 이 때문에 제 각각의 법들이 끼워 맞춘 것처럼 된 것이, 복제를 제한하거나 금지하느냐 말아야 하느냐, 한다면 어떻게 해야 하느냐에 관한 과학적·윤리적 문제들로 이미 혼란스러워진 전국적인 상황을 더욱 복잡하게 만들었다고 이 문제와 관련된 각 방면의 사람들은 말한다. 연방의회 의원들과 마찬가지로 주 의회 의원들도 복제 아기의 전망에 대해 우려하고 있다고 말한다. 또한 연구를 위한 인간배아 복제의 윤리성에 관한 의견도 분분한데, 인간배아 복제 지지자들의 말로는, 질병 치료를 위한 폭넓은 길을 밝게 해준다고 하고, 반대자들의 말로는, '배아 농장' 의 악몽을 키울 것이라 한다. 동시에 그들(주 의회 의원들)은 연방의회에 실망했고, 그들이 행동을 취하면 결국에는 연방정부가 그대로 따라올 수밖에 없게 되기를 기대한다고 말한다.

12. ①

1. <u>Virtually all socialists agreed on the need for basic structural changes in the economy, but they differed widely on how drastic those changes should be</u>. 1) Some endorsed the sweepingly radical goals of European Marxists; others envisioned a more moderate reform that would allow small-scale private enterprise to survive but would nationalize the major industries. There was still less agreement on tactics. Ⓐ Militants within the party favored drastic, even violent, action. Ⓐ Most conspicuous was the radical labor union calling itself "the Industrial Workers of the World (the IWW)." Under the leadership of William Haywood, the IWW advocated a single union for all workers and abolition of the "wage slave" system. Although small in numbers, the IWW struck terror into the hearts of the middle class with their inflammatory rhetoric and their occasional dynamiting of railroad lines and power stations. Ⓑ More moderate socialists advocated a peaceful change through political struggle, and it was they who dominated the party. They emphasized a gradual education of the public to the need for change, and patient efforts within the system to enact it. It soon became clear, however, that the period before World War I was not the first stage of an effective social movement but the last. By the end of the war, socialism was virtually dead as a significant political force. Party leaders continued to talk of the need for change, but hardly anyone was listening.

중심소재: 경제 구조 변환
1. 도입부 = 주제문
모든 사회주의자는 기본적인 경제 구조의 변화를 요구하지만 사회혁명의 정도는 다르다.
1) 뒷받침 문장
사회주의자들 간의 '사회혁명 정도'의 차이에 덧붙여 어떤 전략으로 혁명을 이끌어낼지에 대한 방법도 다르다.
Ⓐ 예시 부연
호전주의자(militants)의 경우 '과격한 방법'을 선호. Ⓐ에서 구체적 예로 'IWW'를 들고 있다. 이어서 Ⓑ에서 앞에서 제시한 'IWW'와 대조적인 온건 사회주의자(moderate socialist)에 대해 상술하고 있다.

★ 중심내용(controlling idea)에 해당한다.

★ 대조의 글 전개방식을 확인할 수 있다.

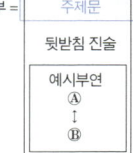

| 해설
첫 번째 문장이 주제문이고, 전체적으로 대조를 이용해 글이 전개되고 있다. 대조의 글에 따라나오는 내용 일치 문제에 접근할 때는 대조되는 각 대상의 특성을 정확히 파악하는 연습을 해야 한다. 시험지의 공간을 이용해 메모 또는 본문에 중요사항을 줄을 그어 각 대상의 특성을 파악하는 연습을 하도록 한다. 보기를 구체적으로 살펴보자.

① Less radical socialists advocated peaceful change.
→ 덜 과격한 사회주의자들은 평화적인 변화를 주장했다(두 번째 단락 첫 번째 문장에 언급되어 있다).
② By the end of World War Ⅱ, socialism was greatly weakened in America.
→ 제2차 세계 대전 종식 무렵 사회주의는 미국에서 크게 위축되었다(본문 마지막에 제1차 세계 대전으로 언급).

③ Moderate socialists insisted on a single union for all workers.
→ 중도 사회주의자들과 'drastic'은 어울리지 않다. 본문의 'radical'이란 단어의 동의어를 사용해 혼동을 일으키려 하고 있다.

| 해석

거의 모든 사회학자가 경제에 있어서 기본적인 구조적 변화가 필요하다는 데 대해서는 의견이 일치했지만 그런 변화가 얼마나 철저해야 하는가에 대해서는 견해차가 컸다. 일부 사람들은 유럽 마르크스주의자들의 철저하게 과격한 목표들을 인정했지만, 또 다른 사람들은 소규모 민영 기업이 생존하도록 허용하는 반면 주요 산업체들은 국영화할 보다 온건한 개혁을 꿈꾸었다. 구체적인 실현 방법 면에서는 더욱 의견이 달렸다. 당 내에서 투쟁적인 사람들은 과감한, 심지어는 폭력적인 조치를 지지 했다. 그 중, 자칭 '세계 산업 노동자 조합(IWW)'이라는 급진적 노동조합이 가장 두드러졌다. 윌리엄 헤이우드의 지도 아래, IWW는 모든 노동자의 단일 노조와 '임금 노예' 제도 폐지를 옹호했다. IWW는 비록 수적으로는 적었지만, 선동적인 웅변과 이따금 감행한 철도 선로와 발전소의 다이너마이트 폭파로 중산층의 간담을 서늘케 했다. 더 온건한 사회학자들은 정치 투쟁을 통한 평화적인 변화를 옹호했으며, 당을 지배한 것은 바로 그들이었다. 그들은 변화의 필요에 대해 대중을 점차 교육시킬 것과 그 변화를 법제화하도록 제도 내에서 끈기 있게 노력할 것을 강조했다. 그러나 제1차 세계 대전 이전의 시기는 효과적인 사회 운동의 첫 단계가 아니라 마지막 단계임이 곧 분명해졌다. 전쟁이 끝났을 때 사회주의는 중요한 정치 세력으로서는 이미 사실상 사멸된 상태였다. 당의 지도자들은 변화의 필요에 관한 이야기를 계속했지만, 귀담아 듣는 사람은 거의 없었다.

13. ①

중심내용(controlling idea) ★

1. As students, we read for many reasons. 1) We read to explore life in certain historical periods, cultures, and regions. We read to examine problems of human justice, to explore basic issues of race, class, sex, and age. By encountering many different and conflicting ideas and beliefs, we learn to think critically, to ask intelligent questions, and to form our own opinions.

중심소재: 독서
첫 번째 문단
1. 도입부 = 단락 주제문
책을 읽는 여러 이유가 있다.
1) 뒷받침 진술

'not A but B'의 강조구 ★
문에서 글쓴이의 주장은 B에 해당한다.

2. Educators should not tell us what to think but should teach us how to think. 1) Rather than flatly stating whether a certain book has value, instructors and school officials should encourage us to read extensively and to decide for ourselves. By encouraging lively debates in the classroom, teachers can help us to clarify what we believe and why. Book censorship, by inhibiting a free and open exchange of ideas, squelches the vitality of our classrooms and threatens our freedom to learn.

두 번째 문단
2. 단락 주제문
학교 내 교육가(교사)의 역할 – 선생은 어떤 책을 읽을 것인지 선정해 주는 것이 아니라 아이가 다양한 책을 읽으며 스스로 책을 선정하도록 장려해야 한다.
1) 뒷받침 진술
교사가 간섭해서 책을 골라주는 검열의 부정적인 측면을 부각하면서 자신의 주장을 강조하고 있다.

| 해설

보기를 하나씩 살펴보자.

① Censorship means that some authors would have to go to prison.
  → 검열은 특정 작가의 경우 감옥에 갈 수도 있다는 것을 의미한다.
② Censorship makes it impossible to have a free exchange of ideas.
  → 검열은 자유로운 사상의 교환을 방해한다.
③ Censorship means that someone else would have to do our thinking for us.
  → 검열은 다른 누군가가 우리의 생각을 대신해 주는 것을 의미한다.
④ Censorship discourages active discussions in our classrooms.
  → 검열은 학교 교실에서 자유로운 토론을 방해한다.

보기 ①만이 언급되지 않은 사항이다. 나머지는 모두 본문에서 파악할 수 있다. 다시 한 번 강조하지만, 어느 문제를 막론하고 주제와 글 전체의 흐름을 파악하는 능력이 기본이 됨을 꼭 기억해야 한다. 보기 ②, ③, ④ 모두 두 번째 단락에 나오는 '교사의 역할' 중 글쓴이가 부정적으로 파악하는 사항과 일맥상통한다.

| 해석

학생으로서 우리는 여러 가지 이유에서 책을 읽는다. 우리는 특정 역사 시대, 문화, 그리고 지역에서의 삶을 탐구하기 위해 책을 읽는다. 우리는 인간 정의의 문제를 검증하기 위해, 인종, 계급, 성별, 연령대의 기본적인 문제들을 탐구하기 위해 책을 읽는다. 많은 다양한 상반되는 이론과 믿음을 마주함으로써, 우리는 비평적으로 사고하고, 지적인 질문을 하며 우리 자신만의 의견을 형성하는 것을 배운다.

교육자들은 무엇을 생각할 것인가를 말해주는 것이 아니라 어떻게 생각할 것인가를 가르쳐야 한다. 교사들이나 학교 당국자들은 어떤 책이 가치를 가졌는지를 단순하게 말하기보다는, 폭넓게 독서하고 스스로 결정하는 자세를 갖도록 장려해야 한다. 교실에서 생생한(활기찬) 토론을 장려함으로써, 교사들은 우리가 믿는 것 그리고 왜 믿는지를 명백하게 밝히는 것을 도울 수 있다. 책에 대한 검열은 사고의 자유스럽고 개방된 교환을 억제함으로써 교실의 생동감을 감퇴시키고 배움에 대한 자유를 위협한다.

14. ③, ③

1. By the fifteenth century, when the European nations were "discovering" America, the continent had been inhabited by millions of natives who had migrated from Asia before. 1) ① Most of the tribes had developed some kind of agriculture or fishing while remaining as hunters and retaining nomadic characteristics. They roamed the high western plains, hunted mountain valleys, and farmed along the rivers from coast to coast. There was considerable diversity and there were several hundred different languages among the wide-ranging tribes. Several tribes, such as the Iroquois, were very successful in achieving political unity and extending their influence.
② The native peoples were well adapted to their environment, and without the aid of the natives, the first European settlers

중심소재: 미 대륙의 첫 정착민
1. 도입부 = 주제문
미대륙은 유럽국가에 의해서 발견된 것이 아니라 이미 아시아 사람들이 이주해 정착한 원주민들이 먼저 발견했다.
1) 뒷받침 진술
① 뒷받침 1
아시아계 이주민들의 사회/경제적 측면에 관한 구체적 부연
② 뒷받침 2
유럽의 정착민들이 오기 이전에 아시아계 이주민은 벌써 북미 환경에 익숙해 있었다고 말하면서 그들이 유럽인들을 도운 내용을 담고 있다(두 번째 문단 포함 유럽인들 이전에 아시아계 이주민이 훨씬 먼저 북미에 들어와 잘 적응하고 있었다는 면을 부각하면서 첫 번째 문단에서 주장한 '미국을 발견한 민족은 유럽이 아니라 아시아계 이주민임을 뒷받침하고 있다).

★ 언제나 첫 번째 문장 분석은 글의 전체적 흐름을 파악하는 데 핵심이다. 'discovering'에 따옴표가 있다는 것은 문자 그대로의 의미로 쓰고 있지 않고, 그 이면에 다른 뜻이 있다는 말이다. 유럽 국가가 미국을 발견하기 전 이미 아시아계 이주민이 살고 있었다고 말하고 있다(이는 유럽 국가에 의해 미국이 발견된 것이 아니라 다른 민족에 의해 이미 벌써 발견된 것이라는 뜻).

207

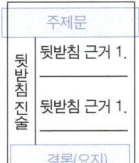
도입부 = 주제문
뒷받침 진술 / 뒷받침 근거 1. / 뒷받침 근거 1.
결론(요지)

might not have survived. Many native vegetables, such as maize and potatoes, became important staples. Moreover, native trackers guided expeditions and taught hunters and explorers the ways of the land.

3. For years, U.S. history began with Columbus, but today the cultures and contributions of the early inhabitants of America are studied and acknowledged. The story of North America begins with the true origin of the continent and its people.

2. 결론(요지)
미국의 역사는 콜럼버스가 아니라 아시아계 초기 정착민임을 다시 강조하면서 글을 마무리하고 있다.

| 해설
글쓴이가 주장하는 요지는 '미국은 아시아계 원주민이 이미 벌써 유럽의 정착민 이전에 살고 있었다.'이다. 문제 1과 문제 2는 모두 글쓴이의 주장과 관련된 내용이 답이 된다. 다시 말해, 내용 일치 문제 중 맞는 것을 고르는 문제는 글의 주장과 밀접한 관련이 있는 사항이 나오는 경우가 많다.

| 해석
15세기에, 유럽 국가들이 아메리카를 '발견'하고 있었을 때, 그 대륙에는 이전에 아시아에서 이주해 온 수백만의 원주민들이 이미 살고 있었다. 대부분 이들 부족은 이미 모종의 농업과 어업을 발전시키면서, 동시에 수렵인으로 유목민의 특성을 유지하고 있었다. 그들은 높은 서부평야를 돌아다녔고, 산의 계곡에서 사냥하였으며, 전국 방방곡곡에서 강을 따라 농사도 지었다. 광범위하게 흩어져 있던 그 부족들 간에서는 상당한 다양성이 존재하고 있었고, 수백 가지의 서로 다른 언어들이 있었다. 이로쿼이 부족 같은 몇몇 부족들은 정치적 통일을 이루고 세력을 확장하는 데 큰 성공을 거두었다.

그 원주민들은 환경에 잘 적응했으며, 이들 원주민의 도움이 없었더라면 유럽에서 온 최초의 정착민들은 생존하지 못했을지도 모른다. 옥수수나 감자와 같은 많은 토착 채소들이 중요한 주식이 되었다. 게다가 원주민 수색하는 사람들이 원정대를 인도했으며, (유럽에서 온) 사냥꾼들과 탐험가들에게 육지의 길을 가르쳐주었다.

오랫동안 미국 역사는 콜럼버스와 함께 시작된 것으로 인식되었다. 그러나 오늘날 아메리카 초기 정착민들의 문화와 공로가 연구되고 또한 인정받고 있다. 북아메리카의 역사는 그 대륙의 진정한 기원과 그곳에 살던 사람들과 함께 시작한다.

15. ③

현상을 드러내는 시그널★을 확인한다.

1. During the past two decades the rise in the real income of manual laborers has been not only great in absolute terms, but also greater in comparison with that of non-manual workers. 1) The effect of this has been to blur the old division between the working and middle classes, many manual workers' families now acquiring habits, tastes, and, to some extent, attitudes which were formerly regarded as "middle class." Due to considerable upward mobility of the working class, social distinctions based on occupation

중심소재: 육체 노동자의 경제적 능력 향상
1. 도입부 = 현상
육체 노동자의 실질 임금이 상승(원인)
1) 주제문(인과 확인)
계층간의 구별이 흐려지면서 과거 중산층이 누리던 습관, 취향, 태도를 어느정도 누리게 되고, 신분에 따른 사회적 구별이 흐려짐.
① 뒷받침 부연

have become less clear-cut. ① Whether they exist and what they consist of depend on what part of the country one is looking at, but people today should not assume that a doctor is regarded as several steps on the ladder above a garage keeper, or that the headmaster of the local state school is regarded as a higher being than the skilled worker who now earns not one quarter of his salary, but just as much as he does, if not more.

| 해설

내용 일치 문제 중 맞는 것을 고르는 문제이다. 많은 경우 주제문에 해당하는 내용과 직간접적으로 관련이 있는 보기가 답인 경우가 많다. 고로, 본문의 주제와 요지를 파악하는 능력은 모든 문제를 푸는 기본이 되므로 이를 파악하는 능력을 꾸준히 길러야 한다.

| 해석

지난 20년 동안 육체 노동자들의 실제 수입 상승은 절대적인 면에서 클 뿐만 아니라 사무직 노동자들의 수입 인상에 비해서도 더 컸다. 이러한 수입 상승의 결과 노동자 계급과 중류 계급들 사이의 오래된 구분이 흐려져서, 이제는 많은 육체 노동자 가족들이 예전에 중산층 계급의 것으로 여겨졌던 습관과 기호, 그리고 어느 정도 태도를 습득하고 있다. 노동자 계급의 상당한 신분상승 때문에 직업에 근거한 사회적 구별은 덜 분명해졌다. 그러한 사회적 구별이 존재하는가, 그리고 그러한 사회적 구별은 무엇으로 이루어지는가는 사람이 그 나라의 어떤 부분을 바라보는가에 달려있다. 그러나 오늘날 사람들은 의사가 차고 관리인보다 몇 단계 위에 있다고 여겨진다거나 지역주립학교의 교장이 숙련 노동자보다 더 높은 사람으로 여겨진다고 생각해서는 안 되는데, 숙련 노동자가 이제는 교장 급여의 4분의 1을 버는 것이 아니고, 교장보다 더 많이는 아니라 하더라도 교장만큼은 벌기 때문이다.

16. ③

★ 고정관념의 부정적인 측면을 다루는 글임을 첫 번째 문장에서 파악할 수 있다.

1. <u>The danger of stereotypes lies</u> **not** in their existence, **but** in the fact that they become for all people some of the time, and for some people all the time, substitutes for observation. 1) ① <u>Worse yet</u>, stereotypes get in the way of our judgment, even when we do observe the world. Ⓐ Someone who has formed rigid preconceptions of all Latins as "excitable," or all teenagers as "wild," doesn't alter his point of view when he meets a calm and deliberate Genoses, or a serious-minded high school student. He brushes them aside as "exceptions that prove the rule." And, of course, if he meets someone true to type, he stands triumphantly vindicated. "They're all like that," he proclaims, having encountered an excited Latin, an ill-behaved adolescent. ② <u>Thus, stereotyping makes people mentally lazy.</u>

중심소재: 고정관념

1. 도입부 = 주제문
'고정관념의 위험성은 관측하는 대상의 대체물이 된다'는 부정적인 관측을 드러내고 있다.

1) 뒷받침 진술
① 관점 1
세상을 관측할 때 정확한 판단력에 방해된다.
Ⓐ 부연진술
① 구체적 예를 통해 '고정관념'에 관한 부정적인 관점을 뒷받침하고 있다.
② 관점 2
사람을 게으르게 한다.

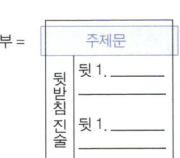

209

| 해설

본문은 '고정관념'을 가지고 그 위험성을 논하는 글이다. 어떤 글을 막론하고 글의 초반부를 집중해서 읽어야 함은 물론, 위 본문에서 글쓴이 주장이 드러나는 첫 번째 문장에서 'not A but B'라는 구문을 사용해 자신이 주장하려는 내용을 효율적으로 강조하고 있다. 강조구문이 나오는 문장은 글쓴이의 주장이 드러나는 부분이므로 절대 놓쳐서는 안 된다. 주제: '고정관념의 위험성'이다. 내용 일치 문제 중 틀린 것을 고르는 문제이다. 보기를 먼저 파악하고 본문을 읽는 것도 좋은 전략이다. 이는 4개의 보기가 모두 옳은 진술이기에 본문에서 전개된 내용의 '요약본'으로 활용할 수 있기 때문이다.

① Stereotyping interferes with our judgment.
→ 고정관념은 우리의 (객관적) 판단을 방해한다(고정관념에 대한 부정적 견해).
② Nobody is free from stereotyping.
→ 누구나 고정관념에서 벗어날 수 없다(고정관념에 대한 부정적 견해).
③ Stereotyping enhances people's mental efforts.
→ 고정관념은 인간의 정신적 노력을 향상하게 한다(고정관념에 대한 긍정적 견해).
④ Stereotyping sometimes makes people overgeneralize.
→ 고정관념 때문에 사람들은 일반화하는 경향이 생긴다(고정관념에 대한 부정적 견해).
⑤ Stereotyping interferes with our observation.
→ 고정관념은 우리의 관측을 방해한다(고정관념에 대한 부정적 견해).

보기 ③이 고정관념에 대한 부정적 견해를 진술한 본문과 가장 거리가 멀다.

| 해석

고정관념의 위험성은 그러한 고정관념이 존재한다는 것에 있는 것이 아니라, 그것이 모든 사람에게 있어서는 일정 기간, 어떤 사람들에게 있어서는 항상 관찰을 대신하는 것이 된다는 점에 있다(보지도 않고 고정관념대로 생각한다는 점에 있다). 더 나쁜 점은 고정관념이 우리가 실상을 목격하고 있을 때조차도 건전한 판단을 방해한다는 점이다. 모든 라틴계 사람들은 흥분을 잘하고, 모든 십 대들은 거칠다는 것과 같은 완고한 선입관을 가진 사람은, 차분하고 신중한 제노바 사람을 만나거나 신중한 고교생을 만나도 자신의 생각을 바꾸지 않는다. 그는 그러한 것들을 '규칙임을 입증해주는 예외'로 치부하고 무시해 버린다. 그리고 물론, 그가 자기 편견에 맞아떨어지는 경우의 사람을 만나면 그는 의기양양하게 주장한다. 흥분하는 라틴계 사람이나, 행실이 나쁜 청소년을 만나면 "그들은 모두 저래"라고 그는 주장한다. 이처럼 고정관념은 사람들을 정신적으로 게으르게 만든다.

17. ③

글의 중심소재는 'corset' 이다.

1. Early-Victorian costume not only made women look weak and helpless, it made them weak and helpless. 1) ① The main agent of this debility was the corset, which at the time was thought of not as a mere fashion item but as a medical necessity.
Ladies' "frames," it was believed, were extremely delicate; their muscles could not hold them up without assistance. ② Well-brought-up little girls were laced into juvenile versions of the corset as early as three or four. Gradually their stays were

중심소재: 빅토리아 시대의 의상 → 코르셋

1. 도입부 = 주제문
1) 뒷받침 진술
① 코르셋을 입었던 배경(이유)
빅토리아 의상 중 '코르셋'을 소개하면서(중심소재 도출) 코르셋을 착용했던 이유를 언급하고 있다.
② 코르셋의 부작용
아주 어린 시절부터 코르셋을 입게 되어 발생하는 부작용을 본문 끝까지 기술하고 있다.

lengthened, stiffened and tightened. By the time they reached late adolescence they were wearing cages of heavy canvas reinforced with steel, and their back muscles had often atrophied to the point where they could not sit or stand for long unsupported. The corset also deformed the internal organs and made it impossible to draw a deep breath. As a result fashionably dressed ladies fainted easily, suffered from digestive complaints, and felt weak and exhausted after any strenuous exertion.

| 해설

본문은 '초기 빅토리아 시대에 코르셋을 입었던 이유와 부작용'을 다루는 글이다. 질문의 요지는 '그 당시 사람들은 왜 여성이 코르셋을 입을 필요성이 있다고 생각했는가?'이다. 본문에 이 점이 정확히 명시된 곳을 찾아야 한다. 다음 문장이 답이 된다.

> Ladies' frames, it was believed, were extremely delicate; their muscles could not hold them up without assistance.

본문의 특정 부분을 문제화하는 경우는 다음과 같은 경우일 때 자주 등장한다.
1) 본문의 가장 핵심적인 내용인 주제문과의 관련성
2) 문장의 구조가 복잡하여 해석이 쉽지 않은 특수구문
3) 다의어가 들어간 문장으로 문맥적 상황을 정확히 파악하여 해석해야 하는 경우

위 문제를 풀기 위해서는 다의어인 'frame'을 여성의 '몸'으로 해석할 수 있는 능력과 삽입구(it was believed = people believed)에 대한 정확한 이해가 있어야 한다.

| 해석

빅토리아 왕조 초기의 의상은 여성들을 약하고 무기력해 보이도록 만들 뿐만 아니라 실제로 여성들을 약하고 무기력하게 만들었다. 이러한 쇠약함의 주된 요인은 코르셋이었다. 그 당시에 코르셋은 단순한 패션 품목이 아니라 의료 필수품으로 여겨졌다.

여성들의 '골격(체격)'은 매우 가냘프게 여겨졌고, 여성들의 근육은 도움 없이는 제대로 몸을 지탱시킬 수 없었다. 좋은 집안의 어린 여자아이들은 3살이나 4살 정도의 나이에 소아용 코르셋으로 (몸을) 졸라맸다. 점차 그들의 코르셋이 길어지고 딱딱해지며 몸에 꼭 끼게 되었다. 그들이 청소년기 후반에 이르렀을 때는 이미 강철로 강화된 무거운 범포천의 코르셋을 입고 있었고, 그들의 등 근육은 몸을 지탱시켜줄 것이 없으면 오랫동안 앉거나 서 있지 못할 정도까지 쇠약해져 있었다. 또한, 코르셋은 체내 장기들을 변형시켰고 심호흡을 할 수 없게 했다. 결과적으로 유행에 맞춰 옷을 입는 여성들은 쉽게 기절하였고, 소화 불량을 겪었으며, 격렬한 활동 후에는 힘들고 지쳐 했다.

18. ③

1. The youngest child in a family often becomes a real charmer, playful or manipulative in his desire to get attention. 1) ① Such children develop strategies to make their presence felt, either by behaving disagreeably or by finding creative or athletic outlets such as writing, drawing, or sports. ② The youngest child's parents are often older, more tired, or more relaxed about rules that seemed important with their preceding children. 2. The youngest child, **therefore**, grows up experiencing fewer family pressures and more independence. **The result** is a more creative, carefree person, which is why the youngest frequently choose careers in the arts, entertainment, and sales.

인과의 시그널을 확인한★다.

도입부 = 중심소재 (막내의 성향)
뒷받침 진술
근거 ① _____
근거 ② _____
결론(요지)

중심소재: 막내
1. 도입부
막내의 성향: 관심을 얻으려고 함
1) 뒷받침 진술
① 아이의 측면
마음에 들지 않는 행동을 하거나 창조적 또는 스포츠와 같은 육체적 통로를 통해 관심을 받으려는 전략을 씀
② 부모의 측면
대부분 나이가 들어 규칙에 엄격하지 않음
2. 결론(요지)
①과 ②의 영향으로 막내는 가족의 압박을 적게 받고, 독립심이 강해 예술, 연예, 영업 쪽의 직업을 주로 선택하게 된다.

| 해설
글 전개 방법은 '인과'이다. 글의 주제는 "막내가 예술, 연예, 영업 쪽 직업을 선택하게 되는 배경"이다. 내용 일치 중 옳은 것을 고르는 문제이다.

① feels more pressures from other family members
→ 글쓴이의 요지와 정반대의 내용이다.

② hardly chooses jobs such as artists and entertainers
→ ①과 마찬가지로 정반대의 기술이다.

③ often behaves in an odd way to get more attention
→ 본문 두 번째 문장에 기술되어 있다.

④ depends too heavily upon his preceding sisters or brothers
→ 글쓴이의 요지와 정반대의 내용이다.

⑤ is usually less important to his parents than older sisters or brothers
→ 글쓴이의 요지와 정반대이다.

오답의 내용을 보면, 모두 글의 요지와 관련되어 오답을 유도하고 있다. 내용 일치 문제는 주제 및 요지를 파악했을 경우, 본문의 내용과 보기를 일일이 다 확인해 볼 필요가 없기에 시간을 아낄 수 있다. 주제와 요지를 파악하는 연습은 어떤 지문이 나와도 선행해야 할 작업이다.

| 해석
가정에서 막내는 정말 매력적인 존재로 관심을 얻으려는 소망에서 장난을 치거나 교묘히 조작하는 성향이 있다. 그러한 아이들은 마음에 들지 않게 행동하거나 그렇지 않으면 글쓰기, 그리기, 스포츠처럼 창조적, 육체적 통로를 찾는 등의 전략들을 개발하여 자신의 존재를 알린다. 막내의 부모들은 더 늙고 지쳐있으며, 손위 형제들에게 중요해 보였던 규칙들에 대해서도 느슨해져 있는 경우가 많다. 그러므로 막내는 가족들의 압력을 덜 받고, 더 독립적으로 자란다. 그 결과 막내는 더 창조적이고, 걱정 근심 없는 사람이 되며, 이것이 바로 막내들이 자주 예술, 오락, 영업 분야의 직업을 선택하는 이유이다.

19. ②, ④

1. But vaccination may have risks of its own. 1) ① The problem lies with the nature of the chicken-pox virus. After you get it, you always have it in your body. Normally you only suffer from chicken-pox once, but the virus can flare up again later in life, producing shingles, a painful skin rash. The vaccine is a weakened form of virus, and it too may be harbored in the body forever. The debilitated virus could conceivably spring to life years after the vaccination, and no one knows what damage might occur. ② Another danger is that the vaccine may not confer life-long immunity and will make a person vulnerable to chicken-pox during adulthood, when the disease can be more serious. "It is impossible in the experimental studies preceeding licensing to study a vaccine's effects for 50 years," says Dr Caroline Hall of the American Academy of Pediatrics. "To the best of my knowledge, the varicella vaccine is safe."

★ 중심소재

중심소재:백신

1. 도입부 = 주제문
백신 자체의 위험성
1) 뒷받침 문장
백신의 위험성을 구체적으로 ①, ②에서 설명하고 있다.
① 약한 형태의 백신이 나중에 힘을 얻어 피해를 줄 수도 있다.
② 백신은 평생 면역을 제공해 주지 못할 수도 있기에 나중에 어른이 되어서 더 심각한 수두에 걸릴 수도 있다.

★ 중심내용(controlling idea)

★ 나열의 글전개 확인

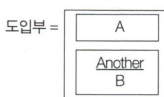

Another로 보아 A의 내용은 B와 같은 맥락의 첫번째 사상의 내용임을 파악할 수 있다.

| 해설
본문은 '백신이 안고 있는 위험성'을 크게 두 가지로 나눠 설명하고 있다. 내용 일치 문제는 언제나 글의 주제와 요지를 바탕으로 접근해야 한다. 문제 1, 2의 보기를 모두 살펴보자.

문제 1.
① can cause later developments of diseases among chickens
 → 닭 이야기가 아니다. 'chicken pox'의 어휘 혼동을 이끌어 내어 오답을 설정했다.
② may have its own problem(s)
 → 본문의 주제문에 해당하는 핵심 내용이다.
③ is tested and proven safe and effective for the life time
 → 글의 요지와 정반대 주장에 해당한다.
④ may be a cause of some deadly diseases
 → 본문의 내용을 과장하여 만든 오답이다.

문제 2.
① Chicken-pox vaccine can reside in the human body only for a short period of time.
 → 본문 중 'you always have it in your body'라고 언급되어 있다. 시간이 지나면서 약해진다는 이야기는 이후 언급되지만 짧은 기간 동안 몸에 머문다는 이야기는 없다.
② Adults are immune to chicken-pox.
 → 어른도 이후 걸릴 수 있다고 했다.
③ Chicken-pox vaccine does not affect human bodies.
 → 본문의 주장과 정반대 내용이다.

④ Chicken-pox vaccination does not give people a complete protection from chicken-pox.
→ 본문의 주장과 일맥상통한다.

정리하면, 내용 일치 또는 구체적 사실 확인 문제는 언제나 글의 주제와 요지를 바탕으로 접근하면 신속성과 정확성을 모두 잡을 수 있다.

| 해석
그러나 백신은 그 자체의 위험성을 갖고 있을 수도 있다. 문제는 수두 바이러스의 성질에 있다. 수두 바이러스를 몸에 갖게 되고 나면, 당신은 늘 그것을 몸 안에 지니고 있게 된다. 보통 사람들은 수두를 단 한 번만 앓지만, 그 바이러스는 나중에 다시 갑작스레 기세를 부려, 대상포진과 고통스러운 피부 발진을 일으킬 수도 있다. 백신은 바이러스를 약하게 만든 형태인데, 이것 역시 몸속에 영원히 숨어있게 된다. 약화된 바이러스는 백신 접종 수 년 후에도 갑자기 살아날 수 있으며, 어떤 피해가 발생할지는 아무도 알 수 없다. 또 다른 위험은 백신이 일생 면역을 부여할 수는 없어서 성인기에 수두에 걸리기 쉬운 상태가 될 수도 있으며, 그때는 이 질병이 더더욱 심각할 수 있다는 점이다. "백신은 인가가 나기에 앞서 진행되는 실험적 연구로 50년 동안 백신의 효과를 조사하는 것은 불가능합니다."라고 미국 소아과 협회의 캐롤라인 홀(Caroline Hall) 박사는 말한다. "제가 아는 한, 수두 백신은 안전합니다."

20. ③

중심소재는 '블랙홀' 이다.★

1. Black holes are more difficult to observe than almost any other object in the universe because they emit no visible light. 1) ① A black hole forms when a large star exhausts the heated gasses (typically hydrogen and helium) that it consumes as fuel during thermonuclear reactions. When this happens, the star becomes very unstable. The forces of gravity cause the dying star to collapse inward upon itself with such intense force that its matter compresses into a single point with a volume of zero and an infinite density. This remarkable point is known as the singularity, because it defies all traditional theories about gravity and the behavior of matter. The singularity is the center of a black hole, but an outer surface called the event horizon surrounds the black hole itself. 2) In fact, the force of gravity is so intense within the event horizon that even ray of light cannot escape. The size of a black hole's event horizon is known as its Schwarzschild radius, after the German astronomer Karl Schwarzschild, who predicted the existence of black holes. Physicists believe that the Schwarzschild radius is proportionally related to the mass of the star that originally collapsed. Thus, theorists claim that a star with a mass ten

중심소재: 블랙홀
1. 도입부
'블랙홀'에 관한 내용이다. 잘 보이지 않는 특성을 근거와 함께 제시하고 있다.
1) 블랙홀의 생성
① 거대한 별이 가열 가스 소모 → 별의 불안정 → 중력 불안정 → 소멸하는 별이 내부로 붕괴하여 물질이 무게는 없는데, 밀도는 무한대인 하나의 점(singularity)으로 모이게 된다. 바로 이 점이 블랙홀의 중심이다(인과).
2) 블랙홀의 특징
블랙홀의 다양한 특징을 본문끝까지 상술하고 있다.

times greater than that of the Sun would form a black hole with a Schwarzschild radius of 18.6 miles (30km).

| 해설

주제는 '블랙홀의 생성과 특성'이다. 틀린 것을 고르는 문제이다. 보기를 먼저 파악하고 문제에 접근한다.

① 블랙홀은 별의 핵융합 반응 과정에서 형성된다.
　→ 'A black hole forms ~ during thermonuclear reactions'에 명시되어 있다.
② 블랙홀의 크기를 재는 단위는 독일 천문학자의 이름을 딴 것이다.
　→ 'its Schwarzschild radius, after the German astronomer Karl Schwarzschild.'
③ 소멸하는 별이 블랙홀이 되는 것을 Schwarzschild radius라 부른다.
　→ 'The size of a black hole's event horizon is known as its Schwarzschild radius'에서 틀리다는 것을 알 수 있다. 즉, 'Schwarzschild radius'는 'event horizon의 크기'이다.
④ 블랙홀의 크기는 원래 소멸한 별의 크기와 비례한다.
　→ 'Schwarzschild radius is proportionally related to the mass of the star that originally collapsed'

| 해석

블랙홀은 눈에 보이는 어떠한 빛도 방출하지 않기 때문에 우주에 있는 어떤 다른 물체보다도 관찰하기가 더 어렵다. 블랙홀은 큰 별이 핵융합 반응 동안 연료로 소비하는 가열 가스(일반적으로 수소와 헬륨)를 다 소모하게 되면 만들어지게 된다. 이것이 일어날 때, 별은 매우 불안정해진다. 중력의 힘은 소멸하는 별로 하여금 너무나 강한 힘으로 안으로 붕괴하게 하여서, 별을 이루고 있는 물질은 부피는 전혀 없는데 밀도가 무한대인 단일점으로 응축한다. 이 놀라운 한 지점은 중력과 물질의 행동에 관한 전통적인 모든 이론을 가지고도 잘 설명되지 않기 때문에 특이점(singularity)이라고 알려졌다. 특이점은 블랙홀의 중심부이지만 사상의 지평선(블랙홀의 바깥 가장자리)이라 불리는 외부 표면이 블랙홀 자체를 에워싸고 있다. 사실, 중력의 힘은 사건의 지평선 안에서 너무나 강력하여 빛의 광선조차도 빠져나갈 수 없다. 블랙홀의 사상의 지평선의 크기는 슈바르츠실트 반경으로 알려졌는데 그것은 블랙홀의 존재를 예측한 독일 천문학자 카를 슈바르츠실트의 이름을 딴 것이다. 물리학자들은 슈바르츠실트 반경이 처음에 붕괴한 별의 질량과 정비례 관계에 있다고 믿는다. 그러므로 이론가들은 질량이 태양의 10배 크기인 별은 슈바르츠실트 반경이 18.6마일(30킬로미터)인 블랙홀을 형성할 것이라고 주장한다.

21. ④

★ 중심소재

1. Malaria is neither a virus like polio nor a bacterium like tuberculosis. 1) Rather, it's a parasite that invades red blood cells and has a three-stage life cycle. ① Infection starts out with a mosquito bite that releases a few of the parasites into the human bloodstream. The invaders travel to the liver where the body's cells hide them from the immune system, allowing them to multiply. Soon afterwards, the parasites burst out of the liver, and attack red blood cells. These, too, eventually burst and release still more parasites, triggering

첫번째 문단

1. 도입부
말라리아에 관한 간략한 정의

1) 단락주제문
말라리아는 적혈구에 침투하여 3단계 생애 사이클을 가지는 기생충

① 뒷받침 진술
말라리아가 모기를 통해 몸속으로 침투하는 과정과 작용에 대해 자세히 다루고 있다.

malaria's symptoms.
2. In the 1950s, malaria was believed to be on the verge of eradication. The introduction of insecticides such as DDT seemed to signal the end of the malaria-carrying mosquito in certain countries.

2. 현상
DDT와 같은 살충제 도입으로 현제 말라리아는 멸종위기 상태

| 해설

두 문단이지만 주로 첫 번째 문단이 주된 내용이다. 내용 일치 문제 중 틀린 것을 고르는 내용은 보기를 먼저 읽어보는 것이 현명하다. 앞에서 언급했듯이, 본문의 내용을 미리 짐작하는 데 큰 도움이 된다. 그리고 내용 일치를 묻는 문제의 보기는 다음과 같은 내용을 바탕으로 오답으로 만드는 경우가 많다.

1) 부분적인 내용을 전체로 확대/과장 해석(일반화 오류)
2) 사실(Fact), 의견(Opinion), 편견(Prejudice)을 혼동하게 하여 오답 유도
3) 강조 부사 또는 극단적 표현을 사용하여 오답 유도
4) 논리적 비약

① A mosquito bite infects a human body with malaria that attacks the bloodstream.
→ 모기가 사람의 몸을 물면 혈류를 공격하는 말라리아에 걸린다.
② Malaria multiplies in the liver, where the body's cells hide it from the immune system.
→ 말라리아는 간에서 번식하는데, 거기에 있는 체세포는 면역 체계에 영향을 받지 않는다.
③ The parasites released into the human blood by a mosquito bite start malaria's symptoms.
→ 모기가 물어 혈액 속에 기생충이 들어가면 말라리아 증상이 나타난다.
④ DDT exterminated the malaria-carrying mosquito in the 1950s.
→ DDT는 1950년 말라리아가 있는 모기를 박멸했다.

보기 ④를 제외하곤 모두 본문에 나와 있다. 본문에서 말라리아 박멸을 'in certain countries'로 일정 국가에 해당하는 내용으로 전개하는 동시에 'seemed'로 보이는 'Opinion'에 해당하는 내용을 보기 ④는 'fact'로 기술하고 있다.

| 해석

말라리아는 소아마비 같은 바이러스도 아니고 결핵 같은 박테리아도 아니다. 오히려, 이것은 적혈구 세포에 침입하며 3단계의 생명주기를 가진 기생충이다. 감염은 모기가 무는 것으로 시작하는데, 그 때문에 몇 마리의 기생충이 인간의 혈류 속으로 들어오게 된다. 그 침입자들이 간으로 이동하고 그곳에서 체세포가 그들을(기생충을) 면역체계로부터 숨겨 이들이 번식하게 된다. 그 후에 곧 기생충들이 간 바깥으로 나와서 적혈구 세포들을 공격하게 된다. 이 적혈구 세포들도 또한 결국 터져서 더욱더 많은 기생충이 나오게 되어 말라리아 증세를 촉발시키게 된다.

1950년대에 말라리아는 거의 박멸되었다고 믿어졌다. DDT와 같은 살충제의 도입이 일부 국가에서 말라리아를 옮기는 모기의 종식을 알리는 신호가 된 듯 보였다.

22. ②

1. Employers sometimes terminate employees due to poor job performance, negative attitudes toward work and co-workers, and misconduct such as dishonesty or sexual harassment. Ⓐ Terminating poor performers is a necessary act, because they lower productivity and employee morale. Co-workers resent employees who receive the same pay and benefits as themselves without contributing fairly to the company's work. 1) <u>Employers need to carefully document reasons for terminating employees.</u> ① According to the Equal Employment Opportunity Commission, almost half of the cases of files against employers involve charges of wrongful dismissal. In recent years, employers have terminated employees through downsizing and outsourcing.

중심소재: 피고용인 해고
1. 도입부 = 현 관행
Ⓐ에서 언급한 이유를 바탕으로 고용주가 피고용인을 해고
1) 주제문
해고를 할 때 정당한 이유를 증명해야 한다.
① 뒷받침 근거
잘못된 사례를 통해 고용주가 해고할 때는 정당한 근거 확보가 중요함을 이야기하고 있다.

도입부 = 현 관행
근거(이유)
주제문
뒷받침 근거

| 해설
본문은 정당한 해고는 필요하다는 내용을 다양한 이유에서 전개하는 동시에 해고할 때는 충분한 근거가 확보되어야 함을 주장하는 글이다.
내용 일치 문제 중 틀린 것을 고르는 문제이다. 보기를 먼저 확인하자.
① Employers terminate employees for different reasons.
 → 고용주는 여러 가지 이유에서 피고용인을 해고한다.
② It is not important that employers terminate poor employees.
 → 고용주가 불량한 피고용인을 해고하는 것은 중요하지 않다.
③ Poor performers lower productivity and employee morale.
 → 실적이 낮은 고용인은 생산성과 피고용인의 사기를 떨어뜨린다.
④ Downsizing and outsourcing are methods of terminating employees.
 → 회사 축소 및 외주는 피고용인을 해고하는 방법이다.

| 해석
고용주들은 때때로 직원을 해고하게 되는데 그 이유는 형편없는 업무 수행, 일과 동료에 대한 부정적인 태도, 그리고 불성실함이나 성희롱과 같은 불량한 행동 때문이다. 업무수행이 형편없는 직원을 해고하는 것은 필요한 행동인데, 이는 그들이 생산성과 직원의 사기를 저하하기 때문이다. 직장 동료는 회사의 일에 그다지 기여하지 않고 그들과 같은 급여와 혜택을 받는 직원을 혐오한다. 고용주들은 직원을 해고하는 이유를 세심하게 문서화해야 한다. 평등고용기회위원회(Equal Employment Opportunity Commission)에 따르면, 고용주들에 대한 소송 중 거의 반이 부당한 해고와 관련된 것이라고 한다. 최근에는 고용주들이 인원 감축이나 외주 등을 통해서 직원을 해고해왔다.

23. ④

'But'을 기점으로 통념비판(Myth-breaking)의 글임을 파악할 수 있다.

1. In the movies, sharks are dangerous predators. They are ready to attack at the first sight of human flesh. 1) **But** as many experienced shark divers and photographers will tell you, real-life sharks don't generally fit their movie image. Most sharks don't swim around the ocean looking for people to eat.

① While you can generalize about various species of shark, it's still true that sharks as individuals have very different personalities. Some are relaxed and laid back. They don't become aggressive even when faced with human intruders. Other sharks are extremely territorial. They are quick to be enraged by an outsider entering their watery world. Yet, on the whole, most sharks are more afraid of human beings than not. Despite sharks' aggressive movie image, only a few species are dangerous.

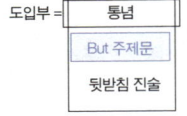

도입부 = 통념
　　　But 주제문
　　　뒷받침 진술

중심소재: 상어 → 상어의 폭력성

1. 도입부 = 통념
영화에서 묘사되는 상어는 인간을 위협하는 약탈자의 모습

1) 주제문
영화속의 상어모습은 실제와 다르다.
① 뒷받침 진술

해설

전체 글은 영화에서 또는 일반인들이 잘못 알고 있는 상어에 대한 Myth를 바로 잡기 위해 쓴 글이다. 글쓴이의 주장은 여느 글과 마찬가지로 'But, Yet' 이후에 전개되고 있다.

제목: 'Sharks in Real-Life'

내용 일치 문제 중 옳은 것을 고르는 문제이다. 대부분 글의 핵심 즉, 주제와 관련된 내용이 답이며, 다른 보기도 주제와 직간접으로 관련성을 보이는 내용이다.

① Unlike their movie image, sharks are very ferocious creatures.
　→ 본문의 요지와 정반대되는 내용이다.
② In summer a few sharks often attack people.
　→ 영화에서 주로 묘사되는 잘못된 생각이다.
③ Sharks reluctantly shun contact with human beings.
　→ 글의 요지와 반대되는 진술이다.
④ Sharks are usually different from their movie image.
　→ 글의 요지와 관련된 옳은 진술이다.

해석

영화에서 상어는 위험한 포식자다. 그들은 인간의 몸을 발견하자마자 공격할 준비가 되어 있다. 그러나 많은 경험 있는 상어 잠수부와 사진사가 이야기하듯, 실제의 상어는 일반적으로 영화 속 이미지와 맞지 않는다. 대부분 상어는 잡아먹을 사람을 찾으면서 바다를 돌아다니지 않는다. 다양한 종의 상어에 대해 일반화할 수 있겠지만, 개체로서의 상어는 서로 매우 다른 성격을 지니고 있다. 일부는 유연하고 여유가 있다. 심지어 인간 침입자와 직면했을 때도 공격적이지 않다. 다른 상어들은 극단적으로 영역에 민감하다. 그들은 수중 세계에 들어오는 이방인에 대해 순식간에 격분한다. 그러나 전반적으로 대부분 상어는 인간을 두려워하는 편이다. 상어의 공격적인 영화 이미지에도 불구하고 위험한 종은 극소수에 불과하다.

24. ④

1. Until a few short decades ago, the notion that love between a man and a woman would lead to marriage was as alien a concept to the Chinese as the assumption that women had any control over whom they would marry. 1) Marrying, according to the traditional Chinese view, was a family business, not the couple's affair. ① Having a daughter was considered a "moneylosing proposition," given the lack of return on the investment. After raising a daughter, to marry her off required a dowry and losing her permanently to another family, for once married, the daughter's identity was with her husband's family. A woman was taught from birth that she must prepare herself for lifelong servitude, to serve her parents and elders while at home, her husband and in-laws once married, and her own sons after the death of her husband. The only redeeming hope for a woman was to become a mother-in-law herself so the cycle could go on.

중심소재: 중국의 전통적 결혼관
1. 도입부
현대와 다른 중국의 결혼관: 사랑에 기반을 두지 않는다.
1) 주제문
결혼은 경제적 관점의 가족사이다. ★중심내용이다.
① 뒷받침 진술
주제문의 중심내용에서 밝힌 사항을 뒷받침 진술이 상술되고 있다.

| 해설

보기 중 세 개가 옳은 진술이다. 보기를 먼저 읽으면서 본문의 내용을 파악해 보자.

① The thought that love between a man and a woman in old China would lead to marriage was uncommon.
→ 고대 중국에서 여성과 남성 사이의 사랑이 결혼으로 이어진다는 생각은 일반적이지 않았다(중국 전통혼례에 관한 이야기인데, 결혼의 이유가 남녀 간의 사랑이 아니라고 말하고 있다).

② Marrying, according to the traditional Chinese view, was primarily a family business, not the couple's affair.
→ 중국의 전통적 관점에서 결혼은 부부 사이의 일이 아니라 주로 가족의 일이었다(결혼에 대한 중국의 전통적 관점).

③ The only redeeming hope for an old Chinese woman was to become a mother-in-law herself.
→ 과거 중국 여성이 유일하게 의존할 수 있던 희망은 시어머니가 되는 것이었다(여성의 관점에서 중국 전통혼례를 이야기하고 있다).

④ An old Chinese woman served her parents and elders, but didn't serve his own sons after the death of her husband.
→ 고대 중국의 여성은 부모와 어르신을 섬겼지만, 남편이 죽은 후 아들은 돌보지 않았다. 즉, 보기만으로 본문에서 '결혼에 대한 중국의 전통적 관점'이 드러나는데, 본문을 통해 좀 더 정확히 쓴다면, '여성의 결혼에 대한 중국의 전통적 관점'이 된다. 보기 ④는 본문의 내용과 일치하지 않는다.

| 해석

수십 년 전까지만 하더라도 남녀 간의 사랑이 결혼으로 이어진다는 생각은 중국인에게는 여성들이 결혼 상대에

대한 통제권을 갖는다는 것만큼이나 생소한 것이었다. 전통적인 중국인의 생각으로는 결혼은 경제적 관념의 가족 사이지 부부의 일이 아니었다. 딸을 갖는 것은 투자에 대한 보답이 없다는 것을 생각하면 '돈을 잃는 일'로 간주되었다. 딸을 기른 후, 그녀를 결혼시켜 보내기 위해선 결혼 지참금이 필요했고, 일단 결혼하면 딸의 신분은 그녀의 남편 가족에 소속되었으므로 딸을 영원히 다른 가족에게 빼앗기는 셈이었다. 여성은 평생 봉사하도록, 즉 집에 있는 동안은 그녀의 부모와 손 위 사람들에게, 결혼하면 그녀의 남편과 시댁 식구들에게, 그리고 남편이 죽은 후에는 그녀의 자식에게 봉사할 준비가 되어 있어야 한다는 가르침을 태어나서부터 받았다. 여성에게 보상이 되는 희망은 그녀가 시어머니가 되어 그 순환이 계속되는 것밖에 없었다.

25. ③

1. There is no reason why philosophers should not be also men of letters. But to write well does not come by instinct; it is an art that demands arduous study. 1) The philosopher does not speak only to other philosophers and to undergraduates working for a degree; he speaks also to the men of letters, politicians, and reflective persons, who directly mould the ideas of the coming generation. They, naturally enough, are taken by a philosophy that is striking and not too difficultly assimilated. ① We all know how the philosophy of Nietzsche has affected some parts of the world, and few would assert that its influence has been other than disastrous. It has prevailed, not by such profundity of thought as it may have, but by a vivid style and an effective form. The philosopher who will not take the trouble to make himself clear shows only that he thinks his thought of no more than academic value.

중심소재: 철학자 → 철학과 글쓰기
1. 도입부
철학자가 글을 잘 못 쓸 이유는 없지만, 글쓰기는 타고 태어나는 것이 아니기에 꾸준한 연습이 필요한 기술이다.
1) 다음 세대의 사상을 형성하는 중요한 사람들은 쉽고 인상적인 철학자의 글에 매료된다고 주장하면서 구체적 예인 ① 철학자 니체를 통해 효과적이고 생생한 쉬운 글쓰기 스타일과 형식의 중요성을 강조하고 있다.

주제 및 제목: Philosophers and Good Writing
주제문: 철학자는 쉽고 인상적인 글쓰기를 할 수 있도록 노력해야 한다.

| 해설
내용 일치 중 옳은 것을 고르는 문제이다. 보기를 하나씩 살펴보자.
① Philosophers can never become good men of letters.
→ 철학자는 글을 잘 쓰는 사람이 절대 될 수 없다(글의 주장과 정 반대이다. '철학자도 꾸준한 노력을 통해서 글을 효과적으로 생생하게 표현할 수 있다'고 말하고 있다).
② Some philosophers are gifted writers who do not need to practice writing.
→ 어떤 철학자는 글쓰기 연습이 필요가 없는 재능을 타고난 작가이다(본문 초반에 글쓰기 능력은 타고나는 것이 아니라 했다).
③ A charming philosophy is one that is impressive and easily understood.
→ 매력적인 철학은 인상적이고 쉽게 이해할 수 있는 것이다(본문에 명시되어 있다: They, naturally enough, are taken by a philosophy that is striking and not too difficultly assimilated).
④ A man's well-written philosophy may be interpreted as his literature.

→ 글과 관련이 없는 사항이다.
⑤ However well a philosopher writes, sometimes he may not be clear.
→ 글의 요지와 반대 주장으로 제시될 만한 문장이다.

정답 ③을 보면, 우선 본문에서 '매료되다'의 표현을 'be taken'으로 사용하고 있지만, 보기에서는 'charming'으로 표현했다. 또한 'striking'을 'impressive', 'not too difficultly assimilated'는 'easily understood'로 표현하고 있다. 말하자면, 본문에서 기본 단어지단 문맥에 따라 의미가 달라지는 'take'와 같은 동사를 얼마나 문맥적으로 잘 해석했는지를 확인하고 있다. 본문에서 까다로운 문장은 내용 일치 또는 유추 문제에 자주 출제되므로 해석에 각별히 주의해야 한다.

| 해석

철학자가 또 문학가가 되어서는 안 될 이유가 없다(철학자도 글을 잘 쓸 수 있다). 그러나 글을 잘 쓰는 것은 본능에 따라 얻어지는 것이 아니다. 즉 그것은 끈기 있는 공부를 요구하는 일종의 기술이다. 철학자는 다른 철학자에게만 그리고 학위 취득을 위해 공부하는 대학생에게만 이야기하지 않는다. 즉 그는 문학가들, 정치가들, 그리고 사려 깊은 사람들에게도 이야기하며, 그들은 다음 세대의 사상 형성에 직접 영향을 미치는 사람들이다. 이들은 당연히 인상적이고 이해하기 너무 어렵지 않은 철학에 빠져들게 된다. 우리는 모두 니체(Nietzsche)의 철학이 세계의 여러 지방에 어떻게 영향을 끼쳤는지 알고 있으며, 그것이 끼친 영향으로 피해가 막심하지 않다고 단언할 사람은 거의 없을 것이다. 그것(니체의 철학)은 그것이 지닌 사고의 심오함 같은 것에 의해서가 아니라 생생한 표현과 인상적인 형식에 의해 널리 보급되었다. 자신의 생각을 남에게 이해시키려고 노력하지 않는 철학자는 단지 학문적으로 가치 있는 사고만을 하고 있다는 것을 보여줄 뿐이다.

26. ③

1. According to anti-consumer and environmental rights organizations, the high consumption lifestyles of affluence cause ① people to be less happy even though they are acquiring more "things." The major negative effect on the environment is that overconsumption is ② depleting the world's natural resources, anti-consumer groups argue.
1) Anti-consumer activist Noam Chomsky, a Massachusetts Institute of Technology professor, points out that the United States has five percent of the world's population, yet consumes forty percent of the world's resources. Chomsky believes that "a lot of that consumption is artificially induced — it doesn't have to do with people's real wants and needs. People would probably be bolter off and happier if they didn't have a lot of those things." ③ Indeed, anti-consumer groups assert that without advertisements by corporations, people would be less likely to overconsume goods.

중심소재: 과소비
1. 도입부 = 주제문(① + ②)
과소비의 부정적인 측면을 두 가지 측면에서 바라보고 있다.

① 물질적으로 더 많은 것을 얻지만, 사람들이 더 불행하다.
② 환경적으로 천연자원을 고갈시킨다.

1) 뒷받침 진술
권위 있는 인물의 말을 인용하여 글쓴이 주장을 뒷받침하고 있다: 세계 인구의 5%인 미국은 전 세계 자원의 40%의 소비를 차지하는데, 이것은 인위적으로 조장된 것이라고 주장하고 있다. 촘스키는 '오히려 사람들은 덜 가지는 게 더 행복해지는 길'이라고 주장.
③ 부연
소비조장의 원인: 광고

| 해설

보기를 살펴보면,

① Without advertisement by corporations, people would be less likely to overconsume goods.
→ 기업의 광고가 없다면 과소비가 줄 것이라는 내용이 본문 마지막에 나온다.

② High consumption lifestyles of affluence cause people to be less happy.
→ 과소비는 사람들을 덜 행복하게 만드는 원인이 된다(글의 요지).

③ Overconsumption makes people feel fulfilled.
→ 과소비는 사람이 온전함을 느끼게 한다(글의 요지와 정 반대).

④ Nowadays, people have an insatiable desire to buy more things.
→ 요즘 사람들은 더 많은 것을 사려는 멈출 줄 모르는 욕망을 품고 있다.
('insatiable'이란 부정적인 단어를 쓰고 있는 글쓴이의 주장과 일맥상통한 진술이다.)

내용 일치 중 옳고 그름의 문제는 언제나 글의 요지와 관련지어 생각하도록 한다.

| 해석

반 소비자 환경 권리 쟁취 기구에 따르면, 풍요로움에 바탕을 둔 높은 소비 성향의 생활방식으로 사람들은 더 많은 '물건들'을 소유하면서도 더 불행해진다고 한다. 환경에 미치는 주된 부정적 영향은 과도한 소비가 세계의 천연자원을 고갈시키고 있다는 사실이라고 반 소비자 단체들은 주장한다.

매사추세츠 공과대학의 교수인 반 소비자 활동가인 Noam Chomsky는 미국 인구가 세계 인구의 5%를 차지함에도 세계 천연자원의 40%를 소비한다고 지적한다. Chomsky는 '그런 소비 중에는 인위적으로 초래된 소비가 많으며, 따라서 사람들이 실제로 원하거나 필요로 하는 것과 아무 관계가 없고, 그런 것들을 많이 갖고 있지 않으면 사람들은 아마도 더 나아지고 더 행복할 것'이라고 믿는다. 실제로 반 소비자 단체들은 기업이 광고하지 않는다면 상품에 대한 과소비가 줄어들 것이라고 단언한다.

27. ③

1. One of the things which separate humans from other animals is the ability to learn from our predecessors. 1) Our knowledge increases because we stand on the shoulders of others who have gone before us. Creativity does not occur in a vacuum. It is usually fueled by studying what other scientists have done. ① For example, when Newton proposed that gravity in the solar system was the same type of force as gravity on the earth, this concept was an extension of the work of Galileo concerning shadows on the moon.

중심소재: 동물과 구별되는 인간의 특징
1. 도입부 = 주제문
동물과 달리 인간은 선조의 지혜를 배울 수 있는 능력이 있다.
1) 뒷받침 문장
① 예시 부연

구체적 진술을 이끄는 시그널 확인
When, If, For example, For instance

도입부 → 주제문 / 뒷받침 진술 / 예시부연

| 해설

주제문이 등장하고 뒷받침 문장을 통해 글쓴이가 전달하려는 내용을 구체적 예를 통해 전개하고 있다. 윗글에서 유추할 수 있는 인간 지식의 특징은 'accumulative'이다. 내용 일치 문제 중 옳은 것을 고르는 문제는 언제나 글의 주제와 요지를 항상 염두에 두고 보기를 본다.

① Galileo was the greatest scientist in the history of the world.
  → 최상급 표현은 조심해야 한다. 본문에 언급이 나오지 않는 이상 '과장'을 이용한 오류 문장일 가능성이 크다.
② Our predecessors are always right.
  → 마찬가지로 'always'라는 일반화는 오류 답안을 유도하는 대표적인 형태이다. 본문에 반드시 언급되어 있어야 한다.
③ It is important to read and build on the work of others.
  → 주제문에서 전달한 글쓴이의 주장과 같은 맥락의 진술이다.
④ Humans learn something from animals.
  → 인간과 동물의 차이점을 기술하는 것이 주된 내용이다.

| 해석

인간과 다른 동물을 구별 짓는 것 중 하나는 앞선 사람들로부터 배우는 능력이다. 우리가 가진 지식은 전에 살았던 다른 사람의 지식을 기초로 하는 것이기 때문에 점점 늘어난다. 창조성은 진공 상태에서는 일어나지 않는다. 그것은 대개 다른 과학자들이 행해왔던 것을 연구함으로써 가능해진다. 예를 들어, 태양계 중력이 지구의 중력과 같은 종류의 힘이라고 뉴턴이 제시했을 때, 이런 개념은 달 위 그림자에 관한 갈릴레오의 연구를 확장한 것이었다.

28. ③

1. Humans are often thought to be insensitive smellers compared with animals, 1) **but** this is largely because, unlike animals, we stand upright. 2) This means that our noses are limited to perceiving those smells which drift through the air, missing the majority of smells which stick to surfaces. 2. **In fact, though**, we are extremely sensitive to smells, even if we do not generally realize it.

1) ① Strangely, some people find that they can smell, for example, one type of flower but not another, whereas other people are sensitive to the smells of both flowers. Ⓐ This may be because some people do not have the genes necessary to create particular smell receptors in the nose. These receptors are the cells which sense smells and send messages to the brain. ② **However**, it has been found that even people who are at first insensitive to a particular smell can suddenly become sensitive to it, if they are exposed to it often enough.

중심소재: 인간과 동물의 후각
1. 도입부 = 통념
인간은 동물보다 후각이 덜 발달됐다고 여겨짐.
1) 원인: 직립보행
① 부연진술
2. 주제문
인간도 특정 냄새에 대해 후각이 아주 발달하여 있다.
1) 뒷받침 진술
① 인간은 사람에 따라 후각이 민감하게 반응하는 대상이 다를 뿐이다.
Ⓐ 이유/근거 제시
② 'However' 이후 잘 인식하지 못했던 냄새라도 오래 노출되면 민감하게 됨.

★ 통념으로 시작하는 글이다. 이후 'But' 또는 'However'가 등장하는지 파악한다.

★ 'in fact'는 'But'과 같이 역접의 역할을 한다.

| 해설

본문은 첫 번째 문단에서 일반적 통념으로 시작하여, 'In fact' 이후 앞의 진술에 대조되는 글쓴이의 요

지를 드러낸 후 이후 문단에서 자신의 주장을 뒷받침하고 있다. '일반통념 비판' 의 글이다. 글의 요지는 'However(In fact)' 뒤에 나와 있다. 틀린 것을 고르는 내용 일치 관련 문제이다.

① Humans mainly detect smells in the air, not on surfaces.
→ 본문 초반에 언급되어 있다(② 참조).

② Different people are sensitive to different smells.
→ ③ 이후 계속 언급된 내용이다.

③ Smell receptors send messages from the brain to the nose.
→ 'These receptors are the cells which sense smells and send messages to the brain.' 에서 틀린 진술임을 알 수 있다.

④ Humans may be insensitive to a certain smell.
→ ③ 이후 계속 언급된 내용으로 ②와 같은 맥락의 진술이다.

| 해석

인간은 동물과 비교해볼 때 냄새 맡는 것에 둔감하다고 흔히 생각된다. 그러나 이것은 동물과는 다르게 우리가 똑바로 서 있기 때문이다. 이것은 우리의 코가 공기 중에 떠다니는 냄새를 지각하는 데 제한되어 있고 지면에 머물러 있는 대부분 냄새는 놓쳐버린다는 것을 의미한다. 그러나 우리가 일반적으로 깨닫지 못하고 있지만 사실 우리는 지극히 냄새에 민감하다.

예를 들어, 이상하게도 몇몇 사람들은 어떤 종류의 꽃향기는 맡지만 다른 종류의 꽃향기는 맡지 못한다는 것을 발견한다. 반면에 다른 사람들은 두 종류의 꽃향기에 모두 민감하다. 이것은 어떤 사람들이 코에 특별한 냄새 수용기를 만드는 데 필요한 유전자를 가지고 있지 않기 때문일 수도 있다. 이런 수용기는 냄새를 감지하고 뇌에 메시지를 보내는 세포이다. 그러나 처음엔 어떤 특정한 냄새에 둔감한 사람들일지라도 그들이 그것에 충분히 자주 노출된다면, 갑자기 그것에 민감해진다는 것이 밝혀졌다.

29. ②

추가강조의 'However' 이후 주제문이 등장하고 이후 뒷받침 진술이 이어지는 패턴을 취하고 있다.

A = B
However A = B = C
뒷받침 진술

역접의 A=B but A ≠ B의 패턴이 아님을 파악한다.

1. Only humans speak. No other animal has anything approaching the complexity of language. 1) However, evidence is accumulating that <u>linguistic ability is also a quantitative rather than a qualitative difference between humans and other primates</u>, especially gorillas and chimps. Wild chimps communicate through gestures and calls.
① Jane Goodall identified twenty-five distinct calls used by Gombe chimps. Each had a distinct meaning and was used only in particular situations. Like people, chimps also communicate through facial expressions, noises, and body movements. Other primates also use calls, which are evoked by environmental stimuli, to communicate messages to other members of the group.

중심소재: 인간 언어능력의 속성
1. 도입부 = 기정 사실
인간에게 유일한 복잡한 언어 속성
1) 주제문(새로운 사실)
동물과 인간의 언어 능력을 따질 때 질뿐 아니라 양적 측면을 간과해서는 안 된다.

① 뒷받침 진술
구체적 실험을 통해 중심내용을 뒷받침하고 있다.

| 해설

옳은 내용을 고르는 내용 일치 문제이다.

① Only humans have communication systems.
　→ 질과 양적인 측면에서 엄청난 차이를 보이지만 여전히 동물도 나름의 의사소통체계가 있다고 말하고 있다.

② There is a quantitative difference in linguistic ability between humans and other primates.
　→ 본문에서 궁극적으로 밝히려는 내용이다.

③ Gorillas use calls only.
　→ 'only'와 같이 단정 짓는 표현은 언제나 내용 일치 문제에서 주의해야 한다. 본문에 명시되어 있지 않는 한 답이 아닐 가능성이 크다. 또한, 본문에서 'only'가 쓰인 곳이 보이는데, 다른 상황에 적용하고 있다.

| 해석

단지 인간만이 말을 한다. 다른 어떤 동물도 인간 언어에 비근할 정도로 복잡한 언어를 가지고 있지 않다. 그러나 인간과 다른 영장류의 동물, 특히 고릴라와 침팬지 사이의 언어 능력 역시 질적인 차이뿐 아니라 양적인 차이라는 증거가 늘어나고 있다. 야생 침팬지는 몸짓과 외침을 통해 의사소통한다. 제인 구달(Jane Goodall)은 탄자니아의 곰비 야생동물 보호 구역에 사는 침팬지가 사용하는 25가지 각기 다른 소리를 밝혀냈다. 각각은 독특한 의미가 있고 특별한 상황에서만 사용되었다. 사람처럼 침팬지도 표정, 소리 그리고 몸 움직임을 통해 의사소통한다. 다른 영장류들 또한 외침을 사용하는데, 이는 환경의 자극으로 일어나는 것이며, 외침을 통해 그 집단의 다른 구성원들에게 메시지를 전달한다.

Test 5 실전 종합문제

[1-3]

1. In a large, crowded hospital in Zimbabwe, a 30-year-old woman was lying on a stretcher about to be wheeled into the operating theater for minor gynecological surgery when Dr. Bingham happened to walk by. Although she'd never seen the patient before—and knew nothing of her medical history—the doctor had a sudden sense of alarm. "I feel I should check her heart," said Dr. Bingham. She put her stethoscope to the woman's chest, and heard a murmur— abnormal blood flow through the heart, a possible sign of mitral stenosis, a heart condition that can cause serious complications if the person is anesthetized. Bingham alerted the surgeons, who cancelled the operation to further evaluate the patient. Tests confirmed that she did, in fact, have the dangerous condition. An amazed surgeon asked Dr. Bingham why she had suspected the disorder. The family practitioner replied that it was "just a hunch." Experience working in Africa had taught her that mitral stenosis was more common there than in the Untied States. In addition, something about the woman had drawn the doctor to her. 1) Like Dr. Bingham, most of us have had remarkably accurate intuitions that seem to spring from nowhere. We call these mysterious flashes of insight hunches, gut feelings, animal instinct, or even a sixth sense. Some people dismiss them as lucky guesses. But several eminent psychologists acknowledge the power of intuition.

1. 구체적 진술
한 여성을 중심으로 구체적 상황이 제기되고 있다: 짐바브웨의 한 여성 환자를 통해 Dr. Bingham이 드러내는 '육감(a hunch)'이 때론 사물 또는 사태를 꿰뚫는 정확한 능력임을 구체적 사례를 통해 드러내고 있다.

1) 일반진술
Dr. Bingham의 구체적 사례를 통해 글쓴이가 궁극적으로 전달하려는 내용을 일반화하고 있다.

주제: 직관의 놀라운 능력

★ 중심소재를 파악할 수 있다. 구체적 사례를 통해서 전달하려는 중심소재는 'hunch' 이다.

★ 구체적 진술(a 30-year-old woman)에서 일반진술(most of us)로 전개되고 있다.

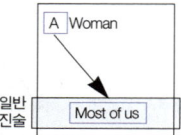

226

1. ⑤

| 해설

구체적 사례를 통해서 궁극적으로 드러내려는 내용이 무엇인지 파악하도록 한다.

2. ④

| 해설

"An amazed surgeon asked Dr. Bingham why she had suspected the disorder. The family practitioner replied that it was 'just a hunch.'" 에서 'family physician' 임을 파악할 수 있다.

3. ⑤

| 해설

내용 일치 문제 중 옳은 것을 고르는 문제 중 글의 요지가 답이 되는 유형에 속한다.

| 해석

짐바브웨의 크고 붐비는 한 병원에 서른 살의 한 여성이 들것에 누워 경미한 부인과 수술을 받으려고 중앙 수술실로 막 들어가려고 했을 때 Bingham 의사가 그 말을 스쳐 들으며 지나가게 되었다. Bingham 의사는 그 환자를 전에 본 적이 한 번도 없었고 그녀의 병력에 대해 아는 것도 없었다. 한데 Bingham 의사는 갑자기 이상한 불안감이 들었다. "그녀의 심장을 진찰해 봐야 할 것 같아요."라고 Bingham 의사는 말했다. 그녀는 청진기를 그 여자의 가슴에 대고 심장으로부터 흘러나오는 비정상적인 혈류의 소리를 들었을 때, 그것은 승모판 협착증이 있을지도 모르는 징후이며, 이런 환자를 마취시킬 때 심각한 합병증을 일으킬 수 있는 심장 상태였다. Bingham 의사는 그녀의 담당 의사에게 주의를 시켜 수술을 취소하게 하고 그 환자를 좀 더 진찰하게 하였다. 검사해본 결과 그 환자는 아주 위험한 상태였던 것으로 확인되었다. 놀란 담당 의사가 Bingham 의사에게 어떻게 하여 그 환자의 질병을 눈치 챘느냐고 물었다. 가정의는 '그저 직감이었다'고 대답했다. 아프리카에서 일했던 경험을 통해 그녀는 승모판 협착증이 미국에서보다 아프리카에서 더 흔하다는 것을 알게 됐다. 게다가 그 환자의 무언가가 그 의사의 주의를 끌게 했다. Bingham 의사처럼 우리 대부분은 어디서 샘솟는지 모르는 대단히 정확한 직감을 지니고 있다. 우리는 이렇게 신비한 순간적인 통찰력을, 본능적 감각, 동물적 본능, 육감이라고 부른다. 어떤 사람들은 그런 것들을 운 좋은 짐작쯤으로 치부해 버린다. 하지만 몇몇 저명한 심리학자들은 직감의 힘을 인정한다.

[4-6]

1) These radiation belts are round the earth area a dangerous barrier during the first part of a space flight. ① They are like invisible reefs. On orbital flights close to the earth, astronauts must steer clear of them, for repeated exposure to such strong radiation would be fatal. On longer missions, men must either avoid radiation reefs or find a quick route through them. 2) Even after a spaceship has passed beyond the reefs

중심소재: 우주비행의 위험요소
1. 도입부 = 구체적 진술
1) 지구 근처에서 비행할 때의 위험요소: radiation belt
① 부연 진술
2) 지구를 벗어난 후 존재하는 위험요소:
death rays(radiation storms)
② 부연 진술
3) solar flares
③ 부연 진술

★ 본문의 특징은 주제문이 생략되고, 구체적 진술만이 존재한다는 점이다. 우주 비행을 하는 데 존재하는 위험 요소를 세 가지 다루고 있는데, 이런 내용을 바탕으로 주제문을 독자가 이끌어내야 하는 'implicit' 유형의 글이다.

227

생략된 주제문
1) 위험요소 1. _____
① 부연진술
2) 위험요소 2. _____
② 부연진술
3) 위험요소 3. _____
③ 부연진술
생략된 주제문

and entered interplanetary space, there is still potential danger from death rays. ② Just as sailors must prepare for storms at sea, space travelers have to be wary of radiation storms that could surround them with a hail of deadly rays. These radiation storms in the sea of space begin on the sun. 3) For reasons still unknown, the sun sometimes shoots off great masses fiery gas into space. ③ These 'solar flares' do no happen often. There are no advance warnings, however. At any time the sun can send a radiation storm sweeping into space.

4. ③

| 해설

주제를 설정할 부분적인 내용만을 전달한다거나, 지나치게 포괄적인 내용을 피해야 한다. 아래의 보기를 보면서 가장 적절한 주제를 설정해 보자.

① Death Rays
  → 위험 요소 중 하나만을 다루므로 주제의 폭이 너무 좁다.
② Space Flight
  → 지나치게 포괄적인 주제에 해당한다.
③ Danger in Space
  → 우주에 존재하는 위험 요소라는 내용으로 본문의 내용을 구체적이면서도 포괄적으로 전달하고 있다.
④ Radiation Belts
  → 부분적인 내용만을 반영한 주제이다.

5. ②

| 해설

"These 'solar flares' **do not happen often**." 에서 보기 ②의 'often' 이 본문과 일치하지 않음을 파악할 수 있다.

6. ①

| 해설

앞뒤 문맥상 가장 적절한 표현을 고르는 문제이다. "These 'solar flares' do not happen often. There are no advance warnings, ____(a)____." 를 보면, 태양 표면의 폭발은 자주 발생하지 않는다. 본문에서

태양 표면의 폭발은 우주 비행에 위협적인 요소이다. 그렇다면, 폭발이 자주 발생하지 않는 점은 안심되는 요소이지만, 아무런 징조가 없이 발생한다는 점은 우주 비행에 큰 위협적인 요소로 작용할 수 있으므로 빈칸에는 역접의 'however'가 가장 적절하다.

| 해석

지구를 둘러싸고 있는 이런 방사능 벨트는 우주 비행 중 겪게 되는 첫 위험한 장벽이다. 그들은 마치 보이지 않는 암초와 같다. 지구 가까이 궤도 순항할 때 우주 비행사들은 치명적인 방사능에 반복적으로 노출되는 것을 피하여 잘 운전해야 한다. 장기 임무 수행 중에 우주 비행사들은 그 방사능 암초를 피하거나 그들을 빨리 피해 갈 수 있는 통로를 찾아야만 한다. 우주선이 그 암초를 지나고 행성 간의 우주 공간에 들어섰다 할지라도 여전히 잠재적 살인 광선의 위험이 존재하고 있다. 바다의 선원이 폭풍을 준비해야 하듯, 우주 여행자들도 그들을 둘러쌀 수 있는 쏟아지는 살인 광선과 같은 방사능 폭풍을 경계해야 한다. 이러한 우주 바다의 방사능 폭풍은 태양으로부터 온다. 아직 이유는 모르지만, 태양은 간혹 우주 공간으로 거대한 화염 가스를 뿜어낸다. 이러한 태양 표면 폭발은 자주 일어나지는 않는다. 그러나 태양 표면 폭발은 미리 예고되지는 않는다. 태양은 언제든지 우주 공간을 쓸어버릴 수 있는 방사능 폭풍을 보낼 수 있다.

[7-9]

1. Determined to prove the doctors wrong, Rocket began rigorous physiotherapy. If he made his left foot move over and over again, he figured, 1) eventually the undamaged cells of his brain would find a way to tell the foot what to do. ① After he learned to stand, he strapped his left foot to the pedal of a stationary bike at the gym then started pedalling. On the first day, he lasted only 30 seconds—but he persisted. It was like doing sit-ups for the brain. Twelve years later, after thousands of hours in the gym, Rocket, danced on both feet. His doctors were amazed. "It was dramatic." says Dr. Robert Willinsky, the neuroradiologist who saved Rocket's life with the clot-buster. "He's a poster child for sure." 2) It turned out Rocket's hunch was right; It is possible to retrain your brain to make up for the part that's out of order. 2. A generation ago, that idea was dismissed as folly by most medical practitioners. They thought the adult brain was like a machine; It couldn't change or grow; all it could do was break down. 1) **But** over the past few decades, brian scans such as the PET and functional MRI have allowed scientists to observe this organ in action. Now they can see that the conventional thinking about the brain was wrong.

중심소재: 뇌의 상실된 기능에 대한 회복능력
첫번째 문단
1. 도입부 = 가설
1) 뒷받침 진술
주인공이 발견한 내용에 대한 구체적 부연
2. 결론(요지)
기능이 상실된 부분을 만회하기 위해 뇌 훈련이 가능하다.

두번째 문단
1. 도입부 = 통념
뇌는 기계와 같아서 다시 그 기능을 회복할 수 없다.
1) 주제문
요지 재진술

★구체적으로 의사의 어떤 점이 틀렸는지를 증명하려는 모습을 본문에서 다룰 것이다. 중심내용(controlling idea)에 해당한다.

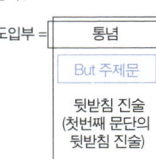

| 본문 분석

어떤 유형의 글이든 역접을 이끄는 'However/But' 이후는 글쓴이의 주장과 직간접적으로 관련이 있으므로 항상 집중해서 읽도록 한다.

7. ①

| 해설

본문에서 주인공은 기존의 의학적 지식과 다른 뇌와 관련된 새로운 사실을 밝혀냈다. 보기 ①이 이러한 사실을 구체적으로 드러내는 주제로 가장 적절하다.

8. ③

| 해설

주인공이 발견한 점은 바로 "the undamaged cells of his brain would find a way to tell the foot what to do"이다. 보기 ③이 이러한 내용을 그대로 반영하고 있다.

9. ④

| 해설

'a poster child'는 '모범, 표본'이란 뜻이다.

| 해석

의사가 틀렸다는 것을 증명하겠다고 단단히 각오하고 Rocket은 엄격한 물리치료를 시작했다. 그는 자신의 왼발을 계속해서 많이 움직이면 결국 손상이 안 된 뇌세포가 발을 사용하는 방법을 찾아낼 것으로 생각했다. 혼자서는 방법을 터득한 후에 그는 자신의 왼발을 헬스장에 있는 운동용 자전거의 페달에 묶고 페달을 밟기 시작했다. 첫날은 겨우 30초 밖에 못했지만, 그는 포기하지 않았다. 이는 마치 뇌를 위해 윗몸일으키기를 하는 것과 같았다. 12년의 세월이 흐르고 헬스장에서 수천 시간을 노력한 끝에 마침내 Rocket은 플로어에서 두 발로 춤을 추었다. 그의 의사는 놀랐다. "정말 극적인 일입니다," 하고 혈전용해제를 이용하여 Rocket의 생명을 구한 신경방사선 의사인 Robert Willinsky 박사는 말했다. "그는 실로 (광고에 나올만한) 대단한 친구입니다." Rocket의 어림짐작이 사실로 드러났다. 즉, 뇌가 고장 난 부분을 보상해 주는 것이 가능하다는 얘기다. 한 세대 전만 해도 의학계 사람들은 그런 생각이 말도 안 되는 어리석은 것이라고 일축했었다. 그들은 성인의 두뇌는 기계와 같아서 성장하거나 변화하지 않으며 오직 망가질 뿐이라고 생각했다. 그러나 지난 수십 년 동안 PET나 기능적 MRI와 같은 뇌 주사 장치로 과학자들은 뇌조직이 활동하는 모습을 관찰할 수 있었다. 이제 그들은 뇌에 대한 전통적인 견해가 틀렸다는 것을 알 수 있다.

[10-12]

1. Work—the very word calls up to many of us ① <u>a picture of sheer boredom; meaningless routines; tiresome activity done only to earn enough money so that existence is possible; something that at least there is a chance to "live."</u> 1) Yes, **despite** this picture—for which perhaps the biblical depiction of work as "the curse of Adam" has some responsibility—not all work, nor work at all times, is so deadly and dull, so lacking is purpose and value. ① For work can provide not only Ⓐ an escape from the worry and loneliness that so many suffer but also Ⓑ material for the realization of our human possibilities. It can be Ⓒ an opportunity to develop toward genuine wholeness also.

중심소재: 일
1. 도입부 = 통념(종교적 의미에서 전통적 관점)
일에 대한 부정적 관점
1) 주제문
현대 사회에서 일은 긍정적 의미를 가진다.

① 뒷받침 근거
Ⓐ, Ⓑ, Ⓒ의 측면에서 뒷받침 내용이 제시되고 있다.

★중심소재는 'work' 이다. 이것으로 무슨 이야기를 하는지(주제) 파악하도록 한다.

★중심내용(controlling Idea)에 해당한다.

도입부 | 통념 A = B
      | But 주제문
      | 뒷받침 진술

| 본문 분석

주제: The Meaning of Work in Modern Society
주장: 기독교적 관점(과거)에서 부정적으로 인식되는 일(Work)은 실제로 '외로움과 걱정을 덜어주고, 인간의 가능성을 실현하게 할 물질을 제공할 뿐 아니라 온전한 완벽함을 위한 기회가 될 수 있다.'는 긍정적 의미를 내포하고 있다는 점이 글쓴이의 주장이다. 첫 번째 문장의 경우, 보기 ②와 ④를 혼동할 수 있는데, 본문이 통념 비판의 글인 점을 파악했다면, 보기 ④가 더 적절한 답임을 쉽게 이끌어 낼 수 있을 것이다.

10. ④

| 해설

일에 대한 부정적 이미지는 과거 성경에 기반을 둔 통념이다. 현대 사회에서 일이란 이와 상반되는 긍정적 측면이 있음을 통념 비판의 유형으로 전개하고 있다.

11. ②

| 해설

"the biblical depiction of work as "the curse of Adam" has some responsibility" 에서 보기 ②를 확인할 수 있다.

12. ⑤

| 해설

"an escape from the worry and loneliness that so many suffer but also material for the realization of our human possibilities. it can be an opportunity to develop toward genuine wholeness also"에서 보기 ⑤의 내용은 파악할 수 없다.

| 해석

일이란 대부분 사람에게 아주 지루한 개념으로 다가온다. 의미 없고, 반복되는 행위로 말이다. 단지 충분한 돈을 많이 벌어 생존을 가능하게 만드는 돈벌이 활동은 아주 지치기만 한다. 단지 거기에는 '살 수 있다'는 기회가 있는 것 정도의 것이다. 맞다. 그러나 일이 성경에서 "아담의 저주"로 생긴 책임감으로 묘사되어 이렇게 해석이 되기는 하지만, 모든 일이 항상 그렇게 힘들고 지루한 것은 아니며, 목적과 가치가 없는 것은 아니다. 왜냐하면, 일은 많은 이가 겪는 걱정과 외로움으로부터의 탈출구일 뿐 아니라 인간 가능성 실현을 위한 물질을 제공해 주기도 한다. (또한,) 온전한 전인격 형성을 위해 나아가는 기회로 작용하기도 한다.

[13–14]

소재의 폭 ↓

Emotions
↓ However
Stress

However 이후 소재의 폭이 좁아짐을 파악한다.

1. Suppose we asked you to keep track of all the emotions you experience in the course of a day. You might report that for brief periods you felt happiness, sadness, anger, relief, and so on. 1) There is one emotion, **however**, that people often report as a kind of background noise for much of their day-to-day experience, and that is stress. Modern industrialized society sets a rapid, hectic pace for living. People often have too many demands placed on their time, are worried about uncertain futures, and have little time for family and fun. ① **But** would you be better off without stress? A stress-free life would offer no challenge—no difficulties to surmount, no new fields to conquer, and no reasons to sharpen your wits or improve your abilities.

중심소재: Emotions Stress
1. 도입부
일상에서 느끼는 다양한 감정 중 특히 Stress 언급(소재의 폭이 Stress로 좁혀짐을 파악한다.)
1) Stress에 대한 부정적 관점
① 주제문
Stress의 긍정적 측면을 강조하며 스트레스가 없는 삶은 "삶의 도전 부재 새로운 분야 상실 능력향상의 이유 부재"로 이어짐을 강조하고 있다.

| 본문 분석

본문을 다시 정리하자면, 도입부에서 인간이 경험하는 '다양한 감정'이란 폭넓은 주제를 설정한 후 그런 감정 중 특히 '스트레스'라는 특정한 감정에 초점을 맞추어 주제를 좁힌 후 일반적으로 사람들이 생각하는 스트레스의 부정적인 측면을 다루는 동시에 'But' 이후 스트레스가 미치는 긍정적인 요소를 역설하고 있다. 주지할 사항은 글쓴이가 궁극적으로 전달하려는 요지는 글의 마지막 부분에 등장하는 'But' 이후의 내용이라는 점이다.

13. ④

| 해설

제시된 문장의 'But'을 활용한다. '스트레스'에 관한 글임을 알 수 있는데, 스트레스가 없다면 상황이 더 좋아지겠는가 하고 묻고 있다. 이를 통해 제시된 문장 앞에는 '스트레스를 받는 상황'이 다뤄졌을

가능성이 크고, 이후의 내용은 스트레스가 없을 때 벌어지는 상황이 된다. 보기 ④가 제시된 문장이 들어가기 가장 적절하다.

14. ①

| 해설

본문 마지막 문장에서 글의 요지를 파악할 수 있다.

| 해석

우리가 다음을 요구했다고 가정해보라. 하루새에 여러분이 경험하는 모든 감정을 한번 따라가 보라고. 여러분은 아마 짧은 기간 동안 행복, 슬픔, 분노, 안심, 그리고 기타 등등을 느꼈다고 얘기할 것이다. 그런데 사람들이 날마다 겪는 것 중 많은 부분을 차지하는 일종의 잡음이라고 종종 말하는 감정이 있으며, 이는 스트레스이다. 산업화한 현대 사회는 삶의 속도가 무척 빠르고 바쁘게 되어 있다. 사람들은 그들의 시간에 종종 지나치게 많은 요구사항을 가진다. 불확실한 미래에 대해 걱정하고, 그리고 가족과의 즐거움을 위한 시간도 거의 갖지 못한다. 하지만 스트레스가 없으면 더 나아질까? 스트레스 없는 삶은 아무런 도전거리도 주지 않을 것이다 — 극복할 어려움도, 정복할 어떤 새로운 분야도 없고 당신의 지혜를 갈고 닦거나 재능들을 향상하게 할 이유도 없는 (삶).

15. ②

1. Teaching is supposed to be a professional activity requiring long and complicated training as well as official certification. The act of teaching is looked upon as a flow of knowledge from a higher source to an empty container. The student's role is one of receiving information; the teacher's role is one of sending it. There is a clear distinction assumed between one who is supposed to know (and therefore not capable of being wrong) and another, usually younger person who is supposed not to know. 1) **However,** ① teaching need not be the province of a special group of people nor need it be looked upon as a technical skill. ② Teaching can be more like guiding and assisting than forcing information into a supposedly empty head. ③ If you have a certain skill you should be able to share it with someone. You do not have to get certified to convey what you know to someone else or to help them in their attempt to teach themselves. 2. All of us, from the very youngest children to the oldest members of our cultures should come to realize our own potential as teachers. We can share what we know, however little it might be, with someone who has need of that knowledge or skill.

중심소재: Teaching
1. 도입부 = 통념
가르침의 일반적 견해
선생 – 전문 직종, 학생보다 많은 높은 지식을 소유한 사람, 이러한 지식을 전달하는 자
학생 – 지식이 전혀 없어(empty) 아는 것이 없는 어린 사람
1) 주제문(=글쓴이의 견해)
① 가르치는 행위는 전문가만의 영역이 아니며 특별한 기술이 아니다.
② 가르치는 행위는 '보조와 안내'의 역할이다.
④ 부연
2. 결론(요지)
글쓴이는 우리가 모두 선생으로서의 가능성을 가진 것으로 주장함(글쓴이의 주장을 드러내는 문장에 자주 쓰이는 'should'를 확인).

★ 중심소재는 '가르침'이다. 가르침에 관한 어떤 내용(주제)을 전개하는지 중심내용을 바탕으로 설정하도록 한다.

★ 통념으로 시작하는 글이다. 이후 전개되는 내용 중 However를 파악한다.

| 해설

"All of us, from the very youngest children to the oldest members of our cultures **should** come to realize our own potential as teachers." 에서 글의 요지를 파악할 수 있다.

| 해석

가르침은 공식인증뿐만 아니라 길고 어려운 훈련을 요구하는 전문 활동으로 간주된다. 가르침의 행위는 더 수준 높은 배움의 원천에서 빈 용기로 지식이 흐르는 것으로 여겨진다. 학생의 역할은 정보를 받는 자의 역할이고, 교사의 역할은 정보를 보내는 자의 역할이다. 알아야 하는 사람 (따라서 잘못될 수 없는 사람)과 모르고 있어야 하는 사람들 (일반적으로는 젊은 사람들) 간에는 추정 상 분명히 구분되는 차이가 있다. 그러나 가르침은 특정 전문 그룹만의 분야일 필요도 없고, 고도의 기술로 여겨질 필요도 없다. 가르침은 비어있을 것으로 추정되는 머릿속에 정보를 강제로 집어넣는 것보다는 지도하고 보조하는 것에 더욱 가깝다. 만약 여러분이 특정 기술을 가지고 있다면, 여러분은 그 기술을 다른 사람들과 공유할 수 있어야 한다. 여러분은 다른 사람에게 알고 있는 것을 전달하기 위해서나 그 사람들이 독학하려고 시도하는 것을 돕기 위해 인증을 받아야 할 필요는 없다. 아주 어린 아이들부터 가장 나이 많은 구성원에 이르기까지 우리 문화 공동체 내의 모두는 우리 자신이 선생님으로서의 잠재력이 있음을 깨달아야 한다. 우리는 알고 있는 지식을 아무리 작은 것이라도 그 지식이나 기술이 필요한 사람과 공유할 수 있다.

[16-18]

1. When journalists hear journalists claim a "larger truth," they really ought to go for their pistols. 1) ① The New Yorker's Alastair Reid said the holy words last week: "A reporter might take liberties with the factual circumstances to make the larger truth clear." ② Oh! large, large truth. Apparently Mr. Reid believes that imposing a truth is the same as arriving at one. But his error is more fundamental still in assuming that larger truth is the province of journalism in the first place. 2. <u>The business of journalism is to present facts accurately</u>—Mr. Reid notwithstanding. 1) For one thing, journalism rarely sees the larger truth of a story because reporters are usually chasing quite small elements of information.

중심소재: 저널리즘의 역할

1. 도입부 = 현상
① '총을 가지러 간다'는 의미에서 알 수 있듯, 'larger truth'는 저널리스트가 해야 할 일이 아니라고 극적으로 표현하고 있다. 그럼 이들의 역할은 무엇인가?

1) 뒷받침 진술
① Alastair Reid의 견해
"작가는 더 거대한 진실을 분명하게 전달하기 위해 사실로 주어진 상황을 자유롭게 다룰 수 있다."
② 글쓴이의 견해(But 확인)
Alastair Reid의 말을 비판하면서 있는 그대로의 사실이 아닌 'larger truth'는 저널리즘의 영역이 아니라고 말하고 있다. 있는 그대로의 사실이 아닌 'larger truth'는 저널리즘의 영역이 아니라고 말하고 있다.

2. 결론(요지)
저널리스트는 있는 사실만 정확히 제시해야 한다.

1) 뒷받침 근거

16. ①

| 해설

기자가 'larger truth'를 언급했을 때, 총을 가지러 간다는 표현은 그러한 말을 하는 사람을 죽인다는 극단적 표현이다. 즉, 기자가 'larger truth'를 논하는 것은 반대하는 표현임을 이끌어 낼 수 있다.

17. ①

| 해설

글의 주제문인 "The business of journalism is to present facts accurately"에서 보기 ①이 정답임을 알 수 있다. 기자는 있는 그대로의 사실을 전달해야지 있는 사실을 'larger' 하게 보도해서는 안 된다'가 글의 요지이다. 참고로, 제목은 'Is there a 'larger, better' truth than just the facts?' 라 볼 수 있다.

18. ⑤

| 해설

앞의 두 문제에서 보기 ⑤를 파악할 수 있다.

| 해석

기자들이 자신이 '더 거대한 진실'을 주장하는 말을 들으면, 기자들은 사실은 총을 가지러 가야 할 판이다. 뉴요커(The New Yorker)지의 알라스테어 레이드(Alastair Reid)는 지난주에 "기자는 전체적 진실을 명백히 밝히기 위해 사실적 상황들을 제멋대로 사용할 수도 있다"는 대단한 말을 했다. 오! 전체적, 전체적 진실이라니. 레이드 씨는 진실을 강요하는 것이 진실에 도달하는 것과 같다고 믿고 있는 것이 분명하다. 그러나 더 근본적인 그의 실수는 전체적 진실이 우선 무엇보다 저널리즘의 영역이라고 가정하는 데 있다. 레이드 씨의 말에도 불구하고, 저널리즘이 하는 일은 사실을 정확하게 제시하는 것이다. 한 가지 지적하자면, 기자들이 대개 아주 작은 정보의 요소들을 추구하고 있기 때문에 저널리즘은 보도하는 기사의 전체적 진실을 좀처럼 보지 못한다.

[19-20]

1. The population of the world has increased more in modern times than in all other ages of history combined. 1) World population totaled about 500 million in 1650. It doubled in the period from 1650 ~ 1850. Today the population is more than five billion. Estimates based on research by the United Nations indicate that it will more than double in the next fifty years, reaching ten billion by the year 2050.

중심소재: 세계인구
1. 도입부 = 주제문
1) 뒷받침 문장
시간의 순서에 따라 구체적 연도와 수치를 통해 뒷받침 문장을 전개하고 있다.

★ 세계 인구에 관한 글이다.

★ 중심내용(controlling idea)을 바탕으로 주제의 폭을 설정한다.

★ 구체적 연도와 수치는 글쓴이의 주장에 대한 객관성 확보역할

| 본문 분석

시간의 글 전개방식을 확인한다.

19. ③

| 해설

1659년대부터 1850년대까지 세계 인구가 이전보다 두 배로 증가했다고 했다. 그 이전까지의 인구가 5억에 해당하므로 1850년대에는 세계 인구는 약 10억에 해당한다.

20. ②

| 해설

문제를 잘 읽어야 한다. 문제에서 요구하는 사항은 2050년대가 되면 세계 인구는 현재의 인구보다 약 얼마의 차로 능가하게 되겠는가 하고 묻고 있다. 현재의 인구가 50억이고, 2050년에는 100억이 된다고 했으므로 50억의 차가 정답이다.

| 해석

세계 인구는 역사의 어떤 시기를 합한 것보다 현대에 와서 더 급격히 증가하고 있다. 세계의 인구는 1650년 약 5억에 달했다. 이는 1650년부터 1850년에 이르는 동안 두 배로 증가했다. 오늘날 인구는 50억 이상이다. 유엔이 시행한 조사를 기초로 한 예상 수치는 다음 반세기 동안 두 배 이상 증가하여, 2050년까지 100억에 달할 것으로 내다봤다.

[21-22]

글의 주제이자 본문에서 구체적으로 다룰 중심내용(controlling idea)이다.

예시를 이끄는 시그널을 확인한다.

도입부 / 주제문
1. For example/ For instance
2. If/when
3. Imagine/consider/ suppose/Let's think
4. 시간의 부사(구)
5. 구체적 대상 선정

강조구문은 글쓴이의 주장이 드러나는 중요한 문장이다.

1. The second point is the more familiar one of the historian's need of imaginative understanding for the minds of the people with whom he is dealing, for the thought behind their acts. 1) ① Take Burckhardt's censorious remark about the Thirty Years' War: "It is scandalous for a creed, no matter whether it is Catholic or Protestant, to place its salvation above the integrity of the nation." It was extremely difficult for a nineteenth-century liberal historian, brought up to believe that it is right and praiseworthy to kill in defense of one's country, but wicked and wrong-headed to kill in defense of one's religion, to enter into the state of mind of those who fought the Thirty Years' War. ② Much of what has been written in English-speaking countries in the last ten years about the Soviet Union, and in the Soviet Union about the English-speaking countries, has been vitiated by this inability to achieve even the most elementary measure of imaginative understanding of what goes on in the mind of the other party, so that the words and actions of the other are always made to appear malign, senseless, or hypocritical. 2. History **cannot** be written **unless** the historian can achieve some kind of contact with the mind of those about whom he is writing.

중심소재: 역사가의 상상력

1. 도입부 = 주제문
주제와 글쓴이의 주장이 드러나는 Topic Sentence: 역사가는 역사적 상상력이 필요함의 중요성을 역설하고 있다.

1) 뒷받침 진술
① 첫 번째 예
글쓴이가 주장한 내용에 대한 구체적 예 중 첫 번째: 글쓴이가 주장한 역사적 상상력이 부족하여 30년 전쟁(종교전쟁)을 오판한 Burckhardt를 예로 제시하고 있다.

② 두 번째 예
냉전 시대에 영어권 국가와 소련에서 쓴 (역사) 책은 대부분 상대방의 언행을 이해하는 역사적 상상력의 부재로 제대로 된 평가가 이루어지지 않음.

2. 결론(= 요지)

21. ④

| 해설

첫 번째 문장에서 답을 이끌어 낼 수 있다. "The second point is the more familiar one of the historian's need of imaginative understanding for the minds of the people with whom he is dealing, **for the thought behind their acts**." 에서 알 수 있듯이 다른 이가 하는 행위 이면에 숨겨진 의미를 제대로 이해하기 위해서는 역사적 상상력이 필요하다고 말하고 있다.

22. ①

| 해설

본문에서 Burckhardt는 역사적 상상의 부재로 30년 전쟁을 제대로 이해하지 못한 구체적 예로 등장하고 있다. 보기 ①이 옳은 진술이다.

| 해석

두 번째 요점은 역사가에게는 자신이 다루고 있는 사람들의 마음, 즉 그들의 행동 배후에 존재하는 생각에 대한 풍부한 상상력이 필요하다는 것으로, 우리에게 더욱더 친숙한 내용이다. 30년 전쟁에 대한 부르크하르트의 비판적 언급을 예로 보자. "가톨릭이든, 개신교이든 종교가 국가의 보존보다 종교 구원에 더 중요성을 부여하는 것은 추한 짓이다." 국가를 지키기 위해 살인하는 것은 정당하다고 칭송받을 일이고, 종교를 지키기 위해 살인하는 것은 사악하고 비뚤어진 것이라고 믿도록 교육을 받은 19세기 자유주의 역사가가 30년 전쟁에 참여한 사람들의 심리 상태에 들어가 본다는 것은 몹시 어려운 일이다. 지난 10년간 소련에 대해서 영어권 국가들이, 그리고 영어권 국가가 구소련에 대해서 쓴 많은 것은 상대방의 마음속에 일어난 것에 대허 가장 기초적인 (역사적) 상상력을 바탕으로 이해하지 못한 무능력으로 인해 훼손되어 왔다. 역사가가 어떤 식으로든 자신이 글로 쓰고자 하는 사람들의 마음과 접촉하지 못한다면 역사에 관해 쓸 수 없다.

[23-25]

1. Historically, women, children, and people of color have been underrepresented in clinical trials. Ⓐ Usually, children are restricted from clinical trials to protect them from the risks of unproven therapies. Unlike adults, children cannot give informed consent. The rationale for excluding women of childbearing age, particularly women who are pregnant, is to protect their developing and future children from possible long-term side effects of unproven drugs. 1) But <u>restricting women and children from clinical trials may also be harmful to them in the long run. Unless they participate in clinical trials, the effectiveness and safety of therapies cannot be rigorously established.</u> ① **For example,** Ⓐ the trials of the effect of zidovudine (also known as azidothymidine, or AZT)

중심소재: 임상실험
1. 도입부 = 현상(현 관행)
여성, 아이들 그리고 유색 인종은 임상시험에서 제해왔다.
Ⓐ 이유/근거 제시
1) 주제문(역접의 but 확인)
여성과 아이들을 임상시험에 참여시키지 않는 것 또한 해가 되면, 이들을 참여시키면서 치료의 효과와 안정성을 높일 수 있게 된다. ← 이후 임상시험이 이들을 참여시키면서 얻게 되는 득이 기술되고 있다.
① 뒷받침 진술
예시 Ⓐ, Ⓑ, Ⓒ을 통해 주제문의 중심 내용을 뒷받침하고 있다.

도입부 = 기존의 관행
  근거
  ↓ but
  주제문
뒷받침 진술
  근거 1. ___
  근거 2. ___
  근거 3. ___

237

* 나열의 시그널 확인

주제문

뒷받침 진술
- For example, _____
- What's is more, _____
- Similarly, _____

on mother-to-child transmission provided important information that has dramatically reduced perinatal HIV transmission. Without the participation of pregnant women in clinical trials, the effectiveness of antiretroviral therapy in preventing mother-to-child transmission of HIV would not be proven. ⓑ What is more, there would be no evidence basis for enhanced public health measures and increased funding to prevent mother-to-child transmission. ⓒ Similarly, the increased inclusion of minorities in trials has provided information on the efficacy and adverse effects in these populations. In addition, it is problematic to take away women's decision-making about research participation simply because they are pregnant.

23. ②

| 해설

(B)를 기준으로 여성과 아이들에 대한 임상시험 참여에 대한 논지가 대조(But)되고 있다는 점을 활용하도록 한다.

24. ①

| 해설

(a)를 기준으로 앞뒤의 내용은 모두 여성과 아이를 임상시험에 참여시킴으로 얻게 되는 유익한 점을 기술하고 있다. 같은 맥락의 두 내용을 이어주는 순접 추가의 접속사로 보기 ①이 가장 적절하다.

25. ③

| 해설

치료의 효과를 높이기 위해 임상시험에 여성과 아이를 참여시켜야 한다는 내용이다.

| 해석

역사적으로 여자들과 아이들 그리고 유색인종들은 임상시험에서 충분히 다루어지지 않았다. 일반적으로 어린아이들은 증명되지 않은 치료의 위험으로부터 보호하기 위해 임상시험이 제한된다. 성인들과는 달리 아이들은 고지에 입각한 동의를 할 수 없다. 가임연령의 여자들 특히 임신 중인 여자들을 배제하는 이유는 입증되지 않은 약물이 가질 수 있는 장기적인 부작용으로부터 태아와 미래의 아이를 보호하기 위한 것이다. 그러나 여자와 아이들의 임상시험을 제한하는 것이 장기적으로 해가 될 수도 있다. 그들이 임상시험에 참여하지 않으면 치료의 효과와 안정

성은 매우 확실하지 않게 된다. 예를 들어 지도부던은 산모에서 태아로의 전이에 미치는 영향에 대한 실험이 출산 전후에 HIV의 전이를 현격하게 줄였다는 중요한 정보를 제공하였다. 은신한 여성이 임상시험에 참여하지 않으면 산모에서 아기로 HIV가 전이되는 것을 막는 반종양 치료의 효능이 증명되지 않을 것이다. 뿐만 아니라 공중보건 대책을 강화하고 모자 간의 전이를 막는 예산을 늘리는 입증 기반을 마련하지도 못할 것이다. 마찬가지로 소수집단을 더 많이 실험에 참여시킨 결과 그들에 대한 효험과 부작용에 더한 정보를 제공해 주었다. 뿐만 아니라 여자들을 단순히 임신했다는 이유만으로 실험 참여에 대한 선택권을 박탈하는 것도 문제이다.

[26-30]

1. Thomas Kuhn made some controversial claims about the overall direction of scientific change. 1) According to a widelyheld view, science progresses towards the truth in a linear fashion, as older incorrect ideas get replaced by newer, correct ones. Later theories are thus objectively better than earlier ones. This 'cumulative' conception of science is popular among laymen and scientists alike, 2) but Kuhn argued that it is both historically inaccurate and philosophically naive. ① For example, he noted that Einstein's theory of relativity is in some respects more similar to Aristotelian than Newtonian theory — so the history of mechanics is not simply a linear progression from wrong to right. Ⓑ Moreover, Kuhn questioned whether the concept of objective truth actually makes sense at all. The idea that there is a fixed set of facts about the world, independent of any particular paradigms, was of dubious coherence, he believed. Kuhn suggested a radical alternative: the facts about the world are paradigm-relative, and thus change. If this suggestion is right, then it makes no sense to ask whether a given theory corresponds to the facts 'as they really are', nor therefore to ask whether it is objectively true.

★ 중심내용(controlling idea)에 해당한다.

중심소재: 토마스 쿤의 과학 변화 이론
1. 도입부(=주제 도출)
과학 변화의 방향
1) 통념(기존의 이론)
일반인과 과학자들이 주장하는 기존의 이론: 과학은 일방향성 선형적 방식으로 진리를 향해 진보함 – '누계적' 특성을 드러냄
2) 주제문(토마스 쿤의 주장)
일방향성 선형적 진보는 잘못된 것이다.
① 뒷받침 진술
Ⓐ 과학(mechanics)의 역사는 잘못된 것에 옳은 것으로의 선형적 진보가 아니였다.
Ⓑ 객관적 진실이란 개념은 없다. 즉, 시대를 반영하는 특정 패러다임에 독립된 세상에 대한 고정된 사실은 없다. 고로 진리는 'paradigm-relative'로 변화하는 것이다.

★ 단락구조

도입부 = 주제도출

통념(기존의 이론)

But 주제문

뒷받침진술

26. ②

| 해설

빈칸 바로 뒤에 이어지는 "This 'cumulative' conception of science"에서 알 수 있듯이 빈칸에 들어갈 표현은 빈칸 앞에서 전개된 내용과 같은 맥락의 'cumulative conception of science'와 일치해야 한다. 과거의 잘못된 과학 지식이 올바른 새로운 지식으로 대체된다는 내용과 같은 맥락의 보기 ②가 정답이다.

27. ④

| 해설

빈칸 앞의 내용을 먼저 살펴보면, 쿤은 글의 도입부에 제시된 과학의 진보에 대한 기존의 관점인 'cumulative conception of science' 가 옳지 않다고 의문점을 제시하고, 이에 대한 구체적 근거(예)를 제시하고 있다. 빈칸 이후 쿤은 추가로 객관적 사실이 존재하는지 의문점을 제시하고 있다. 즉, 빈칸을 중심으로 앞뒤에 전개된 기존의 이론 모두를 의심하고 있다는 점으로 보아 순접 추가 부연의 'Moreover' 가 정답이다.

28. ①

| 해설

'dubious = questionable' 이다.

29. ③

| 해설

빈칸을 중심으로 앞에 전개된 쿤의 주장을 보면, 세상에 관한 정보는 모두 특정 패러다임에 기초한 상대적 진리일 뿐이며 변화한다고 했다. 그러므로 특정 이론이 있는 실제의 객관적 사실과 일치한다거나 그것이 보편적이며 객관적으로 진리라고 묻는 것은 '말이 되지 않음' 을 알 수 있다.

30. ③

| 해설

"The idea that there is a fixed set of facts about the world, independent of any particular paradigms, was of dubious coherence, he believed." 에서 보기 ③은 틀린 진술임을 알 수 있다.

| 해석

Thomas Kuhn은 과학적 변화의 전반적인 방향에 대해 몇 가지 논쟁적인 주장을 펼쳤다. 일반적인 시각에서는 과학은 진실을 향해 선형으로, 즉 낡고 부정확한 사고가 더 새롭고 더 정확한 사고로 대체되는 방식으로 진보한다고 보고 있다. 따라서 나중의 이론들이 객관적으로 그전의 이론보다 우월하다고 할 수 있다. 이런 누적적인 과학 개념이 일반인이나 과학자들 사이에 대중적이었으나, Kuhn은 이는 역사적으로도 부정확할 뿐만 아니라 철학적으로는 순진한 생각이라고 주장한다. 예를 들면, 그는 아인슈타인의 상대성이론이 어떤 면에서는 뉴턴의 이론보다는 아리스토텔레스의 이론과 더 유사하므로 역학의 역사는 틀린 것에서 바른 것으로의 단순한 선형의 진보는 아니라는 것이다. 게다가, 객관적 진실이라는 개념이 맞는 말인지에 대해 의문을 제기했다. 그가 생각하기에 어느 특정한 패러다임과는 독립적인, 세상에 관한 확고부동한 일련의 사실들이 존재할 것이라는 생각은 일관성 면에서 의심스러웠다. 그는 급진적인 대안을 제시했다. 바로 세상에 대한 사실들은 패러다임에 상대적이며, 따라서 변한다는 것이다. 만약 이 주장이 옳다면, 어떤 이론이 있는 그대로의 사실과 들어맞는지를 묻는 것도 이치에 맞지 않으며, 따라서 그것이 객관적으로 진실인지를 묻는 것도 모두 이치에 맞지 않는다는 것이다.

31. ③

1. People are so accustomed to using blankets to make themselves warm that they are surprised to see Ⓐ blankets used to keep ice cold, and to prevent it from melting. 1) Expecting that the same thing will have the same effect, they think that a blanket must make ice warm. ① But what a blanket always does is to prevent heat passing from one side to the other. Thus it keeps the heat of something from passing into the colder air around, and it keeps the air from passing into some objects.

중심소재: 이불, 얼음
1. 도입부 = 주제문(Ⓐ)
Black의 용도: 얼음이 녹지 않도록 담요 사용
1) 통념
몸을 따뜻하게 할 용도로 사용되므로 얼음을 녹일 것이라 생각
① 뒷받침 진술
Ⓐ의 원리 설명

| 해설

얼음과 담요의 관계를 가장 잘 설명한 표현을 고르라는 문제이다. 얼음을 담요로 덮었을 때, 얼음이 녹지 않는 이유는 담요가 외부의 따뜻한 공기를 안으로 들어오지 못하게 차단하는 역할을 하기 때문이다. 이러한 내용을 가장 잘 드러내는 보기는 ③이다.

| 해석

사람들은 자신의 몸을 따뜻하게 하려고 담요를 사용하는 데 너무나 익숙해서 담요를 이용하여 얼음을 차게 유지하여 이것이 녹지 않게 하는 것을 보고 많이 놀란다. 같은 물건(담요)이 같은 효과를 낼 것이라고 기대하면서, 이들은 담요가 얼음을 따뜻하게(고로 녹인다) 할 것이라고 생각한다. 그러나 담요가 일반적으로 미치는 영향은 한 쪽에서 다른 쪽으로 열이 못 나가게 막는 것이다. 고로 이것은 어떤 것의 열이 차가운 공기 주위로 전달하지 못하게 하고, 그래서 이것은 공기가 어떤 물체 안으로 들어오는 것을 막게 된다.

[32-34]

1. The basic principle of broadcasting in our country is that people grant private business the ability to make money while using the public airwaves. In exchange for a license, we demand that broadcasters air programs that serve the public interest, and we ask them not to broadcast indecent material at times when children are likely to be watching or listening. 1) The reason we have special rules for radio and television programming is that the broadcast media is a uniquely pervasive presence in the lives of all Americans.

2. When 100 million Americans, including myself, tuned into the Super Bowl, we allowed a broadcast company to enter the privacy of our homes. 1) We do not expect to agree with our house guests on everything, but we do expect them to

중심소재: broadcasting
첫 번째 문단
1. 도입부 = 중심소재 파악
방송의 규칙 기술
1) 규칙을 지켜야 하는 이유

두 번째 문단
1. 비유를 통해 "문제점 지적-대안" 제시
1) 손님과 주인의 비유를 통해서 글쓴이의 주장을 간접적으로 전달하고 있다: 손님은 아이들이 집에 있을 때 부적절한 말과 행동을 삼가야 한다.

★ 일반적으로 특정 사항의 원칙이 배경으로 제시되면 이러한 원칙이 잘 지켜지지 않는 문제점이 지적되는 내용이 따를 가능성이 크다.

★ 비유를 통해 글의 요지를 간접적으로 전달하고 있다.

| 현상
(문제점 지적)
|
대안(요지)
|
뒷받침 근거 |

show good judgment and to refrain from saying crude and offensive things, especially when children are in the room. ⓒ We expected the Super Bowl broadcast to be respectful of us and our families. Ⓐ **But** what we all got on February 1 was anything but a good guest. Besides the now infamous incident involving Justin Timberlake and Janet Jackson, the half-time show was full of crude and sexually explicit performances. Throughout the game, we were subjected also to some offensive advertising. It is estimated that one in five American children were watching this year's Super Bowl broadcast.

ⓒ 주제문
마찬가지로 가정에서 슈퍼볼 방송을 할 때 우리 가정에 대한 존중을 기대했다.
Ⓐ 뒷받침 예시
구체적 사례를 통해 현상의 문제점을 지적하면서 아이들이 있는 가정 내 방송규칙 준수의 중요성을 강조하고 있다.

32. ①

| 해설

바로 뒤에 이어지는 내용을 보면, 아주 많은 이가 슈퍼볼을 본다는 내용이 나온다. 즉, 방송 미디어는 우리 생활 깊숙이 자리 잡고 있음을 알 수 있다. 우리 삶에 '널리 퍼져/스며 있는'의 보기 ①이 (A)에 가장 적절한 표현이다.

33. ②

| 해설

제시된 문장에서 비유적 표현의 대상으로 '손님'을 언급하고 있는데, 이에 해당하는 대상이 ⓑ 앞의 내용에서 "we allowed a broadcast company to enter the privacy of our homes." 중 'broadcast company'에 해당한다. 제시된 문장 뒤에 이어지는 표현을 보면 "We expected the Super Bowl broadcast to be respectful of us and our families."인데, 우리가 손님을 집에 초대했을 때 기대하는 것과 마찬가지로 슈퍼볼 방송을 가정에 초대했을 때 특정 기대 사항이 있다는 내용이다.

34. ③

| 해설

본문에 비유적인 표현이 나온 다음의 내용에서 보기 ③의 내용을 파악할 수 있다. "we do expect them to show good judgment and to refrain from saying crude and offensive things, especially **when children are in the room**." 참고로 본문의 요지는 '아이가 TV를 시청하는 시간대에 부적절한 내용을 전달하는 프로그램을 규제해야 한다'이다.

| 해석

민간 기업에 공중파를 이용하여 사업하도록 허락하는 것은 미국에서의 방송의 기본적인 원칙이다. 면허를 주는 대가로 우리는 방송국이 공익에 이바지하는 프로그램을 방송하라고 요구하며, 어린아이들이 시청할 가능성이 많은 시간대에는 부적절한 내용을 방송하지 않도록 요구한다. 라디오와 TV 프로그램 편성에 대한 특별한 규칙이 존재하는 이유는 모든 미국인의 삶 속에 방송 매체가 유난히 폭넓게 존재하기 때문이다.

나 자신도 그랬듯이 1억 명의 미국인들이 슈퍼볼을 시청하고 있을 때 우리는 방송국에 우리 가정의 사생활 속으로 들어오도록 허락한 것이다. 우리는 우리 집에 찾아온 손님이 모든 점에서 마음에 들 것을 기대하지는 않지만 적어도 좋은 판단력을 보여주면서, 특히 아이들이 방에 있을 때에는 정제되지 않은 불쾌한 말을 삼갈 것이라고 기대한다. 우리는 슈퍼볼 방송이 우리와 우리 가족들을 존중해 줄 기대했다. 그러나 우리가 2월 1일 슈퍼볼을 시청할 때 이 손님은 전혀 좋은 손님이 못되었다. 저스틴 팀버레이크와 자넷 잭슨이 연루된 이제는 유명해진 사건 외에도 휴식 시간의 쇼는 여과 없이 성적으로 노골적인 공연으로 가득했다. 게임을 보는 내내 우리는 몇몇 불쾌한 광고를 보아야만 했다. 미국 어린아이 다섯 명 중 한 명이 올해 슈퍼볼을 시청한 것으로 추산된다.

[35-36]

1. Automakers are loading up vehicles with more sophisticated technology challenging engineers with how to continue the business boom without further compromising safety. They have made a huge bet that hands-free technology would be the answer. 1) But a recent research shows people talking on cell phones are ① distracted even if their hands remain on the steering wheel. It indicates clear trade-off with hands-free technology. Even though their hands remained on the wheel, study subjects using voice-activated systems ② take longer to dial—a potentially dangerous distraction. Ⓐ To the extent that hands-free technology give drivers a false sense of security and prods them to engage in longer phone conversation, it may even exacerbate the safety problem. 2.Despite the safety concerns, customers' desire to stay connected to the outside world is only expected to increase. 2. Consequently, many organizations have called for the prohibition of mobile phone use by drivers while on the road.

중심소재:
Hands-Free Technology
1. 도입부 = 대안책
자동차 회사들은 안전상에 문제가 없으면서 더 정교한 기술을 탑재한 자동차 생산 → 'hands-free technology'로 타개책 마련
1) 문제점 지적(뒷받침 근거)
① 운전 중 집중력 흐려짐
② 장시간 통화
조사를 통해 드러냄: 'distracted while on the phone.'
Ⓐ 전망(문제의 심각성)
연구 결과와는 달리 자동차 중 전화를 거는 행위는 더욱 늘어날 것으로 보임
2. 결론 = 대안 촉구(요지)
많은 단체가 운전 중 전화 사용에 대한 규제 요구

| 본문 분석

기본적으로 '현상제시 — 문제점 지적 — 해결방안'의 구조를 취하고 있다. 대부분의 이런 글은 '인과'의 글 전개방법을 취하기에 글을 읽을 때, '무엇이(Hands-free technology) 어디에/누구에게(Drivers) 어떤 영향(Distraction while driving → car accident)을 미치는가? 라는 물음에 답하듯 읽어내려 가면 된다.

35. ③

| 해설

앞뒤 문맥을 정확히 파악하는 동시에 'compromise' 라는 동사의 이차적 의미를 알아야 풀 수 있는 문제이다. 우선 'compromise' 에는 '손상하다' 라는 의미가 있다. 본문으로 돌아가, 자동차회사가 시도하는 새로운 기술이 무엇인가? 빈칸 뒤에 나오는 'hands-free technology' 와 'cell phones' 에서 알 수 있듯이, 운전하면서 전화를 할 수 있는 기술을 말한다. 빈칸의 내용에 들어갈 말은 운전하면서 전화를 할 수 있도록 하는 기술을 말하는데, 그러면서 안전상의 문제는 유발하지 않는 그런 기술을 말할 것이다. 고로, '안전에 피해를 주지 않으면서도' 라는 문맥이 되어야 하므로 보기 ③이 가장 적절하다.

36. ①

| 해설

최근 연구를 통해서 밝혀낸 사실은 무엇인가? 자동사 회사들이 제시하는 '안전상에 문제가 되지 않으면서도 운전 중 전화를 할 수 있는 기술' 은 실제 운전 중 집중력을 떨어뜨리고, 운전자가 전화를 더 오래 하도록 하여 사고를 유발할 수 있다는 내용이다. 고로, 연구는 자동차회사들의 기대가 그릇된 것임을 드러낸다고 볼 수 있다. 보기 ①이 정답이다.

| 해석

자동차 제조사들은 안전을 더 해치지 않으면서 자동차 업계의 호황을 이어나갈 방법을 놓고 엔지니어들의 실력을 보여주는 더욱 정교한 첨단 기술을 장착한 자동차들을 생산하고 있다. 제조사들은 핸즈프리 기술이 해답이라고 굳게 장담했다. 그러나 최근의 연구에 의하면 휴대전화로 통화하는 사람들은 손으로 운전대를 계속 잡고 있더라도 주의가 산만해진다고 한다. 이것은 핸즈프리 기술이 분명히 치러야 하는 대가가 있다는 것을 보여준다. 음성 인식 장치를 이용하는 연구 참여자들은 비록 손은 운전대를 계속 잡고 있더라도 전화를 거는 데에 더 오랜 시간이 걸려서 결국 주의가 산만해짐에 따른 잠재적인 위험이 있었다. 핸즈프리 기술 때문에 운전자들이 안전하다고 오해하게 되고 전화 통화를 더 오래 하게 되는 만큼 핸즈프리 기술은 안전 문제를 오히려 악화시킬 수도 있다. 안전 문제에도 불구하고 고객들은 바깥세상과 계속 연결되고 싶은 욕망이 더 커지기만 할 것으로 예상한다. 결국, 많은 단체가 운전 중인 운전자의 휴대전화 사용을 금지하도록 촉구하게 되었다.

[37-39]

첫 번째 문단의 중심소재★ 이자 중심내용(controlling idea)으로 글의 주제로 설정할 수 있다.

1. Speaking of anthropological canards, no discussion of language and thought would be complete without the Great Eskimo Vocabulary Hoax. 1) Contrary to popular belief, the Eskimos do not have words for snow than do speakers of English. ① They do not have four hundred words for snow, as it has been claimed in print, or two hundred, or one hundred, or forty-eight, or even nine. One dictionary puts the figure at two. Counting generously, experts can come up

중심소재: 에스키모 어휘 사기
첫번째 문단
1. 도입부
'에스키모 어휘 사기'
1) 통념 ↔ 주제문
대중이 가지는 일반적 통념과 달리 '에스키모인은 영어 화자보다 눈에 대한 단어가 많지 않다.'고 진술하고 있다.
① 뒷받침 진술
영어에도 에스키모인 만큼 만만찮게 눈에 관한 어휘가 있다고 논박하고 있다.

with about a dozen, but by such standards English would not be far behind, with *snow, sleet, slush, blizzard, avalanche, hail, hardpack, powder, flurry, dusting,* and a coinage of Boston's WBZ-TV meteorologist Bruce Schwoegler, *snizzling*.

2. Where did the myth come from? 1) Not from anyone who has actually studied the Yupik, and Inuit-Inupiaq families of polysynthetic languages spoken from Siberia to Greenland. The anthropologist Laura Martin has documented how the story grew like an urban legend, exaggerated with each retelling. In 1911 Boas casually mentioned that Eskimos used four unrelated word roots for snow. Whorf embellished the count to seven and implied that there were more. His article was widely reprinted, then cited in textbooks and popular books on language, which led to successively inflated estimates on other textbooks, articles, and newspaper columns of Amazing Facts.

두번째 문단
1. 잘못된 통념이 자리잡게 된 배경은? (=단락 주제)
(즉, 이 글은 위와 같이 잘못된 통념이 널리 퍼지게 된 원인/기원을 밝히기 위해 쓴 글임을 알 수 있다.)
1) 구체적 진술(답변)

★ 두 번째 문단의 중심내용 (controlling idea)에 해당한다.

37. ②

| 해설

빈칸의 구가 나타내는 '통념'의 내용이 이후에 한 번 더 이어진다. 'as it **has been claimed** in print, or two hundred, or one hundred, or forty-eight, or even nine"을 참고하도록 한다.

38. ④

| 해설

본문에서 말하는 '통념'이란 '에스키모인은 다른 민족보다 눈을 나타내는 표현이 더 많다' 이다.

39. ②

| 해설

"The anthropologist Laura Martin has documented how the story grew like an urban legend, exaggerated with each retelling."에서 Laura Martin임을 알 수 있다. Boas와 Whorf는 눈과 관련된 에스키모의 어휘가 어떤 식으로 과장 되었는지를 설명하기 위해 언급한 인물에 해당한다.

| 해석

인류학의 헛소문에 관해 말하자면 거대한 에스키모의 어휘 속임수를 빼놓으면 언어와 사상에 대한 어떤 논의도 완벽하지 못할 것이다. 일반인들의 믿음과는 반대로 에스키모인은 영어 사용자들보다도 눈을 가리키는 더 많은 단어를 갖고 있지 않다. 그들은 여러 글에서 알려진 것처럼 눈을 가리키는 단어를 400개도 200개도 100개도 48개도 아닌 심지어는 9개도 갖고 있지 않다. 한 사전은 그 숫자를 두 개로 쓰고 있다. 관대하게 헤아려서 전문가들은 대략 열두 개를 제안한다. 그러나 그런 수준이라면 영어도 'snow, sleet, slush, blizzard, avalanche, hail, hardpack, powder, flurry, dusting' 그리고 보스턴 소재 WBZ-TV의 기상학자인 브루스 슈뵈글러가 만든 신조어인 'snizzling' 등을 갖고 있어서 그에 뒤처지지는 않는다.

이러한 잘못된 통념은 어디서 유래한 것인가? 시베리아에서 그린란드에 이르기까지 통용되는 다종합적 언어들인 유피크 어족과 이누이트 이누피아크 어족들을 연구해 온 사람에게서 그러한 통념이 나온 것은 아니다. 인류학자인 로라 마틴은 어떻게 그 이야기가 매번 다시 이야기될 때마다 과장되면서 도시의 전설처럼 커졌는가를 문헌으로 입증하였다. 1911년에 보애스는 에스키모인들은 눈을 가리킬 때 네 개의 독립적인 어근을 사용한다고 불쑥 언급하였다. 워프는 그 숫자를 일곱 개로 각색하였고 더 많다고 암시하였다. 그의 논문이 널리 재출간되었고 그러고 나서 언어에 관한 교과서와 대중적인 책에서 인용되었으며, 이것이 다른 교과서, 논문, 그리고 신문의 'Amazing Facts' 칼럼 등에서 연속적으로 추정치가 부풀려지는 결과를 초래했다.

[40-42]

도입부
- 현상 – 원인 (주제문)
- 뒷받침 진술
- 주제문에서 밝힌 내용 상술
- 대안 – 이유

1. Languages seem to be converging to a smaller number, as languages like English seem to eat up regional ones. 1) ① The three languages used the most by first language speakers today are Mandarin Chinese, English, and Spanish. English is being used more and more as the main language for business, science, and popular culture. ② Evidence suggests that the dominant languages are squeezing out the local tongues of various regions in the world. Linguists estimate that of the approximately 6,500 languages worldwide, about half are endangered or on the brink of extinction. Ⓐ According to some linguists, the estimated rate of language extinction is one lost in the world every two weeks. If this sounds like the world is losing a species, in a way it is. When a language is lost, meaning no living person can teach another, a world perspective is lost. 2. ① Some foreign language expressions simply cannot be translated. ② Colloquial phrases are pleasant to the ear, not only because they are familiar, but also because they reflect a unique aspect of a culture. Ⓐ Aboriginal languages in Canada and other countries such as Australia have words that reflect a way of life that is connected closely to the Earth. There are

중심소재: 언어 – 언어의 소멸

1. 도입부 = 주제문(현상 –문제점 지적)
영어와 같은 주된 언어가 지역 언어를 잡아삼키면서 그 수가 줄어들고 있다.

1) 뒷받침 진술
① 주된 언어의 종류와 특히 다양한 분야에 영어가 많이 사용됨을 언급
② 구체적 수치를 제시하며 지역 언어의 소멸 위기 언급
문제의 심각성
Ⓐ 2주마다 언어가 사라지고 이는 그 언어가 반영하는 세계관의 소멸이다.

2. 대안 – 이유(요지)
각 지역의 독특한 언어를 보존해야 하는 이유
① 번역 불가능성
② 각 언어는 독특한 문화반영
Ⓐ 부연예시

fifty different words that mean 'snow' in one Canadian native language, and in the Eastern Arrernte language of Central Australia the word nyimpe translates to 'the smell of rain'.

40. ①

| 해설

'squeeze out'은 '짜내다, 밀어내다'는 뜻이다. 즉, 기존에 있던 것을 밖으로 내보낸다는 의미이므로 원래의 것을 '없애다, 제한하다'의 의미로 볼 수 있다.

41. ④

| 해설

빈칸이 들어간 이후 문장의 구조를 보면, "_____ because they are familiar, but also because they reflect a unique aspect of a culture."인데, 'because S V'의 절이 병렬구조로 대치되고 있다. 'but also'로 보아 병렬구조를 가지는 'not only A but also B' 구문임을 쉽게 파악할 수 있다.

42. ③

| 해설

"Some foreign language expressions simply cannot be translated"로 보아 보기 ③은 틀린 진술이다.

| 해석

영어와 같은 언어가 지역 언어들을 먹어 치우면서, (세계의) 언어는 더 적은 수로 수렴되어 가고 있는 듯하다. 오늘날 모국어 사용자들이 가장 많이 사용하는 세 개의 언어는 중국 북경어, 영어, 스페인어이다. 영어는 사업, 과학, 대중문화의 주된 언어로서 점점 많이 사용되고 있다. 증거에 따르면, 이 우위를 차지하고 있는 언어들이 세계의 다양한 지역 언어를 없애고 있다. 언어학자들의 추정에 의하면, 전 세계의 약 6,500여 개의 언어 중에 대략 절반이 위험하거나 멸종될 위기에 있다는 것이다. 어떤 언어학자들에 의하면, 언어가 소멸하는 비율을 따지면, 2주마다 전 세계에서 하나가 없어지는 꼴이라고 한다. 만약 이것이 세계가 생물학적인 종(種)을 하나 잃는 것처럼 들린다면, 어떤 면에선 같은 것이다. 언어가 사라진다면, 그것은 생존하는 어떤 사람도 다른 사람을(그 언어를) 가르칠 수 없다는 의미이고, 세상을 보는 하나의 관점[시각]이 사라진다는 것을 의미한다. 일부 외래 언어의 표현들이 단순히 번역될 수는 없다. 구어체 어구들은 듣기 좋다. 왜냐하면, 그것들이 익숙하기도 하지만, 그들이 한 문화의 독특한 측면을 반영해 주기 때문이다. 캐나다와 오스트레일리아 같은 다른 나라들의 토착 언어들에는 지구와 밀접히 연관되는 생활방식들을 반영하는 단어들이 있다. 캐나다의 한 토착어에는 '눈(snow)'을 뜻하는 50개의 서로 다른 단어가 있으며, 중앙 오스트레일리아의 이스턴 아렌테어(Eastern Arrernte)에는 nyimpe라는 단어가 '비의 냄새(the smell of rain)'라는 의미로 번역된다.

◆ 선택지에서 헷갈리는 2개의 번호에 놓여있을 때 거의 다 풀리는 경험을 하게 되었습니다.

완독 후 시간이 지나도 계속하여 독해에 있어서 막힘이 있을 땐 리딩 이노베이터에서 계속해서 강조해 주었던 독해의 핵심인 중심소제 찾기라는 것!! 을 되새기며 문제를 리뷰할 시 웬만한 문제들은 답이 보입니다. 특히 선택지에서 헷갈리는 2개의 번호에 놓여있을 때 거의 다 풀리는 경험을 하게 되었습니다.

주제 찾기, 제목 고르기, 글쓴이의 주장 고르기 부분에 있어서는 무지했던 저에게 어떠한 문제를 보아도 쉽게 해결 가능하게 해 주었던 책으로써 너무 많은 도움이 되었습니다.

- 독자 서평 (q****3 - 예스24)

◆ 글쓴이의 의도를 파악하는 데 정말 많은 도움이 될 것 같습니다.

이 책은 한마디로 학습자 중심의 영어서적이라는 느낌이랄까? 책의 가장 큰 특징으로 느낀 것은 하나의 영어지문을 본인이 온전히 소화할 수 있도록 구성되어 있다는 점입니다. 학습자가 중심이 되어서 주도적으로 지문을 분석할 수 있도록, 또 책 자체가 그것을 훈련하도록 정리되어 있네요. 그 방법으로 지문을 도식화하여 연습할 수 있게 하는데, 그렇게 하다 보면 글쓴이가 무엇을 이야기하고 있는지 이해하기 쉬워집니다. 저자의 입장에서 내용을 이해하는 눈이 키워질 것 같아요. 여타 독해 책과 다른 점이 바로 이런 글의 구조 파악 부분인데 단순히 어휘 암기의 독해 훈련 방법이 아닌 글이 구조를 이해하고 문제의 접근하는 방식이 신선합니다. 그리고 이렇게 공부를 하면 글쓴이의 의도를 파악하는 데 정말 많은 도움이 될 것 같습니다.

- 독자 서평 (a********7 - 예스24)

◆ 영어를 차근히 공부하고 싶은 사람이라면 이 책을 추천해주고싶다.

우연치 않게 이 책을 알게 되고 바로 구입을 결정했던 이유는, 이 책이 독해를 어떻게 접근해야 하는지 그 방법을 알려주는 책이기 때문이다.

단순히 '지문의 Main idea가 무엇이고, Topic이 무엇이고, Supporting Idea가 무엇이다'라고 읊기만 하는 책이 아니라, 왜 이 부분이 MI인지, 왜 이 부분이 SI인지 알려주고 또 접근하는 방법을 가르쳐 준다.

- 독자 서평 (t*******e - 예스24)

◆ 영어 독해를 어떻게 해야할지 제대로 알려주는 교재

영어 독해 문제를 풀기 위해서 여러 종류의 독해 문제집을 보고 기본서의 독해파트를 보았지만 보통의 영어 독해 문제풀이는 간단한 해설만 있고 해석이 나오는 것이 일반적이고 심지어 해설도 딱히 영어 독해 문제를 풀기 위한 해설인지 의문이 생길 정도로 너무 간략하게 나와서 큰 도움이 안 되는 경우도 많아서 영어 독해문제를 풀면서 많은 갈증을 느꼈는데, 리딩이노베이터 기본편 교재는 영어 독해를 어떻게 해야 할지 제대로 알려주는 교재 구성이 독학으로 영어 독해를 정복하기 좋게 되어 있어서 매우 좋다고 생각됩니다.

- 독자 서평 (k****9 - 예스24)